Pro Oracle Collaboration Suite 10*g*

John Watson

Apress®

Pro Oracle Collaboration Suite 10*g*

Softcover re-print of the Hardcover 1st edition 2006

ISBN-13: 978-1-4302-1181-5

ISBN-13 : 978-1-4302-0235-6 (eBook)

Lead Editor: Jonathan Hassell
Technical Reviewer: Jonathan Ives

Project Manager: Julie M. Smith
Copy Edit Manager: Nicole LeClerc
Copy Editor: Jennifer Whipple
Assistant Production Director: Kari Brooks-Copony
Production Editor: Katie Stence
Compositor: Linda Weidemann, Wolf Creek Press
Proofreader: Liz Welch
Indexer: Brenda Miller
Artist: April Milne
Cover Designer: Kurt Krames
Manufacturing Director: Tom Debolski

For information on translations, please contact Apress directly at 2855 Telegraph Avenue, Suite 600, Berkeley, CA 94705. Phone 510-549-5930, fax 510-549-5939, e-mail `info@apress.com`, or visit `http://www.apress.com`.

The source code for this book is available to readers at `http://www.apress.com` in the Source Code/Download section.

I want to thank the light of my life, Silvia,
for looking after me while I wrote this.
Our cats and dogs tried to help, too.

Contents at a Glance

Contents

About the Author

JOHN WATSON is as English as can be; he just hasn't lived there for years.

Born and educated in Oxford, he started working in IT in London more than 20 years ago. He is enthralled with Oracle technology, and was on their payroll for six years. He says that if you aren't teaching or learning, you're in the wrong job. This attitude has led to him studying all the obscure corners of the Oracle product set and spending time in the classroom teaching Oracle server technologies in between consulting for a wide range of governmental, NGO, and commercial organizations all over Europe and Africa.

At the moment he lives outside Johannesburg, South Africa, on two acres with the people he loves: his wife, cats, dogs, and a few parrots.

About the Technical Reviewer

JONATHAN IVES has worked for Oracle in the United Kingdom for thirteen years, primarily as a principal sales consultant for collaborative products. Prior to that he worked for Digital for four years in a similar role.

He lives in Hampshire, England, and is married with two children. He enjoys good food and sings in a choir. He spends a good deal of time at home providing IT support for his two sons, who are active PC gamers.

Introduction

You don't have to be an Oracle database administrator or an Oracle Application Server administrator to manage an Oracle Collaboration Suite environment. You don't have to be a network administrator or a system administrator either. You don't have to be an expert at managing collaboration services, such as e-mail systems and file servers. But any and all of these skills will help you to manage Oracle Collaboration Suite. The approach I've taken in this book is to provide enough information on all these topics to understand their importance and relevance for the use and administration of Oracle Collaboration Suite and to perform some critical tasks; but I have not attempted to teach you all the skills. There are shops with whole bookcases full of material on these matters (one of them written, and several edited, by me). As you become more deeply involved with managing and using Oracle Collaboration Suite, you will have to do further studying in all of the related subjects.

So what is this book? It is an introduction to an immensely powerful set of applications, which run on the most powerful server technology in the world. I say *introduction* because the applications and the technologies are huge and complex; they each need many books to cover them comprehensively.

Ideally, this book will be read from cover to cover. If you aren't interested in particular topics, you can skip those chapters, but be warned: there are cases where knowledge of earlier chapters is assumed. In particular, a thorough knowledge of the server technologies, architecture, and administration tools (covered in Chapters 2 through 6) is vital to understanding how to manage the application components (covered in Chapters 7 through 15).

Chapter 1 is a quick run through the use and capabilities of the application components. It emphasizes that these components are accessible through several user interfaces, including their own specialized interfaces, generic web interfaces common to all components, and sometimes through Microsoft Outlook or other third-party client tools.

Architecturally Oracle Collaboration Suite is built on the Oracle database and Oracle Application Server. Chapter 2 covers these server technologies in general. Chapter 3 relates them to Oracle Collaboration Suite. There is particular emphasis on the use of the industry standard network communication protocols that underpin the interoperability of the Oracle Collaboration Suite components with each other, with client tools, and with external services.

Chapter 4 outlines some options for deployment, followed by the detail of installation. Oracle Collaboration Suite can run on any mainstream hardware and operating system environment. This chapter includes some platform-specific examples, but for the most part the information is applicable to all platforms.

Chapter 5 describes the management tools available. These are a combination of the standard tools provided by Oracle for administering databases and application servers, and component-specific tools.

The concept of *identity management* is detailed in Chapter 6. All the Oracle Collaboration Suite components make use of the Single Sign-On service and the Oracle Internet Directory (Oracle's implementation of the industry standard LDAP directory server) for identifying and authenticating users. The components also use the Oracle Internet Directory as a repository of access permissions and application roles, and as the source of information for creating and removing accounts.

Configuration and management of the nine application components are covered in Chapters 7 through 15. The chapters are alphabetical by component name—one chapter for each component. It is not necessary to read them in order, but there are some dependencies. For example, the Workspaces component (Chapter 15) is to a certain extent dependent on the Calendar (Chapter 7), Content Services (Chapter 8), Discussions (Chapter 9), and Mail (Chapter 10) components. Where one component is dependent on another, there are forward and backward references to the relevant chapters.

The concluding chapters, 16 and 17, cover ongoing maintenance and designing an environment for scalability and fault tolerance.

CHAPTER 1

Functionality and the User Interface

Oracle Collaboration Suite is a set of many applications known as *components*. This chapter looks at them briefly from the user's perspective, illustrating what they can do and how they all work together to create a collaboration environment with a single point of access.

It is almost impossible to describe Oracle Collaboration Suite without sounding like a salesman—but it doesn't really need selling. Just a description should be enough to convince users to start exploiting the product. But first, it is essential to see how web applications are viewed by end users, which is typically as HTML pages delivered over HTTP, the protocol that enables the World Wide Web.

How Applications Are Delivered with HTTP and HTML

Users connect to web applications (and all of Oracle Collaboration Suite is presented to users as a set of web applications) through browsers, typically Internet Explorer. Browsers issue URLs (Uniform Resource Locators) that retrieve data from a web server for display in the browser. The browser is responsible for managing the application's user interface: local window management, mouse movements, keyboard control.

A URL consists of a number of elements, all but one of which have default values separated by delimiters:

```
protocol://host.domain:port/path/filename.ext?parameter1=value1&parameter2=value2(&...)
```

Table 1-1 shows the elements that make a URL. More parameter-value pairs, each delimited with an ampersand, may be appended to the end.

Table 1-1. *URL Elements*

Element	Default	Delimiter
protocol	http	://
host	none	.
domain	null	:
port	80	/
path	null	/
filename	index (a common default)	.
extension	html (or htm for Windows)	?
parameter	null	=
value	null	&

The only required element is the host—there are defaults for everything else. The defaults for protocol, domain, and port will be provided by the browser; the defaults for the filename, extension, and any string of parameters and values will come from the web server.

Thus, a simple URL that specifies nothing more than a host and a domain, such as `www.oracle.com`, when entered into a browser might be expanded by the browser into `http://www.oracle.com:80`. And when it's received by a web server it might be further expanded to `http://www.oracle.com:80/index.html`.

The page returned to the browser, `index.html` in this example, will be formatted for display to the user by the browser. The page will more than likely contain links in the form of other URLs; or in a more sophisticated application there will be radio buttons, check boxes, and any number of fields to be completed. Eventually, the user will send another URL to the web server, or perhaps a more complicated HTTP message will be composed when the user clicks a "submit" button. The web server will receive this, process it, and return another screen full of information back to the browser for display. As the user navigates through a web application, he may have absolutely no idea what is happening behind his browser window—though if he looks at the address bar he may notice that he is continually issuing URLs and perhaps switching between protocols and hosts as he does so.

The Hypertext Transfer Protocol

The World Wide Web is based on HTTP (Hypertext Transfer Protocol). This was invented in 1989 at CERN, the European Organization for Nuclear Research. HTTP is a layered protocol, which has TCP as its underlying transport. It is optimized for transporting documents typically structured with HTML, as described in the following section, "The Hypertext Markup Language," and is particularly suitable for the Internet environment because of the way it uses TCP ports, and because the connections are stateless.

■ **Note** For those with an interest in science history, *CERN* stands for Conseil Européen pour la Recherche Nucléaire, an organization set up in the 1950s and recently made famous by Dan Brown in his novel *Angels and Demons*. The acronym has remained, though the organization has changed in many ways, including its official name. CERN is and probably always will be the home of the World Wide Web, though its main function is still research into subatomic particles.

All connections to an HTTP server, from any number of clients, are made into the server machine through one TCP port. By contrast, protocols such as telnet use different ports for each session. All telnet client users contact the telnet daemon on the same port (port 23, by default) but each established connection is over a dedicated port assigned by the server's port mapping algorithm at connect time. If HTTP were to use different ports for each user, scalability would be dramatically reduced; there is no operating system on the planet that can handle tens of thousands of concurrent TCP sessions, each on a different port. Multiplexing many sessions through one port solves this problem. It also simplifies firewall security and proxy serving.

The stateless nature of HTTP connections means that it can work over the slow and unreliable connections that typify the Internet. Stateful protocols (telnet is again an example) establish a connection between the client and server processes, and if the connection is broken, even for a fraction of a second, the application will error out. The connection must persist reliably for the duration of the session. By contrast, an HTTP session consists of a series of request-response messages, and the link can be broken between each one. This certainly gives rise to complexities when simulating the maintenance of the state of the session, as far as the application is concerned; but, provided these complexities are handled correctly, the session will be resilient against erratic network performance and outages.

The Hypertext Markup Language

A typical data transfer with HTTP is a URL sent from a client browser to a web server (the request) followed by transmission of a document back to the client (the response). These documents are commonly formatted with HTML, Hypertext Markup Language. This isn't a language at all; it is a set of standards defining how documents should be displayed.

Here is a very simple HTML document:

```
<body>
<b>A Sample Page</b>
<p>
A picture of
<a href=http://jwlnx1.bplc.com:80/photos/jw.gif> John </a>
(not for the faint hearted)
</body>
```

This document uses just four tags:

- <body> to </body> defines the data to display.
- <b> to </b> instructs the browser to use bold face for the enclosed text.

- <p> is a paragraph break.
- <a...> to </a> defines an *anchor*, in this case another URL that will display as a clickable link.

The page generated from the previous code will display in a browser as shown in Figure 1-1.

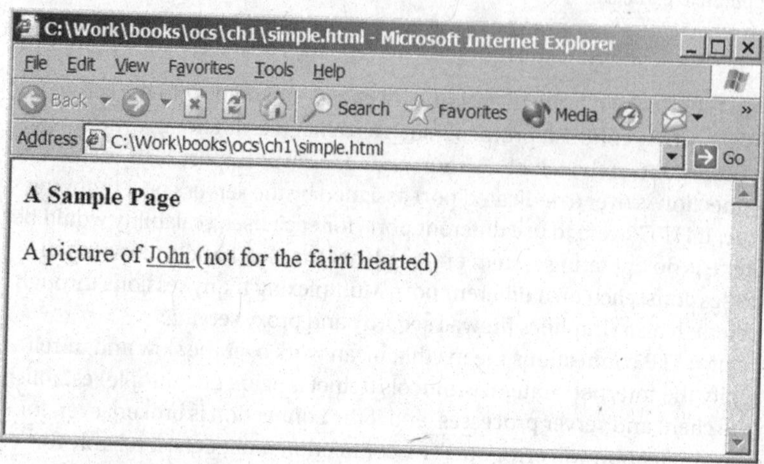

Figure 1-1. *A simple web page*

HTML can get quite complicated. Web pages defined in HTML can include text, tables, all sorts of images, and user interface components such as buttons, drop-down menus, or dialog boxes. Oracle Collaboration Suite applications are presented to end users as a set of connected HTML documents. As you navigate through a web application, you are continually sending HTTP messages from your browser that request different documents.

An HTML document can be a static file stored in the file system of the web server, and indeed many simple web applications consist of nothing more than a series of linked static documents. A more powerful web application will not consist of static files but of documents that are generated dynamically by an application server. Most of these documents will contain information derived from database content.

It is the combination of a web listener and an application server that makes up a true web server. A *web listener* is a process that monitors one or more ports on one or more IP addresses for incoming URLs. On receipt of a URL, it will parse the URL into a filename, locate the file, and copy it back to the browser. This is a very simple process and only suitable for very simple applications. Business data processing needs more: it needs documents that are generated in real time, usually based on information stored within a database in response to requests from each user. A web listener can't do that, but it can be configured to pass the request on to an application server. An *application server* can generate appropriate screens to be returned to the browser in the form of HTML documents.

There are various technologies used in Oracle Collaboration Suite to generate the documents that make up the user interface. These include Java, PL/SQL, and CGI (Common Gateway Interface)—but to the user, the result is just a page of HTML. The user has no means of knowing whether the window he sees in his browser is a static file retrieved from disk by a web listener, or a screen generated specially for him in real time by an application server.

The web listener acts as the front end to an application server, or possibly several application servers. For Oracle Collaboration Suite, the web listener provides a central point of access to the whole suite. The suite may consist of multiple processes on multiple physical machines, but to the end user it appears to be a single application accessed through one URL.

The Case for a Web-Based Collaboration Product

Virtually all organizations with more than a handful of staff have a need for collaboration tools. This need may not be formally defined, but still exists—and usually collaboration facilities are in place, though perhaps in a somewhat unplanned and unstructured fashion.

The most basic collaboration tool is a *file server*, a common datastore where users have shared-access to documents from any terminal and centralized backup. Equally widespread is e-mail. Users always end up combining use of these two: they mail each other documents as attachments. Straightaway, it becomes apparent that combining document management with e-mail enhances the value of both. Another common tool is diary management. The ability to make appointments, to book rooms and other facilities, or to locate staff and resources without resorting to paper systems or telephone calls is a huge timesaver. The ability to combine diary management with mailing lists and document distribution makes it even more valuable. Collaboration tools provide increasing business benefits if the tools are integrated into a suite. As the number of applications, the degree of integration, and the size of the user community all increase, the value of the whole business environment rises; the whole can be far greater than the parts.

To gain maximum benefit, collaboration tools need to be available at all times in all places. This means using wireless devices as well as network-connected terminals and a user interface that is usable on all possible devices. Web technology, enhanced with wireless protocols, fulfills this need.

Oracle Collaboration Suite is not the only product claiming to provide a web-based interface to a range of collaboration products, but it is the only one built on the Oracle technology stack, with its virtually unlimited capabilities for scale and fault tolerance. Also, Oracle Collaboration Suite has an exceptionally large set of products. They are all integrated through use of the Oracle Internet Directory (Oracle's LDAP server) and accessible through a common user interface.

Oracle Collaboration Suite Integration

Oracle Collaboration Suite is made up of a number of separate products, not all of which were written by Oracle Corporation. The most obvious exception to Oracle development standards is Calendar; it doesn't even use an Oracle database to store its data. What Oracle Collaboration Suite does is provide a common user interface to all the applications; a front-end entry point from which one can access all the applications; a security model that synchronizes user IDs in all the applications; and mechanisms for providing transparent data transfers between them. The result is an extremely powerful, superbly integrated suite of applications. End users will never be aware of the undeniable fact that underneath the user interface there are a number of products with different provenance.

The Common User Interface

Oracle Corporation has designed a set of standards for user interface software for web applications. This software can be developed with a number of tools—most probably Java, Forms, or PL/SQL. The various application development tools sold by Oracle Corporation include tool kits to develop applications that conform to these standards. All the Oracle Collaboration Suite products can be accessed through a web front end written in Java, using the UIX user interface toolkit shipped with JDeveloper. JDeveloper is the Java IDE (Interactive Development Environment) provided by Oracle Corporation. JDeveloper was originally based on JBuilder, sold by Borland, but has developed substantially since then. JDeveloper is now downloadable free of charge from Oracle Corporation's web site, though users must study the license conditions to ensure that their use of it is legal.

Using the UIX development environment as a common front end means that all the Oracle Collaboration Suite components appear to be part of one large application, but they are in fact independently developed. This makes it possible for Oracle to maintain different versions of the various products behind the scenes without end users being aware of this. If the suite were in fact one huge application, it would be impossibly large and unwieldy to maintain.

While UIX provides a standard user interface for Oracle Collaboration Suite components when accessed through the Web, the individual components may also have their own client tools. These tools generally follow their own standards, are optimized for the component, and may provide functionality not available through the web interface. It is also possible to link some of the components to the Microsoft Outlook client, which may be helpful for users familiar with that environment.

The Portal Entry Point

Portal is (among other things) a tool for designing web sites that give access to numerous applications from one URL. The Oracle Collaboration Suite applications are all accessed through Portal; each one is presented to the user as a *portlet*, a link that can be clicked. The portlet has code that connects the user to the appropriate service, wherever it may be. In this way, end users are kept unaware of the fact that the components of an Oracle Collaboration Suite installation may be distributed over many machines.

Portal applications make use of the Portal Repository. This exists in an Oracle database and defines the configuration of the web site, customized for each user. The repository schema is created in the database that is installed as part of an Oracle Application Server infrastructure installation.

Figure 1-2 shows the default Portal window that is the entry point to the Oracle Collaboration Suite web interface.

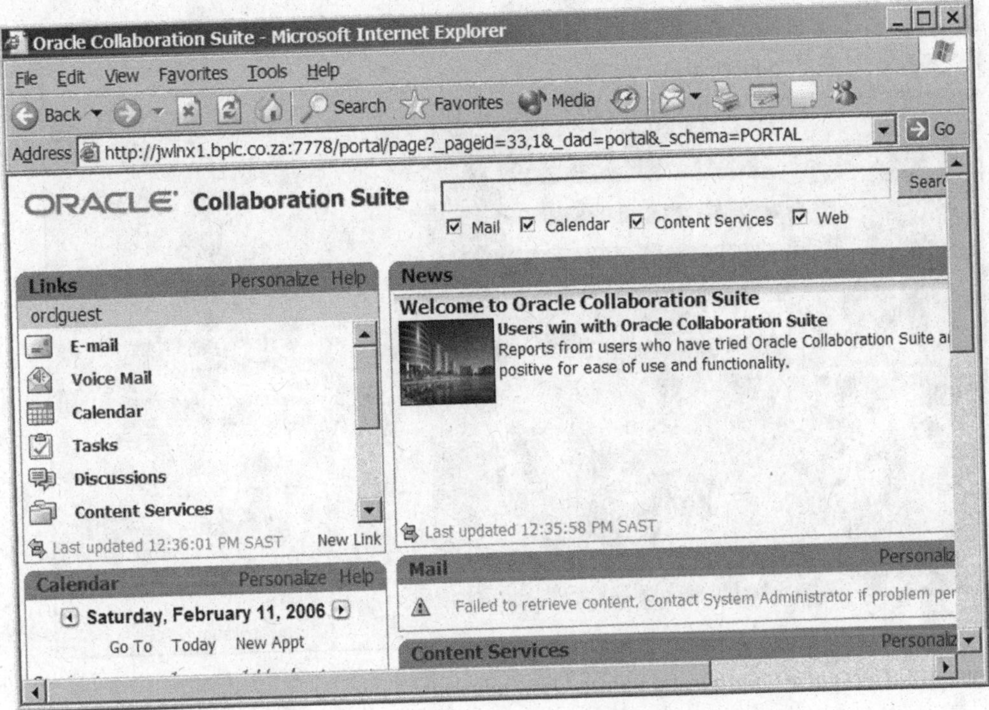

Figure 1-2. *The web interface to the Oracle Collaboration Suite applications*

The Security Model

All Oracle Collaboration Suite component applications share a common security model. This is the critical point of integration. This model is based on the use of Single Sign-On and the Oracle Internet Directory.

Use of Single Sign-On is immediately apparent to the user. When the user first contacts a component through the web interface, he is redirected to the Single Sign-On server, which prompts for a username and password and authenticates these against entries in the Oracle Internet Directory. This authentication service is installed as part of the Oracle Application Server infrastructure, an integral part of the Oracle Collaboration Suite installation. The details of this authentication mechanism are described in Chapter 2. The end result is that a user needs to authenticate himself only once—the first time he connects to a component—and he can then connect to any other Single Sign-On–enabled component without further prompts. This is enabled by a cookie set in the user's browser, which is valid for a certain time span (configured by the administrator) or until the user closes the browser.

Figure 1-3 shows the Oracle Collaboration Suite logon window, to which all users are redirected no matter what component they asked for, and to which they are returned after logging out. This window can, of course, be customized. The default logon window immediately after installation is shown in Figure 1-3.

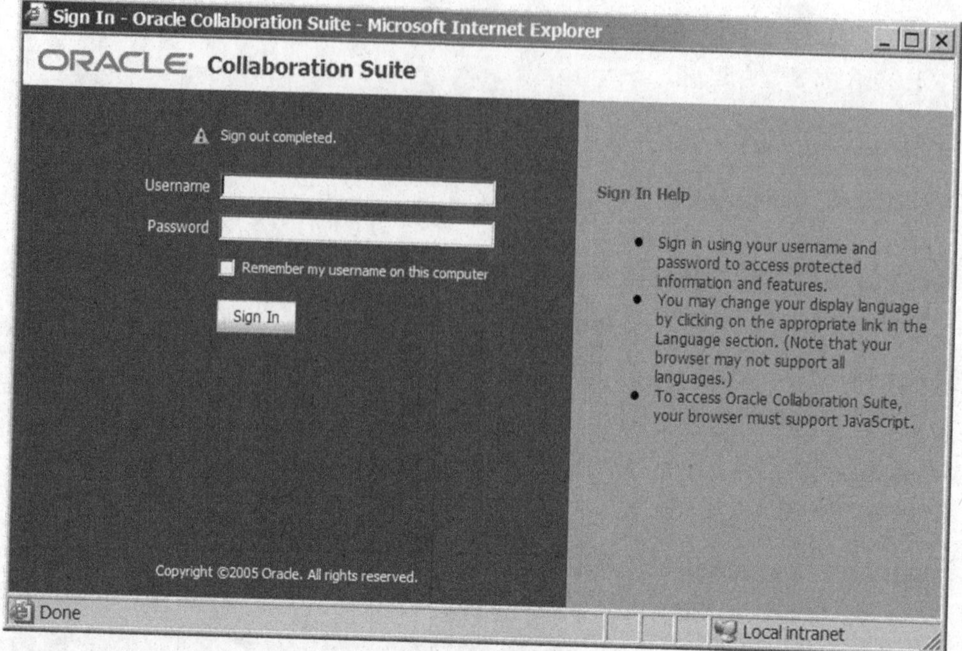

Figure 1-3. *The Oracle Collaboration Suite logon window*

Single Sign-On–enabled applications delegate security to the Single Sign-On server. If the client browser has the Single Sign-On authentication cookie set, the application will permit the user to connect as the user identified in the cookie without any further prompts. Some applications make much more use of the security facilities available within Oracle Internet Directory; they may, for example, use it to store access rights or user profile information. Since the applications do not themselves maintain user passwords, it becomes possible to manage passwords centrally; a user has one password stored in the Oracle Internet Directory. The standards to which the password must conform (such as complexity, interval between changes, policies on reuse) are determined by the Oracle Internet Directory administrator and apply to all applications. This eliminates the requirement for users to maintain many passwords themselves, with different rules for different applications. When a password reaches the end of its lifetime, the next time the user contacts any application, he will be prompted to change it when he is redirected to the Single Sign-On service.

Oracle Internet Directory can automatically provision accounts in Oracle Collaboration Suite components and, indeed, in any other applications written with the appropriate Oracle development toolkits. Account provisioning greatly simplifies user management. For example, it is likely that every employee in the organization will be given accounts for e-mail, file server, and a diary. Account provisioning means that once the user is registered in the Oracle Internet Directory, these accounts will be set up automatically. Then, depending on the characteristics of the user's Oracle Internet Directory registration, accounts in other applications may be provisioned as well. Furthermore, when an employee leaves the organization, Oracle Internet Directory can immediately invalidate all his accounts in all applications; there is no longer any risk of some logins remaining usable.

The Oracle Collaboration Suite Components

This section describes the Oracle Collaboration Suite Components. The descriptions given are very superficial—users will need to study the user guides or follow the online training courses to understand the full capabilities of the various components. The online help is also reasonably complete. Chapters 7 through 15 will cover configuring these various components. In alphabetical order by their official Oracle names (with commonly used descriptions in parentheses) the components are

- Calendar (diary management)
- Content Services (file server)
- Discussions (bulletin board)
- Mail (e-mail)
- Mobile Collaboration (wireless access)
- Real-Time Collaboration (web conferencing and instant messaging)
- Search (web crawling search engine)
- Voicemail and Fax (voice mail and fax)
- Workspaces (grouping subsets of data into projects)

Accessed through portlets in the Portal front end with security controlled by the Oracle Internet Directory and the Single Sign-On service, all the Oracle Collaboration Suite components can be delivered to users through a web interface or through wireless. Many of the components also have their own client tools and development kits. The components work together to provide a collaborative business solution. Thus, when scheduling meetings with Calendar, Mail can distribute the details to participants together with relevant documents from Content Services. While each component fills a useful function in its own right (and some can even be deployed independently of the rest of the suite), it is through exploiting their integration that businesses will gain the most benefit from an Oracle Collaboration Suite deployment. The following sections describe each component.

Calendar

Oracle Corporation could have developed its own diary management package. It didn't. Instead, it bought a well-established and very functional product and adapted it to the Oracle environment. As far as the user is concerned, Calendar is an Oracle product and fully integrated with the rest of the Oracle Collaboration Suite. To an administrator it is still apparent that it is, to a degree, a self-contained product coming from a different development environment. This will become clear in Chapter 7 on Calendar configuration and administration. But to the user, Calendar is part of the suite.

An important point is that Calendar can be installed as an independent product. It comes with its own (non-Oracle) database, and while it can be accessed through the standard Oracle Collaboration Suite web and wireless interfaces, it also has its own desktop client tools. There are also options to control, configure, and monitor Calendar independently of the rest of Oracle Collaboration Suite.

Calendar is a tool for time management and resource scheduling. The information is maintained centrally in real time. And while on the topic of *time*, note that Calendar is fully time-zone aware. Every Calendar user has his or her own diary, known as an *agenda*. Within this agenda, a user can block off time with meetings and also define tasks. Meetings are scheduled events with a start and end time and can last for any period. Tasks keep track of work that should be completed in a certain time frame. Documents can be attached to meetings or tasks, and you can set up reminders for meetings, events, and deadlines. The Calendar Desktop Client can be used to record contact details, as can the Microsoft Outlook address book through the Oracle Connector for Outlook.

Because Calendar data is stored centrally, it can be used as a collaboration tool as well as a personal time manager. It has real-time conflict detection and resolution facilities to aid with scheduling resources and meetings. Both the web and desktop clients (including the Connector for Outlook) can accept a list of required personnel and resources and suggest times available for all attendees. You can also view and update other people's schedules, security rules permitting. In some cases, resources or people may be protected by a requirement for approval from the resource's controller; this is done through generating e-mail requesting the resource.

As with all Oracle Collaboration Suite components, Calendar is integrated with the Oracle Internet Directory. This means that users do not have to request Calendar accounts, and administrators do not have to create them manually; the accounts can be provisioned automatically by the Oracle Internet Directory. If Calendar is deployed independently, it can maintain its own user identities or be connected to a number of third-party LDAP (Lightweight Directory Access Protocol) servers.

There are three mainstream Calendar client programs: the Oracle Calendar Desktop Client, designed specifically for Calendar; the web client; and the Oracle Connector for Outlook. In addition to these, there are facilities for synchronizing Calendar data with PDA or Microsoft ActiveSync devices (such as Pocket PC). As the Calendar data is stored centrally, any user on any platform can query other users' diaries and schedule other users' time irrespective of the platform or client they are using. Use of the various clients is completely interchangeable, though the Oracle Calendar Desktop Client is the most functional user interface. It is available for all popular desktop environments: Microsoft Windows, Macintosh, and (through X Window System) Linux and Solaris. Both the Calendar Desktop Client and the Oracle Connector for Outlook can be downloaded through the web interface.

The following three figures show the Calendar Desktop Client, the Connector for Outlook, and the web client all showing the same data. Figure 1-4 shows the Desktop Client.

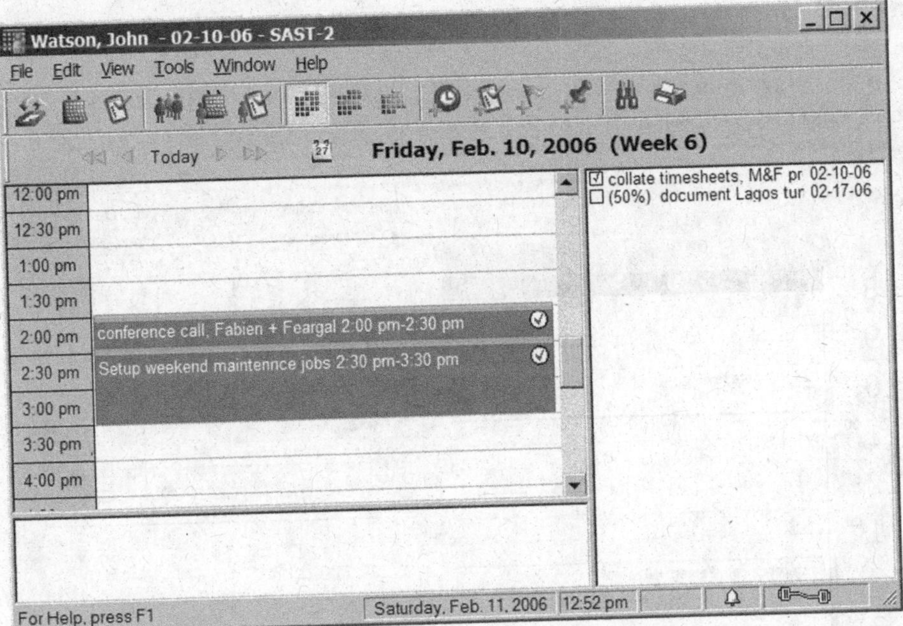

Figure 1-4. *The Calendar Desktop Client showing an appointment and a task*

Figure 1-5 shows the Connector for Outlook.

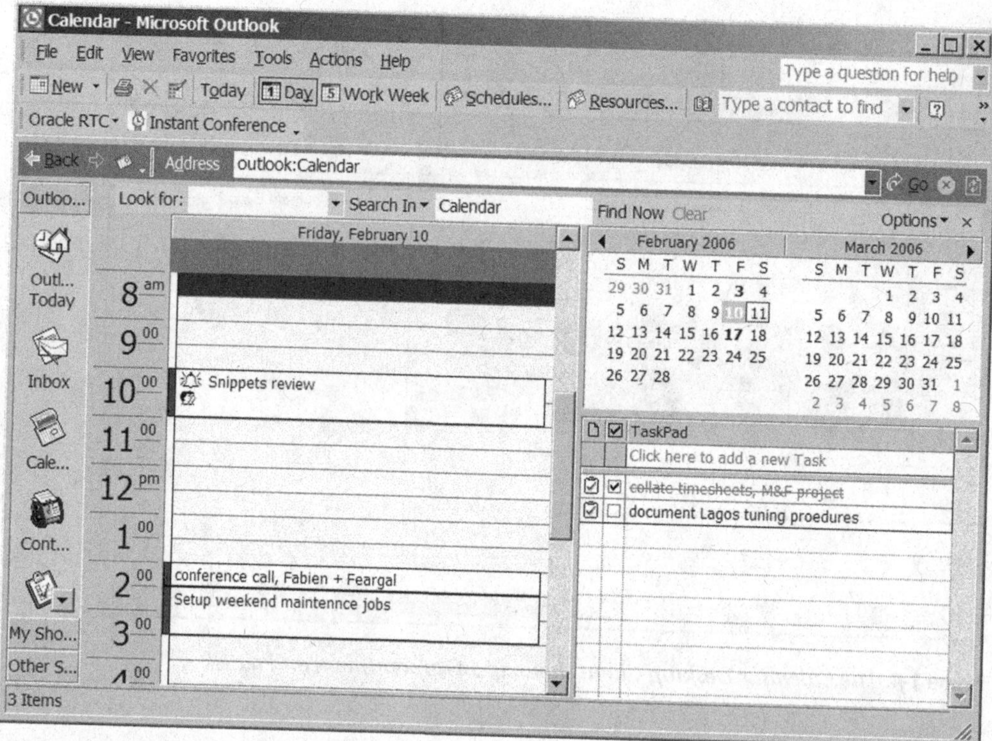

Figure 1-5. *An appointment and task viewed in Microsoft Outlook, enabled with the Outlook Connector*

Figure 1-6 shows the web client.

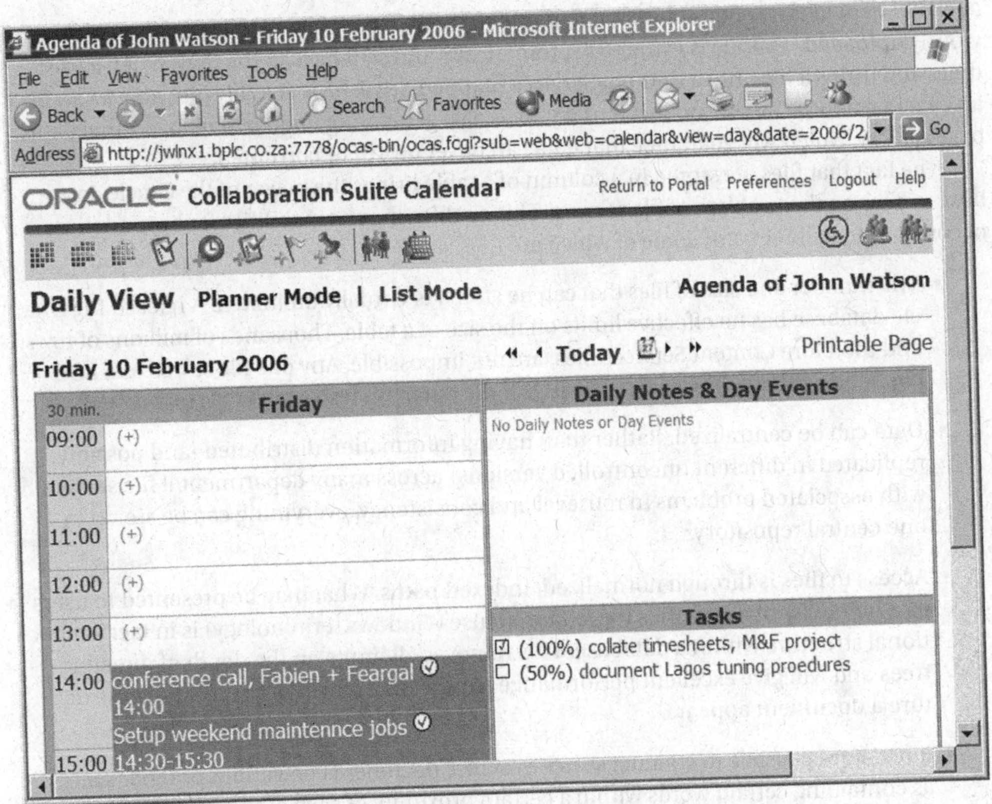

Figure 1-6. *The web interface to Calendar showing an appointment and a task*

Content Services

Oracle Collaboration Suite Content Services is just a file server. But that is like saying that the Stones are just a rock and roll band. Content Services far surpasses the popular conception of a file server.

Yes, Content Services is a standard file server at its most basic. After installing the Oracle Drive client software and configuring a connection to the Content Services server, users on Windows PCs can map a drive letter to the Content Services node using a command such as `net use g: \\"Oracle Drive\jwlnx1"` or the equivalent series of keystrokes involving right-clicking the My Computer icon. Then users can open the file server drive letter, see files and folders, and double-click them to open them, or drag-and-drop files between the file server and their local PC disks. Content Services will appear to be exactly the same as a Windows or a NetWare file server. There will even be the same prompts for username and password. But in the background, things are very different.

All Content Services data is stored in an Oracle database. When a user double-clicks a filename in what he thinks is a file server directory, he is in fact executing a SELECT statement and retrieving a row from a table (SELECT is the SQL command used to retrieve data from a relational database). One column of that row is a LOB (large object) that contains a file previously uploaded. This file is extracted automatically and sent back to the user. When a user drags and drops a file onto a Content Services mapped drive, he is actually inserting a row into an Oracle database table. And incidentally, he is also generating undo and redo: normal database activity, which will guarantee that data can never be lost or corrupted.

The fact that files are stored in a column of a table brings the power of the Oracle database to bear on the problem of file serving. This enables many capabilities far beyond those of conventional file servers, some of which are

- The number and size of files that can be stored is virtually unlimited. A release 10*g* Oracle database has no effective limits on the size of a table. Thousands of millions of rows, and therefore Content Services files, are not impossible. Any one file stored as a LOB could be terabytes big (earlier releases of the database restricted LOBs to *only* 4GB).
- Data can be centralized. Rather than having information distributed (and possibly replicated in different uncontrolled versions) across many departmental file servers with associated problems in retrieval and consistency, everything can be stored in one central repository.
- Access to files is through normalized, indexed paths. What may be presented to users as a hierarchy of directories (or *folders*, to use Windows terminology) is in fact a relational structure within a database. This removes all limits on the depth of directory trees and will give excellent performance irrespective of where in the storage structure a document appears.
- It becomes possible to conduct searches across documents on various criteria (such as containing certain words within a certain proximity of each other) regardless of the applications that generated the documents or the directories in which they are stored; they are all in the same table, so these variations don't really matter.
- Reading a file is done by an intelligent server-side process, not directly by the client. This process can intervene and carry out operations such as format conversion (from perhaps Microsoft Word to WordPerfect) or virus checking before sending the file out to the client.
- Virus attacks can be eliminated. Since the files do not in fact exist as files but rather as a column in a row of a table, the standard methods by which virus programs propagate and cause damage cannot succeed.
- As files are not physically stored in directories, it becomes possible to have the same file appear in many different places with different users being presented with the file in different contexts. What appears to be a directory is in fact a set of pointers to rows in a table. But files never need to be replicated; there need be only one actual copy, which can be seen in several workspaces.
- When a file is retrieved, edited, and saved back to the server this can create multiple versions. Each save of the file can be in a newly inserted row (rather than updating the existing row), leaving the previous version unchanged.

- Through use of different protocol servers it becomes possible for users to retrieve files from Content Services using whatever client they please. Windows users can use the Oracle Drive utility and access files through what appears to be standard Windows drive mapping; alternatively, the content can be presented through FTP or NFS file sharing if the user has the appropriate client tools. HTTP is standard and available on all client platforms.
- WebDAV (Web Distributed Authoring and Versioning) file checkout and check-in facilities with file locking are always available for clients that use it, such as Windows XP users who will get to it through the Web Folders extension to Windows Explorer in the Network Places icon.
- Standard Oracle database facilities for high availability, backup, restore, recovery, and flashback mean that no data will ever be lost; even if accidentally deleted, it will always be possible to recover lost files.

Apart from these advantages to users, Content Services also improves on conventional file servers from the management viewpoint. The scalability means that all the file servers currently in use in an organization can be replaced, with associated savings in hardware, operating system licenses, and administration effort. A single DBA can administer a single database containing files that were previously distributed across hundreds of departmental file servers. This administration will include all the standard performance tuning, backup, and general maintenance work, no matter what platform the database is on. There are no special skills required.

Data stored within Content Services is available to all the other Oracle Collaboration Suite components. It can therefore be used as the source of documents to be distributed with e-mail or referenced by Calendar, Search, or Workspaces.

The following four figures show the same content presented through various interfaces: the web interface, an FTP client, WebDAV on Windows XP, and Oracle Drive (the SMB look-alike). Figure 1-7 shows the web interface to Content Services.

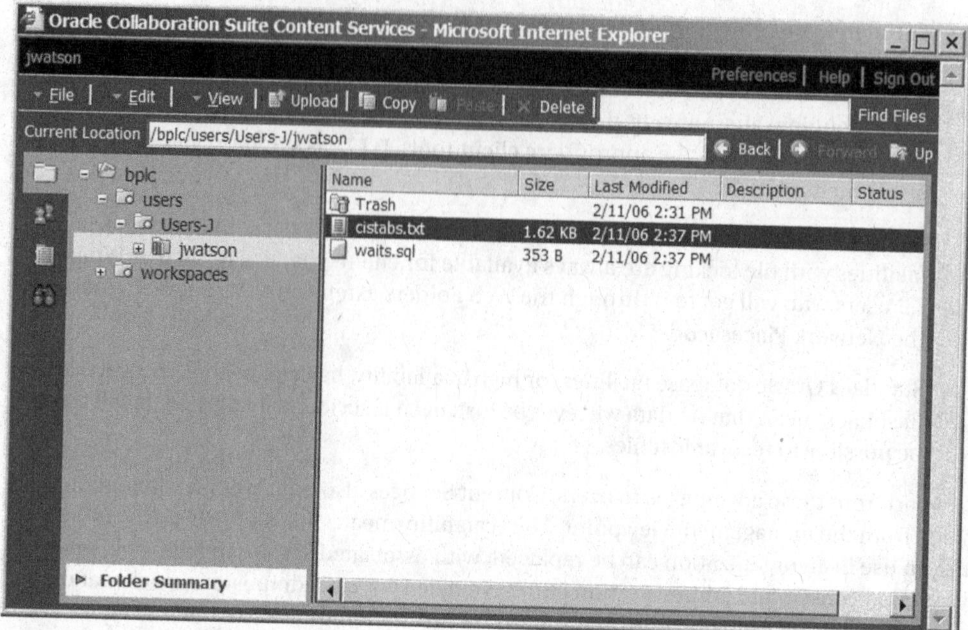

Figure 1-7. *The web interface to Content Services showing two uploaded files*

Figure 1-8 shows the FTP interface to Content Services.
Figure 1-9 shows the WebDAV interface to Content Services.

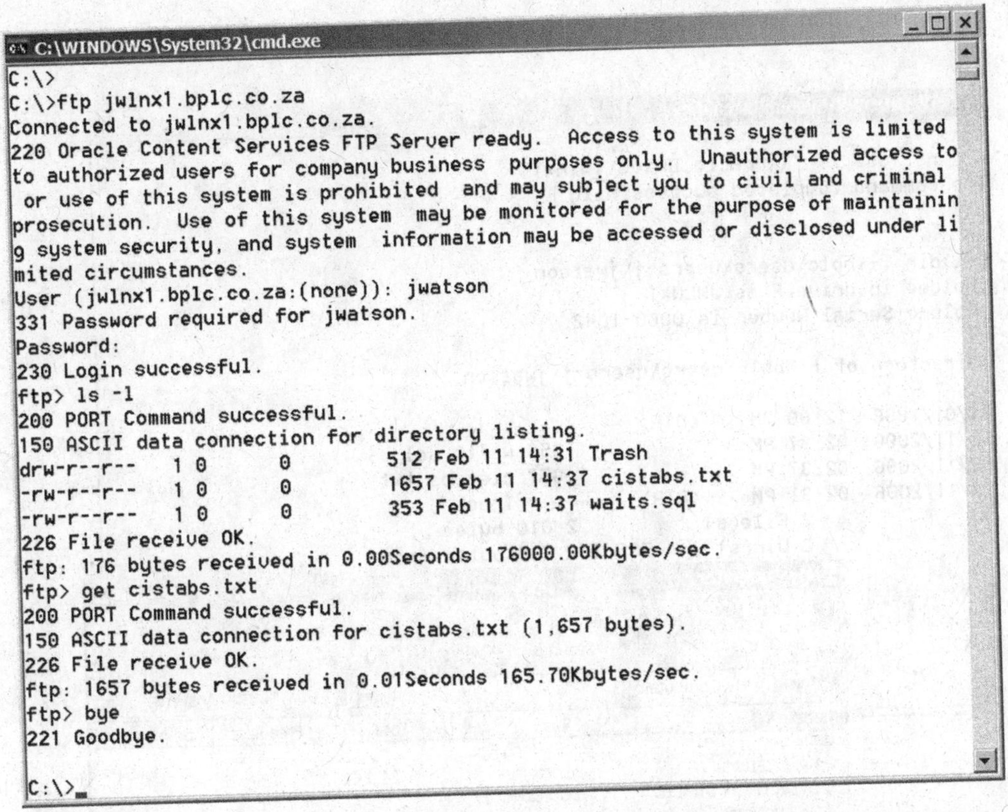

C:\WINDOWS\System32\cmd.exe
C:\>
C:\>ftp jwlnx1.bplc.co.za
Connected to jwlnx1.bplc.co.za.
220 Oracle Content Services FTP Server ready. Access to this system is limited
to authorized users for company business purposes only. Unauthorized access to
or use of this system is prohibited and may subject you to civil and criminal
prosecution. Use of this system may be monitored for the purpose of maintainin
g system security, and system information may be accessed or disclosed under li
mited circumstances.
User (jwlnx1.bplc.co.za:(none)): jwatson
331 Password required for jwatson.
Password:
230 Login successful.
ftp> ls -l
200 PORT Command successful.
150 ASCII data connection for directory listing.
drw-r--r-- 1 0 0 512 Feb 11 14:31 Trash
-rw-r--r-- 1 0 0 1657 Feb 11 14:37 cistabs.txt
-rw-r--r-- 1 0 0 353 Feb 11 14:37 waits.sql
226 File receive OK.
ftp: 176 bytes received in 0.00Seconds 176000.00Kbytes/sec.
ftp> get cistabs.txt
200 PORT Command successful.
150 ASCII data connection for cistabs.txt (1,657 bytes).
226 File receive OK.
ftp: 1657 bytes received in 0.01Seconds 165.70Kbytes/sec.
ftp> bye
221 Goodbye.
C:\>

Figure 1-8. *The FTP interface to Content Services showing how to connect to the server and download a file*

jwatson
File Edit View Favorites Tools Help
Back Search Folders
Address http://jwlnx1.bplc.co.za:7778/content/dav/bplc/users/
Go
Norton AntiVirus
Name
Internet Address
Size
Type
Modified
Trash
http://jwlnx1.bplc.co.za:7778/content/dav...
Web Folder
2/11/200
cistabs.txt
http://jwlnx1.bplc.co.za:7778/content/dav...
1.61 KB
Text Document
2/11/200
waits.sql
http://jwlnx1.bplc.co.za:7778/content/dav...
353 Bytes
SQL File
2/11/200

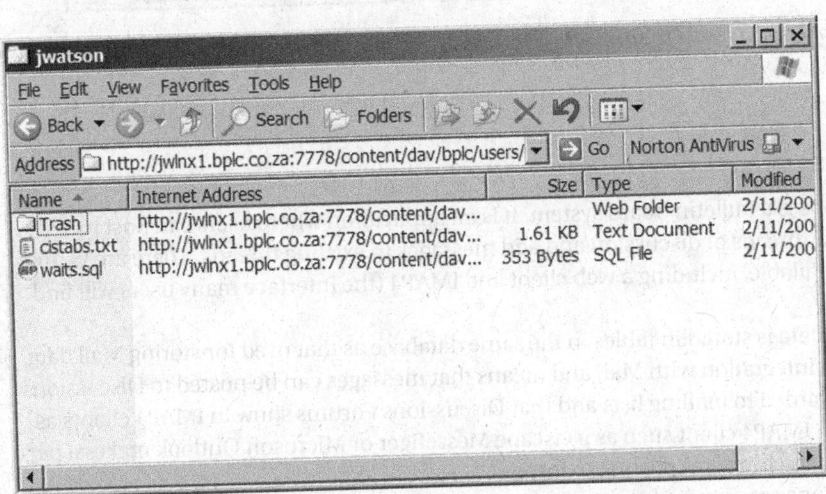

Figure 1-9. *The WebDAV interface to Content Services, accessed from a Windows XP client and displaying like any local Windows folder*

Figure 1-10 shows the Oracle Drive interface from a DOS prompt and from Explorer.

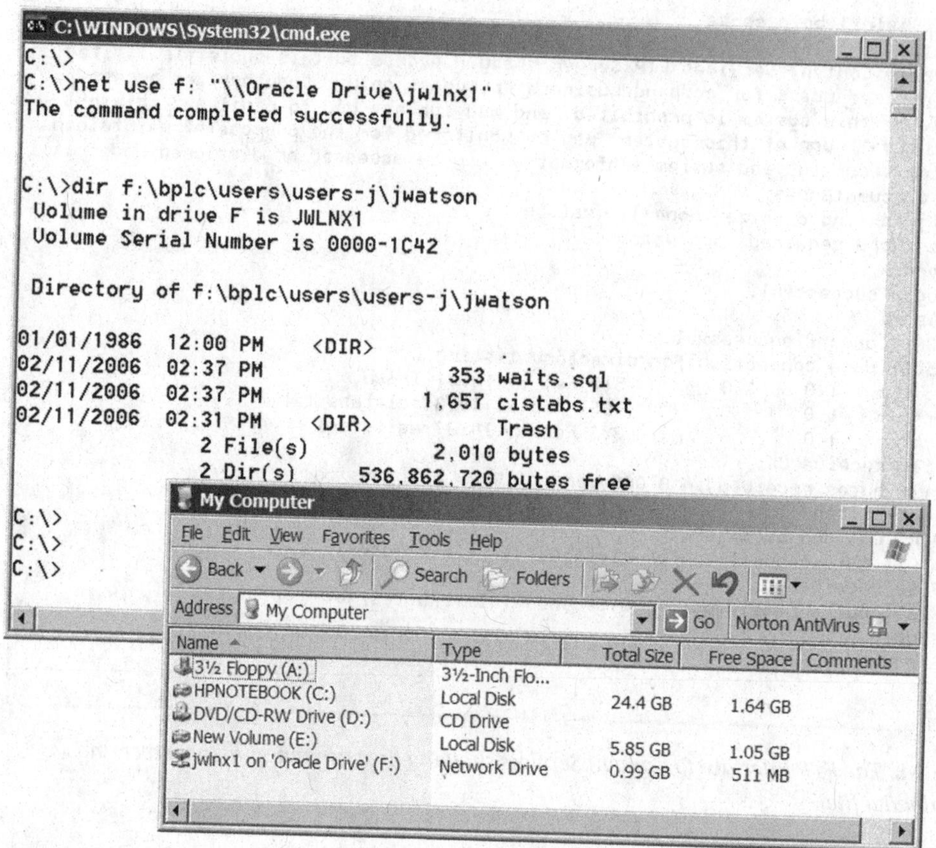

Figure 1-10. *Use of Oracle Drive to simulate Windows drive mapping from a command prompt and through Explorer*

Discussions

Oracle Discussions is a bulletin board system. It is an application where users can post messages to start new threads of discussion and add messages to existing threads. There are various user interfaces available, including a web client and IMAP4 (the interface many users will find most useful).

Discussions data is stored in tables in the same database as that used for storing Mail data. This gives perfect integration with Mail and means that messages can be posted to Discussions from Mail or forwarded to mailing lists and that Discussions Forums show in IMAP4 clients as shared folders. An IMAP4 client such as Netscape Messenger or Microsoft Outlook makes a perfect interface for searching and posting to forums.

The Discussions security and message structure is multitiered. First, there are categories. A *category* can have other categories nested within it, and it can contain forums. A *forum* is the next level of storage, typically, messages on a certain theme. Within a forum, messages are grouped into topics, or threads. Different users have different privileges at the various levels. At one extreme, a category administrator can create other categories and forums in his own category, edit and move messages, and assign privileges to other users. At the other extreme, a user might only be able to view and search a small subset of one forum and have no posting privileges at all. The various privileges include creators, administrators, moderators, writers, and readers.

Discussions has the usual bulletin board features for users (starting new threads, adding to existing threads) and also for management; messages can be vetted for suitability in moderated forums before publishing.

Figure 1-11 shows Discussions in a browser.

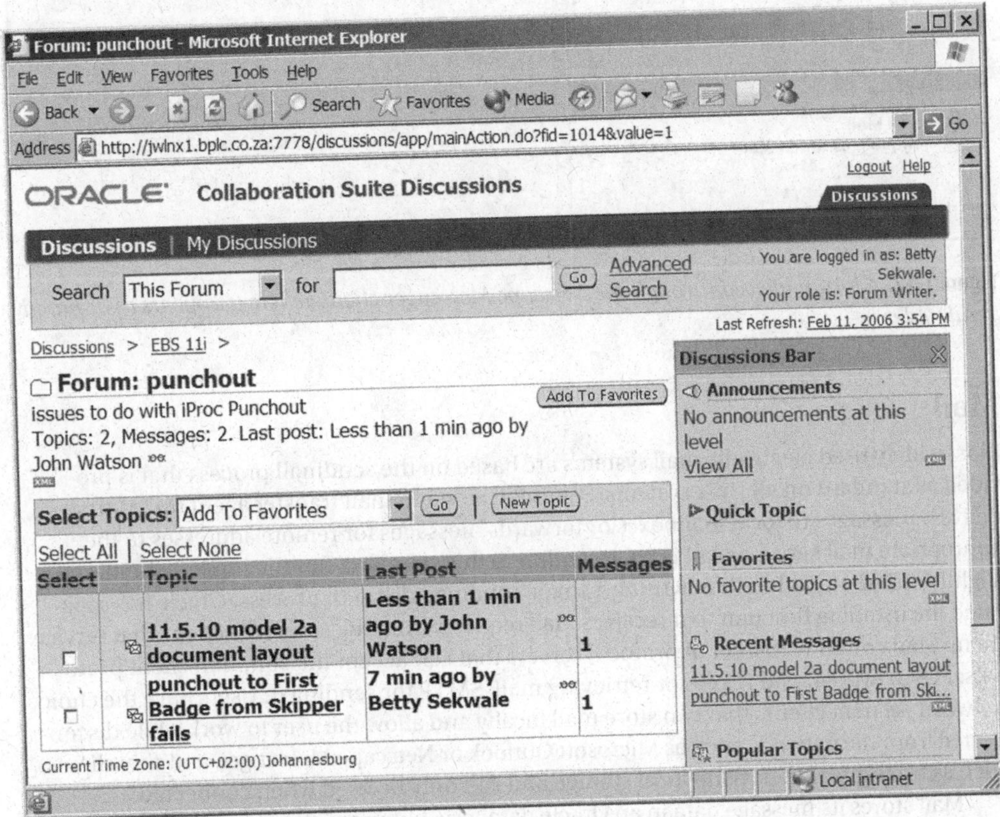

Figure 1-11. *A forum viewed through a browser*

Figure 1-12 shows a forum in the Netscape Messenger IMAP client.

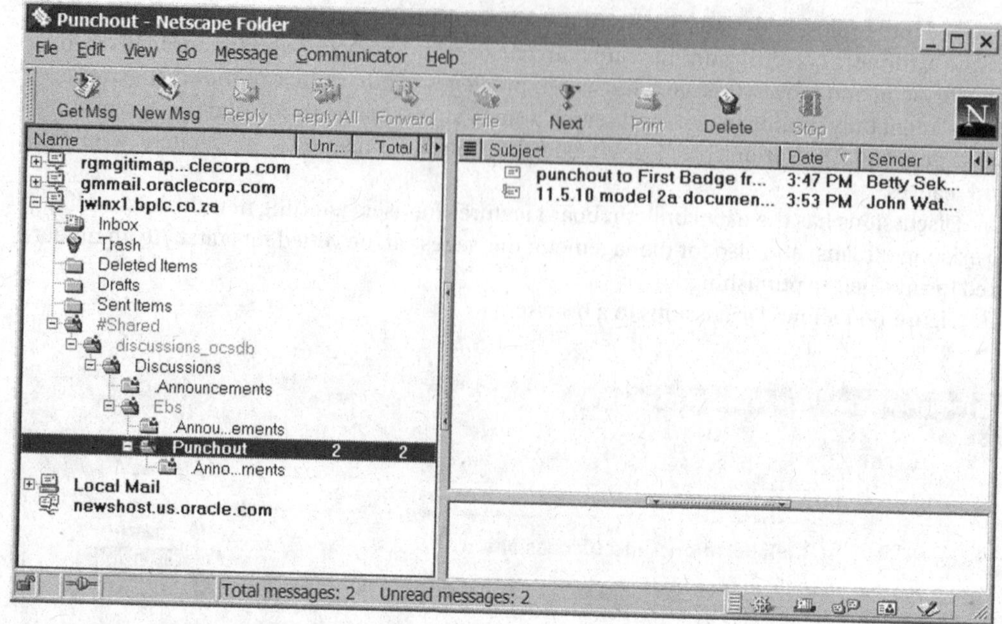

Figure 1-12. *A forum viewed through the Netscape Messenger client, where it appears as a shared mail folder*

Mail

Most widely used electronic mail systems are based on the sendmail process that is provided as standard on all Unix systems. Sendmail acts as a mail transfer agent (MTA) that delivers messages to local mailboxes or forwards messages for remote addresses to the appropriate mail servers. Mail is no exception to this standard, but the implementation is slightly different. Rather than writing a single sendmail daemon process, Oracle has separated the listening function that receives Mail requests from the server functions that service them. Mail comes with a set of protocol servers that can accept the common client protocols: POP3, IMAP4, and HTTP for retrieving mail; SMTP for sending it. Users have the choice between *fat* mail clients that can store mail locally and allow the user to work while disconnected from the network, such as Microsoft Outlook or Netscape Messenger, and *thin* clients, such as browsers that have no local storage and can only be used when connected.

Mail stores its message data in an Oracle database, but users' details are stored in an Oracle Internet Directory. This gives Mail its integration with the rest of Oracle Collaboration Suite. Oracle Internet Directory is used as the store for all distribution lists, address books, and user information.

Mail provides the usual facilities one would expect from any mail server: it will accept messages for remote users and forward them to the appropriate mail server; and it will accept messages for local users and store them until requested. In addition, it can be configured for virus checking and spam filtering. Mail is also the component that manages network news newsgroups. You can use your Mail server to host newsgroups locally and to replicate them with other external network news servers.

The virus check is implemented with the Symantec AntiVirus Scan Engine, or SAVSE. When run on the outbound mail server process, SAVSE can scan all messages being sent out, and scan all messages coming when run on the inbound mail server process. You can also use SAVSE to pass right through the Mail store, checking all existing Mail data. Provided that the virus definitions are kept up-to-date, this should protect users against any virus threat.

Mail protects users from spam with a built-in spam filter. This can be configured to reject mail on three criteria:

- Sender's address and domain
- Recipient's address and domain
- Address and domain of the relaying mail node

Apart from filtering nominated addresses, the filter can be configured to monitor the rate at which addresses are sending mail and automatically block addresses where the rate is suspiciously high. What it cannot do is filter mail based on the content; should that be required, Mail can be protected with third-party products that will block messages before they reach the incoming SMTP server.

There is no limit to the volume of mail that a user can store, or for how long, other than any limits that the administrator chooses to establish. It is not uncommon for users to keep every e-mail they receive plus a copy of every e-mail they send from the moment they join a company to the moment they leave. Mail can handle this and has a special feature designed to make this practical; it can automatically migrate mail data to what is known as *tertiary storage* once it is a certain number of days old. This tertiary storage is a separate tablespace that could be located on storage devices that have reduced performance and fault-tolerance characteristics compared to the higher priced devices used for the more current data. This migration to tertiary storage will happen automatically without users' knowledge. The e-mail will still be accessible through whatever mail client they are using but may take marginally longer to retrieve.

Mail can be configured with rules. A rule has an owner, an event, conditions, and actions. The scope of a rule is determined by the owner. Rules owned by the Mail administrator could apply to all e-mail, or users can create their own rules that will only apply to their own mailbox. Typical triggering events are the receipt or sending of messages, or opening or deletion. It is the use of rules that lets users configure automatic replies and more complex processing. For every rule, there can be a number of conditions (usually based on the content of certain mail header values) with different actions associated with them.

Figure 1-13 shows the Mail user interface through the web client.

Figure 1-14 shows the Mail user interface through the Netscape Messenger IMAP client.

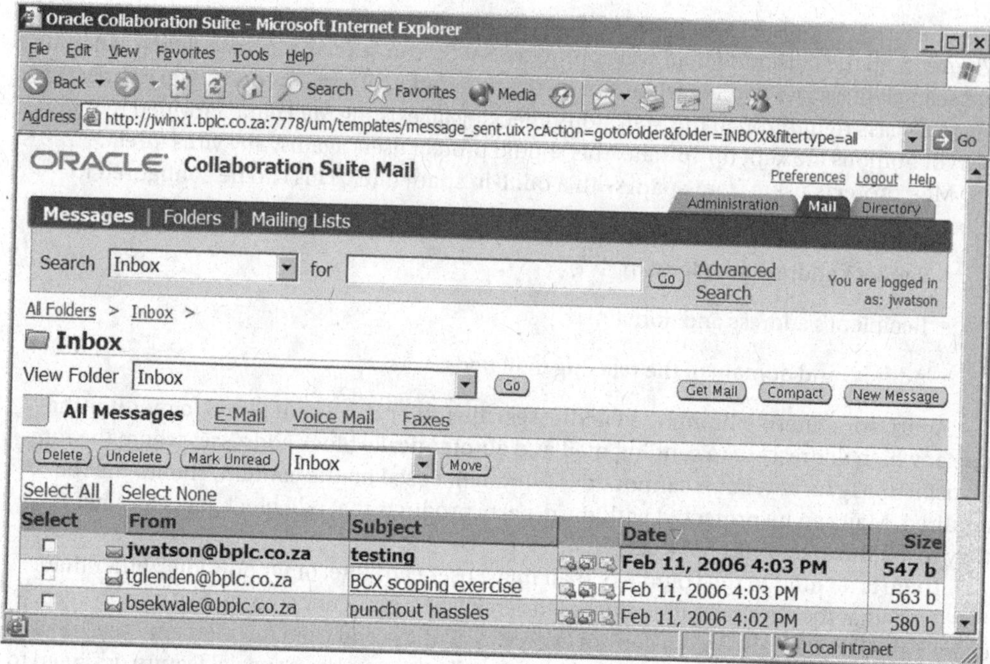

Figure 1-13. *The Mail web client*

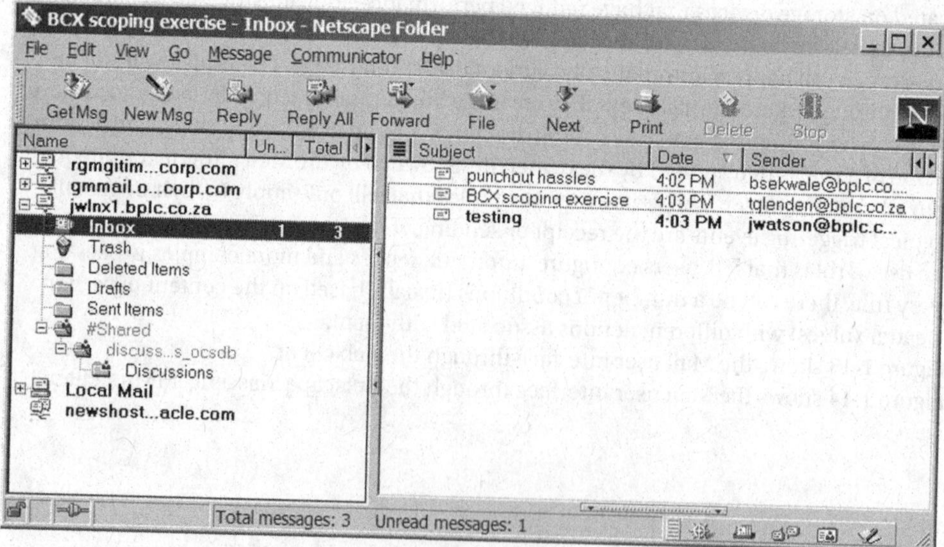

Figure 1-14. *E-mail viewed through the Netscape Messenger client*

Figure 1-15 shows the Mail user interface through the Microsoft Outlook Connector.

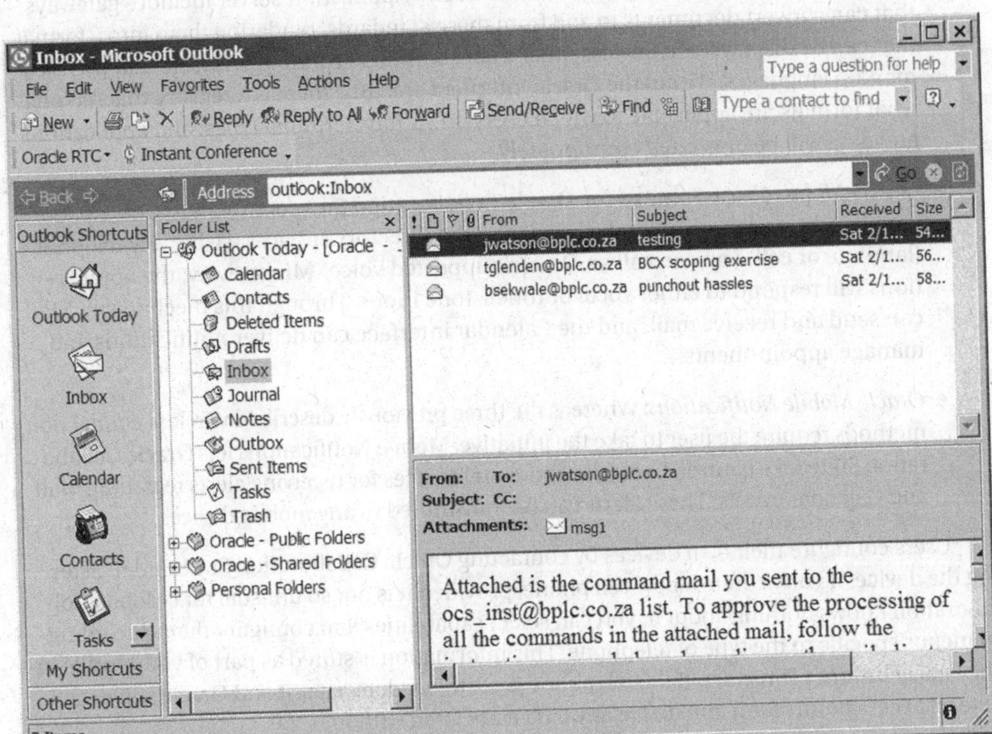

Figure 1-15. *E-mail viewed through the Microsoft Outlook client*

Mobile Collaboration

Oracle Mobile Collaboration gives users access to their mail, files, diary, and corporate directories from any mobile device with wireless access. This access can be on-demand, but by using Oracle Mobile Push Mail (based on the Push IMAP, or P-IMAP, protocol) e-mail can be forwarded automatically in real time as it arrives at the Mail server. If the device is not permanently connected, there are facilities for downloading and resynchronizing data. Thus, you can use a cell phone or a PDA device for receiving and answering e-mail, tracking appointments, transmitting documents, or searching for contact details while working online or offline.

There are four possible technologies for wireless connection to Oracle Collaboration Suite:

- *Oracle Mobile Text*: This is the use of SMS (Short Message Service) messages to send and receive mail. It can also select files for e-mailing or faxing. Directory access lets you search the Oracle Internet Directory, and the integration with Calendar means that you can retrieve, create, and modify appointments.

- *Oracle Mobile Browser*: HTML is not the only standard for displaying documents. Other standards are XHTML, WML, and HDML. Oracle Application Server includes gateways that can convert documents to and from these standards, rendering them into a format that can be displayed on devices other than computers running browsers that use these markup languages. Within the Oracle Internet Directory, there is a registry that records what formats are applicable to which users on various terminal types, and applications and data will be presented appropriately.
- *Oracle Mobile Voice*: Some of the Oracle Collaboration Suite components are voice-enabled, among them Calendar, Mail, and the directory services. Using any telephone (landline or cell) you can call an Oracle-supported VoiceXML gateway; the applications will respond to either vocal or touch-tone input. Through this mechanism, Mail can send and receive mail, and the Calendar interface can deliver notifications and manage appointments.
- *Oracle Mobile Notifications*: Whereas the three previously described wireless connection methods require the user to take the initiative, Mobile Notifications lets Oracle Collaboration Suite take control. Users configure preferences for receiving alerts regarding Mail and Calendar events. These alerts can be transmitted to any mobile device.

Users configure their own devices by contacting Oracle Collaboration Suite and registering the device. If you acquire a new cell phone, provided it is not so unusual that Mobile Collaboration knows nothing about it, you can select capabilities and configure them according to menus specific to the type of telephone. This information is stored as part of your profile in the Oracle Internet Directory. If the telephone gets stolen, deregister it and Oracle will deactivate all access points for it and delete any data associated with it.

Real-Time Collaboration

An electronic mail system uses asynchronous message delivery: messages are sent but may not be received for some time. The recipient may not even be online at the time the message is sent. By contrast, an instant messaging system delivers messages in real time between users who are concurrently connected. Mail is not a tool for real-time collaboration. That requires instant messaging, as delivered by the Oracle Messenger component of Real-Time Collaboration. The other major facility provided by the Real-Time Collaboration component of Oracle Collaboration Suite is Web Conferencing.

It cannot be emphasized enough that Real-Time Collaboration is an exceptionally powerful tool for teamwork and team building in a modern working environment. In many organizations, teams consist of people who are geographically separated. The separation may be simply that some staff prefer to work from home—often a far more productive environment than any office—or it may be that staff are based in different cities and countries. An organization based on virtual teams can be exceptionally versatile. Team members can be assembled for a project from a pool of staff on an ad hoc basis without needing to worry about whether the particular staff members are conveniently located for meetings. When meetings are necessary, Web Conferencing can substitute for physical meetings. During working hours, instant messaging between team members can build up team spirit and keep all members in touch. This is far more effective than using telephone calls, which are usually only between two people. Instant messages can be broadcast across the whole group, keeping everyone involved. They also tend to be less disruptive than telephone calls and can be read offline if a team member is engaged elsewhere.

Real-Time Collaboration is tightly linked to Mail and Calendar. If a meeting is marked as a Web Conference when created in Calendar, it will be scheduled as such in the Real-Time Collaboration client and users will be able to enter the conference directly from the invitation displayed in the Calendar client or from a Mail invitation. Mail clients can send and receive messages through Messenger, and connecting to a Mail client can update your availability as shown to other currently connected Messenger users.

Oracle Messenger is an instant messaging system that lets you have "chat" sessions with individuals or between all members of a group. It has the added capability that any two people can have a normal audio conversation using microphones and loud speakers attached to their PCs; this conversation is carried by the Voice over IP (VoIP) protocol. Users can register themselves as being available for chat, either through the Messenger Console or through Mail. The Console is a Windows client downloadable from Oracle Collaboration Suite. All chat sessions, whether between individuals or groups, are recorded, and both users and administrators can view these recordings.

Note that to use the Real-Time Collaboration components, it is necessary to download and install some client-side software. As of the time of this writing, this was only available for Windows clients.

Figure 1-16 shows a Messenger session displayed in the Messenger Console.

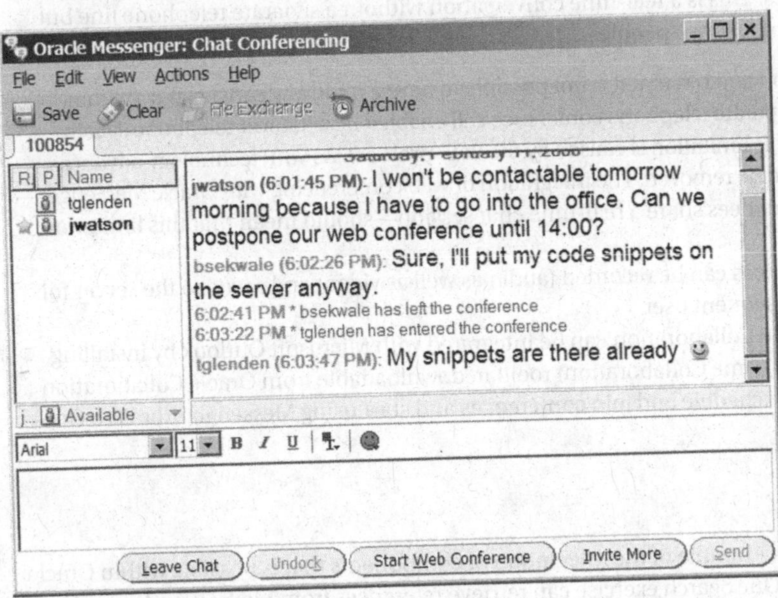

Figure 1-16. *A Messenger chat session in progress*

A *web conference* is two or more users seeing in real time the same windows on their terminals and listening to the same audio. The web conference has one host and any number of attendees. The host controls what is broadcast from his desktop to the attendees. It is not possible for attendees to do anything other than watch, unless the host grants presenting privileges to the other users, in which case they can interact with the host's desktop. This gives the effect of a virtual whiteboard; attendees can take turns editing the content. Attendees can, of course, do unrelated work while attending a conference. The web conference appears in one window and will not impact any other applications that are open.

A web conference includes instant messaging. All attendees can send messages to the conference, which will be displayed in a scrolling window.

The audio aspect of a web conference has restricted capabilities. The restrictions are not caused by limitations of Oracle Collaboration Suite but by limitations in currently available equipment and communication protocols. There are three possibilities for audio:

- Use an external telephone conference call. The call will be recorded as part of the conference for future playback and is thus integrated into the conference. This technique gives the highest functionality and closely simulates a physical meeting; any and all attendees can talk to the whole group.
- Broadcast the host's voice using a microphone on his terminal to all attendees who will listen over speakers attached to their PCs. This uses VoIP and does not require a separate telephone conference call; but the audio communication is only one-way. This mode is ideal for delivering live demonstrations or lectures. Instant messages let attendees give real-time feedback to the conference.
- Use VoIP with microphones and speakers attached to the PCs for a conference of only two attendees. This is a real-time conversation without a separate telephone line but is restricted to just two people.

The limitation on audio is that it is not possible to have a multiway conversation within a group without a separate telephone conference call enabled by whatever telephone switchboard is available. This limitation is caused by the VoIP protocol. As VoIP technology advances, this limitation should be removed. The integration of web conferencing with Oracle Messenger—meaning that all attendees share a real-time chat session—should mean that this limitation is not significant.

All web conferences can be recorded (audio as well as video) and saved to the server for playback by any subsequent user.

Oracle Real-Time Collaboration can be integrated with Microsoft Outlook by installing the Oracle RTC (Real-Time Collaboration) toolbar, downloadable from Oracle Collaboration Suite. This lets users schedule and join conferences and start using Messenger from the Outlook client.

Search

Search is an excellent example of the integration of components that is possible within Oracle Collaboration Suite. One Search exercise can retrieve references from Mail, Calendar, and Content Services, and also from libraries of HTML pages stored externally. This cross-product search capability is based on the Oracle Ultra Search web crawling facility, a standard install in Oracle databases.

Searches are not conducted against live data in real time. They are conducted against indexes built up in advance. These indexes are created by *searchlets*, each designed to search a particular data source. Any one search operation passes through all this indexed content to produce a collated result set. The searchlets update their own indexes from the source data on regular schedules.

The indexed data is based on these attributes for each data source:

- *Content Services*: The contents of files, no matter what application produced them, in public folders and in shared folders accessible to the user conducting the search and his private folders.
- *Mail*: The subjects and (optionally) the body of e-mail in the user's mailbox.
- *Calendar*: The titles and locations of the user's meetings, and the names of his tasks and events.
- *External HTML files*: The title, author, subject, and description tags of all the documents accessible to the Search engine.

Figure 1-17 shows a search conducted from the web client across all sources of data. The only hit is a Mail message.

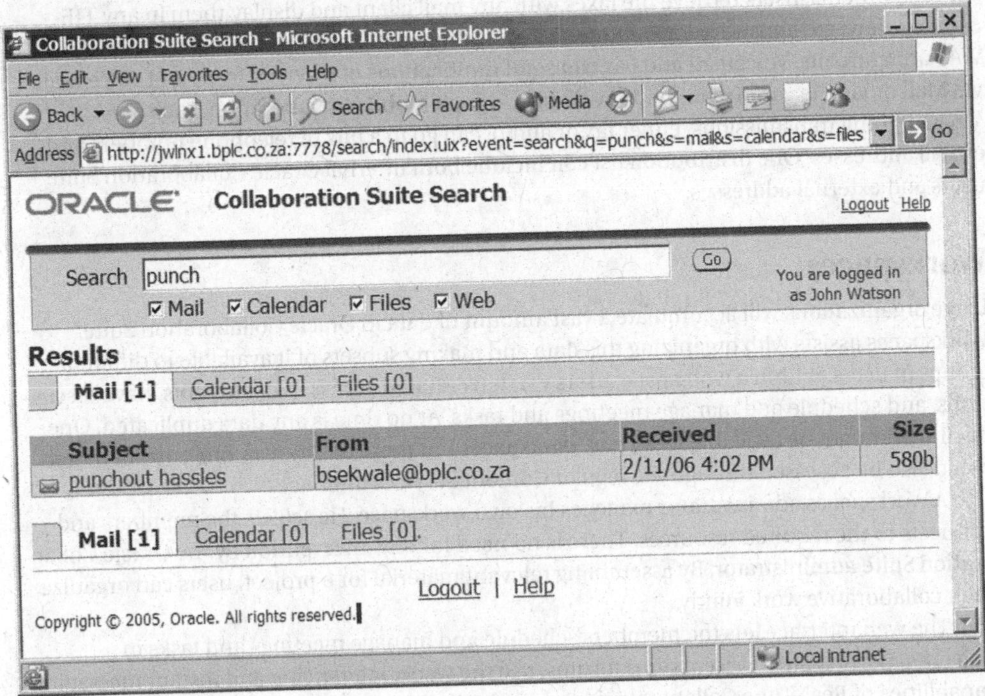

Figure 1-17. *The result of a search for the string "punch" across all components*

Search is based on the Ultra Search product shipped with the Oracle database, with indexes generated by the Oracle Text facility, which can comprehend and index documents in hundreds of different formats. The preconfiguration of Search will let it index data in Mail, Content Services, and Calendar. You can subsequently instruct Search to index data in any data source accessible through a URL, or in any Oracle database. The Search application displays results grouped into Mail, Content Services, Calendar, and Web. This last category includes all the user-defined Search data sources.

Voicemail and Fax

Many organizations will already have centralized facilities for voice mail and fax based on a telephone switch. Oracle Collaboration Suite can work with such solutions or replace them. It will typically give end users greater flexibility in information retrieval than other systems because of its adherence to standards. Voice mail is stored as WAV files, and faxes as TIF files. Browser clients can retrieve them with HTTP; Mail clients can retrieve them with IMAP4 or POP3. This gives users complete freedom in choosing audio players or image display software. All Voicemail and Fax data is stored in the Mail datastore and is therefore available to Search.

Every Oracle Collaboration Suite user should be issued a telephone number that will be recognized by the organization's private branch exchange (PBX). The PBX forwards faxes over a VoIP gateway to Mail. Alternatively if there is no suitable existing PBX, telephony cards installed in a server will work just as well as the entry point for faxes. When saved by Mail as TIF attachments, users retrieve the faxes with any mail client and display them in any TIF-capable viewer. Unanswered telephone calls are handled in a similar manner and saved as WAV attachments. Voicemail and Fax can send notifications of received faxes and voice mail via Mail or via the various methods available through Mobile Collaboration, such as SMS.

Outgoing transmissions, either fax or audio, can go to a mix of telephone numbers and e-mail addresses. One distribution list can include both internal Oracle Collaboration Suite users and external addresses.

Workspaces

Large organizations will accumulate a vast amount of data in Oracle Collaboration Suite. Workspaces assists with organizing this data and making subsets of it available to different groups of users. Within a workspace, users can have shared access to documents, have discussions, and schedule and manage meetings and tasks. At no time is any data duplicated. One document might be available in several workspaces but there is only ever one copy of it that could also be accessed through the regular Content Services interface.

A Workspaces administrator manages his own workspace. He selects the members and connects to the required resources. There is no need for any intervention by the Oracle Collaboration Suite administrator. By assembling relevant material for a project, users can organize their collaborative work jointly.

The web interface lets the members schedule and manage meetings and tasks in Calendar, participate in Discussions forums, use the web conferencing and instant messaging capabilities of Real-Time Collaboration, and use Mail within the restricted scope of their own projects. However, all of a workspace's content is in fact stored in the component where it belongs.

The Whole Is Greater Than the Parts

The preceding run through all the Oracle Collaboration Suite components should have made it clear that while each component is valuable in its own right, it is the fact that they are integrated into a suite that can really empower an organization and its staff. Even though some components have their own client tools, they all share access to the common security model, and they all share common datastores. The exception to this rule is Calendar, which can be deployed independently and therefore has its own datastore; but the flow of information between Calendar and the other components is fully automated and in real time. This behind-the-scenes integration increases the power of each component. The web client is a common interface to all components; this central entry point to the system makes all the applications very accessible and usable.

The interconnection between the application components adds enormously to the value of each one. As an example, when arranging a web conference, the scheduling and diary checking will be done by Calendar; the documents to be discussed will be retrieved from Content Services; the invitations and acknowledgements will be carried over Mail and Mobile Collaboration; and Real-Time Collaboration will pull everything together when the conference takes place. The whole process can take place within the context of a workgroup.

Part of deploying Oracle Collaboration Suite must be an education program to introduce users to the advantages of dumping all existing self-contained applications whose functionality can be provided by Oracle Collaboration Suite. Users must be encouraged to use Oracle Collaboration Suite as a single point for storing and collating information. The more use users make of it and the more they exploit the ability to share information with each other and across components, the greater the benefits they will realize.

CHAPTER 2

Oracle Application Server Architecture and Components

At first sight, Oracle Application Server 10*g* is a huge and terrifying environment within which to work. As you become familiar with it, it will remain huge but no longer terrifying. A problem that beginners to Application Server often suffer from is being unable to see the wood for the trees. There are so many interacting components that it may seem impossible to grasp the overall picture of what is going on. It has to be said that the documentation may not help with this. This chapter will describe the entirety of Oracle Application Server and drill down to the individual components.

Oracle Collaboration Suite is a set of services that run in the Oracle Application Server environment. This introduction to Oracle Application Server will be sufficient for understanding its function as a part of the technology stack that enables the Oracle Collaboration Suite. The initial configuration of Oracle Application Server after an Oracle Collaboration Suite install will work, but to tune a large and complex Oracle Application Server site for optimal performance requires extensive knowledge. At large sites, there will be an Oracle Application Server administrator in addition to the Oracle Collaboration Suite administrator (not to mention the database administrator, the system administrator, the network administrator, the directory administrator, and all the other specialist roles one finds in a large IT installation).

Oracle Application Server Instances, Farms, and Clusters

In Oracle Application Server terms, an *instance* is a set of processes and memory structures created by running the Oracle Application Server executable code installed into an Oracle home. An Oracle *home* is the directory structure created when an Oracle product is installed. One Oracle Application Server Oracle home can only support one Oracle Application Server instance; by contrast, an Oracle home with the database software installed within it can support multiple running database instances (always provided that they have different names).

Although one Oracle home can only support one Oracle Application Server instance, it is possible for one web site to consist of multiple instances, each installed into its own Oracle home, and the homes can optionally be installed on different machines. This gives Oracle Application Server its scalability and fault tolerance. What appears to be one web site with a single point of entry for the end user may in fact consist of multiple Oracle Application Server instances on multiple machines. By enabling load balancing across these instances, and session failover from one instance to another, an Oracle Application Server web site can be configured to support an unlimited number of concurrent users with phenomenal reliability. The possibilities for security are also comprehensive, as different parts of the web site can be located in various locations in a firewall-protected network environment.

Oracle Application Server instances come in two general forms: *infrastructure* instances, and *middle tier* instances. These two overall types of instance have their own variations. It is the middle tier instances that provide services to end users. Middle tier instances run application software, such as the various applications that make up Oracle Collaboration Suite. An infrastructure instance is never used directly by end users; it provides support services to middle tier instances. These support services include user authentication and authorization, configuration management, and directory services.

An Oracle Application Server *farm* consists of one or more middle tier instances connected to a single infrastructure instance. In a large-scale implementation, there may be several middle tier instances, each on its own machine, all controlled by one infrastructure instance. The infrastructure instance may itself have components running from different Oracle homes on different machines for scalability reasons, but a farm contains only one infrastructure. The infrastructure is therefore a single point of failure for an Oracle Application Server environment; but it is possible to configure failover even for the infrastructure, and there are various options for fault tolerance.

It is possible to create clusters within a farm. A *cluster* is a group of one or more middle tier instances configured to run an identical set of Java applications. Note that clustering is not possible for any type of Oracle Application Server service other than Java applications; it is not, for example, possible to cluster a Portal application. Within a cluster, Oracle will guarantee that all instances are the same, or rather, that they are the same as far as end users are concerned. Any configuration change made to one instance will be propagated automatically to the other instances in the cluster. It also becomes possible to distribute end-user connections across the clustered instances, using heuristics that should guarantee an even workload on each instance, and to have end-user sessions fail over from one instance to another should an instance become unavailable. Clusters greatly enhance the manageability and fault tolerance of the web site. The farm/instance/cluster structure can be represented as an entity-relationship diagram, as in Figure 2-1.

The front end to an Oracle Application Server, the process to which users connect, is a web listener, the Oracle HTTP Server (OHS). This is in fact a distribution of Apache. All Oracle Application Server instances, whether infrastructure or middle tier, come with an Apache web listener. This web listener can optionally be front ended by a Web Cache. As a general rule, the Web Cache is used for middle tier instances but not for infrastructure instances. The Web Cache is an acceleration service that will improve response times to end users and may also assist with overcoming some limitations of Apache and security issues. Since Apache is the entry point to an Oracle Application Server web site, that is where this discussion will start.

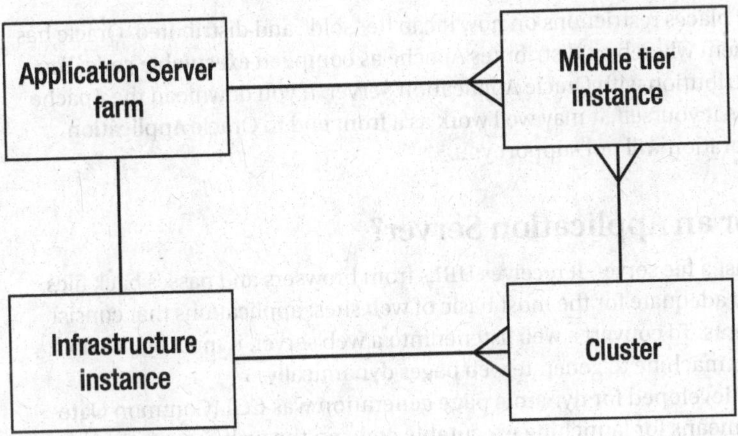

Figure 2-1. *The farm-instance-cluster relationships*

The Apache Web Listener

A web listener is a process that monitors one or more ports on one or more addresses for incoming URLs from browsers. It parses these URLs into filenames, locates the files on disk, and copies them back to the browser. This is a very simple process; you can write your own web listener in a few dozen lines of Java. This is why there are numerous web listener programs that can be downloaded free of charge from any number of sites. It is also why Oracle did not write its own web listener. Instead, it chose to distribute the Apache web listener.

Note that the term *web server* is seriously confusing, as it combines the terms *web listener* and *application server*. For this reason, try to avoid using the term *Apache web server*. The term *HTTP server* is more acceptable (and is frequently used on the Apache Software Foundation web site as a description of the Apache web listener) but in general it is best to use the terms *web listener* to refer to the front-end processes that manage users' web sessions, and *application server* to refer to the back-end processes that run application software.

Apache is a web listener that is available under terms similar to the standard GNU General Public License from the Apache Software Foundation. It has been developed over many years by public-spirited people (and also people who want to show off their skills) who have donated the fruits of their labor to mankind in general. The result is a very powerful product, but also a product that shows many of the problems of software that has been developed by a large and disparate community without much control. You may find that there are odd inconsistencies in the way things are done in the Apache environment and also several ways of achieving the same result. There are also parts of Apache functionality that have fallen into disuse but are still part of the product, and parts that must have been developed for some particular user that no one else will ever use. But in spite of these failings, Apache has become the de facto standard for web listeners. Why pay for a web listener when the one used by 80% (figure for 2005 from the Apache Software Foundation web site) of the world's web sites is available for free? There is also a vast amount of information available on Apache. A decent book shop could have whole bookcases devoted to it.

The Apache license places restrictions on how it can be "sold" and distributed. Oracle has negotiated an arrangement whereby it distributes Apache as compiled executable code. You must use the Oracle distribution with Oracle Application Server. If you download the Apache source code and compile it yourself, it may well work as a front end to Oracle Application Server, but Oracle Corporation will not support you.

A Web Listener or an Application Server?

A basic web listener is just a file server. It receives URLs from browsers and passes back files. This functionality is only adequate for the most basic of web sites: applications that consist of linked HTML documents. To convert a web listener into a web server, it must be possible to run code on the server machine to generate web pages dynamically.

The first technique developed for dynamic page generation was CGI (Common Gateway Interface). CGI is a means for launching executable code on the web listener machine in response to user requests. The URL specifies a filename, but rather than finding the file and copying it back to the browser, the web listener will launch an operating system shell, load the file into the shell, and run it. Clearly, the filename must be an executable program; if the program generates any output, the output, not the file, is sent back to the browser.

CGI works. A CGI program can do anything. But it is not a very efficient processing model. For every CGI invocation, the web listener must launch an operating system shell. This means that a busy web site could be running hundreds or thousands of shells concurrently, launching and terminating them with a frequency that will bring the operating system to its knees. It is also hard to control CGI execution. In principle, the web listener just launches the program and waits. If the program hangs or gets into a loop that consumes 100% of CPU resources, the web listener knows nothing about this. Modern web listeners (and Apache is certainly one of them) do have more efficient ways of running CGI programs: they can monitor the processes and maintain persistent shells. But the inherent inefficiencies of CGI remain. There may also be security issues with CGI; the mechanism was not developed with security in mind. This is why Oracle chose to develop its own facilities for running software for end users—software written in Java and PL/SQL and run in a fashion that will scale to Internet proportions and can provide absolute security.

The Apache license does not permit distributors to modify Apache itself. But Apache does come with a mechanism whereby its behavior can be modified legally by creating Apache modules. An Apache module is a dynamically linked program that is invoked when appropriate URLs are received by the web listener. The web listener parses the URL and, rather than mapping it onto a file for download to the browser, will dynamically load and link the appropriate module and pass the request through to that module for further processing. The mechanism for mapping a URL to a module is based on the path element of the URL. For example, some paths could instruct Apache to launch the module that enables CGI, in which case the file and extension part of the URL will specify the file to be executed through the CGI interface. Another path could be mapped onto the Oracle PL/SQL gateway (in which case the filename and extension will refer to a package and a procedure) or to the OC4J (Oracle Containers for J2EE) module (in which case the file and extension will refer to a Java class). Anyone can write an Apache module to do anything at all. The only difference between the Oracle distribution of Apache and other public domain distributions is in the modules that Oracle has written.

The ability to generate web pages on demand, probably based on database content and constructed in response to user input, is beyond the power of a web listener. For this you need an application server. The combination of a web listener communicating with users over HTTP and an application server behind it that can run software for the end users makes up a web server.

Apache Modules

When Apache is enhanced with modules such as those supplied by Oracle, it becomes a routing process that receives URLs and dispatches them to the appropriate service, which is implemented by the module. If the service generates any output, this is returned via Apache to the browser that invoked it. In this way, the Apache web listener acts as the front end to the Oracle Application Server.

There are a number of Apache modules developed by Oracle Corporation that are shipped with Oracle Application Server. Principal among these are the following:

modplsql: This module accepts URLs that request the running of PL/SQL procedures within an Oracle database. Depending on the path element of the URL, it will use Oracle Net, Oracle's proprietary client/server networking protocol, to connect to a particular database, either with a hard-coded username and password or after generating a login prompt. The filename and extension elements of the URL nominate a PL/SQL package and procedure to be run within the database.

modoc4j: This module accepts URLs that request the running of Java servlets. A *servlet* is a Java program that can be invoked with HTTP and can return a page of HTML. The path element of the URL determines which OC4J instance to pass the request to. The filename and extension nominate the Java class file to run. The Java is not run by modoc4j but by the OC4J instance, which is a process external to Apache.

modosso: This module enables the connection to the Single Sign-On (SSO) service. Single Sign-On–aware applications use modosso to locate the Single Sign-On server and read and write the Single Sign-On cookie.

modossl: Apache can be configured to use secure sockets; there is a public domain module for this. Oracle's implementation of secure sockets, which is integrated with the Oracle Internet Directory (OID), is enabled with this module that replaces the standard Apache secure sockets module.

Every installation of Oracle Application Server comes with an Apache web listener. In the case of an infrastructure instance, Apache is the point of contact for middle tier instances when they need infrastructure services, such as Single Sign-On. For middle tier instances, Apache is the service to which end users' browsers send URLs. Apache dispatches these URLs to appropriate middle tier Oracle Application Server services and then returns whatever output they generate to the browser.

Apache modules are dynamically linked libraries that enhance Apache's capabilities. They run as threads within Apache child processes; some modules carry out work themselves, others are control structures for external processes. modplsql is an example of the first type of module—it logs sessions onto databases and invokes PL/SQL procedures within them. modcgi and modoc4j are examples of the latter type of module. modcgi does not run code; it launches and controls operating system shells that run code. Similarly, modoc4j does not run Java applications; it routes requests through to OC4J instances, external to Apache, that run them. So the Apache web listener is merely a dispatcher process that routes requests to application services provided by modules, which may themselves route requests on to processes that are external to the Apache environment. See Figure 2-2 for this routing model.

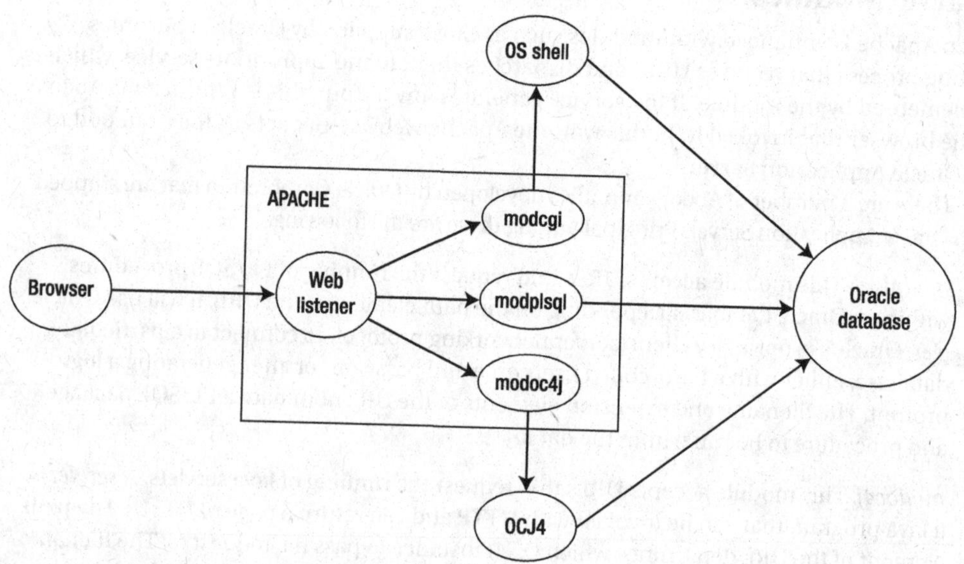

Figure 2-2. *Apache as a router to application services*

The Apache Processing Architecture

The Apache processing architecture is based on a parent process that runs all the time, and child processes that are launched on demand. On UNIX, the child processes are real processes; you can see them at the operating-system level by running the ps command. On Windows, the child processes are separate threads in a single multithreaded process. In either the UNIX or the Windows processing model, the dynamically linked modules run as threads within each child process. The processing model is a child process launched by the parent process whenever a URL is received. It is the parent process that monitors the ports and addresses on which the Apache listener is listening.

In principle, the child process is active only for the duration of the request-response cycle; it is launched on demand and terminated after servicing the request. In practice, Apache will usually be configured to keep the child processes alive for a period during which they can service several requests. Furthermore, Apache will usually prespawn a number of child processes. This can improve performance dramatically, as it reduces the overhead of continually spawning and destroying processes according to user demands. HTTP version 1.1, which is supported by all modern browsers and the current release of Apache, also allows for the possibility of keeping the connection between browser and web listener open for a series of request-response cycles, rather than making and breaking the connection for each request-response cycle, as should be required by the stateless nature of HTTP.

Configuring Apache

Apache is configured with the `httpd.conf` file. The layout of this file and its location are defined by the Apache Software Foundation, and Oracle Corporation has very little freedom to modify this. The file is read when Apache starts, and not subsequently. This means that any changes will not be effected until the listener is restarted.

In all Oracle Application Server Oracle homes, there will be an Apache directory structure that includes (among others) the directories in Table 2-1.

Table 2-1. *Some Apache Directories*

Directory	Description
`ORACLE_HOME/Apache`	Apache root
`ORACLE_HOME/Apache/Apache`	Core Apache files
`ORACLE_HOME/Apache/Apache/bin`	Executable Apache code
`ORACLE_HOME/Apache/Apache/conf`	Apache configuration files

The Oracle distribution includes (among other things) the directories in Table 2-2.

Table 2-2. *Some Oracle-Specific Apache Directories*

Directory	Description
`ORACLE_HOME/Apache/modplsql`	PL/SQL gateway configuration files
`ORACLE_HOME/Apache/modoc4j`	modoc4j configuration files

The `httpd.conf` file, located in the directory `ORACLE_HOME/Apache/Apache/conf`, is a series of directives, all in the form of *token value* pairs. For example, if you want your Apache listener to monitor port number 8000, you would add `Listen 8000` to the `httpd.conf` file, where *Listen* is the token and *8000* is the value. Or to allow Apache to map URLs that include the path `/pub` onto the physical directory `d:\Apache\public`, you would add this directive with the Alias token:

```
Alias /pub "d:\Apache\public\"
```

Note that for this directive the *value* has two attributes: first the virtual path that will be used in URLs, then the physical path that the virtual path will be mapped on to. Following these additions, if a user issues the URL `http://host.domain:8000/pub/index.html` to your `host.domain`, Apache will retrieve the file `index.html` from the physical directory `d:\Apache\public` and send it back to the browser. If the file does not in fact exist in that directory, depending on other directives, Apache may return an "Error 404 – file not found" message, or perhaps some default page, or perhaps a listing of the files that are available in the directory.

A vital directive is `include`, as in

```
include "c:\oracle\ias9i\Apache\Apache\conf\oracle_apache.conf"
```

This instructs Apache to append the file `oracle.conf` to the `httpd.conf` file, and to action all the directives it finds therein. These directives (which are for the most part other `include` directives) are the pointers to the dynamic link libraries that make up the Oracle modules and the files that configure them:

```
# Advanced Queuing - AQ XML
include "c:\oracle\ias9i\rdbms\demo\aqxml.conf"
#OiD DAS module
include "c:\oracle\ias9i\ldap\das\oiddas.conf"
include "c:\oracle\ias9i\Apache\jsp\conf\ojsp.conf"
#Directives needed for OraDAV module
include "c:\oracle\ias9i\Apache\oradav\conf\moddav.conf"
#
include "c:\oracle\ias9i\xdk\admin\xml.conf"
#
include "c:\oracle\ias9i\Apache\modplsql\conf\plsql.conf"
include "c:\oracle\ias9i\Apache\oradav\conf\oradav.conf"
```

Because Oracle Application Server stores configuration data in text files such as `httpd.conf` and in a centrally maintained repository, Oracle does not support manual editing of the configuration files. You should only adjust the Apache configuration by using the management tools provided with Oracle Application Server.

Some directives may well require adjustment from their default settings. The infrastructure instance may also need adjustments. These examples of directives that will usually require changes from default are from the Apache `httpd.conf` file on an Oracle Collaboration Suite middle tier instance running on Linux:

- `StartServers 5`: Specifies that Apache will launch only five child processes on startup. When there are more than five concurrent requests, Apache will have to spawn more processes dynamically.
- `MaxClients 150`: States that Apache will permit only 150 concurrent connections. If more than this is attempted, users will receive Error 500 messages.
- `MaxrequestsPerChild 0`: Limits the number of requests a process will handle before terminating; *zero* means an infinite number. If any libraries have memory leaks, and some do on some platforms, the default of zero (which means an infinite number) will cause problems. Setting it to, for example, 10,000 can do no harm and may help.
- `ExtendedStatus on`: Controls the amount of information returned by the URL `http://host.domain:port/server-status`. *Off* may be less of a security risk than *on*.
- `ServerAdmin you@your.address`: Determines the e-mail address that will be displayed on some pages for users to mail the administrator. This default is not very helpful.

The Infrastructure Instance

An infrastructure instance is optional if the web site is only going to do fairly simple things. But for a complex application environment such as Oracle Collaboration Suite, it is required. An infrastructure instance offers these services to middle tier instances:

- Configuration management
- Oracle Internet Directory
- Single Sign-On
- Certificate Authority

The last three are known collectively as *Identity Management*. It is possible for these services to be distributed over multiple Oracle homes on multiple machines for performance and fault tolerance. The infrastructure includes an Oracle database that is used to store configuration information for all the middle tier instances in the farm, the data maintained by the Oracle Internet Directory, and the repositories required by some middle tier components. The Oracle Internet Directory is an LDAP-compliant directory service used by middle tier applications for maintaining user accounts and privileges, and also for name resolution. The Single Sign-On facility allows end users to connect to many middle tier applications on many middle tier instances after responding to just one logon prompt. The Oracle Certificate Authority can issue digital certificates to enable use of Secure Sockets Layer (SSL) communications and authentication.

The infrastructure instance is front-ended by an Apache web listener, just like any other instance that gives access to these services either by end users or (more frequently) by applications running on middle tier instances.

Configuration Management and the Metadata Repository

A farm has a central repository of configuration data for all its instances. This is known as the *metadata repository* and is stored in an Oracle database. The metadata repository stores information about the overall configuration of the farm and the infrastructure, the various server components configured in each middle tier instance, and the individual applications deployed to these components. A farm has only one metadata repository, but middle tier instance configuration information can in fact be stored in three different locations.

First, the operation of the various components of a middle tier instance is actually controlled by text files in that middle tier's Oracle home. The format and location of these text files is component-specific. For instance, Apache (described earlier in the "Apache Web Listener" section) is controlled by a file `httpd.conf`, whose layout is specified by the Apache Software Foundation. Oracle Corporation has very little control over the format of this file. Alternatively, the Web Cache (described in the "Web Cache" section) is controlled by two files, `webcache.xml` and `internal.xml`, which are formatted with XML (Extensible Markup Language) tags according to Oracle's specifications. Java components are configured with a plethora of XML files; some of these are under Oracle's control, but others must conform to the standards developed by the Java community. It is these text files that are read by the components when they start, but the information within them is echoed out to a central repository.

The second possible location for configuration data is a file-based repository. This is a centrally stored set of XML files containing data for all middle tier instances. The file-based repository does allow central control of multiple middle tier instances, and if an organization does not wish to go to the trouble (and the expense) of creating an infrastructure instance, this may be acceptable if the web site is small and simple. A repository of some kind is a prerequisite for creating Oracle Application Server clusters. The file-based repository is not adequate for managing an Oracle Collaboration Suite web site. For that you need an infrastructure.

The third possible location for configuration data is the database created as part of an Oracle Application Server infrastructure installation. This is a preseeded database containing tables for storing the metadata repository. It also has the schemas needed for storing the Oracle Internet Directory tables, the Single Sign-On code (Single Sign-On does not store any data; it uses Oracle Internet Directory as its data store), and repositories for various middle tier services, such as Portal.

Within a farm, middle tier configuration information is always in two places: the component configuration text files, and the repository. If these two get out of sync with each other, there may be problems. This is a situation that should never occur. But if for example an administrator edits a configuration file by hand, rather than with the management tools that are provided, the two sources of information will differ. This can also happen if an instance is not available when management commands are issued. There are tools provided for propagating changes from the text files to the repository (known as a *configuration update*) and from the repository to the text files (known as an *instance resynchronization*) if the two sources of information have diverged.

The metadata repository database can also be used for storing Oracle Internet Directory data and for the component repositories; the necessary preseeded schemas are always created at installation time. Using the one database for all these functions may give acceptable performance but, if necessary (depending on workload), a separate infrastructure installation can be used to store the directory data, and a third can store the component repositories. Thus, the one infrastructure can be distributed across multiple Oracle homes on multiple machines. If performance and fault tolerance are critical (and they may well be—the metadata repository is vital to the function of an Oracle Application Server web site), the database can be configured as a Real Application Cluster (RAC) database, and also as a Data Guard primary database. Given these two options, it should be possible to configure a zero-downtime and zero-data-loss environment.

Note that the metadata repository database should *never* be used for storing user data, and indeed the license does not permit this legally. Apart from database administration tasks, such as performance tuning and backup, it should not be necessary to ever log on to the metadata repository. But apart from its specialized use, a metadata repository database is a database like any other. As installed out of the box, it is not optimized in any way and will require the usual tuning and other maintenance activities. The exact release of the database shipped with the infrastructure will depend on the release of Oracle Collaboration Suite; there are compatibility issues between Oracle Application Server, the database, and Oracle Collaboration Suite that must be considered before attempting any upgrades.

Oracle Internet Directory

LDAP is the standard for Internet directories. Like HTTP, LDAP is a layered protocol. It runs over TCP and is in fact a TCP implementation of the X500 directory standard. Several global software vendors sell Internet directories. Some major ones are Novell's eDirectory; Sun ONE Directory Server from Sun Microsystems; Microsoft Active Directory; and the Oracle Internet Directory. These have varying degrees of compliance to the LDAP standard, and therefore varying degrees of interoperability.

The information stored in an Internet directory will typically be used for user authentication and authorization and for name resolution. The nature of this type of work is such that there will be many more lookups of data than updates. For this reason, LDAP directories store information in a *tree*. Tree structures are optimal for data retrieval (unlike the structures used in a relational application). A directory tree consists of entries. An *entry* is defined as an instance of an object class. The *object class* defines the structure of the entry in terms of its data attributes. By analogy with a normalized relational database, an entry could be thought of as a row, and the object class as a table. An Oracle Internet Directory stores its data in an Oracle database; the necessary schemas are in the preseeded database created as part of an Oracle Application Server infrastructure installation.

An Oracle Internet Directory instance is implemented as a single listening process that monitors a port for requests from LDAP clients, and a number of server processes that action the requests. These processes must all reside on the same machine, as the communication between them is via whatever IPC (interprocess communication) protocol is provided by the operating system. The LDAP clients can be on any remote machine, since LDAP runs over TCP (though there may be firewall and security issues), and the database storing the information can also be on a remote machine, since the server processes connect to the database using Oracle Net (aka SQL*Net, for those DBAs who still insist on using Oracle 8 terminology). This is illustrated in Figure 2-3.

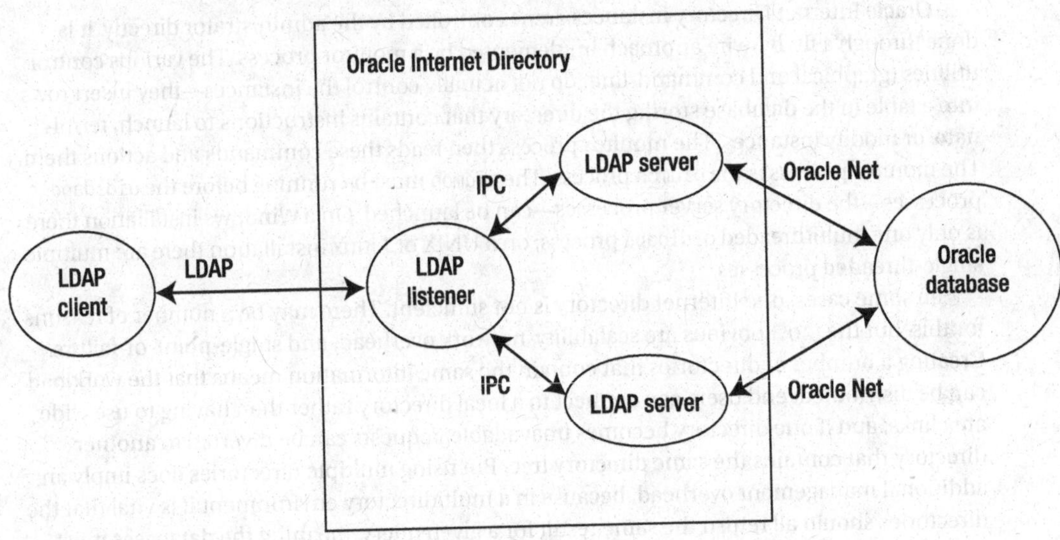

Figure 2-3. *The flow of an LDAP request*

The flow of information for an LDAP request over various protocols is therefore

1. A client process passes a search request to the listener process with LDAP.
2. The listener process passes the request to a server process with IPC.
3. The server process passes the request to the database with Oracle Net.
4. The database executes the query.
5. The database returns the result to the server with Oracle Net.

6. The server returns the result to the listener with IPC.

7. The listener returns the result to the client with LDAP.

A single Oracle Internet Directory instance will be inadequate if it cannot service in a timely fashion the volume of requests being received. Additional server processes can be launched, but the instance only has one listener process that must manage all the concurrent requests. If this is a bottleneck, another instance can be launched on the same machine from the same Oracle home that will monitor a different port, or instances can be launched on separate machines that have an Oracle Application Server infrastructure Oracle home installed. All these Oracle Internet Directory instances can, and in most cases should, connect to the same database; they make up one logical directory server, so that the same set of information can be disbursed by many LDAP instances. In this way, access to a single Oracle Internet Directory can be distributed across a number of physical locations, addresses, and ports, giving both scalability and fault tolerance. Another reason for launching additional Oracle Internet Directory instances is to make use of SSL. If it is necessary to use the SSL implementation of LDAP, a separate Oracle Internet Directory instance (or indeed a separate group of instances) is needed to listen for this variation of the LDAP protocol.

Oracle Internet Directory instances aren't controlled by the administrator directly. It is done through a fly-by-wire approach implemented by a monitor process. The various control utilities (graphical and command-line) do not actually control the instances—they insert rows into a table in the database storing the directory that contains instructions to launch, terminate, or modify instances. The monitor process then reads these commands and actions them. The monitor process is the `oidmon` process. The `oidmon` must be running before the `oidldapd` processes—the directory server processes—can be launched. On a Windows installation there is only one multithreaded `oidldapd` process; on a UNIX or Linux installation there are multiple single-threaded processes.

In some cases, one Internet directory is not sufficient. There may be a number of reasons for this, but the most obvious are scalability, network overhead, and single-point-of-failure. Creating a number of directories that contain the same information means that the workload can be distributed; end users can connect to a local directory rather than having to use wide area links; and if one directory becomes unavailable, requests can be diverted to another directory that contains the same directory tree. But using multiple directories does imply an additional management overhead, because in a multidirectory environment it is vital that the directories should all return the same result for a given query, meaning the databases must contain the same data.

The LDAP standard ensures that multiple directories contain identical copies of the directory tree through the concept of directory replication. Each directory runs an LDAP replication server, which propagates changes made to the entries in its local directory to the replication servers of the remote directories where they are applied. Clearly, mechanisms must exist to handle the possibility of conflicts. Conflicts will arise if the same entry is updated simultaneously in different ways in two different locations. Oracle Internet Directory handles this situation by using the Oracle database and Oracle Net, rather than LDAP. Directory replication is in fact implemented with database multimaster advanced replication for the transport of changes, a standard Oracle database facility that includes automatic conflict resolution capabilities.

Similar in concept to directory replication is directory synchronization. The term *replication* means maintaining identical directory trees in different directories. Replication can only function between identical Internet directories—directories purchased from the same software vendor. *Synchronization* handles the situation where it is necessary to exchange information between incompatible directories purchased from different vendors, or perhaps directories that have different object class definitions. LDAP is supposed to be a vendor-independent standard, so any Internet directory should be able to replicate to any other; but in practice, it doesn't work like that. The various Internet directory vendors have created their own routines for replication that exploit their own platform capabilities and usually do not work with each other. Also, it may well be that different vendors have implemented object classes in different ways. For example, all directories will have an object class that defines a user, but the class could be called *user* in one vendor's directory, and *party* or *person* in another. Furthermore, the different directories will have used different attributes and different data types in the object classes that define their users.

Directory synchronization defines a mechanism whereby changes can be propagated between different directories. The objective is not to keep the directories identical, but merely to ensure that enough information is passed between them to eliminate the need for duplicating the data entry process. For example, if a user changes his password in an application that uses Microsoft Active Directory to store authentication details, the password change should also be reflected in the Oracle Internet Directory, which is used to authenticate the user to Oracle Collaboration Suite applications, so that the password change is automatically reflected there as well. The Oracle Internet Directory implements this capability through the synchronization service. The synchronization routines take certain attributes from entries in one directory and map them on to an LDAP message for transmission to another directory. The actual transfer of information is done automatically over LDAP, but the administrator must manually define the mappings first. Synchronization does mean that basic operations (such as creation or deletion of user accounts) can be propagated between different vendors' directories.

In an ideal world, it would not matter whose directory you used, but it doesn't work like that. For example, there is no way that a Windows file server will accept authentication from an Oracle Internet Directory. Most organizations will end up running more than one directory, but the replication and synchronization services will ease the pain of having to do this. An environment with directories from several vendors, each supporting a different set of applications, can become an administration nightmare—not so much for technical reasons (though these may be an issue) as for political reasons. With user definitions existing in several places with different maintenance procedures, which is to be considered the "source of truth" when they diverge? How long is divergence permitted? Is it legal to make certain updates at all sites? Issues such as these are the subject of business process analysis and must be thoroughly researched and documented by your business analysts.

The Single Sign-On Service

A vital problem of a modern IT environment is that of maintaining user accounts in many applications. This is a problem for administrators and for end users. All end users in a typical organization today will have accounts on different corporate systems for, at least, e-mail, file server, human resources self-service, internal requisitions, and diary management. Then each end user will have more accounts on systems specific to their role in the organization. The end result is that users have a dozen or more usernames and passwords. Not only is managing this situation very time-consuming for the uses, it is also fraught with risk for the organization itself. History shows that a large number of users in this situation resort to practices that are highly dangerous for security, such as

- Using easily remembered (and therefore guessable) passwords
- Keeping hard copies of login details in obvious places
- Using the same password for all accounts

The last possibility is particularly worrying if users reuse the password they select for internal systems when they register with external public services where it may be available to anyone. But even if users are disciplined in maintaining security in this environment, there is a large price to be paid in terms of business efficiency.

Single Sign-On centralizes management of passwords. To the end user, it appears as though he only logs on once, typically to a corporate portal, and then has access to all the application services he is authorized to use without any further login prompts. In reality it is a bit more complicated.

To enable Single Sign-On, first the users must be registered in an Oracle Internet Directory. This is the repository of the users' identities, including their passwords. Then all the applications that are going to use Single Sign-On must be written with the appropriate toolkits provided by Oracle to make them Single Sign-On aware. The applications themselves do not do any user authentication; they delegate authentication to the Single Sign-On service. Authorization is still controlled within the application.

When a user contacts a Single Sign-On application, the application checks the user's browser for a cookie that identifies the user: the Single Sign-On cookie. If this cookie is there, the user is logged into the application immediately, with whatever privileges his username entitles him to. If this cookie does not exist (or if it has expired) the application will redirect the user to the Single Sign-On server. The Single Sign-On server generates a login screen, authenticates the user with a username/password prompt, and if successful sets the Single Sign-On cookie in his browser. The user gets redirected back to the application he originally asked for, the cookie is read, and he is logged on without further prompts. Then for the duration of the cookie's validity he can access any Single Sign-On–aware application in the same manner without any prompts. So although he is in fact being logged on to each application individually, the process is transparent to the user. Since the password is maintained centrally in the Oracle Internet Directory, when it is changed it is changed for all the applications that are using this mechanism. This avoids having separate passwords maintained by each application.

Single Sign-On is written in PL/SQL. It is a set of procedures in a schema created in the metadata repository database. These generate login screens to prompt for a username and password, and then use LDAP to request an Oracle Internet Directory to authenticate the username-password pair. The cookie that is set in the browser is an encrypted, nonpersistent cookie. It should therefore be impossible to hijack a user's session by copying the cookie to another machine. It is also possible (and recommended) to use the HTTPS protocol (which is HTTP with secure sockets) for all communications between browsers and the Single Sign-On service in order to encrypt the password during its transmission from browser to Single Sign-On server.

Figure 2-4 illustrates the Single Sign-On connection cycle, which consists of a number of steps:

1. The browser issues a URL contacting an SSO-enabled service. This request does not include the SSO cookie authentication.
2. The service returns a redirection URL, instructing the browser to contact the SSO server with a logon request.
3. The browser contacts the SSO server with a logon request.
4. The SSO server sends a logon prompt window to the browser.
5. The browser returns a username and password to the SSO server.
6. The SSO server passes the username and password to the OID for validation, using the LDAP protocol. Note that steps 1 through 5 have used HTTP, as will 8 and 9.
7. The OID returns a positive authentication (for the purposes of this example) back to the SSO server, using LDAP.
8. The SSO server sends an SSO cookie to the browser with a redirection URL instructing the browser to contact the service it originally requested.
9. The browser contacts the SSO-enabled service, this time with the SSO cookie, and will be logged in to it without further authentication required.
10. Any URLs contacting other SSO-enabled applications will result in an immediate logon until the lifetime of the SSO cookie expires.

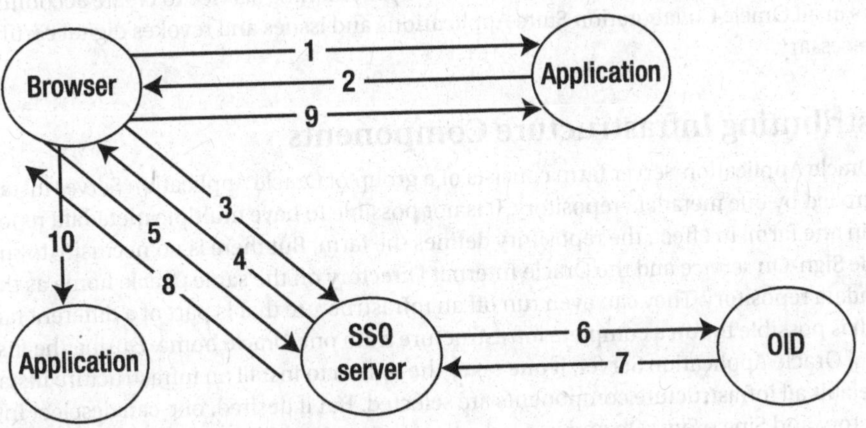

Figure 2-4. *Single Sign-On request flow*

Identity Management and Digital Certificates

The capabilities of the Oracle Internet Directory and the Single Sign-On service can be leveraged by enabling the full Identity Management capability. This uses account provisioning to create, modify, and delete accounts automatically in a number of applications and the certificate issuing authority to generate digital certificates.

Account provisioning centralizes the creation and maintenance of users' accounts in a number of applications. In a typical organization, every employee will have accounts for several organization-wide systems as well as those specific to his job, and possibly for various means of external access. The workload of maintaining these individually is significant and also raises the likelihood of security problems. Enabling account provisioning means that once an employee is registered in, for example, the HR system, he will automatically have accounts created for him in a number of other corporate systems to which all employees should have access. Then when the employee leaves the organization, all his accounts on all systems will be terminated; there will be no danger of any delay in, for example, canceling his dial-in access.

If security is to be based on SSL communication, all users must be given a digital certificate. This is the document identifying who they are, and in an Oracle environment is stored in the Oracle Internet Directory. Managing digital certificates can be automated by using the Oracle Certificate Authority. This is an Oracle Application Server infrastructure service that will generate digital certificates from a parent certificate installed in the infrastructure.

The parent certificate must be purchased from a third-party supplier. This can be from any recognized certificate-issuing authority, though there may be procedural (or even political) reasons for favoring one supplier over another. There will also be cost implications. A certificate for an installation that will have many thousands of users will be far more expensive than a certificate valid for a few hundred users, and the cost does vary from one supplier to another. It is possible to use an Oracle-supplied certificate shipped with the product, but while this will be adequate for internal use (because your own users will trust authentication based upon it) this will not usually be adequate if users will interact with people from external organizations. External users will want to see certificates that can be verified with a recognized certificate-issuing authority.

Oracle Collaboration Suite makes use of the provisioning service to create accounts for users in all Oracle Collaboration Suite Applications and issues and revokes digital certificates as necessary.

Distributing Infrastructure Components

An Oracle Application Server farm consists of a group of Oracle Application Server instances controlled by one metadata repository. It is not possible to have multiple metadata repositories in one farm; in effect, the repository defines the farm. But there is no necessity to run the Single Sign-On service and the Oracle Internet Directory off the same Oracle home as the metadata repository. They can even run off an infrastructure that is part of a different farm.

It is possible to run a complete infrastructure from one Oracle home. During the installation of Oracle Application Server, if one takes the option to install an infrastructure instance, by default all infrastructure components are selected. But if desired, one can deselect Internet Directory and Single Sign-On and instead point the new installation toward an already available Internet Directory and Single Sign-On server.

By distributing the components of the infrastructure, it is possible to provide a highly fault-tolerant and scalable environment. This is discussed in Chapter 17.

Connecting to an Infrastructure Instance

The front end of an infrastructure instance, as for any Oracle Application Server instance, is its Apache web listener. It is not customary to run a Web Cache in front of this listener, as it is very unlikely that that there would be any benefits. Nearly all requests to an infrastructure instance are of such a nature that the Web Cache would have to pass them straight through to Apache without caching the results, so there would be no point.

End users rarely contact an infrastructure instance directly. On contacting a Single Sign-On–enabled application, users will be redirected to the infrastructure for authentication, but that is all. When they are logged in to an application, the application may be continually contacting the Oracle Internet Directory and making directory lookups to check authorizations and retrieve other information, but the user knows nothing of that.

The exception to this rule is the Delegated Administration Service (DAS). This is a Java application deployed to the infrastructure instance that lets users manage their registrations within the Oracle Internet Directory.

The URLs to connect directly to the Identity Management services are

- `http://host.domain:7777/pls/orasso`: This is the URL for the Single Sign-On service running on the infrastructure installed on `host.domain` with an Apache web listener running on its default port of 7777. It will generate a screen with a list of services that have delegated authentication to the Single Sign-On server and a link for a login prompt. While you can issue this URL directly, users will usually be redirected to it by Single Sign-On–enabled applications.

- `http://host.domain:7777/oiddas`: This is the URL for the DAS. This is a self-service application that lets users change their passwords (stored in the Oracle Internet Directory and validated by Single Sign-On) and change various other items of personal information. Users with sufficient authorization can use this tool to manage other users—create or delete them and change their privileges.

Middle tier Oracle Application Server instances connect to their infrastructure whenever necessary. They log on to it using an encrypted password that is derived from (among other things) the hostname of the node they are running on. For this reason there are issues with changing hostnames in an Oracle Application Server environment, but it can be done. If a middle tier instance cannot contact its infrastructure, the effect will depend on the application being used; there is not necessarily an immediate failure. Some application server services may only need an infrastructure service for Single Sign-On. In that case, if the infrastructure is unavailable, users who are already logged on and authenticated can continue working unaffected; only new login requests will fail. Other applications may be making continuous use of the infrastructure, perhaps to construct menus as users navigate through the application; these will fail immediately.

As an administrator you will connect to and control the infrastructure instance through the tools provided as discussed in Chapter 5.

The Middle Tier Instance

A middle tier Oracle Application Server instance runs services that are used by end users whose entry point to the instance is the Apache web listener. Every Oracle Application Server instance has one (and only one) web listener. If the web listener can service the request from a browser by itself (typically because the request is for a static file) it will do so, but if the URL maps onto an Application Server service, identified by the path element of the URL, the web listener will pass the request to the appropriate module.

Middle tier instances come in three forms; the choice is made at installation time. These options (from simplest to most complex) are known as J2EE (Java 2 Enterprise Edition) and Web Cache; Wireless and Portal; and Business Intelligence and Forms. The more complex installations include all elements of the less complex installations; thus, a Business Intelligence and Forms instance will include J2EE, Web Cache, Wireless, and Portal.

The Middle Tier Instance Types

The simplest middle tier instance is the J2EE and Web Cache instance. This is an Apache web listener augmented with the Oracle-supplied Apache modules that enable the PL/SQL gateway and OC4J. It also comes with a preconfigured Web Cache, which can be reconfigured or even disabled if desired. The PL/SQL gateway is a mechanism whereby end users can from their web browsers invoke PL/SQL code that will run within an Oracle database. Java code is compiled to run within a virtual machine—a computer that doesn't actually exist. The Java runtime environment is a simulated environment that supports the Java Virtual Machine (JVM) standard. OC4J is Oracle's Java runtime environment. In addition to the standard Java requirements, it also provides excellent facilities for control, monitoring, and fault tolerance. One middle tier Application Server instance may run many OC4J instances, but it can only have one Apache web listener.

The second possible middle tier installation is Portal and Wireless. This instance type requires an infrastructure to be already available. If during the installation dialog you cannot give the location of an infrastructure instance, the installation will fail. A Portal and Wireless instance includes all the J2EE and Web Cache facilities, plus the Portal and Wireless components. Portal is a tool for developing web sites that can deliver customized content. Portal applications make use of toolkits that enable use of the Oracle Internet Directory and Single Sign-On. Wireless can be used to develop applications that use the standard wireless protocols (such as WML or cHTML) to develop interfaces that make applications usable on any device. For instance, your software will be accessible to users in their cell phones as well as on their PCs.

The third middle tier instance type is Business Intelligence and Forms. In addition to the facilities provided by the J2EE and Web Cache and Portal and Wireless instance types, a Business Intelligence and Forms instance includes the products that were marketed in earlier days under the names Developer 2000 Forms and Reports and Discoverer. Forms is a tool for developing and delivering applications that have a much richer user interface than those possible with web applications based on HTML. The standard web application environment is based on HTML documents, but HTML has limitations. For example, an HTML application can have radio buttons, but it cannot have rolling combo boxes. The HTML standard simply doesn't have tags for creating rolling combo boxes, but Forms does. The term *Business Intelligence* covers Reports and Discoverer. Reports is a facility for scheduling jobs—or running them in real time—that will extract information from an Oracle database and present it in a formatted fashion. Discoverer is a facility for allowing end users to query the database while shielding them from the complexities of the application's relational design.

A J2EE instance can be installed without an infrastructure instance, though during the installation you will be asked if you want to associate the instance with an infrastructure. If you choose not to associate the instance with an infrastructure the instance will not be part of a farm, and it can only operate in a self-contained fashion; there will be no possibility of load balancing or fault tolerance with other instances, and the applications deployed to it will not be able to make use of an Oracle Internet Directory or the Single Sign-On service. The other middle tier types cannot exist without an infrastructure, which must have been installed first.

The PL/SQL Gateway

The PL/SQL gateway is installed with all Oracle Application Server instance types. It is an Apache module that can handle URLs that invoke PL/SQL procedures stored within a database. The procedures can perform any program logic that may be required, but whatever else they do, they will usually generate a page of HTML to be returned to the browser. This page will be created by using the PL/SQL Web Toolkit, a set of packages installed within the database that can be used to produce web pages. These pages can be windows that prompt users to enter data, or windows that display information retrieved from a database, or any combination. The PL/SQL Web Toolkit is a very efficient mechanism for generating HTML applications that use data stored in an Oracle database.

The PL/SQL gateway is enabled by the file `plsql.conf` which is included in the `oracle_apache.conf` which is itself included in `httpd.conf`. A simple file could be as small as just two lines:

```
LoadModule plsql_module c:\oracle\ias9i\bin\modplsql.dll
include "c:\oracle\ias9i\Apache\modplsql\conf\dads.conf"
```

This file nominates the dynamic link library that enables the PL/SQL gateway and has an `include` directive for `dads.conf`. This is the file that creates DADs (Database Access Descriptors). A DAD instructs Apache to direct certain URLs to modplsql by mapping a path in the URL to a database connect string. The DAD can include database login credentials; if it does not include these, a login prompt (in the form of a "403 – Authentication Required" window) is sent back to the browser. The following is a simple `dads.conf` file containing two DADs:

```
<Location /pls/orasso>
    SetHandler pls_handler
    Order deny,allow
    Allow from all
    AllowOverride None
    PlsqlDatabaseUsername orasso
    PlsqlDatabasePassword orasso
    PlsqlDatabaseConnectString infra_as.bplc.co.za:1521:inf
    PlsqlDefaultPage orasso.home
    PlsqlDocumentTablename orasso.wwdoc_document
    PlsqlDocumentPath docs
    PlsqlDocumentProcedure orasso.wwdoc_process.process_download
    PlsqlAuthenticationMode SingleSignOn
    PlsqlPathAlias url
    PlsqlPathAliasProcedure orasso.wwpth_api_alias.process_download
    PlsqlSessionCookieName orasso
</Location>
<Location /hr>
    SetHandler pls_handler
    PlsqlDatabaseConnectString hrdb
</Location>
```

The `<Location>` tags name the DADs and create virtual paths that Apache will recognize as those to be routed to modplsql. In this example, the first DAD is path `/pls/orasso`, which is the standard DAD for connecting to the Oracle Application Server infrastructure Single Sign-On service. The second DAD, `/hr`, is a simpler one that would have been created by the administrator.

If the DAD includes a logon name and password, as in the first DAD, these credentials will be used to log on to the database nominated by the connect string, which can be either a full hard-coded address (as in the first DAD) or an Oracle Net connection identifier (as in the second DAD). If there isn't a username/password, as in the second DAD, modplsql will generate a 403 "Authentication Required" message that will prompt for a username and password. If the URL includes the `file.extension` elements, these will be used to locate a procedure in a package (which must be available to the schema used to log on) to be executed; otherwise, if there is a nominated default procedure (such as the `orasso.home` procedure in the first DAD), then that procedure will run.

To complete the example, if the Apache web listener with the `dads.conf` file listed previously is running on the machine `mid1_as.bplc.co.za`, and the URL `http://mid1_as.bplc.co.za:7777/hr/demo.hello?name=john` is issued by a browser, and there is a PL/SQL package within the database referred to by the connect identifier hrdb created with this code

```
create package demo as
procedure hello(name varchar2);
end;
/

create package body demo
as
procedure hello(name varchar2)
as
begin
htp.print('hello '||name);
end;
end;
/
```

then, following a login prompt, a page will be sent back to the browser that says "hello john." This is a very elementary use of the PL/SQL Web Toolkit (part of which is the htp package) for generating pages of HTML.

Substantial use is made of the PL/SQL gateway throughout Oracle Collaboration Suite. In particular, Single Sign-On is a PL/SQL application invoked through the DAD or virtual path `/pls/orasso`. Try it; if your installation uses the default ports and `host.domain` is the node where your infrastructure is running, the URL `http://host.domain:7777/pls/orasso` will connect you to Single Sign-On. Portal is also to a large extent a PL/SQL web application, as may be the applications Portal connects users to.

Oracle Containers for J2EE (OC4J)

Java applications come in two general forms: Java servlets and Java beans. A *Java servlet* is a Java application that communicates with HTTP. It can be launched in response to a URL from a browser and will usually generate a page of HTML in reply. Java servlets are used for writing user interface code. *Java beans* do not do user interface work. They are software constructs that manipulate data, and you communicate with them by sending them messages that ask them to do something, using protocols such as RMI (Remote Method Invocation) or JMS (Java Message Service).

Java beans then come in several forms. A *session* bean contains code that implements application logic. An *entity* bean represents data; it will be populated with a row from a database. Typically, you communicate with Java beans by sending them messages using the RMI protocol, though there is the variant known as *message-driven beans* (MDBs) with which you communicate with JMS.

While it is possible for a Java servlet to perform application layer functions and to communicate with a database, a more common application architecture would be to use a Java servlet to manage the user interface layer of the applications, and Java beans to manage the data processing layer. The end users will communicate with a servlet by issuing a URL over HTTP. The Apache web listener receives the URL and passes it to the module modoc4j. modoc4j passes it on to the OC4J instance to which the servlet has been deployed. The servlet will generate and manage whatever user dialogs are necessary and eventually pass a request to a session bean, which will manipulate data represented by entity beans that connect to a database. Breaking up an application into many tiers assists developers and maintenance substantially by providing abstraction between the various layers. It becomes possible, for instance, to redesign the user interface without affecting the data manipulation code, or to change the relational structures of the data storage without affecting anything else.

An OC4J instance is a process running externally to Apache. It can launch and control servlets and Java beans, which will run within a JVM. The actual runtime environment, the JVM, is provided by the host operating system. So if your application server is a Solaris machine, you will be using Sun's JVM; whereas if you are using a Linux server you will be using the Linux JVM. Solaris and Linux implement the JVM very differently, but neither your programmers nor Oracle Application Server need to worry about this, because both environments provide a JVM that conforms to the standard API (application programming interface). OC4J is a control structure for starting JVMs and managing the Java applications running within them.

The user's entry point to an OC4J is, as for all Oracle Application Server components, a URL sent to an Apache web listener. The `httpd.conf` file will include a line such as this

```
include "c:\oracle\ias9i\Apache\Apache\conf\mod_oc4j.conf"
```

which points to the file that configures the module modoc4j. The following is a simple version of this file:

```
LoadModule oc4j_module modules/ApacheModuleOc4j.dll
<IfModule mod_oc4j.c>
    Oc4jMount /j2ee/*
    Oc4jMount /hrj demo
</IfModule>
```

This file first specifies the dynamic link library that is the modoc4j code and then creates two virtual paths with the `Oc4jMount` directive. This is a token that takes two values: the first is a virtual path, the second is the name of an OC4J instance to which to send URLs with that virtual path. So if the Apache instance receives this URL

```
http://mid1_as.bplc.co.za:7777/hrj/helloworld?name=john
```

Apache will pass it through to an OC4J instance called `demo`, which will load and run the Java class `helloworld` using the value `john` for the argument `name`. The first `Oc4jMount` directive only has a single value: the virtual path `/j2ee/*`. All URLs that include this path will be dispatched to the default OC4J instance, which is known as the `home` instance.

An Oracle Application Server instance may have many OC4J instances created within it, each optimized for running a particular set of Java applications. The configurable elements include the number of JVMs that the instance will launch; the amount of memory they are allowed to take for Java heap space; and the databases to which the Java applications may connect. It is possible to deploy a Java class as an individual file, but this is rarely done. Java applications that are deployed to an OC4J instance should be packaged as Java archives: these are ZIP files that may contain many class files of Java servlets and beans, as well as static pages of HTML and image files that together make up an application.

If a number of J2EE and Web Cache middle tier instances are part of a farm, it is possible to group them into clusters. Clustering gives Oracle Application Server its fault tolerant capabilities. The infrastructure guarantees that all clustered instances are absolutely identical in three respects: the way modoc4j is configured; the Java applications are deployed to them; and, to a certain extent, the way their Apache web listeners are configured. This means that end users can connect to any instance in the cluster and run the same software. It thus becomes possible to load-balance users across instances by using Web Cache or a third-party tool. Furthermore, within a cluster, the Apache web listener for one instance can route URLs to any OC4J in any other instance, which allows for a second level of load balancing. But even more significant, it is possible to configure clustered OC4J instances to replicate the state of the running applications between one another. This gives fault tolerance; if one OC4J instance crashes, the end users' sessions can be reestablished against a surviving instance without the user being aware of the problem.

There are various communications protocols used in the OC4J application environment. First, end users' browsers use HTTP to send URLs to the Apache web listener. These requests are routed to modoc4j within the Apache executable, then modoc4j uses AJP1.3 (Apache Jserv Protocol version 1.3) to send the request on to the appropriate OC4J instance, which could be running in a different middle tier instance on a different machine. The OC4J instance will load and run the requested Java class, which is probably a servlet. The servlet may then use RMI to contact a Java bean, which could again be running in a different OC4J instance on a different machine. Then the bean might use Oracle Net to contact a database, and LDAP to contact an OID.

Portal

A portal isn't really an application in its own right; it is the front end to many applications. But Oracle Application Server Portal is much more than just a web page with links to a few applications. It is a development environment for designing portals and provides a secure and manageable environment for connecting to enterprise software services and information resources. A portal page makes data from multiple sources accessible from a single location, with personalization for (and by) each user. Portal applications are fully integrated with Single Sign-On and Oracle Internet Directory.

Portal uses a data repository to record the components that can be used to make the web pages it will present to users. These pages are constructed dynamically for each user according to his identity. The Portal repository is a set of schemas in an Oracle database. These schemas are found in the database that is created as part of an Oracle Application Server infrastructure. The workload on the Portal repository database is significant, and for this reason it will often be desirable to have a separate database for this purpose, rather than to colocate the portal repository with the Oracle Application Server metadata repository and the Oracle Internet Directory data.

The applications accessible through a Portal page are reached through *portlets*. A portlet appears to a user as a link. The portlet is generated by Portal according to specifications provided by the application developer. The application must be written with the Portal development kits in order to make it Portal-aware. It will also be integrated with Single Sign-On and the Internet Directory.

Portal is implemented by the Parallel Page Engine (PPE). The PPE is the OC4J application that constructs Portal pages on demand for end users. It uses modplsql to retrieve information from the Portal repository. The PPE is capable of generating pages that can be displayed with standard HTML in a browser, or on a wireless device using whatever markup language is appropriate for the device. It is Portal that makes Oracle Collaboration Suite applications available on wireless devices such as mobile telephones and PDAs.

Forms, Reports, and Discoverer

Forms, Reports, and Discoverer are now shipped as part of Oracle Application Server. Oracle Collaboration Suite does not use them, so this discussion is merely a brief mention in order to complete the description of the Oracle Application Server.

Forms and Reports were distributed in earlier releases as Developer 2000. Forms is an application development environment for building user interfaces. These can be much more sophisticated than those possible in the HTML environment, no matter what tools (Java or PL/SQL, for example) are used to generate the HTML. Forms do not use HTML for displaying information; they use a Java applet downloaded to the user's terminal. This means that the applications are much easier to use, but it also means that the user needs a relatively powerful machine to display them and a fast network because of the additional communication needs of the applet. Forms applications run superbly across an intranet, but the demands they place on the network and the display devices may not always make them suitable for an Internet deployment.

The Forms viewing applet is responsible for local window management on the user's terminal. The Forms logic is run by a Forms runtime engine. This is a process running on the Oracle Application Server machine. Thus Forms applications are truly three-tier: The database tier handles the data access, implemented with SQL; the application server middle tier runs the application, using a Forms Server to launch runtime engines for each concurrent user; the user interface tier in a Java applet on the user's terminal manages interaction with the user. A significant processing capability is needed on all three tiers.

Reports is a tool for retrieving information from a database and formatting it for display. A report is designed by a programmer but run by an end user. The report can be designed to accept numerous parameters, allowing the user a degree of flexibility in information retrieval. The output can be either HTML or PDF, or it can be wrapped up in XML tags. The reports are generated by a Reports server running on the Oracle Application Server middle tier. Unlike Forms runtime engines, which are launched on demand for each user, reports engines are prespawned—a fixed number that waits for requests. If there are more concurrent requests than Reports engines, a queuing mechanism manages the situation.

Discoverer is a tool for querying a database, but unlike Reports the output can be controlled completely by the user. A Reports report can be customized through parameters at runtime, but it must still have been predesigned. A Discoverer report can be designed completely under the control of the user requesting it. The advantage of Discoverer over any other query tool is that it places a layer of abstraction between the database and the user—the Discoverer End User Layer (EUL). The EUL is a set of views that can conceal the complexities of the database design from the user. Rather than having to comprehend a normalized relational structure, the user can design reports based on a simplified view of the database content. It must be remembered, however, that this ease of use comes with a price: the EUL views have to be populated on demand. So while Discoverer makes life easy for end users, it can put extra strain on the database.

Discoverer report definitions, known as *workbooks*, are stored in the database along with the EUL, and the reports themselves are run by Java processes on the middle tier. End users need nothing more than a browser to design, launch, and view ad hoc reports.

The Web Cache

All Oracle Application Server instances are front ended by an Apache web listener. This is all very well for conformance to standards, but there are some limitations in what Apache can do, particularly with regard to performance and scalability. The Web Cache is designed to address these. It can also assist with security issues and resilience against failures. But the most obvious advantage of using a Web Cache is performance: it will accelerate delivery of data to your users.

The ideal situation is that neither end users nor developers will even know that the Web Cache is there. But the users will perceive a performance far greater than if it were not.

Apache's Limitations

An Apache web listener is restricted in terms of the number of concurrent connections that it can service. The standard distribution can only handle 256 connections. It is simple to change this: edit the source code to adjust the limit and recompile. Oracle Corporation has done just that. The Apache distributed with Oracle Application Server can handle 1,024 concurrent connections (the `MaxClients` directive must be changed to enable this). But this does not mean that Apache will be particularly efficient at supporting 1,024 concurrent connections, or that it will handle an overload of requests in an elegant fashion. The Web Cache can address these scalability limitations of Apache in two ways. First, it can handle thousands of concurrent connections. Second, it can distribute these connections across a pool of Apache web listeners. The algorithms used for this distribution can load-balance connections according to the capacities of the machines on which each Apache web listener is running and, if necessary, limit the number of requests sent through to each web listener to avoid overloading.

Apart from issues of scalability, there is also the question of whether it is actually desirable to have Apache handle every request from end users. Access to web sites is typified by many repeated requests for the same or similar information. The most obvious example is the introductory page to a web site, commonly the `index.html` page. Every user who contacts the web site starts with this page, so it must be transmitted unchanged thousands or perhaps millions of times a day. The method by which Apache would do this is not particularly efficient; it may well read the file off disk for every request. The Web Cache can keep copies of popular documents in memory with an indexed access method, and serve them from memory far faster than Apache could serve them from disk. In this way, the Web Cache can improve response times to end users and reduce the workload on the Apache web listener(s).

Web Cache Architecture

The Web Cache is a specialized web listener. It follows the standard web listener processing model of a single process that monitors one or more ports on one or more addresses for incoming URLs, but from there things change. If it can satisfy the URL from its memory cache, it will do so; otherwise, it will pass the request back to a web listener. The web listener will process the URL as it would process one received directly from a browser. It will retrieve the document from disk (or perhaps pass it further back to an Oracle Application Server service) and return it to the source of the URL, in this case, the Web Cache. The Web Cache then returns the document (whether a static file read by Apache off disk, or a file generated dynamically) to the browser. But as it does this, if it is configured with appropriate rules, it will keep a copy of the document in its memory cache. Then the next time the same URL is received, from the same browser or another, the Web Cache can serve it out immediately from memory without having to bother the Apache web listener.

So the Web Cache is the front end to the Apache front end; it routes requests from browsers to the web listener and forwards the responses while keeping copies of them ready for identical requests.

The efficiency of this is limited by the likelihood of repeated requests for the same information. There are also security and data integrity issues. What if a popular document that is in the cache is updated on disk? Will users see the current version from disk, or the old version from cache? What about documents that need to be generated dynamically? There are certainly issues to consider with using a Web Cache, but provided that the rules it uses to determine which documents to cache and for how long are appropriate, it can improve the performance perceived by end users dramatically, reducing the strain on the application server(s) behind it. The default preconfigured rules should be suitable for most sites; they will accelerate delivery of content to users without compromising security or accuracy.

Fault Tolerance and Load Balancing with the Web Cache

A large web site supporting thousands of concurrent connections will consist of several middle tier Oracle Application Server instances, probably part of one farm. All the middle tier instances, including their Apache web listeners, will be configured identically, so that users can connect to any one and access the same applications. They will all be connecting to the same backend database(s) and may even be configured into a cluster.

This is all very well, but a mechanism is required for spreading the incoming URLs across all the web listeners. For this you need a very expensive device: a layer-four switch that can take the incoming connections and redirect them to the various addresses of the web listeners. Web Cache does exactly that, but in a highly intelligent fashion. It can not only do layer-four switching for load balancing but also layer-seven switching. It can direct some URLs (identified with wild cards, using POSIX pattern recognition) to some web listeners (or groups of web listeners), and other URLs to other web listeners, using whatever load-balancing limitations you care to program into it. If a web listener becomes unavailable, the Web Cache will detect this and cease to send it URLs until it is again available.

If your web listeners are overstressed, Web Cache can cover up for this by serving data from its cache, even if the data is out of date, if the rules you configure permit this. This also gives protection against denial-of-service attacks on your site; it is virtually impossible to crash a Web Cache by sending it a flood of requests, whereas conventional web listeners are very vulnerable to this type of overload. The only limitations on the number of concurrent connections a Web Cache can manage are determined by your operating system, and for most platforms this limit is many thousands.

By putting one, or several, Web Caches in front of your web site, you should be able to improve performance and reliability dramatically. For this reason, the Web Cache is enabled by default on all middle tier Oracle Application Server instances. It comes preconfigured with a set of caching rules that will certainly help all web sites; but if you choose to customize these rules to your own environment, the benefits will be even greater.

Oracle Application Server, Web Cache, and Security

All web applications should consider security to be an absolute priority. If e-commerce is to succeed, all users must have complete confidence in the impossibility of hacking the web site. Apart from its capabilities for scaling and accelerating a web site, Web Cache should also be integrated into its security structures.

A vital part of security is the use of firewalls. A *firewall* is, in effect, a router. It is a dual (or more) homed device that connects two (or more) networks. It accepts connection requests from addresses on one network interface and forwards them to addresses on another network interface. But whereas a standard router will forward all requests, a firewall will be configured with rules. These rules can restrict the protocols that will be routed, the addresses from which requests will be accepted, the addresses to which requests will be sent, the ports that can be used, or any combination of these variables. Using several layers of firewall and placing different servers behind the different firewalls can make hacking a web site virtually impossible. Each firewall can be configured with a different set of rules so that traffic that is permitted by one is not permitted by another. In combination, no hacker will be able to get through to server systems storing sensitive data. A general principle is that servers storing data should be in a totally protected zone where they can only be contacted by your own (one hopes secure) systems, but servers offering only processing services can be in a zone of intermediate security where they can be contacted by external clients.

Web Cache can significantly enhance that security of a web site. A possible scenario is illustrated in Figure 2-5.

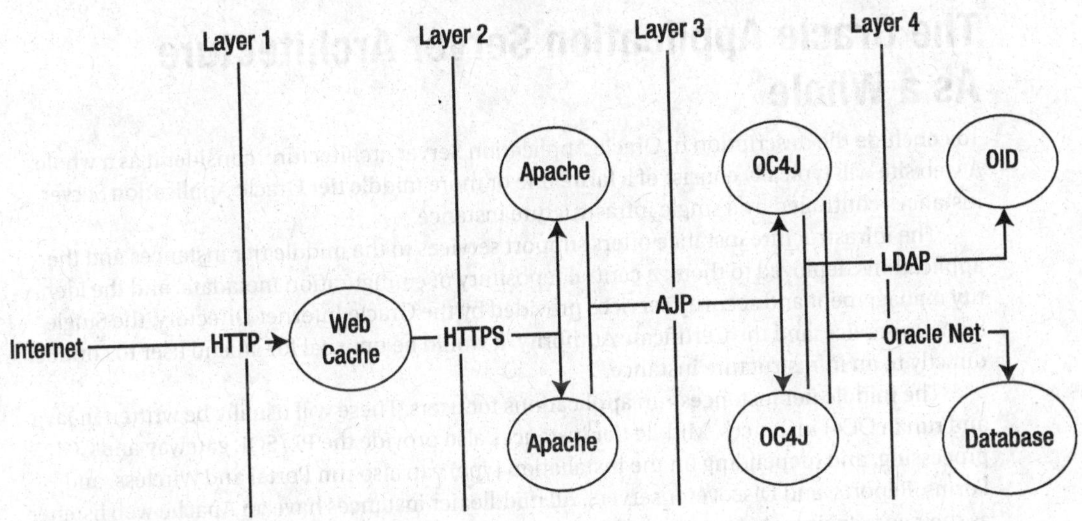

Figure 2-5. *A multilayer firewall topology*

The external firewall is configured to accept only one protocol on one port: HTTP, typically on port 80. It is further configured to route HTTP to only one port on one address, that of the Web Cache. Any other protocol, or any requests for any other addresses, will be rejected. The Web Cache can be configured to forward requests only to the Apache web listeners, behind a second firewall. This firewall will be configured to accept requests from only one address and only one protocol: HTTPS from the Web Cache. It will route these requests only to the Apache web listeners in the next protected firewall zone on the appropriate port. Note that the Apaches can themselves be configured to accept only HTTPS traffic, authenticated with the digital certificate of the Web Cache, from the Web Cache machine. Web Cache will be doing the protocol conversion. The third firewall can be configured to accept only requests from the Apache listeners' addresses; furthermore, these requests would have to be using the AJP protocol, to invoke Java processes in the OC4J instances in the next protected zone, on whatever ports they are monitoring. Yet another firewall could transmit only Oracle Net requests to Oracle database servers, or LDAP requests to OID servers. Both the database and OID servers, which contain sensitive data rather than providing only processing capability, are thus protected by several layers of security.

This four-level firewall is an extreme example. It will be absolutely impossible to bypass all four layers, hacking servers at each stage to fool all the firewall routers into believing that the malicious traffic is legitimate.

The Web Cache is an integral part of the security structure and can indeed replace the first two firewalls. If the Web Cache is installed on a dual-homed device, it can be considered to be a router configured with rules that will allow it to monitor only one or two protocols (HTTP or HTTPS) on one network interface, and to forward them only to a nominated list of addresses (the Apache web listeners) on the other network interface. The Apache web listeners will themselves be configured to reject all traffic that does not come from the Web Cache.

The Oracle Application Server Architecture As a Whole

To conclude the description of Oracle Application Server architecture, consider it as a whole. A web site will typically consist of a farm: one or more middle tier Oracle Application Server instances controlled by a single infrastructure instance.

The infrastructure instance offers support services to the middle tier instances and the applications deployed to them: a central repository of configuration metadata, and the identity management and security services provided by the Oracle Internet Directory, the Single Sign-On service, and the Certificate Authority. It would be unusual for an end user to connect directly to an infrastructure instance.

The middle tier instances run applications for users. These will usually be written in Java and run in OC4J instances. Middle tier instances also provide the PL/SQL gateway and CGI processing, and (depending on the installation type) can also run Portal and Wireless, and Forms, Reports, and Discoverer servers. All middle tier instances have an Apache web listener as their entry point. This routes user requests through to the appropriate application server service by using modules provided by Oracle and dynamically linked to Apache. All the applications deployed to a middle tier instance can make use of Oracle databases.

Web Cache is a transparent front end to one or more middle tier instances. It accelerates delivery of frequently requested content and can also act as a load balancer and be a part of the site's fault tolerance structure.

Figure 2-6 shows the whole picture.

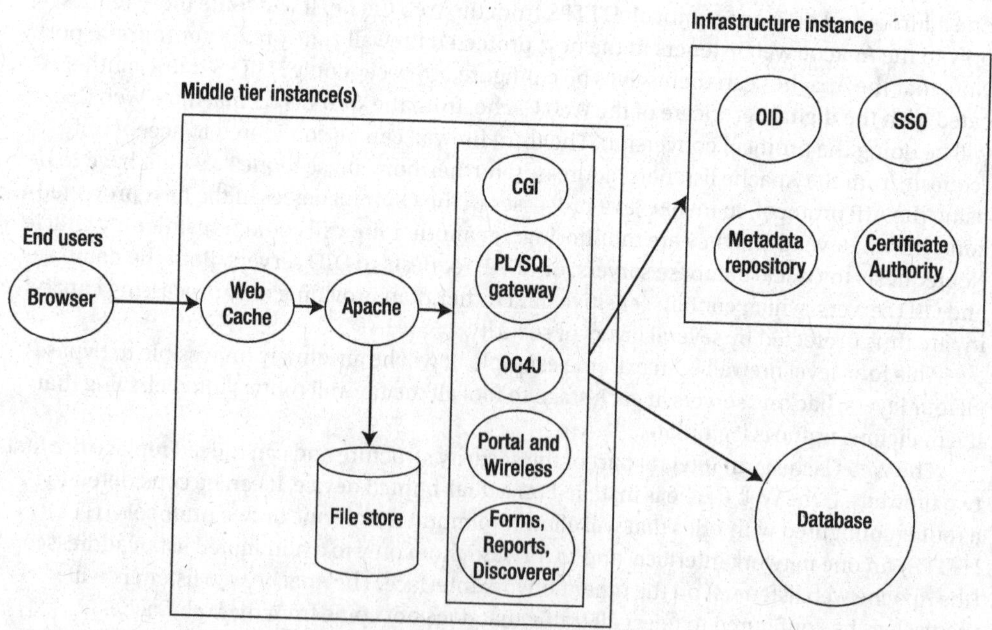

Figure 2-6. *The complete Oracle Application Server topology*

As end users connect to and navigate through applications, they issue URLs or other HTTP requests. These are received by the first layer of the middle tier instance: the Web Cache. The Web Cache returns the document requested if it can, but otherwise will forward the request to the second layer of the middle tier, the Apache web listener. Apache will service the request if it is for a static file, but otherwise it will forward it to the next layer, the appropriate application server service. The service and the applications deployed to it may well make use of the infrastructure instance for security and other purposes and will almost certainly connect to an Oracle database containing the application's data. The document retrieved or generated by the middle tier is returned to the end user's browser via Apache and the Web Cache, completing the HTTP request-response cycle.

CHAPTER 3

Oracle Collaboration Suite Architecture

The components that make up an Oracle Collaboration Suite (OCS) installation run within the Oracle Application Server environment and (with one exception) store their data in Oracle databases. They use a common security model based on the Oracle Internet Directory LDAP server. And most important from the user's point of view, they can all be accessed through a single portal from a browser. But the most important thing from the administrator's point of view is that the architecture is based on the use of industry standard communications protocols that allow components distributed across platforms and servers to work together.

The administrator of an Oracle Collaboration Suite installation has to be familiar with an extraordinary range of products, but the architecture is simple: a database tier that manages the data access, and an applications tier that runs the components that access the data. This model applies to both end-user components and the back-end infrastructure components. The complexity comes in the way many different protocols are used to connect the components together, and perhaps the manner in which different components are distributed across the tiers. But in principle, Oracle Collaboration Suite is just another Oracle Application Server farm that has been preconfigured with a set of applications.

Some of the component applications are implemented with Java and so run completely within the Oracle Application Server environment. Others use external processes, but for the most part they can still be controlled with Oracle Application Server utilities.

Communications Protocols

All the protocols used by the various Oracle Collaboration Suite components are layered protocols—layered on top of TCP. With the exception of Oracle Net they are all international standards defined by the appropriate multinational NGOs (nongovernmental organizations). Oracle Net itself, which is used to maintain connections to an Oracle database, has a published API for C and Java. The use of nonproprietary protocols and the Oracle Net APIs opens up the Oracle Collaboration Suite environment to developers, letting them write their own interfaces to any products they choose. It also should ease the process of migration to Oracle Collaboration Suite, both for end users and administrators.

Following is a description of the protocols and where they are used. Note that many of the protocols have SSL variants. Whether to use SSL is not a decision to be made by the administrator, but by those to whom he reports. Always remember that while SSL communication improves security, it may be detrimental to performance and can be very inconvenient. The following section describes the SSL mechanism; subsequent sections describe each protocol.

Secure Sockets Layer (SSL) Protocol

SSL manages encryption and check summing of data during transmission, and identification of users and services. The mechanism is based on dual-key encryption, also known as PKI (Public Key Infrastructure), and digital certificates.

The principle of dual-key encryption is that every user and every server should be issued with a pair of numbers: one designated as his public key and the other as his private key. The numbers are mathematically linked in such a fashion that if data is encrypted with one number, it can only be decrypted with the other. When one party (say, a user called John) anywhere in the world wishes to send data to another party he will send it via a mail server, called `mail.bplc.com` for this example. He first sends a message to `mail.bplc.com` asking the mail server to send him its public key. The mail server replies with its public key, unencrypted. All SSL users will send their public keys to anyone on demand. John then uses `mail.bplc.com`'s public key to encrypt his data, and sends it to `mail.bplc.com`. The mail server will have access to the matching private key and can use it to decrypt the message. The data is completely protected while in transit: a hacker could certainly intercept the encrypted message and the mail server's public key, but that is useless to him because the message can only be decrypted by the server's private key. As long as private keys really are kept private by the user to whom they are issued, this mechanism is absolutely secure. The problem of private keys becoming known is addressed by lists of compromised keys that are distributed by all digital certificate–issuing authorities, and SSL users should download these lists regularly and install them in their software.

Encryption by itself is not enough. Detecting errors in transmission is also necessary. These could be introduced accidentally or through malicious attempts to disrupt traffic. The SSL protocol includes a check summing algorithm that will detect any such damage.

The problem of identifying network users is solved with digital certificates. A digital certificate is a very simple document stating (among other things) the user's name; the dates for which the certificate is valid; the body that issued the certificate; and the certificate's unique serial number. If one party wishes to confirm the identity of another, it will ask for the digital certificate. To continue the example, the `mail.bplc.com` server can authenticate John by asking for John's digital certificate. John will encrypt his certificate with his private key and send it. The server then sends a request to John for John's public key and uses this to decrypt the certificate and confirm John's identity. The fact that the certificate could be decrypted with the public key proves that it must have been encrypted with the matching private key, to which only John has access. A potential problem is that an imposter could write his own certificate spuriously identifying himself as John and use any pair of keys he has to encrypt it. This is addressed by checking with a hierarchy of certificate issuers. If the server suspects that John's certificate is a fake, it can ask the certificate issuer if he really did give that certificate to John or not. The certificate issuer will also authenticate himself with a digital certificate that can be checked in the same manner, culminating with a top-level issuer who is trusted and assumed to be genuine.

An Oracle Application Server infrastructure instance comes with the Oracle Certificate Authority server. This is a process that generates and issues digital certificates. It is completely self-contained but may not be considered "trusted" by external services and users. To get around this, you should purchase a certificate from an internationally trusted certificate-issuing authority. This trusted certificate will then be the root of all certificates issued to your servers and users. There are a number of such authorities, including Certiposte in France, Thawte in South Africa, or VeriSign in the United States. You can use a certificate purchased from any top-level issuer—shop around for the best deal.

Most of the protocols used in the Oracle Collaboration Suite environment have SSL variants. To use them, you must configure the server processes to monitor a port for the protocol, and the client processes to call that port with the protocol. The encryption, check summing, and certificate exchange are completely automatic.

Certificate management may not be an issue for servers. You can install the files containing your certificates and public/private key pairs on your server computers and protect them with the operating system's security facilities in such a fashion that the server processes can read them but no one else can.

End users face a different problem, because the certificates need to be installed in their browsers. This means that either the user has to install them permanently on each machine that he is likely to use, with the consequent risk that anyone else using the machine may have access to them, or he has to carry the certificate around with him and repeatedly install and uninstall it. Oracle Corporation's enhancement to SSL is the use of *wallets*. These are a means of managing digital certificates. The wallet is a file containing your certificates, which you upload to an Oracle Internet Directory. Whenever you are using a Single Sign-On–aware application, the application can instruct your browser to request a download of the contents of your wallet from the Oracle Internet Directory. To ensure privacy, before this is done you must supply the wallet password; this is protected in transit by encryption with the Oracle Internet Directory's public key. The wallet is never saved permanently in the browser; it is only in the memory cache and is cleared when you exit from the application. Use of wallets is automatic in Oracle Collaboration Suite. When a user is created he is issued a digital certificate and the wallet is stored as part of his directory entry.

Whether and where you choose to enable SSL is a decision to make by agreement with your end users and your network managers. There is no question that SSL will impact adversely on performance, but if your data is sensitive there may be no option. The default Oracle Collaboration Suite installation will use SSL to protect passwords during the Single Sign-On process, but not to protect subsequent traffic. Typically you will not want to use SSL encryption to protect traffic between your servers, as they should be on a network segment that is already shielded from the outside world by one or more firewall routers; but you may wish to protect traffic to and from your end users. You might, for example, choose to use HTTP between your Web Cache and your Apache web listener but use the SSL variant HTTPS between end users and Web Cache.

TCP/IP

TCP (Transmission Control Protocol), with routing capability provided by the IP layer, is the underlying protocol used by all the Oracle Collaboration Suite layered protocols. You cannot run Oracle Collaboration Suite over any other protocol. The only exception is Oracle Net which can use others, such as named pipes on Windows or whatever IPC is provided by your operating system for local connections. The SSL variation of TCP is TCPS.

Historically, Oracle used to support a wide range of protocols (with the exception of NetBIOS/NetBEUI, which has always lacked an adequate routing capability), but in recent years the global market place has standardized on TCP layered protocols, and so has Oracle. As TCP develops, Oracle products will develop in parallel.

Most Oracle Collaboration Suite processes do not use raw TCP. The major exception to this is Calendar. Users connecting to the Calendar server with the client-server tools, either the Calendar Desktop Client or the Oracle Connector for Microsoft Outlook, will be making TCP connections to the `uniengd` server-side process that is supporting their session. Users of the Calendar Application System web client will be using HTTP or HTTPS to connect from their browsers through the middle tier Web Cache and Apache web listener to the `ocas.fcgi` process that generates the Calendar web interface; but the `ocas.fcgi` process will then use TCP for the client-server connection to its `uniengd` process.

HTTP and HTTPS

HTTP, or its SSL variant HTTPS, is used by client processes to contact Oracle Collaboration Suite server processes. It is also used internally between a number of server processes. The stateless nature of the HTTP request-response cycle means that the processes have to make use of session tracking tools such as cookies and HTTP headers to maintain sessions on the applications tier.

Typically HTTP is used by end users with browsers to contact the Web Cache at the front of your middle tier Oracle Application Server instance(s). The Web Cache will forward the request, again using HTTP, to a middle tier Apache web listener. If there is no Single Sign-On cookie in the browser, the web listener will return a redirection URL to the browser, instructing it to contact the Oracle Application Server infrastructure's Apache web listener with the URL for Single Sign-On authentication. This will be over HTTPS. Following authentication and setting the Single Sign-On cookie, the browser will revert to HTTP and return to the middle tier Web Cache, go through that to the middle tier Apache web listener, and from there request application services with whatever protocol is appropriate.

Mail Protocols

The client-server mail protocols are IMAP4, POP3, and SMTP. There is also the NNTP (Network News Transfer Protocol) used for accessing newsgroups. The SSL variants are IMAPS, POP3S, and NNTPS; there is no SSL version of SMTP. To listen for requests on all seven protocols, the Mail server runs one process: the Mail listener. This is launched from the same executable code used to launch the database listener process. The listener will be configured with an entry in the `listener.ora` file in the middle tier instance's Oracle home such as the following:

```
LISTENER_ES =
  (DESCRIPTION_LIST =
    (DESCRIPTION =
      (ADDRESS = (PROTOCOL = IPC)(KEY = ocsapps.jwlnx1.bplc.co.za)))
    (DESCRIPTION =
      (ADDRESS = (PROTOCOL = TCP)(HOST = jwlnx1.bplc.co.za)(PORT = 25))
      (PRESENTATION = ESSMI))
    (DESCRIPTION =
      (ADDRESS = (PROTOCOL = TCP)(HOST = jwlnx1.bplc.co.za)(PORT = 143))
      (PRESENTATION = IMAP))
```

```
(DESCRIPTION =
  (ADDRESS = (PROTOCOL = TCP)(HOST = jwlnx1.bplc.co.za)(PORT = 110))
  (PRESENTATION = POP))
(DESCRIPTION =
  (ADDRESS = (PROTOCOL = TCP)(HOST = jwlnx1.bplc.co.za)(PORT = 119))
  (PRESENTATION = ESNNI))
(DESCRIPTION =
  (ADDRESS = (PROTOCOL = TCPS)(HOST = jwlnx1.bplc.co.za)(PORT = 993))
  (PRESENTATION = IMAPSSL))
(DESCRIPTION =
  (ADDRESS = (PROTOCOL = TCPS)(HOST = jwlnx1.bplc.co.za)(PORT = 995))
  (PRESENTATION = POPSSL))
(DESCRIPTION =
  (ADDRESS = (PROTOCOL = TCPS)(HOST = jwlnx1.bplc.co.za)(PORT = 563))
  (PRESENTATION = ESNNISSL))
)
```

In the previous example all seven protocols have been configured to listen on their default ports on the one address that is the hostname of the node. If the node has multiple network cards, or you want to use nonstandard ports, make appropriate changes to the entry.

End users can make use of thick client tools to access the mail services directly. Possible clients include Microsoft Outlook and Netscape Messenger. The Mail listener routes requests to the Mail server processes, which run in an OC4J component in the Oracle Application Server middle tier instance. An alternative method for users to use Mail is through the Webmail application. This is an OC4J application that users access with HTTP (or HTTPS) through the Web Cache and then the web listener. Webmail contacts the mail server processes and constructs an HTML-based user interface.

As well as the protocols that allow an e-mail client to contact an e-mail server, Oracle Collaboration Suite also supports the P-IMAP (Push IMAP) protocol, as part of Oracle Mobile Collaboration. P-IMAP lets the server take the initiative. Whenever a message arrives in a user's mailbox, rather than waiting for the user to retrieve it the next time he connects to the mail server, P-IMAP will send a message to the user's mobile device: his cell phone, or PDA. This message alerts the user to the presence of a new Mail message. Mail, Content Services, and Calendar can all be configured to alert users with P-IMAP messages whenever certain events occur.

File-Serving Protocols

The Content Services component of Oracle Collaboration Suite now supports four file-serving protocols:

- HTTP
- WebDAV
- FTP
- FTPS

Previous releases of Content Services also supported Windows SMB file sharing and NFS, but these protocols have been dropped with release 10*g*. The four remaining protocols are proving to be the ones that most users are standardizing on, and they should be enough. HTTP and WebDAV are undoubtedly the most user-friendly protocols for end users and include better security. The others are only likely to be used for initial uploads of data, or by users of older systems that do not have HTTP or WebDAV clients.

Calendar Protocols

The international standards for calendar and diary applications protocols are not yet fully developed. The IETF (Internet Engineering Task Force) has defined the iCalendar standard in the request-for-comment paper RFC2445. iCal is intended to assist with deploying interoperable calendaring and scheduling services for the Internet. iCal is supported by Calendar—but very few presently available third-party tools support it. The Calendar software development toolkit can assist application developers in designing interfaces to Calendar using iCal, or they can use the web services interface that is presented by the Calendar Application System.

The lack of adherence to standards by most client tool developers is why Oracle distributes its own Calendar Desktop Client (available for Linux, Solaris, Windows, and Mac) and also distributes the Oracle Connector for Outlook, which gives access to Calendar data from Microsoft Outlook clients.

Many users will download Calendar data to a local client, such as Microsoft Outlook. This allows users to work while disconnected from the Calendar server, but it does raise the question of how locally stored data should be synchronized with centrally stored data. The industry standard for this is the SyncML protocol, which is a layered protocol running over HTTP. Oracle's implementation of SyncML is known as Mobile Data Sync. Any SyncML-compliant client can connect to the Calendar server and transfer Calendar data in both directions. Future releases of Oracle Collaboration Suite will (according to Oracle Corporation) enable the use of SyncML for synchronizing local and central storage of Mail and Content Services data, as well as Calendar data.

LDAP and LDAPS

LDAP and its SSL variant LDAPS are used to send requests to the Oracle Internet Directory LDAP server. This is a set of processes that carry out directory searches and maintenance operations. It is possible for users to contact the LDAP listener process directly, using a tool such as Oracle's Directory Administrator, but in all normal circumstances connections to the LDAP server will be made by middle tier server processes.

Typical use of LDAP is when a user requests authentication from the Single Sign-On server. He will contact the Single Sign-On server with HTTP, and the Single Sign-On server will generate the LDAP request to the Oracle Internet Directory. Components such as Calendar and Mail also generate LDAP requests. The directory is used to store user details, groups, and mailing lists.

Wireless Protocols

Wireless network providers have developed their own proprietary protocols. They should also have a WAP (Wireless Application Protocol) gateway that can convert traffic from the provider's own proprietary protocol to one of the industry standard wireless protocols. Of these, Oracle Application Server supports WML, HDML, and cHTML. Messages in one of these formats can be delivered to the Oracle Application Server Wireless component, which converts them to platform-independent XML documents. These documents are delivered to a Portal process, which acts as the client to the Oracle Collaboration Suite application components. The application component itself is completely protected from the user interface; it has no knowledge of or any need to know the type of device with which the end user is connecting.

Oracle Net

To establish a session against an Oracle database instance, you must use Oracle Net. Even if the user process is running on the same machine as the database instance, the connection is still a client-server connection with some kind of network communication protocol separating the two.

Oracle Net ships with a number of protocol adapters that abstract the Oracle-specific and proprietary layers of Oracle Net from whatever network transport mechanisms are provided by your host operating system. The default configuration is to use the TCP protocol adapter, but you can use others if you wish. Whatever protocol adapter is used, the database sessions are established using platform- and protocol-independent calls through the Oracle Call Interface (OCI) API, which is available for both C and Java. The protocol adapter receives these calls and maps them onto whatever is appropriate for the chosen transport protocol.

Collaboration Suite and Application Server Components

The Oracle Application Server infrastructure instance is used in the usual fashion in an Oracle Collaboration Suite installation: it provides support services to applications deployed to one or more middle tier instances. The infrastructure instance installed with Oracle Collaboration Suite comes with a certain amount of preconfiguration that is specific to Oracle Collaboration Suite. The middle tier is similarly preconfigured with a set of applications.

Infrastructure Components

Oracle Collaboration Suite makes use of all the Identity Management components of the infrastructure. The Oracle Internet Directory is used for storing both user data (such as passwords) and application data (such as Mail mailing lists); all the application component web interfaces are Single Sign-On–aware; and the Certificate Authority is used to generate digital certificates stored in wallets in users' Oracle Internet Directory entries.

The preconfiguration of Identity Management is to enable the provisioning of user accounts in the various application components. The standard installation comes with provisioning set up for Mail, Calendar, Content Services, and Real-Time Collaboration. Whenever you create a user through the OIDDAS application you will be prompted to create these accounts as well; the OIDDAS application is fully described in Chapter 6. A critical difference between a normal Oracle Application Server infrastructure instance and the infrastructure instance for an Oracle Collaboration Suite for installation is the automatic deployment of the modified OIDDAS.

The infrastructure installation comes with an Oracle database. This is preseeded with the usual infrastructure schemas for directory information and for Single Sign-On and for the metadata repository that is required to store all the farm configuration information. These are absolutely standard.

An Oracle Collaboration Suite infrastructure database also has schemas for storing Mail and Content Services data. These are not really part of an infrastructure instance, and in all but very small installations you will not use these—you will run the installer again, probably on a different machine, to create a second database. This is the database toward which you will point your Mail and Content Services applications.

The final use of the infrastructure database is the Portal component repository. The Portal repository is preseeded with the portlet information needed to run the Oracle Collaboration Suite Portal, the user's entry point to the system. You can leave the Portal schemas there or, if the one database is heavily loaded, transfer it to a different database created especially for this purpose.

Middle Tier Components

Virtually all of the Oracle Application Server middle tier services will be used in an Oracle Collaboration Suite installation:

- Web Cache
- Apache web listener
- The PL/SQL gateway
- Several OC4J instances
- Portal and Wireless
- The FastCGI module

The Web Cache acts as the entry point to a middle tier Oracle Application Server instance, sending users' URL connection requests through to the Apache web listener. Apache routes them on to the appropriate application server component. The Forms, Reports, and Discoverer services (collectively known as Business Intelligence) are not used by Oracle Collaboration Suite.

The Web Cache

The Web Cache of an Oracle Collaboration Suite middle tier instance is preconfigured with caching rules that will be applicable for most installations. You can change them if you wish, but this will not usually be necessary. They permit Web Cache to cache static documents—such as images and pages of HTML—for a few minutes before getting fresh copies. Where appropriate, the documents are compressed before transmission.

What you may wish to change is the load-balancing features of Web Cache if you have installed multiple middle tiers. In an environment with more than one middle tier instance, if the instances are symmetrical, you can configure connect-time failover and load balancing between them by registering all the Apache web listeners with all the Web Caches. You can even take this further by putting the Web Caches into a Web Cache cluster. If the instances are asymmetrical—perhaps one for Mail, the other for Content Services—you can still set up a Web Cache cluster, but of course failover and fault tolerance will be impossible.

The default installation will only permit 100 concurrent connections through the Web Cache to the middle tier Apache web listener. This is not a very large number for an Oracle Collaboration Suite site, and you will need to raise it for all but the smallest installations.

If you permit users to connect with thick client tools, such as an IMAP mail tool or an FTP client, they will bypass the Web Cache and contact the appropriate protocol server directly. Users of the Calendar Desktop Client will also bypass the Web Cache.

The Apache Web Listener

Apache will be preconfigured with everything needed for users to access Oracle Collaboration Suite and should not need much (if any) adjustment.

The default configuration can support 150 concurrent connections, as specified with this directive in the `httpd.conf` file:

```
MaxClients 150
```

This amount can be increased up to 1,024 with the version of Apache distributed with Oracle Collaboration Suite. To go beyond that, it is necessary to recompile Apache (which will probably work but is not supported by Oracle Corporation). If you find that user connections are being rejected because the `MaxClients` limit has been reached, change the setting and bounce Apache. Remember that if you edit the file manually, you must subsequently update the metadata repository with the distributed configuration management `dcmctl` utility as follows:

```
dcmctl updateconfig
```

It is probably better to use Application Server Control, which will always update the metadata repository concurrently with the configuration files, and also do some syntax checking.

If you allow Apache to launch too many child processes, operating system performance may degrade. An alternative approach to increasing the number of concurrent users that Apache can support that may avoid the necessity of launching many child processes would be to adjust the keep alive settings. These allow browsers to maintain persistent connections to the web listener, modifying the standard HTTP behavior where each request-response is a new connection. By default, these settings are the following:

```
KeepAlive On
MaxKeepAliveRequests 100
KeepAliveTimeout 15
```

Reducing the number of requests that one session is allowed to make before cutting the connection and/or reducing the amount of time the session will be held open waiting for another request will allow a larger number of concurrent users to be serviced by a smaller number of child processes. But if you find that whatever you do the workload is too great, consider limiting the number of concurrent requests that the Web Cache will forward to Apache. The Web Cache is generally better at handling overloads than is Apache; this is part of its reason for being.

Apache's main function on Oracle Collaboration Suite middle tier instances is to route requests through modplsql to Portal access; modoc4j to one of several OC4J instances that run the Mail and Content Services servers; and modfastcgi for the Calendar Application System processes. On the infrastructure instance, Apache responds to Single Sign-On login requests from users' browsers and connects users to the OIDDAS OC4J application. OIDDAS can be used by users to manage their own accounts in the Oracle Internet Directory, or by administrators to manage and provision anyone's accounts.

The PL/SQL Gateway

The PL/SQL gateway is a method for invoking PL/SQL code execution within a database by issuing URLs from a browser. The gateway is implemented by an Apache module and configured by creating Database Access Descriptors (DADs). A middle tier instance will have one DAD preconfigured: this is the DAD used to access Portal. DADs are defined in the `dads.conf` file, which is included in the `plsql.conf` file which is included in the `oracle_apache.conf` file which is itself included in the `httpd.conf` file. The DAD will typically be configured like this:

```
<Location /pls/portal>
    SetHandler pls_handler
    Order allow,deny
    Allow from All
    AllowOverride None
    PlsqlDatabaseUsername portal
    PlsqlDatabasePassword @BU6ZzULEHHT2qsv1HhCnwmXXpol9uz87iA==
    PlsqlDatabaseConnectString cn=ocsdb,cn=oraclecontext NetServiceNameFormat
    PlsqlNLSLanguage AMERICAN_AMERICA.AL32UTF8
    PlsqlAuthenticationMode SingleSignOn
    PlsqlDocumentTablename portal.wwdoc_document
    PlsqlDocumentPath docs
    PlsqlDocumentProcedure portal.wwdoc_process.process_download
    PlsqlDefaultPage portal.home
    PlsqlPathAlias url
    PlsqlPathAliasProcedure portal.wwpth_api_alias.process_download
</Location>
```

This DAD creates the virtual path `/pls/portal` that will connect to the Oracle Collaboration Suite home page. Studying the various directives shows that this is generated by the procedure `portal.home` in the schema portal whose password is encrypted. This home page redirects the user to Single Sign-On if the Single Sign-On cookie isn't present in his browser.

The infrastructure will also have a DAD defined. This is the DAD used to connect to Single Sign-On and will typically be defined like this:

```
<Location /pls/orasso>
    SetHandler pls_handler
    Order deny,allow
    Allow from All
    AllowOverride None
    PlsqlDatabaseUsername orasso
    PlsqlDatabasePassword @Bby16cA7OllshQY/oLWHQ2vh4sMV4SkZCw==
    PlsqlDatabaseConnectString cn=ocsdb,cn=oraclecontext NetServiceNameFormat
    PlsqlNLSLanguage AMERICAN_AMERICA.AL32UTF8
    PlsqlAuthenticationMode SingleSignOn
    PlsqlSessionCookieName orasso
```

```
    PlsqlDocumentTablename orasso.wwdoc_document
    PlsqlDocumentPath docs
    PlsqlDocumentProcedure orasso.wwdoc_process.process_download
    PlsqlDefaultPage orasso.home
    PlsqlPathAlias url
    PlsqlPathAliasProcedure orasso.wwpth_api_alias.process_download
</Location>
```

Note that as well as the database schema name and password to use to connect to the Single Sign-On server and the procedure to run, there is also the name of the Single Sign-On cookie, orasso, that will be read and set if it is not already set.

The OC4J Instances

A large part of Oracle Collaboration Suite is written in Java servlets and Enterprise JavaBeans deployed to OC4J instances. A middle tier Oracle Collaboration Suite instance will be configured with a number of OC4J instances. The more important ones that should usually be running at all times are the following:

- OC4J_Content: The Content Services application that runs the various file-serving protocol servers.
- OC4J_Mail: The Mail application that runs the various e-mail protocol servers.
- OC4J_OCSADMIN: The Ultrasearch application.
- OC4J_OCSCLIENT: The starting point of the user interface to Oracle Collaboration Suite that must be running if any of the web clients are to be used.
- OC4J_Portal: A PL/SQL application that requires several Java modules, including the PPE that renders the pages to be returned to the user, to be running on the middle tier.

An Oracle Collaboration Suite infrastructure instance will be configured with one OC4J instance that should be running at all times. This is the OC4J_SECURITY instance that runs the OIDDAS application used to provide a web interface for managing Oracle Internet Directory accounts and provisioning application component accounts.

Note that there is also a HOME OC4J instance created in both middle tier and infrastructure instances. It should never be necessary to start this.

The FastCGI Module

The Calendar component has a web interface: the Calendar Application System. Unlike the other Oracle Collaboration Suite components, Calendar can be run independently of Oracle Application Server. For this reason, the Calendar Application System does not use any proprietary Oracle technology, such as OC4J, but rather has been implemented as a CGI application that could, theoretically, be run by any third-party web server.

To avoid the inefficiencies inherent in the pure CGI runtime environment, the Calendar Application System runs in the FastCGI environment enabled by the modfastcgi Apache module. The module itself is enabled with directives in httpd.conf and user access provided through these directives that set up the virtual paths to the Calendar Application System executable code shown here:

```
ScriptAlias /ocas-bin/ "/OCS/product/10.1.1/ocs_1/apps/ocas/bin/"
ScriptAlias /ocws-bin/ "/OCS/product/10.1.1/ocs_1/apps/ocas/bin/"
ScriptAlias /ocst-bin/ "/OCS/product/10.1.1/ocs_1/apps/ocas/bin/"
ScriptAlias /global-bin/ "/OCS/product/10.1.1/ocs_1/apps/ocas/bin/"
Alias /ocas/ "/OCS/product/10.1.1/ocs_1/apps/ocas/htdocs/"
```

These directives are in the `ocal.conf` file which is included in the `oracle_apache.conf` file which is itself included in the `httpd.conf` file. The `ScriptAlias` directives create virtual paths that identify directories of files to be executed. An `Alias` directive creates a virtual path to a directory of files to be transferred.

The Database Tier

It is possible for a fully functional Oracle Collaboration Suite installation to have only one database, but such an arrangement is only suitable for small installations supporting only a few hundred users. Larger installations will have at least two databases: one for the infrastructure components, one for the middle tier components. Even in a single database environment, different schemas are used to separate the data into different areas so that the one database appears to be several. Every Oracle Collaboration Suite database you create through the installation tools will contain all the schemas; you decide which schemas to use in which database.

Apart from the scale of the installation influencing the number of databases required, the different patterns of activity against different groups of data may also make multiple databases advisable. It can be difficult to tune a single database to support several types of workload concurrently; separating the data makes it possible to optimize databases for each kind of usage.

The Metadata Repository

An Oracle Application Server farm requires a metadata repository, which stores information regarding all the OPMN-managed components in the Oracle Application Server Farm, including OC4J instances, Apache web listeners, and application server instances. This repository can be based on a set of operating system files, but for an Oracle Collaboration Suite installation it is always in a database. The metadata repository schema is DCM (Distributed Configuration Management). This schema is created the first time you run the installer and is updated subsequently by configuration changes. These changes are made through the DCM mechanism, invoked either with the command-line utility `dcmctl` or through the Application Server Control tool. It should never be necessary to view or update any data in the metadata repository schemas by any other means.

The Identity Management Schemas

Both Oracle Internet Directory and Single Sign-On require their own database schemas. These schemas are created automatically in the preseeded database installed with an Oracle Application Server infrastructure installation.

The directory schema is ODS. This schema contains the tables that store the directory information tree data. One Oracle Internet Directory can only make use of one database; it is not possible to distribute the directory across multiple databases. To scale the directory to manage a vast number of concurrent requests, you can launch as many servers as you wish, on different machines if necessary, but they can only connect to one database. This limitation is unlikely to be a problem; a well-tuned database on appropriate hardware can handle millions of directory lookups per hour. If the limits of acceptable performance are reached, the database can be scaled up by converting to RAC (Real Application Clusters). If even this is inadequate, additional directories can be created and kept synchronized with replication. These options are discussed in Chapter 17, but they are more likely to be required as part of a fault-tolerance strategy than for reasons of scale.

The Single Sign-On schemas are ORASSO, ORASSO_DS, ORASSO_PA, ORASSO_PS, and ORASSO_PUBLIC. Single Sign-On is a PL/SQL application; it consists of stored procedures. The data storage is minimal. It connects to the Oracle Internet Directory with LDAP to access the information it needs. The workload of Single Sign-On is unlikely to impact seriously on the infrastructure database because the whole idea of Single Sign-On is to limit the authentication workload. Once the Single Sign-On cookie has been set in a user's browser, he need not reauthenticate until it expires. This expiry time is configurable by the administrator, but as it defaults to eight hours it becomes apparent that the Single Sign-On workload should be trivial when compared to the other tasks the database must support.

Oracle Certificate Authority also has schemas in the infrastructure database: OCA and ORAOCA_PUBLIC.

It should never be necessary to adjust any data in the identity management schemas other than through the provided tools.

The Product Schemas

An Oracle Collaboration Suite installation requires database schemas for three products: Portal, Mail, and Content Services. The Portal schemas are the standard schemas found in any Oracle Application Server infrastructure database; the Mail and Content Services schemas are specific to the Oracle Collaboration Suite.

The Portal schemas are PORTAL, PORTAL_APP, PORTAL_DEMO, and PORTAL_PUBLIC. These are preconfigured to support user access to the Oracle Collaboration Suite portlets, and you can adjust them to your own requirements through the Portal configuration tools. This might be to customize the appearance of the various windows, or to include portlets that would link to non-Oracle Collaboration Suite applications. A complex Portal site supporting thousands of users can place a significant workload on the database containing the Portal repository, though the actual volume of data is less likely to be important. If this work does impact on other activity, it is possible to transfer the Portal repository to another database by using export and import routines.

The Mail schema is ESMAIL. This schema contains all the data that makes up your store of Mail messages, including newsgroups, if you have any. This may come to many gigabytes of information, and for an installation of thousands of users will require its own database. If 10,000 users are allowed a mail quota of 100MB each, the total will be a terabyte. And that is before any space is allocated for indexes. Data volumes of this order are no problem for an Oracle database and, if necessary, the database can be converted to RAC; but if performance is seen to drop off, the Mail store can be divided across multiple databases. Then each Mail protocol server can be directed toward a particular datastore.

The Content Services schemas are CONTENT, CONTENT$CM, and CONTENT$ID. The first of these stores the actual data (documents, images, recordings, and anything else that users may want to store in the file server) as large objects. The other schemas are used for communication with other components. There is no limit to the amount of space that end users can take up on file servers, if you do not impose restrictions. The actual level of activity, however, may be comparatively low, and a vast proportion of the data may well be static. One Content Services domain can make use of only one database, and on any installation with more than a few hundred users you may well wish to dedicate a database to this purpose.

The Calendar Datastore

The Calendar datastore is not an Oracle database. It is a proprietary data structure with its own management facilities. It is not impossible that at some future time Calendar data will be stored within an Oracle database, but as of the time of this writing no announcements have been made by Oracle to this effect.

Architecturally, the Calendar datastore is very different from an Oracle database. Perhaps the most significant difference is that there is no equivalent of the redo log. However the Calendar datastore is not difficult to administer and does scale nicely, across multiple machines if necessary.

Note that the Calendar server itself does not run within the Oracle Application Server environment. It can be controlled with OPMN but is in fact a set of processes that run independently of the Oracle Application Server middle tier. It is, however, totally integrated with the Oracle Internet Directory, and it is through this that Calendar becomes incorporated into the Oracle Collaboration Suite.

The separation of Calendar from the rest of the Oracle Collaboration Suite is deliberate and allows it to be run as a self-contained product.

Mapping Application Components to Middle Tier Components

The relationship between the Oracle Collaboration Suite applications as seen by end users and the Oracle Application Server configuration is not always immediately obvious. In a single box site this is not an issue; simply start all the processes on the middle tier and the infrastructure instances, and everything will function. But in a multinode installation, where services are distributed across a number of machines, it becomes necessary to understand which middle tier components need to be running on which nodes to enable the various Oracle Collaboration Suite applications.

If a user requests an application, and a necessary component is not running, it will usually be reported in his browser with an HTTP error 500, the internal server error. As a rule, any components not essential on a node should be disabled, as they will only waste resources.

Figure 3-1 shows all the middle tier components as displayed in Application Server Control. A brief description of each component follows, relating the component to the functionality it provides. In all cases, these components are dealt with fully in later chapters.

Oracle Enterprise Manager - Application Server: ocsapps.jwlnx1.bplc.co.za - Microsoft Internet Explorer

File Edit View Favorites Tools Help

Address http://jwlnx1.bplc.co.za:1810/emd/console/ocs/collabSuiteHome$farm=ocsapps.jwlnx1.bplc.co.za$type=oracle* Go

Select	Name	Status	Start Time	Usage (%)	(MB)	Administration
	Calendar Application System	⇩	Unavailable	Unavailable	Unavailable	N/A
	Calendar Server	⇧	Jan 20, 2006 7:50:58 PM	0.00	4.38	
	Content	⇩	Unavailable	Unavailable	Unavailable	
	Discussions	⇧	N/A	N/A	N/A	
	HTTP_Server	⇧	Jan 20, 2006 4:29:33 PM	0.98	91.45	N/A
	Mail Application	⇧	Jan 20, 2006 5:12:47 PM	0.00	37.95	
	Mobile Collaboration	⇩	N/A	N/A	N/A	
	OC4J_Content	⇩	Unavailable	Unavailable	Unavailable	N/A
	OC4J_imeeting	⇩	Unavailable	Unavailable	Unavailable	N/A
	OC4J_Mail	⇧	Jan 20, 2006 5:13:10 PM	0.00	38.37	N/A
	OC4J_OCSADMIN	⇩	Unavailable	Unavailable	Unavailable	N/A
	OC4J_OCSClient	⇧	Jan 20, 2006 5:13:39 PM	0.00	134.82	N/A
	OC4J_Portal	⇧	Jan 20, 2006 5:15:19 PM	0.00	86.78	N/A
	OC4J_Wireless	⇩	Unavailable	Unavailable	Unavailable	N/A
	Oracle Workflow	⇧	N/A	N/A	N/A	N/A
	Portal:portal	⇧	N/A	N/A	N/A	N/A
	Real-Time Collaboration	⇩	Unavailable	Unavailable	Unavailable	
	Search	⇧	N/A	N/A	N/A	
	Service_Component_Container	⇩	Unavailable	Unavailable	Unavailable	N/A
	Web Access	⇧	N/A	N/A	N/A	N/A
	Web Cache	⇧	Jan 20, 2006 4:29:39 PM	0.004	33.32	N/A
	Wireless	⇩	Unavailable	Unavailable	Unavailable	N/A
	Workspaces	⇧	N/A	N/A	N/A	
	Management	⇧	Jan 20, 2006 4:24:09 PM	1.90	221.32	N/A

Figure 3-1. *The middle tier components as shown by Application Server Control*

Note that most of the components have a check box to their left that can be selected. This is to start or stop the component. If it is not started, it cannot be used. Those with the check boxes grayed out cannot be explicitly started or stopped; they are launched on demand. Typically this is because the component is implemented as a PL/SQL application. PL/SQL procedures are run on demand; they cannot be started and left in run mode waiting for connection requests in the way that other services can be.

The Web Interface

All the Oracle Collaboration Suite applications can be accessed through a web interface. For the web interface to run, the following middle tier applications must be started:

- Web Cache
- Oracle HTTP Server
- OC4J_Portal
- Portal
- OC4J_OCSClient
- Web Access

The Web Cache and HTTP Server (the Apache web listener) manage the HTTP traffic between browsers and middle tier instances. Portal, consisting of the component that generates pages and the parallel page engine, is necessary to construct the web pages seen by end users. The OCS client application is needed to provide the session launch capability against the various application servers.

The Web Access component is also part of the web interface but cannot be independently controlled; it will start and stop with the OC4J_OCSClient.

Calendar

The Calendar server itself consists of a set of processes visible in the Application Server Control window as just one component: the Calendar Server. To see the individual processes, use the `opmnctl` utility:

```
[mid oraocs]$ opmnctl status ias-component=CalendarServer

Processes in Instance: ocsapps.jwlnx1.bplc.co.za
-------------------+--------------------+---------+---------
ias-component      | process-type       |     pid | status
-------------------+--------------------+---------+---------
CalendarServer     | Calendar_CSM       |   26772 | Alive
CalendarServer     | Calendar_CWS       |     N/A | Down
CalendarServer     | Calendar_DAS       |     N/A | Down
CalendarServer     | Calendar_SNC       |     N/A | Down
CalendarServer     | Calendar_ENG       |     N/A | Down
CalendarServer     | Calendar_LCK       |     N/A | Down
```

These processes must all be running to provide the full Calendar functionality, though for a simple installation some can be disabled (see Chapter 7 for details). In the previous example, the only process running is the management process that can be used to start and stop other processes remotely. These processes are all that are required if users connect to the Calendar server only with client-server tools, such as Microsoft Outlook or the Calendar Desktop Client; these tools do not communicate with HTTP and can therefore bypass the web components of the middle tier and contact the Calendar server directly.

To enable the web interface to Calendar, another component must be started: the CGI program that generates the web interface and manages the sessions connections from the middle tier to the Calendar server. This is the Calendar Application System component.

Content Services

Content Services is two components: the server component (that consists of several protocol server processes; see Chapter 8 for details) and a web interface component that runs within an OC4J container. These are shown in Application Server Control as the components Content and OC4J_Content.

The server itself is known as a *node*. There may be several nodes in several Oracle Application Server middle tier instances that together service the Content Services domain. A *domain* is a Content Services schema in one database.

Mail

The Mail application (described in detail in Chapter 10) also consists of two components: Mail Application and OC4J_Mail.

The Mail application is the Mail protocol servers. These are the processes that manage requests received over the POP3, IMAP, and SMTP mail protocols and the NNTP protocol. Not shown in Application Server Control is another required process: the Mail listener itself. This is a process launched from the same executables that run the database listener, the `tnslsnr` program. This is not an OPMN process and can only be managed with the `lsnrctl` utility.

The OC4J_Mail component provides the Mail web interface. This is not necessary of users who only access Mail through thick client tools, such as the Microsoft Outlook client.

Real-Time Collaboration

The Real-Time Collaboration components are OC4J_imeeting and Real-Time Collaboration.

The imeeting component manages the web interface for web conferencing; the Real-Time Collaboration component is the server process that enables real-time communication between users.

Search

The Search component, based on the Ultrasearch web crawling facility that can trawl through database and web content, is accessed through the OC4J_OCSADMIN component. If this is not running it is not possible to execute searches against the content of the various component datastores. Searches are not in fact executed against live data; they are executed against indexes built up in the background. The indexing processes are configurable and are provided by each component. Thus, Search does not search the Mail, Content Services, and Calendar datastores; it merely searches indexes of these datastores that are generated by the relevant server processes.

Workflow

Workflow is a standard database facility consisting of a set of Java procedures (PL/SQL procedures in earlier releases of the database) that can be used for managing the flow of data through a system. A workflow is a set of rules that define inputs to a business process, outputs from it, and what should happen in between. A workflow can have branches, loops, and iterations, all of which are user-defined. Workflows are built into many of the Oracle Collaboration Suite applications and can be used to, for example, manage document control and routing within Content Services. The necessary components for using workflows are Oracle Workflow and Service Component Container.

Workflows can generate e-mail messages and any other form of alert that may be needed, provided the appropriate components are also running.

Wireless

The wireless capability is two components: OC4J_Wireless and Wireless.

The Wireless application follows the standard form of an OC4J process that provides the web interface and a separate server process. The Wireless server acts as the gateway to the many possible processes that may run in the background, providing access to the various third-party wireless service providers.

Web Cache

The Web Cache is two processes: the Web Cache itself and the administration process. They can be individually controlled through the `opmnctl` utility.

Workspaces

Workspaces is implemented in PL/SQL and therefore cannot be controlled through OPMN or Application Server Control.

Management

The Management component is the Enterprise Manager daemon. Since this is the Application Server Control process it clearly cannot be started or stopped through Application Server Control; you must manage it with the `emctl` utility, as described in Chapter 5.

Architectural Summary

The Oracle Collaboration Suite is just another Oracle Application Server deployment. But it is quite a complicated deployment. The simplest installation can be a single node, but most deployments will be more complex than that.

The key to integrating the different components into a suite is the use of the Oracle Application Server infrastructure identity management services. All the components (with the exception of Calendar, if you choose to install it independently) rely on the Oracle Internet Directory for account provisioning, and the Single Sign-On server for authentication.

All the components have web interfaces, accessed through the Oracle Application Server middle tier Web Cache and Apache web listener with HTTP or HTTPS. Some of them can be contacted through client-server tools as well, such as Microsoft Outlook for Mail or an FTP client for Content Services. Whatever client interface is used, it will be running over an industry standard protocol. The web interfaces are implemented as Java applications running in

OC4J containers, with the exception of the web interface to Calendar. This is implemented by the Calendar Application System, which is a FastCGI application.

The application components store their data in one or more Oracle databases, with the exception of Calendar (which has its own datastore). It is possible to use one database for all the infrastructure schemas and the product schemas as well, but this would not be advisable for an installation of more than a few hundred users. Larger installations will have both the infrastructure schemas and the product schemas distributed over several databases.

CHAPTER 4

Planning the Deployment and Installation

There are many options for an Oracle Collaboration Suite deployment. In theory, everything can be changed after the initial installation, but in practice it is advisable to get it right at the beginning. A single box installation can be converted to a multinode installation, but this will involve downtime and a great deal of work. If you suspect that one node will not be enough, use two or more from the beginning. It is, however, a relatively simple matter to add further nodes to a two-node deployment.

This chapter lays out some of the possible deployment models with indications of when they will be necessary, and then goes through the detail of installation. But since all traffic to and between Oracle Collaboration Suite components is over TCP layered protocols, the first point to address is the network and—associated with the network—security.

Network Planning

Most Oracle Collaboration Suite installations will be in organizations with existing networks that already have policies in place regarding protocols and security. Some preexisting factors to consider include the following:

- Network Address Translation (NAT) that abstracts the addresses exposed to the outside world from those used internally
- The name resolution techniques in use for mapping network names to IP addresses, both internally and externally
- What traffic routing services are in use: routers, firewalls, reverse proxy servers, and load balancers
- Permitted e-mail protocols for internal and external access and the existence of SMTP mail relay services
- Virtual IP addresses and service failover

In addition, anticipated traffic volumes need to be considered, and estimates of the network latency need to be made. These two things will have an impact on the performance perceived by end users.

Network Security

Security is a vital aspect of network planning. Typically, organizations will have looser security within their own network than outside. It is assumed that internal users have already gone through a degree of authentication. Thus it may well be that more protocols, including client-server protocols, can be used by internal clients than by external clients. This can mean that internal users will be able to make use of user interfaces with greater function, and perhaps better response, than those coming from outside. For example, internal users might be allowed to use IMAP and POP to reach the Mail servers; the Calendar Desktop Client to reach Calendar; and the Oracle Drive or FTP clients to get to their files stored in Content Services. When coming in from the outside, often the only permitted protocol is HTTP, which restricts users to the web client, which is not as rich a user interface.

Use of the SSL variants of all the network protocols is supported by Oracle Collaboration Suite. However, there can be a severe performance overhead to enabling it. SSL is a peer-to-peer protocol, meaning that as a general rule it is not possible to use it for end-to-end encryption and authentication, but only between individual components of the network. This means that it is possible to take the workload of SSL encryption off the various nodes running Oracle Collaboration Suite services, and instead use SSL accelerators running on dedicated hardware. Alternatively, it may be acceptable to use the faster non-SSL protocols within an organization and only use SSL for external traffic where the increased network latency from use of wide area connections may in any case cover up for the encryption delay.

Name Resolution

One practical point is the node's hostname resolution. It must be possible to resolve the local hostname, and this must be fully qualified with a domain. A common problem is that the `hosts` file is incorrectly configured. If you look at the Internet Engineering Task Force document RFC952 that describes name resolution, it is stipulated that in the local name resolution file (which is `\windows\system32\drivers\etc\hosts` on a Windows machine, and typically `/etc/hosts` on UNIX) the entries should be of the following format:

```
<ip_address>    <canonical_hostname>    <aliases...>
```

For example

```
196.234.78.10   jwlnx1.bplc.co.za   jwlnx1
```

A mistake commonly made by both UNIX and Windows administrators is to place the short name, which is only an alias, before the fully qualified name. This will usually work but has been known to cause problems, so ensure that the order is correct before installing. Also, if at all possible use a static IP address. If your environment assigns IP addresses dynamically, perhaps using DHCP (Dynamic Host Configuration Protocol), assign the server addresses on a long lease. When installing Oracle 10*g* products (either the database or the application server; Oracle Collaboration Suite uses both) on a laptop, assign the machine's hostname to a loopback address, such as 127.0.0.1, so that it will not change, no matter what network the laptop happens to be connected to.

Selecting Ports

An Oracle Collaboration Suite installation requires a number of TCP ports to be used by end users when connecting to the application components and by the components themselves when connecting internally. As it is not possible for two TCP services to use the same port, it is vital to ensure that whatever ports will be used are not already in use by other applications. This matter is complicated by the fact that while the installer can check whether a port it wishes to assign is already in use and return an error if it is, there is no way it can tell that a port which is free at install time may be used later by some unrelated service that might be started subsequently. The common use of the `inetd` method of launching TCP services on demand, rather than having them running continuously, does not help with this.

There are a number of commonly used services where conflicts may occur. The sendmail daemon will be running by default on many UNIX servers, on port 25. This is the port that Mail will attempt to use, but the conflict will only become apparent when you start the LISTENER_ES e-mail listener. The same problem occurs with the Content Services FTP server; it will, by default, attempt to use port 21, which is probably already taken by the system's native FTP server, or it may be taken later on when the `inetd` tries to start it. It is possible to reconfigure the Oracle Collaboration Suite services to use nonstandard ports, but a better solution may be to disable the native services and allow Oracle Collaboration Suite to take the default ports.

There is a documentation file on all systems that should list all assigned ports. It is `/etc/services` on UNIX and Linux, and on Windows it is `\windows\system32\drivers\etc\services`.

This file is supposed to list all ports that are (or may be) in use on the node. The problem is that it is only a documentation file, and while it may have been accurate when the machine was first commissioned, system administrators are notoriously lazy about keeping it updated. Check it anyway. The Oracle Universal Installer (OUI) is supposed to look for and check this file and not assign any ports that are listed. However, do not rely on this. First, the installer will frequently assign ports that are listed, and second there may well be services running (or not running at install time, but which may be running in normal circumstances) that use ports that have not been entered in this file. A good system administrator will keep the services file up to date. After completing your Oracle Collaboration Suite installation, you should certainly update it with all the ports that have been assigned.

To check whether a port is currently in use, use the `netstat` command, which is available on both Windows and Linux. On UNIX or Linux it is

```
netstat -an | grep <port_number>
```

or on Windows it is

```
netstat -an | find "<port_number>"
```

where *<port_number>* is the numeric port you are interested in. This example on a Windows machine is to test whether port 23 is in use:

```
C:\Documents and Settings\Administrator>netstat -an | find "23"
  TCP    0.0.0.0:23              0.0.0.0:0               LISTENING
  TCP    169.254.50.153:1069     169.254.78.10:23        ESTABLISHED
  UDP    127.0.0.1:123           *:*
  UDP    169.254.50.153:123      *:*

C:\Documents and Settings\Administrator>
```

The first line shows that a TCP service is running on port 23 of the host machine; it is a LISTENING service, waiting for incoming connections. This will be the telnet daemon. It will not be possible to start up any other TCP service on this port, unless it is stopped. The second line is not a problem; it shows that port 1069 on the local machine has established a connection to port 23 on a remote node. This will be a telnet session to a remote machine. The third and fourth lines are not a problem; they just happen to include the string 23.

To control the ports assigned by the Oracle Universal Installer, specify them in a file `staticports.ini`, and nominate this file when launching the installer. There is a sample file on the installation DVD in the `response` directory. You do not have to specify ports for all the components; any not specified will revert to default. Then run the installer with one of these options:

```
./runInstaller oracle.ocs.onebox:s_staticPorts=<path_to_your_ini_file>
./runInstaller oracle.ocs.infrastructure:s_staticPorts=<path_to_your_ini_file>
./runInstaller oracle.ocs.midtier:s_staticPorts=<path_to_your_ini_file>
```

These examples are for UNIX. For Windows, substitute `.\setup.exe` for `./runInstaller`.

Whatever is done with port selection, after the installation be sure to check the file `ORACLE_HOME/install/portlist.ini` to see what ports were actually assigned, and update the services file accordingly.

Choice of Platform

Oracle does not recommend particular platforms. Nonetheless, there are certain favored platforms. They are the platforms on which you will get the best support and the platforms for which updates and patches will be developed first. The development platform for Oracle Collaboration Suite 10*g* was Red Hat Linux, which is why the Linux version was the first to be released. It was followed by UNIX versions (Solaris, AIX, HP-UX, and others) with Windows considerably later.

Whatever platform is selected, it is vital to confirm that the exact operating environment is certified. Confirm this by going to the Oracle MetaLink web site at `http://metalink.oracle.com` and searching the platform certifications. It may well be that Oracle Collaboration Suite will run perfectly well on an uncertified platform, but Oracle will not support you in such circumstances. There are also dependencies between the various components, such as the exact release of the Oracle Application Server and the database. Again, you may well be able to run satisfactorily with uncertified combinations, but you will be unsupported.

Note that the choice of platform need not be consistent across all nodes in the installation. It would be perfectly acceptable to use, for example, Solaris on SPARC machines for the infrastructure tier node(s), and Linux on AMD processors for the middle tier node(s). Mixing platforms in this manner may be an excellent technique for providing a highly scalable and fault tolerant environment at a comparatively low cost by using a large number of cheaper and easily replaceable machines for the middle tier and a small number of highly available machines for the back end.

Oracle, in common with several other key players in the IT industry, such as IBM, has made a huge commitment to Linux. It is now the development platform for a number of products and is used for running some major internal systems. The supported Linux distributions are Red Hat and SUSE. The reasons for supporting only these distributions are more historical and political than technical, but the fact remains that they are the only two supported distributions. The choice between these should be immaterial as far the Oracle Collaboration Suite is concerned. Within Oracle, Red Hat is the favored distribution but this is only a historical anomaly. Red Hat has always been an American organization, whereas SUSE was developed in Europe, and the usage of the two distributions does tend to follow their geographical origins. Oracle has development staff working with both organizations, and they are equally good platforms.

If using Linux, the kernel must be untainted. Any kernel modifications or recompilation will result in Oracle refusing to support the installation. Some Linux users object to this restriction, but it is fair. It is impossible to support products effectively if the operating environment is not known, and making modifications to the Linux kernel could have unexpected effects on the operation of the Oracle Collaboration Suite components.

Most large-scale deployments of any Oracle product run on UNIX, usually Solaris on SPARC; HP-UX on PA-RISC; Tru64 on Alpha; or AIX on any processor used by IBM. Support for the less widely used UNIX variants, such as Santa Cruz Operation, or Solaris on Intel, may or may not be provided; check MetaLink to confirm. Historically, Oracle ported its product set to a vast range of platforms, but in recent years the range has been reduced in line with industry trends.

There is a large amount of anecdotal tittle-tattle regarding a supposed enmity between Oracle and Microsoft (and indeed between the founders of the two companies). Do not be concerned by this. It is only rumor and reflects the fact that the two companies are competitors in a number of areas. This competition is a good thing and helps drive development of the products. Windows is a fully supported platform for all Oracle server technologies. Indeed, for some client and middle tier tools, it is the only supported platform. Oracle is as committed to Windows as a server platform as to anything else. It is a perfectly suitable environment for many installations and is sometimes said to be simpler to administer than other platforms. As with Linux, a particular advantage of Windows is that you have a choice of many hardware vendors with a wide range of prices and features.

When making a decision on choice of platform, it is vital to consider what the environment must achieve. All operating systems have strengths and weaknesses. For example, it is sometimes said that Windows is less suitable than UNIX for a 100% uptime environment. But UNIX is certainly not perfect. It may, for instance, have weaknesses with real-time applications, such as flight-control systems. For real-time work, you may need OpenVMS or a mainframe environment. Linux systems are often relatively low-cost solutions but may lack some of the features for control, fault tolerance, and performance that more advanced operating systems offer as standard. There are good and not-so-good points for all the supported platforms, and indeed a mixed environment may be the best option for some organizations.

To conclude, your choice of operating environment should be determined by many factors including but not limited to the following:

- Cost
- Reliability
- Scalability
- Performance
- Support
- Ease of use

And in all cases, avoid making an emotional decision. It is not unknown for IT people to become almost religiously involved with their chosen environment and to ignore all its faults.

Deployment Configurations

As an absolute minimum, an Oracle Collaboration Suite installation must have two Oracle homes: one to support the infrastructure, and one to run the middle tier application services. The infrastructure tier will include a database used as the repository for both infrastructure data and application data. Depending on the scale of the installation and the requirements for high availability, there may be a need for multiple infrastructure instances, multiple middle tier instances, and multiple databases. Each of these must run from its own Oracle home. As all the Oracle Collaboration Suite components communicate over TCP layered protocols, the various middle tier and infrastructure components can be distributed across any number of physical machines running a variety of operating systems, or they can be concentrated on one node.

The requirement for at least two Oracle home directories is sometimes irritating for administrators new to the Oracle environment, but it is a natural result of the complexity of the product. Indeed, release 9*i* of Oracle Collaboration Suite required three Oracle homes, preferably on three machines: one for the infrastructure components, another for the middle tier components, and a third for the component databases. The use of multiple home directories is in fact a feature of the product that makes it possible to run different versions of different components concurrently, and the fact that this is built into even the most basic single-node installation contributes to the scalability and maintainability of the suite.

Single-Node Deployment

The single-node deployment is the simplest configuration. It may well be cost-effective for small organizations having only a few hundred concurrent users, but it has no fault-tolerant capabilities unless some form of hardware failover is used. The single-node installation is perfect for demonstration or training purposes, and many organizations will find it extremely useful to have such an environment available for these purposes, in addition to the live production environment.

A minimal single-node installation can be made on an ordinary PC, provided it has adequate main memory. The system used for development during the course of writing much of this book was a single-node deployment: a PC with a single 1.6GHz Pentium processor and 2GB main memory running on Linux. Such a machine can run the full Oracle Collaboration Suite, but the memory requirements are such that if all the components are started concurrently, it will be paging badly and performance will be atrocious. It would be nowhere near adequate for a production installation. An effective minimum hardware configuration for production purposes would be a twin CPU (or possibly a dual-cored single CPU) machine with 4GB RAM. Such a machine should be capable of supporting an organization with concurrent users numbered in the dozens up to perhaps one or two hundred. A more powerful single-node machine (such as a multiprocessor SMP machine powered by multiple SPARC, PowerPC, PA-RISC, or 64-bit Intel or AMD processors) could support several hundred concurrent users.

The single-node will have two Oracle homes. The infrastructure Oracle home will run an Oracle Application Server infrastructure instance with all the identity management components (Oracle Internet Directory, Single Sign-On server, and the Delegated Administration Service) and an Oracle database. The database will contain the schemas needed to support the identity management services, the Oracle Application Server metadata repository, the product schemas for Portal, and the schemas that make up the Mail and Content Services datastores. This Oracle home will also run a database listener that provides access to the database from the middle tier components. The middle tier Oracle home will run all the application components. It will also run the listener that monitors the Mail protocols and the Calendar node database. Both Oracle homes will run an Apache web listener, but only the middle tier home will run a Web Cache. Even though both Oracle homes are on the same machine, the communication between them is always over TCP.

A decision that must be made with a single-node deployment is where to place the single-node, in terms of the organization's network firewall security structure. A not uncommon arrangement for web application servers is to place the web listener process, and possibly the application process as well, on a server in a firewall DMZ (demilitarized zone)—an area between two firewall routers—and the database(s) used by the application processes in the fully secured internal network. Clearly, this is not possible for a single-node installation. There are two options. First, the node can be placed in the DMZ. This is not always considered to be good practice, because information of record within the database would be in an area that is only partially secured. It does mean, though, that no external users need have access to the internal network. A second solution is to place the single node behind the firewall, in the secure area. Then to avoid the need for external users to connect through the firewall, place a reverse proxy server in the DMZ that will forward all traffic as necessary. If no reverse proxy is available, a stand-alone installation of the Web Cache could fulfill this role.

When deciding where to place the node in relation to the firewall, consideration must be given to the protocols that users will use to access services. As a general rule, reverse proxy servers can only proxy HTTP and HTTPS traffic. This means that the various "thick" client tools will only be usable by users within the firewall who can reach the node directly. These tools include IMAP and POP mailers, such as Microsoft Outlook, the Calendar Desktop Client, and the Real-Time Collaboration Messenger client. External users will be restricted to the web interfaces.

Two-Node Deployment

A two-node deployment will use one node for the infrastructure tier, and one node for the middle tier. The infrastructure node will provide the identity management services and also host the database used for the Content Services and Mail datastores. The middle tier node will run the application components and host the Calendar node database. The volume of traffic between the nodes will be substantial, and network bandwidth should be made available as necessary. Nodes consisting of twin CPUs and 4GB of main memory should be capable of supporting several hundred concurrent users; more powerful servers will be able to support in excess of 1,000 concurrent users.

A significant advantage that the two-node deployment has over a single-node deployment, apart from having the potential for supporting more users, is to do with network security. It now becomes possible to place the middle tier node in the DMZ of the firewall and the infrastructure node behind the firewall in the secure area, as shown in Figure 4-1.

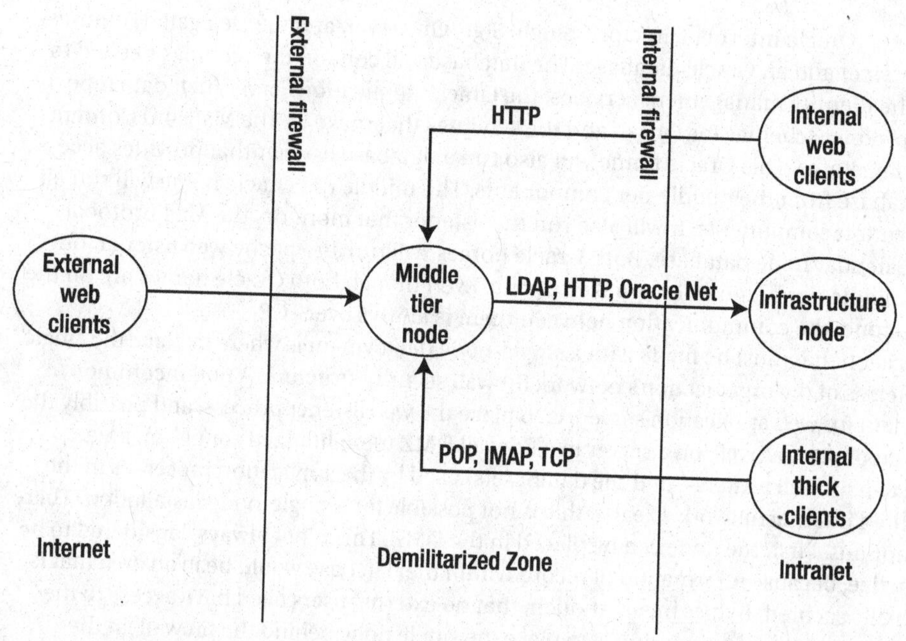

Figure 4-1. *Possible configuration of two nodes and a firewall*

In Figure 4-1, no SSL protocols are shown, but all the protocols do have SSL variants that can be used as well as or instead of those shown.

External users coming on from the Internet can use HTTP to access all services. The external firewall will be configured to accept that one protocol on one port—probably port 80—and will only route connections to the middle tier node, where they will be accepted by the Web Cache. Some organizations may wish to allow IMAP or POP access, in which case the firewall will be configured to accept and pass those protocols, too, on the appropriate ports. The internal firewall will be configured to route LDAP and HTTP traffic from the middle tier node to the infrastructure node; these are necessary for Single Sign-On. It will also route Oracle Net traffic, necessary for access to the Content Services and Mail datastores. Internal users will have to go through the internal firewall to reach the middle tier server, either using HTTP to access the web clients, or (if permitted) IMAP and POP to reach Mail. The internal users will use raw TCP from the Calendar Desktop Client and from the Real-Time Collaboration Messenger client.

Multinode Deployment

An Oracle Collaboration Suite installation can be distributed over many nodes, but before embarking on such a deployment it is vital to be aware of what one is trying to achieve. There are four major reasons for a multinode deployment:

- Scalability
- Performance
- Fault tolerance
- Security

The number of concurrent users that the installation can support will increase by adding more nodes to the various tiers. In the chapters that follow on each application component, there are indications of what CPU and memory resources user sessions require. Clearly, adding more resources will increase the maximum capacities before performance begins to degrade. Depending on the platform chosen, adding nodes may be more cost-effective than adding more hardware resources to an existing node. Adding nodes may also get around certain bottlenecks inherent in the architecture of the product. An example of how additional nodes may be more effective than adding hardware to one node is the scalability of the Oracle database instance. There are points of serialization, such as the generation of redo data that can only be avoided by converting the database from single-instance to a RAC (Real Application Clusters) environment, which requires at least two nodes. RAC is described in Chapter 17.

Apart from Oracle limitations, the platform itself may have limits. For example, the operating system's TCP stack may have problems mutexing a vast number of concurrent HTTP connections through one port, or the preemptive multitasking mechanism may deteriorate as it makes context switches between thousands of processes. Multiple nodes will ameliorate such platform restrictions by spreading the workload across multiple operating system instances.

Any decisions must consider scalability of the infrastructure tier and of the middle tier components. On a large-scale installation, it may be necessary to dedicate entire nodes to Calendar servers, for example. Content Services nodes can be run on different middle tier instances (though they must all share the same datastore), while Mail protocol servers can share the Content Services database or have their own database(s). It is possible to add nodes and middle tier instances to an existing deployment without necessarily incurring any downtime, but adjusting the infrastructure tier configuration is a more drastic action. In particular, it is important to consider the database. A default installation will have one database used for the infrastructure schemas and for the Mail and Content Services datastores. To move the datastore schemas out of this database into another at a later stage would be a large job involving significant downtime, and if it seems likely that the installation will have to support several thousand users it may well be advisable to create a second database for this purpose initially. It does not necessarily have to be on a separate node; a separate Oracle home on the same node would ease the pain of a subsequent migration to a multinode environment.

While a multinode deployment may, depending on circumstances, scale better than a single- or double-node deployment, performance gains are more questionable. The pattern of the work done by users in a collaborative environment tends to be serial in nature; it is usually interactive as users navigate through their e-mail, their diary, and their files. Thus performance gains are likely to come from avoiding bottlenecks caused by increased numbers of users, rather than improved response times for any one request. Network latency is another performance problem with which multiple nodes cannot assist.

For a highly available environment, a multinode deployment is essential. Chapter 17 describes various possibilities for configuring a fault-tolerant system with no single point of failure. All the application components can be configured in multiple Oracle Application Server middle tier instances on multiple nodes, as can all the Oracle Application Server infrastructure components. Alternatively, a vendor proprietary hardware–based failover system could be used.

Security rules for an organization may force a multinode Oracle Collaboration Suite deployment, even if it is not required for technical reasons. If the installation is to be accessible only to internal users on a private network with no Internet connection, then perhaps network security will not be an issue, but for most installations it will be of critical importance.

Security and identity management is discussed in greater detail in Chapter 6, but when planning the deployment it is important to consider whether multiple nodes are necessary to conform to the organization's network security policy.

Internet firewalls come in several forms, but they all follow the same general principle: there can be no direct access to internal systems from the external network; there must be a firewall in between. A firewall may be nothing more than a router that intercepts all traffic, inspects its source, content, and destination, and makes a decision about whether to forward it. Or it may be a much more complicated structure of several layers with different nodes placed at different points. The area within the firewall, between the external public network and the internal private network, is generally referred to as the DMZ; the nodes positioned within the DMZ are known as *bastion hosts*, machines hardened against external attack.

A common rule is that no "information of record" should be stored on the bastion hosts. The bastion hosts may offer processing services, but not data storage. This means that all access to data will be filtered through not only the firewall routers but also the application software, which can apply additional authentication and data access restrictions. Furthermore, any malicious attack will only, in the worst case, bring down the application servers and will not affect the data repositories. It will not compromise the security of information of record. A simple two-node deployment of Oracle Collaboration Suite cannot conform to this model, because the Calendar datastore, in the form of the Calendar node databases, exists in the middle tier Oracle home. Thus, for a two-node deployment, a choice must be made: either the middle tier node is placed in the DMZ, in which case the Calendar data is in an area that is only partially protected, or the middle tier node is placed in the private network, in which case external traffic must be permitted through the DMZ. A multinode deployment can avoid this choice by placing a middle tier server specifically for Calendar in the secured area with access to it through the web listener of a middle tier server in the DMZ.

Preinstallation Work

Oracle Collaboration Suite is installed with the Oracle Universal Installer, as are all current Oracle products. This is written in Java, and so will be the same on all platforms. The installer first makes a few checks of the operating environment and then presents a series of windows that prompt the user for various options.

The installer is reasonably straightforward to use whether or not one has experience. Read the installation guide for your platform, and do what it says: create appropriate user accounts, make any necessary adjustments to kernel settings, and install any required patches. Then copy the installation DVD to a directory and run either `setup.exe` (Windows) or `runInstaller` (all other platforms). If it runs successfully, it will deliver an installation that works.

One perhaps slightly irritating feature is that all components will actually be running at the end of the installation, which can cause problems on a very low specification machine. There may be errors reported by the installer as it tries to start the various components. Poor performance caused by excessive swapping may make some component startups fail with time-outs. Either ignore these or retry them; the installer gives both options. On subsequent startups you can be choosy about which components to start, and you can also reduce the memory requirement by down-tuning the database and some other components if the system is to be used purely for training purposes.

OUI Inventory

The Oracle Universal Installer is so called because it can install any version of any Oracle product. However, different products and versions may well require their own Oracle home directory. This is because all Oracle products are written on top of a set of libraries, known as the *base libraries*, that provide functions common to all products. It is not possible to install two products into the same Oracle home if they use different versions of the base libraries. The OUI is aware of which version of the base libraries a product uses and maintains an inventory of what has been installed. Thus, it can ensure that you never install an incompatible product into an existing Oracle home. If you were to do so, the new installation would overwrite the already installed base libraries and break the products already running off that home.

The Oracle Universal Installer inventory is a set of files that is interrogated and updated by all versions of the OUI whenever you run it. The location of the inventory is platform-specific and can be changed. On Windows, the location of the inventory is fixed by a registry key `HKEY_LOCAL_MACHINE/SOFTWARE/ORACLE/inst_loc` which defaults to `C:\Program Files\Oracle\Inventory`. On Linux, the location is set by an entry in the file `/etc/oraInst.loc`, and on Solaris it is `/var/opt/oracle/oraInst.loc`.

The first time the installer is run on a machine, there will be a prompt for the location of the inventory; subsequent installer sessions will locate and use the existing inventory. The inventory tracks what Oracle homes exist on the machine and exactly what versions of what products are installed in each home. This is the key to ensuring that multiple products can coexist on the same machine without problems. It is also the key to orderly deinstallation.

On UNIX systems, the file pointing to the inventory exists in a directory to which the Oracle user will not usually have access. This is why you will be prompted by the installer to run a script called `root.sh` as the machine's root user. This script will create the `oraInst.loc` file, and may also change the ownership of some other files to root.

Prerequisite Checks

The checks performed by the installer are meant to ensure that the hardware and operating system are appropriate for an Oracle Collaboration Suite installation and should conform to the detail given in the release notes for the platform. They include checks for hardware resources and operating system utilities, permissions, and patch levels. In some cases it may be possible to have a satisfactory installation in an environment that does not pass the checks; but while this might be acceptable for development or training purposes, as it may mean that Oracle Corporation will not support such an installation, it is not usually advisable for production purposes. A case where this might be acceptable is if the environment is more advanced than those that are certified.

There are two sources of data for the installer's prerequisite checks: the `/install/oraparam.ini` file, and various XML files in the `/stage/prereq` directory. The entries in `oraparam.ini` determine whether the installer itself can run, and may include such directives as the following:

```
MIN_DISPLAY_COLORS=256
CPU=450
Windows=4.0,5.0,5.1,5.2
```

These directives (taken from a Windows installation DVD) force the installer to exit with an error message if the display is set to less than 256 colors, or if the CPU's clock speed is less than 450MHz, or if the Windows kernel is not one of those listed. If your server does not conform to any of the limits but you are confident that it can run the product anyway, simply edit the file. A reasonable change might be to add 5.3 to the `Windows` directive, if you are on a later service pack than one of those listed.

The entries in the `prereq` XML files determine whether certain products will run. These may include resource limits and can also specify certain versions of operating system utilities. This example (taken from a `refhost.xml` file on a Linux installation DVD) specifies certain packages and kernel settings:

```
<PACKAGES>
        <PACKAGE NAME="glibc" VERSION="2.2.4-32.17" />
        <PACKAGE NAME="pdksh" VERSION="5.2.14-22" />
        <PACKAGE NAME="sysstat" VERSION="4.0.1-15.2.1as" />
        <PACKAGE NAME="gcc" VERSION="2.96-128.7.2" />
        <PACKAGE NAME="compat-glibc" VERSION="6.2-2.1.3.2" />
        <PACKAGE NAME="libstdc++" VERSION="2.96-128.7.2" />
        <PACKAGE NAME="glibc-common" VERSION="2.2.4-32.17" />
        <PACKAGE NAME="gcc-c++" VERSION="2.96-128.7.2" />
        <PACKAGE NAME="compat-libstdc++" VERSION="6.2-2.9.0.16" />
        <PACKAGE NAME="gnome-libs" VERSION="1:1.2.13-16" />
        <PACKAGE NAME="binutils" VERSION="2.11.90.0.8-12.4" />
        <PACKAGE NAME="make" VERSION="1:3.79.1-8" />
   </PACKAGES>
   <KERNEL>
     <PROPERTY NAME="semmsl" VALUE="256" />
     <PROPERTY NAME="semmns" VALUE="32000" />
     <PROPERTY NAME="semopm" VALUE="100" />
     <PROPERTY NAME="semmni" VALUE="142" />
     <PROPERTY NAME="shmmax" VALUE="2147483648" />
     <PROPERTY NAME="shmmni" VALUE="4096" />
     <PROPERTY NAME="shmall" VALUE="3279547" />
     <PROPERTY NAME="msgmax" VALUE="8192" />
     <PROPERTY NAME="msgmnb" VALUE="65535" />
     <PROPERTY NAME="msgmni" VALUE="2878" />
     <PROPERTY NAME="hardnofiles" VALUE="65536" />
     <PROPERTY NAME="softnofiles" VALUE="4096" />
     <PROPERTY NAME="file-max" VALUE="327679" />
     <PROPERTY NAME="VERSION" VALUE="2.4.9-e.49" />
   </KERNEL>
```

It is almost certain that the kernel settings specified are beyond those actually required and could be edited safely, but forcing the installer to proceed without the package versions listed would be more problematic.

Linux

Linux deserves a special mention with regard to installation. This is because while it is a perfectly reliable platform once it is working, the actual installation can be more awkward than on some other platforms, such as proprietary UNIX releases or Microsoft Windows. The information in this section is generally correct and should suffice, but you must check the release notes and installation instructions for your exact release to confirm details, as there may be platform and version variations.

The installation notes specify a number of packages that must be available and of at least certain versions. You may well have to connect to appropriate web sites to download the requisite packages, which will be packed as RPM files according to the Red Hat standards. Usually you can install the latest version of any RPM equal to or higher than that specified, and Oracle will be happy; but be wary of installing anything too new: you may be committing yourself to installing a lot more than you think, because of package dependencies. Some of the checks are certainly not essential; for example, some products have a "requirement" for some GNOME libraries that aren't actually needed.

Certain operating system limits need to be set appropriately, such as the maximum number of files any one process can open concurrently, and various kernel settings. Some of the specified values are far higher (by orders of magnitude) than any live installation could possibly need, but the checks are there anyway. Either set up your system accordingly, or (if you do not mind putting your installation into a state where an awkward support analyst could refuse to assist you) adjust the limits in the `prereq` files. All these settings should be discussed with your Linux system administrator. As a general rule, do not edit these files; it will usually be preferable to adjust your system to conform to the requirements.

As modification of the Linux kernel is not permitted by Oracle, the kernel settings must be specified in the `/etc/sysctl.conf` file and adjusted dynamically on each bootup. For example, add the following entries:

```
kernel.shmall = 2097152
kernel.shmmax = 4294967295
kernel.shmmni = 4096
kernel.sem = 256 32000 100 142
kernel.msgmni = 2878
kernel.msgmax = 8192
kernel.msgmnb = 65535
fs.file-max = 327879
net.ipv4.ip_local_port_range = 10000 65000
```

The following list describes each entry:

- `shmall` sets the maximum amount of shared memory that can be allocated on the machine in 4KB pages (8GB in this example, which is the default).
- `shmmax` sets the maximum size in bytes of any one shared memory segment and should ideally be at least the size of the largest Oracle instance SGA that is expected. The default is 4GB.
- `shmmni` sets the total number of shared memory segments that can be created. The default of 4096 should be sufficient for any node running any Oracle Collaboration Suite components.

- `sem` controls the semaphores that are used for serializing concurrent access to memory structures and critical code. The example sets four values in one line to the minimum values recommended for an Oracle Collaboration Suite installation:
  - `semmsl` is the number of semaphores per semaphore set and limits the number of processes that can connect to an Oracle instance.
  - `semmns` is the total number of semaphores in the system.
  - `semopm` is the number of operations that can be covered by one use of a semaphore.
  - `semmni` is the number of semaphore sets to create.
- The message queue settings are the minimum recommended for an Oracle Collaboration Suite installation:
  - `msgmni` is the maximum number of message queue identifiers.
  - `msgmax` is the maximum size of a message.
  - `msgmnb` is the number of bytes per queue.
- `fs.file-max` is the maximum number of open files on the system.
- `net.ipv4.ip_local_port_range` assigns the range of IP ports that can be allocated dynamically by the system's port mapper when, for example, launching Oracle server sessions.

The final critical setting is the `ulimit`, which controls the resources that any one Linux user can take up. The default limits per user for the number of processes and the number of open files are not adequate. To show the current settings, run `ulimit -a` and confirm that `open files` is at least 65536 and that `max user processes` is at least 16384.

If these settings are lower, they must be adjusted or the installer will fail on its preinstallation checks. There will be variations in technique on how to do this, depending on your Linux distribution and the security requirements of your system administrators. For example, add the following line:

```
ulimit -u 16384 -n 65536
```

to the file `/etc/rc.d/rc.local` and the limits will be changed for all sessions after the next reboot.

Alternatively, add these lines to the file `/etc/security/limits.conf`:

```
*       soft    nproc   4096
*       hard    nproc   16384
*       soft    nofile  16384
*       hard    nofile  65536
```

and the limits will be changed for all new sessions. It might be better practice to nominate the Oracle owner, rather than to use the * wild card, which refers to all users. You may find, depending on your Linux configuration, that the changes in limits are only effected when running from a session on the node itself and are not effective when running from a remote telnet session. This is because a telnet session will inherit some privileges from the telnet daemon that established the session, and these inherited privileges may not be adequate for changing limits.

Installation

Having configured the node and created a user account according to the installation instructions for your environment, launch the installer by running the `setup.exe` file (on Windows) or the `runInstaller` file (on UNIX or Linux). After running the preinstall checks, the first window prompts for a choice between a "basic" installation and an "advanced" installation. The basic installation will proceed automatically, giving no options other than choosing the directory into which to install the Oracle home and the superuser password. This is the password that will be set for the Oracle Application Server administrator, username ias_admin; for the Oracle Internet Directory administrator, username orcladmin; and the Oracle database administrator, username SYS. The advanced installation will prompt for an installation directory and then present the window shown in Figure 4-2.

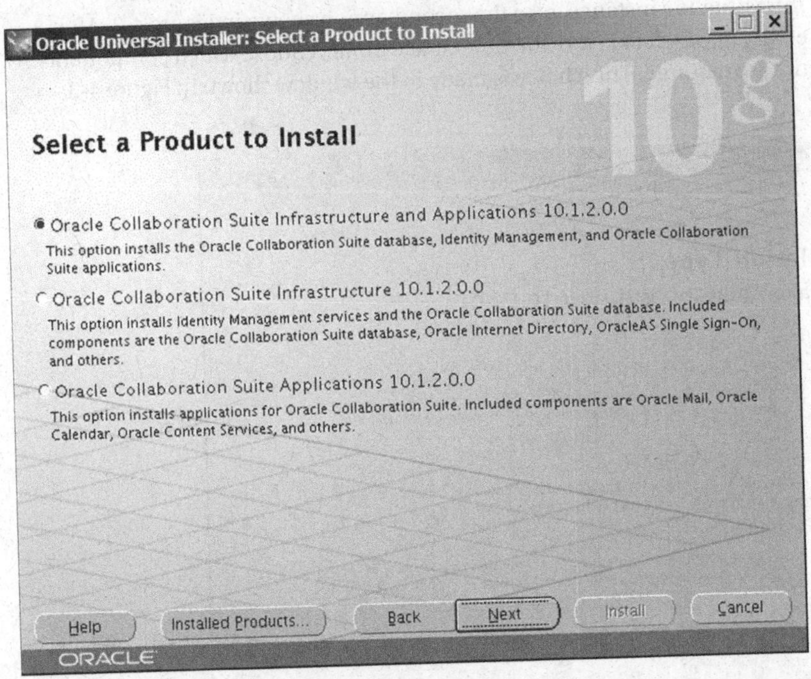

Figure 4-2. *The OUI offering the choice between single- or multinode installation*

From here you can install an infrastructure instance, a middle tier instance, or both. Even through the advanced option, it is not actually possible to prevent middle tier components from being installed; the installer will always install a complete middle tier, though it is possible to stop certain components from being configured.

Single-Node Installation

Selecting the first option shown in Figure 4-2, Oracle Collaboration Suite Infrastructure and Applications, will create a single-node installation consisting of two Oracle homes. These will be in the directories `infra` and `app` beneath the directory specified on the previous window. This is equivalent to selecting the basic installation from the installer's first window.

At the end of the installation, all the infrastructure and middle tier components will be running. The final window shown by the installer will give the relevant URLs and ports, which can also be found in the documentation files `readme.txt`, `setupinfo.txt`, and `portlist.ini`. There will be versions of these files in the `install` directory of both the `infra` and `app` Oracle homes.

Multinode Installation: Infrastructure

A multinode deployment must begin with the creation of an Oracle Application Server infrastructure instance. This will include a database that has the necessary schemas for supporting the farm's metadata repository, the identity management components, and the product schemas. In a two-node deployment this will be the only database you have. Larger installations will usually have a second database on a third node for the product schemas.

To install an infrastructure instance, take the second option shown in Figure 4-2. After nominating a directory in which to create the new Oracle home, choose which components of the infrastructure are required. This choice is made in the window shown in Figure 4-3.

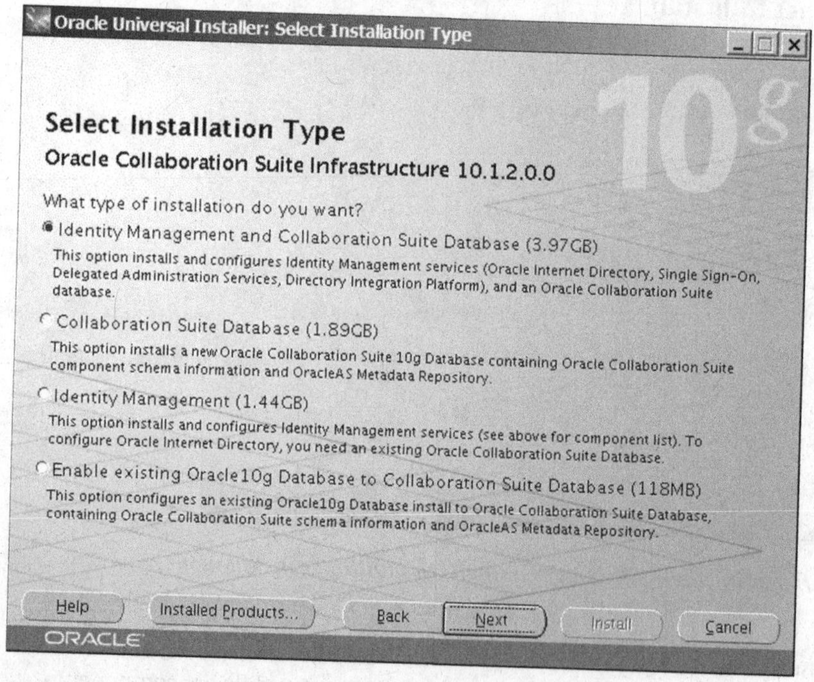

Figure 4-3. *The options for installing infrastructure components*

The options are the following:

- *Identity Management and Collaboration Suite Database*: This will install the complete infrastructure tier: an Apache web listener, an Oracle Internet Directory instance, the Single Sign-On service, and a database with the preseeded schemas for supporting the identity management components, the Oracle Application Server farm metadata repository and the product datastores. This will be the option to take if the deployment is to run with all the infrastructure components on one node; and for a multinode installation it must be taken for the first node to be installed.

- *Collaboration Suite Database*: This will install a database with all the Oracle Collaboration Suite schemas, but nothing else. There must already be a running infrastructure instance, as the new database will need to be registered in the Oracle Internet Directory as a part of the farm. Nominate the address of the Oracle Internet Directory (by IP address and port) when prompted, as shown in Figure 4-4. This second database can be on a different node from the first installation or in a different Oracle home directory on the same node. This is typically to create an additional database to be used for the Mail or Content Services datastores.

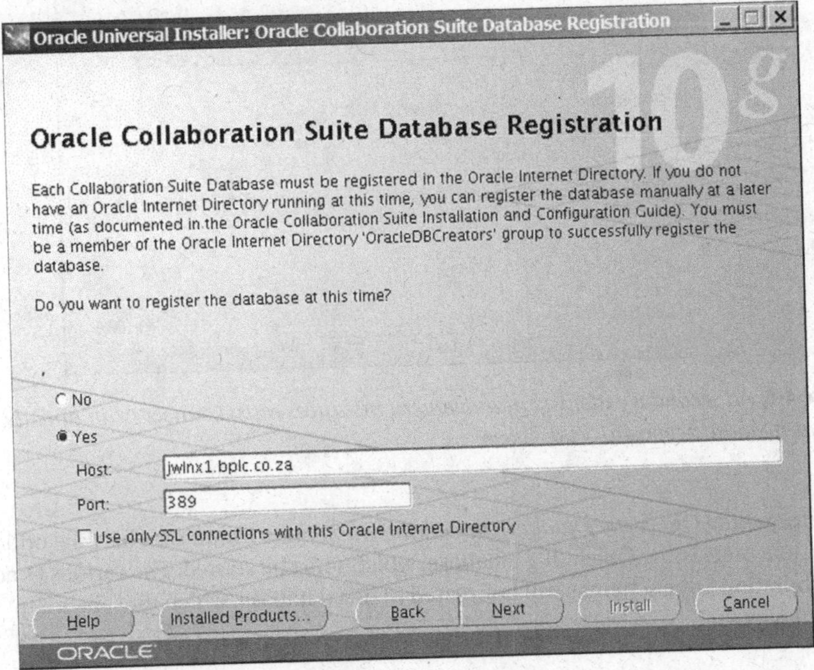

Figure 4-4. *All infrastructure databases must register with an already extant Oracle Internet Directory.*

- *Identity Management*: This will install one or all of the various identity management components: an Oracle Internet Directory instance, a Single Sign-On server, an OIDDAS component, the directory synchronization server, and the Oracle Certificate Authority for generating digital certificates. There will also be an Apache web listener. A metadata repository database must already be available, created with the first option. Nominate the address of this database, as shown in Figure 4-5. This option is typically used to enhance the scalability and the fault tolerance of the identity management services.

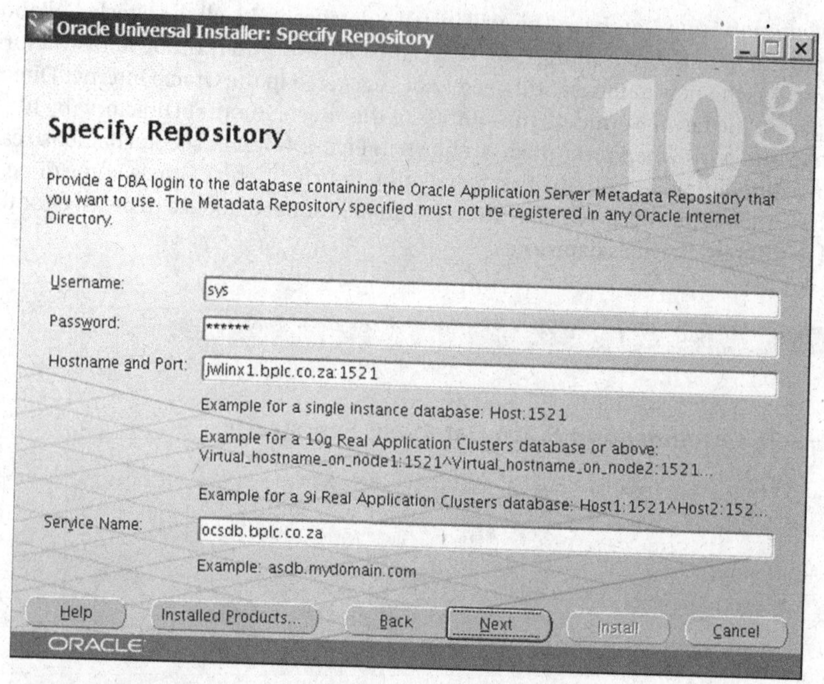

Figure 4-5. *All secondary identity management instances must connect to an already extant metadata repository database.*

- *Enable existing Oracle10g Database to Collaboration Suite Database*: This final option requires a preexisting Oracle 10*g* database, which must be started. The various Oracle Collaboration Suite schemas will be created in this database, which must be a supported release.

Multinode Installation: Middle Tier

To install a middle tier instance, take the third option shown in Figure 4-2. After nominating a directory in which to create the new Oracle home, choose which application components are required. The selections are shown in the window in Figure 4-6.

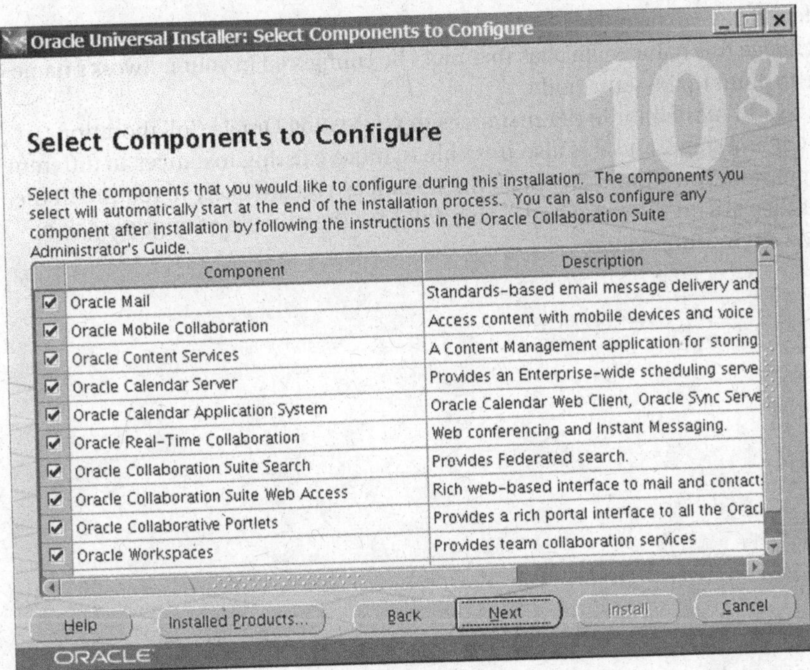

Figure 4-6. *Middle tier component selection*

An infrastructure instance must be available, as the next prompt will be for the address and port of an Oracle Internet Directory server, for which you must provide the orcladmin username and password and the database connect string for the metadata repository database. If there are more than one Oracle Internet Directory instances available, it makes no difference which you nominate; they will all share the same datastore, so the middle tier can register through any of them. There is no choice for the metadata repository; an Oracle Application Server farm can have only one metadata repository.

The next prompt allows you to choose which database to use for each component's application data. This will default to the metadata repository database, but if others are available (having been precreated and registered) they can be selected from a drop-down list for each application component. This is how the datastores can be divided across multiple databases: typically, one database for Mail, and another for Content Services. The other components have relatively small storage requirements but can still be separated if this is considered necessary.

If Mail is selected as a component to install, there will be a prompt for the mail domain to be served. This will default to the root domain of the node's hostname. Subsidiary domains can be created within this Mail instance beneath that domain, but it will not be possible to create a domain with a different root.

Note that when installing a Calendar instance, there is no prompt for the location of the Calendar node database. This will always be a set of files in the middle tier's Oracle home. There will however be a prompt for the name of the Calendar server host, which will default to the primary hostname of the node on which the install is being run. If it is at all likely that the Calendar node will have to be moved later, or that the machine's hostname may change, it is advisable to change this name to an alias that must be configured in your network's name resolution service to point to the same node.

It is possible to add more middle tier instances to an existing Oracle Collaboration Suite deployment at any stage, and it is also possible to move existing instances to different machines; but if possible you should create all the instances you are likely to require in the first place, even if they are on the same node. This will ease the process of migrating to a genuine multinode environment later.

CHAPTER 5

Management and Control Utilities

There are several tools, both graphical and command-line, for managing the Oracle Collaboration Suite technology stack and its various components. This chapter will start with a quick review of the architecture of an Oracle database and the tools for controlling it. It will be a quick review because it is the topic of many other books and educational resources. (Experienced DBAs may want to skip this section.) The chapter continues with a study of the tools for controlling the Oracle Application Server. Most of the Oracle Collaboration Suite components can be controlled through the Oracle Application Server Control utilities, but some of the components have their own startup and shutdown routines. Following a description of these, the chapter concludes with examples of some scripts for automating the startup and shutdown routines on both Windows and UNIX.

Database Startup and Shutdown

All Oracle Collaboration Suite installations will include a database, and most production installations will have more than one. For practical purposes, the minimum is one database for the infrastructure and a second for your datastores. The infrastructure database holds the configuration metadata repository; the Oracle Internet Directory (OID) and Single Sign-On schemas; and the product metadata repositories, such as the Portal repository. The datastore database has schemas for holding data maintained by Mail, Content Services, and other components, but not Calendar data. Calendar uses its own non-Oracle database.

There are three items to consider under the topic of *database*: the database instance, the database itself, and the database listener. The database instance consists of memory structures and processes. It exists in your server's RAM and on its CPUs, and its existence is transitory. An instance can be started, meaning that the memory structures are built and the processes launched and then stopped. The memory is cleared, and the processes are terminated. The database itself is files on disk. Once it is created, it exists until the files are deleted; it is a permanent disk-based structure.

A database (which is a set of files) is opened by an instance (which is a set of memory structures and processes). The instance controls and filters all access to the database. As a general rule, it is impossible for any user or process to get to the database directly; all access is through the instance. There are exceptions to this rule, known as *direct database I/O*, but these are only for a very few operations where high performance is essential. An *open* database is a database to which an instance is currently connected. A database must be open if users are to make use of the data within it. A *closed* database is a database that no instance is using and cannot therefore be accessed. The intermediate stage, a *mounted* database, is usually only a temporary state, between closed and open, during a startup or a shutdown operation, though there is some database maintenance work that can only be done in the mount mode.

Lastly, the database listener is an independent process that lets users connect to the instance, and (through the instance) to the database. The listener monitors ports on the server machine's network interface addresses for incoming connection requests and establishes connections against the instance.

Starting an Instance and Opening a Database

To start an instance, the memory structures must be built and the processes launched. These are configured by an *instance parameter file*, a list of settings that control such factors as the size of the various memory structures and how the processes will behave. The parameter file also specifies limits, such as the maximum number of concurrent sessions that the instance will accept. The default name and location of the parameter file is `$ORACLE_HOME/dbs/spfile<INSTANCE_NAME>.ora` on UNIX, or `%ORACLE_HOME%\database\SPFILE<INSTANCE_NAME>.ORA` on a Windows system, where *<INSTANCE_NAME>* is the name of the instance.

This file is a binary file, but some editors will display the contents in a readable form. By all means use one to look at it, but do not attempt to edit it. During startup, the parameter file is read and its contents used to build the instance in memory. The next step is to mount the database; the *mount* is when the instance locates the controlfile of the database and reads it. The location of the controlfile is specified by a parameter in the parameter file. The controlfile (of which you should have multiple copies for safety) contains, among other things, pointers to the files that make up the rest of the database. After reading the controlfile, the instance can open the database by locating and opening all these files. Once the database is open, it is possible for users to connect.

The SQL*Plus Utility

The command-line utility you can use to start an instance and open a database is `SQL*Plus`. This is `$ORACLE_HOME/bin/sqlplus` on UNIX, or on Windows there is a character version, `%ORACLE_HOME%\bin\sqlplus.exe`, and a graphical version, `%ORACLE_HOME%\bin\sqlplusw.exe`.

To connect with permissions that allow you to start and open a database, you must have a *privileged* connection. Normal users are authenticated against the data dictionary, which is stored within the database. There are rows in data dictionary tables that say who the user is, what his password is, and what he is allowed to do. But if the database is not already open, these tables cannot be read. A privileged connection is one authenticated by one of two methods that are available when the database is closed and the instance not started: *operating system authentication*, or *password file authentication*.

To connect with operating system authentication, you must be logged on to the operating system of the server machine as an operating system user who is a member of the operating system group that owns the Oracle software. You will then be able to start and open a database without any need to provide a password or username; Oracle will delegate the security to the operating system. To connect with password file authentication, your Oracle username and password must have been transferred into a special file, the password file, that exists independently of the database. You provide your username and password, and if they exist in the file, you can then issue the startup or shutdown commands. The advantage of password file authentication is that you do not need to log on to the server machine; it allows you to start up the database remotely from across a network. Use of these authentication methods is syntax-driven. See Figure 5-1 for examples of using first operating system authentication and then password file authentication on UNIX.

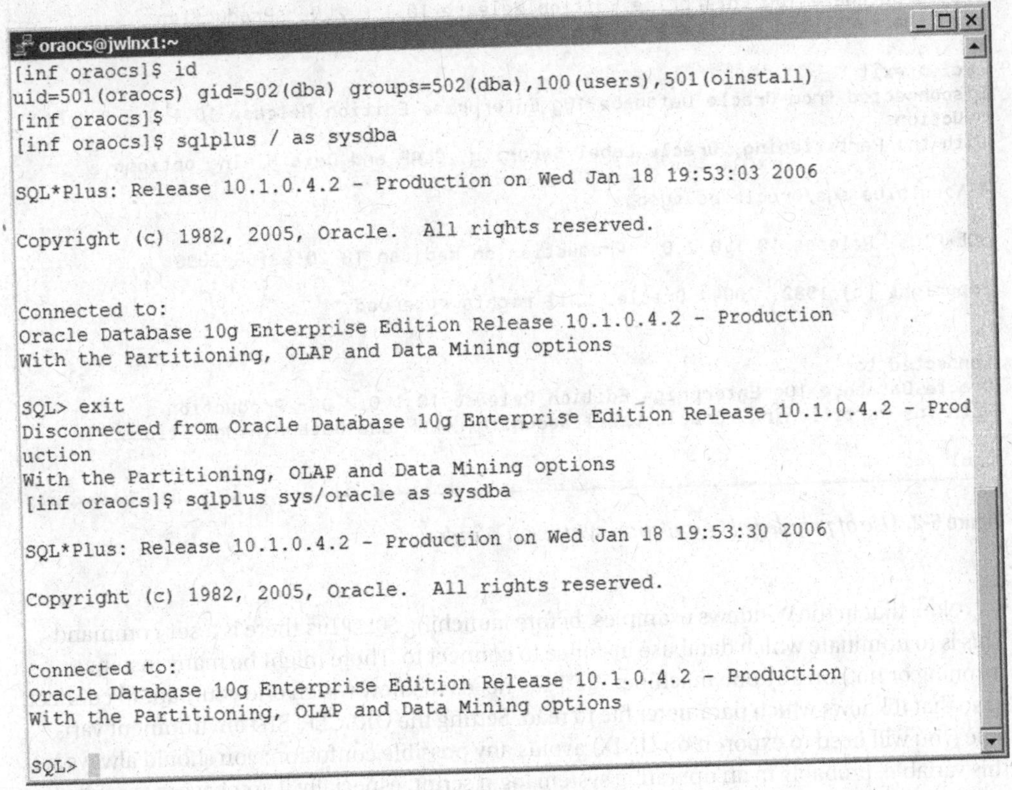

oraocs@jwlnx1:~
[inf oraocs]$ id
uid=501(oraocs) gid=502(dba) groups=502(dba),100(users),501(oinstall)
[inf oraocs]$
[inf oraocs]$ sqlplus / as sysdba
SQL*Plus: Release 10.1.0.4.2 - Production on Wed Jan 18 19:53:03 2006
Copyright (c) 1982, 2005, Oracle. All rights reserved.
Connected to:
Oracle Database 10g Enterprise Edition Release 10.1.0.4.2 - Production
With the Partitioning, OLAP and Data Mining options
SQL> exit
Disconnected from Oracle Database 10g Enterprise Edition Release 10.1.0.4.2 - Prod
uction
With the Partitioning, OLAP and Data Mining options
[inf oraocs]$ sqlplus sys/oracle as sysdba
SQL*Plus: Release 10.1.0.4.2 - Production on Wed Jan 18 19:53:30 2006
Copyright (c) 1982, 2005, Oracle. All rights reserved.
Connected to:
Oracle Database 10g Enterprise Edition Release 10.1.0.4.2 - Production
With the Partitioning, OLAP and Data Mining options
SQL>

Figure 5-1. *Use of privileged connection syntax on UNIX*

First, note the output of the id command: the user is a member of the group dba, which was used to install the software. The syntax / as sysdba instructs Oracle to check this, and having satisfied this criterion, the user is connected. The second example uses sys/oracle as sysdba to specify a username and password that must exist in the password file. In both cases, sysdba instructs Oracle to make the connection as an administration session that might be used for startup and shutdown commands rather than as a normal user session. Figure 5-2 shows the same commands from the Windows character-based tool.

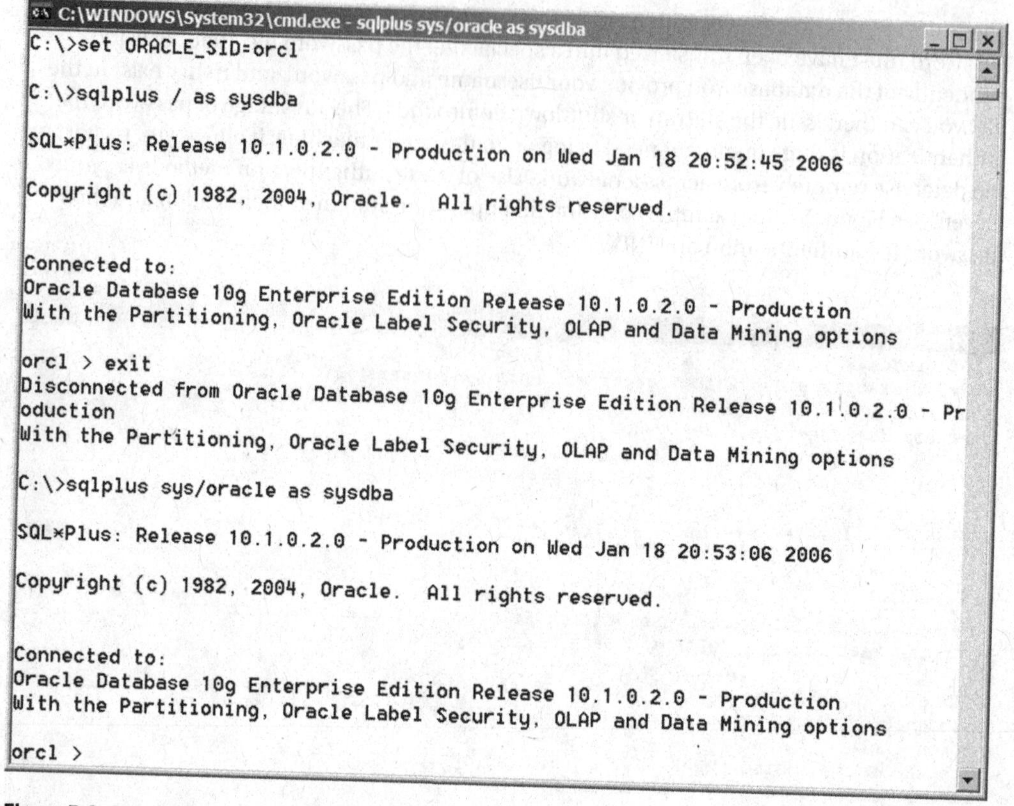
C:\WINDOWS\System32\cmd.exe - sqlplus sys/oracle as sysdba
C:\>set ORACLE_SID=orcl
C:\>sqlplus / as sysdba
SQL*Plus: Release 10.1.0.2.0 - Production on Wed Jan 18 20:52:45 2006
Copyright (c) 1982, 2004, Oracle. All rights reserved.
Connected to:
Oracle Database 10g Enterprise Edition Release 10.1.0.2.0 - Production
With the Partitioning, Oracle Label Security, OLAP and Data Mining options
orcl > exit
Disconnected from Oracle Database 10g Enterprise Edition Release 10.1.0.2.0 - Pr
oduction
With the Partitioning, Oracle Label Security, OLAP and Data Mining options
C:\>sqlplus sys/oracle as sysdba
SQL*Plus: Release 10.1.0.2.0 - Production on Wed Jan 18 20:53:06 2006
Copyright (c) 1982, 2004, Oracle. All rights reserved.
Connected to:
Oracle Database 10g Enterprise Edition Release 10.1.0.2.0 - Production
With the Partitioning, Oracle Label Security, OLAP and Data Mining options
orcl >

Figure 5-2. *Use of privileged connection syntax on Windows*

Note that in the Windows examples, before launching `SQL*Plus` there is a `set` command. This is to nominate which database instance to connect to. There might be many instances (running or not) on any one machine; `SQL*Plus` needs to know which one you want to connect to so that it knows which parameter file to read. Setting the ORACLE_SID environment variable (you will need to export it on UNIX) avoids any possible confusion; you should always set this variable, probably in an operating system login script, especially if you have more than one database on one server.

Having acquired a privileged connection, you can issue startup or shutdown commands. There are variations possible for the startup command, but these are only used when doing maintenance work. For normal usage, a simple `startup` will do, as shown in Figure 5-3, issued from the graphical version of `SQL*Plus` after connecting with operating system authentication.

There are variations in the `shutdown` command. Without any argument, `shutdown` will wait until all users have voluntarily disconnected. This is not going to happen in an Oracle Collaboration Suite environment; there will always be processes logged into the database, whether it is an infrastructure database or a datastore database. The argument you need to make the `shutdown` command succeed, rather than hang as it waits, is one of `transactional`, `immediate`, or `abort`.

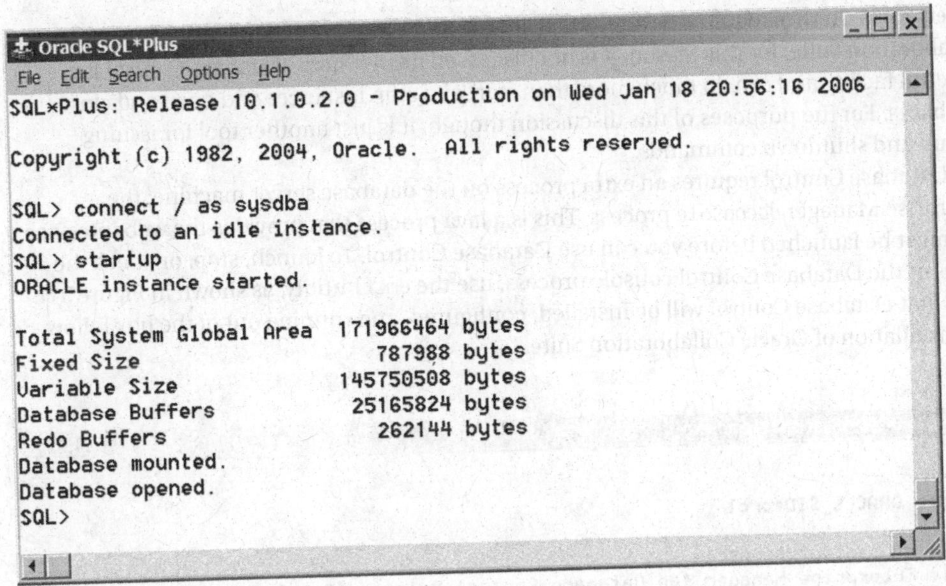

Oracle SQL*Plus
File Edit Search Options Help
SQL*Plus: Release 10.1.0.2.0 - Production on Wed Jan 18 20:56:16 2006
Copyright (c) 1982, 2004, Oracle. All rights reserved.
SQL> connect / as sysdba
Connected to an idle instance.
SQL> startup
ORACLE instance started.
Total System Global Area 171966464 bytes
Fixed Size 787988 bytes
Variable Size 145750508 bytes
Database Buffers 25165824 bytes
Redo Buffers 262144 bytes
Database mounted.
Database opened.
SQL>

Figure 5-3. *Database startup on Windows*

The `transactional` shutdown will disconnect all sessions that aren't doing anything but let other sessions finish their currently running statement or transaction before disconnecting them. This is the "polite" way to shut down a database.

An `immediate` will disconnect all users immediately and roll back any currently active transactions. Either of these shutdown methods is *clean*. After the shutdown there are no incomplete transactions and all work is saved to the database.

An `abort` will terminate the instance right away; no work is written to disk, no incomplete work is rolled back. The effect is exactly as though the power had been cut off or the server rebooted. There is nothing wrong with an `abort`, except that some maintenance work (such as backups) may not be possible until the instance recovery mechanism (invoked automatically after the next startup) has repaired the damage. An `immediate` or `transactional` shutdown may take a long time; `abort` is always virtually instantaneous. The fastest way to achieve a clean shutdown is first, abort the instance. Second, start it up in the restricted mode. This will trigger the instance recovery mechanism but prevent anyone from logging in. Third, shut down cleanly with `immediate`. A `SQL*Plus` script to do this is the following:

```
connect sys/oracle as sysdba
shutdown abort
startup restrict
shutdown immediate
```

Enterprise Manager Database Control

Enterprise Manager is Oracle's web tool for administering all server-side processes. It comes in two forms: Database Control and Grid Control. Database Control is designed to manage a single database; Grid Control can manage any number of databases and also application servers. Grid Control requires an additional license and is not installed as part of Oracle Collaboration Suite; for this reason, it is not discussed further here. Database Control is a powerful facility and can do much more than start and stop instances and open and close databases. For the purposes of this discussion though, it is just another tool for issuing startup and shutdown commands.

Database Control requires an extra process on the database server machine: the Enterprise Manager `dbconsole` process. This is a Java process that provides the web interface and must be launched before you can use Database Control. To launch, stop, or check the status of the Database Control console process, use the `emctl` utility, as shown in Figure 5-4. Note that Database Control will be installed, configured, and running out of the box following installation of Oracle Collaboration Suite.

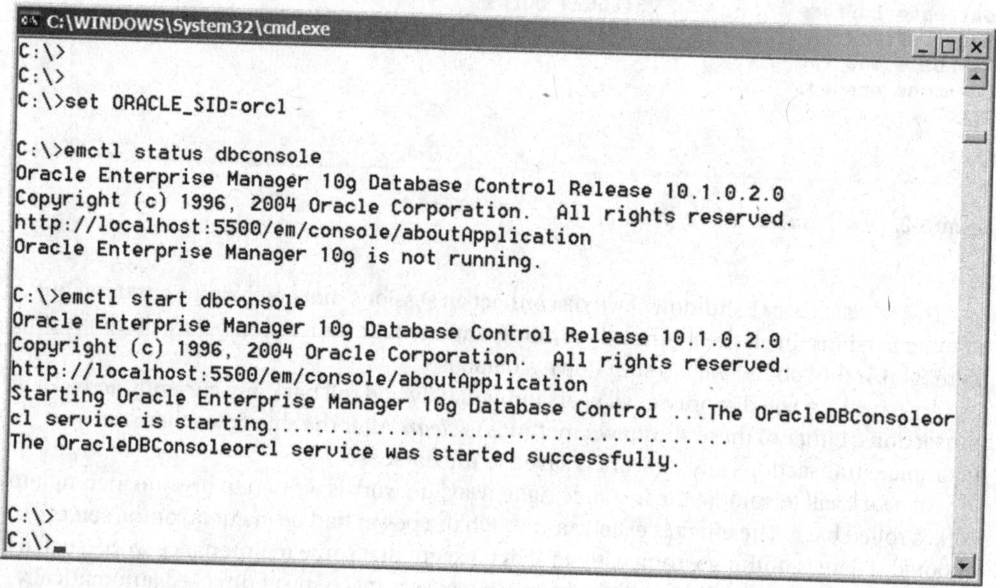

Figure 5-4. *Use of the emctl utility*

The utility is identical on Windows and UNIX. Note that the utility shows the URL being used to contact the process; you will use a similar URL in your browser to contact it once it is running. To contact the Database Control process, use the URL `http://host.domain:5500/em`, substituting the host and domain of your server machine. The port will typically be 5500, but to confirm this, look at the `portlist.ini` file in the `ORACLE_HOME/install` directory. For example, on UNIX, `grep Console < $ORACLE_HOME/install/portlist.ini`, or on Windows, `find "Console" %ORACLE_HOME%\install\portlist.ini`, will extract the Database Control port from the `portlist.ini` file. If this command does not return anything, you are in the wrong Oracle home, or perhaps the ORACLE_HOME environment variable hasn't been set at all.

Request a privileged connection, as shown in Figure 5-5, to reach the Database Control database home page, which includes a button for shutdown (or startup, if it is already shut-down) as shown in Figure 5-6.

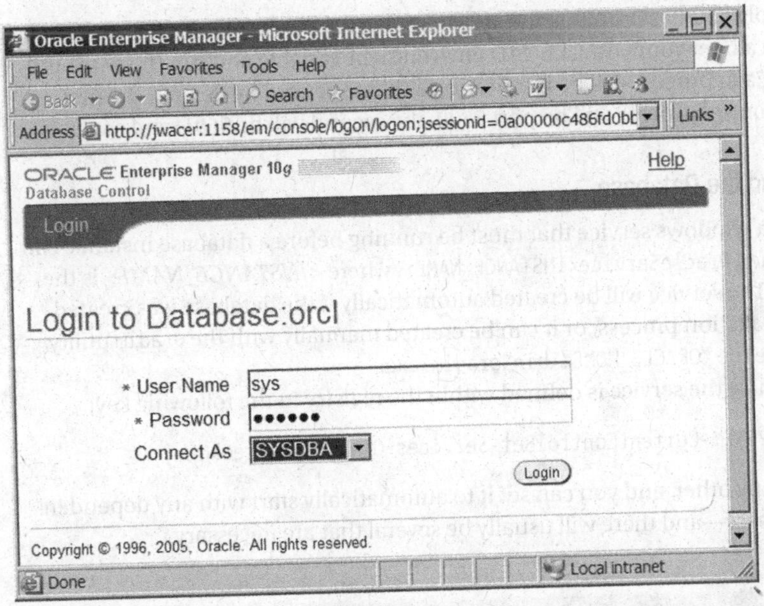

Figure 5-5. *How to connect to Database Control with a privileged connection*

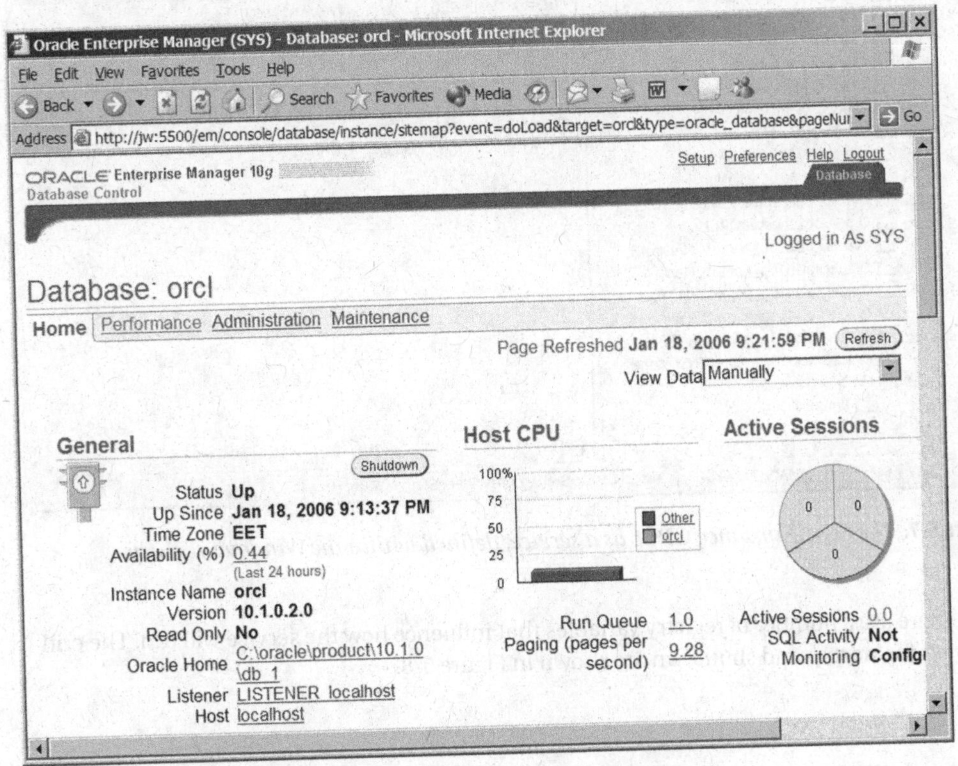

Figure 5-6. *The database home page, with shutdown/startup button*

If there are multiple databases on the one server, each will have its own Database Control process. To start them all, set your ORACLE_SID environment variable and run the `emctl` utility for each instance. Each process will be monitoring a different port; by default, the first instance's Database Control process will be port 5500, the second will be 5501, and so on.

Windows Services and the Database

On Windows, there is a Windows service that must be running before a database instance can be started. This is named `OracleService<INSTANCE_NAME>`, where *<INSTANCE_NAME>* is the name of the instance. The service will be created automatically if the database was created through an Oracle installation process, or it can be created manually with the `oradim` utility, which is the executable file `%ORACLE_HOME%\bin\oradim.exe`.

Figure 5-7 shows how the service is defined within the registry in the following key:

```
HKEY_LOCAL_MACHINE-SYSTEM-CurrentControlSet-Services-OracleServiceORCL
```

It is a service like any other, and you can set it to automatically start with any dependencies that may be necessary—and there will usually be several that are necessary.

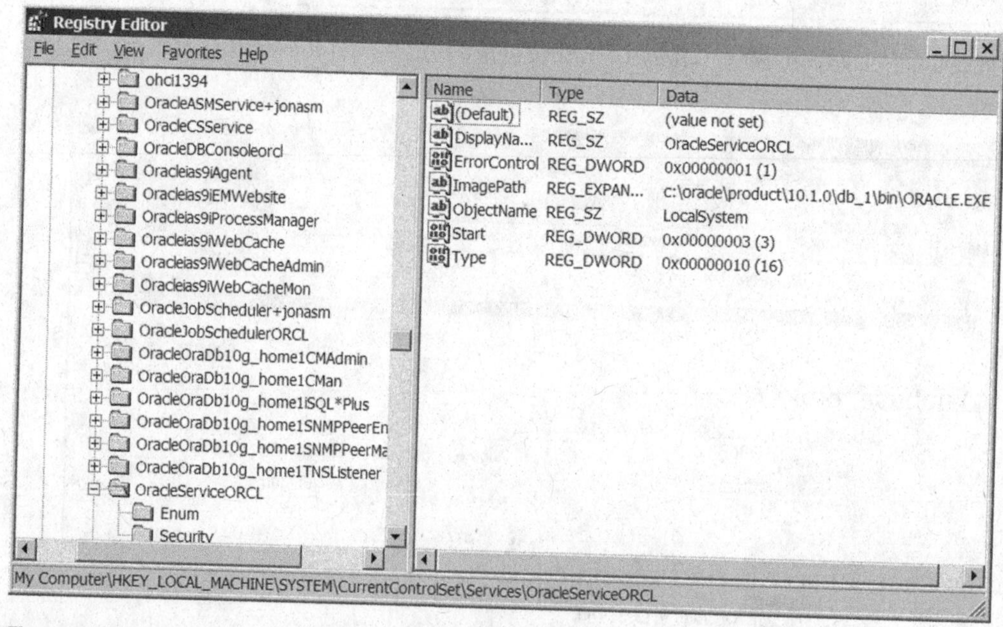

Figure 5-7. *The Oracle instance ORCL as a service, defined within the Windows registry*

There are a number of registry variables that influence how the service will run. The critical ones for startup and shutdown are shown in Figure 5-8.

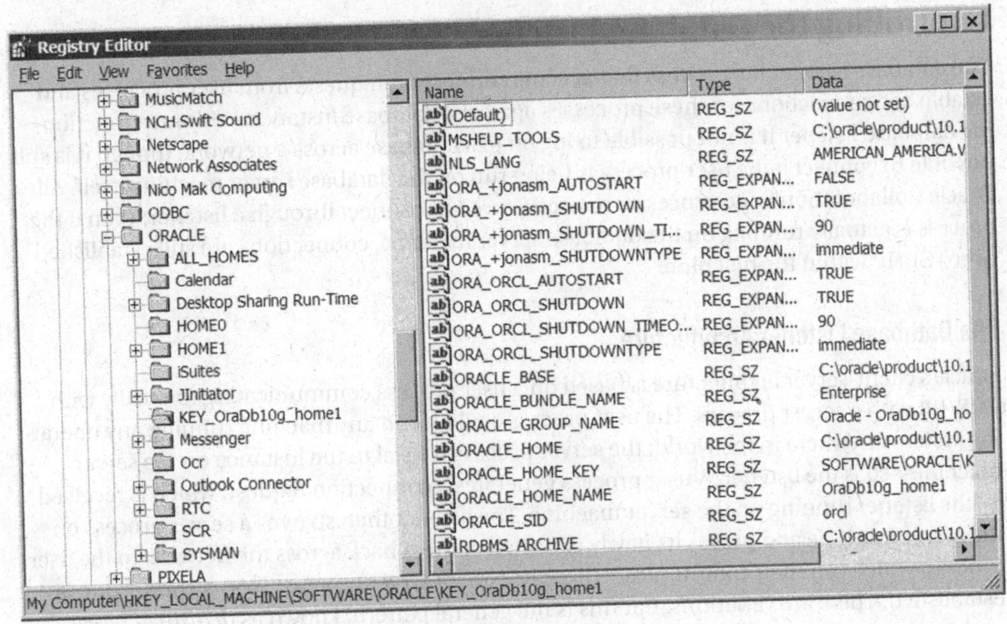

Figure 5-8. *Registry variables for an Oracle instance*

There will be a key for each Oracle home installed on the machine. In the example shown, it is the following:

```
HKEY_LOCAL_MACHINE/SOFTWARE/ORACLE/Key_OraDb10g_home1
```

Note the values for these three keys:

- `ORA_ORCL_AUTOSTART: TRUE`
- `ORA_ORCL_SHUTDOWN: TRUE`
- `ORA_ORCL_SHUTDOWNTYPE: IMMEDIATE`

The first specifies whether Windows should start the instance and open the database when the service is started. The second specifies that when the service is stopped Windows should also stop the instance. The third determines what type of shutdown will be initiated when the service is stopped—in this case, an `immediate` shutdown.

Use of services to start and stop instances can simplify administration on Windows systems quite substantially, because critical variables, such as the name of the instance and the path to the Oracle home directory, are stored in the registry, and the service will have access to them. When using command-line tools, you will often have to set these variables as environment variables first.

Note that the Database Control process also runs as a service; the service `OracleDBConsoleorcl`, shown in Figure 5-7, can be started and stopped from the Windows Services/Control Panel rather than with the `emctl` utility.

Controlling the Database Listener

The database listener is a process that accepts connection requests from user processes and establishes connections for these processes against a database instance. Without a functioning database listener it is not possible to log on to a database across a network, though it is still possible to connect if the user process is being run on the database server machine itself. All Oracle Collaboration Suite processes are configured to connect through a listener; even if the process is actually running on the database server machine, connections are still established over TCP/IP within the machine.

The Database Listener Architecture

Oracle's client-server architecture is based on a user process communicating (typically with TCP/IP) with a server process. The user process could be on any machine running any operating system anywhere in the world; the server process is local to the instance on the server machine—so is the listener. A user process generates a connection request, which is received by the listener running on the server machine. The listener then spawns a server process on the server machine and passes its newly allocated address back across the network to the user process, which can then communicate directly with its server process. Thus a connection is established. There are variations, but this is the general pattern; known as *dedicated server architecture*, one server process is launched for each session and is dedicated to executing the SQL generated by its user process. This is the client-server split: user processes generate SQL, server processes execute SQL.

Once a session has been established by a listener, the listener has nothing more to do with it. You can even stop the listener and this will not affect already established sessions—though, of course, no one else will be able to connect until the listener is started again.

There may be several database listeners running off the executables installed in one Oracle home, but usually they will all be controlled by one file which is

```
$ORACLE_HOME/network/admin/listener.ora
```

on UNIX, and on Windows,

```
%ORACLE_HOME%\network\admin\listener.ora
```

It is possible to relocate this file, in which case you would usually set the TNS_ADMIN environment variable to point to the new location. For example, if you decide to relocate all the Oracle Net configuration files to a directory specially created, on UNIX you could use this command:

```
set TNS_ADMIN=/oraclenet; export TNS_ADMIN
```

On Windows you can set the variable by right-clicking the My Computer icon and then navigating to Properties➤Advanced➤Environment Variables.

Each listener defined in the file will monitor one or more ports on one or more addresses and will have its own name. If there are multiple listeners defined in the one file, all commands issued with the `lsnrctl` utility will have to specify which one. A standard Oracle Collaboration Suite installation will use only one listener per database server machine, which will run on the default port of 1521, and listen on one address—that returned by the `hostname` command. This can be changed later, but using this default does simplify administration.

Before a listener can establish sessions against a database instance, it must know that the instance exists. With earlier versions of the Oracle database, it was necessary to hard code instance details in the listener's configuration file, but later versions use a more intelligent method: when an instance starts, it will locate the listener and register with it. It therefore makes sense to start the listener before the instance. But if the start is done in the other order, or if the listener is stopped and restarted, this is not disastrous because the instance will attempt to reregister periodically.

If the listener is running on the default port of 1521, no database instance configuration is needed. Unless instructed otherwise, an instance will always look for a listener with TCP on the local host address, port 1521. If the listener is using some other port, the instance parameter LOCAL_LISTENER (stored in the instance parameter file) should be set to specify the address of the listener. This can be done through Database Control or from the SQL*Plus prompt using the following commands:

```
SQL> alter system set local_listener=➥
'(address=(protocol=tcp)(host=jwlnx1.bplc.co.za)(port=1522))';
SQL> alter system register;
```

The first command informs the database that there is a listener waiting for TCP connections on the IP address identified by jwlnx1.bplc.co.za, port 1522. The second command instructs the instance to locate the listener and register with it. Variations in the syntax for setting the LOCAL_LISTENER parameter can take account of the need to register the database instance with several listeners on several network addresses.

The lsnrctl Utility

The command-line utility to control a database listener is lsnrctl. On UNIX, it is $ORACLE_HOME/bin/lsnrctl, and on Windows it is %ORACLE_HOME%\bin\lsnrctl.exe.

Assuming that the listener is using the default configuration (which is a requirement for the initial Oracle Collaboration Suite installation), simple start and stop commands are all that is needed. Figure 5-9 shows the use of the lsnrctl utility to start a listener.

Note the details in Figure 5-9 for the listening addresses; this listener is monitoring port 1521 on address jwlnx1.bplc.co.za for TCP, and it is also listening with the IPC protocol for the key EXTPROC. The TCP listening address will be used for launching server processes to support regular user connections. The IPC address will be used for launching processes that can run code in dynamically linked libraries, known as *external procedures*. The services summary at the bottom of Figure 5-9 shows that the listener is prepared to accept connections to a service, PLSExtProc; this is the logical name of the external procedure service. There are no database services registered with the listener at this time.

Figure 5-10 shows the output of the lsnrctl status command a short time (7 minutes and 57 seconds, to be exact) after the listener was started.

Note that the services summary now shows two more services. This is because the database instance ocsdb has now located the listener and registered with it. The service ocsdb.bplc.co.za is the database service that users will use for normal sessions; the service ocsdbXDB.bplc.co.za is used for the XML database capability.

```
oraocs@jwlnx1:~
$ lsnrctl

LSNRCTL for Linux: Version 10.1.0.4.2 - Production on 18-JAN-2006 20:36:00

Copyright (c) 1991, 2004, Oracle.  All rights reserved.

Welcome to LSNRCTL, type "help" for information.

LSNRCTL> start
Starting /OCS/product/10.1.1/ocs_1/infra/bin/tnslsnr: please wait...

TNSLSNR for Linux: Version 10.1.0.4.2 - Production
System parameter file is /OCS/product/10.1.1/ocs_1/infra/network/admin/listener.ora
Log messages written to /OCS/product/10.1.1/ocs_1/infra/network/log/listener.log
Listening on: (DESCRIPTION=(ADDRESS=(PROTOCOL=tcp)(HOST=jwlnx1.bplc.co.za)(PORT=1521)))
Listening on: (DESCRIPTION=(ADDRESS=(PROTOCOL=ipc)(KEY=EXTPROC)))

Connecting to (DESCRIPTION=(ADDRESS=(PROTOCOL=TCP)(HOST=jwlnx1.bplc.co.za)(PORT=1521)))
STATUS of the LISTENER
------------------------
Alias                     LISTENER
Version                   TNSLSNR for Linux: Version 10.1.0.4.2 - Production
Start Date                18-JAN-2006 20:36:02
Uptime                    0 days 0 hr. 0 min. 0 sec
Trace Level               off
Security                  ON: Local OS Authentication
SNMP                      OFF
Listener Parameter File   /OCS/product/10.1.1/ocs_1/infra/network/admin/listener.ora
Listener Log File         /OCS/product/10.1.1/ocs_1/infra/network/log/listener.log
Listening Endpoints Summary...
  (DESCRIPTION=(ADDRESS=(PROTOCOL=tcp)(HOST=jwlnx1.bplc.co.za)(PORT=1521)))
  (DESCRIPTION=(ADDRESS=(PROTOCOL=ipc)(KEY=EXTPROC)))
Services Summary...
Service "PLSExtProc" has 1 instance(s).
  Instance "PLSExtProc", status UNKNOWN, has 1 handler(s) for this service...
The command completed successfully
LSNRCTL>
```

Figure 5-9. *Using lsnrctl on UNIX to start a listener*

```
oraocs@jwlnx1:~
LSNRCTL> status
Connecting to (DESCRIPTION=(ADDRESS=(PROTOCOL=TCP)(HOST=jwlnx1.bplc.co.za)(PORT=1521)))
STATUS of the LISTENER
------------------------
Alias                     LISTENER
Version                   TNSLSNR for Linux: Version 10.1.0.4.2 - Production
Start Date                13-OCT-2005 16:46:17
Uptime                    0 days 0 hr. 7 min. 57 sec
Trace Level               off
Security                  ON: Local OS Authentication
SNMP                      OFF
Listener Parameter File   /OCS/product/10.1.1/ocs_1/infra/network/admin/listener.ora
Listener Log File         /OCS/product/10.1.1/ocs_1/infra/network/log/listener.log
Listening Endpoints Summary...
  (DESCRIPTION=(ADDRESS=(PROTOCOL=tcp)(HOST=jwlnx1.bplc.co.za)(PORT=1521)))
  (DESCRIPTION=(ADDRESS=(PROTOCOL=ipc)(KEY=EXTPROC)))
Services Summary...
Service "PLSExtProc" has 1 instance(s).
  Instance "PLSExtProc", status UNKNOWN, has 1 handler(s) for this service...
Service "ocsdb.bplc.co.za" has 1 instance(s).
  Instance "ocsdb", status READY, has 1 handler(s) for this service...
Service "ocsdbXDB.bplc.co.za" has 1 instance(s).
  Instance "ocsdb", status READY, has 1 handler(s) for this service...
The command completed successfully
LSNRCTL> stop
Connecting to (DESCRIPTION=(ADDRESS=(PROTOCOL=TCP)(HOST=jwlnx1.bplc.co.za)(PORT=1521)))
The command completed successfully
LSNRCTL>
```

Figure 5-10. *Using lsnrctl on UNIX to stop a listener*

Controlling the Listener with Database Control

Database Control can control listeners as well as databases. Toward the bottom left of Figure 5-6 there is a link labeled Listener. Clicking this will navigate to the window shown in Figure 5-11, where you can start and stop the listener, as well as adjust its configuration and observe its performance.

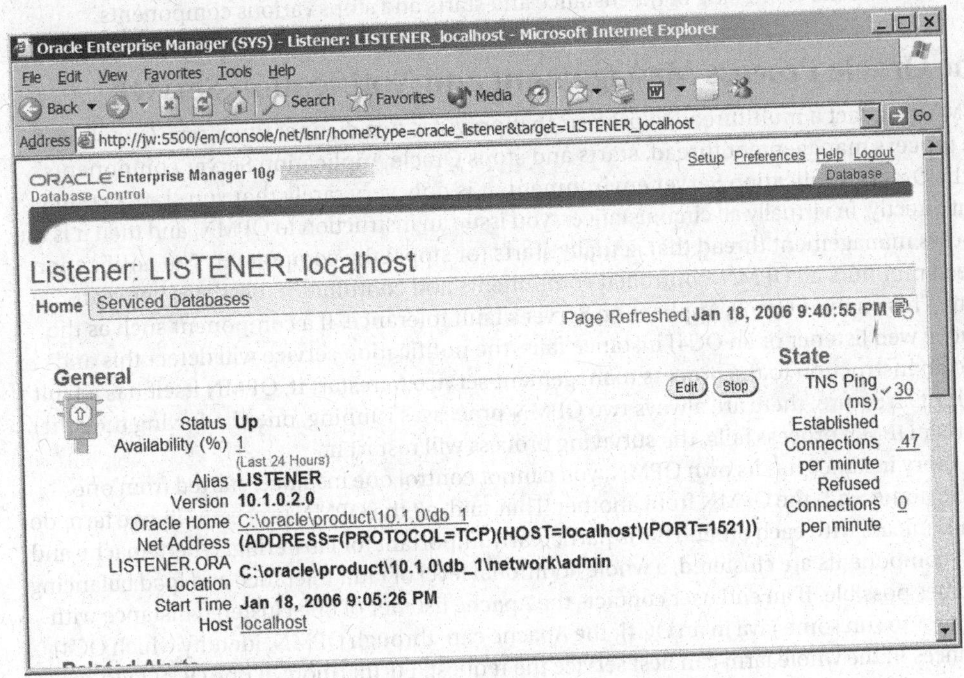

Figure 5-11. *The Database Control listener management facility*

Windows Services and the Database Listener

On Windows systems, listeners run as Windows services. There is no significant configuration that can be done to the service, and the first time the listener is started (either with the `lsnrctl` utility, or through Database Control) the service will be created automatically. The service does, however, provide a convenient way of automating the listener startup; and by configuring appropriate dependencies you can ensure that the listener starts before the database and before any other processes that may need to connect to the database.

Application Server Startup and Shutdown

Chapter 2 covers the architecture of the Oracle Application Server. An infrastructure instance consists of a database, an Apache web listener, and various preconfigured components that provide security and support services to middle tier instances. A middle tier instance consists of a Web Cache, an Apache web listener, and various components you configure to your own needs. An Oracle Collaboration Suite installation is an infrastructure and one or more middle tier instances with the various collaboration applications deployed automatically. For a successful startup of an Oracle Application Server web site, certain components must be available and started in the correct order: first the infrastructure, then the middle tier(s). There are both graphical and command-line tools for doing this.

The heart of any Oracle Application Server instance, whether middle tier or infrastructure, is the Oracle Process Management and Notification service (OPMN). This is the service that monitors the well-being of the instance and starts and stops various components.

The Oracle Process Management and Notification Service

OPMN is in fact a multithreaded process that provides two distinct functions. One thread, the process management thread, starts and stops Oracle Application Server components. In the Oracle Application Server environment, it is only very rarely that you start a component directly; in virtually all circumstances, you issue an instruction to OPMN, and then it is the process management thread that actually starts (or stops) the component. The notification thread monitors all OPMN-controlled components and coordinates messages between them. This enables Oracle Application Server's fault tolerance. If a component such as the Apache web listener or an OC4J instance fails, the notification service will detect this and send an instruction to the process management service to restart it. OPMN itself has a fault tolerant structure; there are always two OPMN processes running, one shadowing the other. If either OPMN process fails, the surviving process will restart it.

Every instance has its own OPMN; you cannot control one instance, started from one Oracle home, with the OPMN from another. That said, all the OPMN processes in one farm do communicate with each other. This is particularly important for clustering. When Apache and OC4J components are clustered, a whole additional level of fault tolerance and load balancing becomes possible. If an end user contacts the Apache listener of one clustered instance with a request to run some Java in an OC4J, the Apache can, through OPMN, identify which OC4J instances in the whole farm can best service the request. Furthermore, if one OC4J fails, sessions can be reinstantiated against a surviving OC4J elsewhere. All this, with the fault tolerance, is enabled by the OPMN services.

To start the OPMN, use the `opmnctl` utility, `$ORACLE_HOME/opmn/bin/opmnctl` on UNIX, and `%ORACLE_HOME%\opmn\bin\opmnctl.exe` on Windows. The utility is very simple to use. The commonly used commands are shown in Table 5-1.

Table 5-1. *Commonly Used opmnctl Commands*

opmnctl Command	Description
`opmnctl status`	Shows the status of the OPMN and its managed services
`opmnctl start`	Starts the OPMN service but nothing else
`opmnctl startall`	Starts the OPMN service and all managed services
`opmnctl startproc <attr>=<value>`	Starts one managed service
`opmnctl stopproc <attr>=<value>`	Stops one managed service
`opmnctl stopall`	Stops all managed services and OPMN itself

Figure 5-12 demonstrates the use of the `status` command and the `opmnctl start` command to start the OPMN service itself but no other components. Note that after starting OPMN, the HTTP_Server (the Apache web listener) immediately starts initializing, too.

```
oraocs@jwlnx1:~
$
$ opmnctl status
Unable to connect to opmn.
Opmn may not be up.
$ opmnctl start
opmnctl: opmn started
$ opmnctl status

Processes in Instance: ocsinfra.jwlnx1.bplc.co.za
-------------------+--------------------+---------+---------
ias-component      | process-type       |     pid | status
-------------------+--------------------+---------+---------
DSA                | DSA                |     N/A | Down
LogLoader          | logloaderd         |     N/A | Down
HTTP_Server        | HTTP_Server        |     N/A | Down
dcm-daemon         | dcm-daemon         |     N/A | Down
OC4J               | OC4J_SECURITY      |     N/A | Down
OID                | OID                |     N/A | Down

$ ps -ef|grep opmn
oraocs    5174     1  0 20:57 ?        00:00:00 /OCS/product/10.1.1/ocs_1/infra/opmn/bi
n/opmn -d
oraocs    5176  5174  1 20:57 ?        00:00:00 /OCS/product/10.1.1/ocs_1/infra/opmn/bi
n/opmn -d
```

Figure 5-12. *Use of the opmnctl utility*

The other components listed are those automatically deployed to an infrastructure instance, in particular the Oracle Internet Directory. Finally, using `ps` shows the two OPMN processes, one shadowing the other. Both will be running a process management thread and a notification thread. On Windows, OPMN runs as a service, but the Windows Task Manager will still display the two individual processes.

OPMN is configured with an XML file:

```
$ORACLE_HOME/opmn/conf/opmn.xml
```

This contains details of the managed services and how they are configured. Very occasionally it will be necessary to edit this file by hand, but only under precise instruction from the Oracle documentation or from Oracle Support Services.

Infrastructure Instance Startup

Critical to an infrastructure is the metadata repository database. Without this, and the listener that lets processes connect to it, the infrastructure is useless. This database must be started first. In a normal database startup, typically the listener is first and then the database.

First make sure that your operating system session has environment variables set appropriately for the infrastructure instance such as the following on UNIX:

```
export ORACLE_HOME= /OCS/product/10.1.1/ocs_1/infra
export PATH=$ORACLE_HOME/bin:$ORACLE_HOME/opmn/bin:$PATH
export ORACLE_SID=ocsdb
```

or for Windows

```
set ORACLE_HOME=d:\OCS\product\10.1.1\ocs_1\infra
set PATH=%ORACLE_HOME%\bin;%ORACLE_HOME%\opmn\bin;%PATH%
set ORACLE_SID=ocsdb
```

Then start the listener:

```
lsnrctl start
```

Then launch SQL*Plus, with a privileged connection:

```
sqlplus / as sysdba
```

and start the database from the SQL*Plus prompt:

```
SQL> startup
```

Now start the infrastructure instance, from the operating system prompt:

```
opmnctl startall
```

and confirm that the instance has started with the status command, as shown in Figure 5-13.

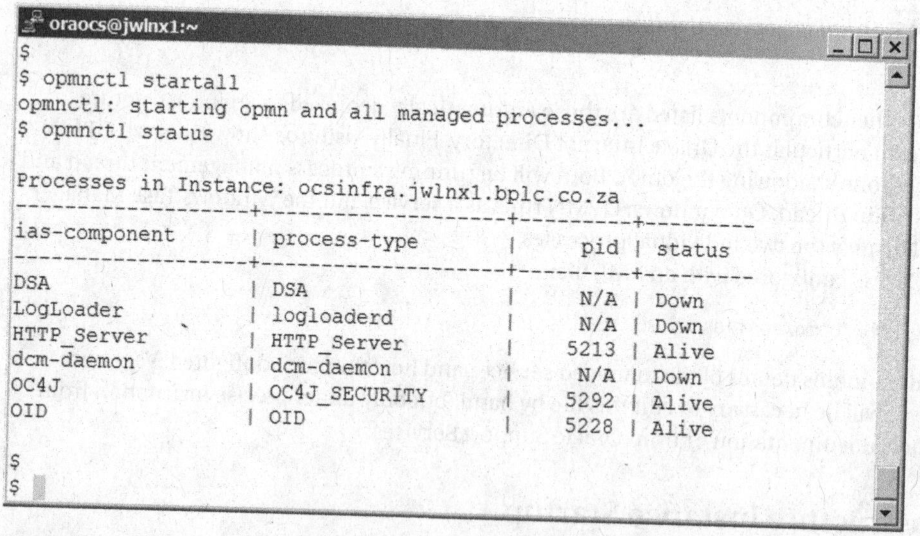

```
oraocs@jwlnx1:~
$
$ opmnctl startall
opmnctl: starting opmn and all managed processes...
$ opmnctl status

Processes in Instance: ocsinfra.jwlnx1.bplc.co.za
-------------------+--------------------+---------+---------
ias-component      | process-type       |     pid | status
-------------------+--------------------+---------+---------
DSA                | DSA                |     N/A | Down
LogLoader          | logloaderd         |     N/A | Down
HTTP_Server        | HTTP_Server        |    5213 | Alive
dcm-daemon         | dcm-daemon         |     N/A | Down
OC4J               | OC4J_SECURITY      |    5292 | Alive
OID                | OID                |    5228 | Alive

$
$
```

Figure 5-13. *Startup of an infrastructure instance with opmnctl*

The critical components are the HTTP_Server (the Apache web listener), the OC4J_Security process (which is part of the Identity Management function), and the OID. The other components are not essential and are usually only started when required. They are DSA, part of OracleAS Guard, the high-availability and disaster-recovery option; the LogLoader, a utility for transferring logging messages from all components into a common repository; and the dcm-daemon, the Enterprise Manager Application Server Control utility.

Middle Tier Instance Startup

Following the infrastructure instance startup, the middle tier instance(s) can be started. These may be located on the same node as the infrastructure instance, or on one or more remote nodes.

The prerequisite for the middle tier instance startup is that the infrastructure instance must already be running. If it is not, some middle tier components may be able to start anyway, but any that rely on an infrastructure, for example, Single Sign-On authentication, will fail. The middle tier components will also require access to the database(s) that stores their information. These must also have been started. If these prerequisites have been met, set your operating system session's environment variables for ORACLE_HOME and PATH to point to the middle tier home, and then start all components with this command:

```
opmnctl startall
```

This command may take some time to complete. Following completion, use the status command, as shown in Figure 5-14.

Note that the first three processes are not running. This is to be expected, as they are not usually configured to start by default. Of the remaining processes, most are Alive, but some are Down. In this particular case, the reason is that the machine is a little underpowered to run a full middle tier of Oracle Collaboration Suite, and the startup routines timed out because of slow response. To start any such components subsequently, use the startproc command. Using the example in the figure, the commands would be the following:

```
opmnctl startproc process-type=email_imap
opmnctl startproc process-type=email_smtp_in
opmnctl startproc process-type=email_smtp_out
opmnctl startproc process-type=Node
```

If you want to start several processes that are part of the same component, such as the Down processes that are all part of e-mail, an alternative command would be

```
opmnctl startproc ias-component=email
```

which will start all Down processes of the e-mail component in parallel. Note that the name of the process or component specified when using the startproc or stopproc command is case-sensitive; the status command lists all the components and processes with their correct names, case included.

```
oraocs@jwlnx1:~
[mid oraocs]$ opmnctl status

Processes in Instance: ocsapps.jwlnx1.bplc.co.za
-------------------+--------------------+---------+---------
ias-component      | process-type       |     pid | status
-------------------+--------------------+---------+---------
DSA                | DSA                |     N/A | Down
LogLoader          | logloaderd         |     N/A | Down
dcm-daemon         | dcm-daemon         |     N/A | Down
OC4J               | OC4J_Mail          |    5686 | Alive
OC4J               | OC4J_OCSClient     |    5687 | Init
OC4J               | OC4J_OCSADMIN      |    5688 | Alive
OC4J               | OC4J_imeeting      |    5689 | Alive
OC4J               | OC4J_Portal        |    5690 | Init
OC4J               | Service_Component~ |    5691 | Alive
HTTP_Server        | HTTP_Server        |    5693 | Alive
WebCache           | WebCache           |    5702 | Alive
WebCache           | WebCacheAdmin      |    5694 | Alive
wireless           | performance_server |    6338 | Alive
wireless           | messaging_server   |    6339 | Alive
wireless           | notificationevent~ |    6340 | Alive
wireless           | notification_serv~ |    6341 | Init
wireless           | OC4J_Wireless      |    6342 | Init
email              | email_housekeeper  |    5712 | Alive
email              | email_imap         |    5703 | Alive
email              | email_listserver   |    5704 | Alive
email              | email_nntp_in      |    5705 | Alive
email              | email_nntp_out     |    5706 | Alive
email              | email_pop          |    5707 | Alive
email              | email_smtp_in      |    5708 | Alive
email              | email_smtp_out     |    5709 | Alive
email              | email_virus_scrub~ |    5710 | Alive
Content            | Node               |    5711 | Stop
Content            | OC4J_Content       |    5713 | Alive
```

Figure 5-14. *Middle tier status following a partially successful startup*

Application Server Control

The graphical tool to manage Oracle Application Server is known as Application Server Control. It is similar in design to the Database Control tool described previously in this chapter, and does in fact predate it. Application Server Control was first shipped with the 9*i* release of Oracle Application Server, whereas Database Control only appeared with release 10*g* of the database.

To use Application Server Control, you must start the daemon that provides its web interface. For this, you use the same `emctl` tool as for starting Database Control. Each Application Server instance will have its own daemon running on its own port. The default port for Application Server Control is 1810 for the first instance on a machine. The second instance will take 1811, and so on. Check the `portlist.ini` file in the `ORACLE_HOME/install` directory to confirm the port number that was assigned at installation time.

A variation from this standard that you will notice with Oracle Collaboration Suite is that the infrastructure Application Server Control runs by default on port 1156; however, middle tier Oracle Collaboration Suite Application Server Control daemons run on 1810 (or the next available port) as one would expect.

Figure 5-15 shows how to check whether Application Server Control is running with the `emctl status dbconsole` command and how to start it with the `emctl start dbconsole` command. Note that both commands show the port the process will run on. Finally, Figure 5-15 shows that you can use `opmnctl` to verify that the `ias-component dcm-daemon`, which is the Application Server Control process, is now running for your current instance.

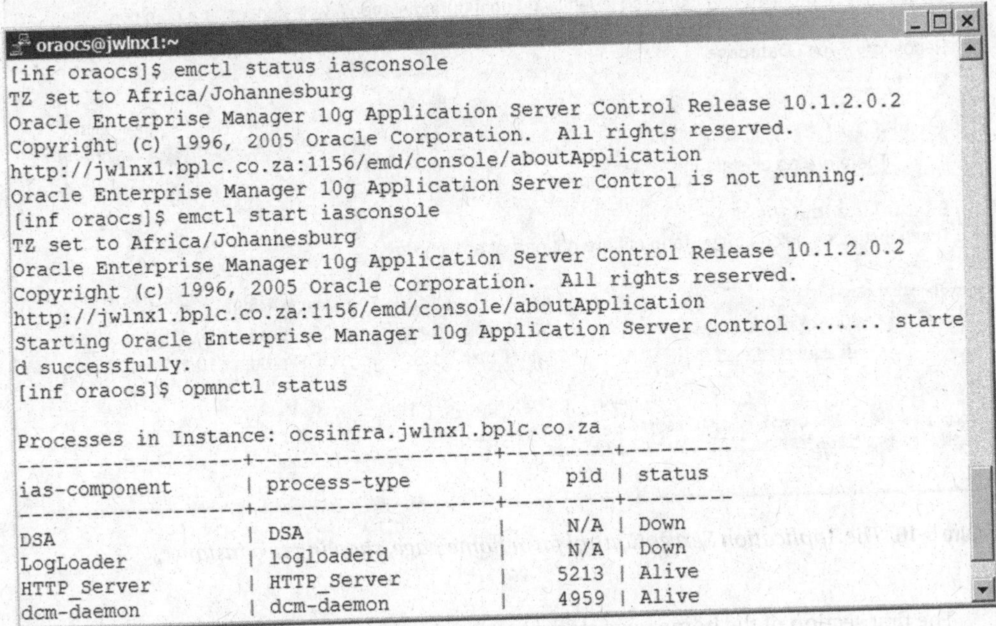

```
oraocs@jwlnx1:~
[inf oraocs]$ emctl status iasconsole
TZ set to Africa/Johannesburg
Oracle Enterprise Manager 10g Application Server Control Release 10.1.2.0.2
Copyright (c) 1996, 2005 Oracle Corporation.  All rights reserved.
http://jwlnx1.bplc.co.za:1156/emd/console/aboutApplication
Oracle Enterprise Manager 10g Application Server Control is not running.
[inf oraocs]$ emctl start iasconsole
TZ set to Africa/Johannesburg
Oracle Enterprise Manager 10g Application Server Control Release 10.1.2.0.2
Copyright (c) 1996, 2005 Oracle Corporation.  All rights reserved.
http://jwlnx1.bplc.co.za:1156/emd/console/aboutApplication
Starting Oracle Enterprise Manager 10g Application Server Control ....... starte
d successfully.
[inf oraocs]$ opmnctl status

Processes in Instance: ocsinfra.jwlnx1.bplc.co.za
-------------------+--------------------+---------+---------
ias-component      | process-type       |     pid | status
-------------------+--------------------+---------+---------
DSA                | DSA                |     N/A | Down
LogLoader          | logloaderd         |     N/A | Down
HTTP_Server        | HTTP_Server        |    5213 | Alive
dcm-daemon         | dcm-daemon         |    4959 | Alive
```

Figure 5-15. *Starting Application Server Control and verifying its status with emctl and opmnctl*

Having started the Application Server Control daemon, connect to it with a browser at the URL `http://host.domain:port`, where the *host.domain* is the address of the server running the instance, and the *port* is the port being used by the daemon process—by default, 1156 for an Oracle Collaboration Suite infrastructure instance, and 1810 (or the next available) for a middle tier instance. You will be prompted to log in. This login screen is generated by your browser in response to a standard error 401 (Authentication Required) HTTP message. You must log in as username ias_admin, giving the password you specified for the instance when you installed the product. At a later stage, you can change the password, but not the username.

Application Server Control has a number of home pages. The first is shown in Figure 5-16, the farm home page.

It doesn't matter which Application Server Control you contact; if it is part of an instance that is part of a farm, you will always be taken to the farm home page. In this case, the URL in the Figure 5-16 refers to port 1156, so you can see that this is the infrastructure's Application Server Control. But that doesn't matter; the middle tier's Application Server Control would construct and return the same page.

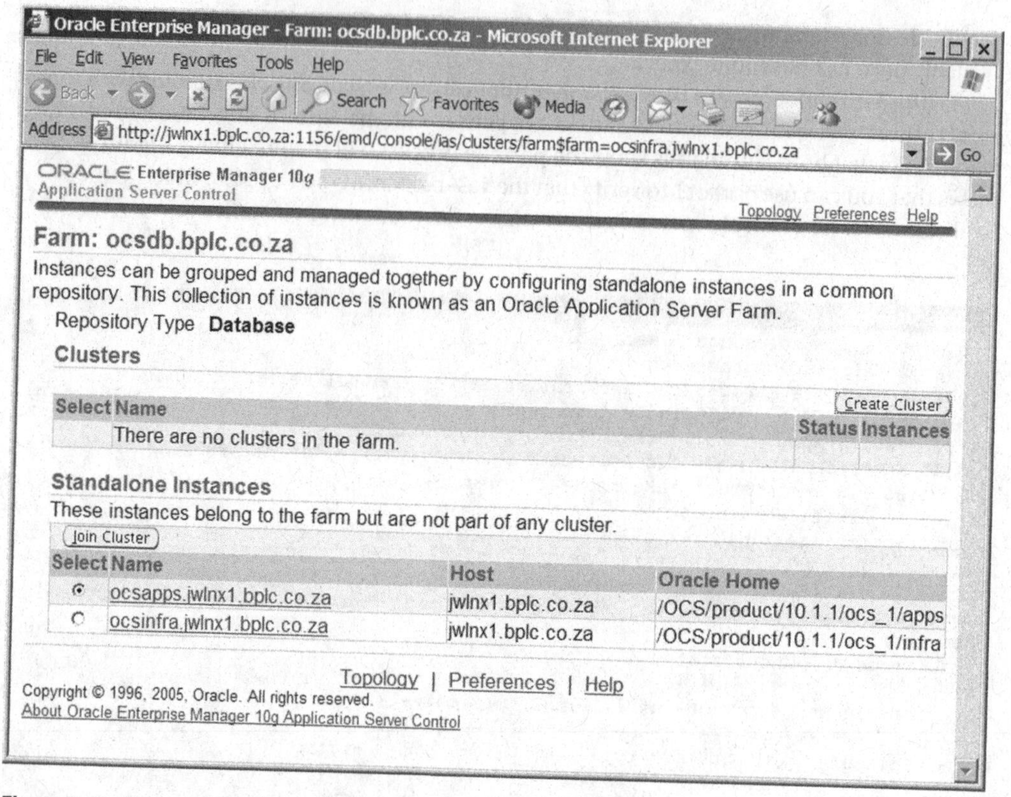

Figure 5-16. *The Application Server Control farm home page, showing two instances*

The first section of the home page is for clusters; there are no clusters in this farm. A *cluster* is a group of two or more middle tier instances that are configured identically for fault tolerance and load balancing. The second section of the home page lists the stand-alone instances. *Stand-alone instances* are part of the farm (their configuration is stored in the metadata repository) but they are not clustered; they are managed independently and may have different applications deployed to them.

The farm shown in Figure 5-16 is the smallest possible configuration for Oracle Collaboration Suite—only two instances. One of these will be the infrastructure instance, the other will be a single middle tier instance. The farm home page does not identify which is which, though the naming convention does make this clear. Each instance has a name, which is a name specified at install time suffixed with the name of the host on which the instance resides. Then there is the actual hostname and the path to the Oracle home. As can be seen, this installation consists of just one machine, though, of course, the infrastructure and middle tier instances are in separate home directories.

To connect to any one instance, double-click the link with its name. This will cause your browser to contact the Application Server Control daemon for that instance with a request for the instance's home page. If the daemon for that instance is not running, the browser will generate an error message saying that the host cannot be contacted. It is therefore necessary to start the Application Server Control daemon for every instance in your farm if you intend to use this tool. Each time you link to an instance, you will be prompted for the ias_admin password for that instance before being shown the instance's home page. All instance home pages begin with similar header information, as shown in Figure 5-17.

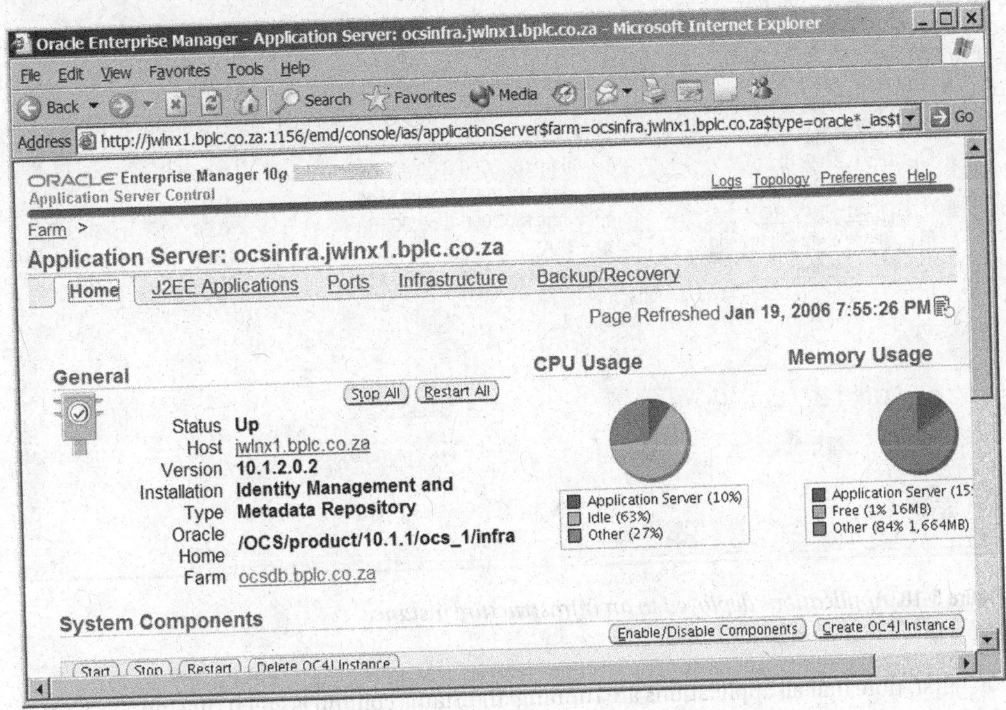

Figure 5-17. *Header part of an instance home page*

In the General section, first note the traffic light symbol (readers in some parts of the world may prefer the term *robot* to *traffic light*), which has a green tick. If all components deployed to an instance are running, this will be green. If any are not running, it will be a red cross. Following that is summary information about the type of instance it is—an infrastructure instance running both the metadata repository and the identity management components, in the example—and basic information about the host machine's CPU and memory usage (very high, in the example).

The Stop All button will stop all components, except the OPMN itself. Application Server Control issues commands to the OPMN in the same way that `opmnctl` does, but unlike `opmnctl`, it cannot issue a command to shut down OPMN. The Restart All button would bounce all currently running components.

The lower part of the instance home page shows the state of the applications deployed to the instance and will be very different for an infrastructure instance and a middle tier instance. Figure 5-18 shows the infrastructure instance home page, a continuation of Figure 5-17.

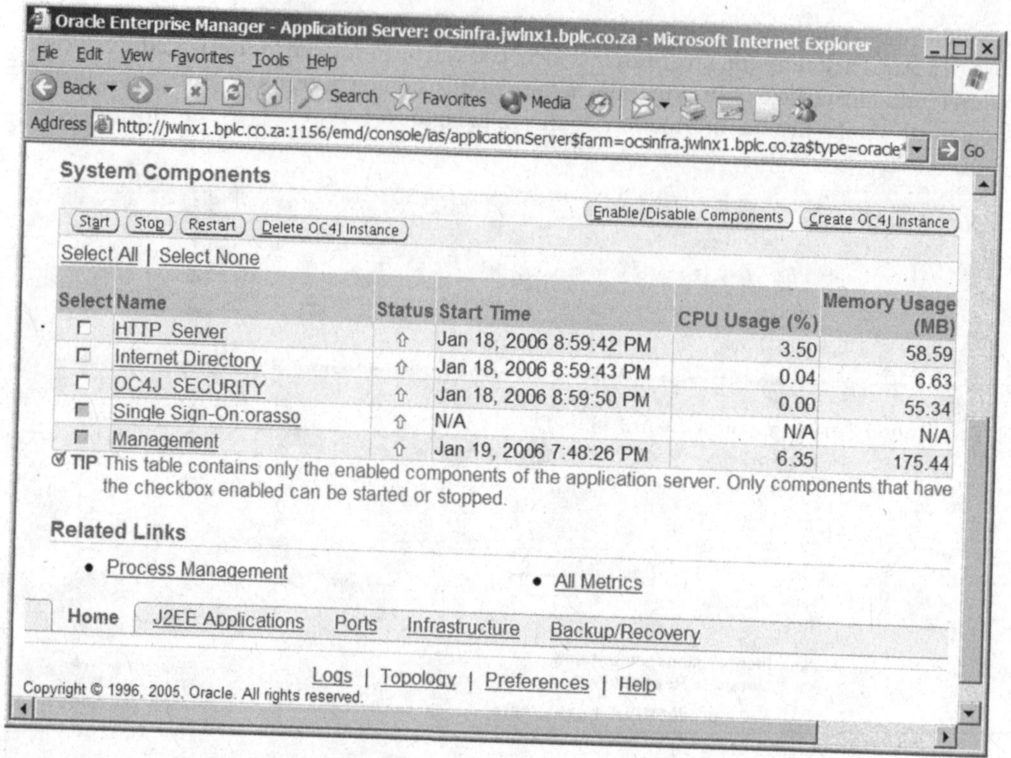

Figure 5-18. *Applications deployed to an infrastructure instance*

First, note that all applications are running: the Status column is green. To stop, start, or restart any of the first three components, select its check box and use the appropriate button.

The first application is HTTP_Server. This is the Apache web listener for the infrastructure instance. Clicking the link lets you reconfigure Apache and is the recommended way to do this. Configuration changes made through Application Server Control will update Apache's own configuration files and make sure that the changes are simultaneously propagated to the metadata repository. There are also links to various monitoring functions. The second application is Internet_Directory. This is the Oracle Internet Directory. Taking this link will let you carry out limited configuration work on the directory; you may need other tools for more advanced operations. The third application is OC4J_Security. It should never be necessary to reconfigure this; it is a predefined application that provides graphical web interface to Oracle Internet Directory and to the account provisioning service.

The last two applications cannot be selected for stop and start; their check boxes are grayed out. This is because they are not applications that run within the instance; they are applications that run in the database. Single Sign-On:orasso is the Single Sign-On application. This is written in PL/SQL. The PL/SQL procedures that make it up are invoked on demand, either by end users from browsers or by applications running in middle tier instances, but either way results in HTTP messages being sent to the infrastructure's web listener. These messages are then routed through modplsql to the database. So Application Server Control is telling us that Single Sign-On is there and working, but it is not something that it can control. The last application, Management, refers to the Application Server Control daemon itself; this must be running or it would be impossible to reach the tool in the first place.

Figure 5-19 shows part of the listing of applications for a middle tier Oracle Collaboration Suite instance, all of which are shut down. The first point to note is that the two applications that make up Calendar can be selected for start and stop, but there is no link to configure them. Calendar is an application that can be installed and run without Oracle Application Server, and it has its own configuration tools. Second, Discussions and Mobile Collaboration have their check boxes grayed out; these are applications that run purely in the database.

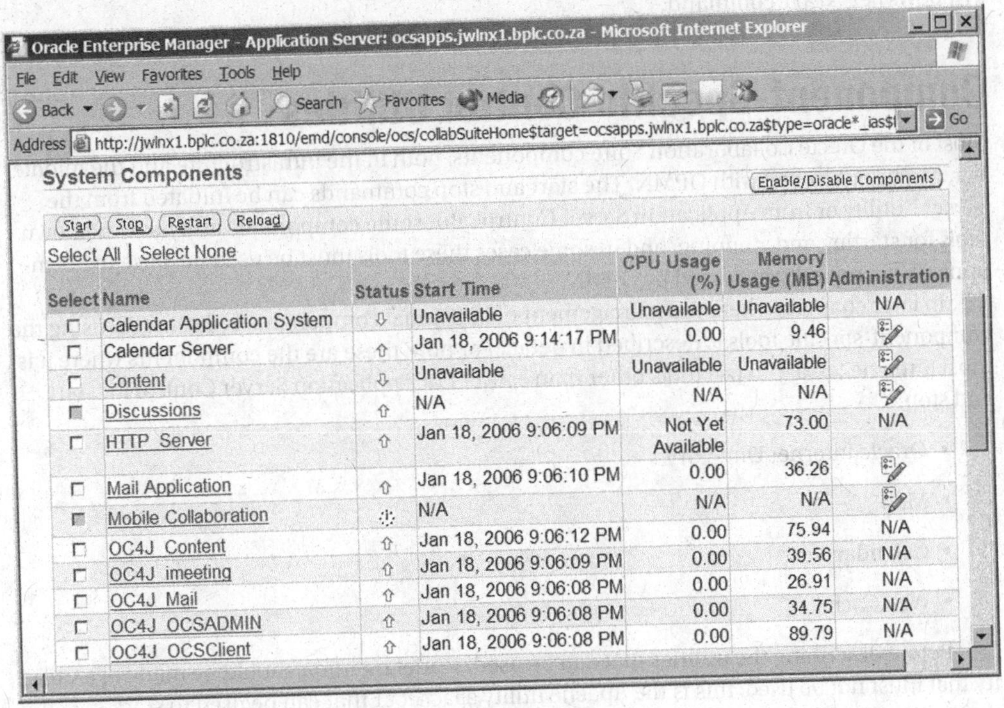

Oracle Enterprise Manager - Application Server: ocsapps.jwlnx1.bplc.co.za - Microsoft Internet Explorer

Address http://jwlnx1.bplc.co.za:1810/emd/console/ocs/collabSuiteHome$target=ocsapps.jwlnx1.bplc.co.za$type=oracle*_ias$l

System Components

Enable/Disable Components

Start | Stop | Restart | Reload

Select All | Select None

Select	Name	Status	Start Time	CPU Usage (%)	Memory Usage (MB)	Administration
☐	Calendar Application System	⇩	Unavailable	Unavailable	Unavailable	N/A
☐	Calendar Server	⇧	Jan 18, 2006 9:14:17 PM	0.00	9.46	
☐	Content	⇩	Unavailable	Unavailable	Unavailable	
☐	Discussions	⇧	N/A	N/A	N/A	
☐	HTTP_Server	⇧	Jan 18, 2006 9:06:09 PM	Not Yet Available	73.00	N/A
☐	Mail Application	⇧	Jan 18, 2006 9:06:10 PM	0.00	36.26	
☐	Mobile Collaboration		N/A	N/A	N/A	
☐	OC4J_Content	⇧	Jan 18, 2006 9:06:12 PM	0.00	75.94	N/A
☐	OC4J_imeeting	⇧	Jan 18, 2006 9:06:09 PM	0.00	39.56	N/A
☐	OC4J_Mail	⇧	Jan 18, 2006 9:06:08 PM	0.00	26.91	N/A
☐	OC4J_OCSADMIN	⇧	Jan 18, 2006 9:06:08 PM	0.00	34.75	N/A
☐	OC4J_OCSClient	⇧	Jan 18, 2006 9:06:08 PM	0.00	89.79	N/A

Figure 5-19. *Applications deployed to a middle tier instance*

Both Figures 5-18 and 5-19 show an Enable/Disable button. This lets you control whether applications will be started when you use the `opmnctl startall` command or the Start All button in the General section of an instance home page. Disabling a component means that these commands will not attempt to start the application, though it can still be selected individually and started with Application Server Control, or you can start it with the `opmnctl startproc` command.

Oracle Application Server and Windows Services

Both infrastructure and middle tier instances have many processes that run as Windows services. The services are created automatically at install time and should not need any reconfiguration. The exception to this is dependencies, particularly if you have both the middle tier and the infrastructure on the same machine. Some of the processes that run as services are the following:

- The Web Cache
- The Apache web listener
- The Oracle Internet Directory
- The Oracle Process Management and Notification service
- The Application Server Control daemon

All of the services can be set to autostart, or you can start them manually with the Windows `net start` command.

Component-Specific Control Utilities

Most of the Oracle Collaboration Suite components, both in the infrastructure and the middle tier, can be controlled with OPMN. The start and stop commands can be initiated from the `opmnctl` utility or from Application Server Control. But some components also have their own tools for starting and stopping, and in some cases these tools must be used because the components are not fully managed by OPMN.

In later chapters where the management of individual components is discussed, using the component-specific tools is described in detail. For now, these are the components where it is most often necessary to use tools other than `opmnctl` or Application Server Control for start and stop:

- Oracle Internet Directory
- Mail
- Calendar
- Web Cache

Before describing the utilities that can be used, a brief mention should be made of a utility that must not be used: this is the Apache utility `apachectl` that can be used to start and stop the Apache web listener. This utility is part of the Apache distribution but it is not aware of the OPMN control structures, and if you use it, the runtime environment will become somewhat confused.

Oracle Internet Directory

Oracle Internet Directory is a perfect example of the fly-by-wire approach taken for many Oracle Application Server components. You do not start and stop it yourself; you ask a control process, the monitor, to start and stop it for you. This can be done with `opmnctl`:

```
opmnctl startproc process-type=OID
opmnctl stopproc process-type=OID
```

or through Application Server Control. But both these methods will start Oracle Internet Directory according to its default stored configuration. There will be occasions when you want to start it with a different configuration, perhaps to handle an unaccustomed workload or to test a configuration before making it permanent. It may also be that the standard tools are simply not available to the Oracle Internet Directory administrator; many sites will not run the Application Server Control daemon at all, or it may be that for security reasons the Oracle Internet Directory administrator does not have permission to use the opmnctl utility.

An Oracle Internet Directory server is a listening process that monitors a port for LDAP requests and sends them to a server process, which actions the request by running queries against an Oracle database, which stores the directory entries.

Typical tuning considerations are the number of listening processes to launch and the address:port combination on which each will listen; the number of server processes to launch for each listener; and the number of concurrent connections each server process can make to the database.

To start the Oracle Internet Directory, the database and database listener must already be running. Then you must start the monitor process. This is an executable residing in the infrastructure Oracle home. The syntax to control the monitor is the following:

```
oidmon [connect=cc] [host=hostname] [sleep=nn] start | stop
```

An example of starting the monitor is the following:

```
oidmon connect=ocsdb host=jwlnx1.bplc.co.za sleep=10 start
```

This example launches the monitor on the network address jwlnx1.bplc.co.za. If the host argument is omitted (as it usually is) the monitor will start on the local host.

The monitor will log on to the database nominated in the connect argument, in this case the database identified by the Oracle Net alias ocsdb. This alias must be resolvable by a tnsnames.ora file. If this argument is omitted, the monitor will log on to whatever instance is specified by the ORACLE_SID environment variable using IPC.

The monitor will poll the database at regular intervals to see if any commands have been inserted that it needs to action according to the number of seconds specified by the sleep argument. This defaults to ten seconds.

Finally, the only required argument is start or stop.

Once the monitor is running, you can use the oidctl utility to place commands in the database that the monitor will action. The oidctl utility is an executable in the infrastructure Oracle home. The syntax is the following:

```
oidctl connect=cc server=ss instance=nn ➥
[host=hostname] [configset=cc] [flags=ff] start | stop
```

An example of using oidctl is the following:

```
oidctl connect=ocsdb server=oidldapd instance=1 ➥
host=jwlnx1 configset=1 flags='-p 3062 -servers 4' start
```

In this example, the connect argument instructs oidctl to log on to the database identified by the Oracle Net alias ocsdb and insert the start command into the appropriate table. Clearly, this argument must match the database specified for the monitor process.

There are three possible types of server in an Oracle Internet Directory. In this case, the server argument starts an oidldapd server, the actual LDAP daemon that listens for LDAP requests. The other server types are `oidrepld`, the replication server that manages replication between different Oracle Internet Directories; and `odisrv`, the Oracle directory integration server that can propagate data to non-Oracle LDAP directories.

It is possible to start multiple `oidldapd` listener processes, provided they are running on different network addresses or on different ports on the same address. Each listener must have a unique instance number. In this case, it is instance number 1. This number will be used with subsequent `stop` commands to identify which listener to stop.

The `host` argument nominates the network address on which the LDAP listener should run; if it is omitted, this defaults to the local host.

The `configset` is a pointer to an entry in the Oracle Internet Directory that controls the configuration of the directory; the Oracle Internet Directory is in effect controlled by the Oracle Internet Directory (isn't recursion a wonderful thing?). Figure 5-20 shows the detail of configset 1, as displayed by the Oracle Directory Manager tool (this tool is fully described in Chapter 6).

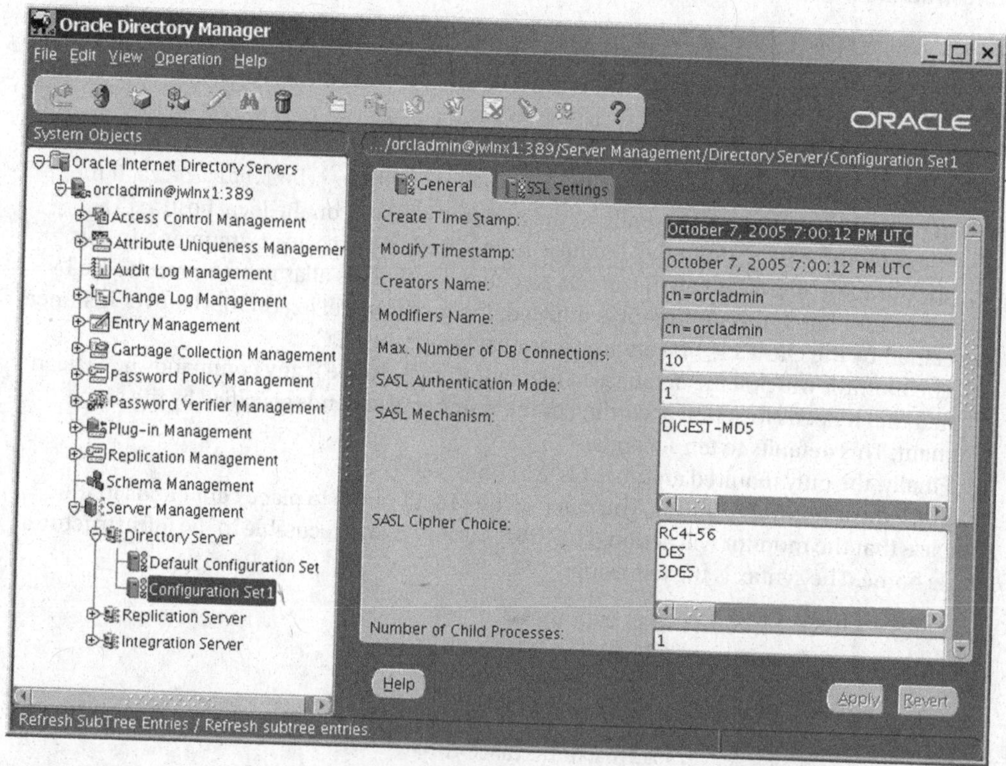

Figure 5-20. *The Oracle Internet Directory configset 1, as shown by the Oracle Directory Manager tool*

Note that configset 1 shown in Figure 5-20, created by the default Oracle Collaboration Suite installation, can have only one server process (the Number of Child Processes setting) but this process can log on to the database with up to ten concurrent connections (and should therefore be able to satisfy ten concurrent requests) and the LDAP listener process will run on port 389. If the `configset` argument is not specified, the directory server will start according to the Default Configuration Set (listed but not selected in the tree on the left of Figure 5-20), which is more limited in its capabilities. You can use the Oracle Directory Manager to create as many configsets as you wish and use them to start different LDAP listeners.

The `flags` argument lets you modify the configset used to start the LDAP processes. In this example, the port number that the listener process will run on will be 3062 and there will be ten server processes launched:

```
oidctl connect=ocsdb server=oidldapd instance=2 host=jwlnx1 ➥
configset=1 flags='-p 3062 -servers 10' start
```

To conclude, if you start the Oracle Internet Directory using `opmnctl` or Application Server Control, it will start the monitor process and then instruct the monitor to start a single LDAP listener process on the local host address configured according to configset 1. By using the `oidctl` utility, you can start and stop additional LDAP listener processes, perhaps on different addresses and using different configsets.

Mail

The Mail component consists of a listening process that monitors port:address combinations for connection requests on various protocols, and a number of protocol server processes that action the requests. The protocols run completely within the Oracle Application Server environment, but the listening process is external.

The Mail listener is based on the same code that is used for the database listener, and you start and stop it with the same `lsnrctl` utility. The Mail listener's name is, by default, LISTENER_ES. To start it, with your environment set to the middle tier Oracle home, use the following command:

```
lsnrctl start listener_es
```

This will launch a listening process that will (unless you have adjusted the default configuration) monitor these ports for the e-mail protocols in Table 5-2.

Table 5-2. *Listening Ports and Protocols for Listener*

Port	Protocol
25	SMTP (Simple Mail Transfer Protocol)
110	POP3 (Post Office Protocol)
119	NNTP (Network News Transport Protocol)
143	IMAP4 (Internet Mail Access Protocol)
563	NNTP with SSL
993	IMAP with SSL
995	POP with SSL

On some UNIX platforms, the listener will fail to start without some further configuration. This is because of UNIX port security. On Windows all ports are treated equally, but on UNIX it is generally not possible for any user other than the root user to start a process that uses a port with a number lower than 1024. All the standard mail ports are less than 1024, so the listener will not start if you attempt to start it as the owner of the Oracle installation. There are platform variations, but in general there are two techniques to work around this.

Starting the LISTENER_ES

You can start the Mail listener as the UNIX Oracle owner if you use the sticky bit file mode attribute to run the listener as a root-owned process. The *sticky bit* is a file attribute that allows a user to run the file with the privileges of the file owner, rather than with his own privileges. The following steps will allow you to start the listener process in the standard manner through OPMN:

1. Log on to the middle tier as the Oracle owner; set the environment to the middle tier.
2. Switch user to the root user, but retain the Oracle owner's environment by using the `su` (rather than the `su -`) command.
3. Change the ownership of the listener executable with the command `chown root $ORACLE_HOME/bin/tnslsnr`.
4. Change the access modes to set the sticky bit with the command `chmod 6751 $ORACLE_HOME/bin/tnslsnr`.
5. Exit back to the Oracle owner ID.
6. Start the listener as the Oracle owner: `lsnrctl start listener_es`.

Some sites consider this technique to be a security risk. It should not be if UNIX is configured correctly, but the use of sticky bits to allow users to launch root-owned processes may not be permitted by your system administrators. In that case, you can start the listener as the root user, but instruct it to take on the identity of the Oracle owner after startup:

1. Log on to UNIX as the Oracle owner; set the environment to the middle tier.
2. Identify your user number and group number with the `id` command.
3. Switch user to the root user, but retain the Oracle owner's environment by using the `su` (rather than the `su -`) command.
4. Start the listener as root, specifying the user number and group number for the Oracle owner: `$ORACLE_HOME/bin/tnslsnr -user <user number> -group <group number> &`.

This technique avoids the use of sticky bits, but it does mean that you have to log on to UNIX as the root user. Furthermore, you will not be able to start the Mail listener through OPMN; you will always have to perform this step rather than being able to control the listener from within the Oracle environment.

Stopping SMTP Service from Preventing Startup

Another issue that can prevent the Mail listener from starting on UNIX systems is the existence of the mail service provided by the operating system. This is not usually an issue on Windows because the default Windows installation does not include an e-mail server, but most UNIX and Linux distributions come with an e-mail service that runs automatically on boot up.

The operating system's mail service, known as the sendmail daemon, will start up on port 25. This means that the Mail listener will not start, because it will (by default) attempt to use port 25, detect that it is in use, and terminate. To check whether your server has started a mail service, see if there is a sendmail process running. A command such as this should do:

```
ps -ef|grep sendmail
```

To be certain, also check whether port 25 is in use:

```
netstat -ln |grep 25
```

If there is a sendmail process running, kill it and edit the appropriate files to prevent it starting automatically on boot up.

Calendar

Calendar, as shown by Application Server Control, consists of the two deployed applications shown in Figure 5-19. The reality is rather more complicated than this because each of these two applications consists of several processes. Furthermore, Calendar's provenance as a third-party application that has been retrofitted into the Oracle Collaboration Suite becomes apparent when you look at the control facilities.

Running opmnctl status will show that there are six process-types that make up the Calendar Server ias-component. These are shown in Table 5-3.

Table 5-3. *The Calendar Server Processes*

Process-Type	Process Name	Function
Calendar_ENG	uniengd	Accepts and services Calendar requests
Calendar_LCK	unilckd	Serializes concurrent access to data
Calendar_SNC	unisncd	Manages connections between Calendar nodes
Calendar_DAS	unidasd	Manages connections to directory servers
Calendar_CWS	unicwsd	Transmits data between nodes and to e-mail services
Calendar_CSM	unicsmd	Enables remote administration of a node

It is these six processes that make up the one application displayed as Calendar Server in Application Server Control; stopping or starting Calendar Server will stop or start all six. The first two are always necessary; they make up the core of the Calendar server. The last four are optional and might not be needed in a small, simple installation. If this is the case, use Application Server Control to flag them as Disabled.

Calendar ships with a set of command-line utility programs. These are located in the directory $ORACLE_HOME/ocal/bin on UNIX, and in %ORACLE_HOME%\ocal\bin on Windows. Included in these are unistart and unistop, and unistatus. The default behavior of unistart is to start all six processes, but by using switches you can limit the effect. For example,

```
unistart -nocws -nosnc -nocsm -nodas
```

will only start the two core processes. The unistop utility has similar switches to stop only certain processes, but the default behavior is to stop all that are running. Both utilities can also be directed at remote nodes, but for this to work the Calendar_CSM process-type must already be running on that node, started either with

```
opmnctl startproc process-type=Calendar_CSM
```

or

```
unistart -standby
```

either of which will start the remote management service but nothing else. The `unistatus` utility will report on which of the six processes are active.

Calendar Application System, shown in Application Server Control, is a set of three applications implemented by CGI programs. The applications are the following:

- *Oracle Calendar web client*: The web user interface that lets users share agendas, schedule meetings, and reserve rooms and other resources through browsers.
- *Oracle Mobile Data Sync*: The tool that enables two-way synchronization between Calendar and client devices that are not permanently connected; you can download your schedules to a local compliant device.
- *Oracle Calendar web services*: A set of web services that programmers can use to construct their own tools that will interact with Calendar.

These processes cannot be started with `opmnctl` and are not even displayed by the `status` command. The reason is that they are implemented with CGI, and OPMN cannot manage CGI processes. These CGI processes are invoked, on demand, by Apache through the modfastcgi module; OPMN knows nothing about them.

The Oracle Calendar Application System is controlled by the `ocasctl` utility, in the `ORACLE_HOME/ocas/bin` directory. Figure 5-21 demonstrates the critical commands.

First, the `status` command returns nothing; the Oracle Calendar Application System has not been started either with `ocasctl` or with Application Server Control.

Then the utility is run with an instruction to launch four CGI servers. The default number, five, is of course configurable.

Following this, the `status` command shows that four servers are running and also shows their process ID numbers. The same information can be obtained by using the UNIX `ps` command.

Finally, the `stopall` command terminates the servers as if Application Server Control had been used to stop the Calendar Application System application.

To conclude, Calendar is a third-party product that has been forced into the Oracle Collaboration Suite. It is perfectly integrated with the security model. It uses Oracle Internet Directory and Single Sign-On, but it can still be installed as an independent product. For this reason it has a separate set of control utilities. The Calendar Application System is not OPMN-enabled, because it is implemented as CGI programs. If these programs were ported to the Oracle Application Server OPMN environment (by, for example, rewriting them as OC4J applications), it would become impossible to install Calendar as an independent product. The effect of this on the Oracle Collaboration Suite administrator is positive; he can separate the Calendar administration domain from the rest of the product set. It becomes possible to delegate Calendar administration to staff who do not have administrative access to the whole of Oracle Collaboration Suite.

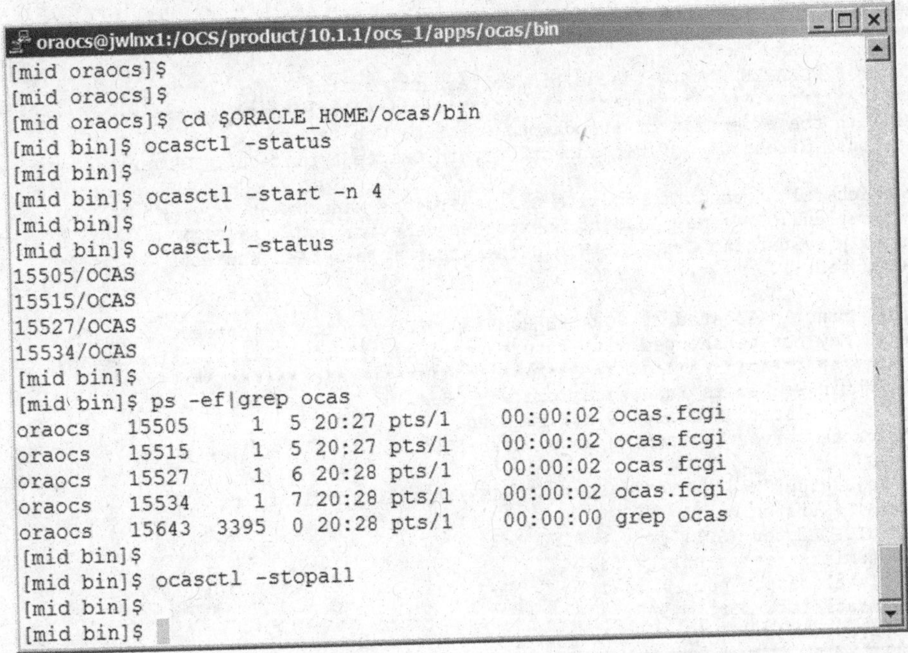
```
oraocs@jwlnx1:/OCS/product/10.1.1/ocs_1/apps/ocas/bin
[mid oraocs]$
[mid oraocs]$
[mid oraocs]$ cd $ORACLE_HOME/ocas/bin
[mid bin]$ ocasctl -status
[mid bin]$
[mid bin]$ ocasctl -start -n 4
[mid bin]$
[mid bin]$ ocasctl -status
15505/OCAS
15515/OCAS
15527/OCAS
15534/OCAS
[mid bin]$
[mid bin]$ ps -ef|grep ocas
oraocs   15505     1  5 20:27 pts/1    00:00:02 ocas.fcgi
oraocs   15515     1  5 20:27 pts/1    00:00:02 ocas.fcgi
oraocs   15527     1  6 20:28 pts/1    00:00:02 ocas.fcgi
oraocs   15534     1  7 20:28 pts/1    00:00:02 ocas.fcgi
oraocs   15643  3395  0 20:28 pts/1    00:00:00 grep ocas
[mid bin]$
[mid bin]$ ocasctl -stopall
[mid bin]$
[mid bin]$
```

Figure 5-21. *Controlling the Oracle Calendar Application System with the command-line utility*

Web Cache

All middle tier Oracle Application Server installations come with a preconfigured Web Cache; Oracle Collaboration Suite middle tiers are no exception. There are two tools additional to `opmnctl` and Application Server Control that can be used to start and stop the Web Cache: the command-line utility `webcachectl`, and the graphical Web Cache Manager.

Figure 5-22 shows how to run the `webcachectl` tool, using the `status` command to check whether the Web Cache is running. The output is unequivocal; this tool should not be used to control a Web Cache that is part of an Oracle Application Server instance. It should only be used with a Web Cache that has been deployed independently, perhaps as a front end load balancer that acts as a single point of contact to a web site and will spread incoming connections across a number of identical Oracle Application Server middle tier instances. The problem with using `webcachectl` is that it is not OPMN aware and may conflict with what OPMN is trying to do.

The output of the `webcachectl status` command shown in Figure 5-22 shows that the Web Cache is running as process ID 5702. It also shows that the Web Cache autorestart facility is not running; this is a process that will monitor the Web Cache and restart it if it fails. In an OPMN-managed environment it is not usually necessary to start this process, as OPMN will perform this function. It also shows that the Web Cache admin server is running as process ID 5694. The Web Cache admin server process is the graphical Web Cache Manager tool. To contact the tool, you must use a browser. To identify the port on which the Web Cache Manager is running, look at the `portlist.ini` file created at installation time. The second command in the figure uses `grep` to extract the detail of all the ports used by Web Cache; 9400 is the port where the Web Cache Manager can be contacted. The equivalent Windows command would be the following:

```
find "Web Cache" %ORACLE_HOME%\install\portlist.ini
```

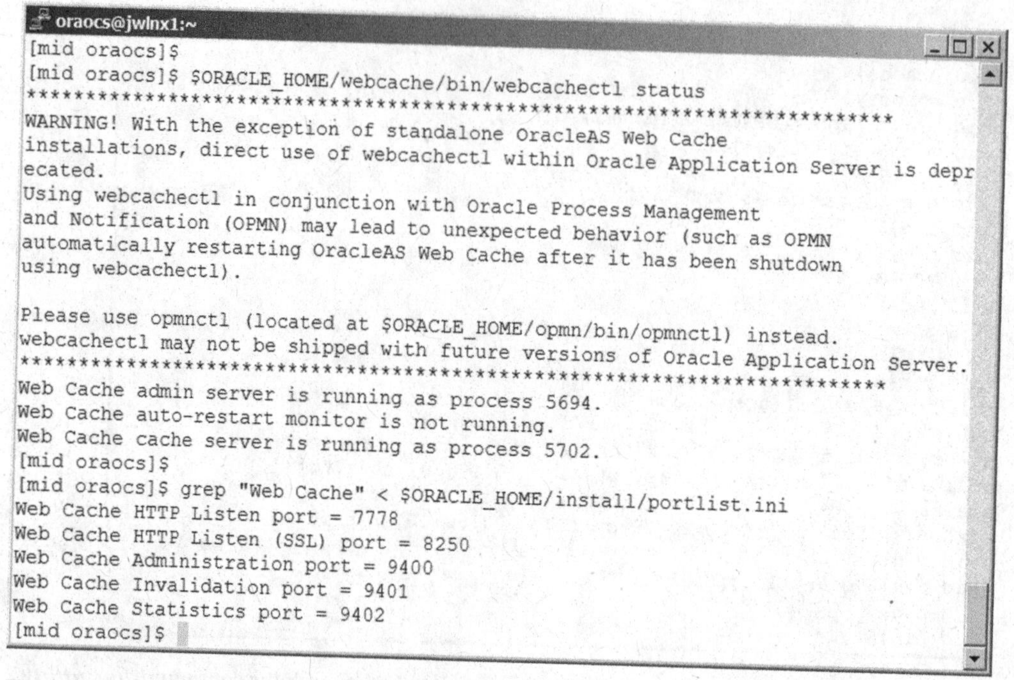

Figure 5-22. *Use (or not) of the webcachectl utility*

Note that 9400 is an Oracle Collaboration Suite default; the usual default port for the Web Cache Manager is 4000.

The Web Cache Manager will prompt for a username and password; these default to username *administrator* (note, neither ias_admin nor orcladmin will work here) and the password will be that specified at installation time. The URL to contact the Web Cache Manager, following the example shown in Figure 5-22, is `http://jwlnx1.bplc.co.za:9400/webcacheadmin`. This will take you to the window shown in Figure 5-23.

Note the Start, Stop, and Restart buttons. These will start and stop the Web Cache itself, but it is not possible to start or stop the Web Cache Manager from here. This can only be accomplished by OPMN, with `opmnctl` or Application Server Control (or, if you do not mind going into unsupported territory, with the `webcachectl` tool). This is the `opmnctl` command:

```
opmnctl startproc process-type=WebCacheAdmin
```

Many sites will not run the Web Cache Manager by default; it can be flagged as Disabled in Application Server Control so that it will only start when specifically requested. It will, however, be needed for some advanced configuration and monitoring work that cannot be done through Application Server Control. There may also be security issues. In some circumstances you might give junior administrators access to the Web Cache Manager through the web without wanting to give them access to Application Server Control or the Oracle Internet Directory. Even though the Web Cache Manager administrator password defaults to that used for ias_admin and orcladmin, you can change it after installation by clicking the Security link shown at the bottom of Figure 5-23.

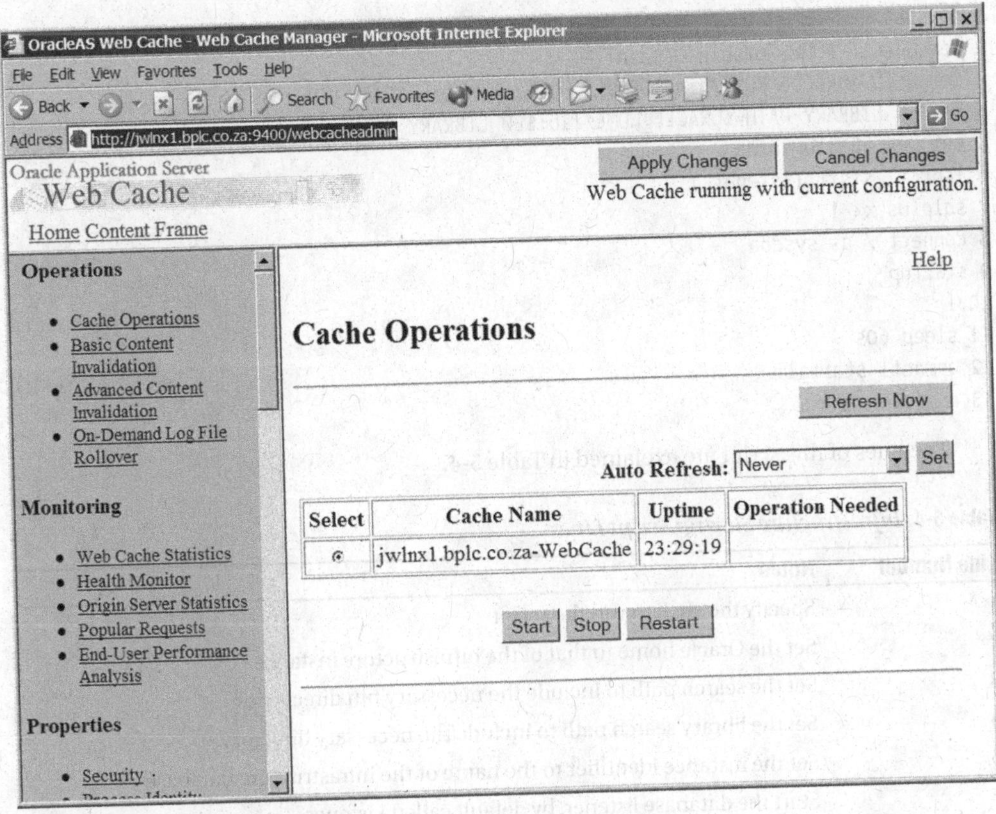

Figure 5-23. *The Web Cache Manager*

Startup and Shutdown Routines

The startup and shutdown of Oracle Collaboration Suite can be completely automated. Care needs to be taken that the various components are started in the correct order. Shutdown is less important; you could just switch off the server nodes without shutting down anything, and the installation will survive, but this is not good practice. One point to emphasize is that no matter what you do, you cannot corrupt the Oracle database(s). The Oracle database has a recovery mechanism that makes it absolutely impossible to lose or damage data, provided that the DBA has taken appropriate precautions. If you are in any doubt about this, study the mechanisms of redo and undo and instance recovery. The configuration of the Oracle Application Server instances is stored in static files and in the metadata repository database, both of which can survive disorderly shutdowns. Orderly routines should generally be followed, but in an emergency you can skip them.

Startup Scripts for UNIX

To start an infrastructure, you must first start the database listener, then the metadata repository database, then the Application Server instance itself. A shell script like the following (the lines are numbered for clarity) will do:

```
1 #!ksh
2 set ORACLE_HOME=/oracle/ocs/inf
3 set PATH=$ORACLE_HOME/bin:$ORACLE_HOME/opmn/bin:$PATH
4 set LD_LIBRARY_PATH=$ORACLE_HOME/lib:$LD_LIBRARY_PATH
5 set ORACLE_SID=infdb
6 lsnrctl start listener
7 sqlplus << !
8 connect / as sysdba
9 startup
10 !
11 sleep 60s
12 opmnctl startall
13 opmnctl status
```

The lines of this script are explained in Table 5-4.

Table 5-4. *Infrastructure Startup Script Lines*

Line Number	Notes
1	Specify the shell to run the script
2	Set the Oracle home to that of the infrastructure instance
3	Set the search path to include the necessary bin directories
4	Set the library search path to include the necessary directory
5	Set the instance identifier to the name of the infrastructure database
6	Start the database listener, by default called Listener
7	Launch SQL*Plus, piping in commands until a "!" symbol is encountered
8	Connect with privileged connection
9	Issue a startup command
10	Stop piping commands, and exit from SQL*Plus
11	Pause for a minute to let the system settle down
12	Launch the complete infrastructure Oracle Application Server instance
13	Confirm that everything is running

This script assumes that all required components have been enabled, so that none need to be started individually. Remember that the Application Server Control daemon is one component that by default is not enabled for automatic start. The script will be edited by your system administrators to catch return codes and to direct its output to a log file. It must be run under the operating system user who owns the infrastructure Oracle home. For example, a command that could be run as a root cron job would be the following:

```
su - oraocs -c startinfra.sh
```

This will switch the effective user ID for running the script to the owner of the instance, oraocs, and then run the script.

If there are other Oracle Application Server instances that are a part of the infrastructure, such as instances that host product metadata repositories, they should be started in a similar fashion.

To start the middle tier instances(s), use a similar script, specifying the details of the middle tier Oracle home, and the listener and database(s) used as product datastores. An example would be the following:

```
1 #!ksh
2 set ORACLE_HOME=/oracle/ocs/mid
3 set PATH=$ORACLE_HOME/bin:$ORACLE_HOME/opmn/bin:$PATH
4 set LD_LIBRARY_PATH=$ORACLE_HOME/lib:$LD_LIBRARY_PATH
5 set ORACLE_SID=middb
6 lsnrctl start listener
7 sqlplus << !
8 connect / as sysdba
9 startup
10 !
11 $ORACLE_HOME/ocas/bin/ocasctl start -n 5
12 lsnrctl start listener_es
13 opmnctl startall
14 opmnctl status
```

The lines of this script are explained in Table 5-5.

Table 5-5. *Middle Tier Startup Script Lines*

Line Number	Notes
1	Specify the shell to run the script
2	Set the Oracle home to that of the infrastructure instance
3	Set the search path to include the necessary bin directories
4	Set the library search path to include the necessary directory
5	Set the instance identifier to the name of the component datastore database
6	Start the database listener by default called Listener
7	Launch `SQL*Plus`, piping in commands until a "!" symbol is encountered
8	Connect with privileged connection
9	Issue a startup command
10	Stop piping commands, and exit from `SQL*Plus`
11	Launch five Calendar Application System servers
12	Start the Mail listener, called ES_LISTENER
13	Launch the complete middle tier Oracle Application Server instance
14	Confirm that everything is running

Startup Routines for Windows

There are two techniques for Windows: using services, or starting the processes directly. The installation will have created a number of Windows services that will launch the various components that make up the infrastructure and middle tier instances. There is no reason not to rely on these services to start all the necessary processes.

The installation routine will have set the Windows services to automatic start. These services will be configured with appropriate dependencies, so that they will start in the correct order. If you do not want the services to start automatically whenever the machine is booted, set them to manual start and launch them with a series of `net start <service_name>` commands. These commands can be placed in a batch or a command file.

To start the processes without using the `net start` interface to Windows services, set the services to manual start and launch the processes using batch or command files similar to those listed previously for UNIX.

The Supplied Startup Script

A startup and shutdown script is supplied with the standard installation. This is `ocsctl_sample`, which will be found in the `ORACLE_HOME/bin` directory of both infrastructure and middle tier instances. The script calls a Perl script, `ocsctl_sample.pl`. The syntax for using the utility is the following:

```
ocsctl_sample -{start|stop} {infra|apps}
```

The script requires that the PATH, ORACLE_HOME, and (for an infrastructure instance) ORACLE_SID environment variables are set appropriately. When run from an infrastructure Oracle home, the script will start the database listener, the database itself, the Application Server Control daemon, and the OPMN processes. OPMN will then start the Oracle Internet Directory and the Apache web listener. When run from a middle tier instance, the script will start OPMN (which will start the various OPMN-controlled application components) and the Application Server Control daemon. It will also start the non-OPMN managed components: the Calendar Application System and the Mail listener.

As the name of the script implies, it is provided as a sample. There is no reason not to edit it for local usage. Edits would be necessary if, for example, the middle tier was not going to run a Calendar node.

CHAPTER 6

■ ■ ■

Applications, Users, and Identity Management

An administration problem faced by all large organizations is that of identity management. From a management workload perspective, this is important; from a security point of view, this is critical. Considerations include how to authenticate users when they request a connection to an application, and then how to restrict their access to data within the application. The complications expand exponentially as more applications come into use and more points of access are established. The emerging industry standard for managing user identities is the LDAP directory. Oracle Application Server uses this standard, as implemented by the Oracle Internet Directory, and has further enhanced it with capabilities for Single Sign-On and account provisioning. The architectural model for establishing end-user sessions against Oracle Collaboration Suite applications is based on connection pooling, with authentication managed by the Single Sign-On service, and account creation (known as *account provisioning*) managed by the Oracle Internet Directory.

Authentication, Sessions, and Connection Pooling

In a client-server database application, authentication is relatively straightforward. The user connects to a database service with a client application, the service can prompt for authentication details, the user provides them, and thus the database server knows who the user is. For example, when connecting to an Oracle database with a tool such as SQL*Plus, the user process establishes a session against the database by logging on with a username and password. In the three-tier web environment, the situation becomes more complicated. The complications come because the user will be authenticating himself to the middle tier, and the middle tier will then have to authenticate to the database.

Authentication and Web Applications

The simplest form of authentication in a three-tier environment is for the middle tier to establish a dedicated session against the database for each user connection to the middle tier. This makes it possible for the middle tier to pass the users' authentication request through to the database and let the database take care of security. This is the model used by the modplsql PL/SQL gateway to invoke PL/SQL procedures within a database. The flow is the following:

1. The user, with his browser, issues a URL to the Apache web listener that requests execution of a procedure through a DAD.
2. Assuming that the DAD does not have a database username and password embedded within it, Apache will respond with the HTTP status code "401 – unauthorized message" including a `WWW-Authenticate` header. This header (one of many headers defined by the HTTP protocol) causes the browser to generate a window that will prompt for a username and password.
3. The browser returns the username and password via Apache to modplsql.
4. modplsql will log on to the database identified by the DAD with the username and password supplied from the browser and issue a PL/SQL execute command for the nominated procedure.
5. The database will execute the procedure, fetch any results back to modplsql, and terminate the session.
6. modplsql, via Apache, will return the results to the browser for display.

For example, consider this URL: `http://jwlnx1.bplc.co.za:7778/hr/empsearch?empid=1000`. If there is a DAD that creates the virtual path `/hr` (see the example in the section "The PL/SQL Gateway" in Chapter 2), after a logon prompt a session will be established against the database, the procedure `empsearch` (which must be available in the schema of the username given) will execute with the parameter `empid` set to the value `1000`, and the results, which the procedure should format as a page of HTML, will be displayed by the browser. Since the browser will cache the username and password given, all subsequent URLs to the same DAD—no matter what procedure they request—will execute without further prompts. As far as the user is concerned he has only logged on once and appears to be in a continuous session. Note that while this is an example using modplsql, the same method can also be used for CGI or Java applications.

This mechanism, where each browser request establishes a dedicated session against the database, means that the database is fully aware of who the user is and has complete control of security. But it has three major problems: password transmission, session management, and user account management.

With regard to password transmission, for each URL sent to the web listener, Apache will generate a 401 message. The first time the user will provide a username and password; for all subsequent URLs the browser will retransmit the username and password transparently. As a user navigates through the web application his authentication details are being retransmitted any number of times without his knowledge. The default configuration is that they will be transmitted in clear text. This certainly has security implications. A mechanism is required whereby the username and password are transmitted only once, and they should be protected by Secure Sockets Layer encryption.

Sessions in Web Applications

The session management issue is one that will cripple performance and limit scalability dramatically. Each contact with the database requires establishing a session. In the Oracle environment this means contacting the database listener, launching a server process, allocating a block of private memory for the session, and going through the logon routine. Only then can the procedure be executed. Then the session must be terminated. The whole cycle might take one or two seconds of which only a few hundredths of a second are actually executing the procedure. This is an appalling waste of resources. A means is needed whereby the database sessions can be persistent and reused for a series of many execution requests, rather than sessions being repeatedly established and terminated.

User account management is a dreadful workload for systems with many users. It is possible for each user to have his own schema within the database, but that means creating hundreds or thousands of database users, each of whom will have to be given appropriate privileges. The database itself can then enforce security on a personal basis for each user. But all this work must be done by the database administrator who may know nothing about the actual applications and the data within them, and what access rights are applicable to different users. A means is needed for devolving the workload of managing user access rights to the various application administrators.

Connection Pooling for Web Applications

To get around the problems of authentications and session management, web applications should not as a rule establish separate sessions against the database for each connection. Furthermore, they should not rely on the database maintaining separate accounts for each user. Instead, a web application's architecture should be based on connection pooling. The application software, running on a middle tier server, will itself log on to the database using a username that has access to all the data and code in the application. This database user is very powerful and the password must be strictly controlled; certainly no end users will know it.

The session established by the application software will be persistent; it is created when the application is started up on the middle tier and remains established until the application is shut down, independently of whether any end-user sessions from browsers exist. In practice, one database session is not usually enough. The application will log on several times, creating a pool of sessions. This solves the performance and scalability issues caused by a need to establish a database session for each user contact with the middle tier. As long as the pool of connections is large enough to satisfy the concurrent request workload, the end users will never have to wait for a connection and there will be no overhead from having to spawn database sessions dynamically.

In effect, the connection pooling mechanism is a technique for multiplexing many transient, stateless connections to an application server over a small number of persistent, stateful connections to a database. This is shown graphically in Figure 6-1, where four applications users (with applications usernames bsekwale, tglenden, igama, and jstrudel) share a connection pool of two sessions, both logged on to the database as database user apps_owner.

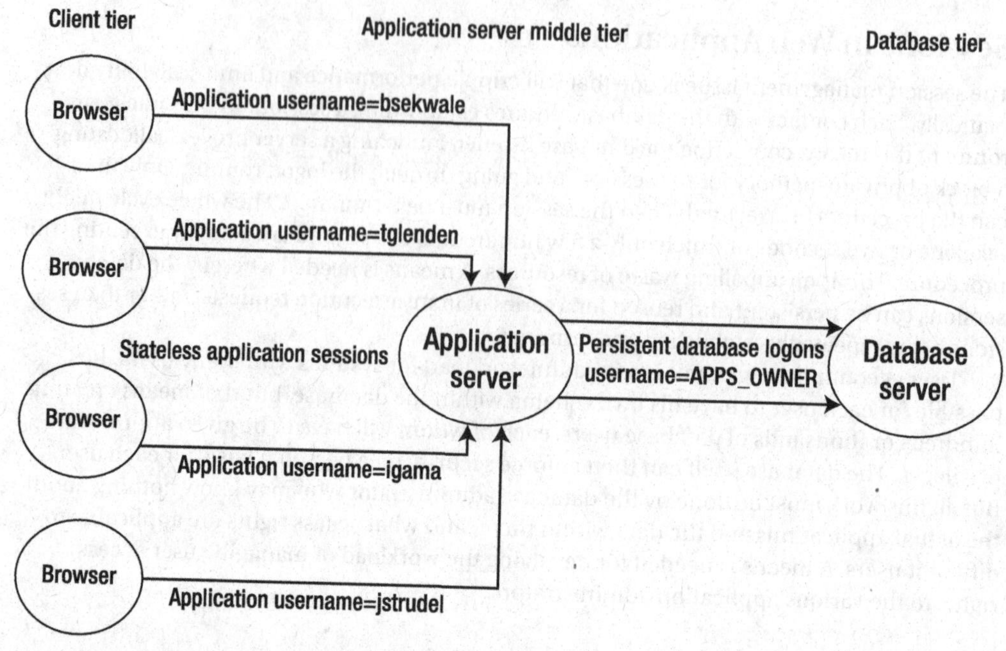

Figure 6-1. *Use of database connection pooling*

End users do not have a database username at all; they have an applications username. On first contacting the middle tier, the application will generate a login prompt to identify who the user is. Then the application can pass the procedure invocation request through one of its existing database sessions for execution, passing the end user's applications identity through to the database as a parameter. The database will then execute the necessary code and modify the execution according to the username provided. As a simple example, consider this PL/SQL procedure:

```
procedure show_sales_total(app_user_name varchar2)
is
  sales_total number;
begin
  select sum(value) into sales_total from sales where salesman=app_user_name;
  htp.print('Your sales total is '||sales_total);
end;
```

When the application invokes this procedure, it will run with the privileges of the application's database logon and should exist in this schema, but the results are filtered according to a parameter app_user_name, which will be the applications username of the end user. This applications username will be known to the middle tier, either because the application prompted for it, or because the browser sent it in a cookie. Thus, many application users, each with a different applications username, can invoke exactly the same code through a shared database session, but each will see different results. The middle tier will have to make sure that the output is sent back to the correct browser. Again, this example uses PL/SQL, but the concept is equally applicable to CGI or Java code.

This technique—where the application authenticates itself to the database to create a pool of persistent connections and end users' applications usernames are maintained on the middle tier—also solves the problem of the database administrator having to manage hundreds or thousands of database accounts. Each application administrator can maintain his own users, granting access according to whatever business rules are built into the application.

The final problem is that of repeatedly transmitting username/password pairs from the browser to the middle tier. This should be solved by simulating a persistent connection between browser and middle tier. To do this, the initial contact with the middle tier will prompt for authentication details; there is no way out of this. But if the middle tier then returns a cookie to the browser that states who the end user is, all subsequent contacts from browser to middle tier need only transmit the cookie, not the actual authentication details. Note that the application should always check that the cookie has come from the IP address of the machine to which it was originally sent, otherwise it would be possible to hijack the session by intercepting the cookie. The cookie then can be used to simulate a stateful connection between browser and application server and will contain the session identifying information that can be passed through to the database over a pooled database connection.

Maintaining user accounts within applications rather than within the database does raise the issue of end-to-end authentication and tracing. The database no longer has any idea of what any one person is doing. In fact, it does not even know that different users exist; all it knows about is the application schema. For this reason, it is vital that the application itself provides full tracing and monitoring facilities.

The Oracle Collaboration Suite web applications all make use of connection pooling and application users. When, for instance, the Content Services application starts up, it logs on to its datastore with a number of persistent connections. These sessions use the CONTENT schema username, whose password is never known to end users. Then within the Content Services application, there are end user accounts. These are merely rows of data in tables that say that a certain person exists and has permissions to see certain other rows and to run certain procedures. Connection pooling is implemented with standard Java procedures, or in C with appropriate OCI (Oracle Call Interface) calls. The use of cookies to simulate stateful connections is part of the Single Sign-On service. In effect, the use of cookies in this manner is to overcome the problem that HTTP is a stateless protocol; the state of the session can be established by interrogating the content of the cookie. Cookies are not perfect and their transmission to and fro can place an additional workload on the network, but they are a standard technique for stateful applications in a stateless environment.

Account Provisioning

In the Oracle Collaboration Suite environment no end users have database logons. The only database logons are those used for administration purposes and the various application schemas. End-user accounts exist only within the applications themselves and are maintained by the application administrators. An Oracle Collaboration Suite user may have accounts in up to four applications:

- Mail
- Content Services
- Calendar
- Real-Time Collaboration

The remaining Oracle Collaboration Suite applications (Discussions, Mobile Collaboration, Search, Voicemail and Fax, and Workspaces) make use of the accounts in these four primary applications.

A user's four application accounts cannot exist in isolation. They must be *provisioned* from an account in the Oracle Internet Directory. The concept behind account provisioning is that the Oracle Internet Directory is the single source of truth for all applications, and that an account created within it will trigger the creation of the necessary application accounts. Removal of the account within the Oracle Internet Directory will force the removal of all dependent application accounts, and updates will also cascade from the directory to the applications. The work of provisioning accounts is carried out by the applications themselves, not by the Oracle Internet Directory. The application will be configured to connect to the Oracle Internet Directory on a regular schedule to check whether any accounts have been created, updated, or removed, in which case it will take appropriate action. There may therefore be a time lag between making the directory change and seeing it reflected in the applications.

Provisioning Profiles

To enable account provisioning, each application registers itself with the Oracle Internet Directory and creates a provisioning profile for itself. This profile defines the configuration information required for the application, and once this is done the application becomes a provisionable target. The mechanism for creating an account and the account's attributes will vary from one application to another. The profile provides the necessary abstraction between the generic user attributes in the Oracle Internet Directory and the application-specific attributes.

The profile consists of a provisioning policy that states the circumstances under which accounts should be created (or removed) and a template with the user account attributes applicable to the application that needs to be populated when the account is provisioned. The policy can inspect directory attributes to determine whether the user should have accounts in particular applications, according to appropriate business logic.

The policies and templates for the Oracle Collaboration Suite applications are installed automatically into the Oracle Internet Directory during the installation process. If your organization has other applications that it needs to bring into the account provisioning process, you must create appropriate documents (formatted as LDAP Data Interchange Format files) and upload them with the `oidprovtool` provisioning registration utility.

Maintaining Provisioned Accounts

The Identity Management service guarantees that the Oracle Internet Directory is always the single source of truth for user information. Any changes made to a user's account in the Oracle Internet Directory will be propagated to all dependent accounts in provisioned applications.

Perhaps the most vital part of this service is deprovisioning: if an employee leaves the organization, disabling his Oracle Internet Directory account will remove all his access to all applications; there will not be any danger of any accounts remaining active.

There are two models for actioning provisioning events: notification-based or on-demand. The notification model can be thought of as *push-provisioning*. According to a schedule, the Oracle Internet Directory will notify the application that there is a change to be made, and the application will then take appropriate action immediately. This means that accounts will be created within a short period of time after registering the user in the directory. The alternative is *on-demand*, which is a pull-provisioning mechanism. The account is not actually created until the user first connects to the application. This avoids creating accounts that may never be used but does mean that the user may experience a delay the first time he tries to use the account. There is no reason not to enable both models if the application permits this.

The following tools can be used to create or modify a user's details within the Oracle Internet Directory and therefore his details in provisioned accounts:

Oracle Human Resources: This is a module of the Oracle E-Business Suite. From release 11.5.10 onward, Oracle Human Resources can be integrated with Oracle Internet Directory. This makes it possible, for example, to register a new employee in the HR module and automatically create his Mail and other accounts. When employees are terminated, they can be deactivated. This removes the necessity for clerical procedures to make sure that IT administrators are aware of personnel changes such as this, or of updates such as name changes.

Third-party directories and utilities: Through the LDAP directory synchronization standard, the Oracle Internet Directory can receive updates from and transmit updates to external sources, such as a Microsoft Active Directory. Due to differences in the manner in which vendors have implemented the LDAP "standard" it is possible that a large organization will find that it needs to run LDAP directories from different vendors to support different application environments. In this circumstance, it is necessary to ensure that changes made in one directory do propagate to the other, and thence to dependent applications.

The Oracle Internet Directory Delegated Administration Service (OIDDAS): This is described in detail in the section "The Delegated Administration Service: OIDDAS" later in this chapter. The OIDDAS is a graphical web-based tool for creating, modifying, and deleting user accounts in the Oracle Internet Directory, which also includes (in the version shipped with Oracle Collaboration Suite) the account provisioning console for managing accounts in the dependent applications.

The Oracle Directory Manager: This is described in detail in the section "The oidadmin Utility." The Oracle Directory Manager is a pure LDAP tool available for Windows and the various UNIX and Linux platforms, for connecting to an Oracle Internet Directory and viewing and editing its contents.

As a general rule, the source of a change to the Oracle Internet Directory entries should make no difference to the effect; the provisioning mechanism should ensure that it cascades appropriately to dependent applications. It is, however, important to remember that there may be time delays before it universally takes effect, particularly if there are communications with third-party directories to consider.

Provisioning Calendar Accounts

Apart from uploading a user's provisioning profile into the Oracle Internet Directory, the application itself may need some configuration for a user. The only Oracle Collaboration Suite application where this may often be necessary is Calendar. The reason is that, unlike the other applications, Calendar can run as a self-contained application, independently of the Oracle Internet Directory. The default installation will be configured for account provisioning, but the configuration will usually have to be adjusted later. If there is an existing Calendar installation that is to be brought into the Oracle Collaboration Suite environment it will have to be adjusted. It may also be necessary to synchronize the Calendar accounts with the Oracle Internet Directory periodically; this would be necessary if, for example, a Calendar node database is restored.

Calendar is configured for provisioning through directives in the file `ORACLE_HOME/ocal/misc/unison.ini`.

The default directives following installation are the following:

```
[PROVISIONING]
policy.default = 1:(objectclass=*)
enable = TRUE
```

This enables automatic Calendar account creation, according to a policy that states that all the accounts will be created in the node with Node-ID of 1, no matter what attributes the user may have in the Oracle Internet Directory. In a large-scale installation, with more than one Calendar node, it will be necessary to adjust this—details of why and how are given in Chapter 7.

Calendar accounts can be created both on-demand and through notifications. By default both are enabled. The directives in the `unison.ini` file are the following:

```
[ENG]
ondemandprov_enable=TRUE

[CWS]
dirprovenable=TRUE
```

The first directive, in the [ENG] section of the file, enables on-demand provisioning, which is carried out as necessary by the `uniengd` engine process that is launched for each client session against the Calendar server. The second directive, in the [CWS] section of the file, instructs the `unicwsd` corporatewide services background process to contact the Oracle Internet Directory and pick up any changes that need to be actioned.

If there is a possibility that the Calendar accounts have diverged from the Oracle Internet Directory accounts, use the `unidsdiff` and `unidssync` utilities (described in Chapter 7) to bring them back into synchronization. Due to the independent nature of Calendar and the asynchronous communications with the Oracle Internet Directory, minor divergence is always a possibility, and the `unidssync` utility, which will ensure that account details are the same, should be run regularly to take account of this. The `uinidsdiff` utility, which can create and delete accounts, is only likely to be needed after something drastic, such as a Calendar node database restore.

Provisioning Mail Accounts

Mail is configured for both notification and on-demand account provisioning. If when creating a user with the OIDDAS tool the administrator chooses not to create a Mail account, it is also possible to create Mail accounts through the Webmail client. To do this, log on to Oracle Collaboration Suite as a Mail administrator (see Chapter 10 for details on how to create a Mail administrative account) through the usual URL, and click the link for the Webmail interface. Select the Administration tab, which is not visible to regular Mail users, and the User subtab as shown in Figure 6-2.

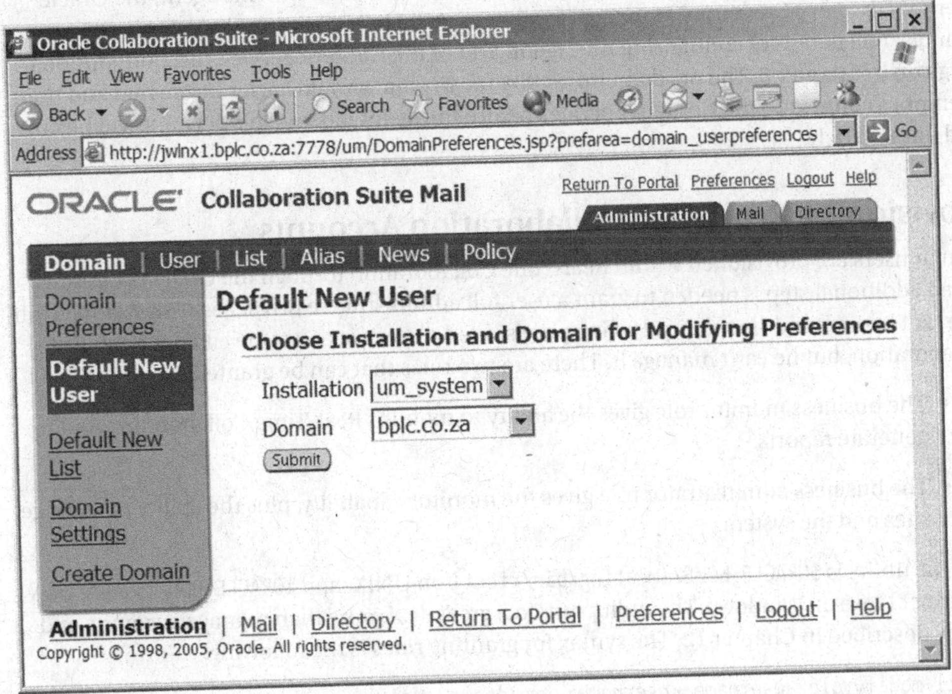

Figure 6-2. *Creating a Mail user through the Webmail client*

There will only be one option for the installation, UM_SYSTEM, and the domains offered will be those already created, either at installation time or subsequently (see Chapter 10 for details on creating additional e-mail domains). The next window will let you select a user (who must already exist within the Oracle Internet Directory and may not already have a Mail account) and set his various Mail attributes (such as space quota and which database to store his mail in) as detailed in Chapter 10.

The Mail account is also used as the base for Voicemail and Fax accounts. Voice mail and faxes are in fact stored in the user's Mail inbox. Once Voicemail and Fax servers have been set up (see Chapter 14 for details on this) it becomes possible to provision all Mail users with a number of Voicemail and Fax accounts. They will have one such account for each site (typically a site will be a physical office with a telephone switchboard) at which they have a telephone number, but all Voicemail and Fax accounts for one person are stored in the same Mail account.

Provisioning Content Services Accounts

Content Services is configured for both notification provisioning and on-demand provisioning through the OIDDAS console. Unlike the other applications, the account creation is actually carried out by an Oracle Internet Directory agent; the other applications may receive notifications from the directory, but they create their own accounts. This agent, the Oracle Internet Directory Credential Manager Agent, is specific to Mail. It runs by default every 15 minutes. Full details of configuring this agent, and of the Content Services account options, are given in Chapter 8. The on-demand facility means that should a user be created and then attempt to connect to the Content Services before the agent has run, his account will be created immediately.

Provisioning Real-Time Collaboration Accounts

Regular users are provisioned within Real-Time Collaboration through the OIDDAS console, but an additional step is needed to grant a user full administrative privileges. This is done with the `rtcctl` command-line utility. Having provisioned a user's account, he can use Real-Time Collaboration, but he can't manage it. There are two roles that can be granted:

- The business monitor role gives the ability to monitor Real-Time Collaboration and to generate reports.
- The business administrator role gives the monitor capability, plus the ability to manage sites and the system.

The utility is `$ORACLE_HOME/imeeting/bin/rtcctl` on UNIX, and `%ORACLE_HOME%\imeeting\bin\rtcctl.exe` on Windows. The utility can do a great deal more than manage accounts and is fully described in Chapter 12. The syntax for granting roles is the following:

```
rtcctl modifyrole -username <username> -rolename <rolename> [-siteid <site-ed>]
```

The options for *<rolename>* are `enduser`, `businessadmin`, and `businessmonitor`. Thus, to make user jwatson an administrator for the default site, after provisioning his account through the OIDDAS tool, run the following:

```
rtcctl modifyrole -username jwatson -rolename businessadmin
```

Then when jwatson connects to Real-Time Collaboration he will see the tabs Monitor, Reports, Sites, and System that are not visible to other users.

Single Sign-On Sessions and Components

All the Oracle Collaboration Suite application components have web interfaces that are Single Sign-On–enabled. Note that the various client-server user interface tools are not Single Sign-On–enabled: Single Sign-On uses HTTP, or HTTPS, and is therefore not available to any tool that does not use a browser as its presentation layer. This means that users of, for instance, IMAP and POP mail clients, the Calendar desktop application, or the Messenger client will not gain the benefits of Single Sign-On. This is a major reason for using the web interfaces to the applications whenever possible.

The Single Sign-On Process

The Single Sign-On mechanism is described in Chapter 2. In summary, it works as follows:

1. A user issues a URL from his browser that requests an Oracle Collaboration Suite application.
2. The web listener detects that the browser does not have a Single Sign-On cookie set, and so returns a redirection URL to the browser that forces the browser to contact the Single Sign-On server.
3. The Single Sign-On server generates a logon prompt.
4. The user supplies a username and password.
5. The Single Sign-On server validates the username/password against the Oracle Internet Directory and sets the Single Sign-On authentication cookie in the user's browser.
6. The browser reconnects to the Oracle Collaboration Suite service.
7. The web listener finds the cookie and passes the connection through to the application component as an authenticated session, using the user identity embedded in the cookie.
8. All subsequent requests for Oracle Application Server application components will be accepted automatically as long as the cookie is valid (by default, for eight hours). The browser will jump from step 1 to step 7.

It appears to the end user that he is only providing credentials once, no matter how many applications he logs on to and how many times he connects and disconnects. In fact, every component application does demand authentication, but as they are all written to be Single Sign-On–aware, they accept authentication as given by the contents of the Single Sign-On cookie. The initial transmission of the username and password is protected by SSL; the redirection URL in step 2 will specify HTTPS, not HTTP. The Single Sign-On cookie is encrypted and includes within it the IP address of the machine to which it was originally sent. This makes it impossible to hijack a session by copying the cookie to another machine. A final point is that the cookie is a nonpersistent cookie that should never be saved to disk by the browser. If the browser were to save it (and Oracle Collaboration Suite has no control over what a browser may be programmed to do) the SSL encryption means that it would be useless if reused, as the encryption key would not be valid in a different session.

A Single Sign-On session is started when a browser takes a user through the process described previously. It persists until the browser is shut down, or the cookie expires, or the user issues a logout URL, which will close any running application sessions and clear the cookie.

The Single Sign-On Components

The client side of Single Sign-On is nothing more than a browser. A corollary of this is that only web applications accessed with HTTP and displayed in a browser can be Single Sign-On–aware. Thus, a user can connect to the Oracle Collaboration Suite web client, authenticate himself, and then navigate through all the applications with no further login prompts as long as he stays within the browser session; but if he launches a thick client tool, such as Microsoft Outlook, he will have to authenticate again.

The middle tier Single Sign-On component is the Apache web listener with the modplsql module. All Single Sign-On–aware applications will instruct Apache to redirect browsers that do not have the Single Sign-On cookie set to the Single Sign-On service. This service is presented to the world through a URL that requests a PL/SQL procedure that runs the authentication code. The following is a typical Single Sign-On login URL:

```
https://jwlnx1.bplc.co.za:4443/pls/orasso/orasso.wwsso_app_admin.ls_login
```

This URL contacts the Oracle Application Server infrastructure web listener using the secure HTTPS protocol, and requests the running of a procedure LS_LOGIN in the package WWSSO_APP_ADMIN in the database schema ORASSO. The virtual path `/pls/orasso` identifies the database access descriptor (which will include an Oracle Net connect string) that will connect to the database hosting the Single Sign-On service. The Single Sign-On URLs are all configured in files included in the Apache configuration file `httpd.conf` and should only be edited by hand in exceptional circumstances.

The infrastructure tier components of Single Sign-On are the PL/SQL procedures that are invoked by Single Sign-On requests through the web listener, and the Oracle Internet Directory that stores the authentication details. Note that these do not have to be in the same database. It is quite possible to run the Single Sign-On service composed of PL/SQL procedures in one database and run the Oracle Internet Directory off a different database. The database objects are in different schemas (the Single Sign-On schema is ORASSO, the Oracle Internet Directory schema is ODS) and they communicate indirectly with LDAP calls through the Oracle Internet Directory server.

The management component of Single Sign-On is a Java application running on the Oracle Application Server infrastructure instance. This is the OIDDAS application. The OIDDAS runs in the OC4J instance `OC4J_SECURITY`, as shown in Figures 5-13 and 5-18 in Chapter 5. This is configured automatically in the infrastructure instance.

The Single Sign-On session itself is nothing more than a cookie. This cookie is set by the Single Sign-On browser, and so long as it is valid, Single Sign-On–aware applications will accept it as an authenticated user identifier who can be logged on with no further prompts. The lifetime of the cookie is configurable but defaults to eight hours. The cookie will identify the browser user as an applications user with an identity stored within and authenticated by the Oracle Internet Directory.

The oidadmin Utility

The use of the Oracle Internet Directory is transparent to end users, and often to administrators. As a rule, interaction with it is through application software. Thus, when a Mail user creates a mailing list within whatever e-mail client he chooses to use, he has no way of knowing that mailing lists are in fact objects created and stored within the Oracle Internet

Directory. Administrators will usually interact with the directory through the OIDDAS tool to create, edit, and remove user accounts and manage the account provisioning process. But there will be occasions when it is necessary to update the directory directly. This is where the `oidadmin` utility comes into use.

The `oidadmin` utility is a client-server tool for connecting to an Oracle Internet Directory and for managing its contents. It is a pure LDAP tool, available for both Windows and UNIX. On UNIX systems you need an X Windows server running, because `oidadmin` is a graphical tool. The utility is installed in the `ORACLE_HOME/bin` directory of both infrastructure and middle tier instances. To launch it, run `oidadmin`. The first prompt is for a username and password (use orcladmin or a similarly powerful user for full access to directory entries) and the address and port of your Oracle Internet Directory server. By default this will be port 389 on your infrastructure machine for the standard LDAP listener, or port 636 for the SSL LDAP listener. Confirm which ports have been assigned by looking at the `ORACLE_HOME/install/portlist.ini` file on the infrastructure instance, though always remember that this file is only a documentation file; if the Oracle Internet Directory server is adjusted to listen on different ports after installation, or if additional server instances have been launched, this file will only be updated if the administrator remembers to do so.

The `oidadmin` utility is not a tool for controlling the Oracle Internet Directory. For that you must use the `oidctl` utility to pass instructions to the OID monitor—the `oidmon` process—as described in Chapter 5. To use `oidadmin`, the directory server must already be running; then you can use `oidadmin` to view and edit the contents of the directory.

The `oidadmin` navigation tree is shown in Figure 6-3.

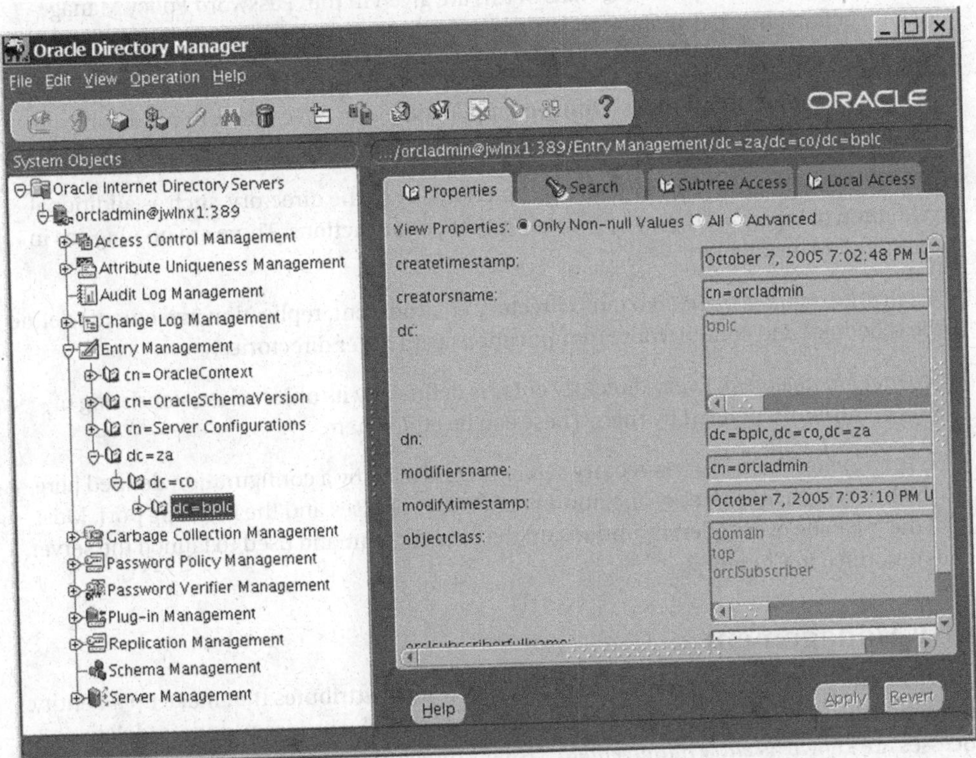

Figure 6-3. *The oidadmin navigation tree*

The `oidadmin` navigation tree has the following top-level branches for each directory server to which it is connected:

Access Control Management: This is where you set up access control policies (ACPs) within the directory to limit the entries that different users, including anonymous or unauthenticated users, can see and modify. There are dozens of preconfigured ACPs.

Attribute Uniqueness Management: This enforces unique constraints on attributes of entries. This is not often needed, because as a general rule uniqueness can always be guaranteed by the fact that an entry's distinguished name is always unique. There is one preconfigured constraint on the Wireless account number. This is because one user can have multiple Wireless accounts.

Audit Log Management: This specifies the events and actions within the directory that will be audited, such as attempts to bind (or log in) to the directory.

Change Log Management: This is the audit trail of all changes to directory entries.

Entry Management: This is where administrators spend most of their time—in the directory information tree itself. Details are given in the next section, "Entry Management."

Garbage Collection Management: This specifies how to purge various data automatically from the directory. Jobs are preconfigured to purge the activity statistics, the change log, and the audit log.

Password Policy Management: Details of this are given in the "Password Policy Management" section later in this chapter.

Password Verifier Management: This defines how the directory will authenticate uses to other application components. Different applications can have different rules; for example the Mail verifier always converts passwords to lowercase.

Plug-in Management: Plug-ins can add functionality to the directory, such as additional validation of input, or "trigger" processing after certain actions. There are no plug-ins in the standard installation.

Replication Management: In a multidirectory environment, replication agreements define the schedules and content for communications with other directories.

Schema Management: Every directory entry is defined by its object class, consisting of a set of attributes defined by rules. These can be edited here.

Server Management: Every directory server is controlled by a configuration defined here, which sets such attributes as the number of child processes and the listening port. Most of these can be overridden by options on the `oidctl` command used to launch the server, as described in Chapter 5.

Entry Management

A directory entry is (by analogy) a record in a table—a set of attributes that make up an entity. Entries must be inserted and then may be updated or deleted. The insert/update/delete processes are known as *entry management*. Usually directory entries are managed by the

Oracle Collaboration Suite applications or by the OIDDAS tool, but sometimes it will be necessary to edit entries by hand. Typically this will only be necessary for user entries or for the Oracle Net connection details used for locating database services.

To view and edit a user's directory entry with the `oidadmin` utility, locate his entry by navigating down his distinguished name. This gives access to the full data, not just the subset visible in the OIDDAS tool. For example, a user's entry includes an attribute carLicense, which OIDDAS does not show, which will be useful if you deploy an application module that manages employees' rights to parking spaces. Figure 6-4 shows editing a user entry.

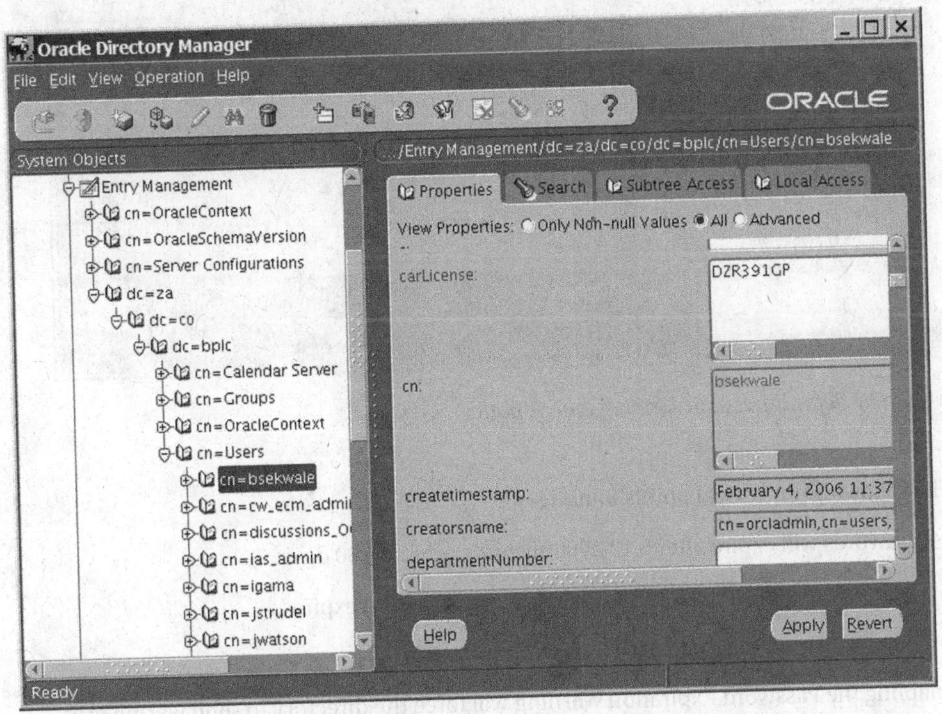

Figure 6-4. *Locating and editing a user definition with the oidadmin utility*

In Figure 6-4, the user being edited has the distinguished name

```
cn=bsekwale,cn=Users,dc=bplc,dc=co,dc=za
```

which is used as the navigation path in Entry Management to locate her entry.

Password Policy Management

A password policy can be applied to a realm. A *realm* is a set of users managed by the same identity management policies. After a standard installation, Oracle Collaboration Suite will consist of one realm. Figure 6-5 shows the password policy for the realm `bplc.co.za` created on installation.

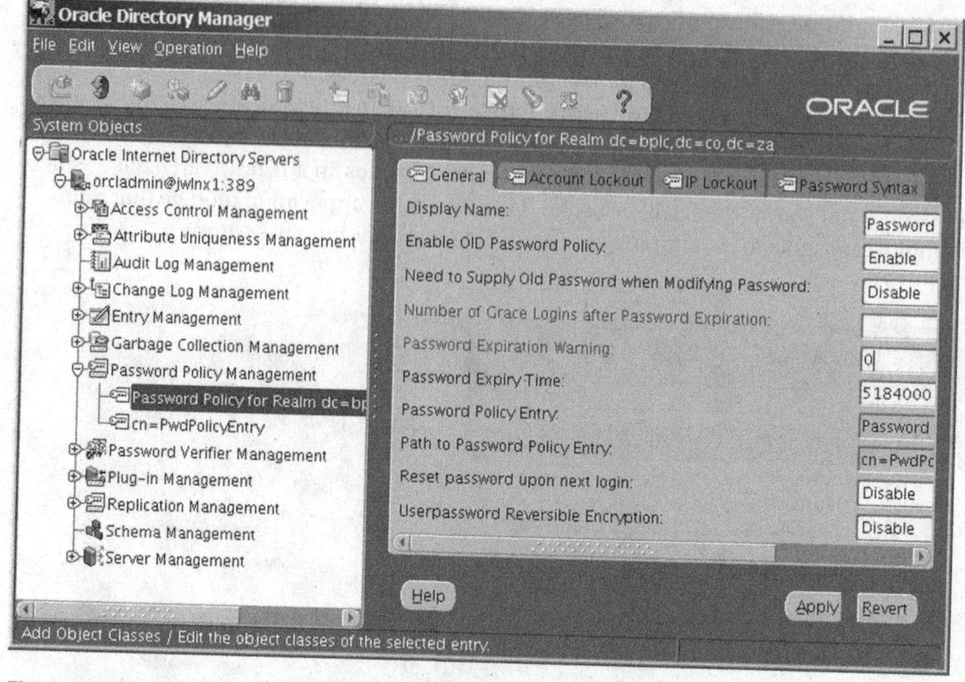

Figure 6-5. *The default password management policy*

The following are critical points to note:

- Passwords will expire after 5,184,000 seconds, which is 60 days.
- There are no grace logins permitted after the password expires.
- There is no warning that passwords will expire soon.

Enabling the Password Expiration Warning will force the directory to send warnings at every logon for the three days before the password expires. The application must be configured to handle this message correctly; Oracle Collaboration Suite Applications will do this automatically.

The Account Lockout tab configures locking accounts after failed logins due to incorrect passwords. The default is that after ten failures, the account will be locked for one day. The IP Lockout tab gives finer control by restricting the lockout to an IP address.

The Password Syntax tab lets you define a minimum number of characters for passwords, a minimum number of numeric characters, and the number of passwords to be stored as "history." The default settings are five characters, one of which must be numeric; there is no history, so users can "change" their password to a previously used one.

In most installations, it will be necessary to adjust these defaults. It is common practice to permit grace logins and warning messages. Clearly there is no point in forcing password changes without setting a history count, but the details of these changes are, of course, a matter for agreement with the organization's security group.

If a user does get locked out, either because of password expiry or inaccurate login attempts, his password can be reset by a directory superuser (such as orcladmin) through the OIDDAS application.

However, a final point to emphasize is that the OIDDAS superuser, orcladmin, is himself covered by the password policy for the realm. He has an entry along with all the other users. His distinguished name is the following:

```
cn=orcladmin,cn=Users,dc=bplc,dc=co,dc=za
```

He will therefore be locked out after 60 days just like everyone else and will no longer be able to connect to the directory as orcladmin through OIDDAS. He will, however, be able to connect to the directory as orcladmin through `oidadmin`, because then he is entering at a level above the realm settings that include the password policy. Once connected, in Entry Management navigate to the previous distinguished name entry and change the userpassword attribute. Enter a clear text password, which will be concealed for subsequent displays. This will re-enable regular access for orcladmin through OIDDAS.

The Command-Line Utilities

There will be circumstances when it is necessary to use command-line utilities to manage the content of the Oracle Internet Directory. This might be because no suitable graphics terminal is available (which is often the case when using a Microsoft Windows PC to manage a UNIX installation, since Microsoft Windows does not ship with an X Windows server) or when managing large amounts of data (such as a bulk upload of many users).

Some of the more important utilities, located in the `ORACLE_HOME/bin` directory, are the following:

- `ldapadd`: Create directory entries from data in an LDIF file.
- `ldapdelete`: Delete the entries listed in an LDIF file.
- `ldifwrite`: Write entries out to an LDIF file.
- `ldapsearch`: Retrieve an entry.

The files passed as arguments to the utilities are LDIF (LDAP Data Interchange Format) files.

This command will write out user jwatson's details to file `jw.ldif`:

```
ldifwrite -c orcl -b "cn=jwatson,cn=users,dc=bplc,dc=co,dc=za" -f jw.ldif
```

The arguments are the name of the database storing the directory, the distinguished name of the entry to write out, and the name of the file to generate.

This command will display jwatson's entry:

```
ldapsearch -D cn=orcladmin -w oracle1 -h jwlnx1 -p 389 "uid=jwatson"
```

The arguments are the username with which to connect (or "bind") to the directory; the password for that user; the host where the directory is running; the port on which it is listening; and the attribute value for which to search.

The Delegated Administration Service: OIDDAS

It is possible to manage user accounts by working within the Oracle Internet Directory directly, but this will be done very rarely. It is not a user-friendly environment. Most day-to-day user management will be through the OIDDAS console. To connect to the console, use the URL `http://<host.domain>:<port>/oiddas` where *<host.domain>:<port>* is either the listening address of the Apache listener for the infrastructure instance, or the listening address of the Web Cache of a middle tier instance. Whichever address you use, the infrastructure Identity Management services must be running:

```
[inf oraocs]$ opmnctl status
```

```
Processes in Instance: ocsinfra.jwlnx1.bplc.co.za
-------------------+-------------------+---------+---------
ias-component      | process-type      |     pid | status
-------------------+-------------------+---------+---------
DSA                | DSA               |     N/A | Down
LogLoader          | logloaderd        |     N/A | Down
HTTP_Server        | HTTP_Server       |    2719 | Alive
dcm-daemon         | dcm-daemon        |     N/A | Down
OC4J               | OC4J_SECURITY     |    2804 | Alive
OID                | OID               |    2732 | Alive
```

The entry screen is shown in Figure 6-6.

Click the Login link at the top left to connect. The user orcladmin, created at install time, should be used for the first logon to the OIDDAS console, but subsequently you should delegate user management privileges to other users and reserve the orcladmin account for operations that no one else can do. The login screen will prompt for a username and a password, and (if multiple realms have been created) a company name as well.

All users see the same four tabs:

- The Home tab takes you to the window shown in Figure 6-6.
- The My Profile tab is the self-service option that lets users change their passwords and adjust their personal information (contact details, address, time zone, etc.) and upload a photograph if they wish.
- The Configuration tab can be selected by all users, but only highly privileged users can do anything on it. Orcladmin can adjust some Oracle Internet Directory configurations here.
- The Directory tab will let all users search the directory and view users' details and let privileged uses edit and create user accounts. Figure 6-7 shows the result of a directory search (using % as the wild card, to retrieve all users) performed when logged in to OIDDAS as orcladmin.

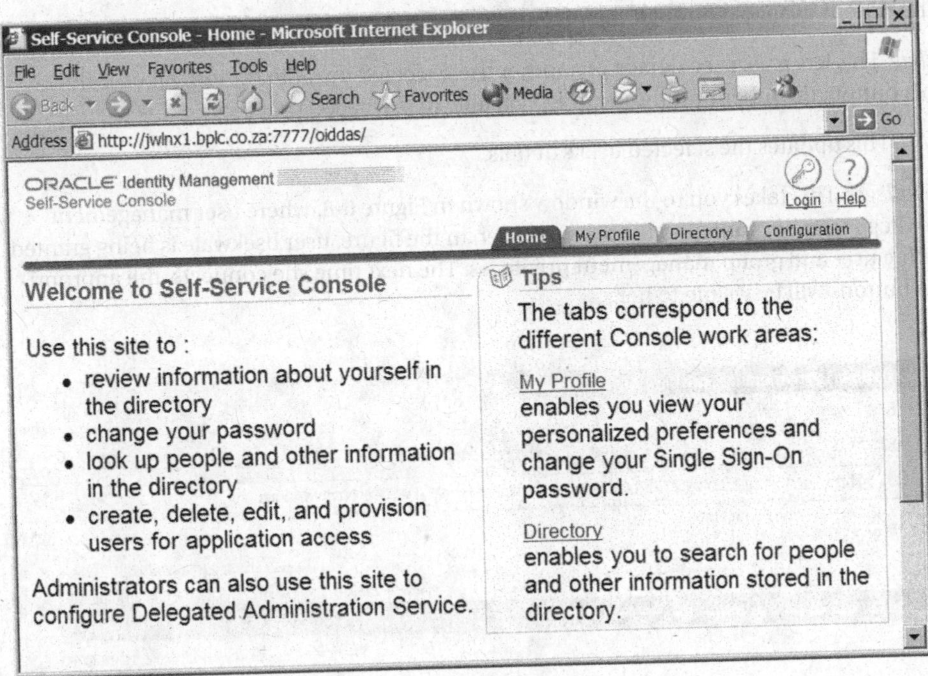

Figure 6-6. *The entry point to the OIDDAS console*

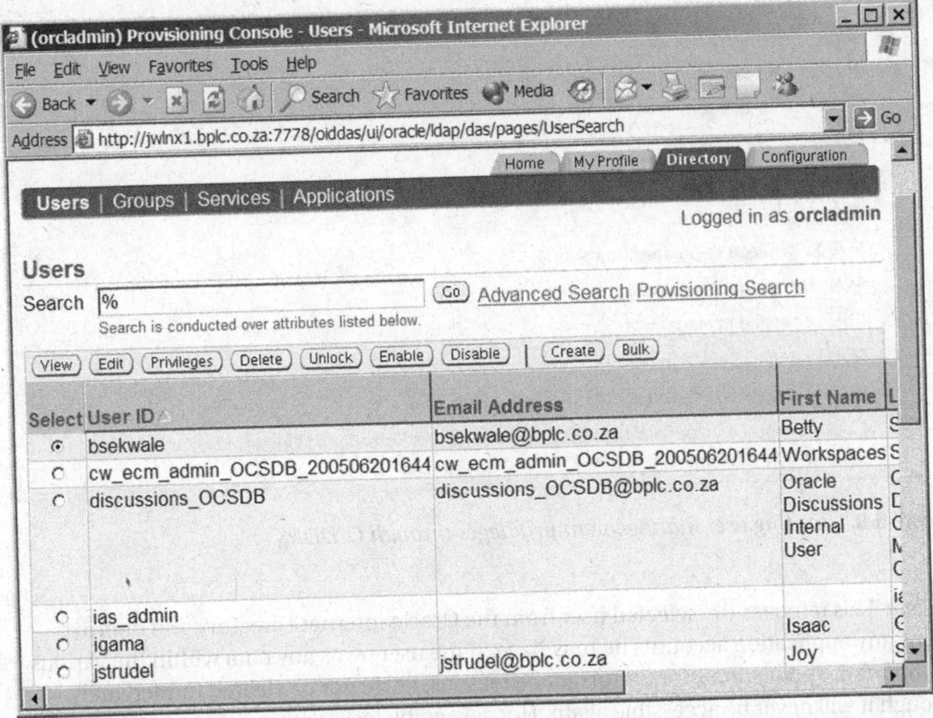

Figure 6-7. *A directory search through the OIDDAS console*

The actions available through the various buttons are the following:

View: This lets a user see details of another user selected by radio button. All users have this button; the other buttons are only available to privileged users.

Edit: This updates the selected user's details.

Privileges: This takes you to the window shown in Figure 6-8, where user management privileges can be granted to the selected user. In the figure, user bsekwale is being granted all the user and group management privileges. The next time she connects, the appropriate buttons will be visible to her.

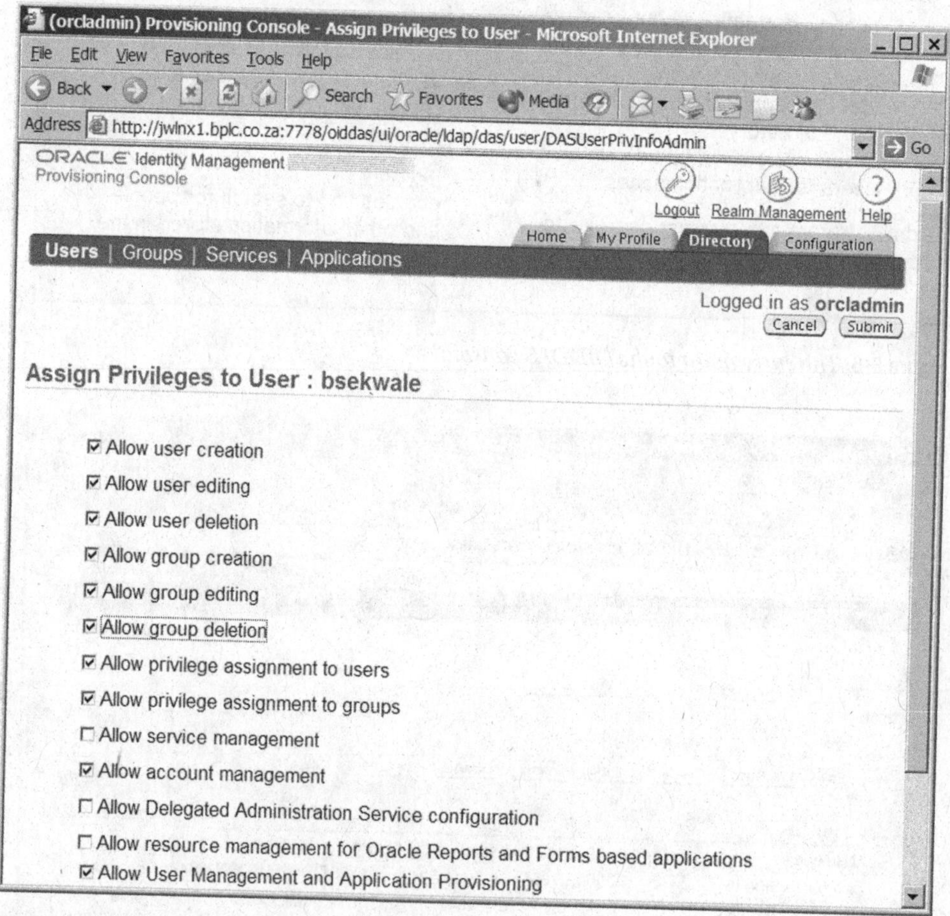

Figure 6-8. *Granting user management privileges through OIDDAS*

Delete: This removes the selected user from the Oracle Internet Directory and deprovisions any application accounts he may have. If the user owns any data within the various component applications, for performance reasons, it will not be cleared immediately, though it will never be accessible again. Housekeeping tasks within the application will clear up the data later.

Unlock: If an account has been locked because of failed login attempts with an incorrect password this button will unlock it.

Disable and Enable: These buttons will make an account temporarily unavailable for use. The user still exists while disabled and can, for example, be scheduled for meetings in Calendar and can be sent mail, but he cannot log on until it is enabled.

Bulk: This button will prompt for an LDIF file containing a list of users to be created, edited, or removed. This is an alternative to using the command-line utilities `ldapadd`, `ladapdelete`, and `ldapmodify` for large-scale operations within the Oracle Internet Directory.

Create: This launches the wizard for creating users and provisioning their application component accounts. The first window of the wizard is shown in Figure 6-9. Detail of provisioning accounts for each application will be given in later chapters, but the wizard is self-explanatory. It walks you through the process of creating the user, selecting which applications he should have accounts in, and setting various application defaults.

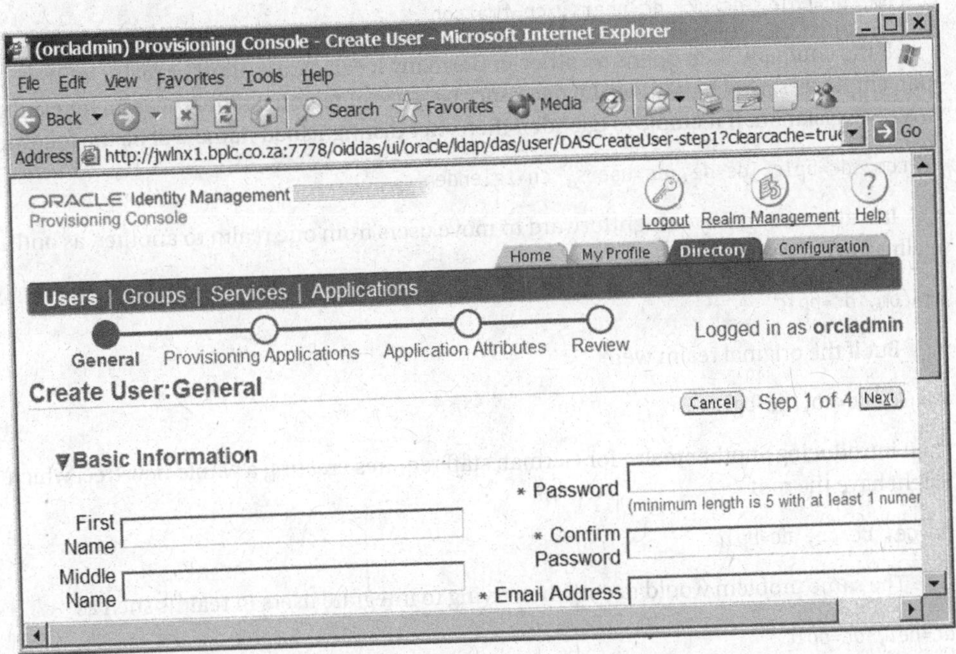

Figure 6-9. *The account provisioning wizard*

The OIDDAS delegated administration service is the central point for managing all user accounts. Furthermore, it allows end users to administer themselves. The self-service management capabilities that let users maintain their own personal data and change their password remove a huge workload from the application administrators, and all users should be encouraged to make use of this.

Oracle Identity Management Realms

As stated previously, a *realm* is a set of users controlled by a set of identity management policies. Within the Oracle Internet Directory, things are a little more complicated. The complexity arises because (all, not just Oracle's) LDAP directory information trees are, as the name implies, trees. A tree grows from the root; all branches within a realm, no matter how long and how tortuous the path, must have the same root.

As long as the realms all have the same root, there is no problem. But if the realms have a different root, the situation becomes more complex; the trees become a forest. For example, if an organization based in England creates its Internet directory with the users stored in this container

```
dc=com, dc=bplc, dc=uk, dc=users
```

the users with common names, senglber and twatson, will have these distinguished names:

```
dc=com, dc=bplc, dc=uk, dc=users, cn=senglber
dc=com, dc=bplc, dc=uk, dc=users, cn=twatson
```

If the company then opens an office in Germany it can create another realm for the German employees, which may well be necessary because of regional differences in, for example, privacy legislation. If it employs tglenden there, her distinguished name will be the following:

```
dc=com, dc=bplc, dc=de, dc=users, cn=tglenden
```

It is also reasonably straightforward to move users from one realm to another, as both realms have the same root:

```
dc=com, dc=bplc
```

But if the original realm were

```
dc=uk, dc=co, dc=bplc
```

then introducing another realm for German staff requires creating a whole new tree, which might have the root

```
dc=de, dc=co, dc=bplc
```

The same problem would occur when trying to integrate users in realms such as

```
dc=net, dc=bplc
```

or

```
dc=org, dc=bplc
```

If an Oracle Application Server installation is only supporting one realm, this is not an issue. If it is supporting multiple realms, when a user requests a login, he must specify which realm he wants to connect to. Because it is not reasonable to expect end users to make use of complete realm names when they request a logon to an application, realms are given a "simple" name. Typically, this will be prompted for on the login screen.

While the Oracle Internet Directory can support multiple realms, whether or not they have a common root, applications may have problems due to their use of the Oracle Context container. An Oracle Internet Directory realm will always have a container called the Oracle Context. This stores application-specific data, such as where an application should look to find its users and groups, and what authorizations the users and groups have. This data must be realm-specific, because users' common names are not unique. Consider an application service provider who is hosting the same application for several companies that happen to have some staff with the same names. The user Isaac Gama who works for the company BPLC has the distinguished name

```
dc=uk, dc=co, dc=bplc, dc=users, cn=igama
```

Another user with the same name works for another company called TLA. He is

```
dc=com, dc=tla, dc=users, cn=igama
```

Clearly, the application must be able to distinguish between the two Isaac Gamas and grant them appropriate privileges when they connect. This wouldn't matter if the users logged on with their distinguished names, but they won't; they probably have no idea what their distinguished names are, and even if they did, the application's login window won't prompt for it. But as long as the application knows which realm the common name belongs to, it can read the appropriate Oracle Context. This is where the root Oracle Context comes in. Figure 6-4 shows the root Oracle Context, the first entry in the Entry Management branch. It also shows a realm-specific Oracle Context, in the realm

```
dc=za, dc=co, dc=bplc
```

The root Oracle Context includes the information needed to allow an application to locate an identity management realm from the realm's common name.

A Word on Security

Security is an issue of vital concern at all sites. All organizations should have a security manual documenting rules and procedures. If your organization does not have such a manual, someone should be writing it—perhaps that someone should be you. In security, there is no right or wrong; there is only conformance or nonconformance to agreed procedures. If administrators follow the rules and advise on what those rules should be, any breach of security is not their fault. But, unfortunately, history shows that when something goes wrong in the security arena, there is a great desire to blame individuals. It is vitally important that administration staff should be able to point to a set of procedures they should follow, and to routines and logs that demonstrate that they did indeed follow them. This devolves the responsibility to the authors of the procedures. If no security manual exists, any problems are likely to be dumped on the most convenient scapegoat. In an Oracle Collaboration Suite environment this is probably the administrator.

Security Risks

Security risks come in many forms. It will usually be useful to group them into categories. Commonly used categories are the following:

- Data confidentiality
- Data integrity
- User authentication
- User authorization

Controlling these areas will ensure that data is only visible to those who should see it, and that those who should see it, can see it.

Data confidentiality is ensured through data encryption. Virtually all networked computer systems will at some point in the network be using a broadcast protocol. This makes it very easy to intercept traffic. For example, there may be point-to-point communication between servers in a machine room, but the rest of the building, where the end users' terminals are, may be using 10MHz Ethernet. Anyone can intercept Ethernet traffic. And when it comes to wireless communications, one needn't even be in the same building to intercept it. For this reason, sensitive traffic should always be encrypted; accept that a malicious person could be reading your data at any time, but rely on the fact that he will not be able to decrypt it. The SSL protocols, described in Chapter 3, guarantee this.

Data integrity ensures that data is valid. Within the applications and the database, integrity is guaranteed by the application and database design. SSL protocols ensure that it is not damaged in transit. The damage could be malicious or accidental—either way SSL guarantees data integrity.

User authentication should be *strong authentication*: authentication based on at least two techniques—for example, not only a password but also a thumbprint. The Single Sign-On server can be integrated with third-party mechanisms that provide strong authentication based on various biometric methods. Strong authentication is also a part of the SSL standard through the use of digital certificates.

User authorization is controlled within each Oracle Collaboration Suite application component, many of which make use of the Oracle Internet Directory as the repository for authorizations that have been granted.

The Security Group

The decisions over what levels of security are needed and what mechanisms should be used to enforce them need to be devolved to a group rather than being the responsibility of an individual. The group should include the following:

- Security administrators
- System administrators
- Application administrators
- Network administrators

- Data and application owners
- Legal experts
- End users
- Senior management

Note that the involvement of users and senior management is vital. Security decisions cannot be acted on and security cannot be enforced purely by technical staff. Commitment and agreement from users and management is essential.

The security group must establish rules on what data needs to be secure and who should have access to what. Following these rules, principles can be established for how data should be protected during storage and transmission. The business decisions must drive the technical solutions, not the other way round.

Security Checklists

A commonly used security concept is a set of *checklists*: general principles established by the security group that can be applied to all systems. There will be a number of such checklists. Some brief examples follow, which can be built up into comprehensive lists for the security manual.

The network checklist includes the following:

- When and where to use SSL
- Use of firewalls
- Permitted protocols
- IP address and routing restrictions

The operating system checklist includes the following:

- Removing or disabling unused accounts
- Password policies
- Removing unnecessary services
- Applying security patches

The Oracle database checklist includes the following:

- Installing only necessary (and licensed) options
- Where possible, locking the default accounts and expiring their passwords
- Changing the default passwords
- Revoking unnecessary privileges
- Applying security patches

The application checklist includes the following:

- Setting up password policies
- Disabling unused accounts
- Defining data access privilege levels
- Grouping users to separate data

Establishing a set of checklists that can be included in a security manual and used as a base for security rules for each data-processing area will ease the process of setting up security procedures. But always remember that it is useless to define all these lists and procedures unless there are associated routines for monitoring whether they are actually followed.

Password Policies

Password policies are always a compromise between security needs and convenience. If a password policy is too restrictive it will cause such inconvenience that users will be tempted to bypass it. The most basic example of this is a policy that requires passwords of such complexity and such frequent changes that users cannot remember them and so store them in an insecure medium (such as sticky notes on their terminals). The password policy used by Oracle Collaboration Suite is configured within the Oracle Internet Directory and applies to a whole realm, as described previously. It is not possible to have different policies for different applications—though the wireless access services will usually have an additional layer of protection for access to the network.

In many organizations there will be a need for users to have multiple passwords: perhaps one for the network, one for Oracle Collaboration Suite, and others for non-Oracle applications. Password management in such environments can become an administrative nightmare and be extremely frustrating for end users. Use of LDAP synchronization to maintain identical passwords conforming to the same policy can help with this, but be wary of taking such integration too far. If the same password is used everywhere and one application is compromised, all applications will be vulnerable.

CHAPTER 7

Configuring Calendar

Calendar is the Oracle Collaboration Suite component for scheduling people, resources, and events. It can be installed as a completely stand-alone product—even without Oracle Internet Directory. But to exploit its full capabilities you need the rest of Oracle Collaboration Suite. The stand-alone installation will not be discussed here in any detail. It is generally simpler than the collaborative installation and provides a subset of the full functionality.

This treatment begins with detail of the Calendar architecture, followed by the setup steps and the various maintenance tasks for the data within Calendar and the Calendar users. First, though, it is necessary to clear up some terminology.

Terminology

There are some terms used in the Calendar environment—*server, host, node*, and *cluster*—that are also used in other contexts but have very different meanings.

Server and Host

A Calendar server is not a computer; it is a set of processes running on a computer. This computer is known as a *host*. Generally speaking, the term *host* is ambiguous. Some people use it to refer to a computer, others to refer to an IP address. In Calendar terms, it means a computer that is running one or more Calendar servers. If a host is running multiple Calendar servers, the servers will each be accessed through a different port on the same address, or perhaps through a different address if the host has multiple network interface cards, and will each be running off a different installation of the Calendar software. Windows is an exception here; the Windows architecture does not permit more than one server per host.

Calendar Node

In normal parlance, a *node* is a computer. In the Calendar environment, a node is a database. One Calendar server will by default connect directly to only one node, but it can make indirect connections through remote servers to any number of nodes, either on the local host or on remote hosts. It is also possible to configure multiple node databases for one server, all on the local host. Every node has a unique number: the Node-ID. Nodes can be linked together into a node network. This means even if your users are spread over several servers and nodes, perhaps on several machines, they can still schedule meetings and events with each other as though they were all on one server and node. Note that all nodes in a node network must use the same Oracle Internet Directory to store user attributes.

A vital point to remember is that the Calendar database is not an Oracle database. It is a disk-based data structure developed over many years before the Calendar product was bought by Oracle Corporation. It is likely that eventually the Calendar database will be replaced with a schema in a regular Oracle database, but this will not happen in the lifetime of Oracle Collaboration Suite 10*g*.

Cluster and Master Node

The common usage for the term *cluster* refers to a group of two or more closely coupled computers with shared access to resources such as disks. A Calendar cluster is nothing like that; it is a node network in which one node is designated as the master node. Use of a master node is not required, but if configured it will provide enhanced facilities for managing the node network, and better performance when handling searches for user accounts across all the nodes, servers, and hosts. For the stand-alone installation, a cluster is optional but it is the default with the Oracle Collaboration Suite installation; when you install a middle tier instance, you are prompted to select whether the installation will be a master node or not. For the installation of your first Oracle Collaboration Suite middle tier, it will always be a *master*.

Calendar Server and Calendar Application System

The Calendar server consists of the server-side processes that give end users access to the Calendar data stored in nodes. It is launched from a set of files in the directory `$ORACLE_HOME/ocal` on UNIX, and in `%ORACLE_HOME%\ocal` on Windows.

The Calendar server can be installed as a self-contained product. It does not require the rest of Oracle Collaboration Suite; it does not run within an Oracle Application Server middle tier; and it need not be dependent on an Oracle Application Server infrastructure instance.

The Oracle Calendar Application System (OCAS) is a set of additional server-side facilities that run in an Oracle Application Server middle tier instance and provides, among other things, the Calendar web client. Users connect to it through the Web Cache and the Apache web listener. The Calendar Application System is installed as part of Oracle Collaboration Suite and is based on a set of files in the directory `$ORACLE_HOME/ocas` on UNIX, or `%ORACLE_HOME%\ocas` on Windows.

The Calendar Application System makes use of the Oracle Application Server infrastructure for Single Sign-On and is fully integrated with the Oracle Collaboration Suite.

Calendar Architecture

The architecture is *client-server*. The user's client process (which could be the Calendar Desktop Client, or Microsoft Outlook enhanced with the Oracle Connector for Outlook) connects to a process launched within the Calendar server. The connection between them is stateful, and persists for the duration of the user's session. An alternative access method is to use the web client. In this case, the connection from browser to web application is *stateless*, a normal HTTP connection with state simulated by the use of cookies and HTTP headers; but the connection from the web client to the Calendar server is a stateful client-server session.

When multiple Calendar servers communicate, they connect via stateful sessions in a similar fashion as when users connect to a server: each server acts as a client to the other servers. The servers use LDAP to communicate with an Oracle Internet Directory and whatever protocols are necessary to connect to e-mail or wireless services for delivering notifications to users.

A point to note is that the international standards for diary-type applications are not yet fully developed. This applies particularly to communications protocols.

Calendar Server Processes

There are six distinct daemon processes that make up a Calendar server, though you may well have several occurrences of each. Only two are always necessary, but you will use all six except in the simplest environments.

The Calendar Engine Process, uniengd

The Calendar engine consists of a listener process and many child processes. The listener process monitors a TCP port for incoming connection requests from Calendar clients. It forks child processes (or threads on a Windows installation) for every session it establishes. Each of these child processes is a `uniengd` process. The child process is dedicated to the one session and handles all requests from its client until the session is terminated. The connection is persistent and stateful. If for any reason it is broken, the client must reconnect and establish a new session. One session (that is to say, one `uniengd` process) connects a user to one node. Even if the node is one of several nodes managed by the same server, the session can access directly only the one node against which it was spawned.

As well as being responsible for all interaction with its client, the `uniengd` process also manages communication with remote Calendar servers on the client's behalf, communication with the directory server, and communication with the local node. It is the `uniengd` that reads and writes data from and to the Calendar node database. Communication with remote nodes, servers, and directories is mediated by the Calendar Synchronous Network Connection server (the `uniscnd` process). Contention problems that would be caused by multiple `uniengd` processes attempting to write to the database concurrently are solved by the Calendar Lock Manager (the `unilckd` process, which is required for the Calendar engine to function).

All users initially contact the server through the listener process on the same port—by default, port 5730.

The Calendar Lock Manager Process, unilckd

The Calendar server can handle many concurrent requests from clients, each serviced by the clients' engine processes, but any requests that require access to the Calendar node database must be serialized. This serialization is handled by the Calendar Lock Manager. The `uniengd` processes contact the `unilckd` process before making any access to the node itself; the `unilckd` process queues up the requests, permitting access in an orderly fashion.

Each node is managed by, at most, one `unilckd` process. If a server has been configured with multiple nodes, there will be multiple `unilckd` processes. By default, the first 10 nodes will be assigned one `unilckd` process each; then an additional process will be launched for every subsequent 15 nodes. The maxnodesperlistener Calendar server parameter can be used to force Calendar to launch additional Lock Manager processes; setting this to 1 will launch one unilckd per node.

The Calendar Synchronous Network Connection Process, unisncd

The Synchronous Network Connection process manages communication between multiple Calendar servers, and communication between the Calendar engine processes and the directory access server. Each server has exactly one unisncd process, no matter how many nodes it is using.

The unisncd process opens up a set of connections to nodes in the other servers in the Calendar network, and (if its local server is managing more than one node) to the nodes being managed by its own server . These are persistent connections that are serviced at the remote end by uniengd processes. Thus, the unisncd process in one Calendar server is a client to the other Calendar servers. In a Calendar node network, every node must have one or more connections to all the other nodes, and any one connection is only one way. As with user sessions, these connections are specific to one node; so even if all the nodes are managed by just one server, the unisncd process must still launch sessions to and from every node.

When a client session against one Calendar node requests access to another node, it contacts its local unisncd process. The unisncd grants a connection to the remote node (which may or may not be managed by the local server) from its connection pool to that node, and the client uses this connection for its request. If there are more concurrent requests than there are connections, the unisncd process will queue them up in a FIFO (first in, first out) queue. Thus the assignation of a connection to one user session is transient, but the connection itself is persistent; there is a close analogy with the method by which Java applications can make use of connection pooling to a database.

The second function of the unisncd is to mediate connection requests to the directory access server within the local Calendar server. This uses the same FIFO queuing mechanism as previously described.

The unisncd process monitors, by default, port 5731 for requests.

The Calendar Directory Access Server, unidasd

To contact the Oracle Internet Directory it is necessary to use the LDAP protocol. The unidasd processes (there will usually be several of these for each Calendar server) perform directory access work on behalf of Calendar client sessions. The session engines request access to a unidasd server through the unisncd process, which will serialize concurrent requests.

'There will be more than one unidasd process: a parent process and a number of child processes, each of which can open a single connection to the Oracle Internet Directory. The total number of connections is controlled by the numconnect Calendar server parameter. The unidasd servers monitor a port for requests—by default, this is port 5732.

Calendar Corporatewide Services, unicwsd

The corporatewide services processes manage replication of data between Calendar servers, communications with external SMTP servers, generation of server-side reminder messages, and a number of housekeeping jobs. The unicwsd processes rely upon the unisncd process to mediate connections to remote servers and to the Oracle Internet Directory, in the same manner as do user session engines. By default there will be two `unicwsd` processes: one to manage interserver replication, and one for all the other tasks.

There are 12 jobs for the `unicwsd` processes. One process can do them all, or you can configure multiple processes for any one job. The jobs are in alphabetical order:

- *ABSync*: Synchronizing the Calendar common address book with the Oracle Internet Directory.
- *ConsistencyScan*: Scanning through the node database to detect corruptions.
- *DirProv*: Provisioning (creating) Calendar user accounts in response to provisioning requests delivered through Oracle Internet Directory.
- *DirSync*: Synchronizing data with the Oracle Internet Directory.
- *EventCalender*: Replicating events to all other servers in the Calendar node network.
- *EventSync*: Propagating changes to configured events between servers in the Calendar node network.
- *GALSync*: Synchronizing the global address list across servers.
- *LogRotation*: Saving and trimming the server log files.
- *Messaging*: Generating messages for transmission by e-mail, by wireless, or through Oracle Real-Time Collaboration (the instant messaging service).
- *Replication*: Managing replication of data between nodes.
- *Snooze*: Handling snoozed requests; these are requests that are not run in real time.
- *SSR*: Generating server-side reminder messages.

Requests for a `unicwsd` job are placed in a queue within the node for processing. It is possible for some types of jobs to back up in the queue. For example, data replication jobs to a remote node, or mail messages will accumulate if the remote service is not available. Once the service becomes available, the queued jobs will be serviced.

The Calendar Server Manager, unicsmd

The Calendar server manager lets you remotely manage Calendar servers and nodes within them. As long as this one process is running, you can issue the following commands from any other server to accomplish the following tasks:

- Startup of the Calendar server
- Shutdown the Calendar server
- Query the status of the Calendar server
- Stop a node of a Calendar server
- Start a node of a Calendar server

For remote management to be possible, the server must be, at least, in what is known as the *standby mode*. This is when all processes are down except the `unicsmd` process. The `unicsmd` process monitors a nominated port for requests; by default, this is port 5734. The three utilities that can use the `unicsmd` process are the `unistart`, `unistop`, and `unistatus` programs.

The Calendar Application System Environment

The Calendar Application System is a set of components that run in the Oracle Collaboration Suite middle tier that enhance the capabilities of Calendar. These components are the following:

- *The Calendar Application System itself*: This is the enabling structure for the remaining components.
- *The Calendar web client*: This is the OC4J component that generates a web interface to Calendar for browser users. Without this, users can only use the Calendar desktop clients, not browsers.
- *The Calendar Mobile Data Sync*: This permits users to transfer Calendar data to and from mobile devices, such as PDAs.
- *The Calendar web services*: These are a set of web services that expose the Calendar functions to the world and can be used to integrate Calendar with third-party applications.

These processes are implemented as CGI programs. Users invoke CGI programs by issuing URLs to the Apache web listener, front ended by the Web Cache. The standard implementation of CGI is that on receipt of a URL that maps on to a CGI program, Apache will launch an operating system shell, load the program into the shell, and run it. This is a seriously inefficient technique because of the necessity for launching new shells and programs dynamically whenever a URL is received. The Calendar Application System uses a more effective implementation. Rather than using the standard modcgi Apache module to run CGI programs, it uses the modfastcgi module. modfastcgi can use prespawned operating system shells and preload the CGI program. This means that the programs, already in run mode, are ready and waiting for execution requests received through URLs.

The Calendar Application System is not an OPMN-managed process and cannot therefore be started by the `opmnctl` utility. To start it, use either Application Server Control for your middle tier instance (it is the first application shown on the middle tier instance home page) or from an operating system prompt, run the `ocasctl` utility:

```
$ORACLE_HOME/ocas/bin/ocasctl start -n 10
```

This command will launch the `ochecklet.fcgi` program (always necessary to enable the Calendar Application System) and ten instances of the `ocas.fcgi` program (the default is five) that will wait to receive user requests. Other switches for the Oracle Calendar Application control utility let you stop processes and see what processes are running and their operating system process numbers. One running instance of the `ocas.fcgi` program can support a number of concurrently connected browser users. Estimates for sizing purposes are that 20 to 40 users can be effectively serviced by one `ocas.fcgi` instance, before the fast CGI performance will begin to degrade.

Servers, Nodes, and Request Flows

Figure 7-1 shows a simple installation: a single Calendar server with a single node.

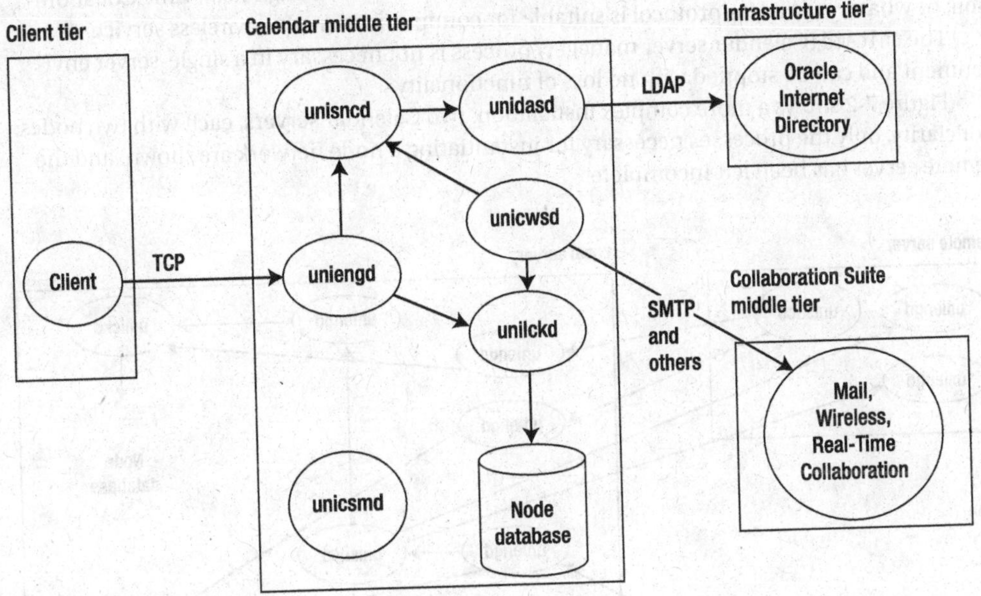

Figure 7-1. *A single server and node installation*

The client tier is either a user client process (which will be the Calendar Desktop Client or the Oracle Connector for Outlook installed in Microsoft Outlook) or a browser. In the latter case, the browser will connect through an Oracle Collaboration Suite middle tier Web Cache to the Apache web listener and on to the Calendar Application System web client running in a modfastcgi container on the middle tier. In either case, the connection from the client tier to the Calendar middle tier is a persistent TCP connection to a dedicated server process, the `uniengd` process spawned for the session. The session is against one node only; in the example, there is indeed only one node.

When the `uniengd` process receives a client request that necessitates reading or writing the node database, it will contact the `unilckd` (Lock Manager) process. Depending on the workload, the request may be queued by the `unilckd` process, but eventually the `uniengd` process will receive permission to access the node.

When the `uniengd` process receives a client request that necessitates use of the Oracle Internet Directory, it will contact the `unisncd` (Synchronous Network Connection) process. Depending on the workload, the request may be queued by the `unisncd` process, but eventually the `uniengd` process will receive permission to connect to a `unidasd` (directory access server) process. This will then action the request by issuing an LDAP call to the Oracle Internet Directory.

The `unicwsd` (corporatewide services) process will connect to the node (via the `unilckd` process) to read and write data as necessary, and to the `unidasd` process (via the `unisncd` process) when necessary for synchronizing node data with directory data. It will also contact the various other Oracle Collaboration Suite components that may be needed for transmitting messages generated by Calendar events. The protocol will depend on the component: SMTP for sending e-mail messages via Mail; Oracle Net for messages through Real-Time Collaboration; or whatever wireless protocol is suitable for communication via a wireless service.

The `unicsmd` (Calendar server manager) process is not necessary in a single-server environment and can be stopped with no loss of functionality.

Figure 7-2 shows a more complex installation: two Calendar servers, each with two nodes. For clarity, only the processes necessary for instantiating a node network are shown, and the remote server has been left incomplete.

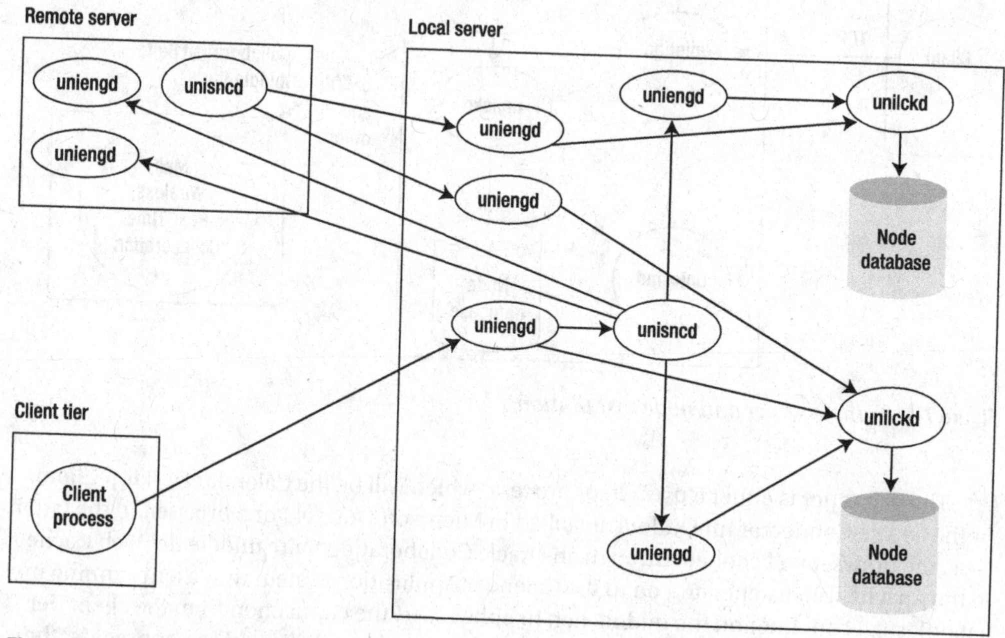

Figure 7-2. *Data flows in a node network between multiple nodes and servers*

On startup, the local Calendar server will launch one `unilckd` process for each defined local node database. Remember that if there are many node databases you can limit the number of `unilckd` processes, in which case each `unilckd` will control access to more than one node.

The `unisncd` process in the local Calendar server will create a pool of connections to `uniengd` processes against every node on the network, both in its local server and in the other Calendar remote server. In Figure 7-2, this pool is just one connection per node but is usually more, so that it can handle concurrent requests. The only exception to this rule is a server managing a single node. In this case, the local `uniscnd` process will not launch a connection to its local node. These connections will be used as the bridge for traffic to other nodes from processes attached to one node. A symmetrical set of connections will be made from the remote server to the local server for traffic in the other direction.

When a uniengd process (which may be servicing either a user session or a connection from a remote unisncd process) requires access to the node against which it has been spawned, it will contact the appropriate unilckd process, which will mediate access to the node. Note that each unilckd process may now have to accept access requests to its node from uniengd processes supporting sessions from local clients, and from the local unisncd process, and from remote unisncd processes.

Figure 7-3 shows the remaining part of a node network.

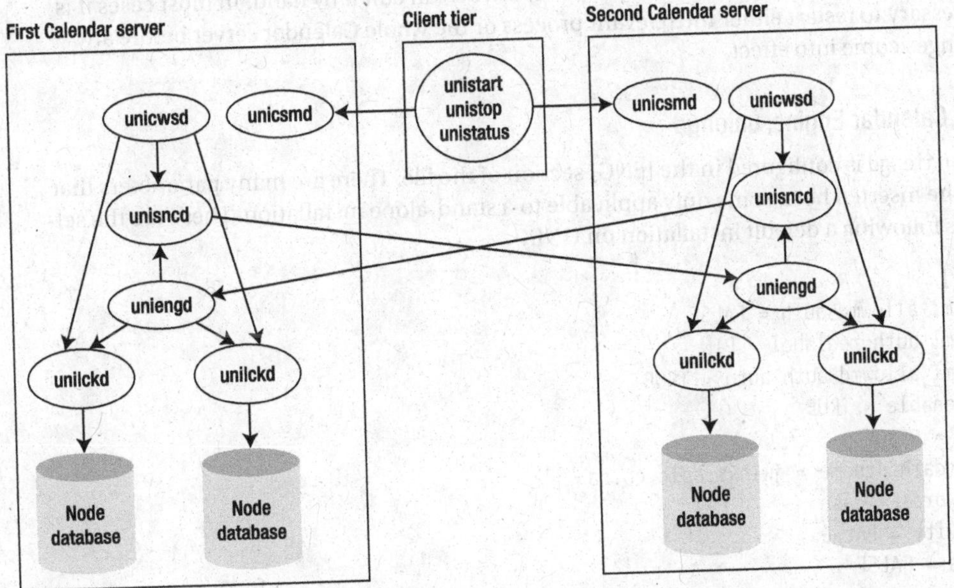

Figure 7-3. *Data flows in a node network between corporatewide services and the Calendar server manager*

The unicwsd processes have to manage communication between the servers necessary to synchronize certain information and to propagate messages regarding events. They communicate with local nodes through unilckd, and with remote servers through unisncd, in the same manner as a uniengd process supporting a user session.

In a multiserver environment, the unicsmd process takes on the role of accepting administration commands from remote servers. The client tools for starting, stopping, and querying the status of a Calendar server can be run from any host and, using TCP, can connect to the unicsmd process of any server.

Configuring the Calendar Server

A Calendar administrator must configure the runtime environment of the server processes that support end-user sessions and create the nodes that store users' data. Then they must manage the accounts they will use and the automation possible through the alert system.

Managing the Server Processes

The six process types that make up a Calendar server are configured in the `unison.ini` file. The term *unison* (or abbreviations thereof) occurs many times in the Calendar environment; it is a historical anomaly referring to the original product name before Oracle acquired it. The file will be `$ORACLE_HOME/ocal/misc/unison.ini` on UNIX, or `%ORACLE_HOME%\ocal\misc\unison.ini` on Windows.

The Calendar administration tools (either Application Server Control, or the Calendar command-line utilities) can modify this file, or you can edit it by hand. In most cases it is necessary to restart either the relevant process or the whole Calendar server before any changes come into effect.

The Calendar Engine, uniengd

The `uniengd` is configured in the [ENG] section of the file. There are many parameters that can be inserted here, some only applicable to a stand-alone installation. These are the settings following a default installation on UNIX:

```
[ENG]
syncml_allowmd5auth = FALSE
syncml_authcredlabel = PIN
syncml_allowmd5auth_auto = TRUE
cab_enable = TRUE
port = 5730
calendarhostname = jwlnx1.bplc.co.za
passwords = case
activity = FALSE
stats = FALSE
standards = {ICAL2.0,CAPI}
allowresourceconflict = FALSE
maxsessions = 2500
```

These are the parameters:

- *syncml_**: Specifies some security settings. Ignored when using an infrastructure.
- *cab_enable=TRUE*: Allows the use of a common address book.
- *port=5730*: Sets the port on which the server will accept user connections.
- *calendarhostname*: Nominates the address on which the server will listen.
- *passwords*: Determines whether passwords are case-sensitive. Ignored when using an infrastructure.
- *activity=FALSE*: Disables logging of user sign-on and sign-off.
- *stats=FALSE*: Disables logging of sessions' CPU usage, wait time, and other figures.
- *standards*: Names the protocols that are required by the Calendar Application System.
- *allowresourceconflict=FALSE*: Instructs Calendar to reject double-booking attempts.
- maxsessions: Limits the maximum number of concurrent connections.

The Lock Manager, unilckd

The Lock Manager is controlled by the [LCK] section. There is only one legal parameter in this section, which is not set by default:

```
[LCK]
maxnodesperlistener
```

This parameter controls the number of Lock Manager processes that will be launched. Calendar will compute the number by dividing the number of nodes the server is using by this parameter and rounding up. If not set, there will be one Lock Manager launched per node up to ten, and then an additional Lock Manager launched per fifteen additional nodes.

The Synchronous Network Connection, unisncd

The Synchronous Network Connection process is controlled by the [SNC] section. The default installation has only one parameter in this section:

```
[SNC]
port = 5731
```

This parameter sets the port the process will monitor for requests from `uniengd` and `unicwsd` processes when they require access to a remote node for data or to a `unidasd` process for directory access. Another parameter that may be of interest is enable. This controls whether to launch the `unisncd` process. It defaults to true. If set to false, it will not be possible to use a directory, multiple nodes, or corporatewide services.

The Directory Access Server, unidas

Calendar can be used with or without a directory server. The Directory Access Server manages the communication with the directory server. When installed with Oracle Collaboration Suite, Calendar will always use the Oracle Internet Directory directory server. Use of the directory is controlled by three sections in the `unison.ini` file: [DAS], [LDAP], and [<*hostname*>,unidas]. Following the default installation these read as follows:

```
[DAS]
dir_updcalonly = TRUE
dir_service = LDAP
so_backlog = 0
enable = TRUE
port = 5732

[LDAP]
applicationentitydn = orclApplicationCommonName=Calendar44283,cn=Application ➥
Entities,cn=Calendar,cn=Products,cn=OracleContext
admindn = cn=Calendar Instance Admin 94975, ➥
cn=Admins,cn=Calendar,cn=Products,cn=OracleContext,dc=bplc,dc=co,dc=za
```

```
attrpreservelist = { "mobile", "employeeNumber", "givenName", ➥
"middlename", "mail", "ou", "C" }
attr_uid = "uid"
eventcalrelativedn = cn=EventCalendars,cn=Calendar,cn=Products,cn=OracleContext
resourcerelativedn = cn=Resources,cn=Calendar,cn=Products,cn=OracleContext
basedn = "dc=bplc,dc=co,dc=za"
security = TRUE
secure-port = 636
port = 389
host = jwlnx1.bplc.co.za
dsa = OID

[jwlnx1,unidas]
numconnect = 50
enable = TRUE
```

The critical entries in the [DAS] section are the port the `unidasd` process will monitor for directory access requests, and the restriction on directory updates, which limits Calendar users to updating only directory entries relevant to Calendar. The [LDAP] section gives the distinguished names of the various entries Calendar needs to search the directory, and the address of the directory server where these searches will be made. The [<*hostname*>,unidas] section specifies the number of connections to make to the directory server and enables use of the directory.

Corporatewide Services, unicwsd

The corporatewide services process is controlled by the [CWS] section. Following a default installation, this section reads as follows:

```
[CWS]
smtpmailprogram = oesmua.sh
smtpmailpath = /OCS/product/10.1.1/ocs_1/apps/ocal/sbin
smtpmail_url = smtp://jwlnx1.bplc.co.za:25
smsnotifyprogram = /OCS/product/10.1.1/ocs_1/apps/ocal/sbin/sendalert
smtpmailpath_auto = TRUE
smtpmailprogram_auto = TRUE
smtpmail_url_auto = TRUE
banner = TRUE
```

These settings specify how the `unicwsd` process should make use of the Mail server. There are many other possible parameters to control—for example, the frequency of consistency scans of the node database (once a week by default); the frequency of common address book synchronization (four times a day by default); and the use of the Oracle Internet Directory for Calendar account provisioning (enabled by default).

The Calendar Server Manager, unicsmd

The Calendar server manager is controlled by the [CSM] section. The default installation has only one parameter in this section:

```
[CSM]
port = 5734
```

There is an optional password parameter that lets you specify a password required for remote administration. You should encrypt this with the `uniencrypt` utility before entering it into the file.

Other Sections in the unison.ini File

The [CLIENT] section can be used to control client behavior. The default installation does not create a [CLIENT] section at all, but some parameters may be of interest. There is a group of parameters that control the frequency with which clients can refresh their display of data. By default, they are all set to 15 minutes. This is a compromise between the need to show data in real time, and the strain put on server resources if hundreds or thousands of clients submit refresh requests with great frequency. If you consider that your users' agendas are sufficiently volatile that a 15-minute lapse between (for example) one user creating appointments and other users being informed of the appointments is too great, you could reduce the refresh intervals. The display of such information will always be real-time when a refresh is requested. This delay will only apply to passive sessions.

The [LIMITS] section places controls on what users can do. The default configuration will, for example, allow attachments to agenda items but restricts their size to 2MB. It is also possible to control the use of wild cards in searches (which can have a disastrous effect on directory performance), the number of people that can be included in mailings, and the number of occurrences of a repeating event.

The [NOTIFY] section controls whether Calendar can send alerts by SMS and wireless. The actual SMS program is specified in the smsnotifyprogram parameter in the [CWS] section. For wireless notifications, the URL to be used to contact the Oracle Collaboration Suite wireless services is specified in the alert_url parameter. This will have been set correctly by the installer.

Logging can be controlled per server process type, but there is also a [LOG] section. The default configuration is

```
[LOG]
rotation_enable = TRUE
rotation_sizetrigger = 10
rotation_periodtrigger = Sunday
rotation_periodtime = 04:30
rotation_atticmaxsize = 200
rotation_atticage = 120
rotation_exceptions = {stats.log,act.log}
```

Logging records are written to the `$ORACLE_HOME/ocal/log` directory. Each process will produce its own log file. Setting the rotation_enable parameter to true enables the automatic moving of log files to a separate storage area known as the *attic*. The attic is the directory

$ORACLE_HOME/ocal/log/attic, and the movement of files will occur, in the default configuration shown previously, when a file reaches 10MB, and the files will be deleted from the attic when the attic contains more than 200MB of files. Files more than 120 days old will also be deleted from the attic. The rotation maintenance is set to happen early on Sunday mornings.

Managing Nodes

The nodes, or databases, to which a server will attach are defined by entries in both the unison.ini file and the nodes.ini file. The relationship between server and node is one-to-many. It is not possible for a node to be accessed directly by more than one server, though through the communications bridge established by the Synchronous Network Connection process a user session against one server can retrieve data from a node managed by a different server. The characteristics of the nodes are defined by sections in unison.ini; the connections between them are defined in nodes.ini. Every node in a network has a unique node number, and every node must be connected to every other node. This is a many-to-many relationship but is not necessarily a relationship between equal peers. Defining one node as the *master* node is not required but will improve management and performance.

The Node Definition

The node database is a set of files in the directory $ORACLE_HOME/ocal/db/nodes/<*node_name*> where <*node_name*> is the node's name. The node created by the default Oracle Collaboration Suite installation has the name N0 (uppercase *N*, number zero) and the unique identification number (Node-ID) of 1. The node name is used for the directory name, but as a general rule nodes are referred to by their Node-ID number. Following the default installation there will be these two sections in the unison.ini file:

```
[1]
name = N0
version = A.06.10
timezone = SAST-2

[CLUSTER]
masternode = 1
```

and this entry in the nodes.ini file:

```
+ H=jwlnx1.bplc.co.za:5730/N=1
all:3
```

The section [1] instructs the server to look for the node database with a Node-ID equal to 1, and then sets certain characteristics for the node. These characteristics are the following:

- *name*: Each node has a name, following the form of a letter and a digit. Names are assigned automatically, the digit incrementing to 9 then the letter incrementing to Z then A to M. Thus the maximum number of names is 260.
- *version:* This must never be changed!

- *timezone*: Apart from scalability, one reason for creating multiple nodes is so that users can be registered in a node appropriate to their time zone. Oracle DBAs may be irritated to discover that the time zone format is not the same as that used within an Oracle database. The example shown in the previous unison.ini file extract is South Africa Standard Time: two hours ahead of GMT, no daylight saving time.
- *aliases*: Lets you define one or more aliases for the node.
- *lck_dedicated*: Controls the spawning of a Lock Manager process. If set to true (default is false) the server will always spawn a Lock Manager (the unilckd process) specifically for the node, rather than possibly assigning it to a Lock Manager that is servicing multiple nodes as controlled by the maxnodesperlistener parameter in the [LCK] section.
- *maxsessionsfornode*: Limits the number of concurrent user sessions against the node. Defaults to the maxsessions parameter specified in the [ENG] section.
- *localnodes*: Nominates a list of Node-IDs whose resources will appear to users as though they were in the one node to which they are connected. This allows for scalability that is completely transparent to the users.

Each node you create subsequently will have its own section in unison.ini identified by the Node-ID number.

The [CLUSTER] section of unison.ini can include two of these three parameters:

- *masternode*: Nominates the node, by its Node-ID, which is the master node of the node network. It must be a node on the local server, not a remote server. It can only be set on one server.
- *remotemasternode*: Specifies, by Node-ID, the master node of the node network. This parameter should be set on servers other than the server that has the master node.
- *excludednodes*: Nominates a list of nodes (by Node-ID or alias) that the server will not create user accounts on. This can be used to prevent further user registrations on nodes that are already overstressed, or to prevent administrators connected to one server from creating accounts in nodes managed by a remote server. It can also prevent creation of user accounts on the master node, which may be considered to be bad practice.

Defining the Node Network

The nodes.ini file specifies to which nodes in the node network each server's Synchronous Network Connection daemon (the unisncd process) should instantiate connections and how many such connections it should instantiate. The ideal situation is that there will be enough connections, in both directions, between nodes such that users will always be able to obtain the connections they need without launching so many connections (each of which is persistent and requires a uniengd process) that the system is overstressed.

The nodes.ini file should exist on only one server. For an Oracle Collaboration Suite Calendar installation, this will be the server created for your first middle tier installation, which is also defined as the master node. It consists of a series of lines that establish the node network. They instruct which nodes the servers' unisncd processes should establish sessions against, and how many sessions to establish. The following is a simple example:

```
+ H=bplc.co.za:5730/N=1
+ H=bplc.co.za:5730/N=2
+ H=bplc.co.uk:5730/N=3
+ H=bplc.co.de:5730/N=4
+ H=bplc.co.de:5731/N=5
all:2
```

This file will create a node network of five nodes. The network consists of three hosts, four servers, and five nodes. One server is running on the host bplc.co.za port 5730, and supports two nodes. The second server, supporting one node, is on the host bplc.co.uk port 5730. The third and fourth servers are running on host bplc.co.de ports 5730 and 5731 respectively and support one node each.

The `all:2` directive instructs each server's `unisncd` process to launch two sessions against each remote node, and if it is supporting more than one local node, two connections against each of them, too. Thus, the server bplc.co.za:5730 will instantiate a total of ten connections: two each against its two local nodes (Node-IDs 1 and 2), and two against each of the remote nodes (Node-IDs 3, 4, and 5). The other three servers will launch eight sessions each: two against each remote node. While there is no reason not to have symmetry like this, in many cases you will want an asymmetric situation based on the likely traffic volume between nodes. For example, it may be that if you have multiple nodes in one country (perhaps distinguished by time zone) there may well be more traffic between them than between nodes in one country and another—so you would configure additional connections between them.

To include a node in the network, add a line conforming to this syntax:

```
+ H=<hostname>:<port>/N=<Node-ID>/GR=<groupname>
```

To exclude a node from the network, prefix the line with a hyphen (-) symbol rather than a plus (+) symbol. The *<hostname>* can be an IP address, but this is considered to be bad practice. The *<Node-ID>* can be the numeric value or an alias, as defined by the aliases parameter in the [Node-ID] section of the `unison.ini` file. An alias may be helpful to users, as there are places in the Calendar client where this value is visible, and unlike a sensibly chosen alias, Node-IDs do not convey any meaning. The use of groups is optional but may help with subsequent directives referring to the number of connections to make; several nodes can be referred to with one directive, rather than requiring a directive for each.

The number of connections is controlled by a set of directives, the simplest of which is the `all` directive used in the previous example of a `nodes.ini` file. Other directives may be either relative in that they add or remove connections already specified by, for example, `all`, or absolute in that they specify a precise number of connections between two nodes. Consider this example:

```
+ H=bplc.co.za:5730/N=HeadQuarters
+ H=bplc.co.za:5730/N=Development
+ H=bplc.co.uk:5730/N=UK
+ H=bplc.co.de:5730/N=Frankfurt/GR=Germany
+ H=bplc.co.de:5731/N=Munich/GR=Germany
all:2
UK:4
```

```
Development:1
HeadQuarters => Development:2
Development_=> HeadQuarters: 2
Germany:+1
```

This example uses aliases rather than Node-IDs throughout. It also puts the two nodes in Germany into a group, both of which are running on the same host but in different servers. The first directive on connection numbers is an instruction to launch two connections to each node. Then this overall instruction is modified. There will be four connections established to the UK node from each of the other nodes. There will only be one connection from each server to the Development node, except that the server hosting the HeadQuarters node will launch two connections to the Development node, and vice versa. Finally, after applying the preceding rules, the last rule says to add one more connection to each node in the Germany group. The end result of this for the bplc.co.za:5730 server will be that shown in Table 7-1.

Table 7-1. *Number of Connections from Server bplc.co.za:5730 to the Five Nodes*

Server	Node	Connections
bplc.co.za:5730	HeadQuarters	2
bplc.co.za:5730	Development	2
bplc.co.uk:5730	UK	4
bplc.co.de:5730	Frankfurt	3
bplc.co.de:5731	Munich	3

Figure 7-4 is a graphical representation of Table 7-1, showing the connections between the server and its local nodes, and the external connections to the nodes managed by the remote servers.

Not shown in the figure are the connections from the remote servers within and between each other . There will be three incoming connections to the bplc.co.za:5730 server from each of the other three servers (two to the HeadQuarters node, and one to the Development node) and also two connections each way within the server for the communication between the Development and the HeadQuarters nodes.

You can create the node network by editing the `nodes.ini` file by hand, or by using the `uninode` command-line utility. The `uninode` utility will create an empty `nodes.ini` file and can connect to each server (you will have to nominate the servers) and interrogate them to identify what nodes each server is running. The utility will then populate the `nodes.ini` file with lines for each node. If, subsequently, you want to exclude a node from the network, prefix the line with - `H` rather than the + `H` prefix used above.

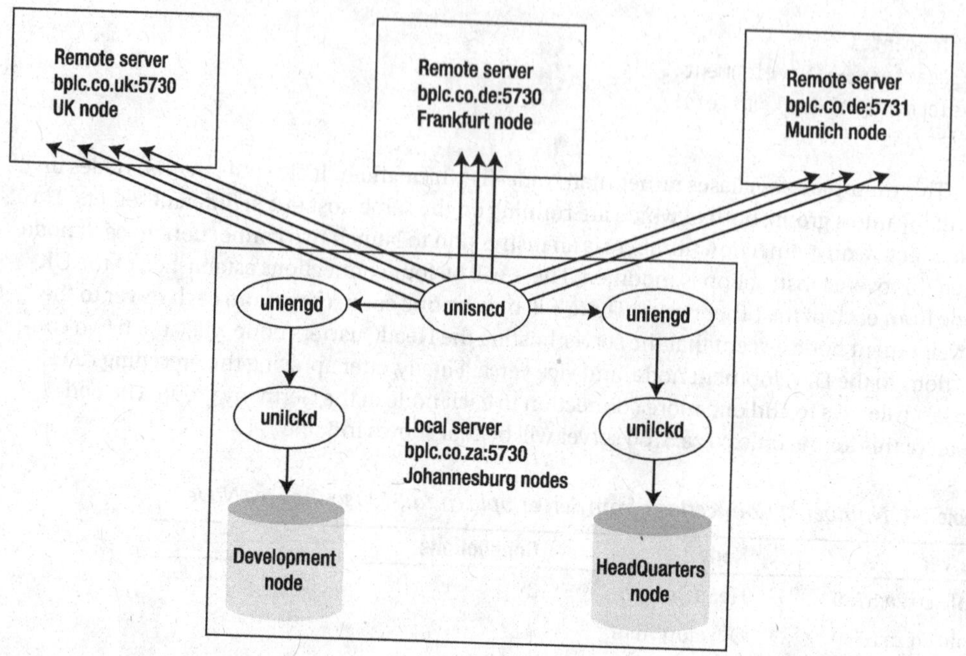

Figure 7-4. *Server-to-node connections to instantiate a node network*

Creating Nodes

To create a new node, you must use the command-line utility `uniaddnode`. It is not possible to create nodes through the Application Server Control Calendar Administrator, and, furthermore, the server must not be running while you create a new node. There are two forms of the command. The first will create a single new node:

```
uniaddnode [-n <node-id>] [-t <timezone>] [-a <alias>]
```

The three arguments are all optional. If no Node-ID number is specified, the Oracle Internet Directory will generate one; however, while this is the documented behavior, you may receive an error unless you specify a Node-ID number. If no time zone is specified, the time zone will be picked up from the host operating system. If no alias is specified, you will only be able to reference the node by its Node-ID. Note that the time zone specification is case-sensitive and must conform to the Calendar standard; you can obtain a list of valid time zones with the `unitzinfo` utility.

The second form of the command can create a set of nodes with one command:

```
uniaddnode -sn <node-id> -num <number>
```

Both arguments are required. The first argument is the Node-ID number of the first node to create, and the second argument is the number of nodes to create. They will be consecutively numbered, and the command will fail if any of the numbers are already in use. It is not possible to specify aliases or time zones for the nodes at this time, though you can add an alias later by editing the `nodes.ini` file. It is not possible to change the time zone after creation. If you discover later that the time zone is inappropriate, you must create a new node and move any existing users into it and delete the old node.

This command adds a second node to the default server created within Oracle Collaboration Suite by the installer. It is being given a nominated Node-ID (which must not already be in use on the node network), the United Kingdom time zone, and an alias:

```
[mid oraocs]$ uniaddnode -n 2 -t GMTOBST -a London
Please enter Sysop password:
uniaddnode: Database initialization done
uniaddnode: node [2] has been successfully initialized
[mid oraocs]$
```

The command will prompt for the SYSOP password, which will be the password selected at install time for all the Oracle Collaboration Suite components' superuser accounts. The SYSOP user is the superuser for Calendar. The command then creates the skeleton node database in the host's file system in a directory named after the generated node name and adds this section to the `unison.ini` file:

```
[2]
name = N1
version = A.06.10
timezone = GMTOBST
aliases = London
```

The `uniaddnode` utility does not make any edits to the `nodes.ini` file; to bring the new node into the node network you must add a line (or lines) manually, the simplest way is to insert the second line shown below:

```
+ H=jwlnx1.bplc.co.za:5730/N=1
+ H=jwlnx1.bplc.co.za:5730/N=2
all:3
```

This will force the server to create a node network of the two nodes, with three Synchronous Network Connection sessions against each node. This very small node network exists entirely within one server. Having created your new node and edited the `nodes.ini` file as above, start the Calendar server in the normal fashion and you will see the `uniengd` processes spawned automatically by the `unisncd` process.

To confirm creation of the node, you can use this command to list all the nodes, and whether they are running:

```
unistatus -n
```

User, Resource, and Event Accounts

Because Calendar can run as a self-contained product, there are often alternative tools for management: either the Calendar command-line utilities, or the facilities provided by Oracle Collaboration Suite. Whatever tools you choose to use, you will usually need to connect to the Calendar server(s) as an administrator. This is the SYSOP account created at install time, which you will use to create accounts for users, resources, and events.

The SYSOP Account

The Calendar user SYSOP is the Calendar administrator. Unlike regular users, the SYSOP user does not exist as an Oracle Internet Directory user; he exists purely in the Calendar environment. At install time the SYSOP password is initialized to the password specified for the other superusers, such as orcladmin for the Oracle Internet Directory, or ias_admin for Application Server Control. To change the password subsequently (necessary to separate the Calendar administration domain from the Application Server administration domain) use the operating system utility `unioidconf`. This lets you bind to the Oracle Internet Directory as the orcladmin user, give the password, and then set a new password for the SYSOP Calendar user. The dialog is

```
$ unioidconf -setsysoppassword -D cn=orcladmin
Enter a bind password:
Enter new administrator password:
Re-enter new administrator password:
```

Do not attempt to change the SYSOP password with the `unipasswd` utility! This is designed for the stand-alone implementation of Calendar and will not update necessary Oracle Internet Directory entries. You can also manage the SYSOP directly in the Oracle Internet Directory by using the `ldapmodify` command-line utility or the Oracle Internet Directory Administrator, as shown in Figure 7-5. The distinguished name of the entry is of this form:

```
cn=Calendar Instance Admin ➥
94975,cn=Admins,cn=Calendar,cn=Products,cn=OracleContext,dc=bplc,dc=co,dc=za
```

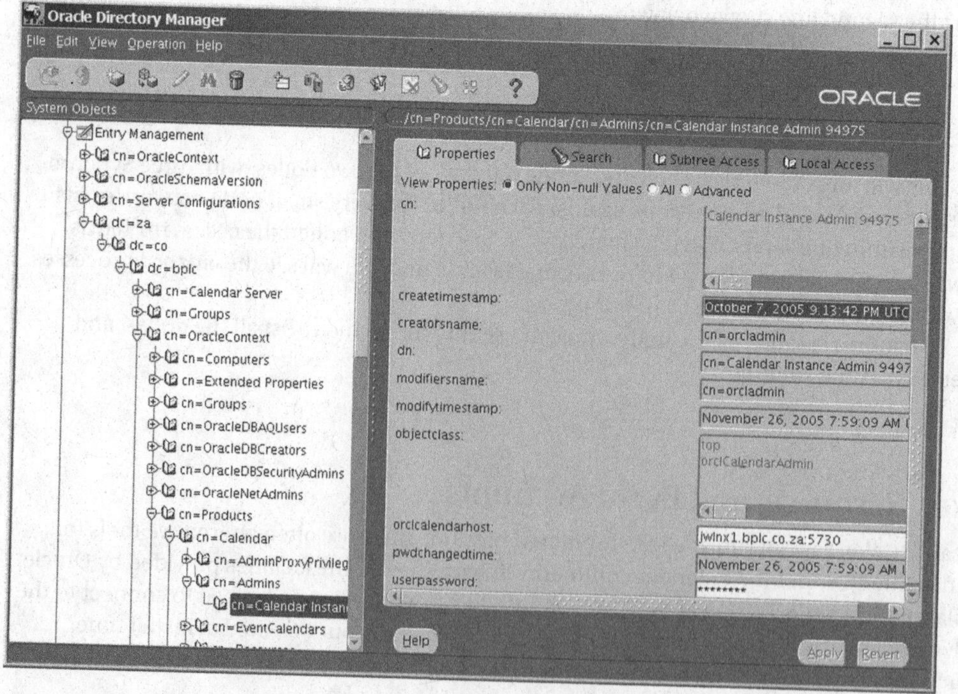

Figure 7-5. *The Calendar Administrator entry in the Oracle Internet Directory*

The first domain component (in this example, it is cn=Calendar Instance Admin 94975) includes a system-generated unique identifier for each Calendar server administrator.

To connect as SYSOP through Application Server Control, click the Administration button for the Calendar Server component on the far right (shown in Figure 5-20 in Chapter 5). You will be redirected to the Single Sign-On window, where you must give an Oracle Internet Directory username and password. This does not have to be a particularly powerful user—anyone will do, as long as Single Sign-On can authenticate him. It cannot be SYSOP, because SYSOP is not an Oracle Internet Directory user. Then you will be presented with the Calendar Administrator login window, as shown in Figure 7-6.

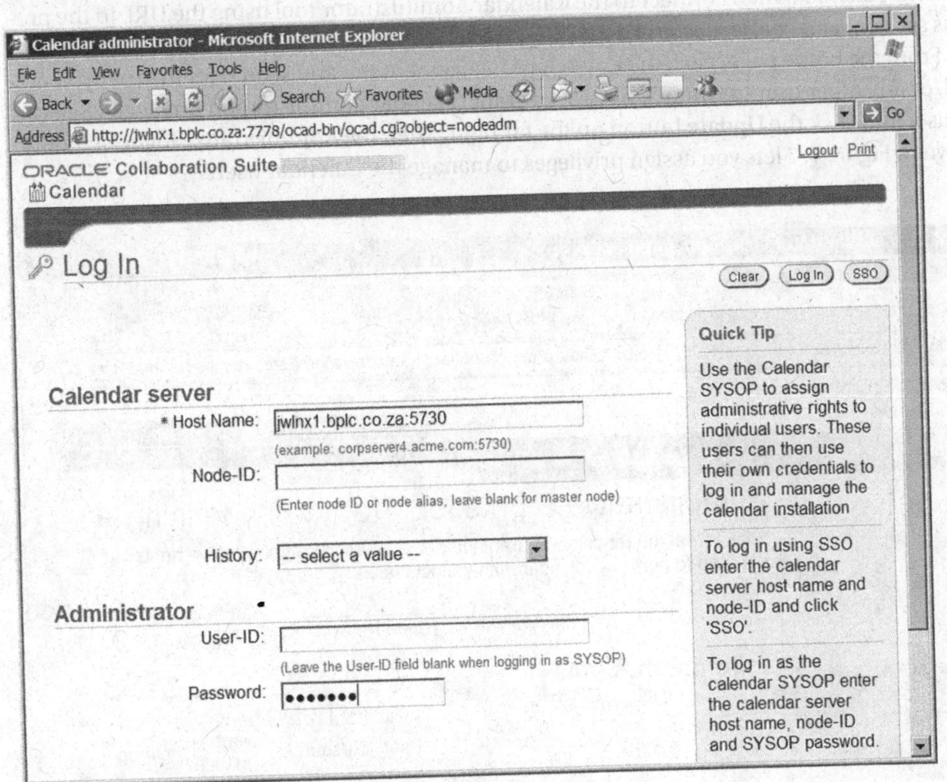

Figure 7-6. *The Calendar Administrator login window*

In the figure, the Node-ID has been left blank; this will connect you to the master node, which is Node-ID number 1. Leaving the username blank defaults to the SYSOP account, and will take you to the Calendar Administrator graphical interface home page. The home page has two tabs. The Server Administration tab will let you start and stop the node or the whole server, and also gives a facility for editing the node and server characteristics; this is equivalent to editing the `unison.ini` and `nodes.ini` files. The Calendar Management tab lets you work with users, groups, resources, and events; these are the four possible Calendar account types.

An alternative navigation path to the Calendar Administrator is to issue a URL, `http://<host.domain>:<port>/ocad-bin/ocad.cgi?object=nodeadm`, that will connect to it directly, where *<host.domain>:<port>* are the address and port of the Web Cache for your middle tier Oracle Collaboration Suite installation.

Creating an Administration Account

You will not want to use the SYSOP account for day-to-day administration. To create a regular account for this purpose, create the user as normal in the Oracle Internet Directory through the OIDDAS tool, and select the options to have the usual applications provisioned, including Mail and Calendar. Then connect to the Calendar Administrator tool using the URL in the previous section, and connect as user SYSOP.

From the home page, click the Calendar Management tab and search for the user you created, or any other user to whom you wish to grant Calendar administration privileges. Select the user and click the Update button on the far right. Then the Administrative Rights window shown in Figure 7-7 lets you assign privileges to manage the Calendar users.

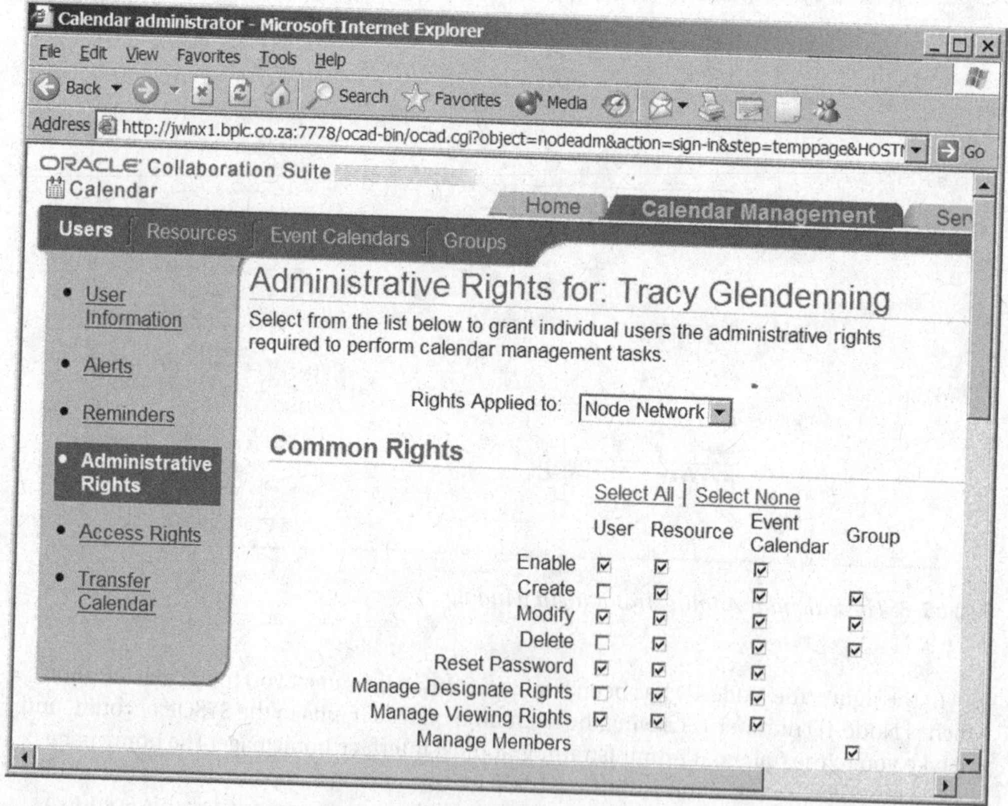

Figure 7-7. *Assigning Calendar management privileges*

In Figure 7-7, user Tracy Glendenning is being given complete privileges to manage resources, events, and groups and all privileges for users except for creation and deletion. These are usually managed through the Oracle Internet Directory. Note that this user has been given these rights across the whole node network; if you wish you can grant privileges per node, letting you distribute the administration capability.

User TGLENDEN will now be able to log on through the Calendar Administrator and manage users (with the exception of creation and deletion) and resources, events, and groups. She will not see the Server Administration tab that lets you start and stop servers and nodes; that is only visible to the SYSOP user.

User Account Provisioning

User accounts can be created in Calendar using several techniques. The default method is automatic account provisioning when creating a user in Oracle Collaboration Suite through the OIDDAS application. For any one user, the administrator can choose not to provision a Calendar account, in which case it can be provisioned later. An alternative, though similar in concept, is on-demand provisioning.

To enable automatic account provisioning, relying completely on defaults, this section is needed in the `unison.ini` file:

```
[PROVISIONING]
policy.default = 1:(objectclass=*)
enable = TRUE
```

This section is created by the default installation. It enables automatic Calendar account creation, according to a policy that states that all the accounts will be created in the node with Node-ID of 1, no matter what attributes the user may have in the Oracle Internet Directory. If you enable automatic account provisioning, you will certainly want to nominate which node the accounts will be created within. A more complicated example based on the nodes described earlier would be the following:

```
[PROVISIONING]
policy.1 = 1:(ou=ManagementTeam)
policy.2 = 2:(ou=Development)
policy.3 = 3:(country=gb)
policy.4 = 5:(country=de,city=Munich)
policy.5 = 4:(country=de)
policy.default = 1(objectclass=*)
enable = TRUE
```

A *policy* assigns a user to a node based on the values of one or more of the attributes in the Oracle Internet Directory that define him. If a user matches several policies, the policy with the lower number takes precedence. This set of policies states that any user whose `ou`, or organizational unit, is the management team will have his account created in node 1, which is the headquarters node. Then staff in the development unit will go to node 2. Staff with the country attribute set to `gb` will be created in node 3, the UK node. Staff with country `de` and city `Munich` will have their accounts created in node 5, while all other users with country `de` will go to node 4.

Finally, all users not caught by higher priority policies will have accounts in node 1. If there is no policy.default policy defined, users who do not match any of the defined policies will not have an account created for them.

If you already have a populated Oracle Internet Directory, you can create Calendar accounts in bulk. This situation could arise if you are only implementing Calendar after implementing other Oracle Collaboration Suite components, or if you are populating the Oracle Internet Directory from an existing third-party directory, such as a Novell eDirectory or a Microsoft Active Directory. There are two techniques: through the Calendar administration GUI, or using a command-line utility.

To provision accounts in bulk using the Calendar administration tool, connect to Application Server Control and navigate to the Calendar Administrator. Click the Calendar Management tab, the Users button, and then the Provision Account for Users button. Perform a search without entering any filter and you will be presented with a list of all users registered in the Oracle Internet Directory who do not yet have Calendar accounts. Select those for whom you want to provision accounts, as shown in Figure 7-8.

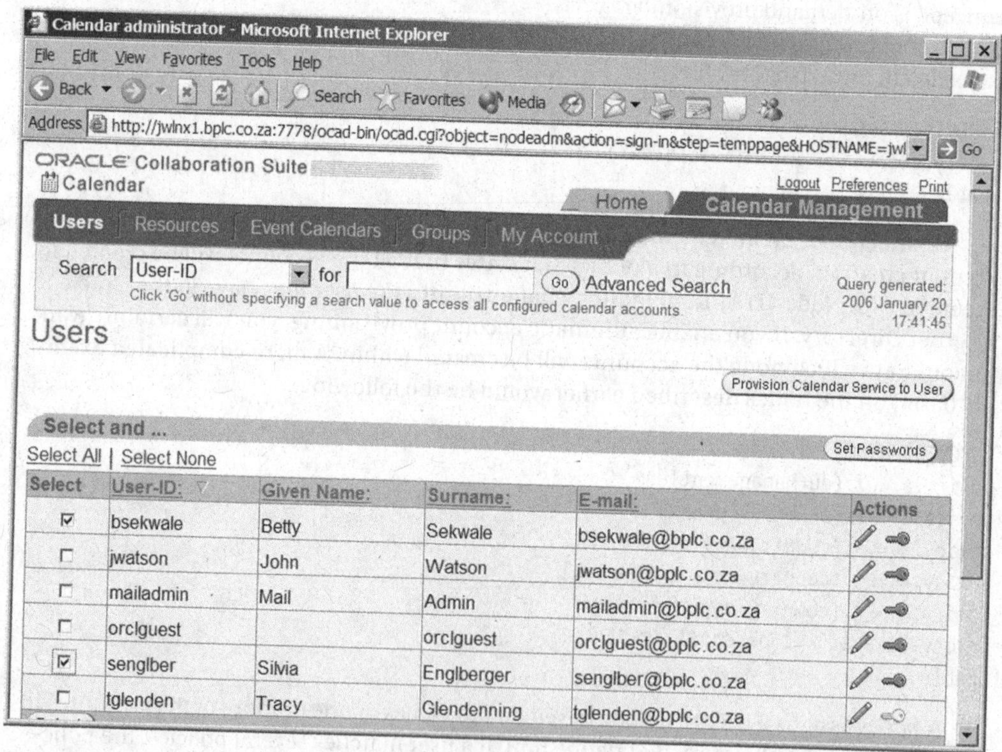

Figure 7-8. *Provisioning accounts through the Calendar administrator*

Alternatively, the `uniuser` command-line utility can load users either from a file or from an LDAP directory.

At any time you can provision an account for an individual user through the OIDDAS application. Connect to the application with a URL of the form http://<host.domain>:7777/

`oiddas` where *<host.domain>* is your infrastructure host (which will have its Apache web listener running on port 7777 by default) and log on as a privileged user, such as orcladmin. Click the Directory tab, search for your user, and in the Edit User wizard select Calendar for account provisioning, as shown in Figure 7-9.

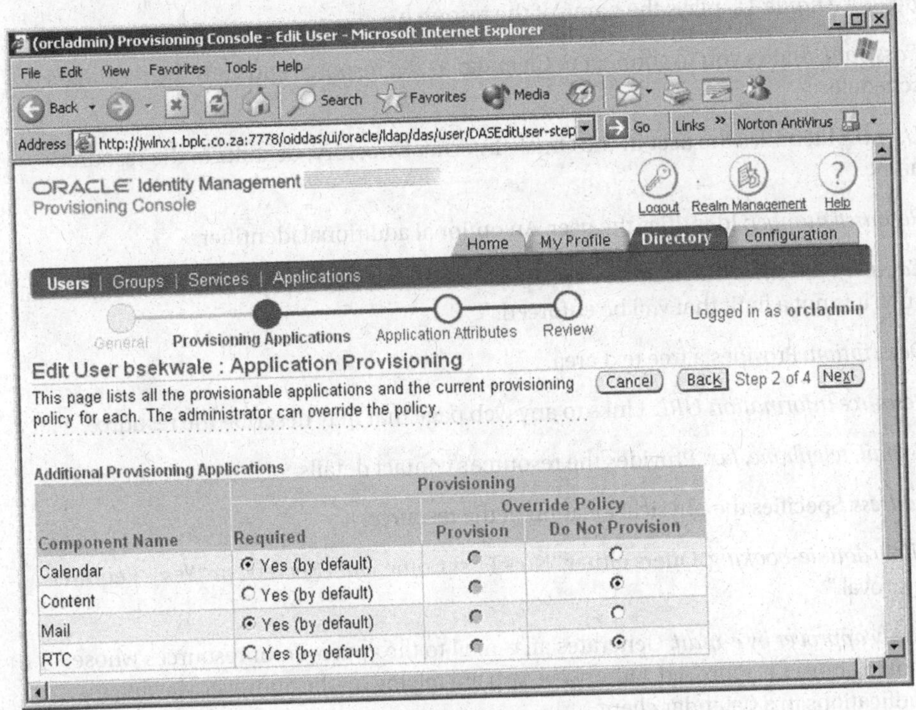

Figure 7-9. *Provisioning an account through the OIDDAS application*

Figure 7-9 shows that Betty Sekwale, username BSEKWALE, was originally created in the Oracle Internet Directory with no accounts in the Oracle Collaboration Suite. Now she is being given accounts in Calendar and Mail, but not for Content Services or Real-Time Collaboration.

Resource Accounts

In Calendar terms, a *resource* is an inanimate object that has an account within the server. Examples are rooms, vehicles, or items of equipment. They can be "invited" to meetings just as users can be, which is the equivalent of booking them. Resources can be managed by users who have to approve requests for booking them, or be available on a simple first come, first served basis with no need to ask approval from the user who manages the resource. As with regular users, you can choose whether to permit double-booking.

Resource accounts also manage diaries for enterprisewide information, such as travel schedules. If you create a resource called Travel Plans, for example, users can "invite" this resource to their schedule with details of what and when the travel is. Then by querying the Travel Plans resource you can see an overall picture of corporate travel arrangements. A Holiday resource can be used in a similar fashion.

To create a resource, connect to the Calendar Administrator as a suitably privileged user. On the Calendar Management tab, click the Resource button, and click Create. When you create a resource you specify some or all of these attributes:

- *Enable account*: Allows the use of the resource if checked.
- *Resource name*: Displays the name of the resource.
- *Password*: Allows you to connect to Calendar as the resource and view the resource's schedule.
- *User ID*: Identifies the user in the Oracle Internet Directory; defaults to the resource name.
- *Resource number*: Identifies the user. An optional additional identifier.
- *Capacity*: Specifies the number of people the resource can accept. This is informational only; it is not a limit that will be enforced.
- *Description*: Provides a free text area.
- *Resource information URL*: Links to any web page that may describe the resource.
- *E-mail, telephone, fax*: Provides the resource's contact details.
- *Address*: Specifies the physical location of the resource.
- *Allow double-booking*: Offers either "No – First Come, First Served" or "Yes – Requires Approval."
- *Notify approver by e-mail*: Generates an e-mail to the approver for resources whose booking must be approved. Otherwise, you are relying on the approver viewing his notifications in a Calendar client.
- *Approver e-mail*: Provides the address to which to send booking notifications.
- *Availability*: Shows availability of the resource. Every resource can have two times between which it is available, which may be different for each day of the week. The default is all day, every day.
- *Resource time zone*: Specifies the time zone displayed to users when they make bookings. The resource will pick up the time zone of the node if you don't specify a different one.

By default any user can book a resource. To make a resource restricted so only certain users or groups can book it you must navigate to the resource's Access Rights page and clear the Can Invite Me check box. This means that only nominated users and groups can book the resource by "inviting" it to a meeting.

To control who can book a resource click the Modify Access Rights button on the resource's Access Rights page. There you can select users and groups whose members will be allowed to book the resource by clicking the Grant Rights button.

It is also possible to create resources through the `uniuser` command-line utility as shown here:

```
uniuser -resource -add R=HQcanteen/PSW=password1 -n 1
```

This will prompt you for the SYSOP password and then you can add a resource called HQcanteen (with a password set to password1) to the node with Node-ID 1. All other attributes will be on default. Other options of the utility let you configure all aspects of the resource; but unless you have a compelling reason to do this it will usually be easier to use the Calendar Administrator tool.

Event Accounts

An event Calendar account informs users about pending scheduled events. Users have read-only access to the event account but can copy events from it into their own schedules. An event account is conceptually just another user with a schedule, as is a resource.

To create an event, connect to the Calendar Administration tool and click the Event Calendars button on the Calendar Management tab. Then to schedule occurrences of the event, either connect to the Calendar Administrator, select the event, and click the Manage Events icon or, using a desktop client (not the web client), connect as the event itself.

As with resources, it is also possible to create and manage events with command-line utilities.

Alerts: Reminders and Notifications

Calendar alerts come in one of two forms: a *reminder*, which is a message regarding a pending scheduled happening; or a *notification*, which is an informative message regarding something that has happened. In either case, they are delivered by corporatewide services, the `unicwsd` processes. Delivery methods are e-mail, SMS, and whatever wireless services are provided by your Oracle Collaboration Suite installation. Alerts will also be displayed in the various Calendar clients.

When creating a meeting or any other event, you can select whether you want a reminder and when you want to receive it. The client-server tools can deliver this reminder as a pop-up window; the web client can only accept it as an e-mail. When a user receives an invitation to a meeting, he can similarly choose to set up a reminder. The person scheduling the meeting cannot force invitees to have reminders set.

A notification of, for example, a meeting invitation can be delivered by e-mail or by wireless, but the method is not under the control of the user setting up the meeting. All he can do is specify the users and request e-mail notification. The logic behind this is that the user creating the meeting will not be aware of which invitees have wireless capability configured. Each user must decide for himself, using his client program, whether he wants to be notified through wireless services when meetings or events are created, modified, or deleted.

Configuring the Calendar Application System

The Calendar Application System is the web interface to Calendar. It is not as rich a user interface as that available through the client-server tools, which are the Calendar Desktop Client and the Oracle Connector for Microsoft Outlook; but it has many advantages associated with web applications.

The Calendar Application System consists of three services: the web client, web services, and Oracle Mobile Data Sync. Each of these is enabled through the Calendar Application System itself. Access to the Calendar Application System services is through the Web Cache and Apache web listener of an Oracle Collaboration Suite middle tier instance.

The Calendar Application System Architecture

The Calendar Application System has several architectural advantages over the client-server tools for both the end users and the system administrators.

From the end users' point of view, first, the client-server tools require a local installation of the software. This is not a major exercise, particularly as the Oracle Collaboration Suite web interface includes links for downloading it, but the tools will not be available on public terminals such as those in Internet cafés. Second, the client-server tools restrict usage to computers. You can't run them on, for example, a mobile telephone. The Oracle Connector for Microsoft Outlook is particularly restricted as it can only run on a Windows PC; the Calendar Desktop Client is also available for Linux or Macintosh. Third, the client-server connection must be persistent. If it is broken, the session will be lost. Users also need a fast and reliable network connection to the Calendar server.

On the server side, the client server tools require a dedicated server process, a `uniengd` engine, for each session. This is expensive in machine resources. At any given moment a typical user is not actually doing anything; of hundreds or thousands of logged-on users, it may be that only a few are actively using Calendar. It is in the nature of the application that users will remain logged on all day, but will only make use of it intermittently. However, the nature of multitasking operating systems such as UNIX and Windows is such that even if a process is idle, it must still be brought on and off CPU regularly, according to the operating system's pre-emptive multitasking algorithm. This process, known as a *context switch*, is very expensive in CPU terms. Registers must be loaded from main memory to rebuild the state of the process; there may be paging activity; and then there will certainly be CPU activity as the process checks whether it has to do anything. Then when the process relinquishes the CPU, the registers must be saved back to main memory, and so on. This activity occurs even if the Calendar user is not doing anything. Context switches between hundreds or thousands of idle processes are a major cause of performance degradation on operating systems such as UNIX or Windows, though other operating systems with more sophisticated time-sharing algorithms may not necessarily suffer from this problem.

Calendar Application System users connect to the Calendar server from a browser through a CGI program running on the middle tier. From the users' point of view, this solves the problems of the client-server tools. The only software the user needs is some kind of web client, and the user's connection to the middle tier is over HTTP, which does not use stateful connections. This makes it usable over the slow and unreliable links that typify the Internet. The connections from the Calendar Application System to the Calendar server are persistent and stateful, but these will be over a reliable local area network connection, or even within the same host.

The Calendar system administrators will also appreciate the use of the Calendar Application System because it does not create one Calendar session and therefore launch one `uniengd` process for each connected user. The Calendar Application System is a CGI program, the `ocas.fcgi` executable controlled by the modfastcgi Apache module. Each `ocas.fcgi` instance can support a number of end-user browser sessions, but it will only open one persistent connection to the Calendar server. Therefore, it will only launch one `uniegd` process. In effect, several browser sessions to the Calendar Application System are multiplexed through one session to the Calendar server, with the middle tier keeping track of the state of each end-user session. Experience shows that 20 to 40 sessions can be serviced by one `ocas.fcgi` process. This architecture will reduce dramatically the number of processes and context switches required on the host. There may also be memory savings, as detailed in a later section.

The Calendar Application System Components

The enabling structure for the Calendar Application System is running instances of the CGI program `ocas.fcgi`, controlled by the `ochecklet_fcgi` program. The components are the web client, web services, and Mobile Data Sync.

The web client is the user interface to Calendar. Users connect to it from a browser. The client has two aspects, the end-user interface and the Calendar Administrator, and has been extensively described already.

The web services offer an interface that third-party applications can use. A web service is a process that can accept SOAP (Simple Object Access Protocol) requests and make appropriate responses. SOAP is a layered protocol that runs over HTTP. It defines a mechanism for issuing requests to processes that conform to a standard format and generating standard format replies. SOAP should provide complete abstraction of the implementation of a process from its presentation to the outside world. When you issue a SOAP request to a web service and get a SOAP reply, you have no way of knowing whether the service is implemented by, for instance, a Java servlet running in an Oracle Application Server instance, or by a secretary with a card index. As long as the service is concealed by a WSDL (Web Services Description Language) wrapper, a SOAP-compliant application can use it. By offering the Calendar server to the web as a web service with publicly defined capabilities, Oracle Corporation has provided a mechanism whereby any developer can interrogate and update Calendar data and integrate the Calendar functions into his own applications.

The Calendar Mobile Data Sync facility opens up Calendar data to any SyncML-compliant device. SyncML is a standard markup language comprehensible to many mobile devices, though each vendor will have its own proprietary implementation. Oracle Collaboration Suite ships with hundreds of device drivers that can make Mobile Data Sync work with virtually all mobile devices—certainly all popular cell phones and PDAs. This means that users can synchronize data in their Calendar accounts with data stored locally in whatever mobile device they happen to use, with data transfer in both directions.

The Configuration Files

The Calendar Application System is configured with five files, all residing in the directory `$ORACLE_HOME/ocas/conf`. They are the following:

- `ocal.conf`
- `ocas.conf`
- `ocwc.conf`
- `ocws.conf`
- `ocst.conf`

The `ocal.conf` file is included in the `httpd.conf` file (described in Chapter 2) and configures the middle tier Apache web listener to accept URLs for the Calendar Application System. It has a set of directives that create the virtual paths used by end users to access the Calendar Application System and maps them onto the `ocas.fcgi` program. This is an extract from a typical file:

```
ScriptAlias /ocas-bin/ "/OCS/product/10.1.1/ocs_1/apps/ocas/bin/"
ScriptAlias /ocws-bin/ "/OCS/product/10.1.1/ocs_1/apps/ocas/bin/"
ScriptAlias /ocst-bin/ "/OCS/product/10.1.1/ocs_1/apps/ocas/bin/"
ScriptAlias /global-bin/ "/OCS/product/10.1.1/ocs_1/apps/ocas/bin/"
Alias /ocas/ "/OCS/product/10.1.1/ocs_1/apps/ocas/htdocs/"
<Directory "/OCS/product/10.1.1/ocs_1/apps/ocas/bin/">
        SetHandler fastcgi-script
        AllowOverride None
        Options None
        Order allow,deny
        Allow from all
</Directory>
```

The ScriptAlias directives create virtual paths, but unlike an Alias directive that creates a path for serving files, a ScriptAlias creates a path for executing files. All the ScriptAlias directives point to the same physical directory, which is defined by the <Directory> directive in the previous example. The SetHandler directive within the <Directory> directive states that the fastcgi-script module will run the files that are invoked, and then some security directives disable all the options that can weaken security.

The ocas.conf file configures the Calendar Application System, as implemented by the ocas.fcgi program. It contains pointers to the various dynamically linked shared object libraries (files suffixed with .DLL on Windows or with .so on Unix) that make up the system, and controls the ocas.fcgi processes themselves with settings for such factors as startup times and logging levels.

The remaining three files configure the three components: the web client, the web services, and Mobile Data Sync. It should never be necessary for an administrator to edit these files by hand, but if your installation requires custom developments it will be necessary for your developers to understand and perhaps adjust the directives within them.

Sizing the Calendar Installation

Critical to a successful implementation of Calendar is providing enough resources for the anticipated workload. Since Calendar does not use an Oracle instance and database, the standard facilities for estimating resource requirements are not available. These guidelines will give an indication of the resources required: disk space, memory, and network connections. The figures are based on numerous implementations of Calendar, though many are from its previous incarnation as the CorporateTime product marketed by Steltor.

Disk Space

Every Calendar account (whether a user, a resource, or an event) requires space for its persistent data, and active sessions require storage for transient data as well. A typical user will accumulate 2.5MB of persistent space per year, and a typical session will require an additional 2MB of temporary space. These figures will vary dramatically depending on use, but they do give a starting point. One particular contributing factor is the use of attachments to meeting invitations. The default installation permits attachments but restricts their size to 2MB; see the [LIMITS] section of the unison.ini file to confirm this. The persistent data and temporary data are stored in these directories:

```
$ORACLE_HOME/ocal/db/nodes/<node_name>
$ORACLE_HOME/ocal/db/tmp/<node_name>
```

The temporary data is more volatile than the persistent data but is not required after a session terminates. This means that your system administrators may want to adjust their logical volume striping strategy to give the temporary data device higher performance and the persistent data device higher fault tolerance.

To complete the arithmetic, consider an installation with 2,000 users in total, of whom 1,000 are expected to be online at any moment. If the installation is planned to store data for three years, the nodes will require 15GB of disk space for permanent data and 2GB of disk space for temporary data.

Main Memory

The Calendar processes run in virtual memory. They do not know or care if this virtual memory has been paged out to swap space or is currently mapped into the host's main memory (or RAM), but performance will deteriorate dramatically if the host is having to swap. Memory is used for three purposes: for each logged-on user; for Calendar background processes; and (on some platforms) for disk caching.

Wherever possible, the Calendar processes will use shared memory. This means that it doesn't make any difference whether one user is connected or a thousand; their uniengd processes will be mapped onto the same shared memory segments. But to maintain each session, there is also a need for private memory that cannot be shared. It is this requirement that needs to be calculated.

Calendar users running a client-server tool (either the Calendar Desktop Client or the Oracle Connector for Outlook) will require about 1MB of nonshared server memory each. This is divided between 750KB taken by the session's uniengd process and 250KB used by the other server processes. Users connecting through the web client may need significantly less. This is because the web client, as implemented by the ocas.fcgi program, can in effect multiplex a number of end-user sessions from browsers through a small number of sessions against the Calendar server. Whereas the client-server tools require a one-for-one relationship between currently connected end users and Calendar sessions—that is, one uniengd process per connection—the web client only requires one Calendar session, or one uniengd process, per ocas.fcgi process. The number of browser sessions that can share a single ocas.fcgi process before the fast-CGI performance begins to degrade is a matter for experiment, but typically 20 to 40 users can share an ocas.fcgi process. Even though each ocas.fcgi process will require about 15MB of memory, the overall memory demand is therefore lower for web client users than for users of the client-server tools.

Continuing the previous example of 1,000 concurrently connected users, if 500 are using the Desktop Client or the Oracle Connector for Outlook they will require 500MB of memory on the server. If the remaining 500 are using the web client, and 20 ocas.fcgi processes are launched, they will require a further 300MB of memory.

The requirement for disk cache memory will be platform-specific. Operating systems such as Linux, typically running on relatively unsophisticated hardware, will use any spare memory as a disk cache. Experience shows that 250KB of cache memory per session will significantly improve performance. More advanced platforms will have caching managed by the disk controllers themselves, so this is less important, but assuming a Linux-type environment this comes to another 250MB.

So for 1,000 concurrent users, the nonsharable server memory requirement could be of the order of 1GB. In a multinode environment, there will also be 1MB required for each process launched by the Synchronous Network Connection processes. The number of these processes is discussed in the following section.

Network Connections

There are two categories of network connections to consider: those from incoming user sessions, each of which requires a `uniengd` process; and those between the servers launched by the `unisncd` processes.

The first category is simple to calculate: one connection per concurrent user of a desktop client, plus one per `ocas.fcgi` process. So in the previous example, there will be 515 `uniengd` processes required, apportioned across hosts, servers, and nodes according to the strategy chosen for segmenting users. The number of connections required between servers will depend on the number of requests from users that require access to a remote node, within their own server or hosted by a remote server. The closer the assignment of users to nodes matches the needs for users to communicate with each other, the lower the number of internode connections that will be required.

As a guideline for sizing the number of connections, the absolute minimum is one connection from each server to each node. For a small installation (with less than 250 concurrently connected users per node) two connections each may be adequate; for a larger installation (250 to 1,000 connected users per node) four may be adequate.

Taking the previous example of 1,000 concurrent users, assume them to be connected to eight nodes managed by two servers: four nodes managed by each server. Further assume that the traffic between nodes is even, so that the connections can be symmetrical. Each server will need two connections to each node, making 32 in total. If, however, each node were managed by its own server, the requirement would expand to 128, which is a significant overhead on top of the 550 sessions required for users and would need to be included in the memory calculations.

Command-Line Utilities

Because Calendar can be installed as a stand-alone product, it comes with a completely self-contained set of management tools. These are delivered as a set of command-line utilities. When running Calendar within the Oracle Collaboration Suite environment, many of these are not essential but there will be times when they are very convenient. The more important ones are described in the following sections. All the utilities reside in the `$ORACLE_HOME/ocal/bin` directory and have names prefixed with `uni`.

This is only a brief description of some of the utilities and why you would use them. Refer to the Calendar Reference manual for the full list, with complete information on their capabilities and syntax.

unistart, unistop, and unistatus

The `unistart` and `unistop` commands control the various background processes that make up a Calendar instance. By default, the whole server is started or stopped, but with syntax variations you can choose to start or stop just some of the processes. Also by default, all the nodes associated with the server will be started or stopped, but syntax variations let you start or stop individual nodes if necessary. The `unistatus` command shows which processes of the server are running and can also give information on individual node activity.

It is possible to start and stop the whole server or individual processes using the `opmnctl` utility or Application Server Control, but neither of these tools can start or stop an individual node. Also, you can use the operating system security facilities to give your Calendar administrator access to these command-line utilities without giving him access to `opmnctl`, which would let him manage the whole of Oracle Collaboration Suite.

unib2lendian and unil2bendian

It is possible to move a node from one host to another host and start a server on the new host that will open the node. In principle, all that is required is to copy the node's files into a directory on the new host with a name that reflects the node name, and copy the relevant section of the `unison.ini` file from the original server to the new server.

A problem that can arise when doing this is that some platforms are little endian and others are big endian. This distinction defines how the operating system interprets a byte: should it be read from left to right, or from right to left? When copying a node from a host that uses one endian format to a host that uses the other endian format, you must convert the node using either `unib2lendian` or `unil2bendian`.

Table 7-2 shows the endian format used on some of the more popular platforms.

Table 7-2. *Endian Formats Used by Different Platforms*

Platform	Endian Format
Solaris SPARC (32-bit)	Big
Solaris SPARC (64-bit)	Big
Microsoft Windows IA (32-bit)	Little
Linux IA (32-bit)	Little
AIX-based systems (64-bit)	Big
HP-UX (64-bit)	Big
HP Tru64 UNIX	Little
HP-UX IA (64-bit)	Big
Linux IA (64-bit)	Little
HP Open VMS	Little
Microsoft Windows IA (64-bit)	Little
IBM zSeries-based Linux	Big
Linux 64-bit for AMD	Little
Apple Mac OS	Big
Microsoft Windows 64-bit for AMD	Little

uniaddnode

This is the command to create a new node database or to reinitialize an existing database. The initialization will fail if the utility detects that there are user accounts in the node; these must be removed first. Variations in syntax let this command create just one node or many nodes in one operation. Once the nodes are created, they must be brought into the node network, either by editing the `nodes.ini` file by hand, or by using the `uninode` utility.

uninode

This is the tool for setting up and administering a Calendar node network. You can only run `uninode` on the server that is (or will be) storing the `nodes.ini` file. This should be the master node in the cluster, which for an Oracle Collaboration Suite installation is always the first middle tier instance. As a simple example, consider an organization with offices in London, Harare, and Munich. Each office has been running its own Calendar server, some with multiple nodes, but after setting up a fast and reliable corporate network that can link the offices, you want to connect the servers into a network. You have decided that the London office will be the master node in the cluster from where you will run your administration commands.

The first point to check is that all the nodes across all the servers have different Node-ID numbers; you cannot put two nodes with the same Node-ID into a network. If any Node-IDs are duplicated, you will have to add a new node (choosing a Node-ID that is not already in use) with `uniaddnode` and move the users from the old node into the new node with the `unimvuser` utility, whose purpose is for moving a user from one node to another. (The nodes can be on different servers.) Then delete the old node.

To create the node network, take the following steps:

1. Log in to the London host, `london.bplc.com`.
2. Create the `nodes.ini` file with the `uninode -init` command.
3. Add the nodes from the three servers:

```
uninode -add -host london.bplc.com:5730
uninode -add -host harare.bplc.com:5730
uninode -add -host munich.bplc.com:5730
```

4. The `nodes.ini` file will be populated with all the nodes, but they will not be included in the network:

```
- H=london.bplc.com:5730/N=1
- H=london.bplc.com:5730/N=2
- H=harare.bplc.com:5730/N=3
- H=munich.bplc.com:5730/N=4
- H=munich.bplc.com:5730/N=5
```

5. Edit the file to include the nodes, with whatever aliases, groups, and Synchronous Network Connections are required:

```
+ H=london.bplc.com:5730/N=1/ALIAS=HeadQuarters
+ H=london.bplc.com:5730/N=2/ALIAS=Development
+ H=harare.bplc.com:5730/N=3/ALIAS=Harare
+ H=munich.bplc.com:5730/N=4/ALIAS=DE-Sales/GR=Germany
+ H=munich.bplc.com:5730/N=5/ALIAS=DE-Support/GR=Germany
all:2
```

6. Force the servers to contact each other and implement the network:

```
uninode -apply
```

unidbbackup and unidbrestore

You can back up a Calendar node with operating system utilities, but this must never be done while the node is in use and therefore requires downtime. The `unidbbackup` utility can back up a node while it is running. The backup includes all the files in the node's directory, as well as the server's configuration files. The `unidbrestore` utility will extract a node's data and (by default) the server configuration from a backup made with `unidbbackup`.

unitzinfo

Calendar uses its own format for time zones. No variations (not even in case) are acceptable. The `unitzinfo` utility can list all the acceptable time zones (which should be enough for anyone) or show the time zone for any one node.

unidsdiff and unidssync

Calendar accounts (for users, events, and resources) should always be synchronized with user accounts in the Oracle Internet directory, but it is possible for them to diverge. This could occur if, for example, a Calendar node were restored independently of the Oracle Internet Directory. It could also happen that certain user attributes could be changed in the directory and not propagated to Calendar because the Calendar server was not running.

`unidsdiff` will pass through the node's users matching them to user accounts in the Oracle Internet Directory and where it finds differences correct them. The corrections are made on the assumption that the source of truth is the Oracle Internet Directory. If an account exists in Calendar and not in the Oracle Internet Directory, it will be removed from the Calendar node. If an account exists in the Oracle Internet Directory but not in Calendar, the account will be adjusted to show that it has not been provisioned in Calendar. This utility should be run after a node restore or an infrastructure database point-in-time recovery.

`unidssync` will correct directory-related information in Calendar, such as address books, so that it matches information in Oracle Internet Directory. This utility should be run as part of a regular maintenance schedule to refresh the common address book and the global address list, as follows:

```
unidssync -absync [-n <node_list>]
unidssync -galrefresh [-n <node_list>]
```

The optional `<node_list>` argument can be set as a list of Node-ID numbers; this is required if the server is running more than one node.

Monitoring and Statistical Utilities

There is a set of utilities that give comprehensive reports on Calendar activity, both current sessions and historical data. There are also utilities that report on memory usage and process activity. The information you can glean from these reports will be more than adequate to assist with tuning and deciding upon the optimum server and network configuration. These utilities, which can take a large number of arguments to control the output, are unistat, unistats, and unistatus.

CHAPTER 8

Configuring Content Services

Content Services is the file-serving component of Oracle Collaboration Suite: one of the most impressive parts of the product. It is also one of the most complicated. No one ever said that powerful applications had to be simple. From the users' point of view, Content Services is simplicity itself, but the configuration is a different matter. Once successfully configured, Content Services is to a large extent self-administering but there are various maintenance tasks for both content and users.

This treatment begins with detail of the Content Services architecture, followed by the setup steps.

Content Services Architecture

An Oracle Collaboration Suite installation will typically include one Content Services domain. A *domain* is a combination of an Oracle database that stores the Content Services data, and one or more Oracle Application Server middle tier instances that host the Content Services nodes. End users connect to a node to access the data. It is possible to support multiple domains within one Oracle Collaboration Suite, but since it is not possible to share data across domains (other than by duplicating it through manually initiated procedures, such as large-scale copying) there is little point in this unless the domains are supporting groups of workers who are completely separate in business terms, in which case, they may well have their own Oracle Collaboration Suite installations anyway.

The Content Services Database

All Content Services data is stored in an Oracle database. This requires creating a schema to hold the data and the code used to manage it. A *schema* is a container for data objects (such as tables) and procedural objects (such as PL/SQL procedures). You connect to a schema by logging on to the database as the schema owner or as another database user who has been given permission to access the schema. The Content Services data is stored by default in the schema CONTENT, with two other schemas whose names are derived from this, CONTENT$CM and CONTENT$ID, that are used for integration purposes.

The installation process creates the Content Services schemas: the tables that will store the files themselves; the tables that store metadata about the files; and the code for managing the files and access to them. These schemas are created in every Oracle Collaboration Suite infrastructure database when installing the Oracle home, along with the schemas for the metadata repository, the Identity Management components, and other product data schemas.

It is possible to use just the one database for all these purposes, but such an arrangement would only be suitable for a relatively small-scale installation. In most circumstances, the schema will be in a database created specially for this purpose and tuned accordingly. The installer can create the database, or the schema can be created in a preexisting database.

There is no effective limit to the amount of data, in terms of the number of files or their size, that can be uploaded into Content Services. The files are stored as large objects (known as LOBs) associated with regular tables. LOBs can be very large indeed. Release 10*g* of the Oracle database places no real restrictions on the size of any one LOB; terabyte LOBs are theoretically possible. The number of files is limited by the maximum number of rows that can be inserted into a table. Again, there are no real limits on this; thousands of millions are possible. A database with a Content Services schema that contains millions of files will be a challenge to the database administrators, but even though it may well be terabytes big, standard administration procedures will apply. If a single database instance can't provide adequate response times, RAC can take the scalability to whatever is required. It is however not possible to spread one domain's data across multiple databases.

There are several tablespaces used for storing Content Services data:

- `CONTENT_IFS_MAIN`: This stores the tables that hold metadata describing documents.
- `CONTENT_IFS_LOB_N`: This stores the BLOB (binary large object) columns that hold the actual documents for nonindexed documents.
- `CONTENT_IFS_LOB_I`: This stores the BLOB columns that hold the actual documents for indexed documents.
- `CONTENT_IFS_CTX_I`, `CONTENT_IFS_CTX_K`, `CONTENT_IFS_CTX_X`: These tablespaces store the indexing data used by Search, which is described in Chapter 13.

The Content Services Nodes

A *node* is the Content Services application software. This is written in Java and runs on an Oracle Application Server middle tier instance in an OC4J component. Nodes monitor addresses on certain protocols for connection requests from users who may connect with a variety of tools. There is no necessity for a node to run on the same machine as the Content Services database, and indeed this would usually be detrimental for performance. If one node is not sufficient, the domain can be expanded to include many nodes on different middle tier Application Server instances on different machines. The default Content Services installation includes two nodes: a regular node and an HTTP node.

A regular node runs FTP and FTPS protocol servers. These monitor one or more ports on one or more addresses of the host machine for FTP and FTP with SSL requests. To the user, a regular node looks like a regular FTP server; you can even run it on the standard ports (port 21 for FTP, port 990 for FTPS), provided that the server does not already have its own native FTP services running at the same time. Note that Content Services does not include a protocol server for SFTP; to clear up any possible confusion, FTPS is FTP with SSL, whereas SFTP is the file transfer element of Secure Shell. Earlier versions of Content Services—when it was known as iFS, the Internet File System, an acronym that still persists in a number of administration areas—could support additional protocols, including SMB and NFS. With the current release, support has been restricted in line with current Internet standards to FTP and HTTP.

An HTTP node runs the Content Services web application. This is a servlet that presents the Content Services web interface to browser users, including WebDAV calls (remember that WebDAV is a layered protocol which runs over HTTP). Access to an HTTP node will be through whatever port(s) the middle tier's Apache web listener is monitoring, and will usually be front-ended by a Web Cache.

Regular nodes also run the Content Services agents. *Agents* are processes that carry out certain tasks according to predefined schedules or events. A number of agents are preconfigured, such as the agent that can delete content that is older than an expiry date, and the agent that calculates whether users have reached their space quota; and there are toolkits for developing custom-designed agents.

Identity Management and Sites

Content Services relies on the Oracle Internet Directory for authentication and account provisioning. Creating a user in the directory will create an account in Content Services, configured according to whatever defaults are set up for the site. A site is based on an Identity Management realm, a *realm* being an area, including users, defined within the directory. Users in one site do not have access to data stored in another site. There is a default site created at install time, based on the default realm. This may be all that many organizations ever need, but if the one site does not give adequate separation, you can create additional realms within the directory and sites within Content Services later. Each site can then have its own rules for space quota or content expiration, for example.

The process that creates Content Services accounts from Oracle Internet Directory accounts is the Oracle Internet Directory Credential Manager Agent. This runs by default every 15 minutes. However, you can configure on-demand provisioning, so that if a user attempts to connect to Content Services before this time is up, the account gets created straightaway.

Preinstallation Planning

You can install Content Services totally on defaults and then configure to requirements later—but clearly, it is better to have an idea of what will be needed at the time of installation. Perhaps the most vital decisions are about selection of protocols and sizing. These will determine what nodes (and how many) to create. There is also the question of whether to implement Oracle Records Management.

Clients and Protocol Support

The FTP and FTPS protocol server node should be usable by any client with the appropriate client tools; virtually all client machines will have an FTP client installed by default, whether they are using Windows, Macintosh, Linux, or any desktop UNIX. Whether you wish to enable FTP is a different matter. It is a very efficient file transfer protocol, but may have bad security implications. For this reason, it is disabled after the standard installation. You may wish to enable it for an initial migration of files from existing file servers (Oracle recommends FTP for bulk transfers) and then disable it later.

The problem with FTP is that it transmits passwords unencrypted. If the Content Services FTP protocol server were to prompt for and validate the users' Oracle Internet Directory Single

Sign-On passwords, the whole security structure would be blown apart; a malicious user could monitor the network traffic, intercept a user's username and password as transmitted with an FTP connection request, and then use them to access the user's complete Oracle Collaboration Suite environment, and indeed any other Single Sign-On–enabled applications. This is not Oracle's problem—it is a problem with the FTP protocol—but the FTP protocol server does provide a way around it. Before a user can connect to an FTP protocol server, he must create a separate FTP password. It is this password, not his Single Sign-On password, that he must provide when using FTP with Content Services. The FTP password is stored within the Oracle Internet Directory and has no other purpose. Users set their own FTP password through the Oracle Internet Directory Self-Service Console. If this password is ever intercepted, the access thus gained will be limited to the data accessible to the user with FTP. It is important that when selecting an FTP password, users do not use their same password as for Single Sign-On; this should be mentioned as part of user training.

An alternative to this use of a separate FTP password is to enable the FTPS protocol server. This will apply the usual SSL public key encryption mechanism, so that the user's password is encrypted before transmission. The FTPS protocol server is accessed with the Single Sign-On password and will usually be much more convenient, but it does require all users to have an FTPS client.

The HTTP protocol server uses the standard Single Sign-On security model: it will check for the Single Sign-On cookie within the client browser and accept the connection if the cookie is present and valid. If it isn't, the user gets redirected to the Single Sign-On server. Subsequent data transfers to and from the protocol server will be over HTTP, or HTTPS if the middle tier Application Server instance has been configured accordingly.

The WebDAV protocol, layered on top of HTTP, lets users lock documents when they download them. It is also possible to enable *versioning*, so that saving the document back to the server will create a new version while retaining the previous version. This functionality is not available with FTP. To use WebDAV, users need an appropriate client. Probably the most commonly used WebDAV-capable client is Windows XP Explorer, through the My Network Places desktop icon.

WebDAV is also used to implement a drive-mapping capability for Windows users. From the user's point of view, this simulates SMB (Server Message Block) file sharing; he can map a drive letter to what appears to be a file server share and treat it as he would any shared folder on a Windows file server. This functionality is enabled through Oracle Drive, a utility the user must download and install. The download is available to all users from the first window seen after logging on to the Portal front end to Oracle Collaboration Suite.

Server Sizing

The Oracle Collaboration Suite Deployment Guide gives examples of sizing for middle tier Content Services nodes and for the content Services database. The examples are all based on the Content Services installation used within Oracle Corporation. This has about 40,000 registered users and uses multiple Linux machines for the middle tier and a Solaris machine for the database server. What is not made clear is that users of this system have often been disappointed with its performance. The major problems have been with space quotas enforced on users and with access speeds.

Quotas are a matter for each system administrator to determine based on discussions with the user community, and by hardware cost and availability. It is often said that the economics of high-speed disk storage are now such that there need be no limits on the space made available to each user, but when you are talking about the terabytes required for an organization of thousands of staff, each of whom require many megabytes (or even gigabytes) of file space, quotas will be required. Access speeds are largely dependent on network bandwidth. If users in a geographically distributed organization are used to having local file servers, they will notice a drop in performance when all the data is migrated to a Content Services installation and the local servers are decommissioned. However, these two problems pale into insignificance when compared with the management benefits of having central storage, backup, and administration, and that is even before considering the collaboration advantages of centralizing data where it is available to members of geographically distributed project teams.

Extrapolating the figures derived from Oracle's internal implementation leads to these (very approximate) conclusions:

On the middle tier machines, 200 concurrently connected users can saturate one CPU. It makes little difference whether the CPU is Intel CISC architecture or a RISC architecture processor such as SPARC or PowerPC; the higher clock speeds typically found in Intel processors compensate for the pipelining of the RISC chips. 1GB to 2GB of memory will be adequate to support this workload. Disk space is minimal: only a few gigabytes for the Oracle home. On the database server machine, CPU and memory equivalent to the sum of the middle tier machines will be more than adequate. Disk space will be 10GB for the Oracle home and the seed database (including temporary and undo space), and the anticipated volume of files to be stored plus 20 percent.

Thus, for a small organization with 500 Content Services users, half of whom are active at any time, twin CPU machines (which will typically come with 4GB of RAM) will be fine for both the middle tier and the database server. If each user on average uses 100MB of file storage, 80GB of disk will be adequate for the Content Services database. Of course, there will also be a machine required for the infrastructure and resources on the middle tier for running other Collaboration Suite components.

Use of Oracle Records Management

All organizations have a need to store *records*: data usually in the form of a file that must be available to certain users for a certain time frame, with certain access restrictions. Apart from operational needs, there will be legal requirements as well. For example, the rules regarding the retention and control of financial or medical data are, in most countries, defined by legislation. Oracle Records Management is an application shipped with Content Services that some sites may decide to implement to manage their records. Oracle Records is installed by default, but enabling it is a matter of choice.

Oracle Records ensures that record data is authentic, retrievable as necessary, and neither destroyed prematurely nor retained longer than needed. The facilities let users declare data as records, control access to records, dispose of records, and manage policies. Policies may cover retention periods, disposition actions, record freezes, and record searches. There are integration points for use of BPEL (Business Process Execution Language) applications, and also hardware retention policies. The hardware integration is either to Network Appliance SnapLock devices or to EMC Centera devices.

If your organization decides to enable Oracle Records Management, there is documentation relating to this.

Content Services Content Management

The Content Services application component is a file server, but much of its superiority over conventional file servers stems from the fact that the data is not stored as files on disk, but as rows in a database. This means that all user access is filtered through an intelligent layer of application and database processing. When a user accesses a file that is stored in Content Services, he is not reading or writing the server's disk system: he is executing `select`, `insert`, `update`, and `delete` commands against a database. These commands are wrapped up in many layers of code that let Content Services offer such capabilities as virus checking, transparent data archiving (known as *aging*), versioning, and intelligent use of different document formats. It is also possible to index files stored in Content Services, with the indexes crossing over all the document types; this is described in Chapter 13, which details the Search component.

Virus Control

Content Services is integrated with SAVSE, the Symantec AntiVirus Scan Engine. The code is part of Content Services, but to use it there must be a SAVSE server available. This server will maintain virus definitions and control the operation of the SAVSE engine. This can be the same server that is used by Mail. When installing the SAVSE server according to Symantec's instructions, or configuring an existing SAVSE server for use by Content Services, these points should be remembered:

- *SAVSE can use two communications protocols*: ICAP (Internet Content Adaptation Protocol), or SAVSE Native Protocol. Content Services can only use ICAP (unlike Mail, which can use either), and the SAVSE server must be configured accordingly.
- *SAVSE can run in four modes*: scan only; scan and repair; scan and delete; and scan and repair or delete. Content Services can only use the first two modes.
- *SAVSE must be configured to issue ICAP403 responses*: enabled with a setting in the SAVSE server configuration file.

Having installed and configured a SAVSE server appropriately, you must configure its operation within Content Services. From the Application Server Control home page, click the Content link (as shown in Figure 5-19 in Chapter 5) to reach the Content Services home page, shown in Figure 8-1.

Virus control is done in two phases. First, there is the scan. Once scanning is enabled, all documents will be scanned for viruses in real time whenever they are opened, if they have not been scanned previously with the current set of virus definitions. Any documents found to be infected are quarantined and cannot then be opened until they have been repaired. The repair happens asynchronously.

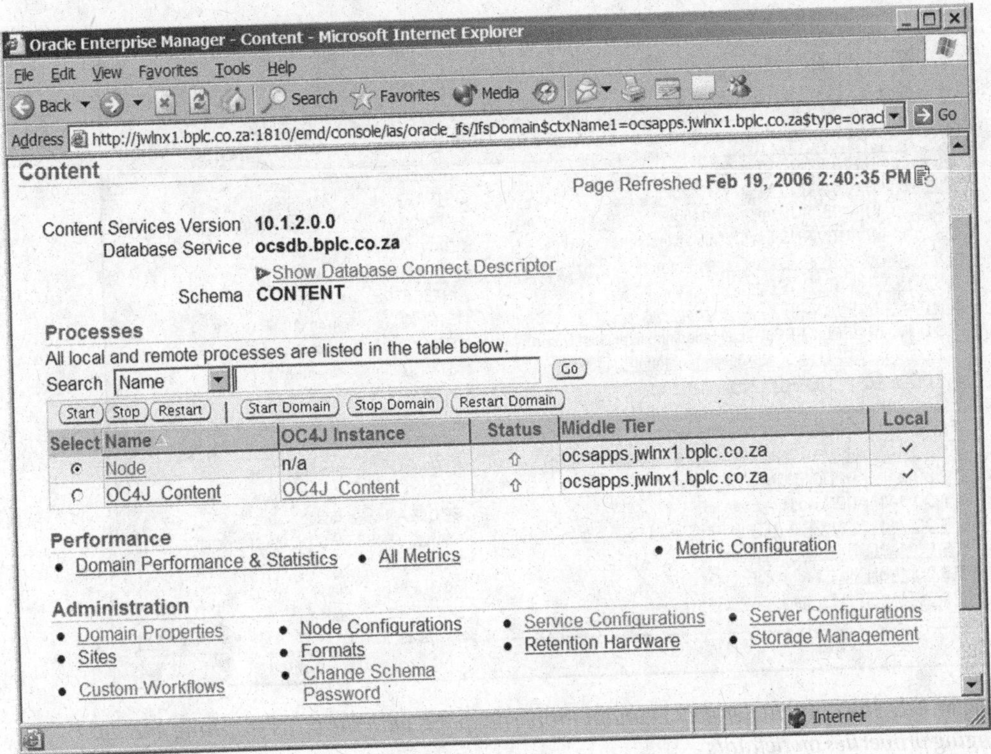

Figure 8-1. *The Content Services Application Server Control home page with both the Node service and the user access component running*

Clicking the Domain Properties link (toward the bottom left of Figure 8-1) will take you to the Domain Properties window, where several dozen properties (all with names prefixed IFS.DOMAIN) can be set (as shown in Figure 8-2). There are six properties that control scanning by SAVSE:

- `IFS.DOMAIN.ANTIVIRUS.Enabled`: This defaults to false, and must be set to true to enable virus scanning.
- `IFS.DOMAIN.ANTIVIRUS.Host`: This defaults to localhost, and should be set to the address of the SAVSE server.
- `IFS.DOMAIN.ANTIVIRUS.Port`: This defaults to 7117, which is the port the SAVSE server will be running on unless configured otherwise.
- `IFS.DOMAIN.ANTIVIRUS.MaxRepairAttempts`: This defaults to 10, and controls the number of times SAVSE will attempt to repair a quarantined file before giving up. If this figure is reached, the file will only be scanned and (perhaps) repaired with manual invocations of SAVSE.
- `IFS.DOMAIN.ANTIVIRUS.Implementation`: This cannot be edited and points to the Java class file that implements SAVSE.
- `IFS.DOMAIN.ANTIVIRUS.LastDefinitionUpdate`: This cannot be edited and is reset with every update of the virus definitions received from the SAVSE server.

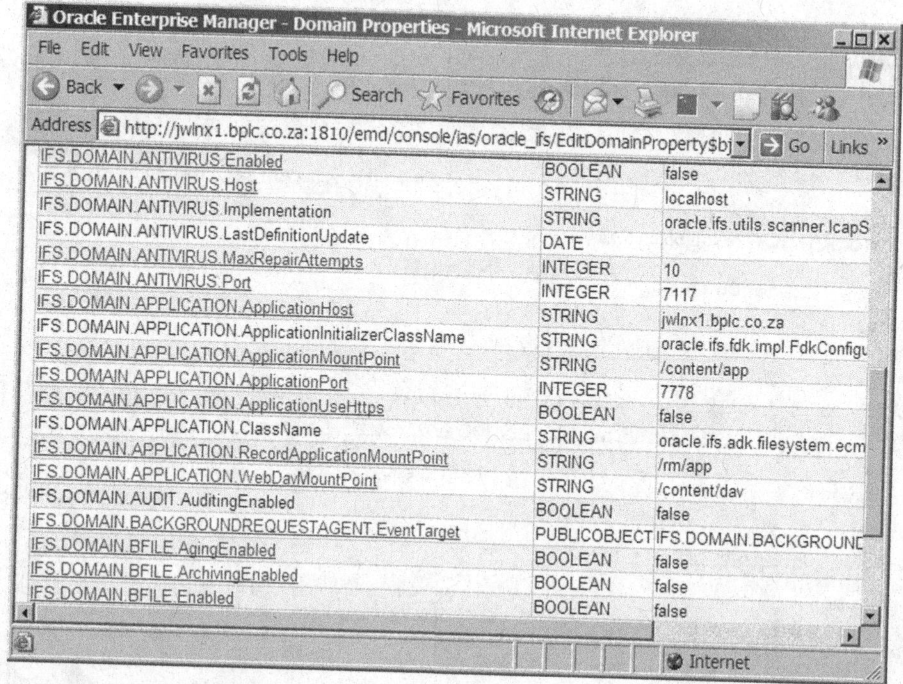

Figure 8-2. *The Content Services Domain Properties page, with the virus scanning and data aging properties on defaults*

Following any changes, restart the Content Services domain, either from an operating system prompt with

```
opmnctl restartproc process-type=Node
```

or through Application Server Control with the Restart Domain button visible in the middle of Figure 8-1.

Once configured, the Virus Repair Agent will start automatically. To confirm this, from the Content Services home page take the Node Configurations link. Select the node on which you want to run the agent (there will only be one node available, with the display name Node, unless you have created additional nodes) to reach the node's home page. All the possible agents are listed, and you will see that the agent named Virus Repair Agent is set by default to initial start.

Content Services will attempt to repair quarantine files according to a schedule. This defaults to once every 24 hours; the assumption is that virus definitions are unlikely to be updated more frequently than this, so there is no point in attempting repairs more often. To configure the virus repair process for more frequent attempts, take the Server Configurations link (toward the bottom right of Figure 8-1), and from the Server Configurations home page click the link for the Virus Repair Agent Configuration and adjust the property `IFS.SERVER.TIMER.ActivationPeriod`. This property value should be formatted as a number followed by a unit indicator, which may be *h* for hours, *m* for minutes, or *s* for seconds. The default is 24h. Whenever the Virus Repair Agent activates, according to this property, it will first contact the SAVSE server and retrieve any updates to the virus definition files and then attempt a repair of all quarantined items.

Virus scanning can have a significant impact on performance, but it may be possible to reduce this. First, certain file types can be excluded from virus scanning. The file types are identified by their MIME type (for those who need to know what every acronym means, MIME is Multipurpose Internet Mail Extensions, a standard for identifying the content of a file by its filename suffix) which can be used to prevent SAVSE from checking certain files that are unlikely to contain viruses. This can improve performance substantially. For example, files suffixed with .ZIP or .EXE are far more likely to contain a virus than files suffixed with .CAB or .DBF. Second, controlling the frequency of virus definition updates will reduce the number of scans. Once the definitions have been updated, *all* files opened (with the exception of those excluded by MIME type) will be scanned; there may therefore be a significant performance hit after the definition update until all popular files have been opened. Third, there is the performance of the SAVSE service; this is often said to be the most significant factor.

But overall, the performance impact of virus scanning is dependent on the pattern of access to the data in the file store. If the nature of the access is such that a large proportion of file reads are of files that have not been opened previously, the scanning impact will be far greater than if many files are read repeatedly. It follows from this that as a general rule there will always be a performance degradation after a virus definition update. But this should reduce as files that are accessed frequently are opened for the first time with the new definitions; the first user to open the file will take the performance hit of the scan, all other users will open the file without any scan taking place.

Data Aging

The default method for storing Content Services data is as BLOBs. BLOBs can be very large indeed; earlier release of the database restricted them to "only" 4GB, but the release 10*g* database used for Oracle Collaboration Suite 10*g* can theoretically store terabyte-size BLOBs. There is therefore no effective limit to the size of the documents that can be stored within Content Services. A BLOB is an Oracle internal data type used for defining a column of a table, but whereas other data types (such as NUMBER or VARCHAR2 for numeric or text columns) are stored inline, BLOBs are stored out of line. A column defined by an *inline* data type stores its data within the row of the table; an *out of line* data type stores only a pointer within the row that points to a location within a separate segment. The BLOB data resides in this second segment, not within the row itself. But even so, it is still within the database. Content Services stores its BLOBs in tablespaces dedicated to this purpose; a good DBA will monitor these tablespaces and store them on appropriately configured devices.

This technique enhances performance substantially, because the pattern of access to BLOB data tends to be very different to the pattern of access to other columns. Consider a simple example of uploading all your music CDs into a database. The table that stores the CDs will have a number of columns describing the music (artist, title, genre, etc.) followed by a column that stores the CD itself. Access to the descriptive columns will generally be small random reads as users fly all over the table using various indexed search criteria to identify the CD they want. But then once they have identified the CD of interest, there will be a continuous read of 600MB as it is downloaded. The Oracle BLOB data type lets the database administrator separate the one logical table into two physical segments; one segment contains the small columns, the other contains the BLOB column. Each segment can be configured appropriately for its typical access and stored on devices optimized for this.

Content Services uses the BLOB architecture but also makes use of an extension of the principle: the use of the BFILE data type. BLOBs are stored within the database, albeit in a manner that separates them from the transactional data with which they are associated. BFILEs take this further: the data is stored in operating system files external to the database. As far as programmers are concerned, a BFILE column is just another column, but the database administrator and the system administrator know that they are actually independent files stored in the database server's file system. All that remains within the database is a pointer to their physical location. This gives the administrator the freedom to store the BFILE data on any devices, even within tape libraries or on optical devices that would normally be unusable for an Oracle database.

Use of BFILEs gives you the ability to migrate a large part of the data stored within Content Services to comparatively low-cost and high-volume devices. A multiterabyte Content Services datastore might be uneconomical to maintain on high-speed disks, but if the actual data (not the indexing information) could be migrated to tape, it becomes feasible. Clearly, a sophisticated tape management system is necessary. For example, the ADSM (Adstar Distributed Storage Manager) tape library software from IBM can migrate files to tape if they have not been accessed for a certain period of time, while leaving them visible in the file system's directory; they are transferred back from tape to disk on demand, transparently to the process that demanded them. A number of other manufacturers have devices with a similar capability. Making use of such facilities gives Content Services the ability to store an effectively unlimited volume of data without the need for an unlimited amount of disk space.

The Content Services data aging facility automatically extracts data from BLOB columns stored within the database and converts it to BFILE columns stored as external files. The extraction criterion is when the data was last accessed. The server's operating system and hardware can then manage the files, transparently migrating them to tape if appropriate. But the moment the data is requested, Content Services will retrieve the data from the BFILE (which may involve the operating system extracting it from tape; Content Services will be unaware of this) and load it into a BLOB. This is necessary because BFILE data is read-only as far as the database is concerned; to make it read-write, it must be transferred back into a BLOB. All this will occur without the user's knowledge; he has no way of telling if the file he requested was stored as a BLOB within the database, or if it had been migrated to low-cost tape storage, though he may notice a minimal delay if the tape management system is overloaded.

To enable data aging, navigate to the Content Services Domain Properties window, as already described for enabling virus scanning, and set the two properties `IFS.DOMAIN.BFILE.Enabled` and `IFS.DOMAIN.BFILE.AgingEnabled` (shown in Figure 8-2) to true. For the change to take effect, the domain must be restarted.

Having enabled use of BFILEs, take the Storage Management link from the Content Services home page, at the bottom right of Figure 8-1. It is not possible to get to this page if the properties have not been set. There are two settings for BFILE storage management:

- The base path for the BFILE storage must be set. This is the directory off which the folders containing the BFILEs will be created. It can be an absolute path, or by prefixing it with `./` it will be a path relative to the database's Oracle home directory. The default is named after the Content Services datastore schema name, ./ifsbfiles/CONTENT.
- The BFILE policy determines whether to remove the file physically from disk if the document is deleted from within Content Services (this is the default) or whether it should remain available as operating system files after deletion. This would be necessary if the files are on a write-once, read-many-times medium, such as an optical device.

Then configure the Content Agent. This is the process that will manage the migration of data between BLOBs and BFILEs, transparently as necessary. From the Content Services home page, take the Server Configurations link, shown in Figure 8-1. From the Server Configurations page, take the link for Content Agent Configuration. The Content Agent's properties are shown in Figure 8-3.

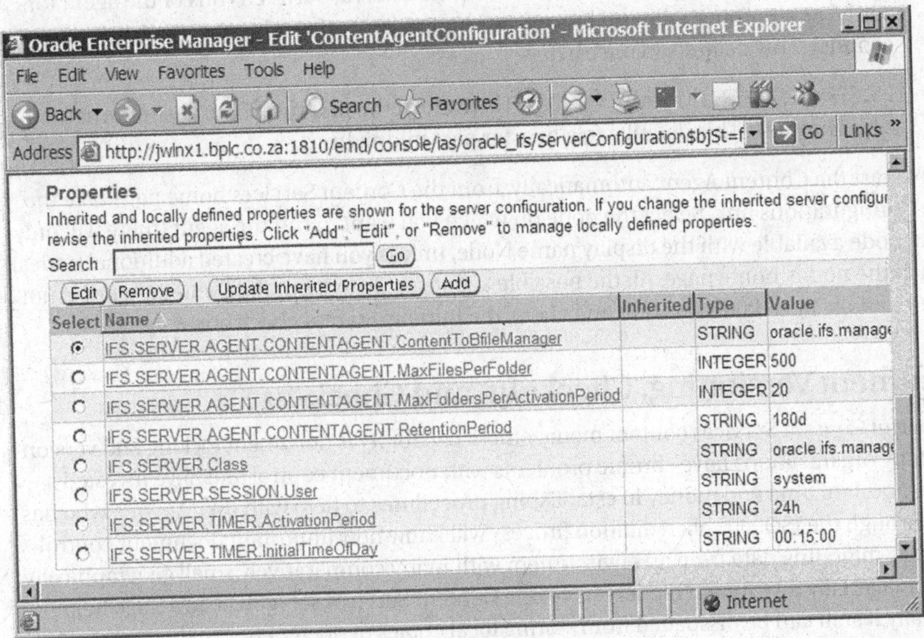

Figure 8-3. *The Content Agent's properties, with the shared properties that apply to all agents*

Only the first four properties shown are specific to the Content Agent:

- `IFS.SERVER.AGENT.CONTENTAGENT.ContentToBfileManager`: The Java class that implements data aging and should not be modified.
- `IFS.SERVER.AGENT.CONTENTAGENT.MaxFilesPerFolder`: The maximum number of files to be written for every path created for BFILE storage. This should be adjusted according to optimal values for the file system and hardware of the node running the database.
- `IFS.SERVER.AGENT.CONTENTAGENT.MaxFoldersPerActivationPeriod`: The maximum number of folders (or directory paths) that may be created by each run of the agent.
- `IFS.SERVER.AGENT.CONTENTAGENT.RetentionPeriod`: The period for which a file will be kept within the database, unaccessed, as a BLOB before migration to a BFILE. The default of 180 days may be excessive for many sites.

The other four properties are shared across other agents, such as the Virus Repair Agent described earlier:

- `IFS.SERVER.Class`: The Java class that instantiates the Content Services server process. This should not be adjusted.
- `IFS.SERVER.SESSION.User`: A database user with full administration rights within the database. This defaults to the SYSTEM user.
- `IFS.SERVER.TIMER.ActivationPeriod`: The time interval between runs of the agent formatted as a number followed by an *h* (for hours), an *m* (for minutes), or an *s* (for seconds). This defaults to once a day.
- `IFS.SERVER.TIMER.InitialTimeOfDay`: The time of the first run of the agent formatted as hh24:mm:ss. This defaults to a quarter past midnight.

To start the Content Agent automatically, from the Content Services home page take the Node Configurations link. Select the node on which you want to run the agent (there will only be one node available with the display name Node, unless you have created additional nodes) to reach the node's home page. All the possible agents are listed, but the Content Agent is not started initially by default; select it, and check the Initially Started check box.

Document Versioning, Checkout, and Check-In

A powerful Content Services content management capability is document locking and versioning. Many organizations have chronic problems with document control and have invested a large amount of time and money in establishing procedures to help with this. Anyone who has been through the ISO9000 accreditation process will know how important document control is. Simply migrating data from an environment with many comparatively small geographically and managerially distributed file servers to one Content Services server will be a huge help—especially if staff can be dissuaded from storing local copies of documents on their own terminals—but enabling the document versioning and locking capabilities of Content Services will complete the solution.

Content Services makes use of the WebDAV protocol. This is a layered protocol on top of HTTP, which is itself layered on TCP. The main features of WebDAV are the ability to "check out" a document and to create versions of it. Once a document is checked out by a user, it will still be visible to other users, but they will not be able to update it until it is checked back in to the file store. Optionally the original precheckout version of the document can be retained after the check-in as a noncurrent version. Use of WebDAV should guarantee that there is no confusion about which version of a document is current and that there is no possibility of one user's updates being overwritten by another user's updates, as can happen all too easily when documents are maintained concurrently by several users in a group. WebDAV will force serialization of changes. It is still possible to have uncontrolled copies of documents in circulation, but only if users deliberately create them; they will have to check out the document, then save a copy to private storage before checking it back in. Clearly, such activity should be discouraged.

The DAV capability is enabled at the folder (or directory) level and then applied to all documents within the folder. It is, however, possible to modify the settings for individual documents. Such settings might include the number of versions to keep before purging, or whether to version it at all. Figure 8-4 shows the end user's view of DAV through the web client.

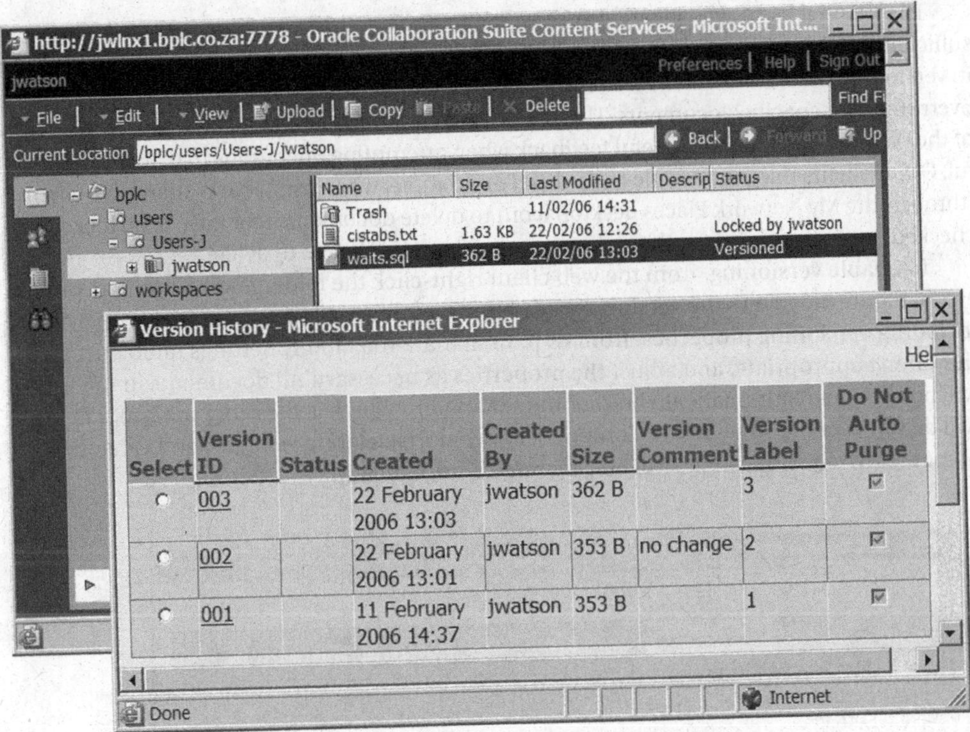

Figure 8-4. *Use of DAV facilities to lock documents and to create versions*

Figure 8-4 shows the Content Services folder `/bplc/users/Users-J/jwatson`, which contains two files. Right-clicking a file will give a pop-up menu with the following options in addition to those that one would expect for a document on a conventional file server:

- *Checkout*: Marks the document such that other users will not be able to update it; only your user ID will be able to edit and save changes, no matter what client tool is used.
- *Check-in*: Returns the document (changed or not) to general use.
- *Lock*: Applies a lock to the document. It cannot be updated or deleted until it is unlocked.
- *Unlock*: Releases a previously applied lock.
- *Submit for Workflow*: Applies a predefined workflow process to the document.
- *Cancel Workflow Request*: Stops the application of a workflow to the document.
- *Version History*: Displays all stored versions of the document.

In Figure 8-4, the status of the document `cistabs.txt` shows that this file is currently locked, and the status of the document `waits.sql` shows that this file is versioned. Right-clicking `waits.sql` shows that it is currently on its third version.

The manual locking facility is always available through the web client, provided one has sufficient privileges; and while other users can read a locked file, they cannot save changes to it. Versioning must be enabled for the whole folder and will then occur automatically unless overridden for specific documents. The Oracle Collaboration Suite web client gives full control of the WebDAV facilities and useful feedback when attempting operations that are unsuccessful. Other clients may not be able to do this. For example, when using the Windows XP client (through the My Network Places desktop icon) to delete documents that have been locked or checked out by another user, the error message is simply "Unable to delete."

To enable versioning, from the web client right-click the folder and bring up its properties. Figure 8-5 shows the versioning window. The folder will have inherited properties, including versioning properties, from its parent; mark the Modify Settings radio button if they aren't appropriate, and adjust the properties as necessary. All documents in the folder will be versioned automatically (rather than manually, which is the other option). There will be ten versions kept before Content Services starts deleting versions, and version names (suffixed with a digit) will be generated automatically.

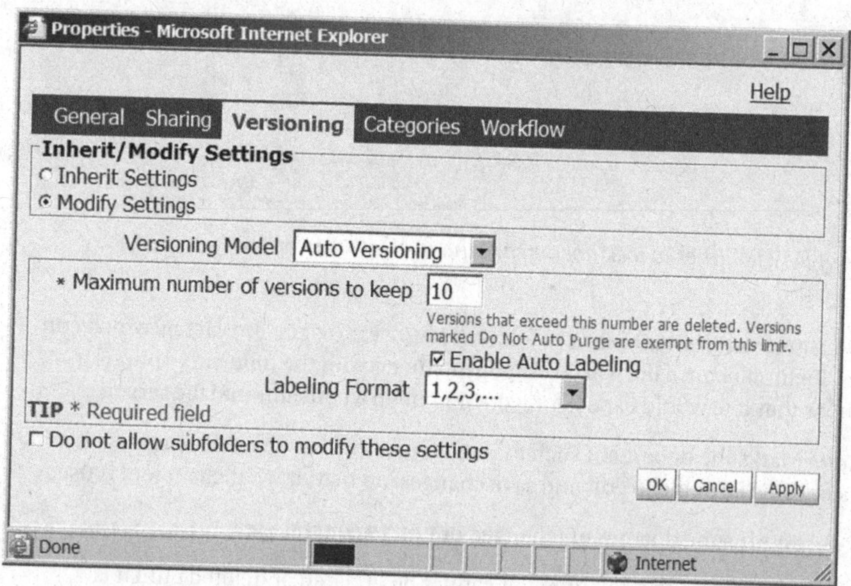

Figure 8-5. *Specifying versioning for a folder*

Document Formats

Ideally, all the documents stored in Content Services will be associated with a format. Formats are related to MIME types but take them further by including options to control whether Content Services should index the file content or scan it for viruses.

The purpose of a MIME type is to allow a file server process (such as an Apache web listener) to send appropriate instructions with a document when it is downloaded, in order that the client process will be able to handle it correctly. When a browser user double-clicks a link to a PDF file, the file is transferred by the web listener to the browser, and the file opens in the

Acrobat Reader. A common misapprehension is to think that the browser launches the Acrobat Reader because the file is suffixed .PDF. That is not the case. What happens is that the web listener, on the server side, looks at the file suffix and uses this to identify the file type. On UNIX systems, this lookup is generally done by searching a file `/etc/mime.types`, which maps suffixes to MIME types. The match must be exact; if you want files suffixed with .PDF, .pdf, and .Pdf to all be associated with the Acrobat MIME type, you will need to have entries for each variation of the suffix in the `mime.types` file. The MIME type is sent to the client with the document, and the client then looks up the MIME type (not the filename suffix) locally to work out how to open it. On UNIX, this second lookup is done in the file `/etc/mailcap`. To take a Linux example, there might be entries like this in the `mime.types` file to identify Acrobat documents and Microsoft Word documents:

```
application/pdf    pdf    PDF    Pdf
application/msword    doc    DOC    rtf    RTF
```

These entries will map several file suffixes to the appropriate MIME type. The `mailcap` file could then include these lines to control how to open such documents:

```
application/pdf;    xpdf %s
application/msword;    ooffice %s
```

The first entry instructs UNIX to use the X Windows version of the Acrobat Reader, `xpdf`, to open files of MIME type `application/pdf`; the second says to use OpenOffice, `ooffice`, to open Word documents. On Windows, this resolution of file suffix to application via a MIME type is done with entries in the registry, beneath the key `HKEY_CLASSES_ROOT`. The MIME types can be edited in the registry directly or from any folder by navigating to Tools ➤ Folder Options ➤ File Types.

In some cases, the MIME type mapping provided by default by the operating system may not be adequate. There is no reason not to edit the operating system's `mime.types` file to add references that will create the MIME types you need, but many applications will ship with their own `mime.types` file. The Apache web listener as shipped with an Oracle Collaboration Suite middle tier instance includes in its configuration file, `httpd.conf`, a directive `Types.Config` that points to a `mime.types` file installed in the Apache configuration directory; this file is reasonably comprehensive, but if you find that your end users' browsers are opening documents with inappropriate tools, or perhaps that they are receiving prompts to save a file to disk and not open it at all, adding entries to this file should fix the problem.

A Content Services format takes MIME types a step further. Every document should be associated with a format, which has five attributes:

- *MIME type* (such as `application/pdf` or `text/plain`): This is for instructions to be sent to the browser.
- *Extension type*: This is the list of filename suffixes to which this format should apply.
- *Binary setting*: This determines whether this format is for binary files.
- *Omitted from virus scan*: This specifies that, by default, files of this format will not be scanned by SAVSE when opened.
- *Indexed*: This determines that all file formats can be indexed and therefore included in Search output. For some the indexing is optional; for others it is required.

To manage formats, click the Formats link from the Content services home page in Application Server Control, shown in Figure 8-1. This will show the already extant formats, as shown in Figure 8-6.

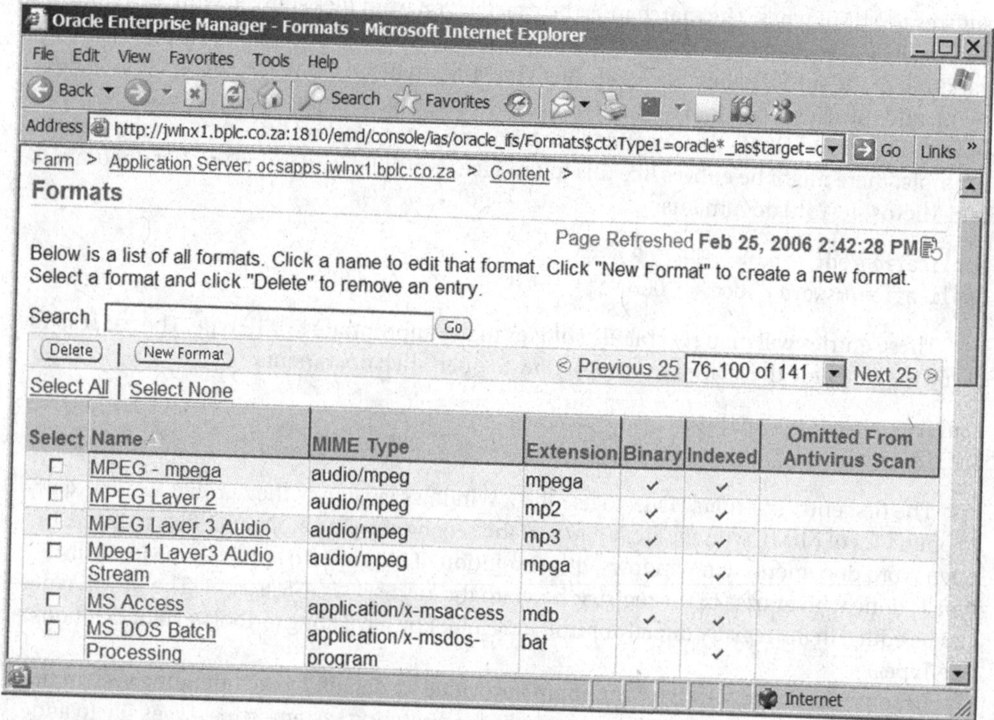

Figure 8-6. *The precreated formats, each mapping an extension to a MIME type*

This listing is in fact derived from a table in the CONTENT schema, CONTENT.ODM_FORMAT, which is where Content Services stores this information. To add a format, click the New Format button. Figure 8-7 shows adding a format that will associate the .CMD suffix with the MIME type that will instruct browsers to run the file as a Windows shell script. The MIME type and the extension can be selected from drop-down boxes of MIME types and extensions already known to Content Services (because they already exist in the ODM_FORMAT table) or new ones can be registered. In this case, the MIME type was selected from the list, but the extension is new.

If a file is not associated with a format because it has a suffix that is not recognized, the Oracle Collaboration Suite Apache web listener will make an attempt to identify the type of file by inspecting its contents; this is done by the Apache mime_magic module. If this fails, the result will typically be to apply the `text/plain` MIME type (that a Windows browser will open with Notepad) to nonbinary data, or the `application/octet-stream` MIME type to binary data, that will cause most browsers to generate a prompt suggesting that the file should be saved to a local disk.

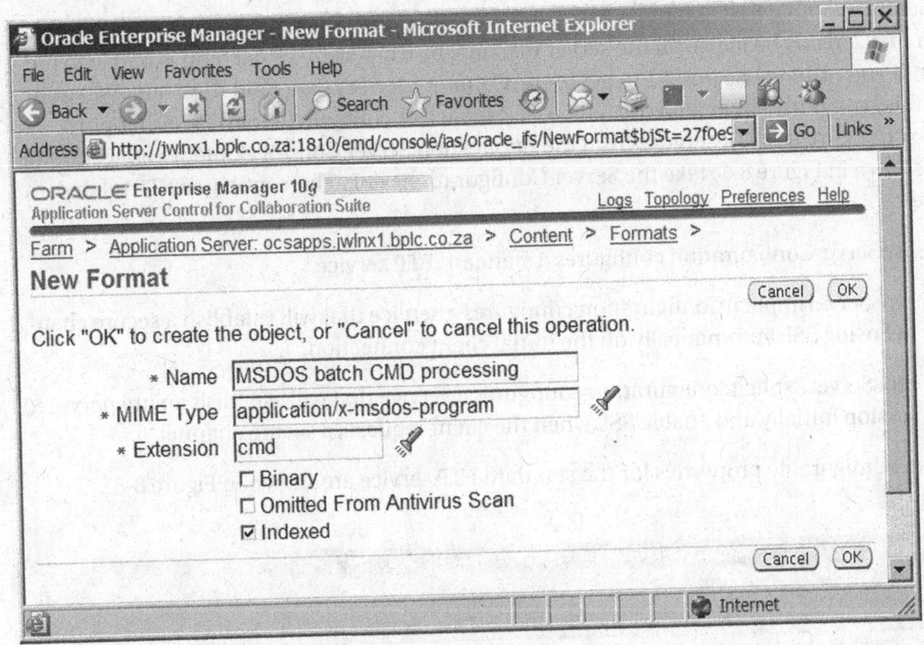

Figure 8-7. *Creating a format that will cause .CMD files to be executed by browser clients*

It must be emphasized here how important it is to educate users about downloading files from unknown servers. It should be apparent by now how dangerous this can be, because what the browser will do is not dependent on the filename suffix; it is dependent on how the server has been configured. Of course, a well-configured (and ethically configured) server will never associate a potentially dangerous MIME type with an innocuous looking suffix, and a well-configured client will have additional checks before allowing a browser to run a downloaded file.

Protocol Support and the Client Tools

The current release of Content Services is by default configured to accept HTTP only. As its name, Hypertext Transfer Protocol, implies it was originally designed for file serving, but it is limited in its capability. For that reason, Content Services will also, by default, accept WebDAV. This is layered on top of HTTP and gives the versioning, locking, and check-in/checkout capabilities. Many organizations will also want to use FTP to get to their Content Services data, but this must be explicitly enabled. The SSL variants of all these protocols can be used as well.

Enabling FTP

FTP, which is layered on top of TCP, is the most lightweight protocol in common use for file transfer. Virtually all client machines will have an FTP client program, and it is usually very fast when compared to other protocols such as SMB, NFS, or indeed HTTP and WebDAV.

Before enabling FTP, you must decide on the port to use. The default FTP port is port 21, which may already be in use on the server machine by whatever FTP daemon is native to the server. If you want to use port 21 to get to the Content Services data (and most sites will want to do this) you must either stop the native FTP service or configure it to use another port.

To configure the FTP service, from the Application Server Control Content Services home page, shown in Figure 8-1, take the Server Configurations link. There are three FTP related services:

- FtpServerConfiguration configures a standard FTP service.
- FtpsServerImplicitConfiguration configures a service that will establish a secure channel using SSL automatically on the initial client connection.
- FtpsServerExplicitconfiguration configures a service that will establish an unencrypted session initially and enable SSL when the client requests a secure channel.

The configurable properties for the standard FTP service are shown in Figure 8-8.

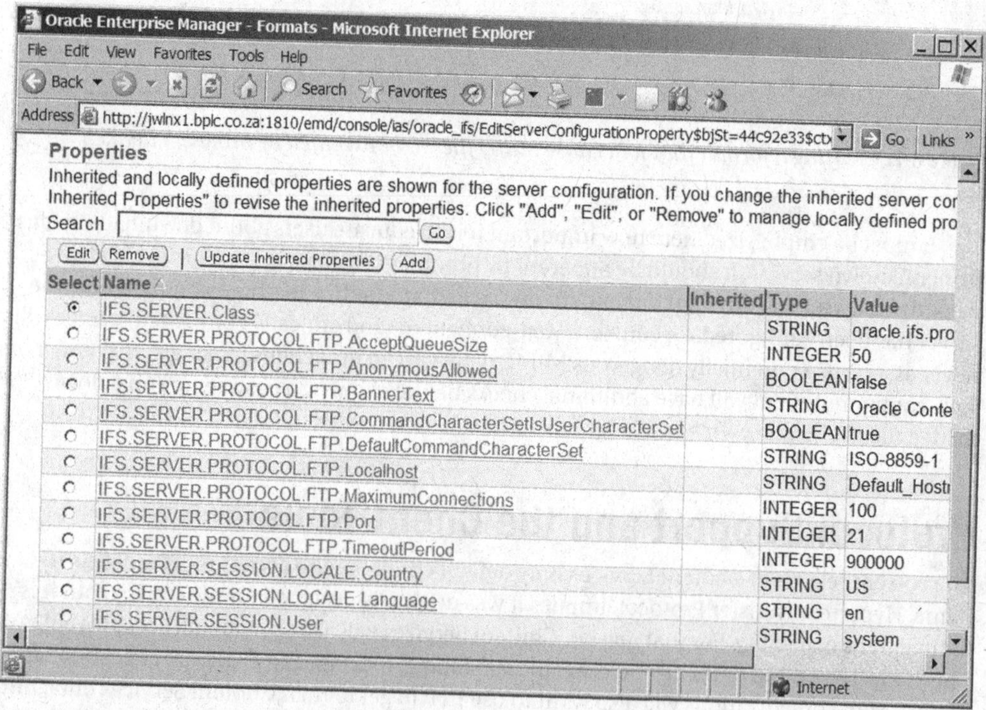

Figure 8-8. *Properties for the standard FTP service*

Most of these properties can be left on default, but some should be considered:

- `IFS.SERVER.PROTOCOL.FTP.AnonymousAllowed`: By default, anonymous FTP is disabled. To enable it, set this property to true and then grant public access to one or more folders.
- `IFS.SERVER.PROTOCOL.FTP.BannerText`: This is the message sent to users when they connect to the server. The message will need to be changed to reflect the details of the installation.

- `IFS.SERVER.PROTOCOL.FTP.MaximumConnections`: The default of 100 should be more than adequate for most sites but deserves consideration.
- `IFS.SERVER.PROTOCOL.FTP.Port`: This must be changed from default if there is already an FTP server running on the server machine on this port.
- `IFS.SERVER.PROTOCOL.FTP.TimeoutPeriod`: This, in units of milliseconds, is how long the server will permit an idle connection to remain established.

To start the FTP service, return to the Content Services home page and take the Node configuration link (shown in Figure 8-1) and then the link for the node where you want to start the service. Following a default installation, this will be the node with the display name Node. In the list of servers offered by the node, select the FtpServer and set it to Active and Initially Started, as shown in Figure 8-9.

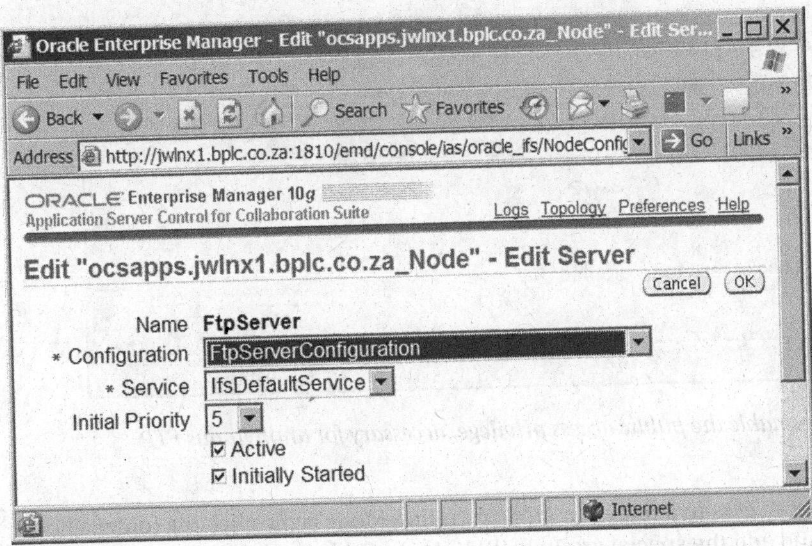

Figure 8-9. *Set the FtpServer to automatic start on the node called Node.*

Before allowing public access to folders, and therefore anonymous FTP, the property `IFS.SERVER.PROTOCOL.FTP.AnonymousAllowed` described previously must be set and the ability to grant public access enabled at the site level. Only a Content Services user with the superuser privileges can do this—either the orcladmin user or another user to whom these privileges have been granted (as described in Chapter 6). Navigate to the Content Services administration system either through the end-user web interface or by clicking the Administration icon for the Content component from Application Server Control (shown in Figure 5-19 in Chapter 5), and click the Switch to Administration Mode tab. Right-click the root site folder (or a lower level folder if you do not want the operation to apply to the whole tree) to bring up its properties. Click the Sharing tab, check the Allow Public Access to Be Granted check box, and apply the change, as shown in Figure 8-10. Note that this does not actually enable public access to anything, but it does allow superusers to enable public access to folders subsequently.

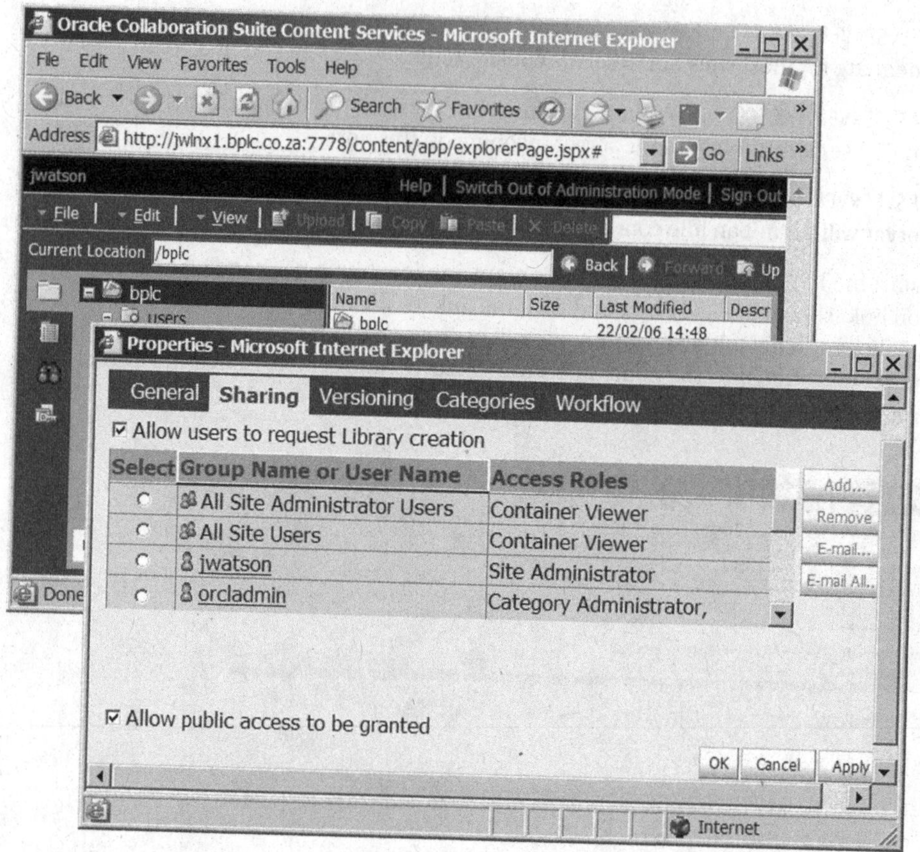

Figure 8-10. *How to enable the public access privilege, necessary for anonymous FTP*

To grant public access to a folder, in Administration Mode right-click the folder, click the Sharing tab, and add the special group PUBLIC to the folder with READER privilege, and AUTHOR as well if you want to let anonymous FTP users upload files as well as download them.

Enabling FTP with SSL (FTPS)

Note that FTP with SSL is the FTPS protocol, not the SFTP protocol. The former is FTP with public key encryption and digital certificates; the latter is the FTP variant of Secure Shell. Oracle Collaboration Suite does not offer Secure Shell protocol in any form.

Enabling FTPS is essentially the same process as enabling FTP. First set the properties for the service, such as the listening port, and then start the server.

There are two FTPS services: the implicit service, and the explicit service. The *implicit service* will use SSL from the moment the connection is requested and runs by default on port 990. The *explicit service* runs by default on port 21 and will normally be run instead of the standard nonsecure sockets FTP service. It has the capability to use SSL, but the switch from clear text is only made when the user explicitly issues an AUTH command requesting this.

Both the FTPS services must have the `IFS.SERVER.PROTOCOL.FTPS.WALLET.Location` property set, pointing toward the location of a wallet file with the server's digital certificate. This can be a physical path or it can be an LDAP address if the wallet has been uploaded to the Oracle Internet Directory. The wallet should be generated in the usual manner, using the Oracle Wallet Manager.

Client Access and End-User Tools

The most functional interface to Content Services is the web interface. This gives full access to the WebDAV capabilities. From the Oracle Collaboration Suite portal interface, click the Content Services link. This will bring up the Content Services web interface, as shown in Figure 8-11. The folder tree will show only those folders on which the user has some sort of permission; the tab Switch to Administration Mode will only be visible to users with appropriate permissions.

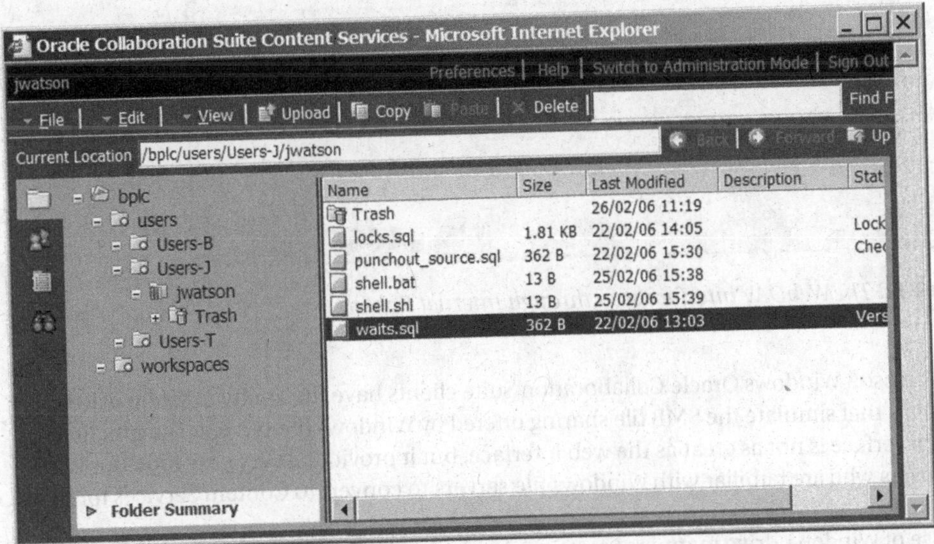

Figure 8-11. *The Content Services web interface, as seen by a user with administrator privileges*

Double-clicking a document will open it with whatever tool is appropriate to its MIME type; right-clicking it will give access to the DAV functions of locking, check-in/checkout, and versioning. To upload files, take the Upload tab, which will generate a window for browsing the local file system and selecting files for upload.

The WebDAV browser interface is accessed through any browser. Issue the following URL:

```
http://<host.domain>:<port>/content/dav
```

where *<host.domain>* is the address of the middle tier node and *<port>* is the port of the middle tier's Web Cache listener. Following a Single Sign-On login prompt you will be presented with a window that lets you navigate around the Content Services directory tree, as shown in Figure 8-12. This interface certainly works, but is very limited; the limitations are not caused by Oracle Collaboration suite, they are a result of the limited functions provided by the HTTP protocol. The Launch button will launch the web interface, shown in Figure 8-11, and users will need a very good reason (such as a terminal with minimal graphics capability) not to use this.

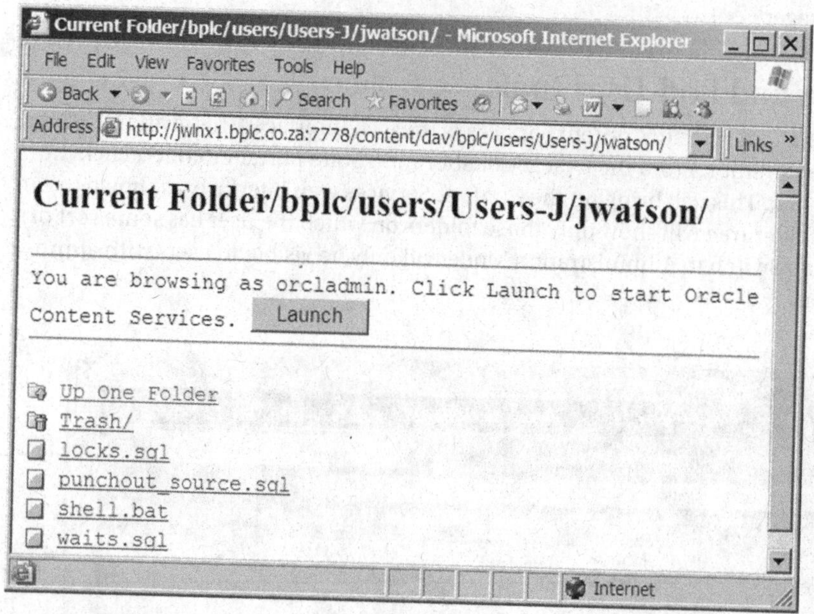

Figure 8-12. *The WebDAV interface seen through Internet Explorer*

Microsoft Windows Oracle Collaboration Suite clients have the ability to set up drive mappings that simulate the SMB file sharing offered by Windows file servers. The functionality of this interface is not as great as the web interface, but it provides a very easy route for Windows users who are familiar with Windows file servers to convert to Content Services for their file storage.

Use of Windows drive mappings requires the user to download and install a small application: Oracle Drive. This is available to all users at `http://<host.domain>:<port>/clientsdl/OracleDrive/ODriveSetup.exe` where *<host.domain>* is the address of the middle tier node and *<port>* is the port of the middle tier's Web Cache listener. There are links to this URL from the first Oracle Collaboration Suite window (take the Oracle Desktop Access link and navigate from there) and from various places within the web interface. Running this file will install the Oracle Drive application. The standard installation will create shortcuts on the user's Start menu, desktop, and taskbar. To create a drive mapping, run the program by clicking one of the shortcuts. The Oracle Drive window will appear and prompt you to choose a service. Define a new service by giving the details of your Oracle Collaboration suite middle tier, as shown in Figure 8-13.

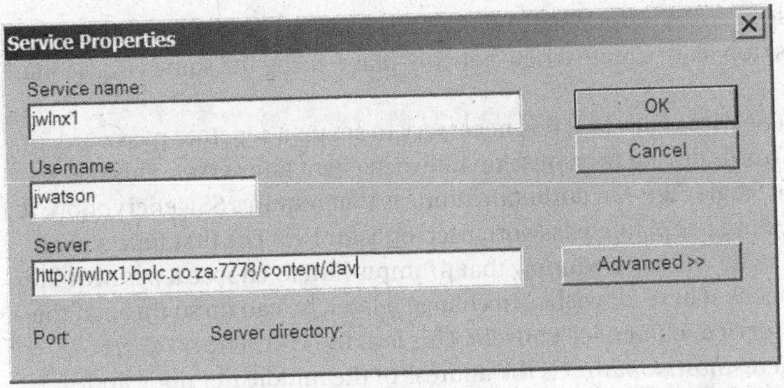

Figure 8-13. *How to define a Windows drive mapping to Content Services*

In Figure 8-13, the port and directory have been specified on the server URL; an alternative is to specify them in the Advanced properties. The directory given will cause the drive mapping to be from the root of the Content Services file system. Clicking OK will prompt for the Single Sign-On password, and the drive mapping will then be completed. By default, it will take the next available drive letter. Data can then be accessed through the Windows Explorer using the normal double-click to open files and drag-and-drop to copy files. Right-clicking a file will give access to the usual file properties, plus the ability to lock or unlock the file. The Oracle Drive client has options for working offline, with a synchronization facility for automatically transferring updated files between local and remote storage.

Access from an operating system prompt to an Oracle Drive mapped file is as for any other disk device:

```
C:\>dir g:\bplc\users\Users-J\jwatson
 Volume in drive G is JWLNX1
 Volume Serial Number is 0000-1C42

 Directory of g:\bplc\users\Users-J\jwatson

01/01/1986  12:00    <DIR>          .
22/02/2006  13:03               362 waits.sql
25/02/2006  15:39                13 shell.shl
25/02/2006  15:38                13 shell.bat
22/02/2006  15:30               362 punchout_source.sql
22/02/2006  14:05             1,851 locks.sql
26/02/2006  11:19    <DIR>          Trash
               5 File(s)          2,601 bytes
               2 Dir(s)     536,862,720 bytes free

C:\>
```

Also available to Windows users is the WebDAV interface provided by Windows through the My Network Places desktop icon. Create a new network place, using the same URL as that given to Oracle Drive.

To connect to Content Services with FTP, it is necessary to set up a separate password. FTP does not encrypt passwords during transmission between client and server. This means that it is not possible to use Single Sign-On authentication, as that requires SSL encryption. It is therefore necessary to choose a separate password used only for FTP. The first time a user connects to Content Services he will see a window that prompts him to choose a password for FTP access. If he doesn't specify it here, or wishes to change it later, he can do so through the Delegated Administration Service self-service console. This is at the URL http://<host.domain>:<port>/oiddas where *<host.domain>* is the address of the middle tier node and *<port>* is the port of the middle tier's Web Cache listener. After logging in (with the Single Sign-On password) click the My Profile and the Change My Password subtab. In the Application Passwords section there is an option to set (or update) the password for Content. This means the Content Services FTP password; it will not affect any other client tool, because all the others use Single Sign-On.

Having set an FTP password, use any FTP client to connect to Content Services, as shown in Figure 8-14.

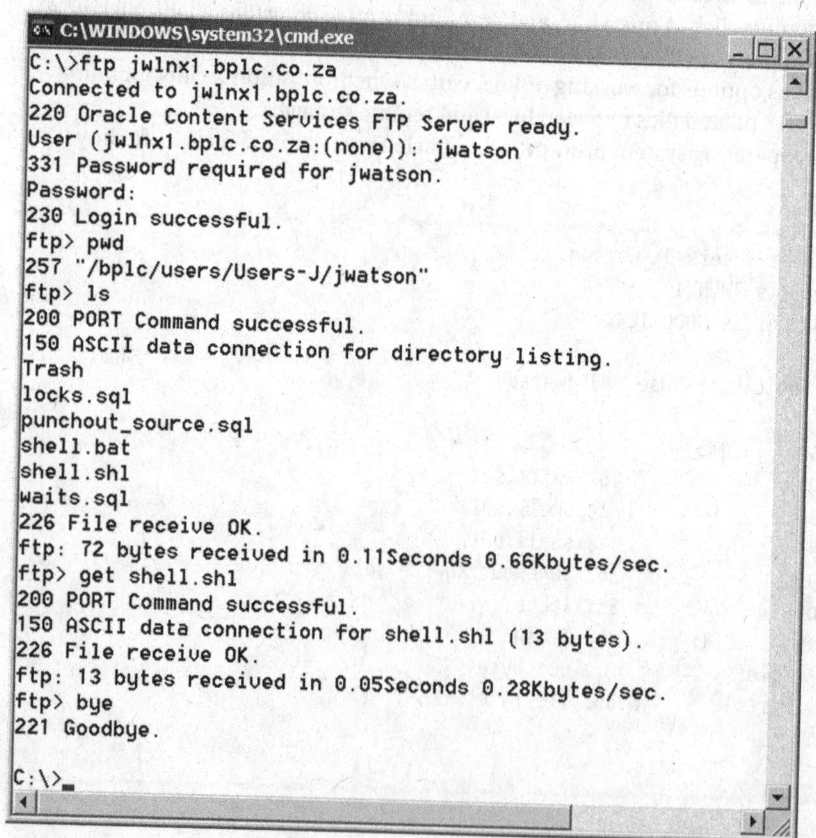

Figure 8-14. *How to use an FTP client to access Content Services data*

Using FTPS does not require setting up a separate password, because FTPS will encrypt the password during transmission.

File Sharing with Content Services

The default security with Content Services gives each user full control over the contents of his home folder and no access to any other folder except for the Container Viewer privilege on the folders above him in the tree. This Container Viewer privilege is necessary for him to be able to navigate down the tree to his home folder, but even with this privilege he will not see any other folders. Once a user is given any sort of privilege on any other folder, he will be able to see it through the Container Viewer privileges and, depending on what rights he has been given, he will be able to manipulate the files in the folder. It is possible to assign rights at the file level, but this is generally considered to be bad practice as it involves a huge amount of work. If possible, assign rights at the folder level.

Figure 8-15 shows user tglenden connected to Content Services through the web client. She can see the folders bplc, users, users-B, users-J, users-T, and workspaces. However, the only actual user home folders she can see are her own and jwatson's. There are other home folders in the tree, but she has been given no permissions on them and therefore does not even know that they exist. Jwatson has given her access to his folder, which is why she can see it. She can see the workspaces folder (discussed in Chapter 15) but, again, she cannot see any of the workspaces within it.

If tglenden wishes to make the contents of her folder available to others, she can right-click to bring up its properties. Clicking the Sharing tab will let her search for select groups and users and grant them appropriate privileges. In Figure 8-15, users jwatson and bsekwale are being given the reader privilege on her folder, which will let them open her files but nothing else. The full list of possible privileges is extremely long and provides for very fine granularity of access.

While it is certainly possible to share files and folders by this method, a far better technique is through the use of Workspaces. Configuring and using Workspaces is the subject of Chapter 15.

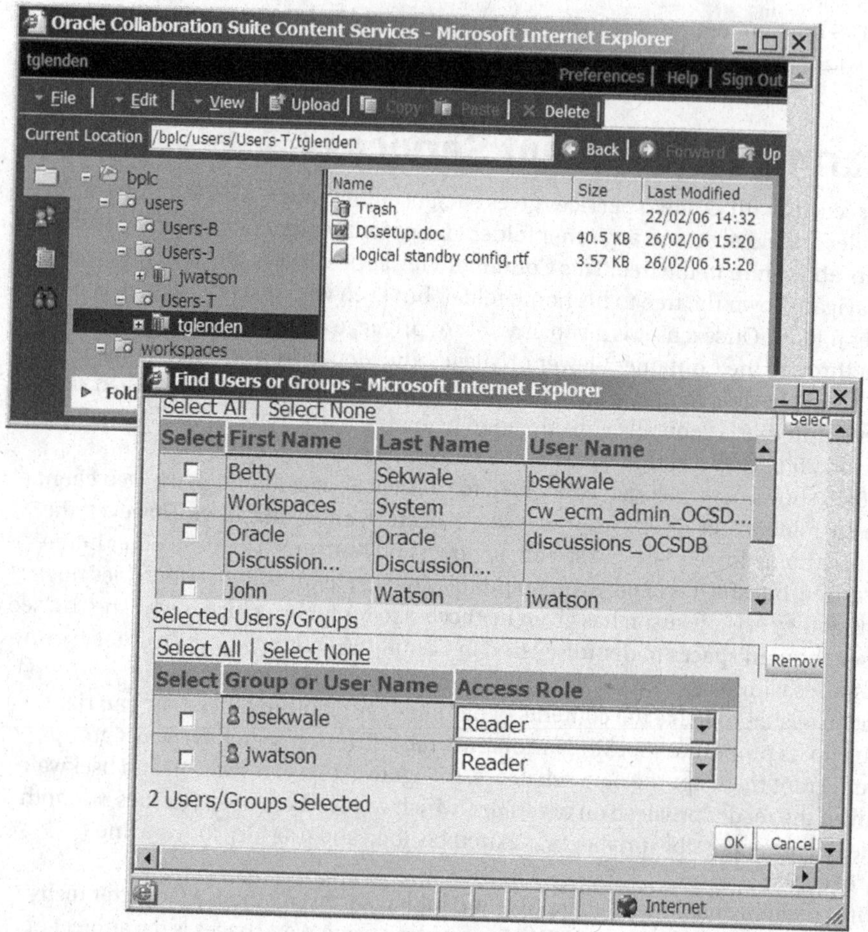

Figure 8-15. *Granting access to folders through the web client*

Using Workflows with Content Services

A *workflow* is a control and monitoring mechanism for managing business processes. There are any number of types of workflow that could be usefully associated with documents. Perhaps the most obvious are those relating to creating and deleting documents. In any organization where documentation and version control are taken seriously, there should be automated procedures that control these functions. Content Services provides a framework for workflows that will govern these and other related functions, but it is also possible to develop workflows that can integrate any number of business processes with the documents on which they are dependent.

The Workflow Architecture

Workflow is an Oracle product that is shipped with a number of applications but can also be installed as a self-contained product. It is a tool for defining, controlling, and monitoring business processes. The processes can have branches, iterations, and multiple entry and exit points.

Workflow is extensively used in the Oracle 11*i* E-Business Suite, such as for controlling the process whereby an employee requisitions an item: the requisition is raised, it is approved by his manager, a purchase order is generated to an appropriate supplier, the goods are received, and so on. Alerts built into the workflow could redirect the approval to an alternate approver if it has not been dealt with within two days, or require multiple approvers if the value of the requisition is over a certain limit. The workflow would generate appropriate e-mail at various stages to keep interested parties informed of progress. Earlier releases of Workflow were written in PL/SQL, but it is now a Java application. It makes extensive use of Advanced Queuing, another product that has been migrated from PL/SQL to Java. There are two sides to Workflow: the Workflow engine, which is built into the database, and the Workflow designer, which is part of Application Server.

While Workflow is a very powerful tool for modeling and implementing business processes, a potentially superior tool is the Oracle BPEL Process Manager. BPEL is a language designed for developing applications that make use of processes and data maintained by disparate systems that is emerging as the standard for web-based integration projects. BPEL applications use XML and web services to integrate discrete business functions into complete applications. The web service architecture is fully supported by Oracle Application Server, and the Java development toolsets associated with Oracle Application Server include all the class files needed to create web services and publish them to the network. The Oracle E-Business Suite ships with hundreds of predefined web services that can be used to expose the business processes of an organization to the web; other products from other publishers may have similar facilities. Use of BPEL means that the business data processing systems can be fully integrated with the office automation systems offered by Oracle Collaboration Suite.

The potential of BPEL to integrate business data processing functions with office automation functions is enormous and can have huge benefits for large organizations. To take a simple example, it makes it possible to combine the human resources processes for managing and recruiting staff with the document management processes for storing CVs and job advertisement copy.

Oracle has made a huge commitment to the BPEL standard, and it is likely that the Workflow product will eventually be migrated into a BPEL application; but for the time being they are separate, and both have their place in Content Services.

The Default Workflow Processes

There are two preconfigured workflows that can be applied to documents stored in Content Services: serial approval and parallel vote. The actions on a document that can trigger either of these are the following:

- Check-in
- Checkout
- Copy
- Upload
- Delete
- Move
- Read
- User request

The parallel vote workflow causes the triggering event to notify all approvers of the action concurrently; the serial approval notifies each one in turn.

To activate these workflows, in the web client right-click a folder to bring up its properties and navigate to the Workflow tab. If a folder were configured with a workflow, as in Figure 8-16, which requires the approval of jwatson and bsekwale before a document can be deleted, an attempt to delete the document will result in the message "A request to delete your files has been submitted. The files will be deleted after your request has been approved." The document will then be flagged as "locked for workflow." The approvers can be notified by e-mail if the Workflow engine has been configured for e-mail notifications, or they can view their outstanding requests by taking the View tab on the Content Services web interface, and navigating to Reports and My Requests, as shown in Figure 8-17. Clicking the request will pop up the approval box.

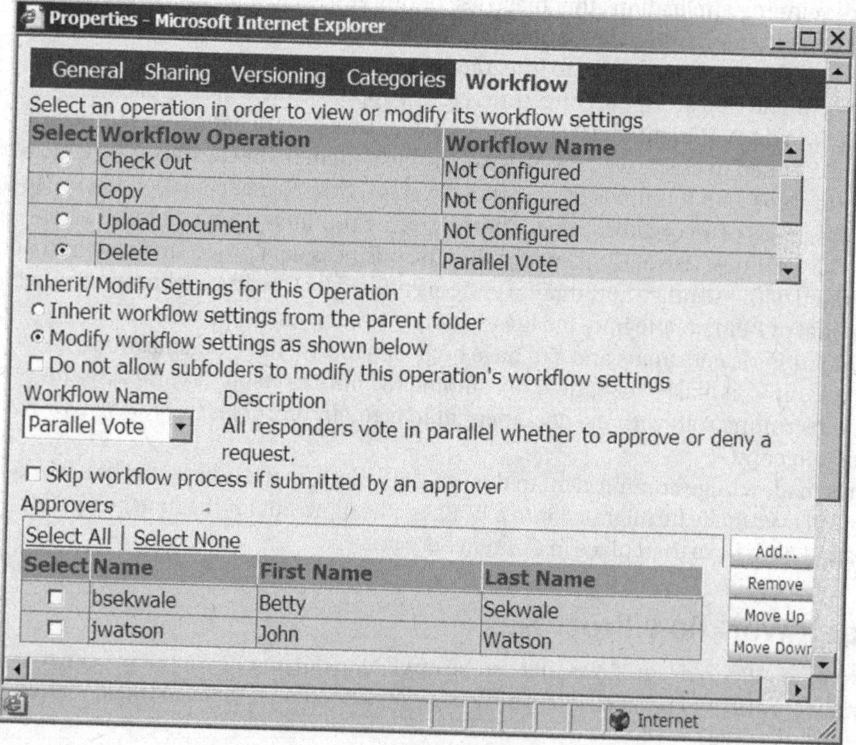

Figure 8-16. *Defining a workflow for document deletion*

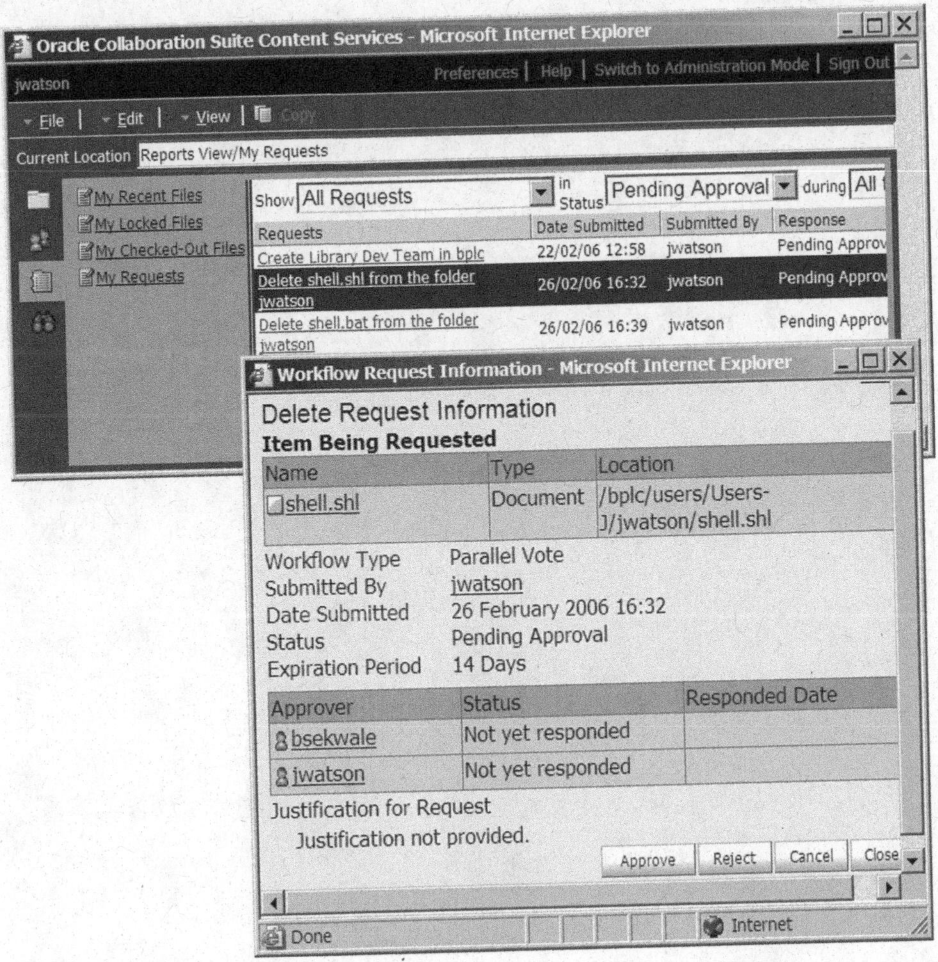

Figure 8-17. *View oustanding Workflow requests, and then approve (or reject) them.*

Custom Workflows

Designing custom Content Services workflows can only be done with Oracle BPEL Process Manager, not with the simpler Workflow product. The creation of a workflow will specify the triggering event(s), the cancel event(s), the arguments used for input at various stages, and the outputs, as well as define the actions performed during the process. Once created, the BPEL workflow must be registered with Content Services and associated with a folder.

To design and use BPEL custom workflows, Oracle offers the BPEL Process Manager and Process Connect products, which together can generate applications that integrate processes and data from any source that conforms to the Web Services standards.

CHAPTER 9

Configuring Discussions

Discussions is the bulletin board component of Oracle Collaboration Suite. Architecturally it is based on Mail; it uses the Mail asynchronous message delivery system, and it stores its data in Mail folders within the Mail datastore database.

There is a component-specific user interface accessed through the Oracle Collaboration Suite web client. This will give the greatest functionality. It is also possible to use any IMAP capable e-mail client as an interface to Discussions data. A third possibility is to use the RSS (Really Simple Syndication) protocol to include Discussions data in user-defined portals.

Discussions Architecture

Discussions is to a large extent based on the Mail component, described in detail in Chapter 10. Indeed, a standard IMAP e-mail client, such as Microsoft Outlook or Novell GroupWise, can be used as the Discussions user interface. Discussions will appear within such clients as shared mail folders. There are other possible interfaces: a web client, accessible from any browser; an RSS interface; and a Java API. Discussions data is stored in the Mail datastore database, and all access is controlled through Single Sign-On with the Oracle Internet Directory used for authentication.

For Discussions to be running, the Mail component must also be started, including the Mail listener, since the SMTP and IMAP servers are required for posting and retrieving messages to and from forums.

Data Storage

The Mail application component includes the facility for shared folders. Shared folders are a feature of IMAP mail servers. With IMAP, data can be managed centrally; this is not the case with POP3 mail servers, where mail must be downloaded to local clients before any management beyond the most basic is possible. This central storage makes it possible to give multiple IMAP users access to the same folders. Note that any end users who are using POP3 will not be able to access Discussions data through their e-mail client.

Discussions messages are grouped in a hierarchy. Any one message is posted to a forum, and the forum is in a category. A category can contain a number of forums or other categories, in a multilevel structure. Discussions works with Mail and creates a shared folder for each category, and shared subfolders for each forum (or category) within it. Then the messages sent to a forum become e-mail messages in the shared folder.

All the Discussions categories, forums, and messages are just Mail data in the Mail datastore database. It is possible to distribute Mail data across multiple databases, and in some cases it might be considered advisable to dedicate a database to Discussions data, but there is certainly no requirement for this.

Use of IMAP

Discussions is built around IMAP folder management. IMAP lets users store and manage mail on the mail server. By contrast, POP3 can really only understand one folder: the mailbox into which messages are delivered. All that can be done to incoming messages is reading them, downloading them, and deleting them. An IMAP mail server lets users create a directory system of folders and subfolders into which mail can be organized.

As a rule, IMAP users will download mail to local clients, though it is not necessary as long as the mail server administrator does not object to storing an unlimited amount of mail centrally. Most sites will, however, impose a space quota on users, and often this is extremely low, perhaps only 50MB or 100MB. In this case, users will have to download mail in order to store it permanently, probably by subscribing to their folders, so that new messages are downloaded automatically every time they connect to the server. Then a deletion policy can be applied on the server without losing the mail. End users will need an IMAP-capable client, such as Microsoft Outlook, Novell GroupWise, or Netscape Messenger, to do this.

The concept of *subscribing* to a folder is critical to the use of Discussions if users wish to view the Discussions content offline. IMAP folders are stored on the e-mail server, and their content—the messages—can be viewed from an IMAP client. Subscribing to a folder causes the client to download the folder and its contents to the user's local machine, where it can be viewed offline. This lets users maximize the efficiency of their network connections. The client need only connect periodically to download all new messages as a batch to view later, rather than remaining connected continuously in order to see the messages.

Discussions data will generally be handled differently from regular mail. An active bulletin board may receive hundreds or thousands of postings a day—far more messages than a regular user would receive, and it is not reasonable to expect all bulletin board users to subscribe to folders as busy as this, though they certainly can if they wish. It is possible to restrict the size of a Discussions folder, but since the folders are shared by many users they do not count against any one user's Mail quota.

As with regular mail, there is no need to have an IMAP client installed on the local terminal. There is a web client available through the standard Portal interface to Oracle Collaboration Suite.

Postings to a Discussions forum arrive in the form of an SMTP incoming mail message. This is processed as any other incoming mail; the Mail listener by default monitors port 25 for SMTP, receives the message, and sends it to the SMTP incoming mail server, which saves it to the appropriate folder in the Mail datastore.

The manner in which incoming Mail messages are handled by the SMTP incoming mail server and retrieved through the IMAP server is described fully in Chapter 10.

The Web Interface

The Discussions web interface is accessible from the Oracle Collaboration Suite Portal front end and provides the most functional interface. From here, if one has appropriate permissions, one can create new categories and forums, read from and post to existing forums, and manage access rights.

Each user can make adjustments to the way the web interface presents the information, controlling whether to show messages in a forum sorted chronologically or grouped into topics (also known as *threads*) and how many messages to display per page.

There is no Oracle Collaboration Suite component that must be started specifically to make Discussions available through the web interface. The application consists of Java servlets that are part of the OC4J_OCSClient component. These servlets will be launched by the OC4J container in response to user requests if this component is running. For this reason, the `opmnctl status` command does not show any Discussions component, as it is not a separately managed OPMN (Oracle Process Manager and Notification) process. Within Application Server Control, there is a link to a Discussions component (shown in Figure 5-20 in Chapter 5) but it cannot be selected for startup and shutdown. Clicking this link will show a page of information on how the application is performing and the rate at which messages are being processed.

As with any web interface, Discussions is available on any browser or HTTP-compatible device.

Really Simple Syndication (RSS)

The Really Simple Syndication protocol is a relatively new Internet protocol being developed primarily for news web sites and web logs. In years to come it may well be seen as a replacement for the Network News Transfer Protocol (NNTP) as news web sites increase in popularity over the older network news services. Like so many of the more recent Internet protocols, it is layered on top of HTTP.

At the top level, an RSS document is an element with a mandatory attribute called *version* that specifies the version of RSS that the document conforms to. Subordinate to the element is a single element that contains information about the channel (the metadata) and its contents. RSS lets a web developer publish his web site in a form that can be easily understood by another program. It repackages the web site as a list of data items with metadata describing them. This metadata will include information such as the date of the item, its version, a description, and its URL. An RSS client can then check the web site according to various search criteria and download or display any new or updated articles. The end result is that users do not have to visit repeatedly their favorite web sites to check for changed articles. The RSS client will check the sites and store and display new pages locally. RSS aggregators, also known as *feed readers*, can trawl RSS source sites extracting articles of interest. The feeds can then be made available on any other web server.

RSS clients can connect to Discussions forums through the supplied RSS servlet that is a part of the Discussions application that is deployed to the OC4J_OCSClient component. It thus becomes possible for third-party developers of RSS applications to include Discussions forums in their sources of information, along with other RSS feeds. Some popular RSS sites are Yahoo, the BBC, and NASA. There are many more. The ability to publish Discussions content through RSS is an important capability for disseminating information.

The Discussions Security Structure

All Oracle Collaboration Suite users must have Mail accounts before they can use Discussions. It is, however, possible to configure a forum for public access. Such a forum will accept postings from the outside world and can be read by anonymous users. Within these general principles there is a complex security structure that allows for some forums to be uncontrolled, while others can be tightly monitored and moderated. Security is based on Discussions roles.

Discussions categories and forums make up a hierarchy similar in concept to a directory tree. Roles are granted to a particular category or forum and apply to the whole subtree beneath that point. The various roles also make up a hierarchy—from the Global Administrator who can do anything, down to the Forum Reader who can do nothing more than view postings in the forum(s) on which he has been granted this privilege.

As a general rule, each role subsumes the capabilities of the roles below it, and users with a role can pass that role on to other users. There are two exceptions: the Category Writer role (which cannot be granted by Forum Moderators or Creators) is simply a quick way to grant the Forum Writer role on all forums in a category; and neither Forum Writers nor Readers can pass on their roles.

If a role is revoked from a user, and the user has previously passed on his role to other users, the revoke will not cascade to the other users: the grantees will still have the role, even though the grantor no longer has it.

Different users, according to their roles, have different tasks to perform within Discussions. Following is a list of the roles in descending order of power. Some of the roles only apply to categories; others apply only to forums.

- *Global Administrator*: Has full administration rights, including creating other Global Administrators (through OIDDAS) and the root-level categories that will contain all the subcategories and their forums, and granting the Category Administrator role to the users who will manage the root categories.
- *Category Administrator*: Manages the settings and properties for his category, and grants either Category Creator or Forum Creator to users for this category, depending on whether he wants to set up a multilevel structure. He can delete his category, recursively deleting all its subcategories and forums.
- *Category Creator*: Creates categories within his category and within these subcategories, and grants the Forum Creator role. He can also grant the Category Writer role as a shortcut to grant Forum Writer across all forums in the category.
- *Forum Creator*: Creates the bulletin boards and grants either the Forum Moderator role or the Forum Writer and Reader roles, depending on whether the forum is to be moderated.
- *Forum Moderator*: Manages forum content, including editing and hiding postings; moving postings between topics; deleting, clipping, and moving topics; locking topics or the whole forum; approving postings before they are made public; and posting announcements. He grants the Forum Writer and Reader roles.
- *Forum Writer*: Creates new topics and responds to existing topics. Depending on the way the forum is set up, he may be able to edit his own postings.
- *Forum Reader*: Browses and reads any forums to which he has been granted access.

A user's roles on the various forums are stored within the Oracle Internet Directory, and they are determined when the user first connects to Discussions. Then, for performance reasons, they are cached by the Discussions servlet on the Oracle Collaboration Suite middle tier rather than being read from the directory with every subsequent access. Whenever a write operation, such as posting a message, is attempted, Discussions will revalidate its cached list of roles; but for read operations, Discussions relies on the cached information. The effect of this is that if a user's roles are adjusted while he is connected to Discussions, the changes will be immediate for posting, but changes to his read permissions will only be effective after he logs out and logs back in. Thus, if a user is given permission to access a new forum, he will not see it until he reconnects; but if he is downgraded from Writer to Reader, he will immediately get an error when he attempts to post.

Using Discussions

This section uses an example to demonstrate how Discussions might be used. In this example, an IT organization has decided that it needs a set of bulletin boards for its support services division. Some will be public, and therefore accessible to third parties; others will be internal. Some will be moderated; others will not be.

The following list shows the roles and the actions for which the users will be responsible:

1. ORCLADMIN creates an APPSADMIN user and grants him the Mail System Administrator role.
2. APPSADMIN creates the root-level category SUPPORT, and grants JWATSON Category Administrator.
3. JWATSON creates the category EXTERNAL, grants Forum Creator to SHART, creates the category INTERNAL, and grants Forum Creator to IGAMA and TGLENDEN.
4. SHART, IGAMA, and TGLENDEN create the ANNOUNCEMENTS forum in EXTERNAL for public read-only access and create the PARTNERS forum for the public with moderated read-write access, and grant Forum Moderator to JSTRUDEL. In INTERNAL, they create whatever forums are needed, granting reader and writer privileges as appropriate.
5. SHART, IGAMA, and TGLENDEN monitor the forums, taking action as necessary to move, clip, and lock topics; lock entire forums; edit messages; and adjust access rights.
6. JSTRUDEL moderates the content of the PARTNERS forum.

The following steps show how to set up the forums using the previous example.

Step 1: Create the Discussions Global Administrator

Connect to the OIDDAS component and log on as the orcladmin user. Click the Directory tab and either create a new user (by clicking the Create button) or search for an existing user and click the Edit button. Either way, in the Provisioning Applications window make sure that the user has a Mail account, and then in the Mail section of the Application Attributes window, shown in Figure 9-1, change his role from the default of User to either System Administrator or Domain Administrator. The former role has administration capabilities over the whole Mail system; the latter is restricted to just his own domain.

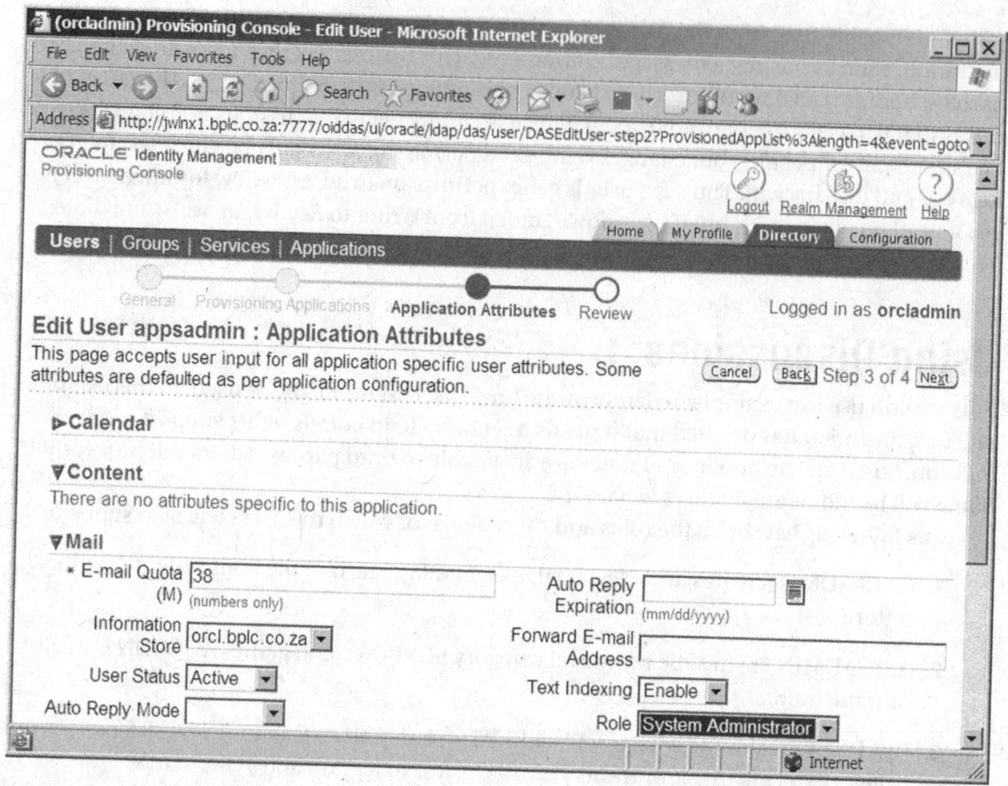

Figure 9-1. *Create a Mail (and Discussions) superuser with the OIDDAS provisioning console.*

Granting this privilege creates a Mail superuser, which includes the ability to manage Discussions. In Figure 9-1, the user APPSADMIN is being created specifically to be the superuser for all applications, and he is therefore being granted the System Administrator role.

When a user with this role connects to Discussions by taking the appropriate link from the Oracle Collaboration Suite Portal page, he will see a window that looks like that shown in Figure 9-2. Note that on the right-hand side of the window there is an Administration tab, not visible to normal users, and below this is an indication that the user is a Global Administrator. There are also buttons to create new categories and forums.

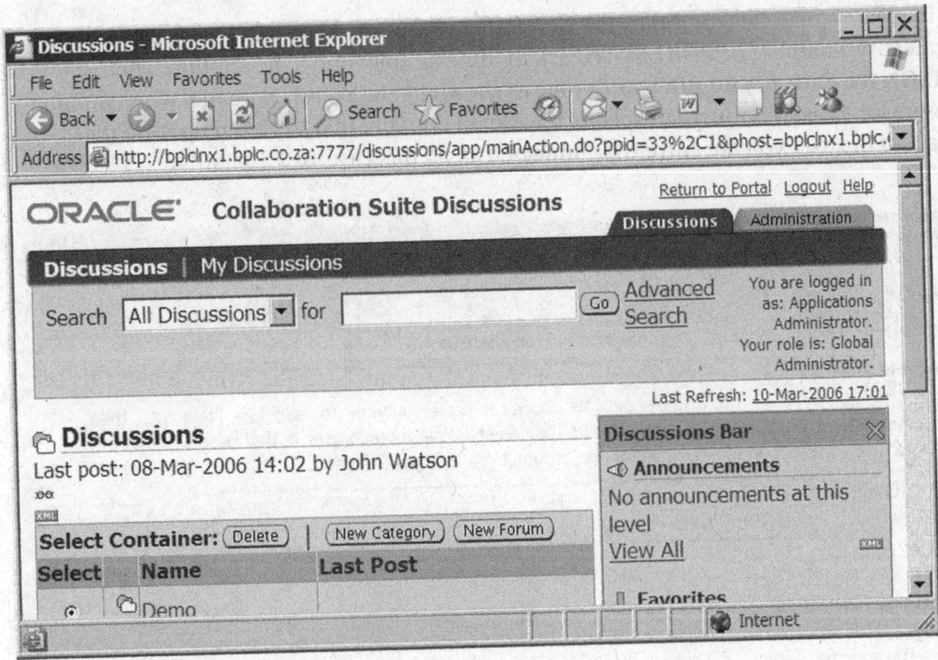

Figure 9-2. *The Global Administrator's initial Discussions window*

Step 2: Create the Root-Level Category

After logging on to the Single Sign-On server as user APPSADMIN and navigating to the window shown in Figure 9-2 you may wish to adjust certain systemwide defaults that will be applied to all new forums; do this by clicking the Administration tab. The defaults are the following:

- Attachments to postings are permitted, but only up to 10KB.
- Replies to postings will quote the original message.
- Writers can edit or hide their postings, but only if there have been no replies.
- Users of the web interface will see all messages in a forum sorted in descending chronological order; the alternative is to group messages into threads.
- Postings will be formatted with HTML tags; the alternative is to use plain text formatting.
- Access to a forum will be restricted to those who have been granted the reader or writer role. The alternatives are to permit public read access, with or without public write access.
- E-mail messages to the forum will be ignored. The alternatives are to accept and post e-mail from anyone, or to accept and post e-mail only if it comes from a Forum Writer.

All of these settings can be overridden for any particular forum.

To create a new category, click the New Category button, shown in Figure 9-2, and give the category a name (SUPPORT SERVICES, in this example) and a description. Then grant JWATSON the Category Administrator role, as shown in Figure 9-3. Note that when nominating users for roles, you must not specify the e-mail domain; that is picked up from the domain of the user you are currently connected as (in this case, APPSADMIN).

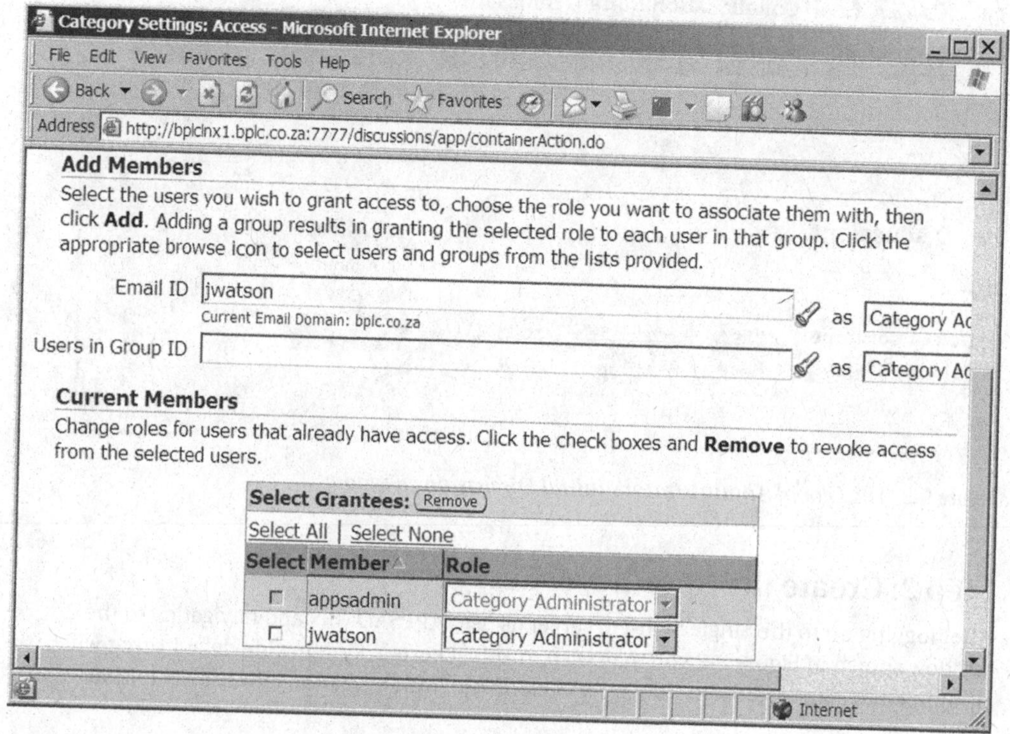

Figure 9-3. *Grant a user the Category Administrator role.*

Step 3: Create the Subcategories

Log out from the APPSADMIN session, and connect as JWATSON. Open the SUPPORT SERVICES category, and create two new categories within it: the INTERNAL category, and the EXTERNAL category. For each of these, click the Settings button and the Access tab. Grant Forum Creator roles to the appropriate users.

Step 4: Create the Forums

Connect to Discussions as SHART, navigate to the EXTERNAL category, and create the two required forums.

To create the ANNOUNCEMENTS forum, click the New Forum button, give it a name, and on the Access tab select the radio button for "Enable public access without anonymous posting." This will allow anyone on the planet to view the postings to the forum, but (unless more users are granted Forum Writer) only SHART can post to it.

Then create the PARTNERS forum, and on the Email tab select the "Open – Email messages sent to the forum e-mail address will always be posted to the forum" radio button, so that outside users will be able to e-mail the forum as well as use the web client to post messages. This is necessary because the external users will not have a Single Sign-On username, which is required to get to the web client. You must also specify an e-mail address for the forum, such as `partners@bplc.co.za`. Then on the Access tab select the "Enable public access with anonymous posting" radio button. This will allow anyone to mail messages to the forum. Clearly, moderating the content is an important task.

The e-mail address of a forum is in fact an alias onto a Mail user with a name of the form `discussions_<db_name>@<default.domain>` where *<db_name>* is the name of the Mail datastore database, and *<default.domain>* is the default Mail domain. This user is automatically created at install time; details can be seen in OIDDAS. The aliases are created for you when you enable a forum for e-mail posting. To see the details of all the aliases that have been set up for enabling e-mailing to forums, go to the Alias Management window of the Mail web client, as shown in Figure 9-4. Full information on managing Mail aliases is given in Chapter 10.

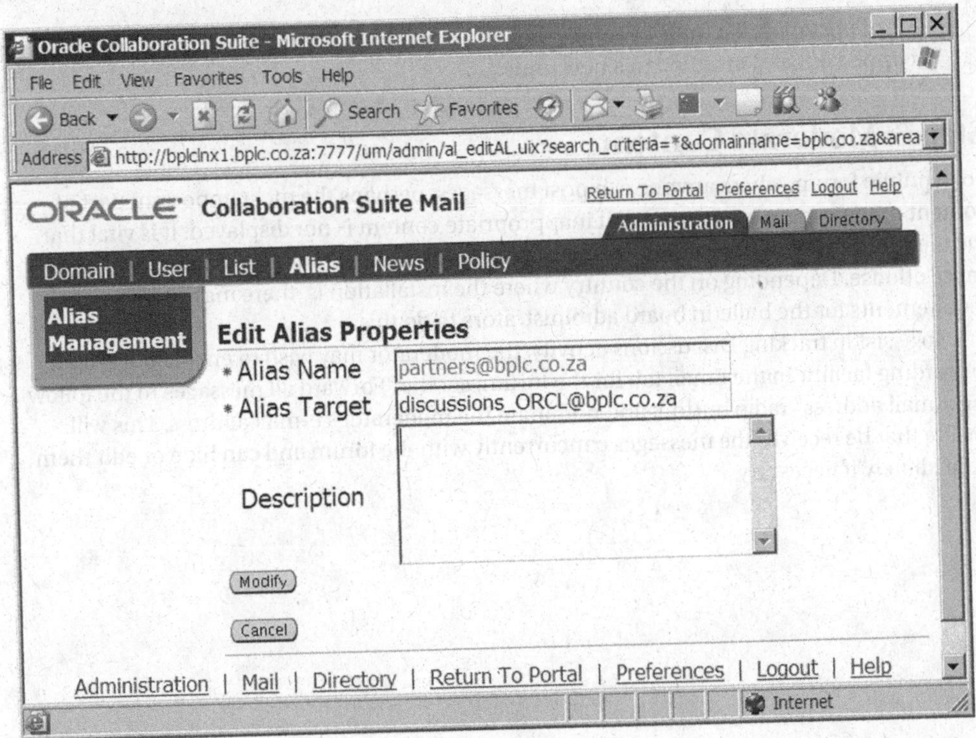

Figure 9-4. *Use of a Mail alias to route e-mail to a forum via the Discussions Mail account*

Step 5: Monitor and Manage the Forums

The creator of each forum (or the moderator, if this responsibility has been devolved) should monitor the activity within the forum. Actions necessary may include the following:

- *Editing or hiding inappropriate posts*: By default, Forum Writers can edit or hide their own postings, but only if there have not been any replies. The Forum Creator or Moderator can edit or hide any post. A hidden post will appear to Forum Writers and Readers as a "Message Deleted" message; the moderator will see it with strike-through characters.
- *Locking forums and topics*: Individual topics can be locked, meaning that no further messages can be posted to it; or whole forums can be locked. The end result is that the topic or forum becomes read-only, except that moderators can still post and edit. Reasons for doing this might be that there is another topic or forum on the same subject making the first one redundant, or perhaps a topic has become too large to be viewed as a whole with ease.
- *Moving topics across forums*: It is possible to relocate a topic from one forum to another, provided the person doing this has the moderator role on both the source and target forums. This is done to move postings to a forum that is more appropriate for the content.
- *Clipping topics*: If a topic becomes too long or wanders off the subject, postings can be clipped out and assigned to a new topic.

Step 6: Moderate Content

For a public forum, where anyone can post messages, perhaps the most important part of content management is ensuring that inappropriate content is not displayed. It is vital that the moderator should track closely what is being written and remove messages that could cause offense. Depending on the country where the installation is, there may even be legal requirements for the bulletin board administrators to do this.

To assist in tracking Discussions activity, the moderator may wish to enable the e-mail forwarding facility. In the Email tab for the forum, set the "Forward all messages to the following e-mail address" radio button, and nominate the moderator's e-mail address. This will ensure that he receives the messages concurrently with the forum and can hide or edit them immediately if necessary.

CHAPTER 10

Configuring Mail

Mail is the electronic mail component of Oracle Collaboration Suite. Mail uses industry standard interfaces and protocols. There is no reason for any Mail user to be aware of the fact that his e-mail service is being provided by Oracle Collaboration Suite rather than by any other e-mail service provider, but if he is aware of this he can exploit the collaborative possibilities of integration with other components.

There is more to Mail than e-mail. There are voice mail and fax capabilities, and the user terminal does not have to be a PC running an e-mail client. The scalability of Mail is effectively unlimited. It can be configured as a simple two-tier system with an e-mail server servicing a few thousand clients. A middle tier of several protocol access servers between several Mail databases and the users means Mail can support a virtually unlimited number of clients.

This chapter describes the Mail architecture and request flow before going on to configuring Mail for use. Finally, some of the command-line utilities are described.

Mail Architecture

Mail follows the standard model for e-mail servers. E-mail mail transfer agents (MTAs) receive messages, either from another remote MTA or from a user process. If the message is to an address local to the mail server, the MTA will send it to its local datastore. If it is for a remote address, it will route it on to another MTA. The MTA arrives at a decision on where to send remote mails by interrogating a DNS server. DNS servers maintain not only the name resolution records that are used for mapping `host.domain` names onto IP addresses, but also Mail Exchange (MX) records that determine where messages to remote addresses should go.

Users make use of an e-mail client to retrieve mail and to generate messages to be sent to the local MTA. The popular protocols for e-mail clients are POP3 and IMAP4. Note that it is possible for a user to communicate directly with the MTA for sending messages, but this is rarely done and will never occur in a standard Oracle Collaboration Suite installation. For generating mail, the e-mail client separates the user from the MTA; it presents him with an interface for creating the message and carrying out associated work such as searching address lists, then formats the message appropriately for transmission by the MTA. For retrieving mail, the e-mail client presents an interface for searching the mail datastore and displaying messages.

A web mail client means that users do not need any e-mail client software on their local machine; they can reach their e-mail server purely through HTTP. This simplifies e-mail usage dramatically and means that mail can be accessible from any web-enabled device without any of the firewall or security issues that can arise when using a (relatively) thick e-mail client that makes use of the mail protocols. It also means that mail data can be centrally stored and managed, which is generally much more secure than having users store their own data, both for confidentiality reasons and for minimizing data loss.

Mail makes extensive use of the Oracle Internet Directory. The directory is used for storing all user identification data, including e-mail addresses, and also for such Mail-related data as mailing lists.

Figure 10-1 shows the components that make up an Oracle Collaboration Suite Mail server. Note the three-tier structure of end users making use of end-user protocols that run on client devices, typically PCs, but they don't have to be. The protocol servers run on the Oracle Application Server middle tier instance(s) that provides the Mail service, and the Oracle Application Server infrastructure instance(s) is used for directory services and data storage.

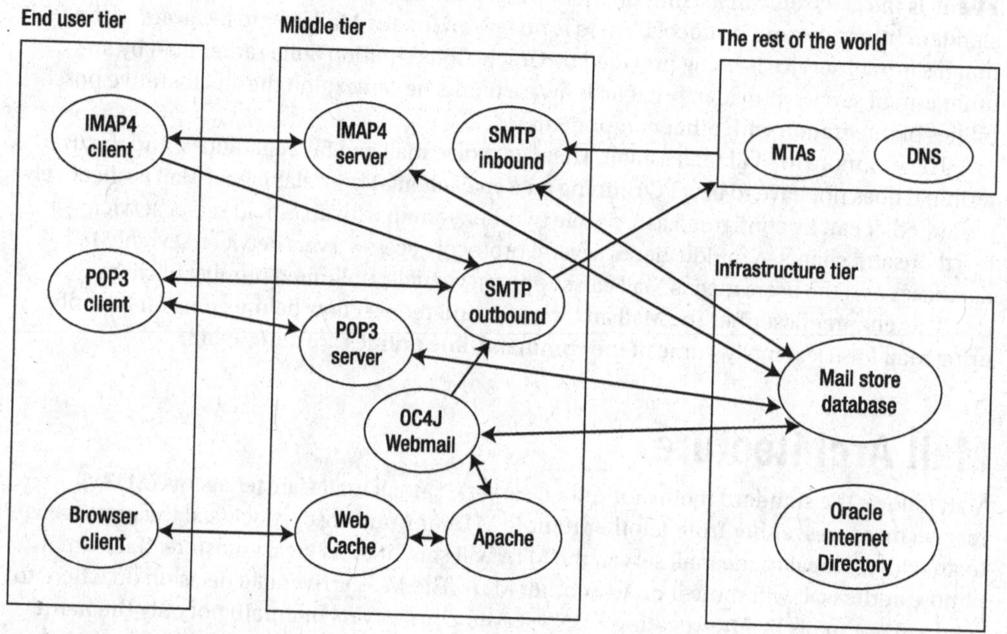

Figure 10-1. *Mail architecture*

The Mail Protocols

It is important to be clear on the protocols used in the Mail environment; they are listed in Table 10-1. All the protocols are layered on top of TCP/IP and can, if necessary, be protected by adding an SSL.

Table 10-1. *The Mail Protocols*

Protocol	Where Used
IMAP (Internet Mail Access Protocol)	Between client process and IMAP protocol server
POP (Post Office Protocol)	Between client process and POP protocol server
SMTP (Simple Mail Transfer Protocol)	All communications to and from the SMTP outbound server; incoming messages to the SMTP inbound server
Oracle Net	All communications to and from the Mail datastore database
LDAP (Lightweight Directory Access Protocol)	All communications to and from the Oracle Internet Directory (not shown in Figure 10-1)
HTTP (Hypertext Transfer Protocol)	Between browser and Web Cache, and between Web Cache and Apache
AJP (Apache Jserv Protocol)	Between Apache and the Webmail process running in an OC4J instance
NNTP (Network News Transport Protocol)	Between the Oracle Collaboration Suite network news server and external network news servers and users' network news clients (not shown in Figure 10-1)
SOAP (Simple Object Access Protocol)	Between the OCS client and the Webmail web services (not shown in Figure 10-1)

The Mail Datastore

The database installed with an Oracle Collaboration Suite infrastructure is preseeded with the schemas used by Mail. It is possible for Mail to share the same database as other Oracle infrastructure components: the metadata repository, the Oracle Internet Directory, and the product schemas for Portal, as an example. This database could even be used as the Content Services datastore, too. However, an installation like that, with all components residing in one database, will not be suitable for many sites. Even though one database can support an extraordinarily high workload, it will often be advisable to divide the workload across several databases on several machines. This will also facilitate tuning. The pattern of activity against the Oracle Internet Directory tables (numerous searches and a relatively small amount of insert/update/delete data manipulation actions) is very different from that against a Mail datastore or a Content Services datastore.

To install a separate database for Mail, use the Oracle Universal Installer to create the infrastructure Oracle home, and point it toward an already installed Oracle Internet Directory and Single Sign-On service. Shut down all the infrastructure services except for the database itself and the database listener. Then in your middle tier instance's Oracle home, create an entry in the `tnsnames.ora` file that will connect to the new database and adjust the configuration of the protocol servers (or create additional protocol servers) to connect through this entry to the new Mail datastore.

The Protocol Servers

The middle tier Oracle Application Server instance installed with an Oracle Collaboration Suite will come with all the protocol servers preconfigured, along with all the other Oracle Collaboration Suite components. As with the database, it is perfectly possible to run all the components in one middle tier instance, but this may not be advisable. Many sites will have one or more middle tier instances dedicated exclusively to Mail. To achieve this, install multiple middle tiers, all connected to the same infrastructure instance, and disable the components that you do not wish to run; all components will be enabled by default.

There are four protocol servers. These servers run as processes in the Oracle Collaboration Suite middle tier Oracle Application Server instance(s).

The SMTP inbound server is the reception point for mail reaching your site. The worldwide system of DNS servers must be configured with MX records that will direct mail addressed to users in your mail domain to the address of your SMTP inbound server; this will be the IP address of the machine hosting the middle tier Oracle Application Server instance. It will save all received mail to the Mail datastore. The SMTP outbound server is responsible for accepting mail generated by your clients and forwarding it to whatever remote MTA is identified by the MX records in the worldwide DNS system.

The POP3 server listens for connections from POP3 clients; the IMAP4 server listens for IMAP4 requests. A typical client would be Microsoft Outlook or Netscape Messenger. The POP3 and IMAP4 protocol servers generate a user interface for clients that can be used for searching the mail store database, and for generating mail to be dispatched to the SMTP outbound protocol server.

The Webmail application is a Java application that runs in an OC4J instance. Any browser (at least, any reasonably modern browser that conforms to standards) can be used as a Webmail client. As far as the client is concerned, Webmail is just another web application: clients contact it with HTTP through the middle tier's Web Cache and Apache web listener. The Webmail application retrieves mail from the Mail datastore and forwards outgoing mail to the SMTP outbound server.

All the protocol servers make use of the Oracle Internet Directory. Directory entries are used for identifying and validating local e-mail addresses for security and for storing distribution lists. The Webmail application is Single Sign-On–aware and will also use the directory through the Single Sign-On service.

The Mail Listener

The various protocol servers all monitor, or listen on, particular TCP ports for connection requests. Oracle already has a process designed for listening on TCP ports for connection requests: the database listener. Rather than write a whole new set of processes to listen for the mail protocols, Oracle uses the database listener, modified to handle the mail protocols. This mail listener is configured in the same manner as a database listener, with a file. On Windows, it is

```
%ORACLE_HOME%\network\admin\istener.ora
```

or on UNIX it is

```
$ORACLE_HOME/network/admin/listener.ora
```

The ORACLE_HOME referred to is the home directory for the middle tier installation, not the home directory for the infrastructure. A typical entry in the listener.ora file to create a Mail listener is the following:

```
LISTENER_ES =
  (DESCRIPTION_LIST =
    (DESCRIPTION =
      (ADDRESS = (PROTOCOL = IPC)(KEY = ocsapps.jwlnx1.bplc.co.za))
    )
    (DESCRIPTION =
      (ADDRESS = (PROTOCOL = TCP)(HOST = jwlnx1.bplc.co.za)(PORT = 25))
      (PRESENTATION = ESSMI)
    )
    (DESCRIPTION =
      (ADDRESS = (PROTOCOL = TCP)(HOST = jwlnx1.bplc.co.za)(PORT = 143))
      (PRESENTATION = IMAP)
    )
    (DESCRIPTION =
      (ADDRESS = (PROTOCOL = TCP)(HOST = jwlnx1.bplc.co.za)(PORT = 110))
      (PRESENTATION = POP)
    )
    (DESCRIPTION =
      (ADDRESS = (PROTOCOL = TCP)(HOST = jwlnx1.bplc.co.za)(PORT = 119))
      (PRESENTATION = ESNNI)
    )
    (DESCRIPTION =
      (ADDRESS = (PROTOCOL = TCPS)(HOST = jwlnx1.bplc.co.za)(PORT = 993))
      (PRESENTATION = IMAPSSL)
    )
    (DESCRIPTION =
      (ADDRESS = (PROTOCOL = TCPS)(HOST = jwlnx1.bplc.co.za)(PORT = 995))
      (PRESENTATION = POPSSL)
    )
    (DESCRIPTION =
      (ADDRESS = (PROTOCOL = TCPS)(HOST = jwlnx1.bplc.co.za)(PORT = 563))
      (PRESENTATION = ESNNISSL)
    )
  )
```

This listener will listen for the seven supported protocols on their standard ports, as shown in Table 10-2.

Table 10-2. *The Default Mail Protocol Ports*

Port	Protocol
25	SMTP
110	POP3
119	NNTP
143	IMAP4
563	NNTP with SSL
993	IMAP with SSL
995	POP with SSL

To start the Mail listener, use the `lsnrctl` utility:

```
lsnrctl start listener_es
```

Note that you must specify the name of the listener, LISTENER_ES, because it is not the default name of LISTENER (listener names are not case sensitive). On some UNIX platforms the listener will fail to start without some further configuration. This is because of UNIX port security. On Windows all ports are treated equally, but on UNIX it is generally not possible for any user other than the root user to start a process that uses a port with a number lower than 1024. All the standard mail ports are less than 1024, so the listener will not start if you attempt to start it as the owner of the Oracle installation. The techniques to bypass this security feature are detailed in Chapter 5. In brief, you must change the operating system ownership of the listener executable to the root user, and then set the sticky bit on the file as follows:

```
chown root $ORACLE_HOME/bin/tnslsnr
chmod 6751 $ORACLE_HOME/bin/tnslsnr
```

These changes will allow you to take on the root user's privileges for the purpose of starting the Mail listener. An alternative approach (also described in Chapter 6) is to start the listener as the root user, and then have the process take on the identity of the Oracle owner once it is running. To do this, as the root user, run

```
$ORACLE_HOME/bin/tnslsnr -user <user number> -group <group number> &
```

substituting the user number and group number of the Oracle owner. Both these methods have pros and cons as far as your system administrators are concerned, and which to use is a matter for discussion with them.

Once started, this listener will monitor several addresses, each using a different port for a particular protocol. Study the file and you will see the various protocols (referred to as PRESENTATION) and the ports on which they will be accepted. The IPC listening address is not used for mail services, but for administration commands.

To test whether a given protocol is actually working, attempt to make connection with telnet. There are two possible errors. First, the Mail listener may not be running; this will generate an "Unable to connect to remote host: Connection refused" message, as the telnet client will not get any response. Second, the protocol server may not be running; this will generate a "Connection closed by foreign host" error as the listener fails in its attempt to forward the request to the protocol server. Figure 10-2 shows the output of testing the availability of the SMTP protocol server, on port 25, with telnet at various stages. Note that this example is using the telnet client supplied with Linux; other telnet clients (notably, that supplied with Microsoft Windows) may not display the messages in the same way.

```
oraocs@jwlnx1:~
[mid oraocs]$
[mid oraocs]$
[mid oraocs]$ telnet jwlnx1.bplc.co.za 25
Trying 127.0.0.1...
telnet: Unable to connect to remote host: Connection refused
[mid oraocs]$
[mid oraocs]$ telnet jwlnx1.bplc.co.za 25
Trying 127.0.0.1...
Connected to jwlnx1.bplc.co.za (127.0.0.1).
Escape character is '^]'.
Connection closed by foreign host.
[mid oraocs]$
[mid oraocs]$ telnet jwlnx1.bplc.co.za 25
Trying 127.0.0.1...
Connected to jwlnx1.bplc.co.za (127.0.0.1).
Escape character is '^]'.
220 server ready. Unauthorized Access Prohibited.

500 5.5.1 Command unrecognized
```

Figure 10-2. *Using telnet to test the availability of the SMTP protocol server*

The first use of telnet in Figure 10-2 fails with an "Unable to connect…" message because the listener has not been started. After starting the listener in another window, the second use of telnet fails with a "Connection closed…" message; the listener is running but the protocol server is not. After starting the protocol server with

```
opmnctl startproc process-type=email_smtp_in
```

in another window, the third use of telnet succeeds; the "220 server ready" message indicates that there is a service there (though, being an SMTP service, it can't understand a telnet client). The different protocol servers, running on their various ports, will generate different messages at this point.

Mail Processes

Incoming and outgoing mail goes through various processes and over various protocols during its passage through Mail. The external interfaces (IMAP4, POP3, SMTP) are perfectly conformant to standards, and an Oracle Collaboration Suite Mail e-mail server will fit into an existing e-mail system with no problems. Internally, Mail makes extensive use of Oracle proprietary products. There are development toolkits that let programmers develop applications that use Mail through published APIs, if for some reason the standard Mail facilities are not adequate.

The Mail processes are all controlled with OPMN. As displayed by the `opmnctl status` command (see Figure 5-14 in Chapter 5) they are the following:

- `email_housekeeper`
- `email_imap`
- `email_listserver`
- `email_nntp_in`
- `email_nntp_out`
- `email_pop`
- `email_smtp_in`
- `email_smtp_out`
- `email_virus_scrub~`

Figure 10-3 shows them as seen through Application Server Control.

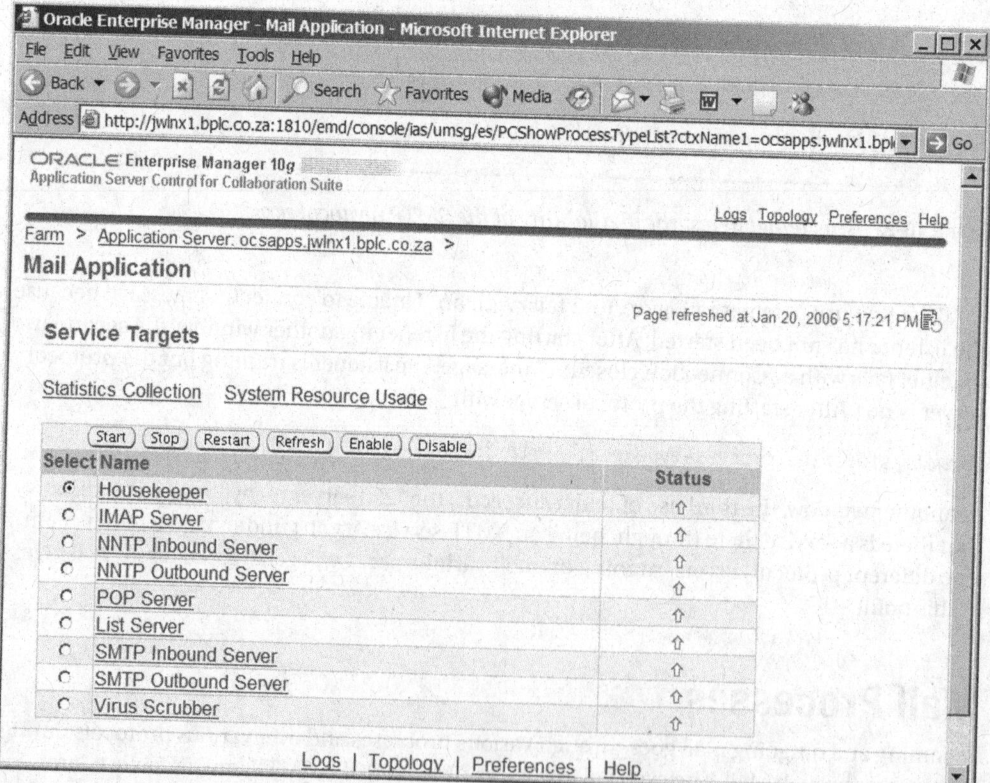

Figure 10-3. *The Mail server processes, partially started*

The Housekeeper

The housekeeper servers (in a production system there will be several of them) perform three major functions:

Garbage collection: When users delete a message, for performance reasons, it is not actually deleted in real time from the Mail datastore. It is merely flagged for deletion and actually deleted at some later point by the housekeeper. At the same time, the housekeeper can also clean up (control) messages sent between Mail servers that have been left on queues. A housekeeper configured for garbage collection is created automatically for every Mail server.

Text indexing: It is possible to index message bodies, headers, and attachments for fast searching, but this is a time- and resource-consuming process. For this reason it is not done in real time. Messages that need to be indexed are queued up for indexing on a schedule by a housekeeper server that you configure for this purpose after installation. A housekeeper configured for indexing can also do statistics cleanup and Text index optimization.

Tertiary storage: Many users retain a large amount of mail in their mailboxes indefinitely; most of this will be static and rarely if ever accessed. In order to optimize performance for live data and the use of hardware resources, you can configure a housekeeper server to migrate older messages to a set of tablespaces created for this purpose.

Regardless of the size of the installation, Oracle recommends creating at least three housekeeper servers, one for each of the previous functions.

The IMAP and POP Servers

Typically, a site will run either IMAP or POP and disable the other. The IMAP or POP server maintains a pool of worker threads for servicing client requests, and a pool of database connections shared by all the worker threads. One worker thread is assigned persistently to each client connection; the threads acquire and release database connections whenever they need to read from or write to the Mail datastore.

It is possible to configure multiple Mail datastores, all of which can be accessed by any one POP or IMAP server; and by installing multiple Oracle Collaboration Suite middle tier instances you can create additional POP and IMAP servers all connecting to the same Mail store database(s).

The default ports used are the following:

- Port 110, POP
- Port 143, IMAP
- Port 993, IMAP with SSL
- Port 995, POP with SSL

The List Server

List servers manage public and private distribution lists. Users create their own lists to be used for mass distributions of mail and documents or as discussion forums. There is a supported API that lets developers integrate lists with third-party messaging services and applications.

The list server does not need a TCP port; it makes use of the SMTP service for delivering its messages.

The Network News Server

The Network News Server is two processes, one for incoming NNTP messages, one for outgoing. A network news site is one or more NNTP servers connected to a local datastore of NNTP articles. Sites can exchange locally posted articles with each other, thus establishing a "replication" type environment where many NNTP servers have content in common.

The NNTP inbound server accepts articles from clients and posts them to its own newsgroups stored within the Mail datastore database; the outbound server manages exchange of these articles with other NNTP sites anywhere in the world that have been configured as peers.

The default ports used by the news server are the following:

- Port 119, NNTP
- Port 563, NNTP with SSL

The SMTP Server

The SMTP server is two processes, one for incoming SMTP messages, one for outgoing. Each server connects to only one Mail datastore database, but multiple server-database pairs can be configured to scale the Mail site. Address rewriting rules ensure that even though mail boxes for different users may be managed by different servers and stored in different databases, the Mail site appears to be one server and can be one mail domain.

The SMTP server can handle mail within the domain, mail from internal users directed to addresses outside the domain, and mail received from outside the domain for internal users. It can also act as a relay server, forwarding externally generated mail to another mail server, and will work with the list server if a destination address is in fact a mailing list.

Note that the SMTP server can (and should) be configured for virus detection and spam filtering.

The SMTP server uses, by default, port 25.

The Virus Scrubber

The virus detection carried out by the SMTP server should detect all virus threats in incoming mail, but unfortunately this is not good enough. The rate at which viruses are developed means that it is inevitable that at some time infected mail will be received before the virus definition routines used by the SMTP server are updated to detect the problem, so you will have infected files in your Mail datastore.

The Virus Scrubber service will scan the entire Mail datastore or a subset according to rules and a schedule. Both the Virus Scrubber and the SMTP virus detection use detection and cleanup software from the Symantec AntiVirus Scan Engine (SAVSE).

Mail Request Handling

However mail is originally created, received, or accessed, it is all stored in an Oracle database: the Mail datastore. This means that users can pick up mail with any tool they please; they are not tied to one client or one protocol. In his own office, a user could use Microsoft Outlook with the Oracle Connector for Outlook installed for added functionality and connect to the local Mail server with IMAP. Then, provided he does not delete his messages from the server as he copies them to his Outlook client, he can continue working later from any Internet café or from home using the Webmail application.

Incoming Mail

In most organizations, mail servers are protected from the outside world by placing them behind a firewall. Depending on how sophisticated this firewall is, there may be a certain amount of processing of incoming mail before it even reaches Mail. Messages will typically pass through virus scanners and spam filters running on the firewall, and all traffic may be proxied rather than getting to the Mail SMTP inbound server directly. But as a Mail administrator, you need not be concerned with that; as far as Mail is concerned, mail from external organizations and e-mail services will be routed to the SMTP inbound mail server. The routing is done according to MX records in DNS servers that map your mail domain to the address of the machine where you have installed your Oracle Collaboration Suite middle tier.

The SMTP inbound server will, unless you configure it otherwise, be listening on port 25. This is the port to which external MTAs will be sending messages. When a message is received, formatted according to the SMTP protocol, the SMTP inbound server will first connect to the Oracle Internet Directory, using LDAP, to validate the address and confirm that it is in fact for a registered user within your Mail domain. If the address passes this test, the SMTP inbound server will connect to the mail store database, using Oracle Net, and save the message in the appropriate mailbox, where it will wait for user pickup, or possibly for further routing and final delivery.

Outgoing Mail from POP3 or IMAP Clients

The user client process (such as Microsoft Outlook) constructs the message according to the SMTP standards and sends it to the SMTP outbound mail server, using the SMTP protocol. The SMTP outbound mail server connects with LDAP to the Oracle Internet Directory and validates the address details. If the address is an internal address, the SMTP outbound server forwards the message to the SMTP inbound server. The SMTP inbound server then processes it as it would any other incoming message and saves it to the Mail datastore. There is no difference between processing mail from an external source and mail from an internal source. If the address is for an external mail domain, the SMTP outbound server will consult the DNS system for MX records that will instruct it on where to forward the message. The message is then sent on its way to the destination MTA, possibly going through a number of "hops" as the MX records route it from one MTA to another before it reaches the MTA that will recognize the destination address as being for one of its local users.

Note that the POP3 and IMAP4 protocol servers are not involved in delivering outgoing mail at all.

Retrieving Messages with IMAP4 and POP3

The choice between IMAP4 and POP3 is a matter of personal preference, though most users will prefer IMAP4. Both protocols allow users to connect to a mail server to send, retrieve, and store mail, and also to transfer mail from the server to local client storage. The IMAP protocol is rather more efficient in terms of the volume of data transferred than the POP protocol, and also allows much more sophisticated management of e-mail on the server; POP3 will generally only be used in an environment where it is customary always to transfer mail to the client immediately, rather than store and manage it on the server.

Either protocol requires a relatively thick client, such as Microsoft Outlook or Netscape Messenger. Users configure the client with the address of the protocol server: the IP address or hostname of the middle tier machine. The standard listening port for IMAP is 143; for POP version 3 it is 110 (though it was 109 for POP version 2).

On receiving a client connection request, the protocol server will authenticate the user against the Oracle Internet Directory. It is not possible to use Single Sign-On authentication, because that requires HTTP; even if users have already connected to Single Sign-On, they will receive another logon request generated by the Mail protocol server and displayed in their e-mail client. This login prompt (but not the login itself) can of course be avoided if users connect with a client that allows them to save login names and passwords.

Once the user has been authenticated, the protocol server will retrieve any and all messages from the user's mailbox and transmit them to the client process. Depending on the user's settings, the protocol server may or may not delete the messages from the Mail datastore as it does this.

The Webmail Application

The Webmail application is a J2EE application consisting of Java servlet web services; it does not include any Enterprise JavaBeans. It runs in an OC4J container hosted by an Oracle Application Server middle tier instance. Like all web services, it communicates with SOAP messages: XML documents. The name of the application, as shown with the `opmnctl status` command or in Application Server Control, is OC4J_Mail.

As with all Oracle Application Server middle tier web applications, the standard access method is from a browser through a Web Cache to an Apache web listener. If the browser has not yet been authenticated by Single Sign-On, Apache will redirect the browser to the Single Sign-On server. Once authenticated, Apache will forward the request through modoc4j to the Oracle Collaboration Suite web client, which will connect the user to the Webmail web services. End users do not contact Mail directly—they rely on the Oracle Collaboration Suite web client to do this for them. The Mail development toolkits can assist programmers in constructing their own processes that can use the Webmail web services directly, but regular users are shielded from the complexity of having to construct their own SOAP messages.

For the Webmail application to be available to end users, several Oracle Collaboration Suite middle tier components must be running:

The Web Cache: This is the users' point of entry to the Oracle Collaboration Suite.

Apache: Web Cache will route all requests to the Apache web listener. Apache will forward them to the Oracle Collaboration Suite client component.

Oracle Collaboration Suite client: The OC4J_OCSClient component generates the user interface for Mail (and other applications).

The Webmail application: The OC4J_Mail component runs the web services that make up the Webmail application.

The SMTP protocol server (part of the Mail application component): Without this, Webmail can retrieve mail from the Mail datastore, but it cannot send mail, and no new incoming mail will be accepted.

The Webmail application displays messages by reading data directly from the Mail datastore. It sends messages by transmitting them to the SMTP outbound service from where they are managed as normal. There is no interaction between Webmail and the IMAP or POP protocol servers.

Mail Object Administration

There are a number of objects within the Mail environment that can be seen by users. Principal among these are the following:

Domains: These are the site addresses used by your various Mail users—the part of an e-mail address that follows the @ symbol.

Users: These are the accounts you create in Mail, based on users created in the Oracle Internet Directory. In addition to users, you can create aliases for users.

Distribution lists: These are mailing lists stored within the Oracle Internet Directory and used by the users.

Newsgroups: These are the bulletin boards hosted locally that can replicate with external network news servers.

All these objects are used by your Mail users, but in some cases they must be created by the Mail administrator.

Creating a Mail Administrative User

The simplest way to create your Mail administrator is through the OIDDAS facility. This is an application that runs in the Oracle Collaboration Suite infrastructure instance; connect to it through the infrastructure's Apache web listener and create the user. The URL will be similar to `http://jwlnx1.bplc.co.za:7777/oiddas`.

The `host.domain` is that of your Oracle Application Server infrastructure instance; the port is the default port for an infrastructure's Apache web listener. Log in as the orcladmin user, click the Directory tab, and click the Create button to create a new user. Be sure to give him the System Administrator role in the Mail application's attributes section when working through the Create User wizard.

Having created your Mail administrator, log out from OIDDAS and connect to your middle tier instance using the newly created username. The Webmail interface will have an Administration tab, which is not shown for regular users. This account will be used for most Mail administration work.

Managing Domains

A *domain* identifies an e-mail account as belonging to a particular organization. E-mail domain names (which need not be related to DNS domains, though they often are) are unique worldwide and must be registered through an organization that offers domain name registration services, such as an ISP. Within a domain, the user's name must be unique. The worldwide DNS system is responsible for maintaining MX records that ensure mail for a particular domain reaches the correct mail server.

To manage domains you must connect to the Mail web client as a Mail user with either the System Administrator privilege or the Domain Administrator privilege; a Domain Administrator can only manage his own domain, whereas a System Administrator can manage all domains and create new domains.

One e-mail domain will have been created at install time. In fact, depending on the domain you specified at install time, you may have created several. If, for example, the domain specified at install time was `bplc.co.za`, there will have been three domains created: `za`, `co.za`, and `bplc.co.za`. These default domains may be all you ever need, but you can create additional domains later. These must be "child" domains of one of the existing domains. Thus, if your default domain is `bplc.co.za`, you might create child domains called `gp.bplc.co.za` (for staff based in Gauteng Province), `ec.bplc.co.za` (for staff in the Eastern Cape), and `kzn.bplc.co.za` (for staff in KwaZulu Natal).

Apart from creating multiple domains to separate users into groups—typically groups that will follow organizational structure—different domains can also be configured with different default settings: attributes such as the user's space quota. If your installation of Oracle Collaboration Suite were to provide mail services for a number of companies, you would create separate domains for each company configured according to the standards set by the various service level agreements. However, Mail is the only Oracle Collaboration Suite component that can do this; the others are limited to just one domain, and for this reason use of multiple domains is not recommended by Oracle.

Figure 10-4 shows the Mail administration window. There is no choice for installation; `um_system` is acceptable. Choose a domain to manage. The choice of domain will be your default domain (shown in Figure 10-4) or its parent or grandparent.

The Create Domain link under the Domain button will prompt you to choose a parent for the new domain, which must be one of your existing domains, and then the name to append to the parent. For example, if you select the parent domain to be `bplc.co.za` and enter `kzn` as the domain name, your new domain will be `kzn.bplc.co.za`.

To configure user settings for your various domains, take the default New User link. The attributes that can be configured for each domain are shown in Figure 10-5. In particular, note the option to choose a database. In a large-scale installation, you will create several Mail datastore databases. Each domain can use a different database, or they can share a common database. You can switch a domain over to a different database for all new users without affecting existing users.

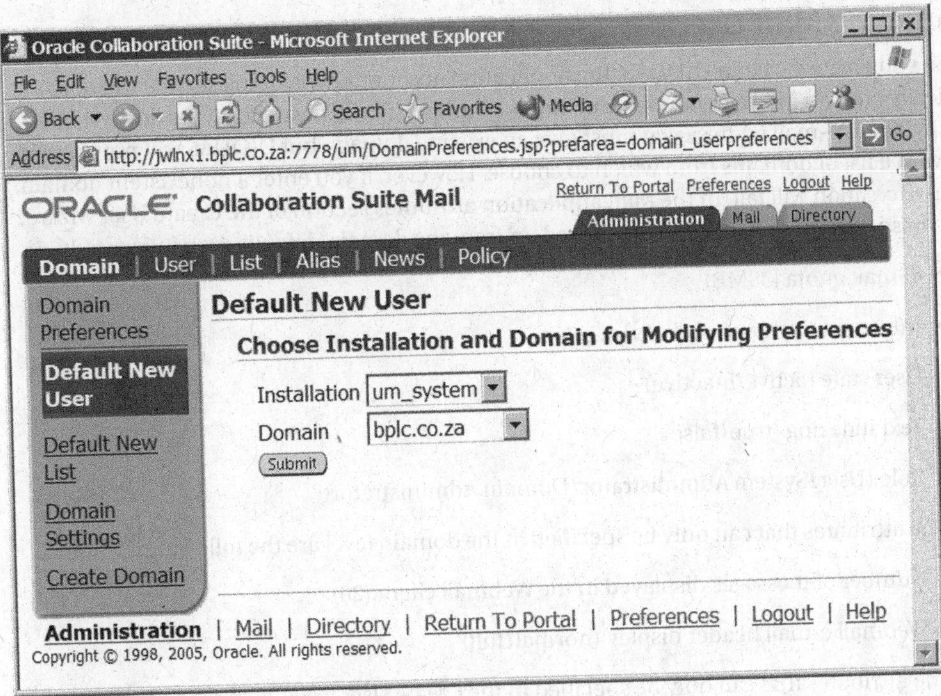

Figure 10-4. *The Mail administration window in the web client*

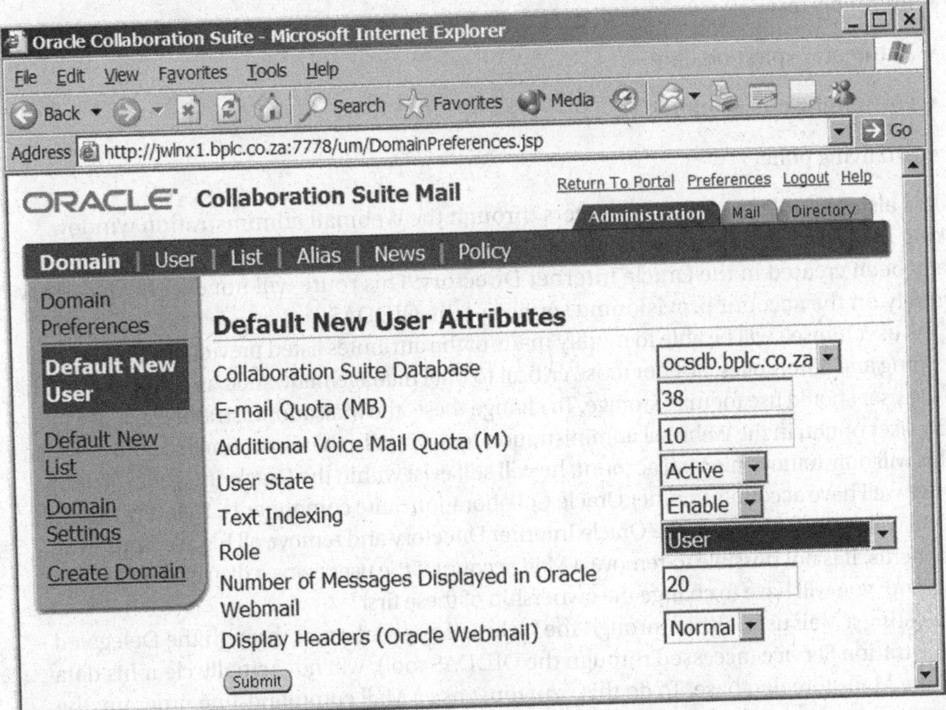

Figure 10-5. *Default user attributes that can be set per Mail domain*

Managing Mail Users

When you create a user in OIDDAS, the application account provisioning service will automatically create a Mail account for him, unless you specifically deselect this option. When specifying his e-mail address you must give an existing domain, but OIDDAS will not present you with a list of domains from which to choose. However, if you enter a nonexistent domain, the user creation will fail. In the Mail application attributes section of the Create User wizard, you can specify these items that are picked up from the domain defaults seen in Figure 10-5:

- E-mail quota (38MB)
- Information store (`ocsdb.bplc.co.za`)
- User state (active/inactive)
- Text indexing (true/false)
- Role (User/System Administrator/Domain Administrator)

The attributes that can only be specified at the domain level are the following:

- Number of messages displayed in the Webmail client (20)
- Webmail e-mail header display (normal/full)

The attributes that can only be specified in the Create User wizard are the following:

- Autoreply mode (echo/reject/reply/vacation)
- Autoreply text
- Autoreply expiration date
- Forwarding e-mail address
- Archiving policy

It is also possible to create Mail users through the Webmail administration window. Clicking the User button shown in Figure 10-4 will let you create a user in Mail if he has already been created in the Oracle Internet Directory. This route will not ever be necessary if you rely on the account provisioning service of the OIDDAS.

The user himself will be able to modify many of the attributes listed previously, such as mail forwarding and autoreplies, but not those critical to Mail management, such as quota or the database the user should use for mail storage. To change these, the Mail administrator must use the Modify User option in the Webmail administration tool. This also has an option to remove a user, but this will only remove his Mail account; he will still exist within the Oracle Internet Directory and may well have accounts in other Oracle Collaboration Suite components. Deleting a user in OIDDAS will remove him from the Oracle Internet Directory and remove all his accounts in all components. It is not possible to remove a Mail account if the user owns a distribution list or a newsgroup; you will have to change the ownership of these first.

Deleting a Mail user, either through the Webmail application or through the Delegated Administration Service (accessed through the OIDDAS tool), will not actually clear his data out of the Mail store database. To do this, you must use a Mail command-line program: the oesucr utility. First, use the utility to obtain a list of all deleted users whose data has not yet been cleared:

```
$ oesucr -list_deleted_users
User igama@bplc.co.za deleted on Sat Nov 05 16:17:22 SAST 2005
User bsekwale@bplc.co.za deleted on Sat Nov 05 16:17:22 SAST 2005
```

Save the list to a file (in this example, called deleted_uses.txt) formatted with a comma-separated list of addresses, like this:

```
mail=igama@bplc.co.za,bsekwale@bplc.co.za
```

Then use the utility to delete all the Mail data that belonged to the deleted users:

```
$ oesucr deleted_users.txt -clean_user_mailstore_data
users delete from mailstore list size=2
user to delete mailstore =igama@bplc.co.za
user to delete mailstore =bsekwale@bplc.co.za
```

Managing Aliases

The alias capability lets you redirect mail from one address to another. Mail to one domain can in effect be redirected to another, or mail addressed to one person can be received by another. An example of when this is necessary is when a user changes his or her name, as frequently happens when people marry. If the user wishes to change his or her e-mail address to reflect the new name, you can make this change and then create an alias for the old address; all e-mail coming to your Mail server that is addressed to the old address will be rerouted to the new one. In this case, the alias will be within one domain. Another case is when restructuring your domain system. For example, if you decide to consolidate several domains into one, you will have to issue users with new e-mail addresses on the new consolidated domain. Setting up aliases for the old addresses that point to the new ones will mean that incoming mail to the old domains will still be delivered. Note that aliases have nothing to do with forwarding; the alias does not exist as an address. An alias merely lets the Mail server accept mail for a nonexistent address and deliver it to an extant address.

To create an alias, click the Alias tab as shown in Figure 10-6. When creating an alias, you must first select the domain in which it will reside. This should be the target domain of the expected incoming e-mail. Then specify the alias. This is the address that the mail will be using; it is an address that does not exist (or perhaps does not exist any longer.) Finally, specify the target; this is the address to which the mail will be delivered. This target address can be in the same or a different domain, but it must be an address that does exist in your Mail installation.

The aliasing capability is also very useful for generic e-mail accounts. Many sites will have nonpersonal accounts, such as a notional user called *support* that is used by clients for reporting problems. If you do not wish to create an e-mail account for this nonexistent person, you could create an alias for it that points to your help-desk manager's account. This should ensure that all support problems are received, without having to expose an internal address to the outside world. When your help-desk manager goes on holiday or is fired, you can edit the alias to point to his replacement.

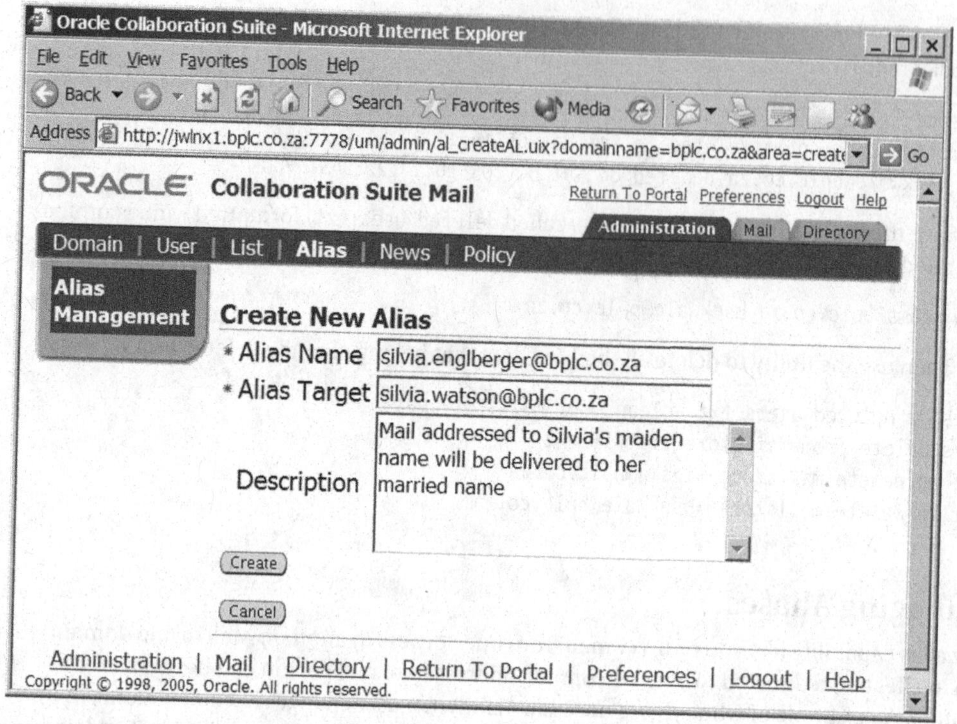

Figure 10-6. *Creating an alias within the bplc.co.za domain*

Distribution Lists

Distribution lists are a set of e-mail addresses. A single e-mail sent to the list is forwarded to all the list's members—all the e-mail addresses of which the list consists. List processing is managed by the Mail list server process.

A distribution list must be defined as being of a certain group type, which defines how mail is accepted and processed; a certain subscription type, which defines who can join the list for receiving mail; and a certain posting type, which defines who can send to the list.

The possible group types are the following:

Announcement: An announcement list is used for sending messages to the list members, with no processing of delivery notifications or autoreplies. This type of list is used for messages where the sender is not concerned with whether any individual receives the messages.

Discussion: A discussion list has the reply-to e-mail header attribute set to the name of the list, so replies will automatically be posted to all list members. Autoreplies and delivery notification are sent back to the sender, though it is possible to configure bounce processing. If this is enabled, autoreplies go to the list server's bounce processor. This is very useful for large lists. It is most disconcerting for a user to send mail to a discussion list and then receive hundreds of "I'm on holiday" type replies.

Edited: An edited list restricts those who can post mail to the list to a configurable list of editors who will be a subset of the list membership. Autoreplies and delivery notification are sent back to the sender, though it is possible to configure bounce processing.

Moderated: All messages sent to a moderated list are sent to the list moderators. These are a subset of the list membership. At least one moderator must approve any message before it is posted to the rest of the distribution list. Autoreplies and delivery notification are sent back to the sender, though it is possible to configure bounce processing.

The possible subscription types are the following:

Open: An open list is available to all Mail users. Anyone can subscribe to the list and receive all mail posted to it.

Restricted: Users must send a request to subscribe to the owner of the list, or any of a sub-list of approvers, and cannot join the list until this request is granted.

Closed: It is not possible to request a subscription to a closed list. Subscribers must be invited by the list's owner.

The possible posting types are the following:

Subscriber: Only the members of the list can post a message to a subscriber list. Mail from nonsubscribers is rejected.

Open: Anyone can post to an open posting list, whether they are members of the list or not.

To create a distribution list, connect to the Webmail client as an administrator, and click the List button on the Administration tab, shown in Figure 10-4. Click the Create List link and you will be asked which domain the list resides in, then whether the list is a Quick list or a List Server list. A Quick list is an Announcement list created with only a subset of configuration options. Assuming that you choose List Server, you can provide the information shown in Table 10-3.

Table 10-3. *Distribution List Attributes*

Attribute	Default Value	Description
List name	default_list	The name used as the e-mail address of the list; will be qualified by the domain
Owner	The current user	The fully qualified e-mail address of the person who will own the list
Maximum message size	0 (unlimited)	You can restrict the size of messages that the list will accept
Topic	Null	A single line describing the content of the list
Invite text	Null	Text for an e-mail used to invite users to join the list
Editors list	Null	The fully qualified e-mail addresses of the editors (applies only to an edited list)

Continued

Table 10-3. *Continued*

Attribute	Default Value	Description
Moderators list	Null	The fully qualified e-mail addresses of the moderators (applies only to a moderated list)
Group approvers	Null	The fully qualified e-mail addresses of the users who can approve subscription requests (applies only to a restricted list)
Information test	Null	A multiline description of the list's purpose
Merge tag	Null	A tag that can be used for mail merge and for scheduling deliveries
Collaboration Suite Database	The current Mail store	The database in which to queue the messages received until the list server processes them
Autoreconfirm	True	A flag to control whether requests to subscribe and unsubscribe should be confirmed by the user
Group type	Discussion	The type of list, which may be announcement, discussion, edited, or moderated
Subscription type	Open	The type of subscription, which may be open, closed, or restricted; this limits who can join the list
Post type	Open	The type of posting, which may be open or restricted; this limits who can post to the list
Unsubscribe not allowed	False	A flag that controls whether members can choose to leave the list
List state	Active	The state of a list, which may be Active (posting permitted), inactive (posting not permitted), or migrating (currently being moved into the installation)
Enable digests	No	A flag to control whether messages are batched up and delivered to members as one message according to a frequency the member chooses
Bounce processing	No	A flag to control whether the bounce processor should catch all failed delivery messages and inform the list owner when one recipient has bounced a certain number of times.
Restrict membership to the domain	Yes	The membership of the list restricted to users in the same domain as the list itself
Edit/view member privilege	Members, owner, approvers, moderators, editors	Types of members who edit and view other members

Attribute	Default Value	Description
Suppress headers	Null	Header information for posts from different types of members can be suppressed
Archive list	False	A list that can be archived to another list

Once the list is created, Mail users can choose to join (or request to join) through the Webmail client and send messages to the list if permitted. The user interface is perfectly self-explanatory.

Newsgroups

A newsgroup is a collection of messages regarding a particular topic. They are posted to a news server and maintained by that server on its local file system. Through the NNTP Usenet system, the contents of a newsgroup can be replicated to a number of news servers, known as *peer* servers. Each peer server accepts local postings and forwards them to other peer servers.

Newsgroups may be public or private. A *public* newsgroup will have worldwide distribution and will be maintained at many new sites; *private* newsgroups are local to one domain and are used as internal discussion forums. Historically, newsgroups were a driving force of the Internet community; to a degree, their importance has now diminished, but being able to act as a network news server is a vital part of Oracle Collaboration Suite's capability.

Network news is enabled by starting two processes: the `email_nntp_in` and `email_nntp_out` processes. Then a Mail administrator must set up peer newsgroup servers that will provide and accept postings and create the newsgroups, either private or public. This is done through the Webmail client.

Figure 10-7 shows the window where you define peer newsgroup servers. Connect to the Webmail client as an Administrator and click the Administration tab and the News button.

To define a network news peer server take the following steps:

1. Enter the name of a server with which you wish to exchange public newsgroup content.
2. In the Inbound Feed section, list the newsgroups for which articles will be accepted. You can use wild cards. If no groups are listed, feed for all newsgroups offered by the peer server will be accepted.
3. List the newsgroups that will be rejected. This second list is checked after the first list, so if (perhaps through injudicious use of wild cards) a newsgroup is listed as both accepted and rejected, it will be rejected.
4. Finally, in the Outbound Feed section (not shown in Figure 10-7) list the newsgroups hosted by your server, which will be propagated to the peer server.

To create a private newsgroup, click the Private Newsgroup Management link shown in Figure 10-7. You will be presented with a list of newsgroups, which will include any mailing lists you have already created. Newsgroups are implemented as mailing lists, with the added functionality that public newsgroups can be propagated to peer servers using the NNTP protocol. To create a public newsgroup, click the Public Newsgroup Management link.

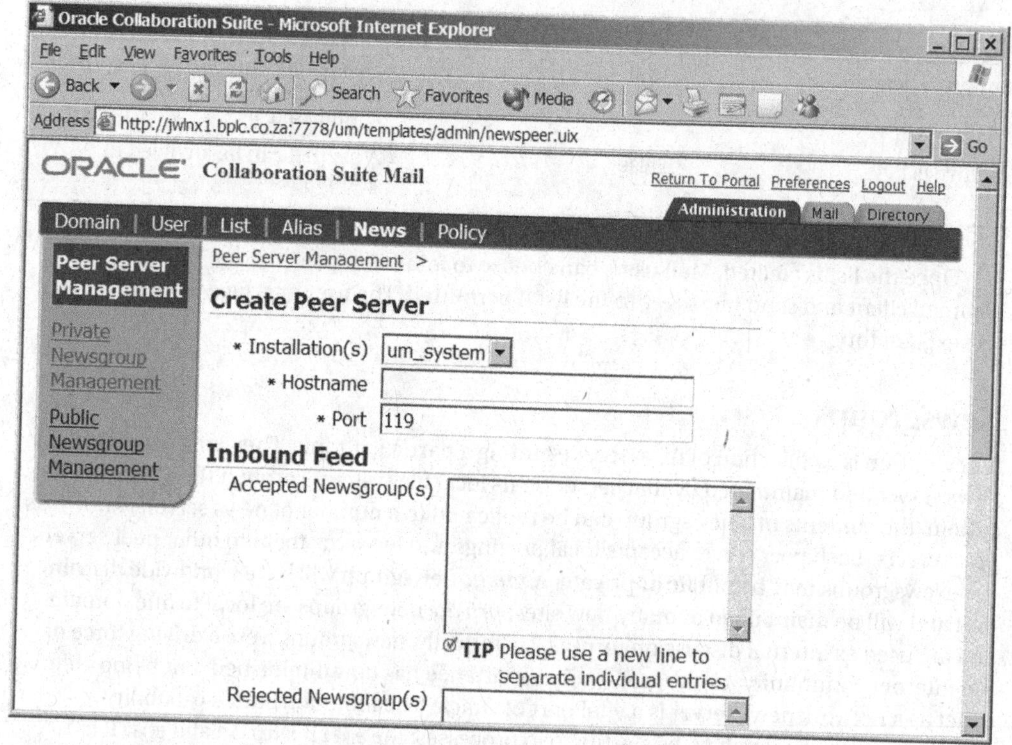

Figure 10-7. *Defining a network news peer server*

Mail Server Configuration

The out-of-the-box configuration of Mail will function, but usually you will want to configure the server environment. The scalability of Mail is controlled by managing its database server connections and the number of Mail server processes. Additional performance can come from indexing documents and enabling archiving.

Database Connections

One Mail datastore database can hold messages for several domains, or one domain's data can be distributed across several databases. When creating a Mail user, you must specify which database will store that user's messages and folders; it is not possible for one user's data to be distributed across databases.

To add a second database to the Mail environment, you must install another Oracle Collaboration Suite infrastructure instance without the identity management components and associate this with the existing infrastructure's Oracle Internet Directory. This will bring it into the Application Server farm and make the database available as a mail store to the Oracle Collaboration Suite middle tier instance(s). Then to modify the Mail server's database connection parameters, use Application Server Control, connect to the middle tier instance, and click the link for the Mail Application component, shown in Figure 10-8.

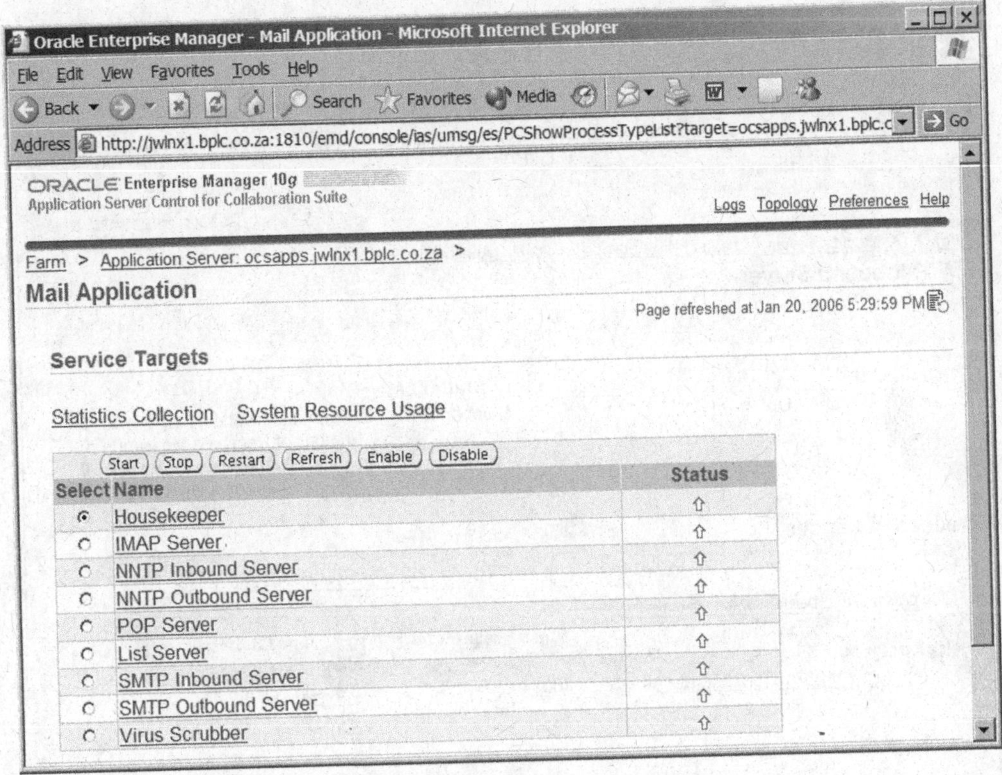

Figure 10-8. *The Mail servers, as shown in Application Server Control*

Click the link for whichever XXXprotocol server process you want to configure to reach the window shown in Figure 10-9. Each protocol server home page has a section called Target with a link for Collaboration Suite Database Connection Parameters.

To make a database available to a protocol server, click the Default Settings link. This will present you with a list of databases that are available in the farm; select those you want the protocol server to be able to use. For each available database, you can configure the number of concurrent connections the server is allowed to make for its connection pool. This is done through the Collaboration Suite Database Connection Parameters link, where for each selected database you can configure the initial number of connections the server will make; the time-out before it will make another connection; and the maximum it is allowed to make. The defaults are one initial connection and a maximum of ten with a one-hour time-out between launching additional connections.

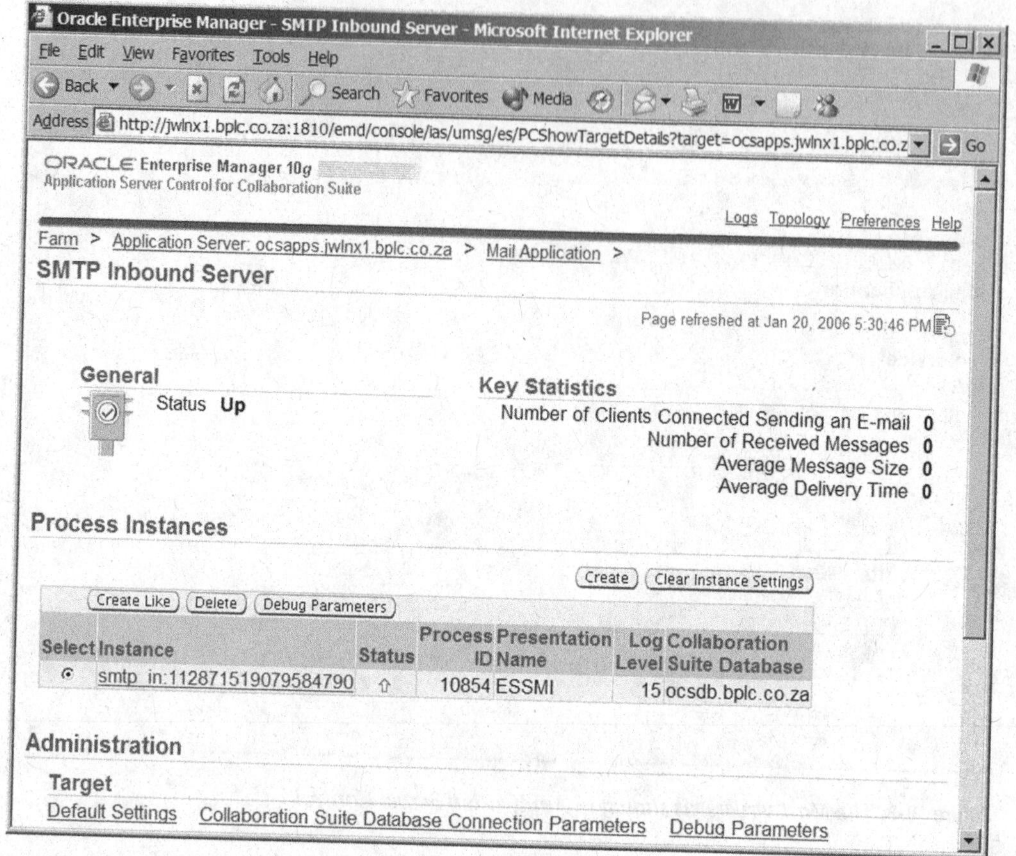

Figure 10-9. *The home page for the SMTP inbound protocol server*

Creating Protocol Server Instances

The default Mail installation will give you one protocol server for each protocol with the SMTP and NNTP servers having separate inbound and outbound processes. Depending on the workload, one server per protocol may be inadequate, no matter how many databases and database connections it is allowed to use. Heavy use by users will require additional IMAP or POP servers if performance is not to degrade; large volumes of incoming or outgoing mail may require additional SMTP inbound or outbound processes if mail is not to back up or be rejected.

To create additional servers, use Application Server Control. In the Mail Application window shown in Figure 10-8, click the link for the server you want to augment. There is a Create button that will create an additional instance of the server configured with defaults, and a Create Like button that will create an instance with the same configuration as an existing instance. There is no reason for multiple server instances to be identical; you could, for example, create one server for each of your mail store databases rather than several servers each connecting to all of your mail store databases.

Creating and Using Housekeeper Servers

The housekeeper servers—you will usually have at least three of them—carry out background maintenance tasks. There are nine distinct housekeeper tasks. One housekeeper server can do more than one task, but you will usually configure multiple housekeeper servers to carry out the different tasks on different schedules.

There are nine tasks (all but one by default disabled) that a housekeeper server can carry out (each with an appropriate suggested schedule):

Collection: This task will remove all messages tagged as being deleted (hourly).

Process control message cleanup: This task will clear expired messages from the process control queues (hourly).

Pruning: This is the only task that is by default enabled. This task will clear the system trash folder and mark unreferenced messages for collection (hourly).

Expiration: This task will move messages to the system trash folder that are more than a certain number of days old (daily).

Statistics cleanup: This task will remove all statistics on housekeeper activity, according to how many days old the statistics are (hourly).

Log mining enablement: This will enable the generation of the additional redo information necessary for using the Log Miner utility to reconstruct and reverse changes made to data. The Log Miner is a feature of the Oracle database.

Tertiary store: This task transfers messages from the live data tablespace to another tablespace (monthly).

Text synchronization: This enables the automatic update of the indexes needed for text searching, so that new messages will be included in search results (hourly).

Text optimization: This will correct the problem of Text indexes degrading with time (daily).

To create a housekeeper server, select the existing housekeeper server created at installation time. This link is selected in Figure 10-8. From there, either reconfigure the existing housekeeper, or click the Create button to create a new one. The housekeeper server(s) can be configured to run any and all of the previous nine tasks. It is possible for one housekeeper to perform several tasks, but it is usually advisable to create one housekeeper per task. Figure 10-10 shows a housekeeper configured exclusively for migration of messages to tertiary storage.

It is not possible for a housekeeper server to address multiple databases, though one housekeeper can have several threads connecting to its database; use of multiple threads can be complementary to launching multiple housekeepers.

Oracle recommends creating at least three housekeeper servers:

- A server for collection, process control message cleanup, pruning, expiration, and log mining
- A server for statistics cleanup and synchronizing and optimizing the Text indexes
- A server for migration to tertiary storage

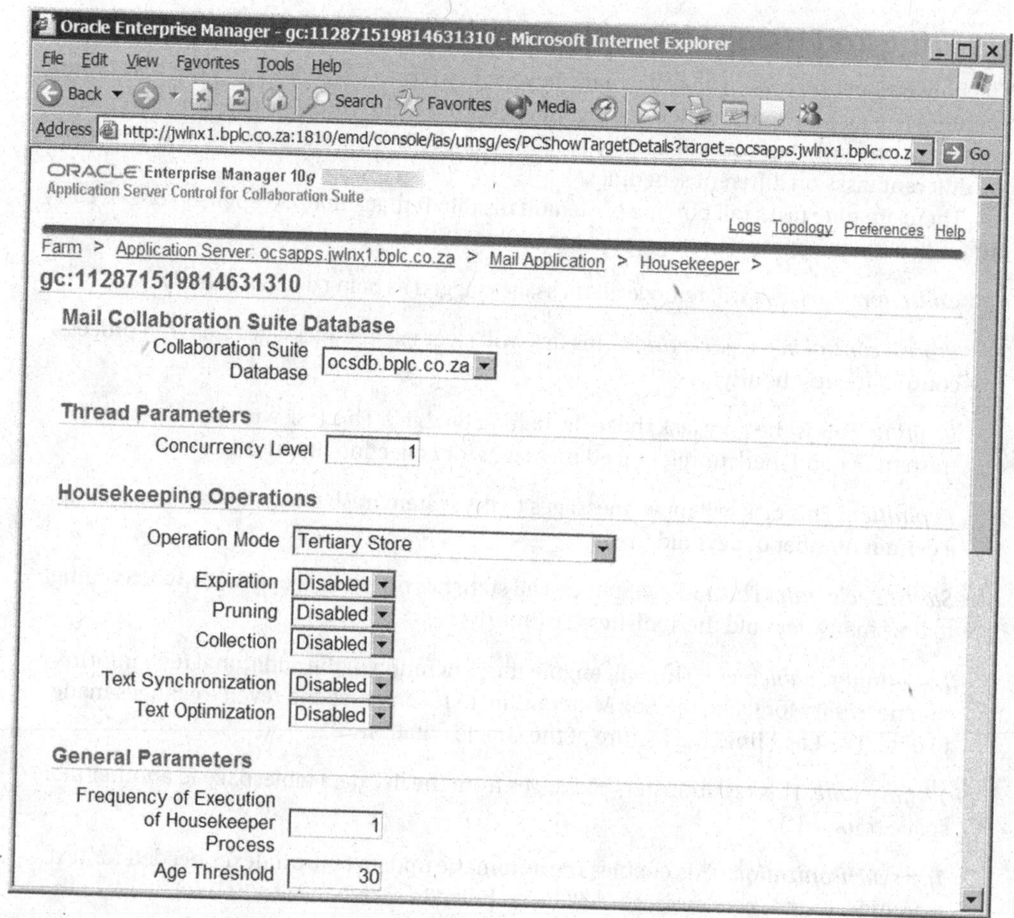

Figure 10-10. *Creating a housekeeper server for migration of messages to the tertiary store*

Garbage Collection

One housekeeper server is configured by default in every mail installation. This is the garbage collection housekeeper. One garbage collector can carry out all the space-related housekeeping tasks (collection, process control message cleanup, pruning, and expiration) or you can configure several.

When users "delete" messages from their mailboxes, the message is not in fact deleted—it is only tagged for permanent deletion later on. The deletion occurs during the collection process. This is for performance reasons. In the Oracle database environment, deletion of data is an expensive process, involving the generation of undo data and redo data, as well as the actual deletion of data. Do not worry about this; generation of undo and redo are a vital part of the Oracle architecture and a major reason for using the Oracle database rather than a database published by any other vendor. Rather than have interactive end-user sessions take the strain of actually deleting messages, Oracle Collaboration Suite delegates this task to the housekeeper server, which can take as long as it needs without impacting end-user sessions.

Process Control Message Cleanup

Another case where out-of-date data can accumulate in a Mail database is in the tables used by the various Mail servers to pass messages between each other. The Mail servers communicate via the Advanced Queuing facility provided as standard with the Oracle database. This is a mechanism whereby processes can enqueue messages into queue tables that can be dequeued by other processes. These messages should be cleared from the queues when all queue subscribers have read them, but it is possible for messages to accumulate unnecessarily. A housekeeper server can check whether any messages are being kept for no purpose and remove them.

Pruning

The pruning process clears the system trash folder and messages that are no longer referenced anywhere. The system trash folder is populated with messages deleted automatically (see the next section, "Expiration"). Unreferenced messages are those for which there are no longer any live pointers. This situation can arise because Mail does not store multiple copies of a message. For example, if a message has been mailed to many users via a distribution list, it will only exist once in the datastore: each user's Mail account will have a pointer to it. Once all users with a reference to a message have deleted their reference, the pruning process will mark the message for collection by the garbage collector.

Expiration

The expiration process can be set up to move all messages older than a certain number of days to the system trash folder, from where they will be pruned and collected. This will limit the amount of data stored within Mail, but may be intensely annoying to end users. This functionality is probably best suited to a POP environment, where as a general rule, users will always download mail to a local client and remove it from the Mail server as they do so. In an IMAP environment, where it is customary to store and manage mail on the server, expiration could destroy data users would expect to be retained.

Statistics Cleanup

This process enables clearing statistical information on housekeeper activities. These statistics can be seen through the All Metrics link on the housekeeper home page.

Log Mining Enablement

The Log Miner is a database facility that can extract information from the redo logs. The redo logs contain a record of all change vectors that have been applied to the database, so that in the event of it being necessary to restore a backup of a data file, the changes can be applied to the backup in order to bring it forward in time and synchronize it with the rest of the database. Thus, Oracle can guarantee that no data will ever be lost even if data files are damaged. Since change vectors applied to both data segments (such as tables) and to undo segments (which record the before-update versions of data, so that uncommitted changes can be rolled back) are logged, analysis of the redo logs lets Oracle reconstruct statements that have been executed against the database, and also construct statements that will roll back these statements.

Using the Log Miner can be difficult, and database administrators do not generally do it unless under extreme pressure from users to reverse user error. Enabling Log Miner–based recovery through a housekeeper process simplifies the use of the Log Miner; the housekeeper process will record additional information that makes recovery of deleted Mail data through log mining a quick and simple operation. As a general rule, to ensure that the Log Miner can work with maximum effectiveness, it is necessary for the database administrator to enable supplemental logging to capture additional data in the redo stream that will guarantee that the SQL statements Log Miner constructs really do refer to the correct rows, even if the database has been reorganized. This is done with the following command:

```
alter database add supplemental log data (primary key,unique index) columns;
```

Note that with this facility enabled, recovery of deleted mail may be possible, but it is never easy.

Text Synchronization

Enabling this process, which is based on the Oracle Text facility bundled with the Oracle Database 10*g* Enterprise Edition, instructs Oracle to generate indexes on all incoming mail message bodies. The default configuration will function with European languages but may not give useful results with some Asian languages, due to the manner in which word breaks are defined. The Oracle database (as of the time of this writing) ships with alternative program components (known as *lexers*) designed to recognize words in Chinese, Japanese, and Korean language groups. If much of your data is in one of these languages, you should enable the appropriate lexer.

To enable a lexer, from your infrastructure Oracle home, connect to your Mail datastore database as database user es_mail. The password will be that selected at installation time for the Oracle Collaboration Suite superuser. Then run a script to rebuild the Oracle Text indexes. The script is

```
$ORACLE_HOME/oes/install/sql/recreate_text_index.sql
```

which will prompt you for the language group for which you wish to set up Oracle Text and the character set that should be assumed for incoming documents.

Enabling Text index synchronization is a necessary precursor for giving users the ability to index their Mail documents. This is a facility that you can enable or disable as a default for all Mail users when you define your domains, while overriding it for individual users.

Text Optimization

The indexes used by Text tend to deteriorate in efficiency as the indexed documents (Mail messages and attachments) are deleted or moved. Enabling the optimization option will improve the performance of the indexes by carrying out appropriate index maintenance.

Migration of Data to Tertiary Storage

The tertiary store task moves old Mail messages from the standard storage area to another presumably cheaper storage area. Setting up the Mail tertiary store is detailed in the next section.

Tertiary Storage

Mail storage tends to increase with time. It never seems to decrease. The only sure way to restrict the space required is to offer only POP3 as the client protocol and to run a housekeeper server that will expire messages on a regular basis. Then by disabling IMAP and the Webmail application, users will be forced to download mail to a local client and manage it there. But this removes a huge amount of functionality from Oracle Collaboration Suite. Assuming that your site does permit IMAP and does allow users to keep an unrestricted amount of mail, your storage requirement will be continually increasing. The use of tertiary storage lets this happen while giving you the option of reducing the cost impact.

The disk systems used for the tertiary Mail store can be slower and less fault tolerant than those used for the live mail. For example, your live data might well be on a RAID 1+0 volume (with striping and mirroring provided by your operating system vendor, or using Oracle's Automatic Storage Management with normal or high redundancy), but the tertiary store could be on an unstripped, unmirrored volume. This can give significant cost savings. Users should not be aware that older messages have been moved to a different storage medium, but accountants certainly will be.

To enable the migration of Mail messages you must create a housekeeper server configured for this purpose. Figure 10-10 shows a housekeeper server that will run once a day and migrate mail more than 30 days old to the tertiary store.

Mail uses ten tablespaces. To see the detail of their creation, study this script in your middle tier Oracle home:

```
$ORACLE_HOME/oes/install/sql/tblspc_mailstore.sql
```

The ESTERSTORE tablespace is that used for messages moved by the housekeeper, according to its Frequency of Execution and the Age Threshold, as shown in Figure 10-10. The tablespace configuration immediately following installation is of no value; all the data files that make up the ten Mail tablespaces will be in one directory. To exploit the tertiary storage capability, you must move the data file(s) that make up the ESTERSTORE tablespace to a different device. This is a perfectly normal database administration exercise that you can accomplish with operating system utilities or (if you are moving them to an Automatic Storage Management device) the Recovery Manager (RMAN).

Virus and Spam Control

Mail provides two levels of virus protection, both based on the Symantec AntiVirus Scan Engine (SAVSE). The SMTP inbound protocol server can scan all incoming messages and also apply spam filters. However, this is often not enough; no matter how frequently Symantec issues updated virus definition files and how diligent you are at applying them, the situation will arise where you will receive infected messages and the SMTP server cannot detect them. For this reason, there is a separate server process supplied that can pass through the entire Mail datastore: the Virus Scrubber server.

Spam Filters

The SMTP inbound server will reject mails from any one source if the number received within a certain time frame exceeds a certain value. To set these and other spam-related parameters, in Application Server Control navigate to the SMTP inbound server and set them in the Rules and Routing Control Parameters section, as shown (with all values on default) in Figure 10-11.

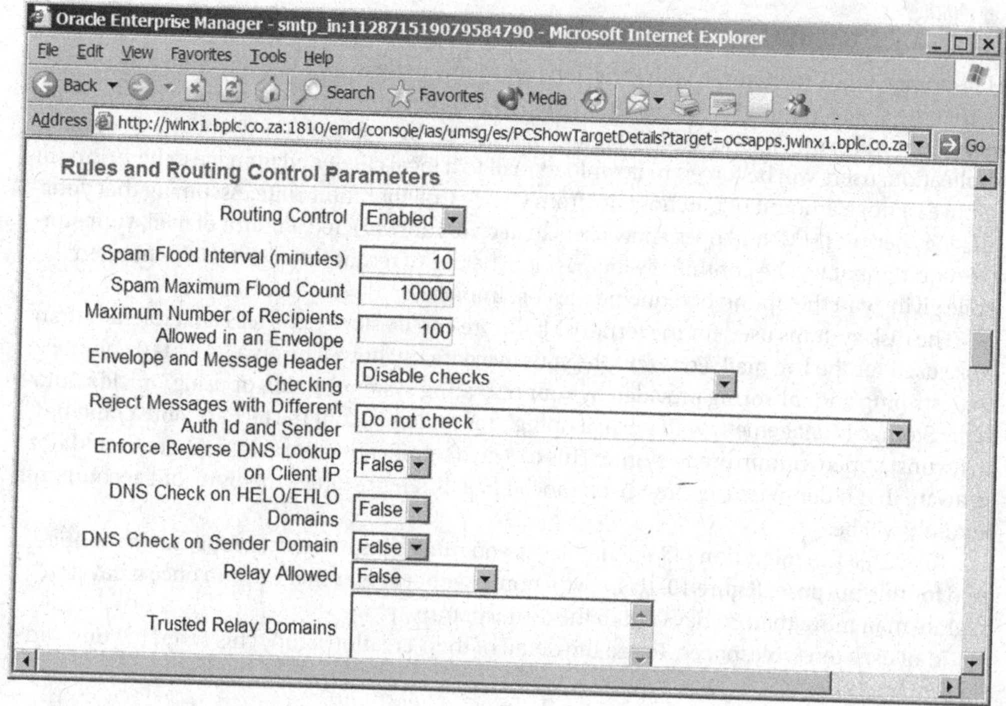

Figure 10-11. *The spam-related values for the SMTP inbound server*

The spam filtering parameters are the following:

Spam flood interval: This specifies a time frame in minutes for tracking the number of messages received from any one address.

Spam maximum flood count: This specifies the threshold for messages received within the spam flood interval after which mail from the source host will be rejected.

Maximum number of recipients allowed in an envelope: This specifies a restriction on the number of recipients for any one e-mail message.

Envelope and message header checking: This rejects mail if the envelope sender does not match the From header, unless the envelope sender is null. This will help detect mail from spammers that purports to come from someone else.

Reject messages with different auth id and sender: This further checks on whether the SASL (Simple Authentication and Security Layer)—a protocol SMTP and IMAP clients and servers can use to validate identities—matches correctly with the envelope sender or the From header.

Enforce reverse DNS lookup on client IP: This controls whether the server will attempt to identify the name of the sending server based on its IP address. This will help detect mail servers that are trying to keep their identity hidden.

DNS check on HELO/EHLO domains: The DNS HELO/EHLO check confirms that the sender's purported mail domain does exist in the DNS MX records. This may help detect mail where the sender is falsifying his identity.

DNS check on sender domain: This is similar to the HELO/EHLO check. It confirms that the sender's purported DNS domain does exist.

Relay allowed and trusted relay domains: These settings permit the server to relay mail on to a list of nominated domains. This should prevent your server from being used as the middleman in a spamming operation.

These parameters can also be configured through the Webmail client. Log in as a Mail administrator, click the Administration tab, click the Policy button, and you will find them on the Routing Control link.

Apart from enabling these controls within the SMTP inbound server, you can also protect your server with a third-party spam filter that will intercept all messages and only forward to the Mail server ones considered valid.

Virus Detection

Virus detection and removal is configured through the Webmail client application. Use a browser to connect to the Oracle Collaboration Suite middle tier, and log in as a Mail administrator. Click the Administration tab and then the Policy button to reach the window shown in Figure 10-12.

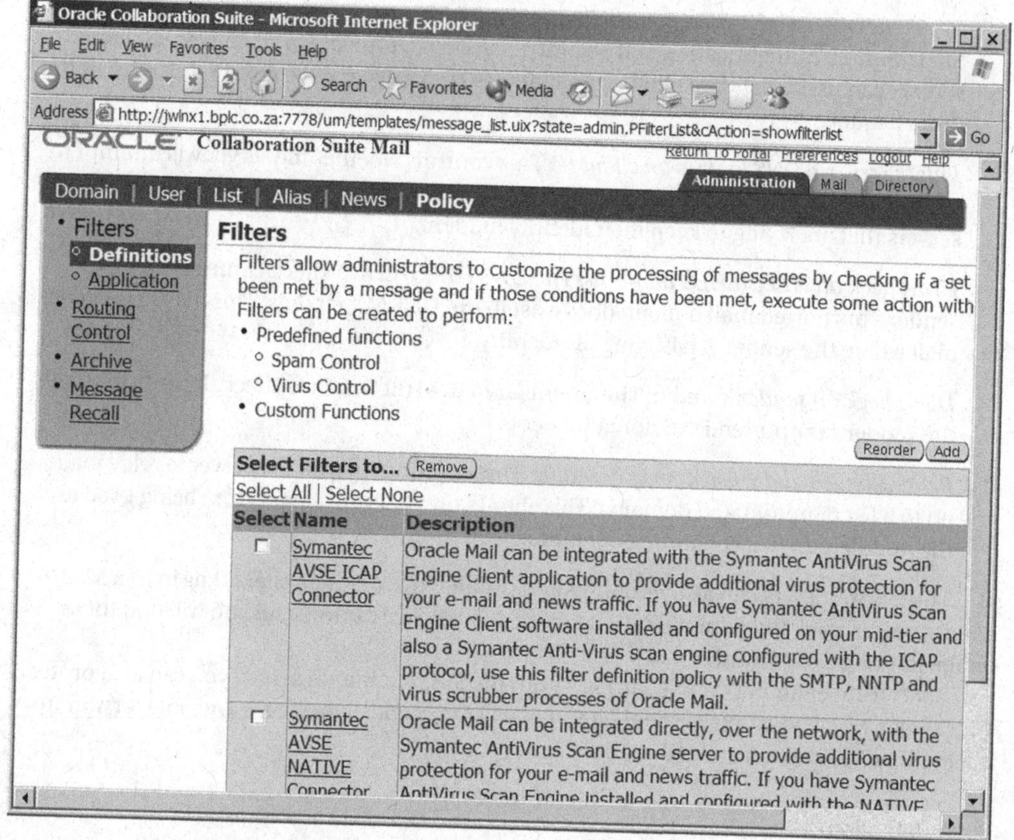

Figure 10-12. *The supplied virus filter definitions*

The virus protection is implemented with SAVSE. You must have an SAVSE server accessible on your network, ideally on or near the middle tier instance that is running your Mail server(s). The SAVSE server will have been installed to use two protocols: either the ICAP (Internet Content Adaptation Protocol), or the Symantec proprietary SAVSE Native protocol. Select whichever protocol is available to reach the virus filter editing window. Figure 10-13 shows the window for the ICAP filter.

The File Name is the name of the dynamic link library that contains the SAVSE client software. Copy this file from the SAVSE host; it will be in the directory `Scan_Engine/Scan_Engine_SDK/Lib/<platform>/dynamic` where *<platform>* is the operating system on which your Oracle Collaboration Suite middle tier is running. Place the copy in the directory `$ORACLE_HOME/oes/lib` on the middle tier.

Continuing with the Edit Filter options, set Active to Yes to enable the filter; it is by default not enabled. Set External Process to Yes if you want the filter to run as a separate process rather than within the process that invokes it. Set Capable of Message Modification to Yes to allow the filter to clean infected messages.

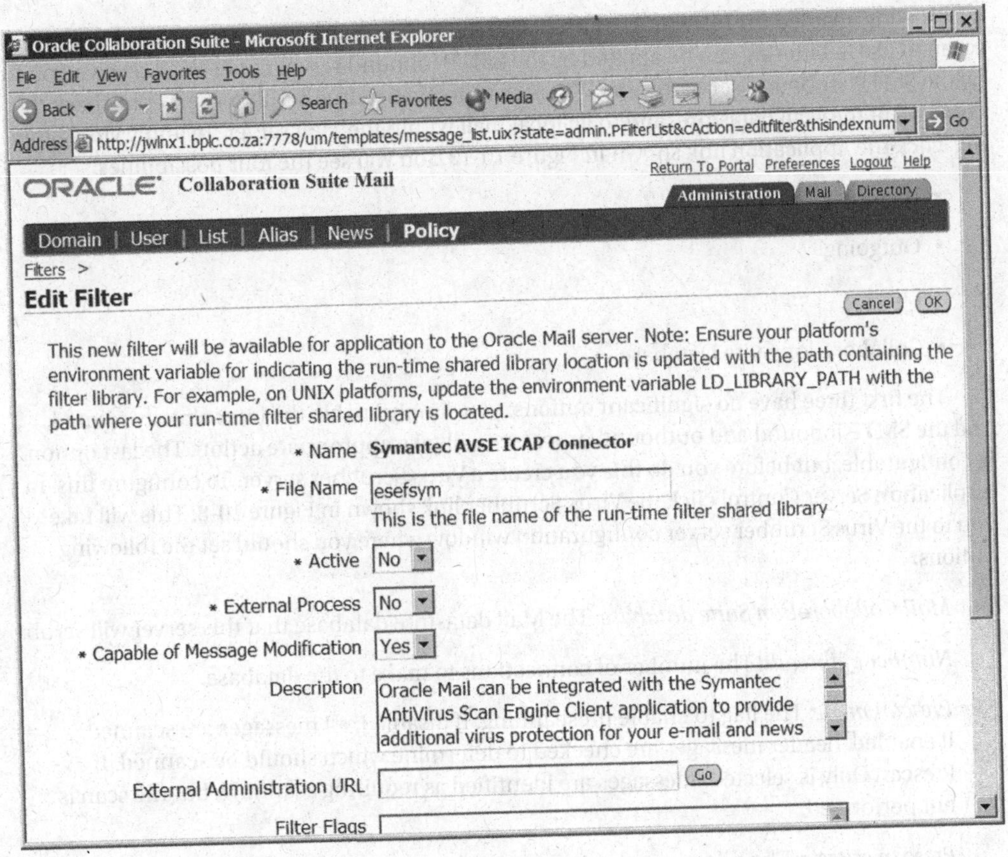

Figure 10-13. *The options for editing a virus filter*

The External Administration URL is the URL to the SAVSE server's administration utility.

The Filter Flags option will differ depending on the protocol being used. If using the Native protocol, it is very simple:

```
(host=<host_name>)(port=<port_number>)(repair=<true or false>)
```

Specify the host and port of the SAVSE server, and repair to TRUE to allow the filter to attempt to clean infected messages. If the clean operation succeeds, it will be the disinfected message that is inserted into the Mail datastore.

If using the ICAP protocol, the Filter Flags option will take this form:

```
(config=Server:IP_address:port_number;;;FailRetryTime:60;;;ReadWriteTime:180) ➥
(policy=ScanOnly:1;;;RepairOnly:1;;;AlwaysReportDefInfo:1) ➥
(tmpdir=directory_for_temporary_files)(lib=libsymcsapi.so.4.x.x)
```

The SAVSE documentation gives full details on the syntax for this option.

Having enabled the filter process itself, you must then instruct the various Mail servers on when to use it. Filtering can be applied by the SMTP inbound server to check all received mail, by the SMTP outbound server to check all mail sent, by the Virus Scrubber server to check the contents of the Mail datastore, and to all local mail within the Mail server. To apply virus filtering, click the Application link shown in Figure 10-12. You will see the four possibilities:

- Incoming
- Outgoing
- Local
- Collaboration Suite Database

The first three have no significant options; you simply enable the filter already created, and the SMTP inbound and outbound processes will take appropriate action. The last option is configurable, but before you do this you create a Virus Scrubber server. To configure this, in Application Server Control click the Virus Scrubber link shown in Figure 10-8. This will take you to the Virus Scrubber server configuration window where you should set the following options:

Mail Collaboration Suite database: The Mail datastore database that this server will scrub.

Number of threads: The number of connections to make to the database.

Prescan mode: The flag to enable prescanning. If disabled, all messages are scanned. If enabled, header messages are checked to determine which should be scanned. If Prescan Only is selected, messages are identified as requiring scanning, but the scan is not performed.

Prescan criteria: The selection criteria to determine which messages to prescan, if prescanning is enabled. Enter here the details to select which messages to scan (such as messages received between two dates, or messages from a certain source).

Scan interval: The frequency to run the Virus Scrubber server.

Repair mode (purge or quarantine): The action to take if a clean operation fails.

Quarantine destination address and folder: The location for storing quarantined messages. This is only applicable to IMAP (because POP3 cannot use folders) and then only if the quarantining repair method is selected. These options specify the mail account and the folder within it to use for storing quarantined messages.

Notification message to the virus recipient and to the virus sender: The notification messages to send to the source of an infected message and the intended recipient.

Having configured the Virus Scrubber server in Application Server Control, apply it in the Webmail client. Click the Application link shown in Figure 10-12, then the Collaboration Suite Database link, then the Configure Filters button to reach the window shown in Figure 10-14.

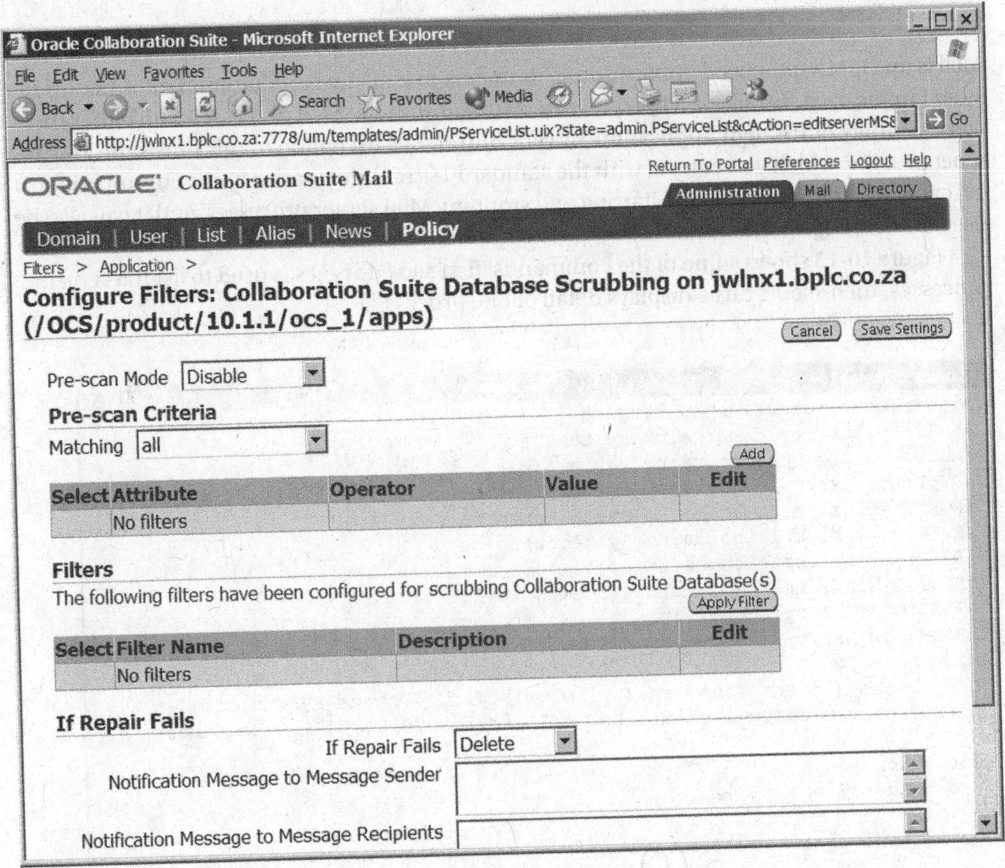

Figure 10-14. *The options for applying a virus filter with theVirus Scrubber*

The first options shown in Figure 10-14 let you override the Virus Scrubber's configuration by selecting which (if any) prescan criteria to apply. Then select which filter (either the ICAP protocol filter or the Native protocol filter, depending on which one you have available) to use. The final options let you override the Virus Scrubber's default behavior if a clean fails.

Mail Command-Line Utilities

There are occasions when you will prefer to use command-line utilities to manage Mail, rather than the graphical tools in the Webmail client and Application Server Control. Typically, this will be for large batch operations or any occasion when you want to manage operations through shell scripts. There is also the possibility of giving your Mail administrator access to the command-line utilities so that he can administer Mail, without giving him access to `opmnctl` or Application Server Control, which would give him administration access to all the other components as well. These are some of the more important command-line utility programs.

oesctl

Mail is an OPMN-managed application. This means that all the configuration information is stored in the `opmn.xml` file and that you can start and stop the Mail processes with either the `opmnctl` utility or through Application Server Control. The exception to this rule is the Mail listener process, which you control with the standard `lsnrctl` database listener control utility. `oesctl` is an alternative tool for starting and stopping Mail server processes, and it can also be used for defining additional servers.

Figure 10-15 shows some of the commands: first `show targets` is used to list the server processes, then `show status` displays detail of one process.

```
oraocs@jwlnx1:~
[mid oraocs]$ oesctl show targets
TARGET: jwlnx1.bplc.co.za:um_system:gc
TARGET: jwlnx1.bplc.co.za:um_system:imap
TARGET: jwlnx1.bplc.co.za:um_system:list
TARGET: jwlnx1.bplc.co.za:um_system:nntp_in
TARGET: jwlnx1.bplc.co.za:um_system:nntp_out
TARGET: jwlnx1.bplc.co.za:um_system:pop
TARGET: jwlnx1.bplc.co.za:um_system:smtp_in
TARGET: jwlnx1.bplc.co.za:um_system:smtp_out
TARGET: jwlnx1.bplc.co.za:um_system:vs
[mid oraocs]$
[mid oraocs]$ oesctl show status jwlnx1.bplc.co.za:um_system:smtp_in
jwlnx1.bplc.co.za:um_system:smtp_in:112871519079584790 ----Heartbeat---
--
[mid oraocs]$
[mid oraocs]$ oesctl -?

OES command line tool V 10.1.1 :

        usage: oesctl  [ [<command>] [<target>|<instance>] ]
```

Figure 10-15. *The oesctl utility; the -? switch will list all the options.*

The targets shown in Figure 10-15 are the various protocol servers. To create, for example, a second instance of the SMTP inbound protocol server, use the following command:

```
$ oesctl create instance jwlnx1.bplc.co.za:um_system:smtp_in
Successfully created a new instance for a total of: 2
```

The `um_system` argument in the previous example is the name of the Mail installation, as shown in Figure 10-4.

One command within `oesctl` that you hope you will never need is the following:

```
oesctl sync_opmn_conf
```

The Mail protocol server configuration is defined in the `opmn.xml` file, but this information is in fact based on entries stored in the Oracle Internet Directory. All the management tools should ensure that these two sources of information are synchronized, but it is possible that some form of unanticipated system failure would cause them to diverge. In this case, use the SYNC_OPMN_CONF command to rectify the situation. It will delete all references to Mail from the opmn.xml file and reinstantiate them from the entries in the Oracle Internet Directory.

oesbkp

Your database administrator can establish backup routines for the Mail datastore database that will make it absolutely impossible to lose any data under any circumstances. A difficulty with the Oracle database is recovering from user errors, such as accidentally deleting mail messages, or even whole folders. As far as the database is concerned, this is a regular transaction that cannot be reversed—but the users may wish to have it reversed, and quickly.

One technique to reverse user error is to use the Log Miner. This is virtually impossible unless you enable a housekeeper server to track information Log Miner needs, and even then it is not a task to embark upon lightly. At the very best, it is slow and difficult. You may need to trawl through many archive log files—which might be no longer available on disk—to locate the data needed. Another technique is to use Flashback recovery. Unlike the Log Miner, this technique uses undo data (not redo data) and can be very quick; but it will only be possible to use Flashback if the error is reported quickly. Undo data is not usually retained for any great period, and you will have to act fast.

The oesbkp utility is another level of protection that the Mail administrator can use to extract Mail data from the Mail datastore and preserve it as operating system files. An example is the following:

```
oesbkp task=backup type=all user=jwatson@bplc.co.za admindn=cn=orcladmin ➥
password=oracle1 ldaphost=jwlnx1.bplc.co.za ldapport=389 ➥
 backupdir=/home/oraocs/jwatson_mail_bak
```

The critical arguments (only a subset of all that are available) are shown in Table 10-4 with their default values.

Table 10-4. *Arguments for the oesbkp Utility*

Argument	Default	Meaning
task	none	The operation to be carried out (backup or restore)
type	all	What to back up or restore (everything, or only the mail, or the address book, or any rules)
user	none	The fully qualified name of the account to which the operation will be applied
admindn	cn=orcladmin	The name to use to log on to the Oracle Internet Directory; this must be a fully privileged user
password	none	The password for the Oracle Internet Directory logon
ldaphost	localhost	The machine hosting the Oracle Internet Directory
ldapport	389	The listening port of the Oracle Internet Directory
backupdir	user.dir	The target (or source) directory for the backup (or restore)

The backup will create a set of files in the target directory. There will be an `ldif` file with the address book information; an XML file defining any routing and filtering rules that the user may have created; and a set of files containing the mail from each of the user's folders. There will also be a file suffixed `foldermap` that maps the folder names to the operating system filenames; this is necessary because names that are legal within the Mail environment may not be legal at the operating system level.

Always remember that `oesbkp` backups are not a substitute for your database administrator's database backups; they are complementary to them and serve a different purpose.

oesutil

The `oesutil` utility has two purposes: to check on whether users are approaching their storage quota within the Mail datastore, and to perform bulk deletions of data.

To check quota usage, use the `CHECK_USER_QUOTA` command:

```
oesutil -check_user_quota domain=<domain> user=<username> quota=<number>
```

The *domain* is the e-mail domain to which the user belongs. The user can be a full e-mail username or a partial name with wild cards. The *quota* is an integer from one to a hundred, expressing a percentage. All users whose addresses match the domain and user arguments will be checked, and any whose percentage usage of their quota is above the number given will be listed.

To delete information, use the `DELETE_DOMAIN` command. This comes in two forms, depending on whether you want to delete a complete domain and everything it contains, or to delete a subset of information from within a domain.

First, to delete a domain, use the following:

```
oesutil -delete_domain type=all domain=<domain> installation=<installation>
```

The *domain* is the domain to delete. The *installation* is the name of your Mail installation. This will have defaulted to `um_system`, as shown in Figure 10-4.

Second, to delete data from a domain, use the following:

```
oesutil -delete_domain type=<value> domain=<domain>
```

The type argument specifies what to delete from the domain. The options are the following:

- *User*: To delete all users from the domain
- *Alias*: To delete all aliases from the domain
- *List*: To delete all mailing lists from the domain
- *News*: To delete all newsgroups from the domain

Bulk Loading Tools

To ease the process of migration to a Mail environment, there are utilities for bulk creation of Mail accounts, newsgroups, and distribution lists. These are the following:

oesucr: This is used for clearing data belonging to deleted users. The Oracle Internet Directory entries for the users must already exist.

Oesng: This will create the newsgroups; they will be populated with the first feed from the peer servers, which can be defined in bulk with the oespr utility.

Oesdl: This creates distribution lists.

These utilities take files with a specified format and create or modify Mail objects accordingly.

As an example of using oesucr to load Mail users, first create a file defining the users. This might be generated from data extracted from whatever user directory information is available. Each entry must have three attributes for e-mail address, space quota in bytes, and the user's distinguished name within the Oracle Internet Directory. Note that the users must exist in the Internet directory. For a migration exercise from a legacy system to Oracle Collaboration Suite, these entries might have been created using the Oracle Internet Directory bulk loading tool. Optional attributes can specify the archiving policy to be applied to the account, whether the user will be granted administration privileges, and any folders to be created in the user's account. The following listing is of a file that creates a regular user named SOMAR with the minimum information, and a second user named PREDDY with archiving-enabled administration privileges and some folders:

```
mail=somar@bplc.co.za
orclmailquota=400000000
baseuserdn=cn=somar,cn=users,dc=bplc,dc=co,dc=za

mail=preddy@bplc.co.za
orclmailquota=400000000
baseuserdn=cn=preddy,cn=users,dc=bplc,dc=co,dc=za
orclmailarchivingpolicyid=default
orclmaildomaincontrolaci=system
folder=personal,admin
```

The archiving policy must already exist (the DEFAULT policy is precreated at install time). The options for administration are SYSTEM, giving control over the whole installation; DOMAIN, giving control over the user's mail domain; or REGULAR, which is the default and has no administration privileges. Any named folders will be created from the user's root folder. Each user must be separated by a blank line.

Then to create the users, run this command:

```
oesucr <file_name>
```

where *<file_name>* is the file listed in the previous code listing.

CHAPTER 11

Mobile Collaboration

The Mobile Collaboration component lets users remain in continuous communication with their corporate systems no matter where they are, provided they have some sort of recognized wireless device. The accessible data includes e-mail, voice mail, diaries, tasks, files, and address books and other directories. Furthermore, this access is not only on-demand; there is a "push" facility, whereby the Oracle Collaboration Suite server will send notifications to users whenever certain events occur. Not only can you remain in contact with your office at all times, but your office will remain in contact with you.

The functionality of Mobile Collaboration is not limited merely to notifications. These are invaluable. Notifications for such events as e-mail being sent to you from certain people, events being added to your diary, or a document being updated can all be sent by SMS or other means. But perhaps equally important is that all the component applications can be accessed from wireless devices—though of course the functionality will be, to a certain extent, determined by the capabilities of the terminal device. It is, for example, possible to e-mail a file stored in Content Services from your cell phone.

The enabling technology relies on international standards for wireless data communications and on the interfaces provided by the manufacturers of wireless devices. The access methods are browser, SMS, e-mail, or voice.

Mobile Collaboration Processes and Architecture

The Mobile Collaboration server can provide access to the Oracle Collaboration Suite application components in three ways. Mobile browser access uses the HTTP-related wireless protocols; mobile text access uses e-mail and SMS; voice access uses speech recognition and a text-to-speech converter. Notifications can be dispatched to users by Mobile Collaboration through a messaging gateway that can use a web service (there is a suitable service hosted by Oracle for anyone to use) or SMS, e-mail, or fax.

At the heart of Mobile Collaboration is the Messaging server. This receives messages from Oracle Collaboration Suite application components and messages from end users through a listening process that must be configured for the various mobile devices being used. Users should do this configuration themselves. There is a messaging gateway that abstracts the mechanism for message delivery from the processes that generate the messages.

Other server processes are the push mail server, which works with the notification system to forward e-mail from a user's account within Mail to his mobile device, and the automatic speech recognition and text-to-speech servers that enable mobile voice access.

The Mobile Collaboration processes are implemented as two Oracle Application Server middle tier components: an OC4J component that has the web-based processes, and a number of stand-alone processes. In the Application Server Control middle tier home page these are called OC4J_Wireless and Wireless. These two components can be managed through Application Server Control or through OPMN:

```
[mid bin]$ opmnctl status ias-component=wireless

Processes in Instance: demomid.bplclnx1.bplc.co.za
-------------------+-------------------+---------+---------
ias-component      | process-type      |     pid | status
-------------------+-------------------+---------+---------
wireless           | performance_server |    4010 | Alive
wireless           | messaging_server  |    4011 | Alive
wireless           | notificationevent~ |    4012 | Alive
wireless           | notification_serv~ |    4013 | Alive
wireless           | OC4J_Wireless     |    4009 | Alive
[mid bin]$
```

The Messaging Server and Notifications

The Messaging server is the hub that accepts requests from end users with mobile devices for application component services, and dispatches notifications to these end users that are generated by the application components. There are four associated processes:

- The Async Listener monitors access points for incoming messages. Access points can accept either e-mail, or SMS, or instant messages, and can be configured to manage requests for various application services. It operates asynchronously; the messages are not necessarily managed in real time.
- The Notification Event Collector gathers notification messages generated by the various application components. As with the Async Listener, the messages are not necessarily managed in real time; they may be queued before transmission to the Notification Engine.
- The Notification Engine dequeues messages received by the Notification Event Collector and sends them to the Messaging server for transmission to end users.
- The Messaging Gateway provides a generic interface to various messaging technologies: e-mail, SMS, voice, and fax. Messages dispatched by the Messaging server pass through this gateway on their way to the end user's mobile device.

Figure 11-1 is a graphical representation of the communication flow for requests and notifications through the Messaging server.

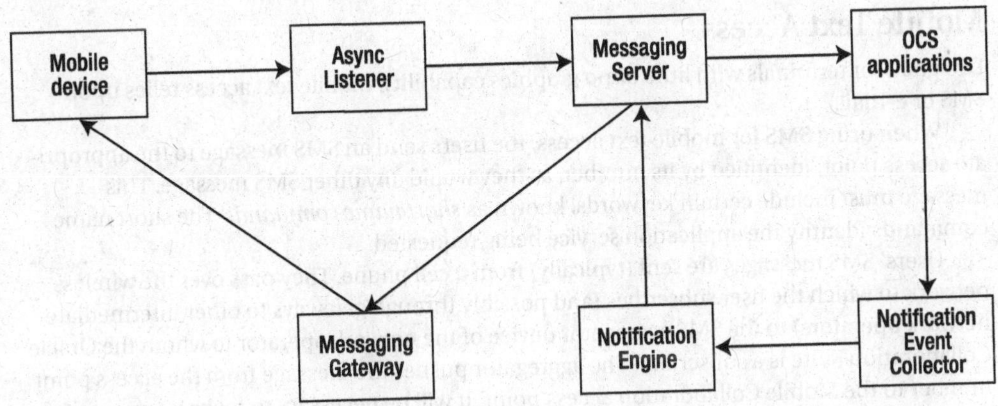

Figure 11-1. *End-user requests follow the flow from left to right; application-generated notifications flow from right to left.*

Mobile Browser Access

Mobile browser access uses the following industry standard markup languages to present a user interface to the Oracle Collaboration Suite application components:

- HTML (Hypertext Markup Language)
- XHTML (Extensible Hypertext Markup Language)
- WML (Wireless Markup Language)
- HDML (Handheld Device Markup Language)

The ability to render data in these formats is an integral part of Oracle Application Server, and following a standard installation of Oracle Collaboration Suite will require no further configuration. Any device that supports a browser that can understand one of these markup languages can be used as a terminal, and all the application components will be available, though clearly the user interface may not be as rich as that provided through a browser such as Internet Explorer.

Mobile browser access does not make use of the Messaging server. It does however need a WAP gateway. There are a number of proprietary protocols used by the various wireless network operators. Any outgoing messages formatted in one of the standard markup languages must be wrapped in the protocol before the wireless network can transmit it, and any incoming messages must be unwrapped before being passed to the Oracle Application Server middle tier. This work is done by a WAP gateway, which should be provided by the network operator and must be able to use one of the industry standard markup languages listed previously. Internally, Oracle Application Server transforms the markup language into device-independent XML. It is this ability to render data into whatever format may be required by the wireless device—which is a standard feature of Oracle Application Server—that makes the Oracle Collaboration Suite applications available on a vast range of mobile terminals.

Mobile Text Access

Designed for terminals with little or no graphics capability, mobile text access relies upon SMS or e-mail.

When using SMS for mobile text access, the users send an SMS message to the appropriate access point, identified by its number, as they would any other SMS message. This message must include certain keywords, known as *short name commands*. The short name commands identify the application service being requested.

Users' SMS messages are sent (typically) from a cell phone. They pass over the wireless network to which the user subscribes (and possibly through gateways to other intermediate network operators) to the SMS aggregator device of the network operator to whom the Oracle Collaboration Suite is a subscriber. The aggregator pushes the message from the access point number to the Mobile Collaboration access point. It will be necessary to make a commercial arrangement with the network operator that takes account of anticipated message volumes and service levels.

The Async Listener parses the SMS request and passes it to the Messaging server. The Messaging server retrieves the desired content from the relevant application component and returns it to the Messaging Gateway. From there, the message passes to the network operator's SMS aggregator and across the airwaves to the user's cell phone.

Figure 11-2 summarizes the request-response cycle for mobile text access by SMS.

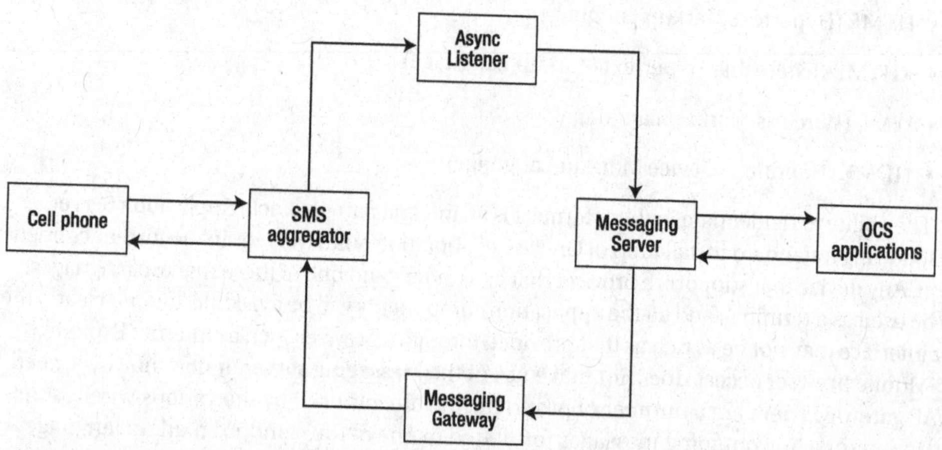

Figure 11-2. *SMS mobile access information flow: The request initiates from a cell phone and moves from left to right; the response from the application component returns from right to left.*

When using e-mail for mobile text access, users send an e-mail message requesting information and receive a text response. The e-mail can be sent from any device—typically some form of desktop device, or a wireless e-mail service such as BlackBerry. The e-mail must be addressed to an e-mail access point configured in the Async Listener and contain appropriate short name commands.

As with any other incoming e-mail message, it will be received by the Mail listener and passed to the SMTP inbound server which will save it to the Mail datastore in the Oracle Collaboration Suite database. The Async Listener contacts the IMAP server to retrieve the mail and decode the message, and the Messaging server will then action the message by retrieving the relevant information from the appropriate application component. The use and configuration of the SMTP and IMAP servers is detailed in Chapter 10; there should be no special setup required for Mobile Collaboration. The Messaging server forwards the response to the Messaging Gateway for onward transmission to the user. The Async Listener polls its Mail account through the IMAP server at regular intervals. The response to a request will therefore be asynchronous, not real-time.

Figure 11-3 is a graphical representation of the request-response cycle for mobile text access with e-mail, showing the flow of the request from the originating wireless device through the Mail component to the Async Listener and the Messaging server.

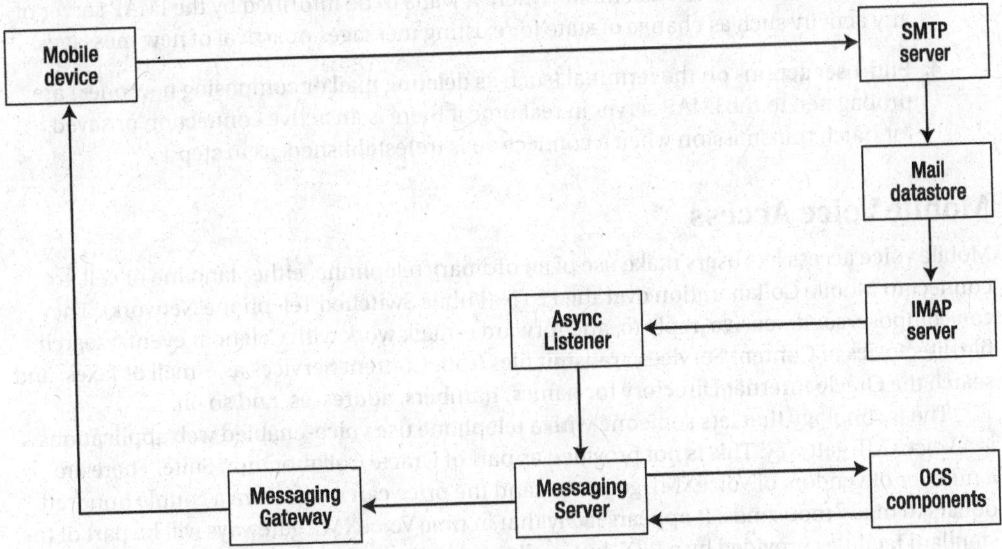

Figure 11-3. *The request-response flow for mobile text access with e-mail*

The Push Mail Server

Push mail is implemented with the P-IMAP protocol. It provides near real-time transfers of e-mail received by the user's Mail account and stored in his inbox folder to his mobile terminal. Push mail requires a client program to be installed on the user's terminal device: this client can store e-mail locally and be used for reading and composing e-mail while connected to or disconnected from Oracle Collaboration Suite. Two-way synchronization routines propagate any changes in the state of the user's mail stored centrally to the mobile client, and vice versa.

The device on which the push mail client is installed must be registered with Mobile Collaboration. This registration includes the username; so when contact is made with Mobile Collaboration from the device, the only required input is a password. The client communications are all over HTTP (or HTTPS) to the OC4J_Wireless component, but there are issues with use of Web Cache that make it advisable to configure the network such that the mobile devices can reach the OC4J_Wireless component by contacting the Apache web listener directly on its listening port rather than through the Web Cache.

The push mail communication flow is the following:

1. The push mail client contacts the push mail server with appropriate P-IMAP commands requesting authentication. The login request includes the device identifier, the username, and a user-supplied password.
2. The client synchronizes its inbox with the user's centrally stored IMAP inbox folder. During this process, any actions (such as e-mail composition or deletion) performed on the terminal while disconnected are propagated to the IMAP server; the headers of any e-mail received are sent to the terminal (message bodies are only sent on demand) along with status changes (such as deletions).
3. The client switches to Push mode, where it waits to be informed by the IMAP server of any activity such as change of state for existing messages or arrival of new messages.
4. End-user actions on the terminal (such as deleting mail or composing new ones) are propagated to the IMAP server in real time if there is an active connection or saved for batch transmission when a connection is (re)established, as in step 1.

Mobile Voice Access

Mobile voice access lets users make use of an ordinary telephone, either landline or cell, to connect to Mobile Collaboration over the PSTN (Public Switched Telephone Network). They can compose, send, receive, reply to, and forward e-mail; work with Calendar events; search file directories in Content Services; transmit files from Content Services as e-mail or faxes; and search the Oracle Internet Directory for names, numbers, addresses, and so on.

The technology that lets someone with a telephone use voice-enabled web applications is a VoiceXML gateway. This is not provided as part of Oracle Collaboration Suite. There are a number of vendors of VoiceXML gateways, and the price can range from a couple hundred dollars to many thousands. It appears likely that in time VoiceXML gateways will be part of the standard facilities provided by a PBX, but until that happens you will have to buy one separately. The VoiceXML standard is being developed under the control of the W3C (World Wide Web Consortium) and is intended to provide a means whereby anyone can access web systems from any telephone. Apart from giving fully abled users access to information at all times, this has important implications for making web resources available to differently abled users who may have problems using conventional PC-type terminals.

All VoiceXML gateways will have these modules:

Telephony interface to the PSTN: This is typically a card capable of connecting one or more T1 lines (or E1 lines in Europe or Africa) to the server node. A T1 line can carry 24 audio channels (the E1 standard can take 30). The telephone link could be a normal analog line, but such a connection would be suitable only for a very small-scale implementation.

ASR (automatic speech recognition) server: This will accept the audio data coming in through the telephony interface and convert it to a form comprehensible by the VoiceXML interpreter.

TTS (text-to-speech) server: This will accept data from the VoiceXML interpreter and convert it to audio for transmission over the telephony interface.

VoiceXML interpreter: Sometimes referred to as a *voice browser*, this module acts as the interface to Mobile Collaboration. It must communicate over HTTP, as does any other browser.

When selecting a VoiceXML gateway, a primary consideration will be compatibility with existing equipment. If your PBX vendor has a VoiceXML gateway, it makes a lot of sense to use it. The next factor is the anticipated volume of connections. Maintaining a channel between the end user and Oracle Collaboration Suite, with the ASR server processing the incoming traffic and the TTS server processing the outgoing responses, requires significant computing resources. It is possible that one T1 line, with its 24 connections, could saturate a single CPU and 1GB RAM. The VoiceXML hardware and software need to be appropriately sized and scalable. Most VoiceXML systems should be capable of scaling to four T1 lines (96 concurrent connections).

A mobile voice access session will go through these steps:

1. The user from a fixed line or mobile telephone calls the number designated as the voice access point for Oracle Collaboration Suite. The call is routed by the PSTN to the number (which will typically be a PBX) and then to the VoiceXML gateway.
2. The VoiceXML gateway sends the connection request over HTTP to Mobile Collaboration, which generates a login request to the Single Sign-On server.
3. The Single Sign-On server returns a login prompt formatted as device-independent XML, which Mobile Collaboration converts to VoiceXML and sends to the gateway.
4. The TTS server generates an audio response from the VoiceXML document, which is sent over the telephony interface to the user. This initiates a verbal dialog between the user and the ASR server which prompts for an account number and a PIN.
5. The account number and PIN go through the VoiceXML interpreter to Mobile Collaboration. These credentials are passed back to Single Sign-On and the Oracle Internet Directory for authentication.
6. Mobile Collaboration launches the Voice Main Menu application, generating pages in VoiceXML that are passed to the TTS server for presentation to the user.
7. A dialog ensues between the user and Mobile Collaboration via the VoiceXML gateway, as the user makes use of the Oracle Collaboration Suite applications.

Mobile Data Sync

Mobile Data Sync is Oracle's implementation of the SyncML standard. This is developed by the Open Mobile Alliance organization, and full details of the current specification can be found at `www.openmobilealliance.com`. SyncML defines techniques that allow people to use applications and data stored on a mobile device, while periodically synchronizing any updates with applications and data stored centrally. The synchronization goes in both directions.

Oracle is a member of the Open Mobile Alliance, and as such is assisting with developing the SyncML standard. The current implementation of SyncML within Oracle Collaboration Suite is only for Calendar, within the FastCGI software that makes up the Oracle Calendar Application System. It requires no configuration. It is likely that later releases of Oracle Collaboration Suite will make all the applications available through SyncML.

Configuring the Mobile Collaboration Services

Configuration requires two steps: First, set up the Mobile Collaboration enabling services and access points, and, second, set up the Mobile Collaboration applications. The first step includes setting up the access points for browser, e-mail, SMS, and voice access; configuring the push mail server; configuring the Messaging Gateway; setting up wireless communications; and setting up fax services. The second step is to set up the Mobile Collaboration applications. These are Mail, Calendar, Address Book, Directory, Short Messaging, Fax, and Files. Once the middle tier Mobile Collaboration configuration has been completed, users can register their mobile devices and use the applications.

Access Points

The browser access point is configured automatically following installation. The URL is `http://<host.domain:port>/ptg/rm` where *<host.domain:port>* is the listening address of the middle tier Web Cache. This URL will prompt for an account number and pin, as shown in Figure 11-4. The account number will be the telephone number entered by the user when he registered himself for Mobile Collaboration. The PIN is that chosen at the same time.

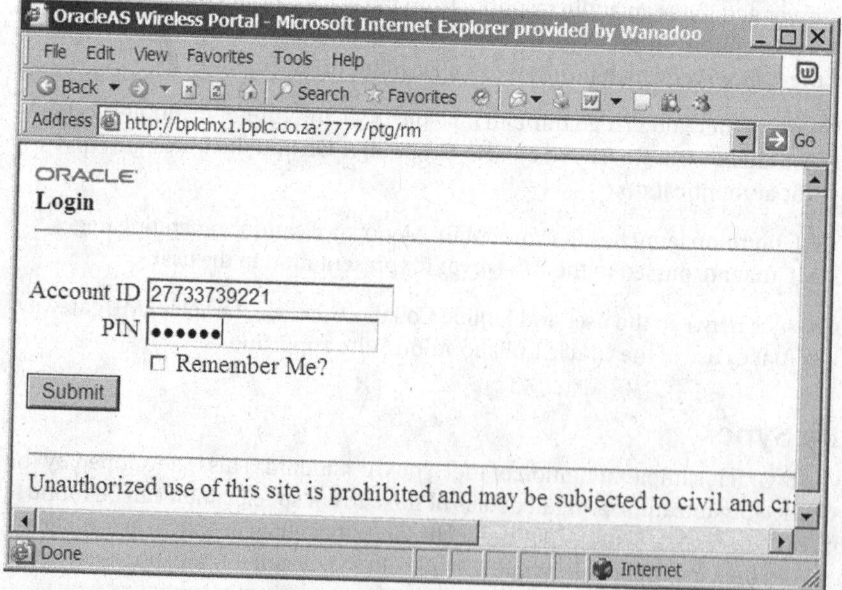

Figure 11-4. *The URL and login mechanism for mobile browser access are preconfigured.*

Following login, the window shown in Figure 11-5 will be returned. The seven applications should work immediately through browser access.

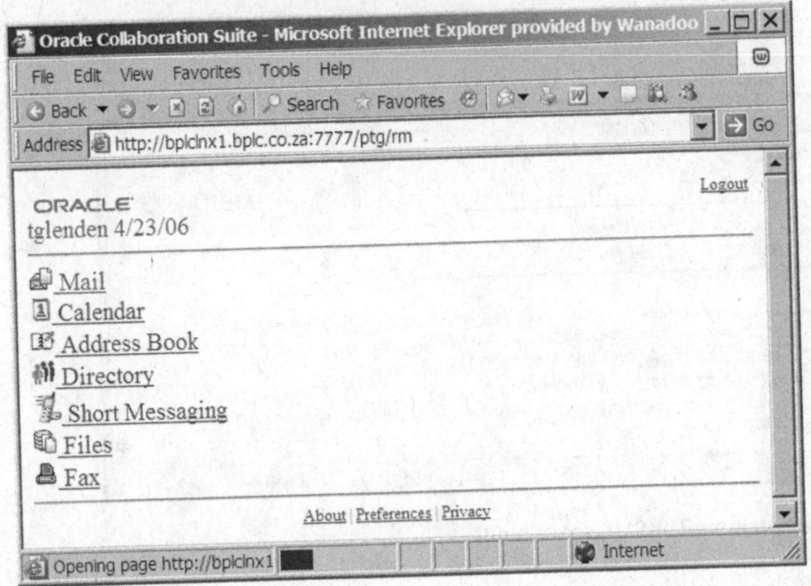

Figure 11-5. *The seven mobile applications, which function through browser access without further configuration*

E-mail and SMS mobile text access points need to be configured through Application Server Control. From the middle tier instance home page, click the link for the component called Wireless. The Wireless home page shows the status of the various processes. To create access points, click the Site Administration tab, then the Access Points link in the Component Configuration section. Initially there will be no access points defined (the browser access point is not shown), so click the Add button to create one. The Add Access Point window, shown in Figure 11-6, prompts for a unique name for the point, then for the delivery type. This may be e-mail, SMS, two-way pager, or IM (instant message); the delivery type controls the format for the address. Following are descriptions of the access points:

An *e-mail access point* requires an e-mail address. This would usually be an account created specifically for this purpose. It does not need any particular distinguishing characteristics, only the ability to receive and send e-mail messages.

An *SMS access point* is identified by its telephone number, including the international code but without any leading + symbol or zero. The same applies to a pager access point. The account will have been set up by the service provider with appropriate routing for messages as described in Chapter 12 on Real-Time Collaboration.

An *IM access point* needs the name of the instant messaging network, then a pipe symbol as a delimiter, then the account. Any Jabber-compatible client can be used to connect. Refer to `www.jabber.org` for further information on the Jabber standards for network naming.

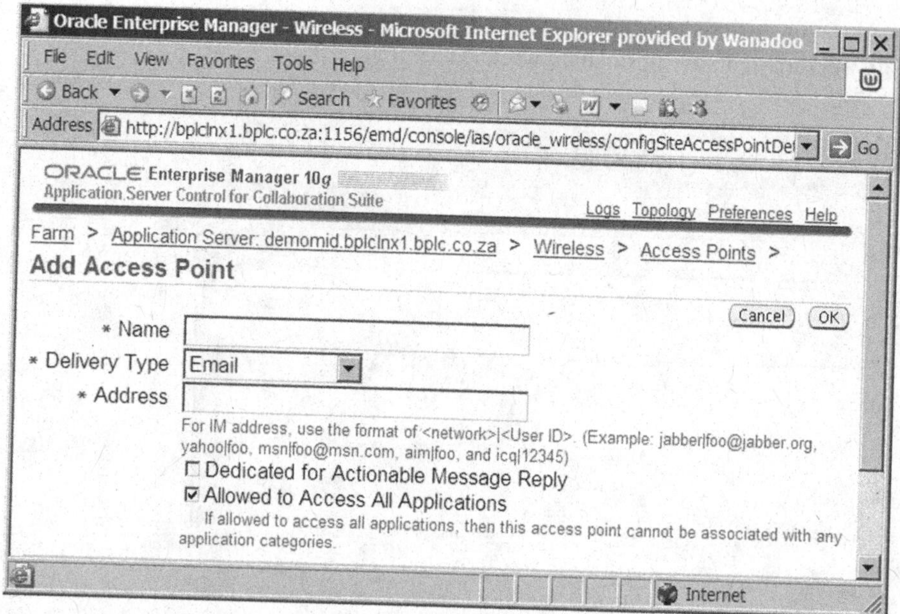

Figure 11-6. *Creating an e-mail or SMS access point*

The Dedicated for Actionable Message Reply check box should be used for an access point that is used for push mail. The outgoing messages sent through such an access point are *actionable*—they can be acted upon by users on receipt. Messages sent in response to user requests, through access points for which this check box has not been selected, are in their final form (they are nonactionable) and cannot be replied to.

The Allowed to Access All Applications check box means just that: the access point can be used to provide a menu of applications, such as that shown in Figure 11-5. Deselecting this check box means that the access point can be tied to just one application. This application need not be an Oracle Collaboration Suite application; it could be any application deployed to the middle tier Oracle Application Server instance. The application can of course make use of Oracle Collaboration Suite if it wishes. This option could, for example, be used in conjunction with high-cost services to users that can be accessed via SMS (such as purchasing and downloading irritating mobile phone ring tones, the files for which might be stored in Content Services).

Push Mail

The push mail process, based on use of the P-IMAP protocol, requires minimal configuration. The only configuration possible is to set the logging level and the maximum number of concurrent users. Figure 11-7 shows the configuration window in Application Server Control, with the settings for Log Level and Maximum Number of Concurrent Users on the default.

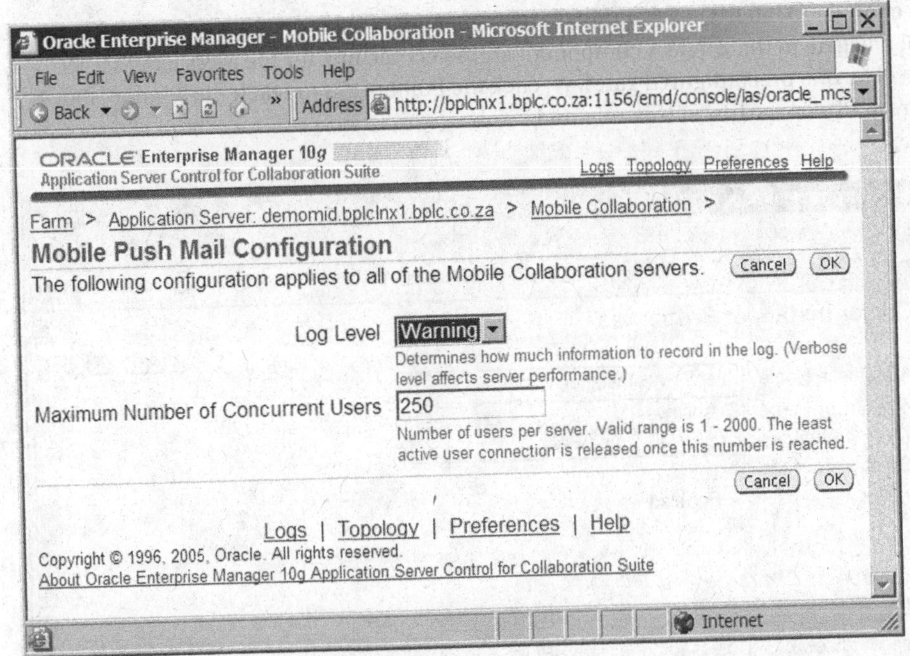

Figure 11-7. *The push mail configuration window with settings on default values*

The options for logging are Warning, Error, and Verbose; the latter will give debug information for all commands received by push mail and may result in such a volume of data being logged as to impact on performance. The log is written to `ORACLE_HOME/wireless/pimap/logs/logs.xml`. It would normally be viewed through Application Server Control by clicking the Logs link, rather than opening it with an editor.

If the number of concurrent users is exceeded, it is handled in a reasonably graceful manner; the connection that has the least activity is disconnected, and the connection is given to the new user. When mail needs to be pushed to the disconnected user, the user will be reconnected (possibly disconnecting someone else in the process). The result should be nothing more than a delay in pushing mail.

The Messaging Server

Notifications, whether by SMS, e-mail, voice, or fax, are dispatched through the Messaging server. These notifications could indicate the arrival of an e-mail from a particular source, Calendar meeting invitations, a Content Services workflow event, or any other event configured by the user. The Messaging server must be configured to pass these notifications to the Messaging Gateway, which will often be provided by a third party.

Oracle hosts a messaging gateway that can be used for testing purposes. It will accept up to 1,000 messages from any one Oracle Collaboration Suite installation. For production use, it will be necessary to contract with a certified message gateway provider. Oracle can supply a list of such providers. Oracle itself uses MultiMode Inc., a Silicone Valley-based provider.

To configure Mobile Collaboration to use a messaging gateway, in Application Server Control navigate to the wireless component and select the link for the Messaging server. There will be one preconfigured gateway; click the Edit button to reach the window shown in Figure 11-8 and see how it is configured.

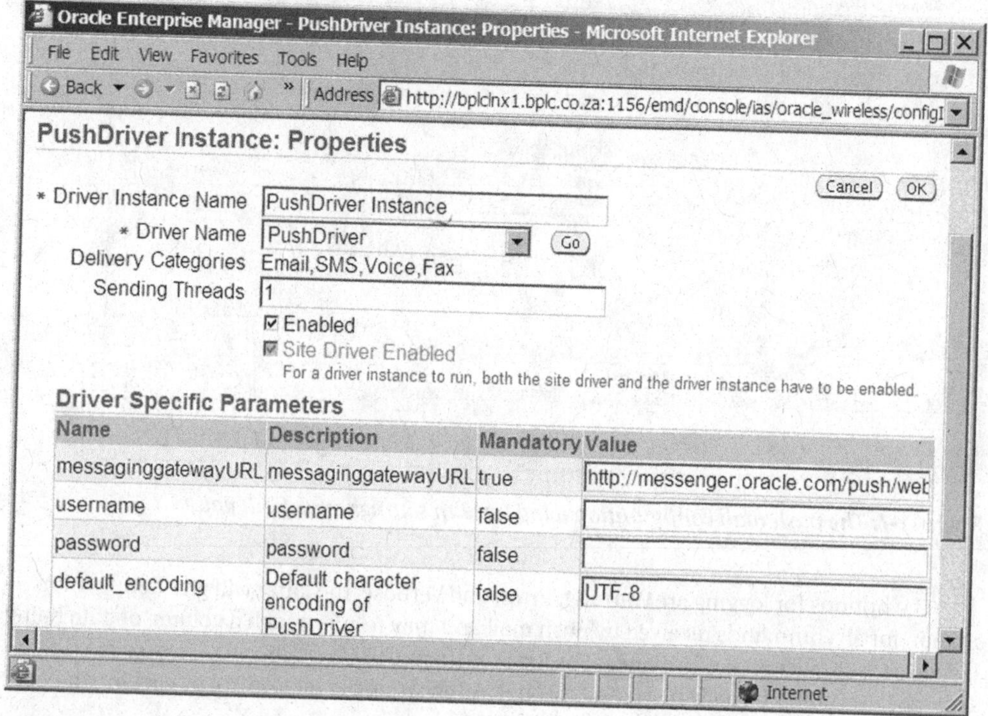

Figure 11-8. *The Messaging Gateway configuration window, showing the initial setup for the Oracle-hosted test gateway*

The Oracle hosted messaging gateway is accessible through the web site `http://messenger.oracle.com`, as can be seen in Figure 11-8. The username and password will be those provided by Oracle for your site and will give you access for 1,000 messages. The driver-specific parameters are the following:

Driver instance name: A unique name for the gateway.

Driver name: The name of the driver. Mobile Collaboration ships with 15 network drivers (as of the time of this writing), which should cover most needs.

Sending threads: The number of processes to launch for sending messages to the gateway.

Enabled: The setting to check if the Messaging server is to run.

Site Driver–Enabled: The setting that enables all Messaging servers that use this driver.

messaginggatewayURL: The URL to the gateway.

Username and password: Logon details for the gateway.

Default_encoding: The character set to be assumed.

The 15 supplied drivers can handle all the usual protocols for delivery of messages by SMS, e-mail, voice, or fax, and in some cases are preconfigured for certain well-known gateway service providers. The gateway provider will supply details of the URL to be used, which will include the protocol and other parameters that may be required. Each driver will have its own specific configuration parameters. Some of the drivers, with examples of the parameters, are the following:

RightFax: The parameters provide the information that will appear on the cover sheet, such as the sender's name and number, and detail how to connect to a RightFax fax gateway. RightFax is a fax server product supplied by Captaris.

VoiceGenie: The parameters include how to manage situations where the message recipient's telephone is engaged or doesn't answer, and various voice prompts. Owned by the French company Alcatel, VoiceGenie offers audio gateway services based on the VoiceXML protocol.

EmailDriver: The parameters include whether to use IMAP or POP3. They also include the folder in which to place mail, and address and authentication details for the incoming and outgoing mail servers. This is a generic driver that should work with any e-mail gateway.

If none of the supplied drivers is adequate for your chosen message gateway service provider, a custom driver can be written and used instead. It must conform to the specifications laid down in the Oracle Application Server Wireless Developers Guide. There is an SDK (Software Development Kit) included with Oracle Application Server that will be of assistance.

The Mobile Collaboration Applications

Mobile Collaboration comes with a set of seven applications that give access to Oracle Collaboration Suite application components:

- Mail
- Calendar
- Address Book
- Directory
- Files
- Short Messaging
- Fax

All of these will function out of the box. Configuration, if considered necessary, is done with the Oracle Application Server Wireless Tools. To reach the tools, from the middle tier's Application Server Control, click the Administration icon for the Mobile Collaboration component. This is shown in Figure 5-19 in Chapter 5. Click the Content tab, then the Publish Content subtab to reach the window shown in Figure 11-9.

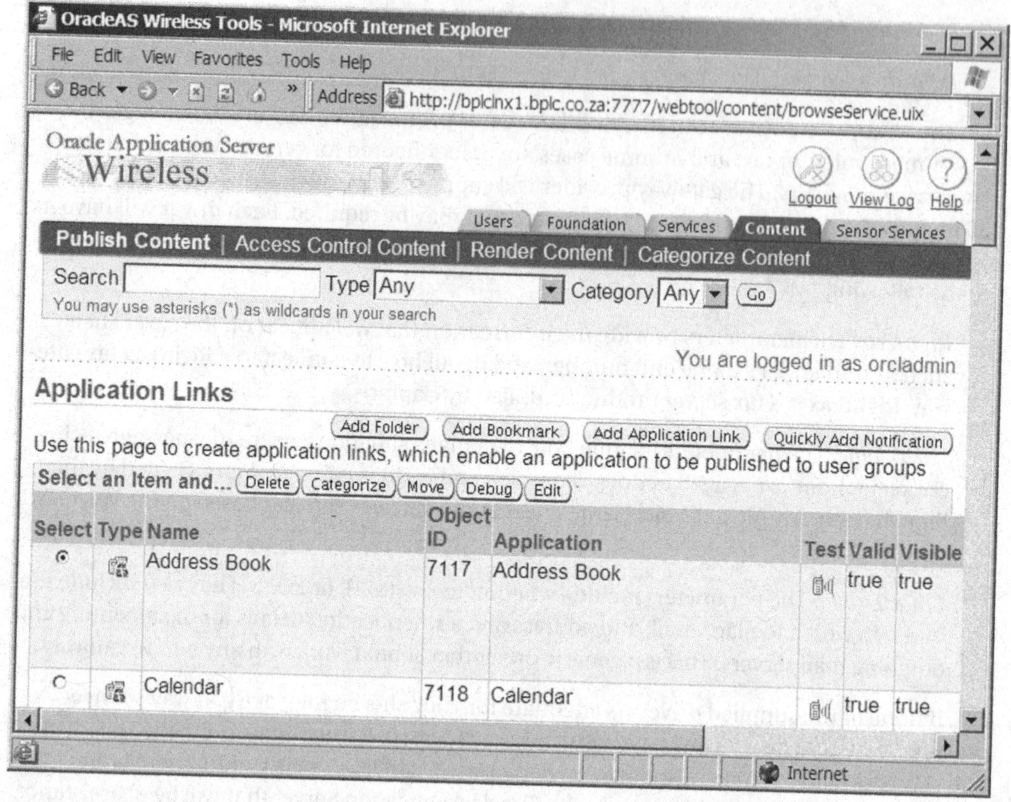

Figure 11-9. *Use the Wireless Tools to configure and test the mobile applications.*

All the mobile applications have configurable parameters, but they all have sensible defaults.

To access the applications, users connect to the configured access points using whatever device they wish. Following authentication, Mobile Collaboration will respond with a menu generated into whatever user interface is appropriate to the device.

It is possible to test the mobile applications without using a mobile device. Clicking the Test icon for an application (shown in Figure 11-9) will launch a wireless PDA simulator, shown in Figure 11-10. The simulator can be used to confirm the applications' functionality, both for using the applications and for receiving notifications.

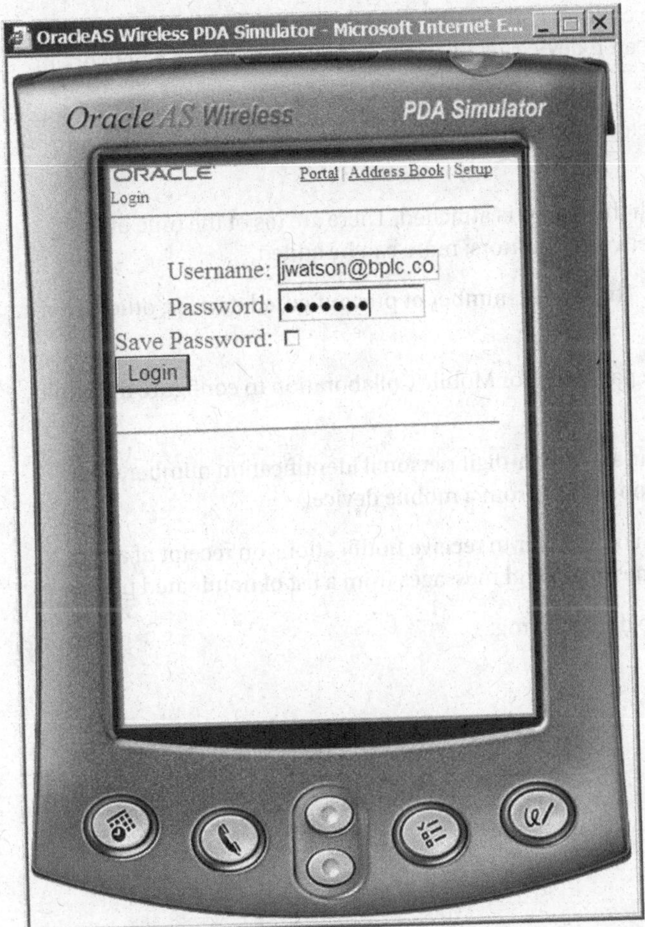

Figure 11-10. *The wireless PDA simulator (note that the username must be the full e-mail address)*

Managing Devices

End users register their own wireless devices with Mobile Collaboration. This is essential so that Mobile Collaboration can present information in a form that is appropriate to the device. Once registered, users can download any software necessary for push mail and Calendar synchronization, and Mobile Collaboration will then maintain the data on the device.

Device Registration

From the Oracle Collaboration Suite portal, accessed from a browser, users should click the Mobile Preferences link. The preferences to be set are the following:

Country code: The telephone country code of the user's device, with a leading + symbol—for example, +1 for a U.S.–located device, or +49 for a device connected to a network in Germany.

Mobile phone number: The telephone number of the device, without any leading zero and including the area code.

Carrier: The network to which the device is attached. There are (as of the time of this writing) ten preconfigured network operators; more can be added.

Model: The telephone model. There are a number of preconfigured devices; others can be added.

Single Sign-On password: The password for Mobile Collaboration to configure the applications to the device.

Create a mobile access PIN: The six- to ten-digit personal identification number used instead of a password when connecting from a mobile device.

Mail preferences: The selection of whether to receive notifications on receipt of any or all voice mails, faxes, urgent messages, and messages from a list of nominated people.

The preconfigured carriers are the following:

- Cingular Blue
- Fido
- Nextel
- O2
- Rogers
- Sprint
- T-Mobile
- TIM
- Verizon Wireless
- Vodafone

There is not a graphical tool to introduce more carriers to Mobile Collaboration; so to do so it is necessary to insert some rows into a table in the Oracle Collaboration Suite database. This is the table CARRIERS in the schema WIRELESS. To inspect and update this table, use SQL*Plus (or any other tool that can be used for issuing ad hoc SQL commands). Every carrier is identified by an ID number (which must be unique) and will have three or four rows giving the carrier's name; whether or not it supports OTA (Over-the-Air) provisioning of software (*T* for true, *F* for false); the time in milliseconds for keeping a session open; and (optionally) the default e-mail domain to use when sending e-mail to the devices. The following example uses SQL*Plus to connect to the database, describe the table, retrieve the details of one carrier, and then insert rows to create a new carrier:

```
[ocsdemo]$ sqlplus system/oracle1@orcl
SQL*Plus: Release 10.1.0.4.2 - Production on Wed May 10 17:02:19 2006
Copyright (c) 1982, 2005, Oracle.  All rights reserved.
Connected to:
Oracle Database 10g Enterprise Edition Release 10.1.0.4.2 - Production
With the Partitioning, OLAP and Data Mining options
SQL> desc wireless.carriers;
 Name                              Null?    Type
 --------------------------------- -------- -----------------------
 ID                                NOT NULL NUMBER(38)
 KEY                                        VARCHAR2(256)
 VALUE                                      VARCHAR2(256)

SQL> select * from wireless.carriers where id=3;
        ID KEY                 VALUE
---------- ------------------- -------------------
         3 name                Vodafone
         3 ota                 t
         3 pingInterval        300

SQL> insert into wireless.carriers values(13,'name','TelkomRU');
1 row created.
SQL> insert into wireless.carriers values(13,'ota','t');
1 row created.
SQL> insert into  wireless.carriers values(13,'pingInterval','600');
1 row created.
SQL> insert into  wireless.carriers values(13,'emailFormat','tru.com.ru');
1 row created.
SQL> commit;
Commit complete.
SQL>
```

This code listing defines a new carrier, TelkomRU, that users will be able to select from now on. In this example, the SYSTEM user account was used to connect to the database. If it is ever necessary to connect as the WIRELESS user, the password can be found in the Oracle Internet Directory. Using either the graphical `oidadmin` utility or the command-line utility `ldapsearch`, query the entry with the following distinguished name:

```
OrclResourceName=WIRELESS,
orclReferenceName=<name of your database>,
cn=IAS Infrastructure Databases,
cn=IAS,
cn=Products,
cn=OracleContext
```

The password will be the attribute orclpasswordattribute. For example, the following command will search the directory on address `jwlnx1:389`, connecting as the user ORCLADMIN:

```
ldapsearch -D cn=orcladmin -w oracle1 -h jwlnx1 -p 389 "orclresourcename=WIRELESS"
```

It will display all the attributes of the entry, including the password. The `oidadmin` utility and the command-line utilities are described in Chapter 6.

The preconfigured telephone and PDA models are the following:

- Audiovox PPC 4100, XV6600
- BlackBerry 6200 and 7200
- HP iPAQ h6300, h6450
- Motorola MPx200
- Nokia 6260, 6600, 6620, 6630, 7610, 9300, 9500
- PalmOne Treo 600/650
- Samsung MITS 700
- Siemens SX56/66
- Sony Ericsson T610, T616, T630, T637, P800, P900, P910a, P10i, K700i, S700i

The definitions are stored in the DEVICES table in the WIRELESS schema, but it should not be necessary to query this table or to insert rows into it as there is a graphical interface for adding devices. In the Wireless Tools (the opening window is shown in Figure 11-9) click the Foundation tab and the Devices subtab, and follow the wizard to create a new device according to the manufacturers' specifications. There is a Clone option that will create a new device based on an existing definition; this will usually be much easier than starting from scratch, unless the new device is completely different from any already defined.

The next window informs the user that his mobile device has been registered and shows the details of how to contact the access points for the mobile applications: the URL for mobile browser access, the telephone number for mobile voice access, and the e-mail address and SMS number for mobile text access. There is also an option to cause Mobile Collaboration to send "bookmark" messages to the user's mobile device with this same information, and send messages that will prompt the user to initiate an OTA download of the client programs.

Client Programs

The Mobile Collaboration component can be used as a source for downloading the client-side software needed to use push mail and the Calendar mobile data synchronization on mobile devices. The software is delivered in the form of a program transferred from the Mobile Collaboration server to the device as an OTA download. The Mobile Collaboration administrator must first upload the program to a program repository, then users select and download whatever software is appropriate to their needs.

Oracle provides some programs for OTA download. Calendar synchronization and push mail clients for Intel-powered Pocket PCs running Windows ME and ARM-powered Palm devices can be found on the middle tier server in the `ORACLE_HOME/wireless/pimap/download` directory; others may be found on the Oracle web site.

To upload a program to the repository, the program (in the form of a ZIP file) must be available on the machine where you are running your browser. Connect to the middle Application Server Control and follow the link for the Mobile Collaboration component. Click the Administration tab and the Client Program Management link to reach the window shown in Figure 11-11 where programs can be uploaded or removed.

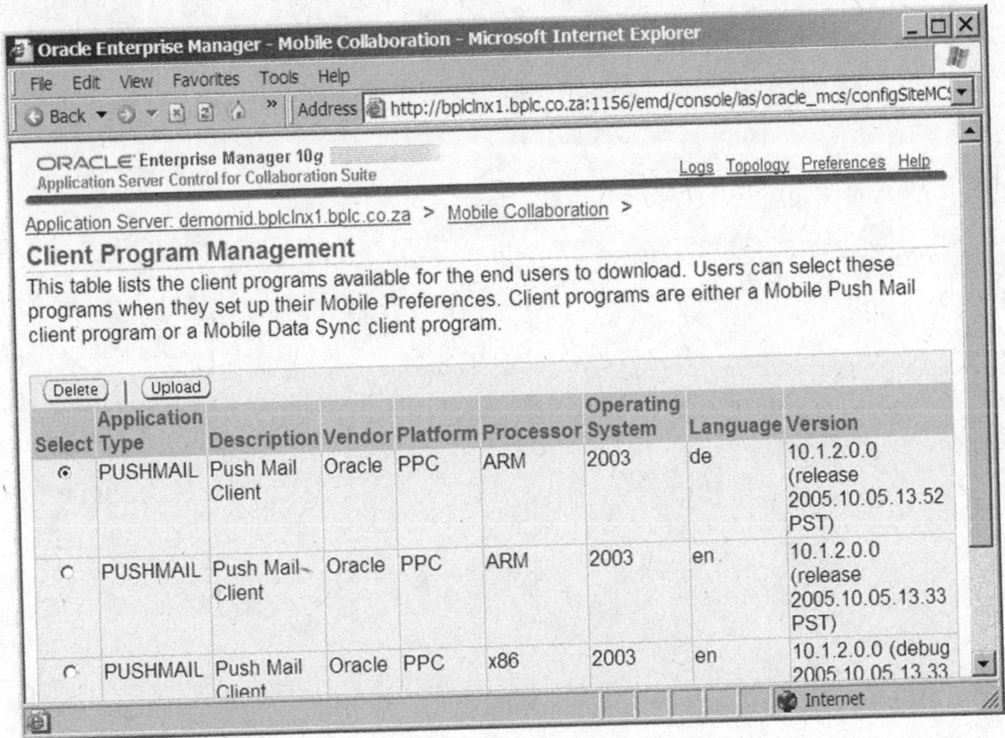

Figure 11-11. *The Client Program Management window, showing the English and German push mail clients for Palm PCs and the English push mail client for Pocket PC*

Device Lockdown

There are circumstances where it will be necessary to disable a device's access to Mobile Collaboration. This is known as *device lockdown*. Reasons could be that an employee has left the organization or the device has been stolen.

The mechanism for device lockdown is for push mail to send an SMS (or whatever other message type is appropriate to the device) that deletes the push mail client program. Following this, the device will not be able to receive push mail messages until the user once again goes to the Oracle Collaboration Suite portal and reregisters the device.

To lock down a device, in Application Server Control navigate to Mobile Collaboration ➤ Administration ➤ Device Lockdown, and select the device to be disabled.

CHAPTER 12

Configuring Real-Time Collaboration

Many users of Oracle products will already be familiar with Real-Time Collaboration through their use of Oracle Support Services; web conferencing is used all the time for customer support. After raising a service request (previously known as a TAR, for those who cling to old terminology) you may be asked to join a web conference that will allow the support consultant to see your PC's screen and control the applications you are running (provided you grant permission). This can dramatically speed up diagnosis and resolution of problems. But Real-Time Collaboration is much more than a tool for remote viewing and control of PCs.

As the name implies, Real-Time Collaboration handles synchronous communications between users. The facilities are instant text messaging, audio transmission using the Voice over IP (VoIP) protocol, and the ability to broadcast windows from one user's PC desktop to others. Combining these facilities enables a collaboration tool that can create a virtual office, where teams can be geographically separate but still communicate in real time as though they were sharing an office.

Being able to assemble virtual teams from a pool of staff without needing to worry about where they are based should deliver huge advantages in efficient use of staff. Rather than having to employ specialist staff at each location, a company can employ a smaller number of specialists and share them across locations as required. One can draw an analogy with the concept of the grid: just as grid computing lets you size hardware resources for average demand rather than peak demand, virtual teams let you exploit staff to the fullest by assigning them dynamically to any project that fits their abilities, no matter where they are based. However, experience shows that without a real-time collaboration facility, such teams tend to be somewhat dysfunctional because they lack the human interaction necessary for developing team spirit. The various Real-Time Collaboration components fill this gap. One should note that some virtual-team environments have had issues with time zones. Real-Time Collaboration can't solve that problem completely, but it does have the ability to record all chat sessions and web conferences, so that team members who miss something can catch up later.

As with all the Oracle Collaboration Suite application components, Real-Time Collaboration is available on wireless and other devices; but to gain its full functionality a PC is needed, preferably a PC running Microsoft Windows. Some of the client tools are only available for Windows, because the various HTTP-related protocols (which would be available on all devices) cannot, as yet, deliver all that is required for a real-time collaborative environment.

There may also be issues with running some of the Real-Time Collaboration components across the Internet, due to wide area network performance and restrictions that may be imposed by firewalls.

The Client Tools

There are two client-side facilities that must be installed by users before they can use Real-Time Collaboration to the fullest. These are the Web Conferencing client and the Messenger client. There is also an add-in for Microsoft Office. As of the time of this writing, these clients were only available for Microsoft Windows. To download the client tools, connect to the Oracle Collaboration Suite portal interface and navigate to the appropriate links. If a user does not have the Web Conferencing client installed at the point of joining a conference, it will be downloaded automatically; usually no user intervention is required, other than enabling ActiveX and disabling any pop-up blocker. Note that the Messenger client is not the only possible client for the instant messaging component of Real-Time Collaboration; instant messaging uses the Jabber protocol, and any Jabber-compliant client should be adequate.

The Web Conferencing client lets users join scheduled or ad hoc online conferences with one other person or with a large group. The conference can include audio streaming direct to the participants' PCs (using attached or built-in microphones and speakers) and sharing of windows or an entire desktop, and a "white board" facility that lets users take turns at broadcasting and modifying windows. There are limitations with the audio streaming, in that the VoIP protocol cannot handle full-duplex communication between more than two terminals. This means that if the conference consists of several people, only one person can broadcast his voice at a time; however, there is a "pass the microphone" facility that will let the conference controller grant control of the voice channel to other people.

The Messenger client is an instant messaging console that sets up chat sessions between any number of people. Features include the ability to invite people to join a chat session, publish your availability for chat, and convert a chat session into a full web conference. Messenger is used to provide full-duplex communication during web conferences as an alternative or addition to the audio streaming.

Note that to connect with the Messenger client, it is necessary to log in with a full e-mail address, such as `tglenden@bplc.co.za`. If a user gives only an unqualified username, he will receive the (not very helpful) message "Unable to connect to the server." It is possible to change this behavior to make the login consistent with the other application components by adjusting certain Real-Time Collaboration properties, as described later in the section "Setting Real-Time Collaboration Properties."

The Real-Time Collaboration add-in for Microsoft Office lets you schedule and start web conferences from within Outlook, share Office documents within the conference, and use the Messenger client for chat sessions from within the Office suite of applications.

Architecture, Networking, and the Hardware Environment

There are two architectural factors that distinguish Real-Time Collaboration from the other Oracle Collaboration Suite application components. First, it has specific network requirements; and second, some functionality can only be provided on one platform: Microsoft Windows.

Neither of these restrictions is likely to be a showstopper for any implementation. There are workarounds for the networking issue, and the requirement for a Windows machine is only for particular functions that will often not be needed and do not impact on the remainder of the installation. Real-Time Collaboration consists of a parent process controlled by OPMN in the standard manner for any Oracle Application Server component that manages a number of child processes that provide the functionality. It is two of these child processes, the Document Conversion server and the Voice Conversion server, that require a Windows environment.

The Document Conversion server is really just left over from previous releases. The purpose of this server is a little like the human appendix, in that it once performed a function that is a little obscure now. Originally the Web Conferencing console had a feature called Cobrowse. This enabled the conference presenter to "lead" the browser of attendees to specific predefined web sites. This is subtly different from desk sharing. Cobrowsing exploits the browser network connection of the attendees. So if the conference convener cobrowses with attendees, he leads their browsers to a web site but the content is downloaded through their own browsers' network, settings, proxy server, and so on. Presentation Mode, which requires the Document Conversion server, was a companion to Cobrowse, as it lets users upload Office files such as PowerPoint presentations to a web server. The Cobrowsing approach of leading the client browser could be used to deliver HTML presentations to customers using their web browser connections and settings.

In reality, simple desktop sharing has proved just as fast and more convenient. The conference convener can share his browser application, and browse using his own network connection, simply sharing this application. The Presentation mode has been retained to support existing customers using this mode, but virtually all web conferences will now share the application, such as PowerPoint, natively.

Network Security

All access to the Real-Time Collaboration applications can be initiated over HTTP or HTTPS, but there is a limitation: the current release does not fully support the use of reverse proxy servers and load balancers. It is therefore necessary to configure the network in such a way that users can contact the Real-Time Collaboration server(s) directly. This is less likely to be an issue for internal users on the same intranet as the server but may be a problem for external users coming in through a corporate firewall.

The initial contact with Oracle Collaboration Suite can be through whatever firewall and reverse proxy server is normally used, but the client-side Web Conferencing and Messenger consoles need to establish connections against the server itself. This can be accomplished either by making the address of the server directly routable by the firewall router, or by using a network address translation (NAT) device with port forwarding to map the server's external address to its internal address. In order to ensure that maximum security is maintained, it may be considered advisable to run the Real-Time Collaboration server on a middle tier node installed specifically for this. It will only be this node that need be directly routable to (or accessible through NAT) from the outside world. The other middle tier node(s) offering the other component application services (and Web Cache, Apache, the Single Sign-On access point, and all the other application components) can be protected by a reverse proxy server and load balancer in the usual fashion.

Figure 12-1 shows a possible configuration that will minimize risk while making Real-Time Collaboration available to external users.

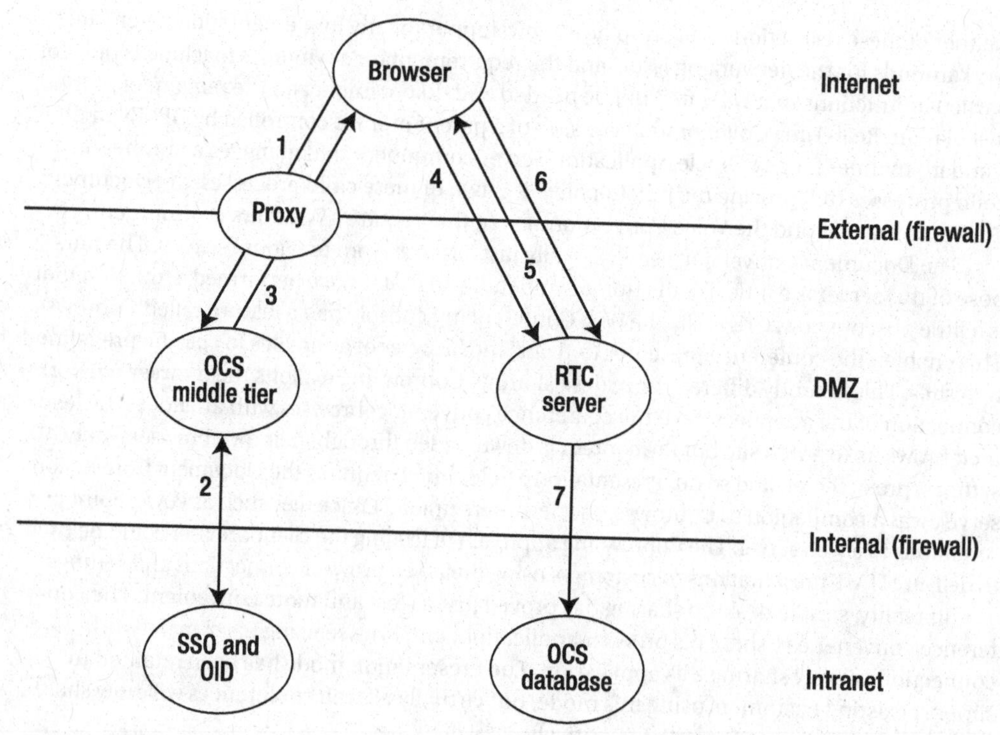

Figure 12-1. *Possible topology to maximize security when deploying Real-Time Collaboration*

In Figure 12-1 the user is running a browser somewhere on the Internet. The Oracle Collaboration Suite middle tier consists of two Oracle Application Server middle-tier instances in the firewall DMZ; one runs only the Real-Time Collaboration server, the other runs all the other components. The infrastructure instance with the Collaboration Suite database is behind the internal firewall. The connection flow is the following:

1. The user's browser, through whatever firewall reverse proxy server is in use, requests a connection to Real-Time Collaboration.
2. If there is no Single Sign-On cookie in the browser, the user is redirected to the Single Sign-On server for authentication. If there is a Single Sign-On cookie, proceed to step 4.
3. The Single Sign-On cookie is sent back to the browser through the reverse proxy server.
4. The user is redirected to the Real-Time Collaboration service that he requested in step 1. This service is running on a different middle tier instance, on a directly routable node.
5. If the user does not have the Web Conference and Messenger consoles installed, the Real-Time Collaboration server generates a download page for these (there is no user intervention required) and they are installed on the client; if they are available, they launch immediately.

6. The consoles establish a session against the Real-Time Collaboration server directly, bypassing the firewall proxy.
7. The Real-Time Collaboration server connects to the Oracle Collaboration Suite component datastore.

The Components of the Real-Time Collaboration Server

As with all the Oracle Application Suite application components, the users' web entry point to Real-Time Collaboration is by issuing a URL that passes through the Web Cache to the Apache web listener. The URL can be issued directly or invoked from the standard Portal front end. Either way, the URL is of the form

```
http://<host.domain:port>/imtapp/app/home.uix
```

where *<host.domain:port>* is the address of the middle tier's Web Cache. The virtual path `imtapp` maps onto the OC4J component OC4J_imeeting, which must be running. This component generates the web user interface. To start it, either use the `opmnctl` utility

```
opmnctl startproc process-type=OC4J_imeeting
```

or take the appropriate link from Application Server Control. The server itself is another component that must be started separately:

```
opmnctl startproc process-type=rtcpm
```

or, again, go through Application Server Control. The server is implemented as an Apache module that acts as a listening process for all Real-Time Collaboration communication, mod_imeeting, and an independent process, the `rtcpm`, the Real-Time Collaboration Process Manager. The mod_imeeting module, deployed as a shared object library, is installed within Apache by including the `mod_imeeting.conf` file in the `oracle_apache.conf` file, which is itself included in the `httpd.conf` file in the Apache configuration directory. It is dynamically linked and runs on demand, as does any other Apache module. The mod_imeeting module acts as a central point for receiving web requests, which it manages by handing off the socket to the `rtcpm` process. It is possible to bypass mod_imeeting and contact the `rtcpm` directly by making use of the supplied SDK.

The `rtcpm` process manages several other processes. First, there are three communication services: the Redirector, the Multiplexer, and the Connection Manager. The Redirector receives all connection requests, whether for Web Conference or for Messenger, and routes Web Conference requests to the Multiplexer, and Messenger requests to the Connection Manager. In a multiserver environment it will apply a load-balancing algorithm to determine which server to send a new request to. All servers will connect to the same database, so it doesn't matter which server any one user establishes a session against; all the Multiplexers and Connection Managers will have access to the same database schemas.

The Multiplexer acts as a communication hub between end users running the Web Conferencing client and three back-end server processes: the Web Conferencing server, the Document Conversion server (if required, which it rarely is), and the Voice Conversion server. The Web Conferencing server manages conferences, maintaining the state of each attendee, enforcing permissions and security rules, distributing real-time data, and managing the recording and archiving of the conferences. The Document Conversion server converts documents from their native format (such as the Microsoft Office formats) to HTML for presentation during the conference if using the Cobrowse facility. The Voice Conversion server supports the conversion of analog audio traffic into a digital stream that can be distributed via the Multiplexer. Both the Document Conversion and Voice Conversion servers are optional, but if installed they require (with the current release) a Microsoft Windows environment. It is however possible to run them on a separate node from the rest of the middle tier, so this does not limit the choice of operating system.

The Connection Manager handles sessions between end users running the Messenger client and the Presence server, which is also sometimes referred to as the Instant Messaging Router. The Presence servers are not unique to the Oracle environment; a number of software vendors have written them, and they are becoming widely used in the networking and communications arena. Presence servers use the SIMPLE protocol, SIP for Instant Messaging and Presence Leveraging Extensions(SIP stands for Session Initiation Protocol). SIMPLE is layered on top of TCP and is becoming the standard for instant messaging applications and much more. The Oracle Presence server manages the publication of user's availability and their membership of chat sessions and distributes messages via the connection manager. A secondary process that may be required by the Presence server is the Voice Proxy server. If the Messenger client is being used for an audio conversation (which is possible, but only between two people) the Presence server sets up a direct connection between the two Messenger clients. If this is not possible, typically because of network protocol and security restrictions, the communication can be via a Voice Proxy server.

To see that the components are running, use the `rtcctl` utility's `listcomponents` command:

```
[mid bin]$ rtcctl listcomponents
ID      NAME              TYPE        DESCRIPTION                 NUM_PROCS
10007   rtc-connmgr       connmgr     IM Connection Manager       2
10000   rtc-confsvr       confsvr     Web Conferencing Server     4
10006   rtc-imrtr         imrtr       IM Router                   1
10008   rtc-voiceproxy    voiceproxyVoice Proxy Server            1
10004   rtcpm             rtcpm       RTC Process Monitor         1
10001   OC4J_imeeting     oc4j        OC4J                        1
10003   rtc-rdtr          rdtr        Redirector                  1
10002   rtc-mx            mx          Multiplexer                 1
10005   rtcctl            rtcctl      RTC Command-Line Control    1
```

The ID number is an internal number, not an operating system process number. Note that the output of the `listcomponents` command includes lines for the OC4J_imeeting process and the `rtcctl` utility itself, as well as the background processes that make up Real-Time Collaboration. To display the actual operating system process identifier numbers (PIDs), use the `getpids` command:

```
rtcctl> getpids
ID      NAME                 COMPONENT TYPE    PIDS
10007   rtc-connmgr          connmgr           12236
10007   rtc-connmgr          connmgr           12241
10000   rtc-confsvr          confsvr           12165
10000   rtc-confsvr          confsvr           12219
10000   rtc-confsvr          confsvr           12213
10000   rtc-confsvr          confsvr           12237
10006   rtc-imrtr            imrtr             12140
10008   rtc-voiceproxy       voiceproxy        12307
10004   rtcpm                rtcpm             12060
10001   OC4J_imeeting        oc4j              10760
10003   rtc-rdtr             rdtr              12214
10002   rtc-mx               mx                12220
10005   rtcctl               rtcctl            24304
```

The background processes are started as necessary by the `rtcpm`, which provides a fault-tolerant environment by restarting them if necessary. Fault tolerance for `rtcpm` itself is provided through the standard OPMN mechanisms.

The command-line utility for managing Real-Time Collaboration is `rtcctl`, which is located in the `ORACLE_HOME/imeeting/bin` directory. This is in fact a shell script that launches a Java process. A point that can cause confusion is that in earlier releases it was called `imtctl`. When searching through web sites and documentation for technical assistance with Real-Time Collaboration, it may be worth searching for both names. In the current Linux release, `imtctl` does in fact still exist; it is byte-for-byte identical to `rtcctl`.

Audio Streaming and the Voice Conversion Server

The limitations of VoIP, as of the time of this writing, that make it impossible to have full-duplex voice communication between all participants in a web conference (though it is certainly possible for any one participant to broadcast to the others) can be overcome by using the PSTN to establish a parallel telephone conference. The audio traffic over the telephone conference will be integrated into the web conference by the Voice Conversion server. This will happen in real time for the benefit of conference participants listening with VoIP, and will be recorded for the archives. These are the possible techniques for audio streaming:

- One-way (single-duplex) communication from a PC microphone broadcast to all other members of a web conference, with PC-attached loud speakers.
- Two-way (full-duplex) communication using PC microphones and speakers between the members of a two-person web conference. Using "pass the mike" in a greater-than-two-person conference, any two can have a two-way conversation with the others listening.
- Two-way (full-duplex) communication using PC microphones and speakers between the members of a two-person Messenger chat session.

- Audio playback of a web conference recording over PC speakers, synchronously with the visual aspects of the conference.
- One-way (single-duplex) communication to all members of the conference with audio from a PSTN source. This source could be one telephone call, or a teleconference.

Services using VoIP and PC-attached loudspeakers and microphones can really only work in one direction: there will be one person, probably the conference owner, broadcasting his voice to the other attendees. The exception to this is a conference of only two people, in which case both of them can talk. To make up for this there is instant messaging available within every web conference. This is of course full-duplex, no matter how many participants there are. For all participants to talk concurrently (which, incidentally, can be very hard to manage unless the conference leader is extremely strict with the other participants), you need a separate teleconference over the PSTN. It is this that requires the Voice Conversion server to stream the audio traffic to those members of the conference who are not in the teleconference and to record the audio traffic as part of the conference for later playback.

Currently, the only supported Voice Conversion server is based on the Intel Dialogic card, with supporting software for Microsoft Windows. A Windows PC is therefore a necessary part of the environment if web conferences are to include full-duplex audio over the PSTN, though all other parts of Oracle Collaboration Suite can, of course, run on other operating systems and platforms. If users are content with single-duplex audio, the Voice Conversion server and the Dialogic card are not necessary. If Voice and Document Conversion servers have been installed (on a Windows machine) they must be started (or stopped) using the `rtcctl` utility.

Note that Dialogic cards are also necessary for deploying the OCS Voicemail and Fax application component, described in Chapter 14.

The Voice Conversion server hardware requirements are not particularly demanding; a PC running Windows 2000 (or later) with a 3GHz CPU and 1GB RAM will be ample for many installations. The more demanding part is the telephone line. This should be a T1 leased line (or the similar E1 line in Europe and Africa). A T1 line can be delivered as copper but is usually an optical fiber. Either way, it comes from the telephone exchange directly into your office. A T1 line can carry 24 audio channels concurrently (the E1 equivalent can carry 30).

It is in fact possible to use DS-0 (Digital Signal level zero) lines, such as the two DS-0 lines delivered by an ISDN (Integrated Services Digital Network) connection, but as these can carry only one audio channel each, they are unlikely to be of any use for anything other than testing or demonstration purposes. A DS-0 line can only deliver 56KB per second. You get two of these with a single ISDN telephone line, but this transmission speed is only adequate for a single voice channel.

The interface between the T1 line(s) and the PC server is the Dialogic card. Intel supplies various cards depending on the capacity needed. For example, a single D/240JCT-T1 Dialogic card can handle one T1 line, one Voice Conversion server, and 12 concurrent audio channels; at the other extreme, a pair of D/480JCT-T1 cards can manage eight T1 lines, four Voice Conversion servers, and 192 audio channels. The comparable E1 dialogic cards are the D/300JCT-E1, which can manage 15 channels, and a pair of D/600JCT-E1 cards, which can manage 240 channels. A T1 line might cost $1,000 a month, depending on your local telecommunications environment; the Dialogic cards will cost several thousand dollars, depending on which model you need.

To install the Voice Conversion server, run the installer program from the Oracle Collaboration Suite DVD. Select the name and destination for the Oracle home to create, select the option to install a middle tier instance, and then select the Real-Time Collaboration and the Voice Conversion server components. You will then receive the usual prompts for connection to the Oracle Internet Directory and the metadata repository that will bring this new instance into the Oracle Application Server farm. Note that the Windows user owning the installation will require full administration privileges on the machine, including the "logon as a batch job" privilege that, by default, not even the Windows Administrator user has.

To control the Voice Conversion server, you must use the `rtcctl` utility, as it is not an OPMN-managed process:

```
cd %ORACLE_HOME%\imeeting\bin
rtcctl start -ct voiceconv
rtcctl stop -ct voicconv
```

User Accounts

Regular users of Real-Time Collaboration have accounts provisioned through the OIDDAS application provisioning tool. These users will be granted the role Enduser and have access to all the facilities offered by Real-Time Collaboration. The other roles can only be granted with the `rtcctl` command-line utility:

- *Business Administrator (Businessadmin)*: There must be at least one user to whom this role has been granted; he will be the superuser for the system.
- *Business Monitor (Businessmon)*: This role can generate reports on system usage and quality of service.
- *Site roles*: By default, there is one site within Real-Time Collaboration. It is possible to create multiple sites and assign the Enduser, Businessadmin, and Businessmon roles per site rather than globally.

To grant these roles, log in to the Oracle Collaboration Suite middle tier server as the Oracle owner and run the `rtcctl` utility. The `rtcctl` utility can do much more than grant roles, but the syntax for this is the following:

```
rtcctl modifyrole [-siteid <site_id>] -username <user_name> -rolename <role_name>
```

If the `siteid` argument is omitted, the role will be granted across all sites. So to make the user APPSADMIN a superuser for Real-Time Collaboration, run the following:

```
$ rtcctl modifyrole -username appsadmin -rolename businessadmin
```

Before a user can be granted any of these roles, he must exist as a user within the Oracle Internet Directory.

When a regular user with the Enduser role connects to the Real-Time Collaboration web interface he will see these tabs:

- *Home*: Join a conference to which you are invited; start an instant conference; download the client tools.
- *Schedule*: Create a new conference and issue invitations.

- *Materials*: Upload documents to your personal document repository within Real-Time Collaboration for viewing and distributing within a conference.
- *Archive*: Set characteristics for archiving your own conferences and view archives of other conferences to which you have access.

These tabs can be seen in Figure 12-2, which shows the initial window when a user connects to Real-Time Collaboration.

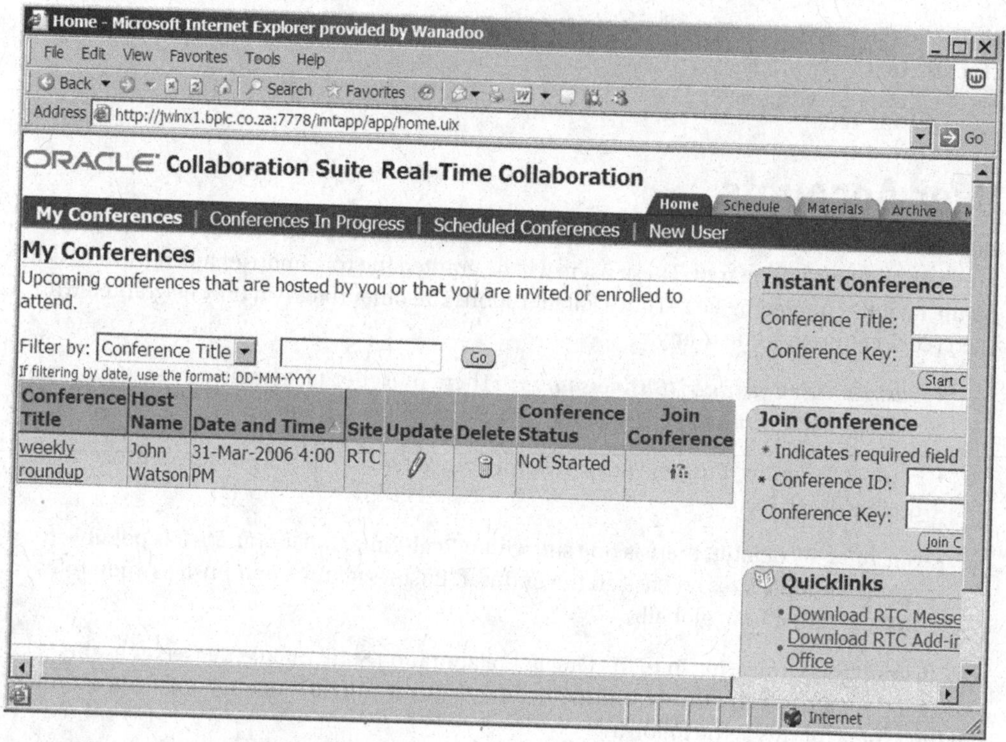

Figure 12-2. *The Real-Time Collaboration initial window*

Once you connect to the web interface as a user to whom the Businessmon role has been granted, you will also see these tabs:

- *Monitor*: See the state of all conferences currently running.
- *Reports*: Generate reports on all completed conferences.

Once you connect to the web interface as a user to whom the Businessadmin role has been granted, you will also see these tabs:

- *Sites*: View details of sites (including the site ID, needed for use of the `rtcctl` utility) and create new sites.
- *System*: View the status and setup of the Real-Time Collaboration environment; view and set properties; control resource usage (such as RAM and CPUs); manage logging.

To revoke an administration role from a user, run the utility again specifying the Enduser role.

As well as users within Oracle Internet Directory, Real-Time Collaboration uses four preseeded schemas within the Oracle database on the infrastructure tier:

- RTC has the database objects (tables, indexes, and PL/SQL packages) that make up the bulk of Real-Time Collaboration.
- RTC_REP has the database objects for storing and reporting on Real-Time Collaboration activity and performance.
- RTC_APP has permissions on and synonyms to the objects in RTC and RTC_REP schemas; access to the data is always through this schema.
- RTC_IM has the objects that implement the Oracle Messenger instant messaging component.

It should never be necessary to connect directly to the database as any of these users during normal operation. One exception is when clearing data from the system after deleting a user from the Oracle Internet Directory. Such deletion will remove the user's Real-Time Collaboration account, but the user's data will still exist and be accessible in Real-Time Collaboration. This is because the fact that a user is no longer valid is no reason to lose all the data (such as web conference archives) that he may have accumulated. To remove his data from Real-Time Collaboration, use a supplied Perl script, in the `ORACLE_HOME/imeeting/install/db` directory on the middle tier. The syntax is the following:

```
delete_user.pl -dbname <db_alias> -rtc_app_user RTC_APP ➥
-rtc_app_password <password>  [-user <user_name>]
```

where *<db_alias>* is the Oracle Net alias of the database hosting the instance, and *<password>* is the RTC_APP schema password (which will be the superuser password entered at install time). The optional `user` argument specifies one deleted user whose data will be cleared. Omitting this argument will clear the data of all deleted users. For example, if user IGAMA has been deleted from the Oracle Internet Directory, which will also deprovision his accounts, the following command will remove his Real-Time Collaboration data from the database:

```
delete_user.pl -dbname orcl -rtc_app_user rtc_app -rtc_app_password oracle1 ➥
-user igama
```

Setting Real-Time Collaboration Properties

After installation, Real-Time Collaboration is configured by setting properties. Properties can be set and viewed with the `rtcctl` utility or through the web interface. They will be set to values that are usually appropriate by the installation process, but some may need adjustment later according to circumstances.

The tools for viewing and setting properties are the `rtcctl` command-line interface and the graphical interface of the Real-Time Collaboration web client. If using these proves too frustrating, they can be bypassed by addressing the relevant database table directly. A query similar to the following may be helpful for displaying all the properties that have been set, ordering them by the scope to which they apply:

```
set linesize 100
column name format a30
column value format a50
column scope_type format a10
column scope_key format a10
select rtc.rtc_admin_properties.name,
rtc.rtc_admin_properties.value,
rtc.rtc_admin_properties.scope_type,
rtc.rtc_admin_properties.scope_key
from rtc.rtc_admin_properties
order by rtc.rtc_admin_properties.scope_type,
rtc.rtc_admin_properties.scope_key,
rtc.rtc_admin_properties.name;
```

Adjusting these properties by executing DML commands would not usually be supported by Oracle Corporation, but querying them can be helpful.

Another source of information on properties and configuration in general is the file `imrtr.xml`, which is in a hidden directory:

```
$ORACLE_HOME/imeeting/im/.etc/imrtr.xml
```

Again, while it is certainly acceptable to look at this file, editing it is a different matter.

Viewing and Setting Properties with rtcctl

All the properties can be displayed and set with the `rtcctl` utility; the finer points of syntax are not always very well-documented, which can make the tool frustrating to use. To launch the utility, change directory to the `ORACLE_HOME/imeeting/bin` directory and run `rtcctl` to enter a simple user interface. Alternatively, run the utility followed by whatever command is required. To set properties, use the `setproperty` command; to view them, use `getproperties`.

A property may have a scope of (in descending order) system, site, instance, or component. The *scope* of a property defines where it is valid and where its value will be applied. There is a hierarchy of scope levels: the *system* is at the top and contains one or more *sites*; a site contains *instances*; an instance has *components*. Some properties can only be set at one level, and their scope is restricted to that level; others are applicable at several levels, in which case the setting at a higher level will be inherited by the lower levels. Following installation, there will be only one instance (consisting of several components) and one site. You can create additional instances by installing additional middle tier nodes for scalability and fault tolerance, and additional sites with different characteristics for different purposes. Some properties can be set at the system level and will be inherited by either the sites or the instances. An inheritable property set at the system level may or may not be modifiable at the lower level, depending on how it is set. Attempts to get or set some properties will fail unless an appropriate scope is specified.

The syntax for setting properties is the following:

```
rtcctl setproperty [-<scope>] -pname <property_name> -pvalue <value> ➥
[-force <force>]
```

`-<scope>` defines whether the property setting will apply to the whole system or to one instance or site. The options are the following:

- -system true indicates a system level property that may be inherited by all instances or sites.
- -siteid <*nnn*> defines a property for one site, where <*nnn*> is the site ID number.
- -i <*instance_name*> nominates an Oracle Application Server instance.
- -cid <*nnnt*> nominates a component of an instance by ID number.
- -cname <*component*> nominates a component of an instance by name.

-pname <*property_name*> -pvalue <*value*> specifies the property by name and the value to which it will be set. There are dozens of properties that control all aspects of Real-Time Collaboration. Each property has a scope within which it may be defined, such as system and site, or system only.

-force <*force*> determines whether an inheritable property can be modified lower down the inheritance tree. The options for <force> are true or false. The default is false, meaning that the setting can be adjusted for individual sites or instances.

To view current property settings there is the getproperties command. In fact, this command does not display all the properties; it did with release 9*i* of Real-Time Collaboration, but with release 10*g* its default output is so restricted as to be almost useless. Figure 12-3 shows the basic documented use of getproperties that shows 11 properties followed by the syntax that will list many more properties (but still not all of them).

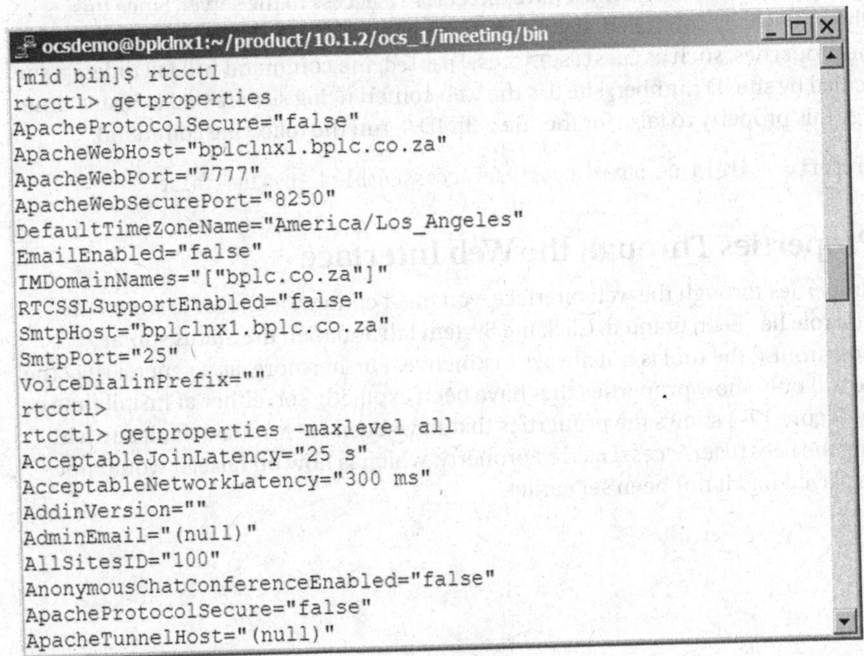
ocsdemo@bplclnx1:~/product/10.1.2/ocs_1/imeeting/bin
[mid bin]$ rtcctl
rtcctl> getproperties
ApacheProtocolSecure="false"
ApacheWebHost="bplclnx1.bplc.co.za"
ApacheWebPort="7777"
ApacheWebSecurePort="8250"
DefaultTimeZoneName="America/Los_Angeles"
EmailEnabled="false"
IMDomainNames="["bplc.co.za"]"
RTCSSLSupportEnabled="false"
SmtpHost="bplclnx1.bplc.co.za"
SmtpPort="25"
VoiceDialinPrefix=""
rtcctl>
rtcctl> getproperties -maxlevel all
AcceptableJoinLatency="25 s"
AcceptableNetworkLatency="300 ms"
AddinVersion=""
AdminEmail="(null)"
AllSitesID="100"
AnonymousChatConferenceEnabled="false"
ApacheProtocolSecure="false"
ApacheTunnelHost="(null)"

Figure 12-3. *Use of the getproperties –maxlevel all command to display all the Real-Time Collaboration properties*

The other options for the command are the following:

- `getproperties -maxlevel general` will display the restricted output shown by default.
- `getproperties -maxlevel advanced` displays 39 properties, some of which are in fact rather basic.
- `getproperties -maxlevel internal` displays 131 "internal" properties.

The `all` option, depicted in the second command in Figure 12-3, is the most useful form of the command: it will list 134 properties. The three properties excluded by the `internal` option are `DocumentConversionDisabled`, `ModImeetingDisabled`, and `VoiceConversionDisabled`, which all default to false. Note that the output of `all` is not all the properties; there are other properties that can only be displayed by specific request with the `getproperty` command.

For example, to view the setting for the property that controls whether guest users who are not registered in the Oracle Internet Directory can make use of Real-Time Collaboration, use the following command:

```
rtcctl getproperty -siteid 0 -pname guestuseraccessenabled
```

This property (which is not shown by `getproperties -maxlevel all`) defaults to true, which will allow anyone, whether or not they are registered in the directory, to use the facilities. While this might be applicable for a site being used for delivering a technical support service to members of the public, for example, you might want to change this for other sites. Note that even with this property on true, the users must have direct HTTP access to the server. Since this access is likely to be strictly controlled, security is not an issue.

For some properties, such as `GuestUserAccessEnabled`, the command will fail unless a site scope is specified by site ID number; site 0 is the web conferencing site created at install time.

To change this property to false for the site with ID 0, run the following command:

```
rtcctl setproperty -siteid 0 -pname guestuseraccessenabled -pvalue false
```

Setting Properties Through the Web Interface

To manage properties through the web interface, you must connect as a user to whom the Businessadmin role has been granted. Click the System tab and then the Status subtab.

Navigation around the tool is not always instinctive. Furthermore, as a general rule, the web interface will only show properties that have been explicitly set, either at install time or subsequently. Figure 12-4 shows the properties that have been set for the default site with ID 0, including the `GuestUserAccessEnabled` property, which is now on false; it would not have been displayed had it not been set earlier.

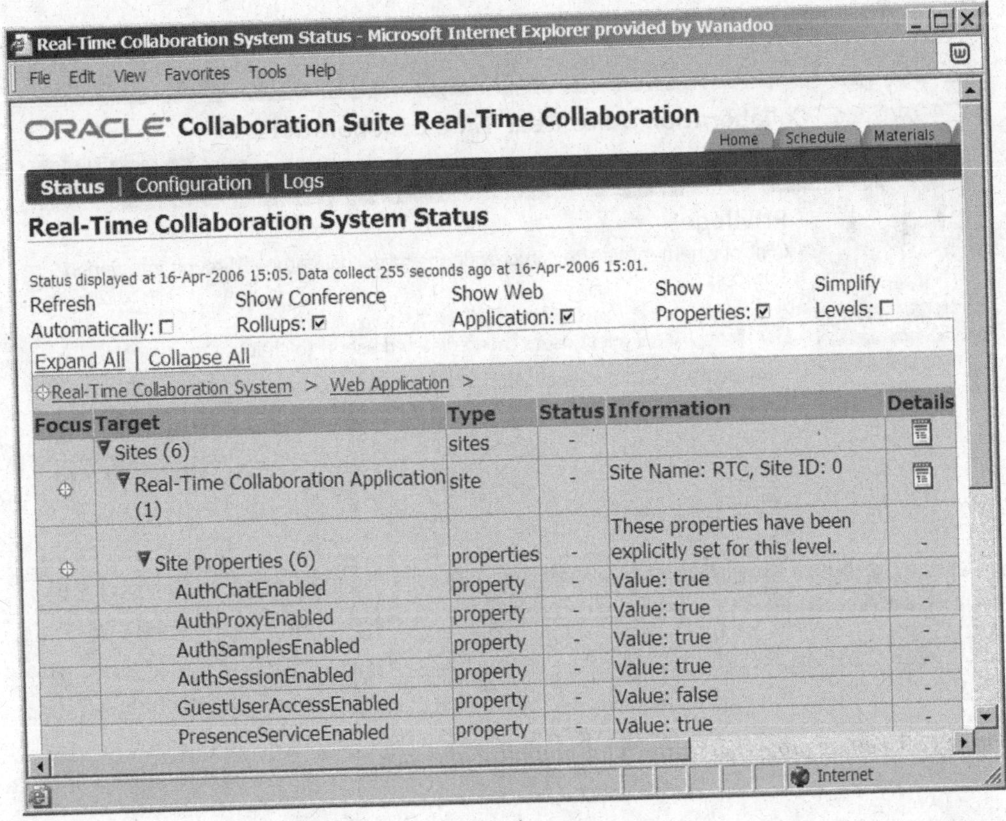

Figure 12-4. *Viewing the properties of a Real-Time Collaboration site through the web interface*

Properties can also be set through the graphical interface. Figure 12-5 shows the window where the `GuestUserAccessEnabled` property can be set; it is the radio button labeled "Allow guest users (nonregistered users) to chat?" which is set on No, for false.

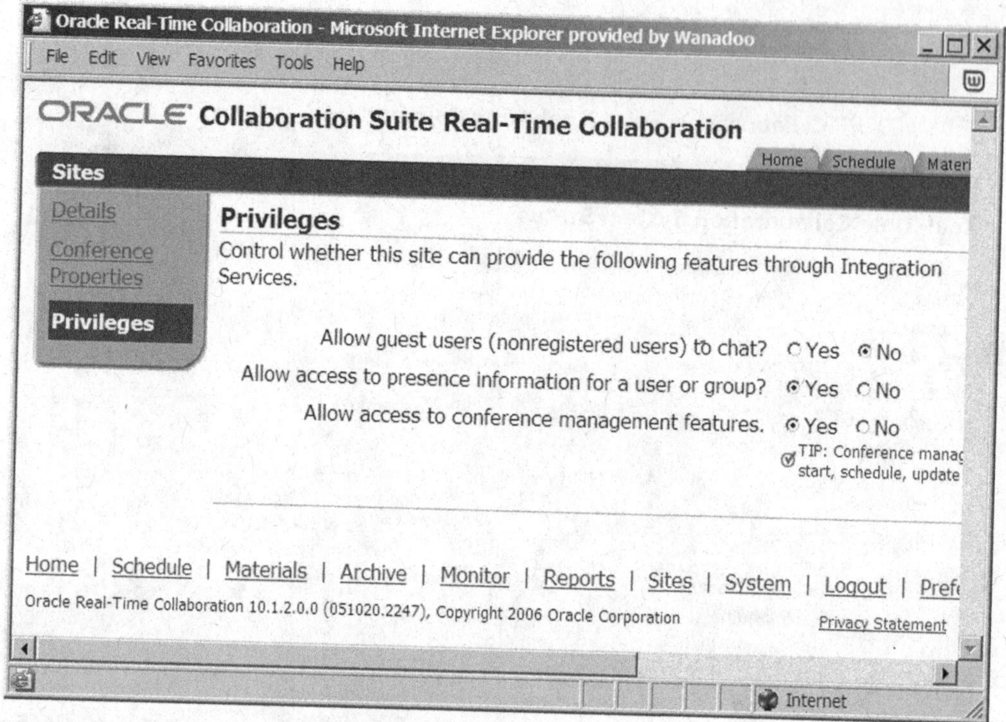

Figure 12-5. *Setting properties through the graphical interface*

Properties Worthy of Consideration

In many cases it will not be necessary to adjust properties from default—but when creating additional sites, it usually will be necessary. A major reason for creating sites is so they will have different properties. It may also be necessary to adjust some of the system-level properties. This section gives descriptions of some of the many properties that control Real-Time Collaboration. Study the Real-Time Collaboration documentation for a full list of properties.

To set or view these properties, there is a choice between the `rtcctl` command-line interface and the web interface. The `rtcctl` utility can be extremely finicky in syntax—for instance, if a property requires a scope, the utility will give you no help on this. You will typically only get an error message stating that the property cannot be set "in this context." You can try using the `geterror` command for further information on the error, but this additional information is unlikely to be helpful. The web interface can be awkward to use because sometimes it is difficult to find the property at all—but it does avoid syntactical or scope errors.

Whatever changes are made with either tool, it is necessary to restart Real-Time Collaboration for the change to take effect. Do this through Application Server Control, or with OPMN:

```
opmnctl restartproc ias-component=RTC
```

or with `rtcctl`

```
rtcctl stop
rtcctl start
```

Some properties that may need to be changed are the following:

`CorpImageName`, default `oracle_ocs_corp.gif`: Set to a path relative to `$ORACLE_HOME/j2ee/OC4J_imeeting/applications/imeeting/imtapp/res/media`. This points to an image file displayed on the user interface windows. Set this to your company logo with this command:

```
setproperty -pname corpimagename -siteID 0 -pvalue "logo.gif"
```

`ChatEnabled`, default true: This allows conference attendees to send messages to conferences. If you want to disable this form of interaction for a site, which will cause the various chat options to be grayed out in the user interface, use this command:

```
setproperty -siteid 0 -pname chatenabled -pvalue false
```

`EnableVoice`, default true: There is little point in leaving this enabled if users do not have appropriate hardware. To disable audio communication and remove the options from the user interface use this command:

```
setproperty -siteid 0 -pname enablevoice -pvalue false
```

`GuestUserAccessEnabled`, default true: This lets people who are not registered in the Oracle Internet Directory attend conferences if the invitation list for a conference also permits this. Disable this with the following command:

```
setproperty -siteid 0 -pname guestuserenabled -pvalue false
```

`RememberPasswordEnabled`, default false. This forces the Messenger client to prompt for a password with every usage, which can be irritating for users and unnecessary if terminals are adequately secured. Allow the client to store the password and transmit it transparently with the following command:

```
setproperty -siteid 0 -pname rememberpasswordenabled -pvalue true
```

`ApacheProtocolSecure`, default false. If the Apache web listener of your middle tier instance(s) is using SSL, Real-Time Collaboration can be configured to use it with this command:

```
setproperty -system true -pname apacheprotocolsecure -pvalue false
```

`ApacheWebHost`, default is the hostname of the middle tier node. The installer will use the node's hostname to contact Apache; but if network aliases are being used or the node has multiple canonical names, this may not be appropriate. Also remember that this name must be directly routable from client machines. Change it with this command:

```
setproperty -system true -pname apachewebhost -pvalue bplclnx1.bplc.co.za
```

`ApacheWebPort`, default is the middle tier's Web Cache listening port for HTTP. The property `ApacheWebSecurePort` is the equivalent for HTTPS. If the Web Cache's port is changed (typically to port 80), this property will have to be adjusted to match with this command:

```
setproperty -system true -pname apachewebport -pvalue 80
```

IMDomainNames, default is the DNS domain of the middle tier node. This is nothing to do with DNS domain or e-mail domain; it is merely a domain (or a list of several possibilities) that must be appended by users to their UID when they log in, if the OIDAuthAttribute is set to UID. The UID is usually the most convenient attribute with which to identify a user; it is specified when the user is created. To allow users to connect without a domain (by entering only their UID) you must set this to the name of the middle tier node. The syntax needs double quotes and square brackets, and (on UNIX) the inner double quotes should be escaped with a back slash. The following is an example of setting this to the middle tier node name:

```
setproperty -system true -pname IMDomainNames -pvalue ➥
"[\"bplclnx1.bplc.co.za\"]"
```

The following is an example of setting it to two values so users can append either value (they must append one or the other) to their UID to log on:

```
setproperty -system true -pname IMDomainNames ➥
-pvalue "[\"bplc.co.za\",\"bplc.co.de\"]"
```

OIDAuthAttribute, default UID: This is the attribute in the Oracle Internet Directory that will be used to identify a user when he connects with the Messenger. By default, users log on with their UID, such as TGLENDEN. Some sites prefer to use the e-mail address, such as tglenden@bplc.co.za, which would be specified with this command:

```
setproperty -system true -pname oidauthattribute -pvalue mail
```

SvrNumProcs, default 4: This controls the number of Multiplexer processes (which route connections to Web Conferencing servers) and Connection Managers (which route connections to the Presence server) that will be launched (by default, one of each) and also the number of Web Conferencing servers that will be launched (by default, four). Use the CT switch to specify Multiplexers or Connection Managers or Web Conferencing servers. To launch two Multiplexers and Connection Managers and eight Web Conferencing servers, use these commands:

```
setproperty -system true -ct mx -pname srvnumprocs -pvalue 2
setproperty -system true -ct connmgr -pname srvnumprocs -pvalue 2
setproperty -system true -ct confsvr -pname srvnumprocs -pvalue 8
```

IMMaxConnections, default 1000: This determines the number of connections that *each* Connection Manager is allowed to route to the Presence server. Remember that there can only be one Presence server per instance. On UNIX there may be operating system limits that will make it preferable to have a higher number of processes, each with a lower number of concurrent connections. To change the number for each started Connection Manager to 500, use this command:

```
setproperty  -system true -pname Immaxconnections -pvalue 500
```

DateFormat, default dd-MMM-yyyy h:mm a: Laid out as a Java date string this specifies the format for date displays in the Real-Time Collaboration web client. To set this to a common European standard, where tea time on the fourth of May this year is 04-05-06 16:00, use this command:

```
setproperty -system true -pname dateformat -pvalue "dd-MM-yy HH:mm"
```

`WelcomeHeaderText`, default "Welcome to Oracle Real-Time Collaboration" and `WelcomeHeaderDescText`, default "Oracle Real-Time Collaboration provides a real-time collaboration environment for your conferences": These make a heading on the prelogin page. To adjust these to something company- and site-specific, use these commands:

```
setproperty -system true -pname welcomeheadertest ➥
-pvalue "BPLC Real-Time Collaboration"
setproperty -siteid 0 -pname WelcomeHeaderDescText -pvalue "Internal Corporate ➥
Site"
```

`IsCalendarOCSInstalled`, default false: Calendar can schedule web conferences. You may wish to make Calendar the only tool for scheduling web conferences, thus ensuring that all such conferences are included in Calendar-managed diaries with appropriate checks for conflicts. To remove the Schedule tab from the Real-Time Collaboration web client windows use this command:

```
setproperty -siteid 0 -pname iscalendarocsinstalled -pvalue true
```

`EmailEnabled`, default false: If conferences are always scheduled by Calendar (see previous entry), this property is not an issue. But if conferences can be scheduled through Real-Time Collaboration, setting this to true with this command will cause the web client to generate e-mail messages with invitations:

```
setproperty -siteid 0 -pname emailenabled -pvalue true
```

`AdminEmail`, default NULL: All the Real-Time Collaboration web client windows have a Contact Us link at the top left. This takes users to a window where they can write an e-mail to the system administrators. It is intended for feedback reports on conferences. This needs to be set as a valid e-mail address for any such messages with this command:

```
setproperty -system true -pname adminemail -pvalue appsadmin@bplc.co.za
```

`SmtpHost` and `SmtpPort`, default Mail SMTP outbound listening address: The default will be fine for a full Oracle Collaboration Suite installation, but if the organization has only purchased the Real-Time Collaboration license, these properties must be changed to the address of the existing third-party e-mail server with these commands:

```
setproperty -system true -pname smtphost -pvalue mail.pub.bplc.com
setproperty -system true -pname smtpport -pvalue 25
```

Managing Sites

Following installation of the Real-Time Collaboration component, there will be one site created for normal use named RTC, with site ID 0. There will be a further six sites created for internal use by other application components. These sites cannot be deleted. You can however create additional sites. Each site can have its own characteristics, set by adjusting appropriate properties, and will host its own web conferences. The characteristics that would be customized at the site level might include security, user interface appearance and behavior, and reporting activity.

Typically, sites will be created for different groups of users, such as the various departments within a company or (if Real-Time Collaboration is used for maintaining contact with external entities) different categories of customers.

To create a site, you must connect to Real-Time Collaboration as a user to whom the Businessadmin role has been granted. After creating the site, you can grant the Businessmon and Businessadmin roles to other users for the new site. Connect to Real-Time Collaboration, either through the Oracle Collaboration Suite portal or directly with a URL such as `http://bplclnx1.bplc.co.za:7777/imtapp/app/home.uix`.

When redirected to the Single Sign-On server, log in as a user with the Businessadmin role. Clicking the Sites tab will show all existing sites (initially only the RTC site and the component sites for Discussions, Workspaces, Portal, Calendar, and Messenger). Click the Create Site button to reach the window shown in Figure 12-6. Fill in the appropriate details.

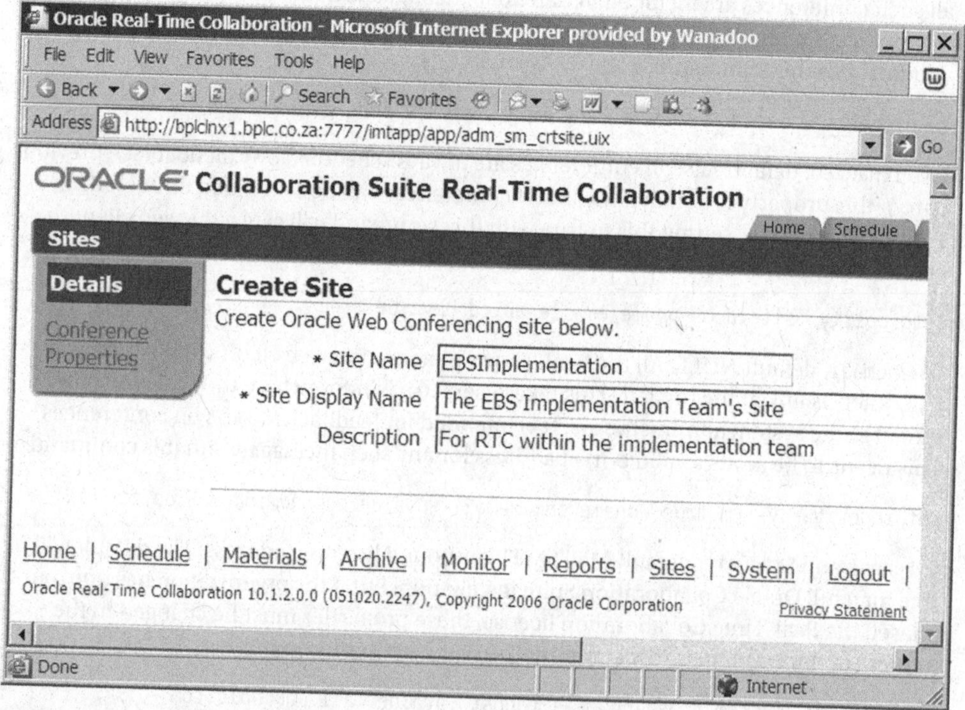

Figure 12-6. *Creating a Real-Time Collaboration site*

Click the Apply button to create the site. A unique site ID number will be generated and you will be returned to the Sites window. Selecting the Details icon for the new site will let you edit some of the properties and privileges for the site. These edits can also be done with the `rtcctl` utility by setting properties with a scope clause that specifies the site's site ID number.

The site ID number can be appended to the previous URL used to connect to Real-Time Collaboration, and following logon, users will only see the conferences scheduled within the site.

Grant the administration role to a site rather than to the whole system by appending a scope clause. For example, if the site ID is 10000867 use this command:

```
rtcctl modifyrole -username tglenden -rolename businessadmin -siteid 10000867
```

Following this, user TGLENDEN will see the administration tabs when she connects to the nominated site but not when she connects to any other site.

Real-Time Collaboration Archives

Real-Time Collaboration is, as the name implies, intended for use in real time: virtual meetings with synchronous communications between attendees. It is important that the information disbursed and developed during these virtual meetings is not lost. This is not only important operationally but may have legal significance as well. Archiving can be critical in many countries where corporate governance standards and corruption are major issues. The default behavior is that all web conferences are archived, but Messenger chat sessions are not.

Web conference archives are stored in the RTC schema of the Oracle Collaboration Suite database. The information for each conference includes the title, date/time, duration, and number of attendees. Information on attendees includes the time each joined and left the conference, their UID (if any), and their e-mail addresses. The recording includes the visual elements, any audio track, and any distributed documents.

The archive is stored under the ownership of the person who convened the conference. The convener has control over who can view or download the archive: attendees, all users registered in the Oracle Internet Directory, or anyone at all.

Messenger archives can be stored either in the Real-Time Collaboration repository or locally by end users with the Messenger client. To enable central storage, set a property with this command:

```
rtcctl setProperty -system true -pname IMArchiveEnabled -pvalue true
```

The local storage is enabled by default. To confirm this, within the Messenger client click the Tools tab, then Options. Select Instant Messages and you will see that the check box for Save Messages has been selected with 4MB of space allocated.

Problem Identification

To assist with problem resolution, Real-Time Collaboration includes some diagnostic tests. As well as the `rtcctl` commands `listcomponents` and `getpids` already mentioned, there is the `runtests` command:

```
rtcctl> runtests
Instance - demomid.bplclnx1.bplc.co.za:
TEST NAME       SUCCESS
mtgtest         true
dbtest          true
apptest         true
```

```
proxytest          false
emailtest          false
imtest             true
servletAccessTesttrue
rtcctl>
```

This test shows that the voice proxy server process cannot be contacted (in this case, because the Voice Conversion server has not been installed) and that the e-mail server to which messages will be sent is not available (in this case, because the `AdminEmail` property has not been set). There are also two tests that can be run from a browser, one for Web Conferencing and one for the audio services. The URL to run the Web Conferencing test is

```
http://<host.domain:port>:/imtapp/app/adm_sa_insttests.uix
```

where *<host.domain:port>* is the address of the middle tier Web Cache.

Figure 12-7 shows the result of the Web Conferencing test.

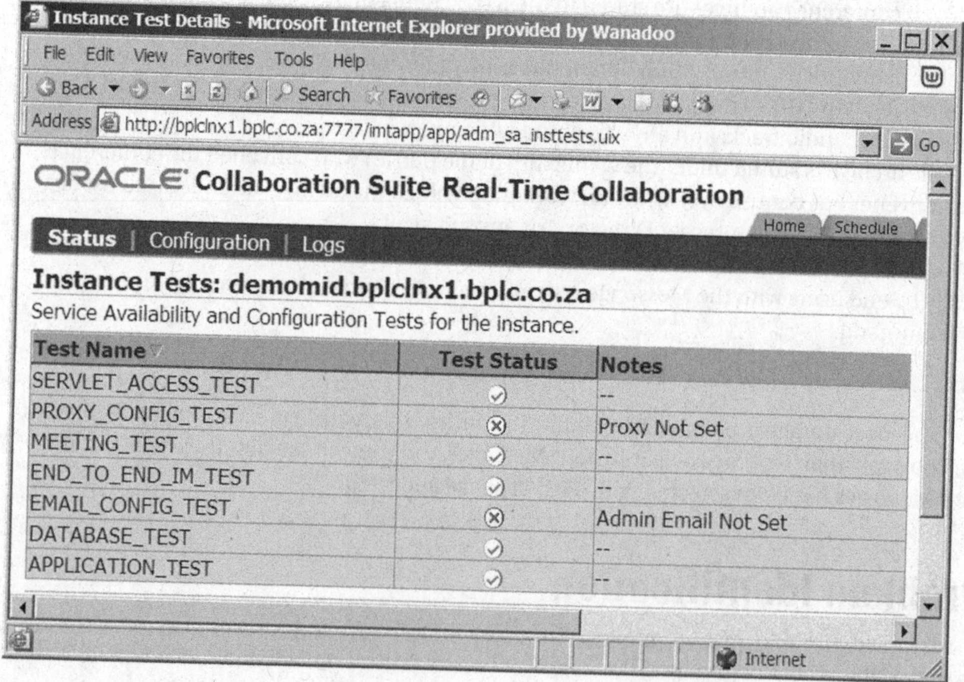

Figure 12-7. *The Web Conferencing self-test*

The second test is on URL

```
http://<host.domain:port>:/imtapp/app/imttests.jsp
```

which gives much more information on the state of the audio services.

Log files are generated by every Real-Time Collaboration process in directories beneath the ORACLE_HOME/imeeting/logs directory. They can also be seen in a browser at the following URLs:

```
http://<host.domain:port>:/imtapp/logs/system.jsp
http://<host.domain:port>:/imtapp/logs/imtLogs.jsp
```

CHAPTER 13

Configuring Search

Most large organizations have information stored in a vast number of formats and distributed over many locations. It may be impossible to collate information that is spread over multiple file servers and databases and managed by different applications. An Oracle Collaboration Suite installation will immediately help solve this problem; all the file servers can be concentrated in one Content Services instance, and all the mail servers migrated to one Mail instance. But there is still the problem of data format. How can you, for example, retrieve all documents containing a certain word, whether the "documents" are e-mail messages, WordPerfect files, Excel spreadsheets, or columns in a database table? The Search component can do this and more.

Search is an application that can retrieve data from many data sources stored in many formats. Its cross-product capability makes it one of the most powerful tools there is for integrating information in a collaborative environment. Architecturally it is based on two products that have been shipped with the Oracle database for some time: the Ultrasearch component that provides web crawling capability for database content and other formats, and the Oracle Text indexing tool. Since these components have historically been part of the database, it is in the database documentation that you will find full details of their configuration and capabilities, rather than in the documentation for Oracle Collaboration Suite or Oracle Application Server.

Search comes preconfigured for searching data in Content Services, Calendar, and Mail. For many sites this will be all that is needed, but it can be enhanced to include any number of web sources, operating system files, and database tables in its search domain. It can understand (as of the time of this writing) more than 100 file formats, including word processors, spreadsheets, and databases—the exact number will depend on the release. If it is necessary to include any additional non-preconfigured data sources and formats in the Search scope there are mechanisms for doing this.

Search Architecture

Search does not itself search any data. It searches precreated indexes on data. Depending on the data source, these indexes may be created by the application that is maintaining the data, or they may be created by Ultrasearch or by Oracle Text. The indexes need to be maintained, which will have performance implications. Generally speaking, the more up-to-date the indexes are kept, the greater the performance implications. To maintain them in real time would put a huge strain on the operating environment.

For the user, there are several points of entry to Search: through individual application components or from the Oracle Collaboration Suite portal front end, both of which require an OC4J component to be running on the Oracle Collaboration Suite middle tier; or from applications external to Oracle Collaboration Suite that make use of the Ultrasearch API. The components that must be enabled on the infrastructure tier are the Oracle Text indexing processes and the Ultrasearch processes. Both of these have a schema within the Oracle Application Server infrastructure database.

Oracle Text

The Oracle database is a relational database management system. Relational databases store and manipulate data in the form of two-dimensional tables, using indexes on columns to relate the tables together and to allow for fast retrieval of rows. The relational paradigm is fine for storing some types of data—typically the data that might be needed for an online transaction-processing system—but it is not optimal for some types of data, and totally inappropriate for others. Types of data that may be difficult or impossible to manage in a relational structure include geographical data, audio and visual data, and text data.

A fundamental problem with all these data types is that they cannot be forced into a two-dimensional structure of columns that can be indexed; it is impossible to normalize the data into a relational structure. Historically, the solution was to use nonrelational structures, such as the inverted structure used by Adabas, or an object-oriented database such as Objectivity/DB published by Objectivity Inc. Over the years, the Oracle database has been enhanced in several ways to make it capable of managing nonrelational data. Oracle Spatial provides facilities for managing geographical data, and Oracle Intermedia manages audiovisual data. Oracle Text is the enhancement for managing textual data. All these enhancements rely on the use of the LOB data types to store the data, and a set of procedures (for the most part implemented in Java) that analyze the content of the LOBs in an appropriate fashion and generate a set of indexes that can be searched with normal SQL code and also with specialized PL/SQL functions and procedures. Thus, Oracle Text makes it possible, for example, to search all documents for those that contain certain words, perhaps within certain proximity of others. The general approach is to pass through the documents, extracting every word, and storing the words in a separate table on which there are normal relational indexes; this is similar to the Adabas inversion.

Applying a set of filters lets Oracle Text decode a wide range of document formats for indexing, and even present the documents in other formats, typically HTML. There is also the ability to add metadata to documents, describing them and their contents, which can also be included in the search criteria. The documents to be indexed can be stored as LOBs within database tables or as files within the operating system's file system or as any location accessible through a URL.

The Oracle Text schema is CTXSYS, which will be preloaded into the Oracle Collaboration Suite database. This schema has the relational tables and indexes derived from the nonrelational data that has been indexed, and the procedures and functions used to manage the indexes. For instance, the package CTX_DDL has procedures for defining the rules to apply when indexing documents, and the package CTX_QUERY can execute queries against the indexes. All the Oracle Text facilities require use of what is known as a *lexer*. A lexer defines the way the text data is structured and is necessary to allow Oracle Text to parse the data correctly. It will include rules for such things as word breaks and how to handle case and accent variations, the language, and much more. Oracle Text ships with lexers capable of managing both European and Asian languages.

The default tablespace for the CTXSYS schema is the SYSAUX tablespace. If extensive use is made of Text, this schema can expand to a significant size, perhaps several gigabytes. The database administrator should monitor the size of the CTXSYS schema, and if necessary move it to another specially created tablespace. This query will show how much space is being used by Oracle Text:

```
select space_used_kbytes from v$sysaux_occupants where occupant_name='TEXT';
```

This procedure call will relocate Oracle Text to another tablespace (which must have been created already) called CONTEXT:

```
execute ctxsys.dri_move_ctxsys(tbs_name=>'CONTEXT');
```

Unlike normal relational indexes, Oracle Text indexes need not be maintained in real time. While this can be done, it generally impacts adversely on performance; inserting a large number of documents into a table (as could happen when, for example, a user drags and drops a folder from his local PC desktop to a Content Services mapped drive) may require a considerable amount of work as Oracle Text updates the relevant indexes. The process of updating indexes to include recent insert, update, and delete activity is known as *index synchronization*. The default configuration of Oracle Text as installed with Oracle Collaboration Suite is such that synchronization is not done in real time as the changes are made. Rather, the synchronization is done asynchronously by invoking the `CTX_DDL.SYNC_INDEX` procedure at regular intervals by running an automatically repeating job, controlled by the `DBMS_JOB` job queue.

By default this job will run every 30 minutes and execute this procedure call:

```
ctx_ddl.sync_index(idx_name=>'IFS_TEXT');
```

An argument that can be passed to the procedure is `MEMORY`. This defaults to 16MB and affects both the performance of the synchronization and the performance of subsequent searches. A larger value will reduce the amount of disk I/O needed for the operation and result in an index that is less liable to fragmentation, so it can be scanned faster but can cause problems if runtime memory is scarce. This procedure call, executed from a SQL*Plus prompt, will use up to 256MB while synchronizing the index:

```
SQL> execute ctx_ddl.sync_index(idx_name=>'IFS_TEXT',memory=>256M);
```

Apart from being synchronized, indexes also require maintenance to keep them efficient. This is known as *index optimization* and is performed by invoking the `CTX_DDL.OPTIMIZE_INDEX` procedure. The optimization process refreshes the relational tables and indexes associated with the documents, removing obsolete data and eliminating any fragmentation. There are five modes of optimization:

- Rebuild mode creates completely fresh data structures. It requires a significant amount of storage space because while the new structures are created, the old ones are still extant.
- Full mode compacts data and removes obsolete rows.
- Fast mode compacts data but does not remove obsolete rows.

- Token mode optimizes all data relevant to a particular token. A *token* can be used to restrict the optimization to those documents containing a particular word. This mode is useful for optimizing access to frequently referenced data without bothering to optimize access to data that is rarely queried.
- Token-type mode optimizes access to documents selected by a metadata item, such as all those owned by a certain user.

Optimization, like synchronization, will occur automatically according to a scheduled job. This will by default run once every 24 hours and execute this procedure call:

```
ctx_ddl.optimize_index(idx_name=>'IFS_TEXT', optlevel=>'FULL', maxtime=>60 );
```

This will perform a full optimization, but will only run for one hour before terminating. The nature of index optimization is such that at the next scheduled run, it will carry on from where it left off.

The details of the jobs can be seen by querying the DBA_JOBS view. If the setup is not considered suitable, make adjustments by using the DBMS_JOB.CHANGE procedure. For instance, the daily scheduling of the optimization will be from the time the instance is started, which may not be sensible. Adjusting it to run during the night might be advisable, because even though the synchronization and optimization operations can be carried out online while the system is in use, they can impact on performance and are better run during periods of low activity.

The default configuration means that the Text indexes could be up to 30 minutes out-of-date. If this is unacceptable, there is no reason not to adjust the job to run more frequently, or it can be run manually at any time from SQL*Plus, where *<job_number>* is the number of the job:

```
SQL> execute dbms_job.run(job=><job_number>);
```

Obtain this by querying the DBA_JOBS view. It must always be borne in mind that indexing Text columns takes a long time, and it is possible that the workload could impact adversely on the performance of user activity. It may be necessary to discuss this with the database administrator and to consider using database facilities such as the Scheduler and the Resource Manager to minimize this risk.

To enable text indexing within Mail, this must be requested per user, either when the user is first created or, if it is not requested at that point, enabled later. Figure 13-1 shows the relevant window in the OIDDAS provisioning console.

Certain types of document can be removed from the indexes entirely. This is done by configuring the document formats, or MIME types, within Content Services. Figure 8-7 in Chapter 8 shows the relevant window in which indexing is being enabled for all files with the .CMD suffix.

If documents that should be retrieved by Search are not being found, first use the OIDDAS provisioning console to check that the user has indexing enabled. Then within Content Services, check that the format (or MIME type) has been selected for indexing, as shown in Figure 8-7. Then run a query against the view CTXSYS.CTX_PENDING:

```
select pnd_timestamp from ctxsys.ctx_pending where pnd_index_name='IFS_TEXT';
```

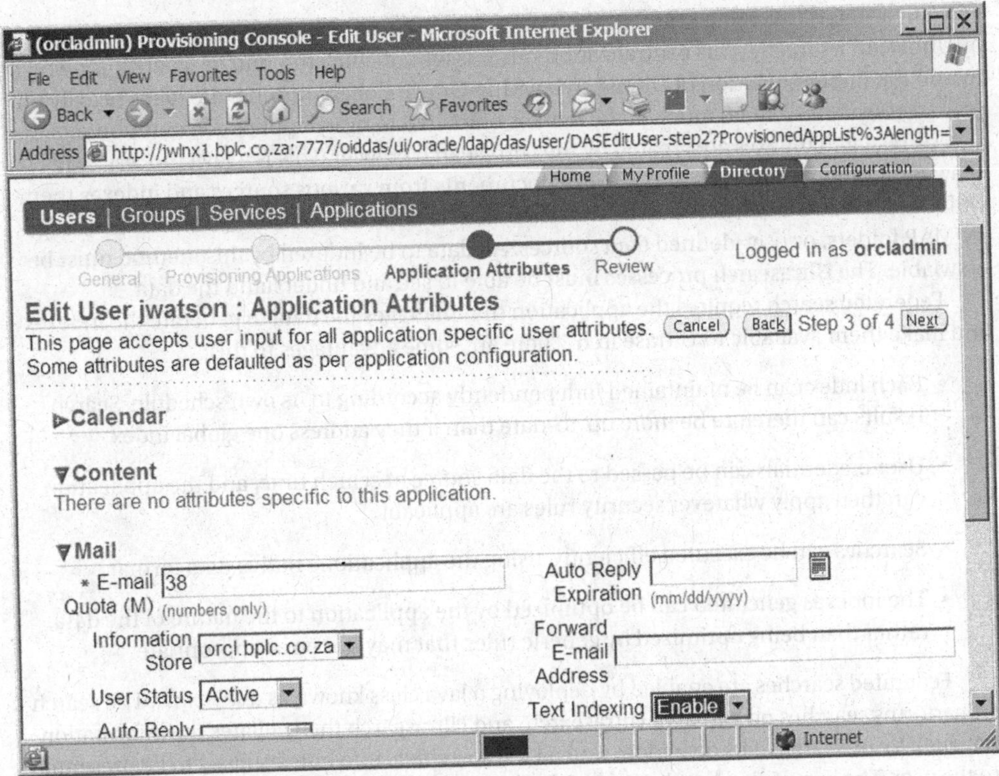

Figure 13-1. *To enable text indexing for a user's Mail, set Text Indexing to Enable in the application provisioning console.*

This lists the creation time of each document that should be indexed but has not been so far. After a scheduled run of the synchronization, it should be empty; there should by default be no entries more than 30 minutes old. If there is a backlog of entries, check that the job that synchronizes the indexes is running:

```
select broken from dba_jobs where what = 'ctx_ddl.sync_index(''IFS_TEXT'');';
```

If the job is "broken," which it will be if it has failed repeatedly, fix it with this procedure call:

```
execute dbms_job.broken(job=>job_number,broken=>FALSE,next_date=>SYSDATE);
```

substituting the number of the job. This call will launch the job immediately and enable the normal schedule thereafter.

Oracle Ultrasearch

The Oracle Collaboration Suite Search component uses Oracle Ultrasearch to search prebuilt indexes. These indexes can be on data from a number of sources indexed using Oracle Text. Earlier releases of Ultrasearch cataloged all the data sources into one index. This was very efficient as far as executing searches was concerned but required everything to be managed by Ultrasearch directly. This centralization raises issues of efficiency and of security, for which reason the implementation of Ultrasearch within Oracle Collaboration Suite relies heavily on *federated* searches, where much of the work is offloaded to other application components.

Ultrasearch indexes are created by the Ultrasearch crawler. This is a Java process that spawns a number of threads that retrieve documents from various sources and indexes them with Oracle Text. The sources can be web sites, Oracle database tables, files on disk, messages in IMAP folders, or user-defined data sources. All data to be indexed by this method must be crawlable. The Ultrasearch processes must be able to see and understand the data.

Federated search requires the application that manages the data to generate the indexes and make them available to Ultrasearch. There are some advantages to this:

- Each index can be maintained independently according to its own schedule. Search results can therefore be more up-to-date than if they address one global index.
- User credentials can be passed to the data source at search time, and the application can then apply whatever security rules are applicable.
- Searches can be executed efficiently, using the application's native data format.
- The indexes generated can be optimized by the application to the nature of the data, rather than being optimized by generic rules that may not be as appropriate.

Federated searches are enabled by deploying a Java class known as a *searchlet*. The searchlet performs searches on behalf of Ultrasearch, and Ultrasearch then collates the information returned by its search of its own index and all the searchlets into one result set to be presented to the user. The out-of-the-box Oracle Collaboration Suite installation will have federated searches enabled for Content Services, Calendar, and Mail.

As with Oracle Text, the default tablespace for Ultrasearch data storage is the SYSAUX tablespace, and if (as is inevitable for a large installation with Ultrasearch configured to index many data sources) this schema expands to several gigabytes, the database administrator should relocate it to another specially created tablespace. The following query will show how much space is being used by Ultrasearch:

```
select space_used_kbytes from v$sysaux_occupants where occupant_name='ULTRASEARCH';
```

The following procedure call will relocate Ultrasearch to another tablespace (which must have been created already) called SEARCH:

```
execute wksys.wk_util.move_wk(tbs_name=>'SEARCH');
```

Following installation, there will be three database schemas in the Oracle Collaboration Suite database related to Ultrasearch. These are WKSYS and WK_TEST and WKPROXY. The WKSYS schema contains all the database objects that make up Ultrasearch and has very high privileges (including the DBA role). The WK_TEST schema is the administrator of the default Ultrasearch instance (called WK_INST) and has only the roles needed to use Ultrasearch: CTXAPP and WKUSER. To create additional Ultrasearch instances, you must first create the schema and grant it the necessary roles. The WKPROXY schema is used by the Ultrasearch administration tool to connect to the database when using the tool on Single Sign-On mode.

Middle Tier Components

The interface to Search provided by Oracle Collaboration Suite requires a Java component to be running on the middle tier: the OC4J_OCSADMIN application. This can be seen in Application Server Control, shown toward the bottom of Figure 5-19 in Chapter 5.

The searchlets are deployed to the middle tier as part of the applications to which they belong. If the application components have not been started, it is not possible to search the associated data.

Connecting to and Using Search

Oracle Collaboration Suite provides the Search component as an interface to Ultrasearch and Oracle Text. This will be adequate for many sites. It is preconfigured for searching Mail, Content Services, and Calendar. Some organizations will wish to extend Search's capabilities to include other data sources: tables in databases, corporate and public web sites, and disk-based file stores. This can be done from within the provided Search interface, but if desired, external applications can be bought or developed that will make use of Ultrasearch and Oracle Text directly. These may provide greater functionality than the Search interface.

The Administration Interface

The Search administration tool is available to Oracle Collaboration Suite users on the URL

```
http://<host.domain>:<port>/ultrasearch/admin_sso/index.jsp
```

where *<host.domain>*:*<port>* is the address of the Oracle Collaboration Suite middle tier Web Cache. This URL will generate a Single Sign-On prompt. Following installation, the only valid logon is orcladmin. In fact, when you connect through this Single Sign-On interface, you are connecting to the database schema WKPROXY.

If Ultrasearch is installed independently of Oracle Application Server (in which case there will be no Single Sign-On facility available), to connect to the administration interface it is necessary to give the database login of the Ultrasearch schema. This URL

```
http://<host.domain>:<port>/ultrasearch/admin/control/login.jsp
```

will connect to the appropriate logon window. The username will be WK_TEST and the password following installation will default to the well-known password of WK_TEST, but the account is locked within the database. Therefore, before connecting in this manner, connect to the database as a user with DBA privileges, unlock the account, and change the database logon password. Here is an example of doing this:

```
[inf ocsdemo]$ sqlplus system/oracle1
SQL*Plus: Release 10.1.0.4.2 - Production on Sun Mar 19 10:40:49 2006
Copyright (c) 1982, 2005, Oracle.  All rights reserved.
Connected to:
Oracle Database 10g Enterprise Edition Release 10.1.0.4.2 - Production
With the Partitioning, OLAP and Data Mining options
```

```
SQL> alter user wk_test account unlock;
User altered.
SQL> alter user wk_test identified by newpassword;
User altered.
SQL> exit
Disconnected from Oracle Database 10g Enterprise Edition ➥
Release 10.1.0.4.2 - Production
With the Partitioning, OLAP and Data Mining options
[inf ocsdemo]$
```

Following the password change, the password stored within the middle tier must also be changed through the Edit Instance option.

Following logon (whether through the `index.jsp` or the `login.jsp`) it is necessary to select which Ultrasearch instance you wish to administer. One Ultrasearch instance is one schema in the database. The schema created for Oracle Collaboration Suite is WK_TEST, configured with the instance WK_INST. This will be the only instance available. The options available as tabs in the administration window are the following:

- *Instances*: Create or delete instances, or switch an instance between read-only and updateable. Specify the instance's database schema password.
- *Crawler*: Configure the resources to be devoted to crawling searchable content and the depth and level of detail of the searches.
- *Web Access*: Define the proxy server to use when connecting to web sources.
- *Attributes*: Define searchable metadata attributes for indexed documents. The preconfigured attributes are the following:
    - Author
    - Description
    - Host
    - Language
    - Last modified date
    - MIME type
    - Subject
    - Title
- *Sources*: Define the sources of information that Ultrasearch should index. The possible sources are the following:
    - Web (accessible with HTTP through a URL)
    - Table (a table and column(s) in an Oracle database)
    - E-mail (an IMAP folder)

    - File (a disk directory on the local host)
    - Oracle sources (the federated sources within Oracle Collaboration Suite)
    - User-defined (data sources crawlable by a nominated Java class)

- *Schedules*: Control the schedules for synchronizing and optimizing the indexes on the various data sources.
- *Queries*: Gather sources into groups of related data; influence the relevancy of different criteria; manage the display of results; configure timeouts for searches.
- *Users*: Create other administrators.
- *Globalization*: Specify the various user-defined fields (such as attributes and data source groups) displayed in Ultrasearch windows with multiple labels, to be used according to different users' language preferences.

These options are shown in Figure 13-2 as tabs in the administration window.

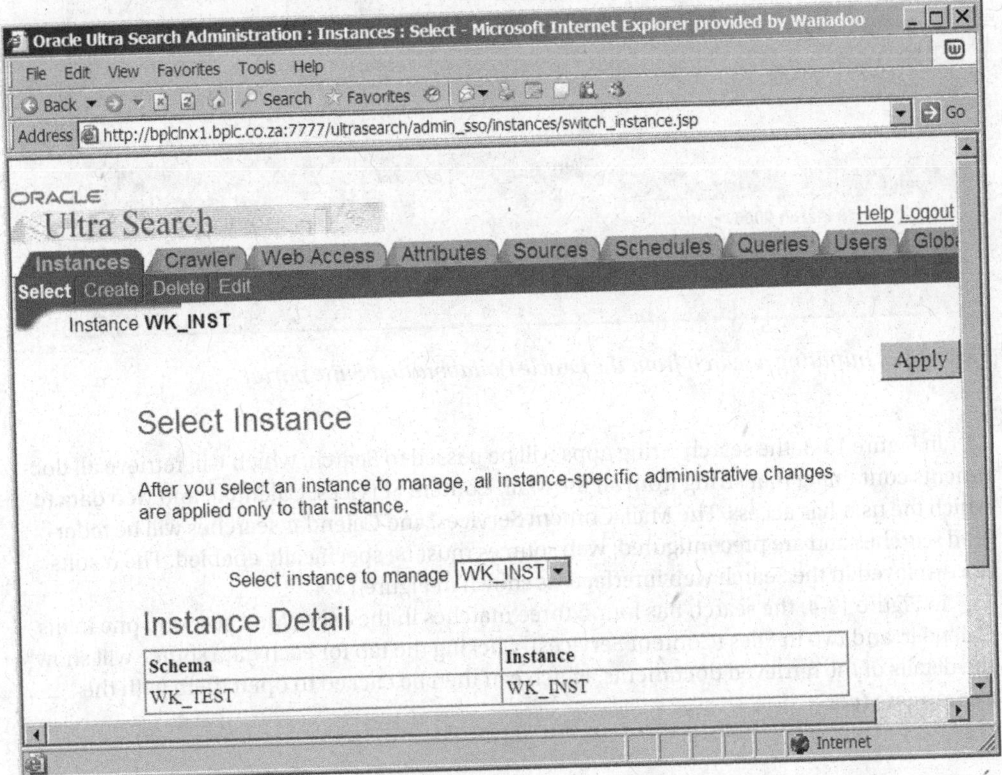

Figure 13-2. *The Ultrasearch administration window, prompting for instance selection*

The User Interface

The Oracle Collaboration Suite portal front end has Search available from the first window, as shown in Figure 13-3.

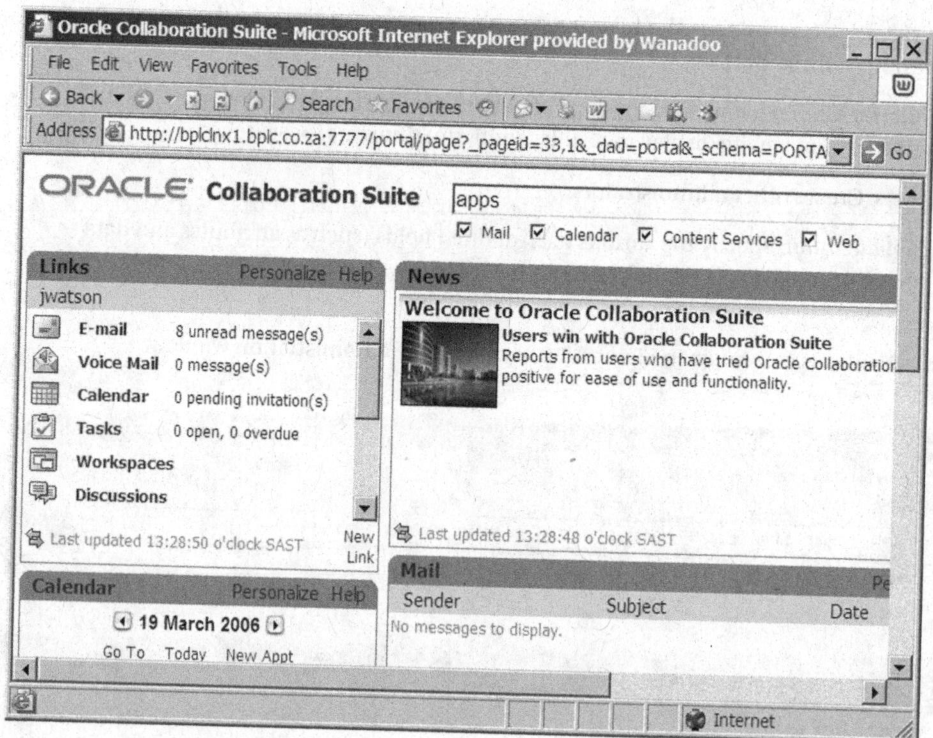

Figure 13-3. *Initiating a search from the Oracle Collaboration Suite portal*

In Figure 13-3, the search string apps will be passed to Search, which will retrieve all documents containing that string from all the Mail, Content Services, Calendar, and web data to which the user has access. The Mail, Content Services, and Calendar searches will be federated searches and are preconfigured; web sources must be specifically enabled. The results are displayed in the Search web interface, as shown in Figure 13-4.

In Figure 13-4, the search has found three matches in the user's Mail account, one in his Calendar, and two in Files (Content Services). Clicking the tab for each data source will show the details of the retrieved documents, which can then be clicked to open them with the appropriate tool.

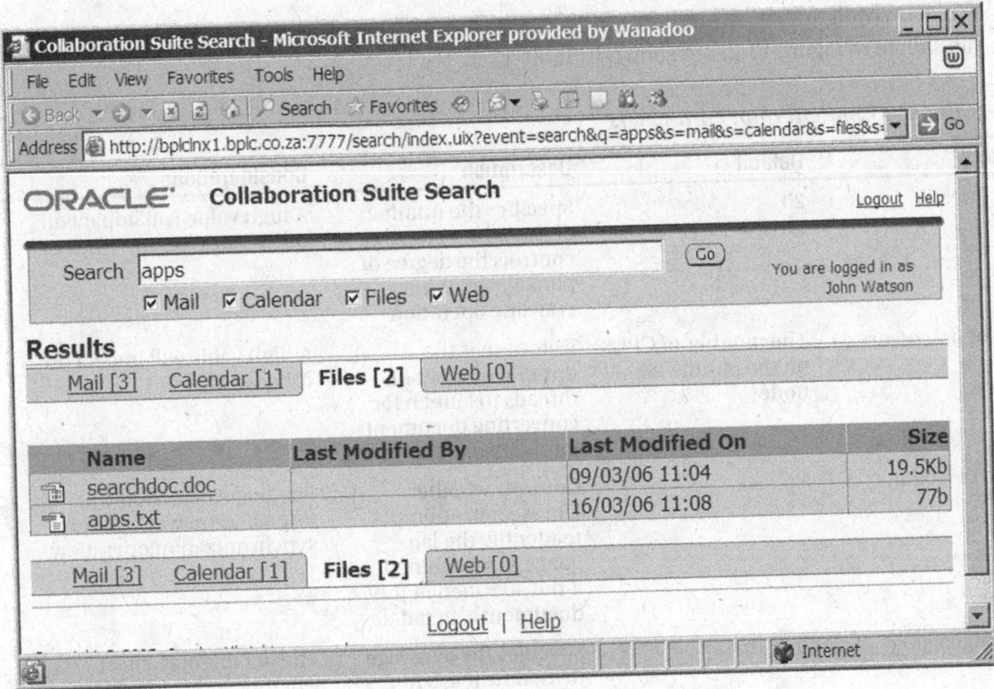

Figure 13-4. *The Search user interface showing a result set*

The Crawler and the Data Sources

The preconfigured Search sources are all Oracle sources: the federated sources that search Mail, Content Services, and Calendar. The other source types must all be set up after installation.

Federated sources are indexed by the source itself, and user-defined sources are indexed by a custom-designed agent, which should be implemented as a Java class. The Web, Table, E-mail, and File sources are indexed by crawler processes, according to predefined schedules. The crawlers navigate around the source, indexing every document they encounter.

End users' searches are not conducted against the actual data. The searches are conducted against the indexes generated for all the sources, and therefore will return results only as up-to-date as the indexes.

The Oracle Collaboration Suite web interface, as installed out-of-the-box, can search the Mail, Calendar, and Content Services federated sources, as well as web sources. To search the other sources, it is necessary to adjust the interface to include appropriate portlets.

The Ultrasearch Crawler

The *crawler* is a multithreaded Java process running on the Oracle Application Server middle tier instance. The threads connect to the data sources, using whatever protocol is appropriate for the source, and read the documents they find into a cache on the local file system. Once the cache is full, the cached documents are indexed by Oracle Text before fetching the next batch of documents. The index itself resides in the Oracle Collaboration Suite database in the Ultrasearch schema.

The configurable parameters for the crawler's operation, accessed through the Crawler tab shown in Figure 13-2, are shown in Table 13-1.

Table 13-1. *Crawler Configuration Parameters*

Parameters	Default	Description	Considerations
Crawler threads	20	Specifies the number of threads to launch; controls the degree of parallelism of the crawling operation	A high value will impact on other work.
Number of processors	The number of CPUs on the middle tier node	Determines the optimal number of threads to launch for converting documents for indexing	A high value will impact on other work.
Language detection	No	Controls whether Ultrasearch attempts to identify the language of a document if not specified in the document's metadata	Language detection will impose extra work on the synchronization operation.
Default language	English	Specifies the language to assume if it is not specified or determined	The default may affect whether some documents are indexed appropriately.
Crawling depth	No limit	Limits the number of nested links to follow	A greater depth will impact on how long the crawl takes; 3 or 4 is typically adequate.
Timeout threshold	30s	Limits the length of time to wait to access a document before giving up	A high threshold will tie up a thread for a long time, but if set too low many documents may not be indexed.
Default character set	ISO Latin-1	Signifies the character set to assume if it is not specified in the document metadata	The default should reflect what the bulk of the data is likely to be.
Cache directory	$ORACLE_HOME/ ultrasearch/cache	Indicates where to cache the documents fetched for indexing	The directory should have adequate space.
Start indexing every	5MB	Indicates how much data should be fetched before indexing it	A larger value may make the indexing more efficient.
Clear cache after indexing	No	Indicates whether to delete fetched documents from the cache	The default will consume space.
Logging	Everything	Indicates whether to log details of events or only summaries	Can also specify the directory and the language for log records.
Database connect string	The infrastructure instance	Indicates the correct database connect string	The default will be wrong if the Ultrasearch schema is in a dedicated database.

The crawler is used for web, table, e-mail, and file data sources. During its first run, it must index everything to build up the index; subsequent runs will only synchronize the index by addressing documents that have been added, deleted, or changed since the last synchronization. When setting the tuning parameters, consider how long a crawl will take, and the impact on both the middle tier instance where Ultrasearch is running and the machine where the crawl is taking place.

Web Sources

A *web source* is an Internet address accessible to Ultrasearch by a URL. To create a web source, click the Sources tab shown in Figure 13-2, then the Web subtab. Give the source a name and one or more URLs (which must use the HTTP or HTTPS protocol) necessary to reach the data.

According to the synchronization schedule, Ultrasearch will launch the specified number of threads and connect to the URLs that make up the source. If a proxy server has been specified, the connection will be through it. The threads will then retrieve the documents found and navigate further through any HTML links in these documents to retrieve more documents, and so on, until the depth of crawling specified has been reached. Ultrasearch maintains a map of URLs, which prevents it from retrieving the same document more than once and from getting trapped in circular relationships.

To restrict the crawling, rules known as *boundary rules* can be set up to limit the URLs that will be indexed and followed. These rules are based on host and domain names and can therefore stop the crawler from following links that would require navigating to remote hosts. Path rules, set per host, can further limit the crawl by specifying whether paths starting with, terminating with, or containing certain strings should be processed. By default there are no rules. The wizard for creating and editing web sources takes you through the process of setting them up.

Many web masters will not want web crawlers to follow and index certain URLs. This is a good thing; if a web master knows that certain virtual paths do not contain any information worth indexing, he will not want external crawlers to take up bandwidth in his web server as they retrieve documents from them, and the owners of the crawling processes will not want to waste time indexing rubbish. Such *rubbish* might include directories of temporary data or previous versions of current data. The standard mechanism for this is to create a file `robots.txt` that lists virtual paths that crawlers should ignore (see the site `www.robotstxt.org` for details of this file) and Ultrasearch will by default observe the rules found in any such files that it encounters.

Table Sources

A *table source* is a table in an Oracle database. The table can exist either in the database hosting the Ultrasearch instance or (through a database link) in any other database. Indeed, if the Oracle transparent gateways have been installed, the table could be in a non-Oracle database. In this latter case, access is through the Oracle Net transparent gateways, and there will be some extra work needed.

Table sources are extremely useful, but they can also be very awkward to set up. The key to avoiding problems is to have a clear understanding of the security model within which Ultrasearch operates and the way database links work. In order to index a table's contents, the crawling process must connect to the database storing the table as a database user with the

SELECT privilege on the table. Therefore it is essential to grant this privilege to the Ultrasearch instance owner, or you will simply be told that the table does not exist when you try to set it up as a data source. If the table is in a remote database (as it always will be in the case of Ultrasearch as installed with Oracle Collaboration Suite) there is the complication of the connection being through a database link. The areas that cause chronic confusion are the setting up of database links and the granting of table access permissions in a manner that will let Ultrasearch see the data to be indexed, but nothing else, while ensuring that security is not compromised for any other users.

A database link is a means whereby a session against one database can connect to another remote database. The session against this second database does not come from the user process that launched the session against the first database. The first database itself becomes a client to the second database. A database link can have two items of information: the connect identifier that identifies the remote database service (specified with the USING clause), and the username and password to connect to the service (specified with the CONNECT TO clause). Links may be *public*, meaning that all database users can see and use them, or *private*, meaning that they are schema objects owned by a user and that only he can see them. It is also possible to combine public and private links. The database administrator can create a public link that defines only the connect identifier; then each user can create his own private link within his schema that defines the username and password. By this means, the DBA can control the network aspect of the connection, while each user controls and protects his own password. It is generally considered to be very bad practice to create public database links that include usernames and passwords.

As an example of setting up a table source, consider this situation: An organization has an Oracle Collaboration Suite instance and a separate database running a human resources application. It is considered necessary to include the employees' CVs in the scope of Search. One solution would be to store the CVs as documents in a Content Services folder, but this has not been done. Instead, in the HR schema of the human resources database, there is a table called EMP with one row per employee that has a column called CV of data type BLOB. Each employee has his CV stored in this column of his row.

In the remote database, connect as a user with DBA privileges (such as SYSTEM) and create a user specifically for Ultrasearch. Using the following commands grant him only the privileges needed to connect and see the one table:

```
create user search_access identified by password;
grant create session to search_access;
grant select on hr.emp to search_access;
```

In the Ultrasearch database, as a user with the CREATE PUBLIC DATABASE LINK privilege, such as user SYSTEM, create a public link. This will be accessible to everyone and therefore for security reasons will not have a username and a password embedded within it. It is to be called HRDB and uses the database connect identifier HRDB. Then connect as the owner of the Ultrasearch instance (by default WK_TEST) and create a private link with the same name that has only the username and password, as in the following commands:

```
connect system/oracle1
create public database link hrdb using 'hrdb';
connect wk_test/wk_test
create database link hrdb connect to search_access identified by password;
```

Then connect to the Ultrasearch administration tool with the URL that will prompt for a database login, such as the following:

```
http://bplclnx1.bplc.co.za:7777/ultrasearch/admin/control/login.jsp
```

Connect as the database user who owns the instance; the default user is WK_TEST. The reason for not using the Single Sign-On login route is that the WKPROXY user (to whom you connect through Single Sign-On) will not be able to see the private database link in the WK_TEST schema. Select the instance (WK_INST, by default) and then click the Sources tab and the Table subtab. Clicking the Create Table Source button will launch the wizard. The first window is shown in Figure 13-5.

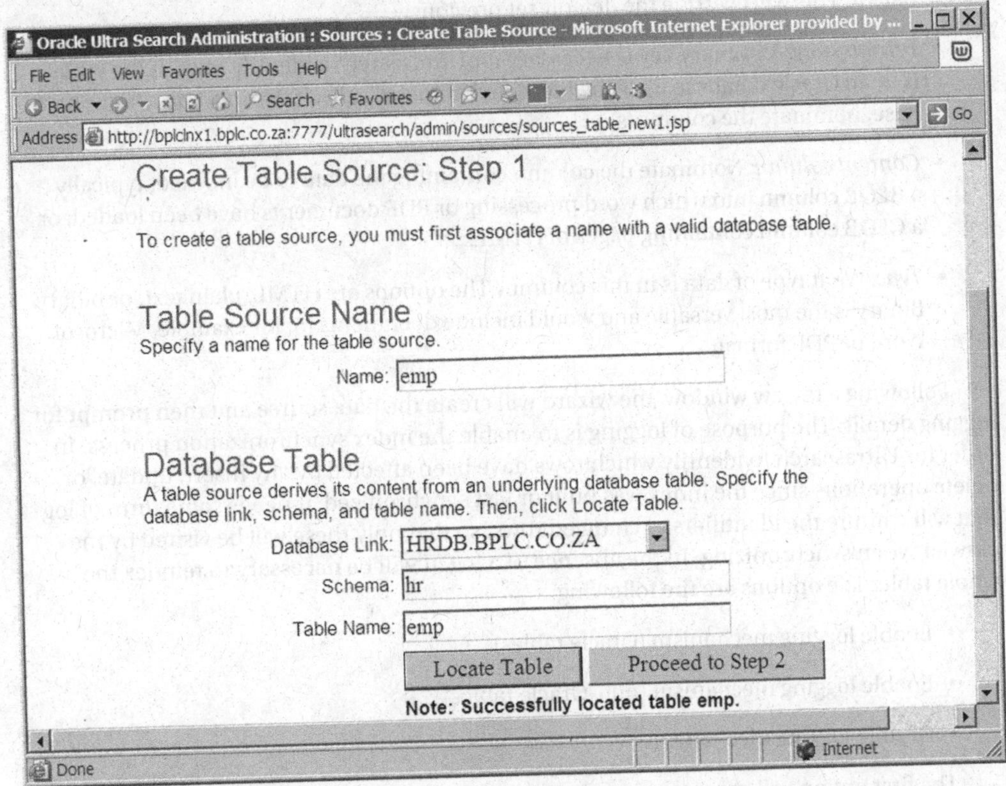

Figure 13-5. *Create an Ultrasearch table source.*

Give the new source a name, and then select the Database Link from the drop-down list. This is where problems often occur: the link you want does not appear in the list. The list will include all public links that were created with both the CONNECT TO and the USING clauses (there should be none of these for security reasons), all the private links in the WK_TEST schema that were created with both CONNECT TO and USING, and all the public links created with USING that have a matching private link created with CONNECT TO. The link shown in the Figure 13-5 is an example of this last case. Note that the link name is suffixed with a domain. If when a link is created you do not specify a domain and the instance parameter DB_DOMAIN has been set, this value will be appended to the link name.

Then specify the Schema in the remote database that has the table, and finally the Table Name. Click the Locate Table button. This is the other point that may have problems: the message "Failed to locate table" is all too frequent and will typically be caused by the username embedded in the database link having inappropriate privileges in the remote database.

The second window of the wizard prompts for these items:

- *Language*: Select the language to be assumed for the content of the column to be indexed.
- *Language column*: If there is a column of the table that specifies the language, nominate it. This will override the default set previously.
- *Primary key*: A primary key is necessary for Ultrasearch to identify rows. If the table is in an Oracle database it will be identified automatically; if it is in a non-Oracle database, nominate the column(s).
- *Content column*: Nominate the column containing the data to be indexed, typically a BLOB column into which word processing or PDF documents have been loaded, or a CLOB column containing pages of HTML.
- *Type*: What type of data is in this column? The options are HTML, plain text, or binary. Binary is the most versatile and would include documents in, for example, Microsoft Word or PDF format.

Following a review window, the wizard will create the data source and then prompt for logging details. The purpose of logging is to enable the index synchronization process. In order for Ultrasearch to identify which rows have been affected by any insert, update, or delete operations since the index was built or last synchronized, it needs some form of log that will capture the identifiers of changed rows, so that only these will be visited by the crawler when synchronizing. In the absence of a log, it will be necessary to reindex the whole table. The options are the following:

- Enable logging mechanism (Oracle tables)
- Enable logging mechanism (non-Oracle tables)
- Disable logging mechanism

The first option will generate a set of statements that can be used to create triggers that will capture the primary keys of changed rows into a table. Following the example being used, the statements generated are the following:

```
create table HR.wk$log_emp (k1 NUMBER,mark char(1) default 'F');
grant all on hr.wk$log_emp to wk_test;
create or replace trigger HR.wk$ins_emp after insert on HR.EMP for each row
begin
insert into wk$log_emp(k1,mark) values(:new.EMPNO,'F');
end;
```

```
create or replace trigger HR.wk$upd_emp after update on HR.EMP for each row
begin
insert into wk$log_emp(k1,mark) values(:old.EMPNO,'F');
insert into wk$log_emp(k1,mark) values(:new.EMPNO,'F');
end;
create or replace trigger HR.wk$del_emp after delete on HR.EMP
for each row
begin
insert into wk$log_emp(k1,mark) values(:old.EMPNO,'F');
end;
```

These statements (or similar) must be executed in the remote database. First, create a table that will store the primary keys of changed rows and grant access to this to Ultrasearch. In the sample code generated, the assumption is that the table is in the local database, hence the use of WK_TEST; this will not work if the table is in a remote database. In our example, WK_TEST would have to be replaced with SEARCH_ACCESS. Then create triggers that will capture the new primary key, the old primary key, or both, depending on the nature of the action performed.

If the table being indexed is on a non-Oracle database, the wizard cannot generate code to enable logging and you will have to write it yourself.

The final step in the wizard is to map columns of the table to the metadata attributes that can be included in the index. These will be the attributes listed previously in this chapter in the section titled "The Administration Interface."

The final windows in the wizard prompt for two optional settings: first, for a URL that will be generated for display of the search results; and second, whether to apply an access control list to restrict the search output.

E-mail Sources

E-mail sources for Ultrasearch are the contents of an inbox folder accessible through IMAP. Typically, this will be a folder of a user—probably not a personal user, but a user created specifically for this purpose—who subscribes to all the mailing lists that are of interest. This means that individuals do not need to subscribe to the lists but can still search them.

As the crawler indexes messages it deletes them from the IMAP folder and transfers them to a directory in the file system of the machine hosting the Ultrasearch instance.

The details to be specified are the following:

- The address of the IMAP server hosting the folder to be crawled
- The username and password to connect to the folder
- The directory (known as the *archive directory*) to which to save messages
- An (optional) access control list to apply

File Sources

A *file source* is one or more directories accessible on the node hosting the Ultrasearch instance through the FILE protocol. This is the protocol that lets a browser navigate around its local file system. For example, entering this URL into Internet Explorer

```
file://c:\tmp
```

will display the contents of the nominated directory. An example of using the FILE protocol to go across a network is the following:

```
file://ocsdemo/oracle1@10.0.0.4/tmp
```

This URL will display the contents of the directory `/tmp` on the host identified by the IP address given, logging on to that host with username OCSDEMO and password oracle1.

The file source wizard prompts for one or more URLs of the forms illustrated previously, taking account of operating system variations in file and directory naming. If the URL specifies a directory, the whole contents of the directory will be crawled and indexed; if it specifies a complete path to one file, only that file will be indexed.

The next step in the wizard lets you refine the search by specifying path prefixes that should be included or excluded from the crawling and indexing exercise. If this is not done, the only limits are those imposed by operating system access permissions. Following this, specify the documents types to be indexed. By default only HTML and plain text files are included; it is common practice to include other standard formats that may be found in the file system, such as PDF or Microsoft Word.

The FILE protocol is reasonably efficient for locating and reading files but is not always appropriate for displaying them. For this reason the wizard will prompt for a *display* URL. This is the path to the service that can best display the files retrieved by an index search. For example, if an Apache web listener is being used for file serving, there could be two routes by which a file can be accessed: the FILE protocol, used by Ultrasearch when crawling; and HTTP, when users actually download the document.

This URL uses the FILE protocol to specify a location within the file system, which will be used to generate and store indexing information:

```
file://d:\home\users\jwatson\pub
```

But this URL might be the way to get to the data through the web listener:

```
https://10.0.0.4:7777/~jwatson/pub
```

In this case, you would specify a file URL prefix of

```
file://d:\home\users\
```

and a display URL prefix of

```
https://10.0.0.4:7777/~
```

which will force Ultrasearch to substitute one string for the other when returning results to users.

Oracle Sources

The *Oracle sources* are the federated sources that search themselves using their own internal search processes (which will be proprietary to each source) and Portal web sites. In either case, they are services for which there is an API known to Ultrasearch. These APIs are implemented as Java classes known as *searchlets* that are specific to the type of source. For example, the Calendar searchlet is `eis/oracle/oracleCalendar/CalendarSearchlet`. The searchlet classes are deployed to the Oracle Collaboration Suite middle tier at installation time.

User-Defined Sources

The user-defined data source mechanism lets developers design routines for searching any data repository not otherwise accessible to Ultrasearch. Examples might be third-party databases for which an Oracle Net transparent gateway is not available, or legacy systems that do not use the standard Internet protocols.

The user-defined source is crawled by a user-designed agent, which must be implemented as a Java class deployed to the Oracle Collaboration Suite middle tier. This agent connects to the data source and passes through its contents, gathering document locator URLs and associated metadata. These will be included in the Ultrasearch index.

Index Maintenance

The Ultrasearch index is updated asynchronously according to the schedules that run the various index generation routines. It is not maintained in real time. It is only updated when the index synchronization jobs are run. If it were maintained in real time, the performance impact on other activity would be considerable. This means that the index is usually out of date. The effect for end users is that Search results may include links to documents that no longer exist or perhaps have been edited so that they are no longer relevant, and new documents that should be in the Search result set may not be included. How significant this is depends on the volatility of the data and how critical it is that searches should be complete.

A related topic is index optimization. The Ultrasearch index is based on the Context indexing facility, which uses nonrelational indexes. These become less efficient (though not less accurate) with time. Optimization will correct this deterioration and can also be carried out according to schedule.

Synchronization

The process of updating the index to take account of changes to the indexed data is known as *synchronization* and is carried out according to user-defined schedules. Different data sources can have different synchronization schedules, and federated data searches will synchronize their own data themselves according to their own schedules. As well as defining automatic index synchronization, the scheduling facility can also set synchronization to "manual only," in which case the data source's index entries will be static until you run the `Execute Immediately` command to synchronize the index on demand.

If the Oracle Collaboration Suite installation does not have any data sources configured other than the federated sources for Calendar, Mail, and Content Services, there is no need to create any synchronization schedules; these are federated sources, with preconfigured maintenance jobs that may well be adequate. But if you have created any additional data sources, they will need synchronization schedules to update the Ultrasearch index. There will also need to be an optimization schedule to tidy up the index. To reach the scheduling tool, connect to the Ultrasearch administration tool, click the Schedules tab, and click the Create New Schedule button to launch the wizard that takes you through the process.

The synchronization schedule wizard will prompt for these items:

- *Name*: Every schedule needs a name.
- *Frequency*: The units for frequency can be monthly, weekly, daily, or hourly, with a starting time.
- *Indexing option*: This controls whether the crawler should gather URLs and include them in the index (which is the default) or stop after the gather. Taking this latter option makes it possible for the administrator to examine the URLs and decide whether to include them in the index.
- *Remote crawler profiles*: If there are multiple Ultrasearch instances (on the same node or different nodes) the schedule can be assigned to one of these remote instances. This lets you spread the workload of maintaining the index across different instances.
- *Sources*: Select the source(s), which may be any combination of file, web, table, and Portal sources, to which this schedule will apply. It is not possible to assign the same source to more than one schedule.

Rather than specifying a frequency, a schedule can be set to manual start only. In this case the sources it manages will only be synchronized if you take the `Execute Immediately` option. It is also possible to disable a schedule.

Optimization

The optimization schedule is preconfigured: it will start every Sunday at 01:00, and will continue to run until the job is finished. However, it is by default disabled. Apart from enabling it and specifying a frequency and start time, you may well wish to set a time limit for its running. If it does not complete within this time limit, it will pick up from where it finished the next time it starts.

The optimization schedule can be disabled and it can also be run manually with the `Optimize Index Immediately` option.

Mail Index Maintenance

As a federated data source, Mail searches are done by the Mail searchlet, a Java application deployed to the OC4J_OCSADMIN middle tier component. It also does its own index maintenance according to its own schedules. A Mail instance will be configured with one (by default) or more housekeeper servers to do this; see Chapter 10 for more details on these, including how to create additional servers.

A housekeeper server can be configured to perform several tasks, or only one. Figure 13-6 shows an example of configuring a housekeeper server specifically for index optimization.

Oracle Enterprise Manager - gc:113951272486835289 - Microsoft Internet Explore...

File Edit View Favorites Tools Help

Back Search Favorites

Address http://jwlnx1.bplc.co.za:1810/emd/console/ias/umsg/es/PCShowTargetDetails?target Go

Text Synchronization Disabled

Text Optimization Enabled

General Parameters

Frequency of Execution of Housekeeper Process 1

Age Threshold

TIP Units for Tertiary Store, Statistics Cleanup are days, for Process Control Message Cleanup are minutes

Run Task On Demand

Index Optimization Level Full

Index Optimization Max Time (hours) 12

Done Internet

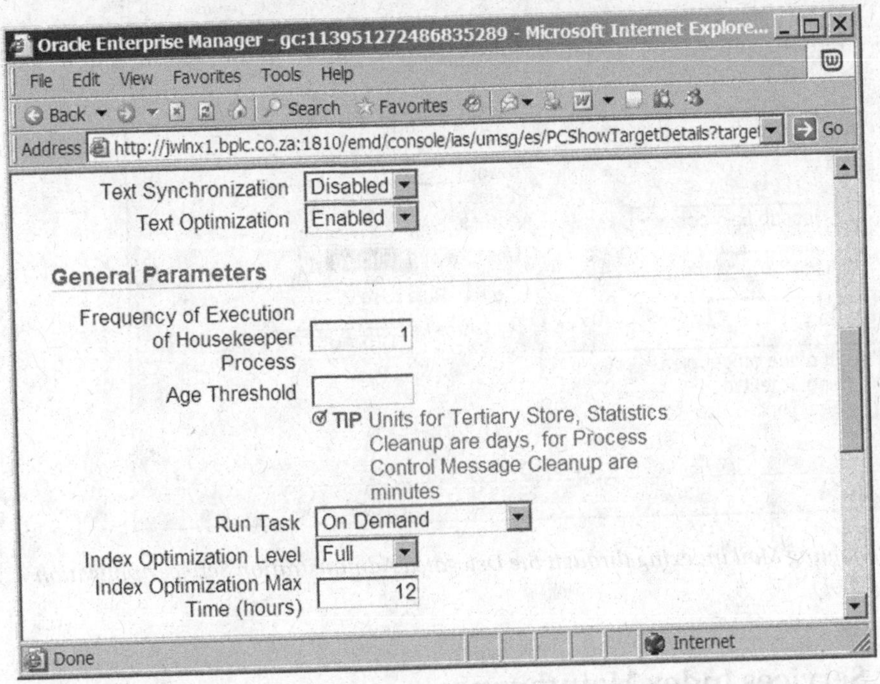

Figure 13-6. *Suitable settings for a Mail housekeeper server intended for index optimization*

In Figure 13-6, only Text index optimization has been enabled, and the housekeeper server is set to run on demand only, rather than according to a schedule. This would be a suitable setting if you only want to run the process during maintenance slots, or perhaps at times when other activity on the server happens to be low. The Index Optimization Level can be set to Full, Fast, or Rebuild. Full will compact the index and free up space by removing obsolete rows, whereas Fast will stop after the compact stage. Rebuild will create a new index. Another housekeeper process would be created that would carry out a synchronization. This process could run automatically, perhaps every 60 minutes.

Mail message subjects are always indexed. Indexing of the body of Mail messages must be specified per user. Figure 10-5 in Chapter 10 shows where to enable this when creating or editing a user through the Mail administration utility. Figure 13-7 shows the same option through the OIDDAS application provisioning console (the OIDDAS is described in detail in Chapter 6).

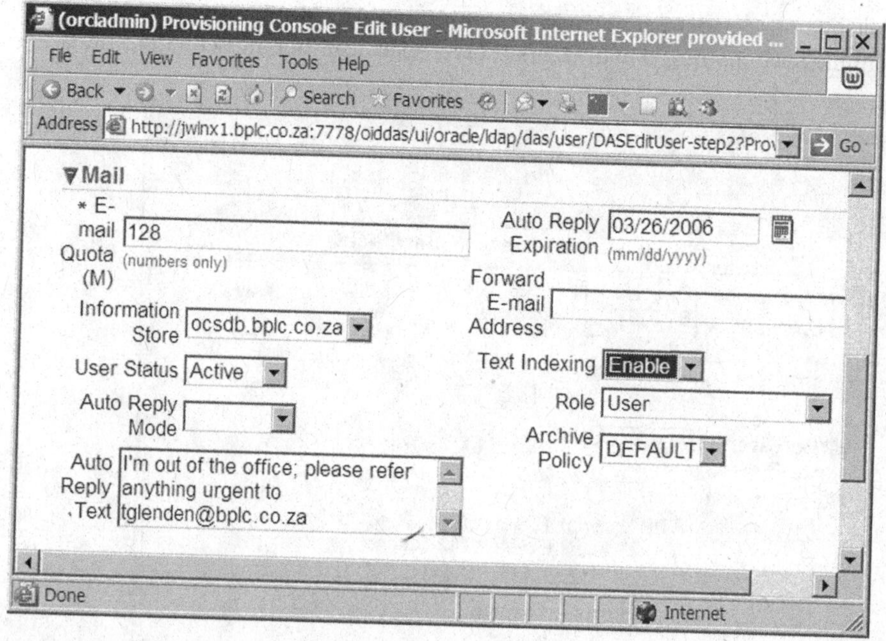

Figure 13-7. *Enabling Mail indexing through the Delegated Administration Service application provisioning tool*

Content Services Index Maintenance

Content Services searches are carried out by the Content Services searchlet; the index maintenance is done by the Text jobs scheduled with the `DBMS_JOB` job scheduler. To determine whether a document uploaded into the file store will be indexed, Content Services will inspect its extension to determine its MIME type, and that will determine the format to apply. Formats and MIME types are described in detail in Chapter 8. One attribute of a format is whether the documents to which it applies should be indexed. Figure 8-6 in Chapter 8 shows which formats will be indexed, and Figure 8-7 shows how to enable or disable indexing for a particular format.

The Content Services data index is synchronized and optimized according to the schedule specified for the two jobs described previously: the job that runs CTX_DDL.SYNC_INDEX (by default every 30 minutes), and the job that runs CTX_DDL.OPTIMIZE_INDEX (by default once a day). These jobs maintain the IFS_TEXT index itself. There is, however, an additional index used only by Content Services searches: this is the (appropriately named) `IFS_LYKE` index that provides extra performance and function for searches involving wild cards. This index is created and maintained automatically with procedures in the package CTX_SUBSTR. This package is in the CONTENT schema rather than the CTXSYS schema. There is a preconfigured job that will run CTX_SUBSTR.INDEXSYNC every ten minutes.

Note that there are two agents within Content Services, the `FolderIndexAgent` and the `FolderIndexAnalyzerAgent` that run (by default) once a day within the Content Services node. These are not related to the Text index used by Search, but rather they maintain the indexes used to generate the folder (or directory) structure through which documents are presented to users.

Calendar Indexes

Because Calendar can be deployed as a stand-alone application independently of any other Oracle product, Search does not rely on the presence of Ultrasearch and Text when searching Calendar node database(s). The indexes are maintained within the Calendar database(s) by the `uniengd` session processes whenever they perform any actions on data. The Calendar searchlet performs searches against these internal indexes and returns the results to the Search user interface for display.

The items within Calendar that are indexed and therefore searchable by the searchlet are the following:

- Meeting titles and descriptions
- Meeting locations
- Task titles and descriptions
- Event titles and descriptions
- Daily notes

CHAPTER 14

Voicemail and Fax

The Voicemail and Fax application component provides facilities for receiving, storing, and retrieving incoming voice and facsimile telephone calls. There are many third-party products that can do this. The distinguishing factors of Voicemail and Fax include that the facilities are very comprehensive, and most importantly that the application and data are integrated with the rest of Oracle Collaboration Suite. This integration means that information managed by Voicemail and Fax is included in the single data model that characterizes Oracle Collaboration Suite, and that services provided by other components (such as Mail and Mobile Collaboration) can be associated with it.

Voicemail and Fax will answer calls routed to it by a PBX (private branch exchange) or the PSTN (Public Switched Telephone Network) and guide the caller through the process of recording a message. Such messages can then be retrieved by the recipient through an e-mail client via his Mail account or on a mobile device over Mobile Collaboration. Facsimiles addressed to the user's fax number will be routed to Voicemail and Fax by the PBX, stored by Voicemail and Fax in the user's Mail account, and can then be accessed through an e-mail client. Integration with Mobile Collaboration means that notifications can be sent to the user's cell phone or PDA when messages are received.

Voicemail and Fax can be used only for simple message taking and retrieval, but it can also be used as the front end to a call center. It is possible to construct complex IVR (interactive voice response) applications that will guide callers through the process of interacting with a call center, and possibly eliminate the need for many of them to speak to operators at all.

Voicemail and Fax Architecture

Architecturally, Voicemail and Fax is dependent on the Mail component of Oracle Collaboration Suite, and an interface to either the PSTN or a PBX. This interface is managed by the Intel NetMerge Converged Communications Server (CCS), which must be separately licensed and installed on a Microsoft Windows machine. For this reason, Voicemail and Fax can only be installed on Windows. The other Oracle Collaboration Suite components can, of course, be on any supported platform. The message storage formats let users retrieve voice mail and facsimiles through a variety of clients.

Message Flow

Voice and facsimile messages enter the system from the PSTN and (in most cases) through a PBX. Figure 14-1 shows the message flow.

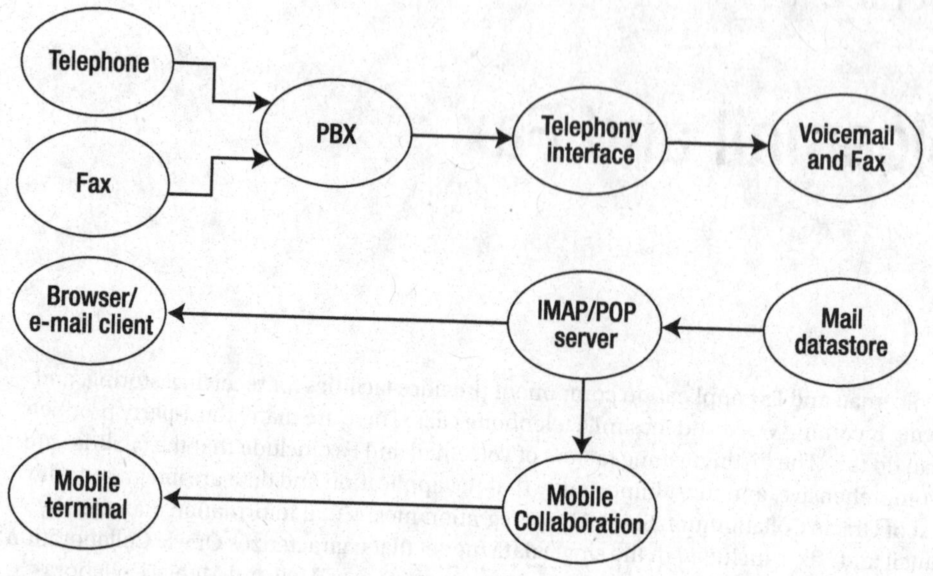

Figure 14-1. *The message flow through Voicemail and Fax from the source through various components to the recipient*

A message goes through these stages:

1. Incoming voice calls are routed by the PSTN to the organization's PBX. The PBX will attempt to route it to the recipient's number. Should this not be answered, the PBX will divert it through the telephony interface to the Voicemail and Fax server.
2. Incoming facsimiles are routed by the PSTN to the organization's PBX. The PBX will route them immediately through the telephony interface to the Voicemail and Fax server.
3. The Voicemail and Fax server receives the call (generating any prompts necessary in the case of a voice call) and saves the message to the recipient's Mail folder in the Mail datastore.
4. On demand from the user, the Mail IMAP or POP3 server will retrieve the message from the Mail datastore.
5. Messages can be retrieved directly by users through the Mail web client or any IMAP or POP3 compliant e-mail client.
6. Messages can be retrieved on mobile devices through Mobile Collaboration.

Not shown in Figure 14-1 is the use of the Oracle Internet Directory. This is used to store relevant user attributes, such as telephone numbers, preferences, and recorded greetings.

The Telephony Interface

The *telephony interface* is a hardware and software component that acts as a gateway between Voicemail and Fax and the outside world. The only supported interface between the Voicemail and Fax server and the PBX (or the PSTN, if the connection does not go via a PBX) is the Intel NetMerge CCS. This is available only for Microsoft Windows 2000 and 2003 (as of the time of this writing). Intel NetMerge CCS is Intel's implementation of the CT (computer telephony) server standard defined by the ECTF (Enterprise Computer Telephony Forum), which is itself part of the CompTIA (Computing Technology Industry Association).

The NetMerge CCS abstracts the detail of different telephony implementations from the generic services that Voicemail and Fax offers. This means that Voicemail and Fax can accept calls from any type of telephone line and any manufacturer's PBX.

The connection between the Intel NetMerge CCS machine and the PBX or PSTN can either be over an Intel Dialogic card to a T1 telephone line (this line type, and the European E1 variant, is described in greater detail in Chapter 11) or other cards that connect to other digital and analog line types, or over a standard Ethernet interface. If using an Ethernet interface, calls will be taken as VoIP traffic. Facsimile traffic can also be accepted over fax cards.

The Intel NetMerge CCS as shipped has the ability to manage a file system: it can store and retrieve messages as disk files. This is not adequate for Voicemail and Fax, which needs to use the Mail datastore. In order to enhance the Intel NetMerge CCS so that it can fulfill the needs of Voicemail and Fax, Oracle Corporation has provided the Oracle Container. This is an extension to the Intel NetMerge CCS API, and it is through this that Voicemail and Fax makes its API calls. The Oracle container is written in C and is linked with the OCI (Oracle Call Interface) libraries, giving it access to PL/SQL and Oracle databases.

Message Storage and Formats

All received messages are stored in the Mail datastore in the user's Inbox folder. Voicemail and Fax identifies for whom the message is intended by interrogating the Oracle Internet Directory, making a lookup based on the information sent to it by the telephony interface.

The messages are delivered as attachments to standard e-mails: voice mails are formatted as WAV files, faxes are formatted as TIF files. Any e-mail client using POP or IMAP that can view TIFs or play WAVs can be used. The Mail web client can also retrieve voice mail and faxes if the user's browser has appropriate plug-ins installed. The body of the e-mail will include such information as the number from which the message came and the time it was received.

Once stored, messages received through Voicemail and Fax are indistinguishable from any other e-mail and can be managed as such. Receipt can therefore trigger notifications through Mobile Collaboration, and they can then be retrieved on mobile devices through push mail.

The Voicemail and Fax Application Services

The Voicemail and Fax application is implemented as a Java application deployed to an OC4J component on the Oracle Application Server middle tier Application Server instance. It offers these services:

- The Routing Service acts as a dispatcher process, directing requests to other services.
- The Retrieval Service manages users accessing their mailboxes by telephone. It authenticates users, and lets them retrieve and respond to voice mail in the Mail datastore.
- The Recording Service manages incoming messages by playing greetings, recording messages, and saving the messages to the appropriate folder in the Mail datastore.
- The Fax Receiving Service accepts incoming facsimiles and saves them to the appropriate folder in the Mail datastore.
- The Telephony Monitor monitors and reports on the performance of the telephony interface.
- Message Delivery Monitor monitors and reports the time it takes to deliver messages.
- The Message Recovery Service provides some fault tolerance. It recovers messages that are not delivered successfully and attempts redelivery.
- The Call Transfer Service manages the transfer of calls to an operator if requested by a caller and permitted by the IVR system.
- The IVR Service runs user-defined applications that guide callers through the application with a series of aural menus that accept oral or DTMF (dual-tone multifrequency) key pad responses.
- The SMDI (Simplified Message Desk Interface) Service is an interface to SMDI-capable PBXs.
- The MWI (Message Waiting Indicator) Service raises and clears the users' "message waiting" indicators.

These services together make up the Voicemail and Fax application.

The PBX Application Cluster

Many organizations will have more than one PBX and more than one Voicemail and Fax application. The reason may be that the organization is geographically distributed, and there are also issues of scalability and fault tolerance. A PBX application cluster defines the relationship between a PBX and one or more Voicemail and Fax applications: each PBX will be associated with at least one Voicemail and Fax application, with more than one if it is generating more calls than one application can service. It is possible for a PBX application cluster to contain multiple PBXs, but only if the connection from the PBXs to the Voicemail and Fax server is over VoIP. Multiple incoming VoIP connections will be interpreted by the Intel NetMerge CCS service as one virtual PBX.

During the installation process, there will be a prompt to create a PBX application cluster. This will be based on the connection through Intel NetMerge CCS to the PBX. After installation, this cluster can be reconfigured, or more clusters can be defined if the physical connections to the PBX have been adjusted.

Note that no matter how the Voicemail and Fax applications are distributed, they will all be running in middle tier Application Server instances associated with the same infrastructure instance, so it will not matter which Voicemail and Fax application a user contacts; he will still be able to retrieve his voice mail.

Installation

The Voicemail and Fax servers are shipped on a separate DVD from that used to install the rest of Oracle Collaboration Suite. This DVD also contains the Voice Conversion Server and the Document Conversion Server, optionally used by Real-Time Collaboration. The installation is a normal Application Server middle tier instance, to which these components are automatically deployed. The installation is a separate middle tier instance from the other Oracle Collaboration Suite components because of its specific requirements. These are the following:

- Windows operating system 2000 or 2003 must be installed. For nonproduction purposes, Windows XP can be used, but this is not certified and the installer will show an appropriate warning.
- 900MB memory must be installed. A warning is displayed if less than 512MB is available.
- Intel NetMerge CCS must be installed. This should be purchased from a third party, not through Oracle Corporation.
- Enterprise Manager Grid Control must be available.
- A Mail instance must already be installed in a different middle tier instance.

If any of these conditions are not met, the installation will not succeed. Figure 14-2 shows some of the checks performed by the Voicemail and Fax configuration wizard.

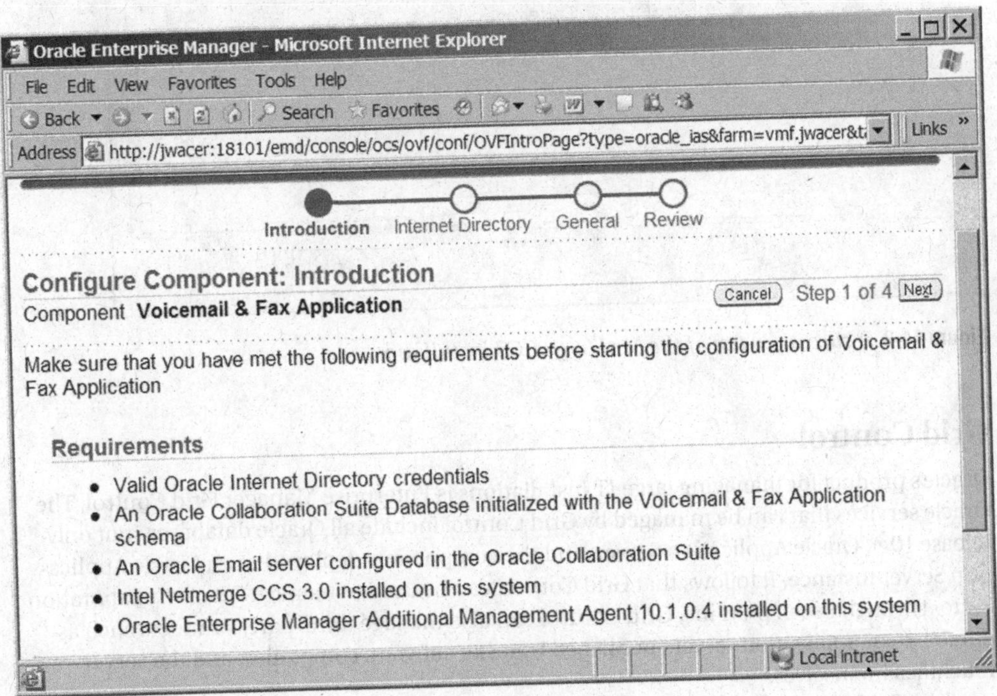

Figure 14-2. *The Voicemail and Fax configuration wizard*

Installing NetMerge CCS

The NetMerge CCS installation is perfectly straightforward and will create a Windows service called Intel NetMerge Converged Communications Server. This service must be running at all times if Voicemail and Fax is to function.

To confirm that the installation is successful, NetMerge CCS comes with a simulator that generates traffic from a popularity contest where votes are phoned in to several different telephone numbers. The installation, and running the simulator test, is fully described in the NetMerge CCS installation manual. Figure 14-3 shows the result of a successful run, which is a tie between contestants Rob Muldoon and David Lange and Invalid Votes.

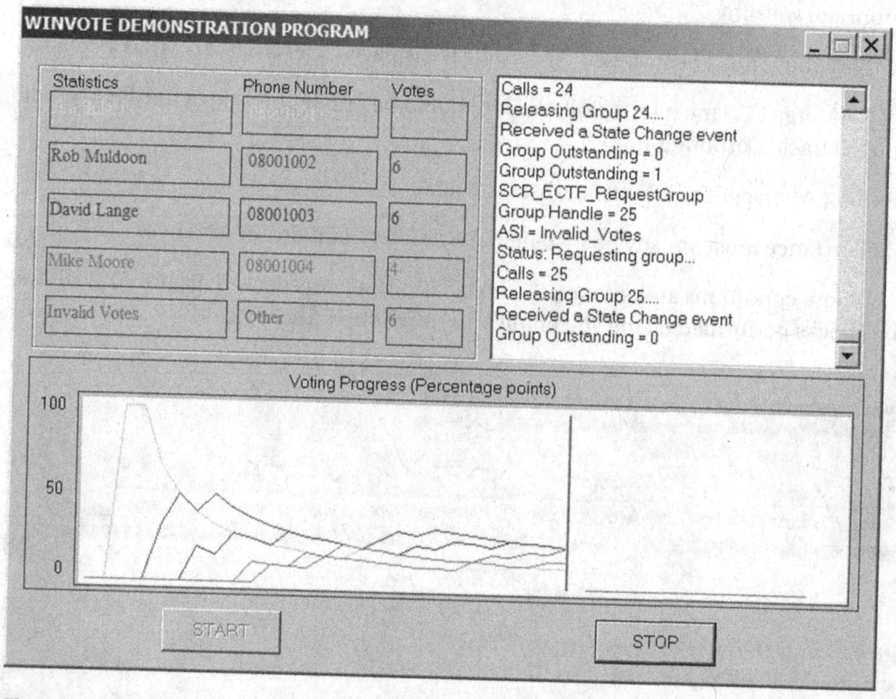

Figure 14-3. *A successful test of the NetMerge CCS installation*

Grid Control

Oracle's product for managing large IT installations is Enterprise Manager Grid Control. The Oracle services that can be managed by Grid Control include all Oracle databases (not only release 10g), Oracle Application Server, and the components deployed to an Oracle Application Server instance. It follows that Grid Control can be used to manage Oracle Collaboration Suite. Through use of plug-ins, Grid Control can also manage third-party products such as databases or application servers published by other software companies, and the server machines themselves.

The Grid Control architecture is a Management Server process that acts as a central point for monitoring and administering all the registered services, with Agent processes running on each node that is running a managed service. The Management Server makes use of a repository database to store configuration and other data. The Agents are responsible for sending monitoring information to the Management Server and for running jobs against the managed services. The Management Server is a central control facility from which the administrator can control and monitor the entire environment.

As Grid Control is not a requirement for Oracle Collaboration Suite in general, it is not discussed here in any detail. But it is required for Voicemail and Fax. The installer will check whether the Grid Control Agent is running and will not proceed if it is not available. At a later point in the installation, while running the configuration wizards, the installer will attempt to register Voicemail and Fax with the Grid Control Management Server. If this registration fails (as it will if there is no such server available) it is not critical, as the registration can be completed later.

Before installing the Voicemail and Fax middle tier instance, it will be necessary to install and start the Grid Control Agent on the machine that is to be used. This is a trivial task that will only take a few minutes. Run the Universal Installer from the Oracle Enterprise Manager 10g Grid Control DVD, and select the option to install only the Agent. The Agent should be installed into its own Oracle home, not an Oracle home used for any other product. This is so that it can exist independently of the products that it is managing.

There will be a prompt for the location and port being used by the Grid Control Management Server. If there is no such server available, leave this on its default setting (which will be port 4889 on the local machine). As there will be no Management Server running, the installer will give a warning at this point. Ignore this warning and the installation will proceed. Following the installation, the Agent will be running as a Windows service. To register the Grid Control Agent with the Grid Control Management Server later, locate the Enterprise Manager properties file, which is `%ORACLE_HOME%\sysman\config\emd.properties`, and edit the property `REPOSITORY_URL` to the address of the machine where the Grid Control Management Server is running. If SSL was enabled for the Management Server, it will also be necessary to edit the properties `emdWalletSrcUrl` and `emdWalletDest`. An example of settings for these properties is the following:

```
REPOSITORY_URL=http://omssrv1.bplc.co.za:4889/em/upload/
emdWalletSrcUrl=http://omssrv1.bplc.co.za:4889/em/wallets/emd
emdWalletDest=/home/oragrid/OracleHomes/oms10g/sysman/config/server
```

If the full Grid Control environment of Agents and Management Server is available, it should certainly be investigated to determine whether it should be used for administering Oracle Collaboration Suite; but if it is not, Application Server Control is a perfectly acceptable alternative. However, there are some Voicemail and Fax functions where there is no choice.

Using the Universal Installer to Install Voicemail and Fax

As any other Oracle product, Voicemail and Fax is installed with the Universal Installer, which is described in Chapter 4. The DVD with Voicemail and Fax also includes the Document Conversion and Voice Conversion servers that can optionally be used with Real-Time Collaboration.

The Universal Installer shipped with Voicemail and Fax should be launched by running the `setup.exe` program. After its initial checks, it will present the available products for selection, as shown in Figure 14-4.

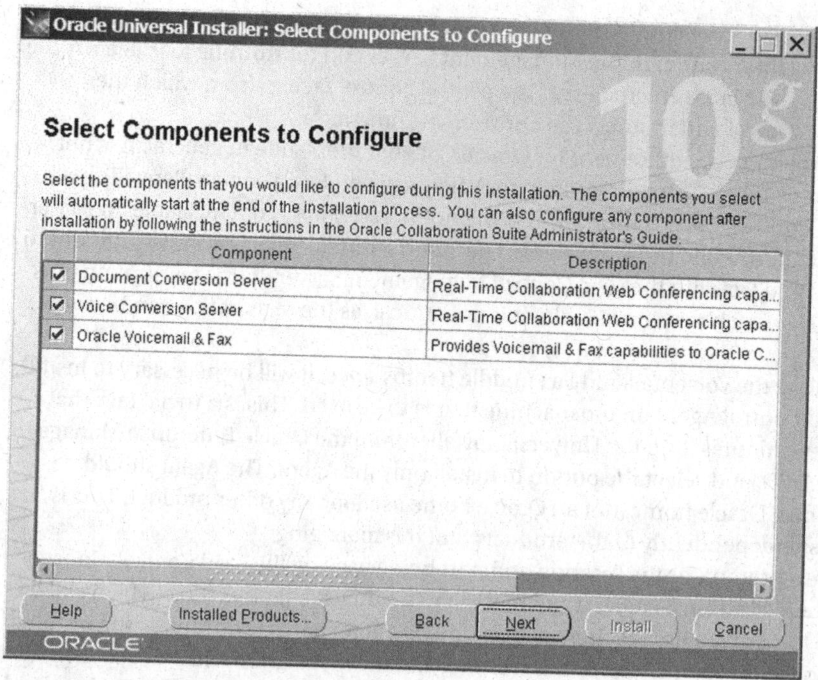

Figure 14-4. *Select the desired products supplied on the Voicemail and Fax DVD.*

The Installer will prompt for the location of the Oracle Internet Directory and the directory superuser name and password. It will then present a list of available Oracle Collaboration Suite databases—one must be selected. In a basic one- or two-node Oracle Collaboration Suite environment there will only be one such database, but in a more complicated environment with multiple databases you can choose which database to use for the Voicemail and Fax data. As Voicemail and Fax has very little data that is exclusive to it (it uses the Mail datastore for user data) this decision is unlikely to have much significance, and the database used for the metadata repository is the obvious choice.

Once the installation has completed, the standard Application Server startup and shutdown routines (using the `opmnctl` utility, or Application Server Control) can be used to manage the instance. Alternatively, because a Voicemail and Fax middle tier will be on a Windows machine, the Windows services interface can be used.

Figure 14-5 shows the output of the `opmnctl status` command following a startup of a Voicemail and Fax middle tier instance.

```
C:\WINDOWS\system32\cmd.exe
D:\product\10.1.2\ocs_7\opmn\bin>opmnctl status

Processes in Instance: ocs7.jwacer
-------------------+--------------------+---------+---------
ias-component      | process-type       |     pid | status
-------------------+--------------------+---------+---------
DSA                | DSA                |     N/A | Down
HTTP_Server        | HTTP_Server        |    5076 | Alive
LogLoader          | logloaderd         |     N/A | Down
dcm-daemon         | dcm-daemon         |    3976 | Alive
WebCache           | WebCache           |    1512 | Alive
WebCache           | WebCacheAdmin      |    2604 | Alive
OC4J               | OC4J_OCSClient     |    5796 | Alive
VoicemailFaxAppli~ | RoutingService     |    4508 | Alive
VoicemailFaxAppli~ | RecordingService   |    1096 | Alive
VoicemailFaxAppli~ | RetrievalService   |    3944 | Alive
VoicemailFaxAppli~ | FaxReceivingServi~ |    1716 | Alive
VoicemailFaxAppli~ | MessageRecoverySe~ |    4664 | Alive
VoicemailFaxAppli~ | CallTransferServi~ |    5956 | Alive
VoicemailFaxAppli~ | InteractiveVoiceR~ |    6072 | Alive
VoicemailFaxAppli~ | MWIService         |    4344 | Alive
VoicemailFaxAppli~ | MsgDeliveryMonito~ |    2268 | Init
VoicemailFaxAppli~ | TelephonyMonitorS~ |    5544 | Alive

D:\product\10.1.2\ocs_7\opmn\bin>
```

Figure 14-5. *The components deployed to a Voicemail and Fax middle tier instance*

Installed and configured with the Voicemail and Fax components are the usual components that are installed with any Oracle Collaboration Suite middle tier instance:

- Oracle HTTP Server
- Web Cache
- The OC4J_OCSClient user interface component
- Application Server Control

Including the web components that generate the user interface means that the Voicemail and Fax instance can be used by end users as an entry point to Oracle Collaboration Suite. It will provide the standard Portal interface, with links to all the components, as would any other middle tier instance.

Incoming Call Management

Incoming calls from Oracle Collaboration Suite users who wish to manage their voice mail accounts can be routed directly to Voicemail and Fax by the PBX, as can incoming faxes. Calls from external users to internal users' extensions will be transferred to Voicemail and

Fax by the PBX if the extension is not answered. Some calls may also be transferred directly to IVR applications.

Any one call may require a number of the Voicemail and Fax services. The initial point of contact with Voicemail and Fax is always the Routing Service, which will forward the call on to the appropriate service for processing. This service may then make use of other services.

Voicemail Management Calls

Calls made for the purpose of managing voice mail will be routed directly through the telephony interface to Voicemail and Fax by the PBX.

The call will be received by the Routing Service, which sends the call to the Retrieval Service. Attached to the call will be the caller's caller ID, if this is available. Typically, calls received from a cellular network will include a caller ID, but calls from the PSTN will not. The Retrieval Service identifies the mailbox being requested (either by prompting the user to provide a box number, or by using the caller ID) and confirms, by querying the Oracle Internet Directory, that the mailbox does exist. The Retrieval Service generates a password prompt, validates the password against the Oracle Internet Directory, and then uses IVR to present a menu with these options to the user:

- Listen to new and saved voice mail messages
- Send a voice mail message to another user
- Reply to the sender of a voice mail message
- Forward a voice mail message to another user
- Conduct administration tasks such as changing the password and recording a greeting message

The Retrieval Service makes use of other services as necessary. It will, for example, invoke the Recording Service if the user wishes to reply to a message. After recording the message, control will return to the Retrieval Service.

Incoming Faxes

Faxes will be routed directly through the telephony interface to Voicemail and Fax by the PBX. The call will be passed by the Routing Service to the Recording Service, which will detect the fax tone and pass it on to the Fax Receiving Service. The Fax Receiving Service will verify that the destination is for a valid user who has the fax facility enabled, and then go through the standard fax routine for negotiating a transmission speed before saving the fax to the user's Inbox.

Incoming Voice Messages

A caller will dial into the PBX and be connected to a user's extension. If the user does not pick up the call within a preconfigured time, or perhaps if the user has enabled automatic forwarding to voice mail, the PBX will transfer the call to Voicemail and Fax for recording a message.

The Routing Service receives the call and sends it to the Recording Service, along with such information as the time and source of the call. The Recording Service will confirm that the destination number is for a user who has voice mail enabled, and then uses the IVR Service to take the caller through the process of recording a message. The IVR greeting will be that recorded by the user or a systemwide default greeting. Once recording is completed, the Recording Service saves the message to the user's inbox.

Transfer to an Operator

As users work their way through the Voicemail application, there will usually be options to request to speak to an operator. If the user takes this option, he will be transferred to the Call Transfer Service. The Call Transfer Service will look up the number for the operator (which may vary depending on the application to which the user is connected) and pass the call back to the PBX for connection.

Note that many call centers will consider transfer to an operator to be a failure of the system. A key objective in modern call centers is to minimize the number of call-center staff required. Well-designed IVR applications can automate the entire interaction with the user, providing him with a service that may be as good as or better than that which he would have received from an operator. It will certainly be a service that is cheaper to provide.

Use of IVR Applications

IVR applications play a major role in many organizations. They can be used to manage functions such as support calls, sales inquiries, report distribution, directory searches, and much more. This can give improved service to the users and great savings to the service provider by letting him use his staff more effectively.

Voicemail and Fax IVR applications are defined by program developers using XML documents. These documents consist of tags that can generate audio menus to which callers can respond either by pressing buttons on a DTMF-enabled telephone or orally. The design of such applications is fully documented in the Voicemail and Fax Administrators Guide, and there is also a graphical interface for designing simple applications. But no matter how sophisticated the application, the callers may show resistance to using it. How effective IVR applications are at replacing human operators is not only dependent on how well the application is designed, but also whether the users are inclined to use it.

The PBX will forward calls for numbers designated for IVR applications directly to the Routing Service. The Routing Service will connect the caller to the IVR Service. Depending on the number requested, the IVR Service will handle the call with the appropriate IVR application. A simple application might generate an audio menu such as "Thank you for calling BPLC. To speak to a salesperson, please press 1. To speak to someone in customer support, please press 2. If you know the extension of the person to whom you wish to speak, please press 3. If you know the name of the person to whom you wish to speak, please press 4. Please press 5 to leave a message, and someone will return your call. To be transferred to an operator, please press 9. Press 0 to repeat this menu."

Menus of this nature can work reasonably well, but there are some general guidelines developers should follow. Careful consideration of matters such as language, accent, and style is vital to encourage the use of IVR. Also, menus that are overlong or that link to other menus are always irritating to callers. But no matter how well designed the IVR application is, some callers will always prefer to speak to an operator immediately. If this happens consistently, there may be a design fault in the application, or the application may not be suitable for its users. There are known geographic and demographic trends that should be studied when designing IVR applications. For instance, it is well-known in the call-center industry that use of such IVR systems does not always come naturally to users in Africa, and that short menus are therefore vital if a large number of calls are not to request transfer to an operator. European and North American callers are more likely to find longer and linked menus acceptable (even though annoying).

Creating IVR Applications

Creating IVR applications is the responsibility of your developers. There are three tasks:

- Specify the hours and days during which the application will be available.
- Create the deployment, consisting of call flows and sound files.
- Map the application to a telephone number.

The first and last tasks are accomplished through Grid Control. Navigate to the Voicemail and Fax component, and enter appropriate values in the PBX application cluster configuration windows.

Creating a deployment is done with a command-line utility, the IVR Manager. This is implemented with a batch file:

```
%ORACLE_HOME%\um\scripts\ivrman.bat
```

A deployment consists of call flows and sound files that must be uploaded into the Oracle Internet Directory with the IVR Manager.

Call flows are XML documents that define the flow control through the application. The call flows also specify the audio messages used, and the mappings of keys pressed by users to the telephone extension numbers to which they will be forwarded. Sound files are the audio messages saved as WAV files. There are sample IVR applications provided that can be deployed for testing or edited for use. The XML files will be found in the directory `%ORACLE_HOME\um\sample\ivr\scripts`. Sound files are in the directory `%ORACLE_HOME%\um\scripts\ivrsound`.

It is possible for developers to reuse the components of IVR applications. For example, the same call flow with a different set of sound files could present an application in different languages.

CHAPTER 15

Workspaces

An Oracle Collaboration Suite installation will accumulate a vast amount of information in the various application component datastores. The sheer volume of information, no matter how well classified, can make it difficult to locate and correlate data. In a large organization with thousands of employees there will be millions of documents in Content Services, similar numbers of e-mails and Calendar data items, and numerous recordings of meetings and web casts in Real-Time Collaboration. Even with the sophistication of the Search application, it can be next to impossible to identify and assemble information relevant to one project, or to one group of staff, in a convenient fashion.

Workspaces are the solution to this problem. They provide a mechanism whereby a subset of information from any and all of the component applications can be brought together and accessed from one point. The possible sources of Workspaces data are Content Services, Calendar, Mail (including voice mail and fax), Discussions, and the Real-Time Collaboration web conferencing and instant messaging archives. By giving a subset of Oracle Collaboration Suite users access to a workspace, it becomes possible for a project team to assemble and share documents, to schedule team meetings and other events, to send each other messages, and to start discussions on relevant topics, for example. Searches with the Search component can also be limited in scope to one workspace.

Within a workspace, information can be grouped into views. This provides a further level of classification. The finest level of classification is provided by defining links between individual information items. Views and links can cut across all the other lines of classification. There are no restrictions on the types of data item that can be grouped in views or linked together or where they are stored in their native storage components and the content of a view. Any one item can appear in any number of views or links.

Workspaces Architecture

Critical to appreciating the power of Workspaces is understanding that it does not store user data. The information put into a workspace exists only in the application component datastore where it was originally placed. Workspaces can be thought of as placing an additional layer of classification and security on top of the existing structures for storing, cataloging, and accessing information maintained by the other Oracle Collaboration Suite applications. There is only ever one source for a given data item, but Workspaces lets data be collated along different dimensions and presented accordingly.

Access to data is always possible through the usual user interfaces, such as the web client or the client-server tools. The Workspaces application, which is deployed to the OC4J component OC4J_OCSClient on the Oracle Application Server middle tier instance, makes use of the various APIs and other facilities provided by the application components to open another channel of access that can group data from the various sources together. Security is, as always, enforced through the Oracle Internet Directory and Single Sign-On. Figure 15-1 is a graphical representation of the relationship between Workspaces, the other application components, and the datastores.

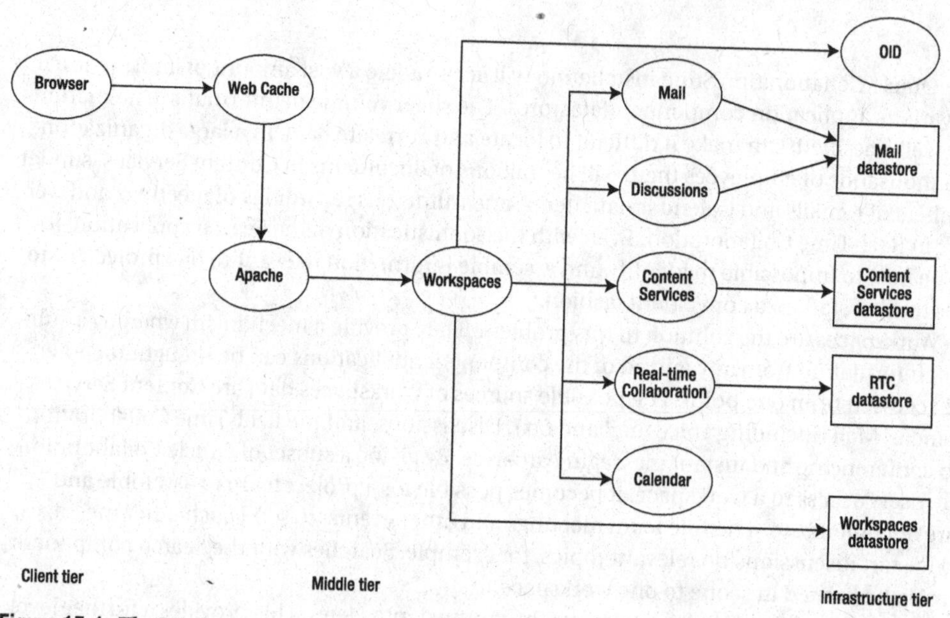

Figure 15-1. *The Workspaces component in relation to the other middle tier and infrastructure components*

End-user access to Workspaces is from a browser, following the usual route through the Web Cache to the Apache web listener. After Single Sign-On authentication when first contacting the middle tier, the user can navigate to the list of workspaces to which he has been given access. The security structures identifying Workspaces users and their privileges are stored in the Oracle Internet Directory. The Workspaces component then generates a user interface which presents the content of a workspace to the user. The documents and other items in a workspace are managed by the application components to which they belong; no data is ever duplicated, and it is also available through the components' standard interfaces. The Workspaces configuration metadata is stored in a schema in the Oracle Collaboration Suite database.

Workspaces is critically dependent on the availability of the other application components. If these are not started, users connected to Workspaces will not be able to access any data. Workspaces can tolerate downtime of an application component in a reasonably graceful manner, but only information stored in the components that are running will be accessible. An attempt to access information in the component that is down results in a message stating that it is temporarily unavailable.

In a deployment with multiple Oracle Application Server middle tier instances, the Workspaces application can be started on one or all of the instances. Multiple instances will give fault tolerance, load balancing, and scalability. The only point to be aware of in such an environment is that the Workspaces application does cache some data within its OC4J container. As the caches are not synchronized in real time, it is possible that users with sessions against one instance will not immediately see changes made by users with sessions against a different instance. The delay varies depending on the type of change. Users' definitions and their workspace memberships and privileges are stored in the Oracle Internet Directory and propagated to Workspaces by the provisioning mechanism. Changes may not be reflected in Workspaces for up to 30 minutes, and different Workspaces instances may pick up the changes at different times. Changes that modify a workspace's content will be picked up immediately by other sessions attached to the instance that made the change; even though content is cached, a change will invalidate all cached data and force Workspaces to refresh it. This invalidation mechanism does not work across instances, but cached content is refreshed in any case after five minutes, and as this refresh is from the component datastores, any changes made will take at most five minutes to propagate to other instances.

Users and Security

The Workspaces application does not have users as such. There is no requirement to provision user accounts, because Workspaces does not have any user data. All the data in a workspace is in fact stored by the application to which it is native. There is a privilege necessary to create a workspace, and within that workspace, users can be given permission to read or write the data. The workspaces roles, in descending order of authority, are the following:

Application Administrator: Users granted this role can manage the entire Workspaces environment. They can grant all roles (including this one), set application-level attributes, define the templates used to create workspaces, and perform any action in any workspace.

Workspace Creator: Users granted this role can create workspaces. They become workspace administrators for any workspaces they create and are therefore able to assign roles to other users for these workspaces and perform any action within them. The Application Administrator can make this role redundant by setting the workspace creation policy to Public, rather than Restricted. If this is done then anyone can create workspaces.

Workspace Administrator: Users granted this role for a workspace can perform any action in the workspace, including controlling membership by granting the Writer and Reader roles.

Writer: Users granted this role for a workspace can create folders, upload files, schedule meetings, create tasks, and manage the relationships between objects.

Reader: Users granted this role for a workspace can view the workspace's content but cannot add to, edit, or delete from the content.

Each role includes the capabilities of the roles beneath it, so there is no need to grant more than one role per workspace per user. The roles granted are stored within the Oracle Internet Directory and are checked whenever a session attempts to do anything. The access privileges will be synchronized across all the Oracle Collaboration Suite application components. For example, if a user has only read access to a file in Workspaces, he will have only read access if he opens it through the Content Services web client.

To create a Workspaces Application Administrator, connect to the Oracle Collaboration Suite middle tier Application Server Control, and click the Administration icon for the Workspaces component. On receipt of the Single Sign-On prompt, connect as the orcladmin user and you will be logged in to Workspaces. Navigate to the Administration tab and the Application subtab, and then Roles. You will see that orcladmin has the Application Administrator role, and no one else has any roles at all. Select a user and grant him the Application Administrator role. This should be the only time it is necessary to connect as orcladmin, and the only time it should be necessary to connect through Application Server Control. All subsequent administration work can be delegated to the nominated user, who will connect through the Oracle Collaboration Suite portal.

The window for assigning the Workspaces application roles is shown in Figure 15-2.

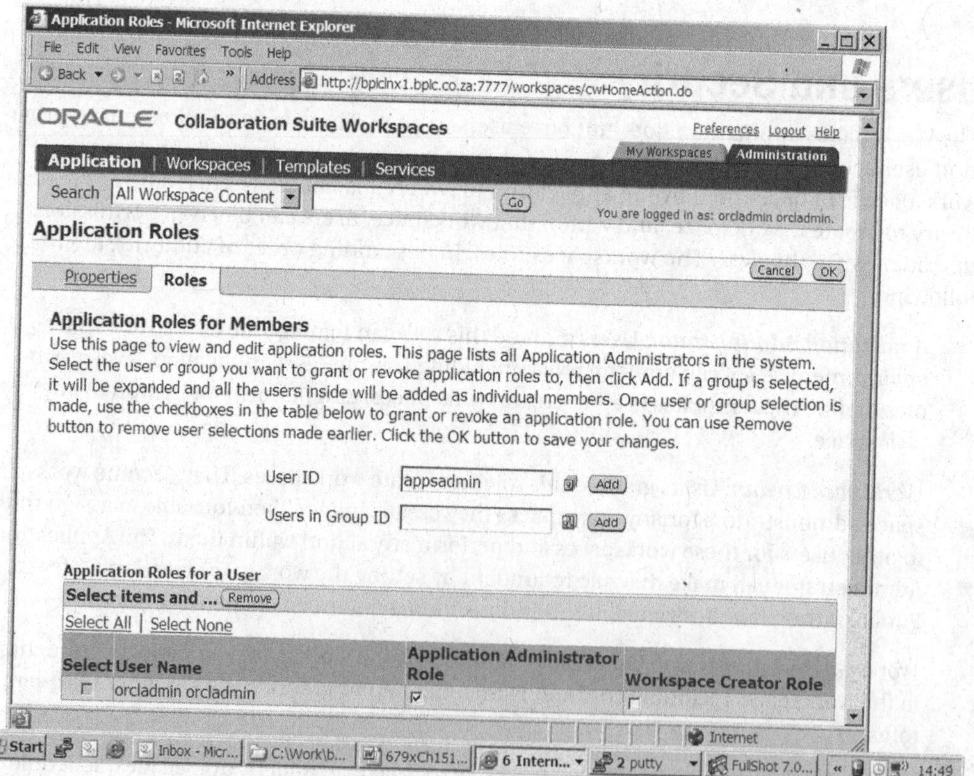

Figure 15-2. *Create a Workspaces Application Adminstrator when connected as orcladmin.*

Managing Workspaces

There are some tasks for the Application Administrator, and others that can be delegated to the workspace creators and administrators. When a user with the Application Administrator role connects to Workspaces through the Oracle Collaboration Suite portal he will see a window with two tabs: My Workspaces and Administration. The Administration tab has four subtabs for the Application, Workspaces, Templates, and Services tasks.

Application Administration

The Application tab on the Administration page is used to set these properties:

Workspace creation mode: This defaults to Public, meaning that anyone can create a workspace. The alternative is Restricted, meaning that users must be explicitly granted the Workspace Creator role. This can often be left on default, since being able to create workspaces does not in fact confer any authorization that the user does not have already in the component applications; it merely lets users make use of an added value service that will make them more productive in their work.

Default workspace template: A template defines the initial structure of a workspace. Following installation there will be a choice of two templates: Basic, which is the default, and Empty. Other templates can be created later.

Enable notifications: If enabled (as it is by default) e-mail will be sent to new and existing members when users are added to or removed from a workspace. The address and port of an SMTP server must be specified—the default is the address and port of the Mail SMTP server.

Notification messages: These are the notification messages that will be sent to the user and other members of the workspace when a user is added or removed. These messages should be customized to the needs of the organization.

The notification messages when users join or leave a workspace can include text and variables. The following is an example of the default message that is sent to a user when he is added to a workspace. The message subject is

```
Welcome to Workspace "${workspace-display-name}"
```

The message body is

```
<html>
<body>
<p>(Automated message from Oracle Workspaces)</p>
<p>${cur-user-name} has added you to workspace "${workspace-display-name}"
as a member with "${new-member-role}" role. Please visit the
<a href="${workspace-url}">workspace</a>
for more details.</p>
<p>_______________________________</p
```

```
p><a href="${cw-home-url}">Oracle Workspaces</a></p>
<p>Questions? Please see the Help/FAQ sections of Oracle Workspaces ➥
 for support information.</p>
</body>
</html>
```

This is a standard page of HTML. If some users have e-mail clients that can't display HTML correctly, the message should be replaced with plain text. There are a number of tokens that can be embedded in the message:

`${cur-user-name}`: The user who performed the addition to or removal from the workspace

`${new-member-role}`: The role granted to a new user

`${new-member-names}`: A comma-separated list of new members to a workspace

`${removed-member-names}`: A comma-separated list of members removed from a workspace

`${workspace-display-name}`: The name of the workspace, as displayed to users, to which the operation applies

`${workspace-url}`: A direct link to the workspace

`${cw-home-url}`: A link to the workspace's home page

These tokens will be expanded to appropriate values when the messages are sent.

Workspaces Administration

The Workspaces tab on the Administration page is used for three maintenance tasks: recovering corrupted workspaces, assigning ownership of a workspace whose owner has been deleted, and taking (temporary) administration rights for a workspace.

It is possible for a workspace to get corrupted. This does not refer to moral corruption, which would be dependent only on the content, but to logical corruption—the metadata describing the workspace in the Workspaces repository can become inconsistent. This should never occur, but in some circumstances it can happen due to the asynchronous nature of some tasks. An example is adding a library to a workspace. A library is stored as a shared folder in Content Services, with pointers to it in the Workspaces metadata repository. The creation of the folder is an operation in Content Services, and the creation of the pointers is an operation in Workspaces.

Ideally, these two operations would be accomplished as a single transaction, terminated in the same way that a database transaction is terminated with a SQL `commit` or `rollback` command. However, because the operations are carried out in two different applications, this is not possible. To continue the database transaction analogy, a two-phase commit would be necessary. It is possible for the creation of the folder to succeed, but creation of the pointers to fail. In this case, the Workspaces repository will be left in an inconsistent state, making the workspace unusable. Any such inconsistencies are detected automatically and the workspace is put into a recovery mode. While in this mode it cannot be accessed by any users. The Recovery window of the administration tool lists all corrupted workspaces and has an option to recover them. The recovery operation will take whatever action is necessary to make the workspace usable. Typically, this would involve backing out those parts of a partially completed operation that did not go through.

A workspace is created and owned by a user. The user is defined within the Oracle Internet Directory, but there is no account provisioning mechanism between the Oracle Internet Directory and Workspaces; all users are always given access to the Workspaces application. This model works because there is no user data in Workspaces, and the user will have already been provisioned in the data-storing components. When a user is removed from the Oracle Internet Directory, his data is not immediately removed from the component applications, though it will become inaccessible. The various applications have routines for permanently removing such data (as described in previous chapters). But in the case of Workspaces, it is more than likely that the data, being the definition of the workspace and the links to its contents, will still be valuable to other members of the workspace. If a user is removed from the Oracle Internet Directory, any workspaces owned by him will be listed in the Unowned Workspaces window of the administration tool, which has an option to assign the workspace to a new owner. In this way the data and access to it can be preserved.

A user with the Application Administrator role can act as the workspace administrator for any workspace, but he will not have this capability when he connects to Workspaces through the usual route. To invoke this capability he must go through the administration tool and select the workspace from the All Workspaces window. This will give the option to delete the workspace or to enter its home page with administration rights as though he were the workspace's creator or a nominated administrator.

Template Administration

A template is a skeleton for a workspace. It can define who the members should be; what files and folders, meetings and tasks, and Discussions forums should be included; whether e-mail should be available; and what views of the content should be presented.

There are two templates provided: the Basic template, which includes all the services, and the Empty template, which includes none. When a workspace is created it can be based on a template and modified, and it is subsequently possible to create a template from a workspace. A typical progression would be to create workspaces from the Basic or Empty templates, modify them by adding and removing users, services, and views, and then save their definition as another template for reuse. In this fashion, templates will be built up that reflect common collaborative needs.

Having perfected your workspace there are various administration options for saving it as a template to be used again. Either the structure can be preserved, or the structure plus the content. Next time you perform a similar task you can take the template off the shelf, but only if you saved the last one. This adds a lot of value, and a typical organization will build up a library of useful project templates. As they are also accessible in XML, the workspace could be generated as part of a workflow or process. The template administration window lets users view template definitions, delete templates, or upload templates from an XML file (the template definitions are stored as XML documents).

Services Administration

The services are the sources of information for Workspaces. The Services Administration window lists them with an indication of their status. The services are the following:

- Library
- Meetings and Tasks
- Discussions
- Inbox

The Library service requires Content Services; the Meetings and Tasks service requires Calendar; the Discussions and Inbox services require Mail.

Figure 15-3 shows the services administration window.

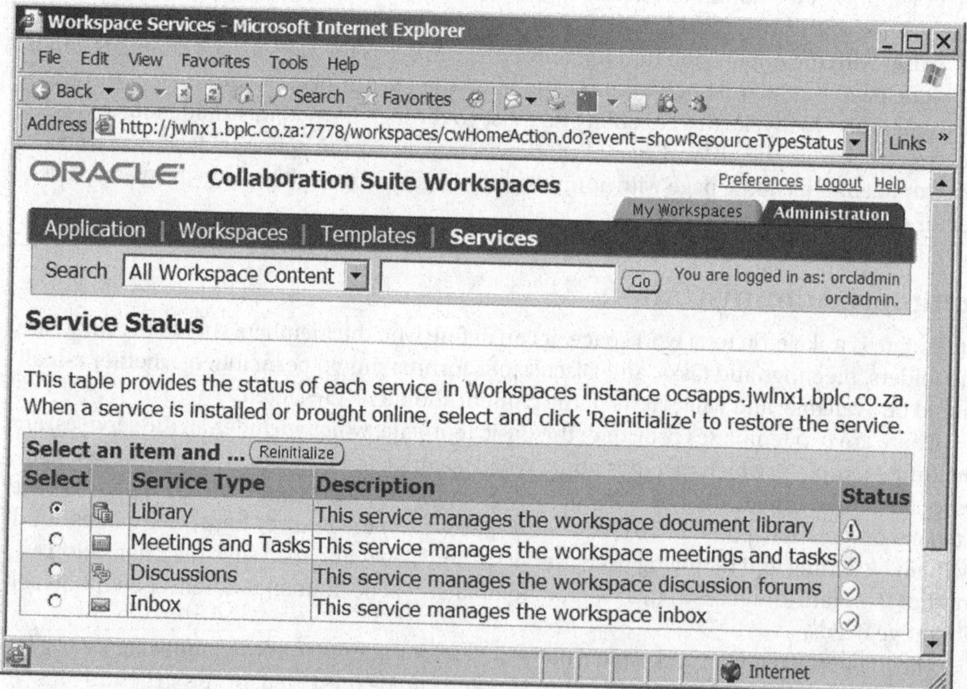

Figure 15-3. *The Workspaces Service Status window*

The Services Administration window does not reflect whether the service is actually running and available for use, only whether it has been configured. If, for example, the initial deployment of Oracle Collaboration Suite did not include setting up the Calendar component, the Meetings and Tasks service would have a status of "warning" rather than "OK." If Calendar is deployed at a later stage, the service should be selected and initialized for use within Workspaces. The service can also be reinitialized if additional middle tier nodes are installed or their addresses are changed. The initialization or reinitialization updates the Workspaces repository with the URLs needed to contact the service. As this information is stored within the Oracle Collaboration Suite metadata repository, no user input is required other than clicking the Reinitialize button.

If some (or all) users are not provisioned for all the Oracle Collaboration Suite component applications, it will be good practice to create templates that exclude the services that are dependent on the nonprovisioned components. This will prevent confusion as users attempt to use a Workspaces service for which they do not have an account in the underlying component.

Creating and Using Workspaces

A workspace is a collection of information stored in various Oracle Collaboration Suite application components presented as a unit to a group of users. The workspace must first be created based on a template, and then its structure and contents will be maintained by the users.

Creating a Workspace

For a user to create a workspace, either the workspace creation mode must be set to Public (as it is by default, meaning that all authenticated Oracle Collaboration Suite users can create workspaces), or the user must be granted the Workspace Creator role. Both of these conditions can be checked and adjusted in the administration tool. The Workspaces home page, accessed through the Oracle Collaboration Suite portal, will have a New Workspace button, which will launch the wizard to create a new workspace.

The first step is to select a template on which the workspace will be based. For the first workspace, there will only be two templates available: the Basic Workspace Template and the Empty Workspace Template. Whichever is chosen, the second step is to set these workspace properties:

Workspace name: The name used internally, which can never be changed and must be unique. This is not case sensitive, but there are some restrictions on the characters permitted.

Display name: The name shown to users, which can be changed subsequently. This is case sensitive and must also be unique.

Description: A text description of the workspace.

Default member role: The role to be granted to new members, unless otherwise specified: Reader, Writer (the default), or Administrator.

Member access: Access for members (the default) or administrators only. The latter setting would usually only be temporary, while performing maintenance work on the workspace.

Membership notification: Notifications of workspace joiners and leavers sent to all members (the default) or affected members or disabled.

Workspace listing: Who can see the workspace. A publicly listed workspace will be visible to all authenticated users or the workspace can be only viewable by members (the default).

Once created, the workspace owner (who will be the only member of the workspace at this point) should enter the workspace through the web interface, set up the initial structures that will be required, and extend the membership.

Defining the Services and Users for a Workspace

Figure 15-4 shows the Overview window of a workspace called EBS Implementers, which was created on the Basic template.

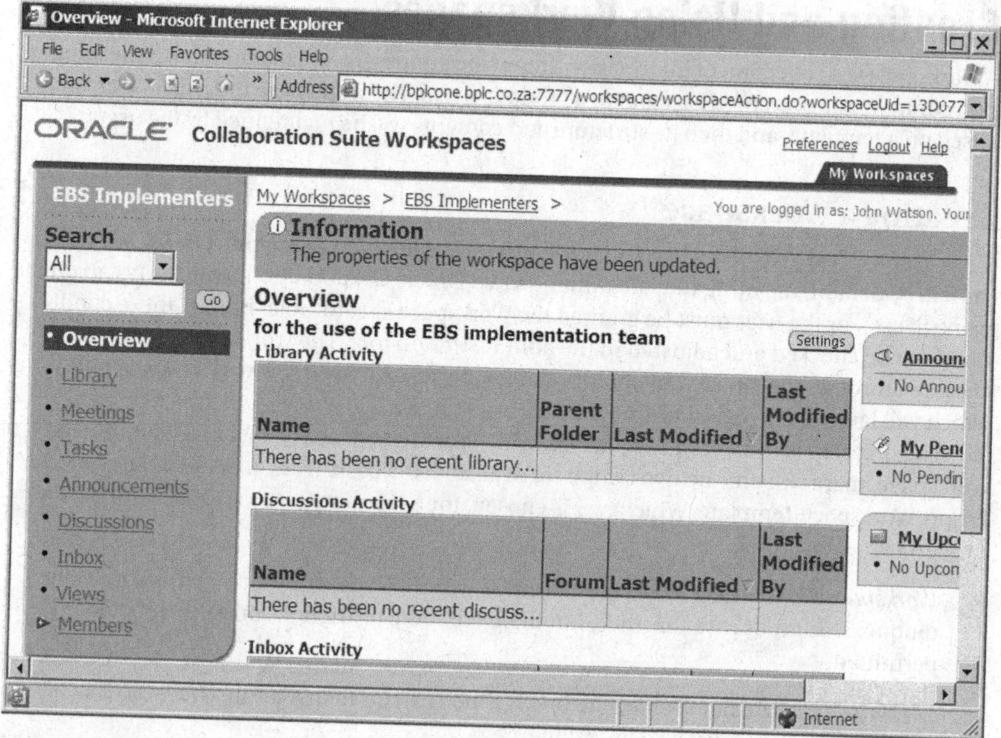

Figure 15-4. *A workspace defined with the Basic template immediately after creation*

The bullets on the left of the Overview window shown in Figure 15-4 show the services available within this workspace. Note that the presentation of the services to users is different from the presentation to administrators: the administrator sees a single Meetings and Tasks service (provided by the Calendar component); the users see two separate services. And where the administrator sees a single Discussions service, the users see both Discussions and Announcements (both provided by the Discussions component).

The workspace in the example shown in Figure 15-4 is based on the Basic template, which includes all the services, and therefore has all the possible services. A workspace based on the Empty template would have only the bullets for Overview, Announcements, and Views.

The Settings button visible toward the right-hand side of Figure 15-4 will let the workspace administrator adjust all the properties, with the exception of the workspace name. It will also present a window where services can be added or removed. The possible services that can be added or removed are Discussions, Inbox, Library, Meetings, and Tasks (these last two come or go together). Announcements, Views, and the Overview are always available.

The Members link on the Overview window (visible at the bottom left of Figure 15-4) presents a window where users can be selected for membership and given the Reader, Writer, or Administrator (for this workspace only) role. Selection is by individual or by group. The groups are those defined within the Oracle Internet Directory with the OIDDAS tool.

The workspace Search capability has its scope restricted to the contents of the workspace. The drop-down box toward the top left of the Overview window can further restrict the scope of the search to the content of files, discussions, or meetings. This corresponds to restricting the scope to workspace content stored in Content Services, Mail, or Calendar. Within the selected scope, the searches are based on keywords and are implemented by the Search application component. To make searches that go across workspaces, it is necessary to use the standard interface to Search, accessible through the Oracle Collaboration Suite portal.

Managing the Content of a Workspace

Workspace members control the content of the workspace. This is one major feature of the component: the Oracle Collaboration Suite administrator need do nothing other than grant the Workspace Creator role; the creator will take on the administration workload from there. The workspace members to whom he grants the Writer privilege will populate the workspace with the information the group needs.

On entering a workspace, users will see the home page shown in Figure 15-5. This page shows links to recent activity, links (on the right of the window) to announcements and the current user's pending tasks and meetings, and (next to the members' names, at the bottom left) icons for sending e-mail and instant messages.

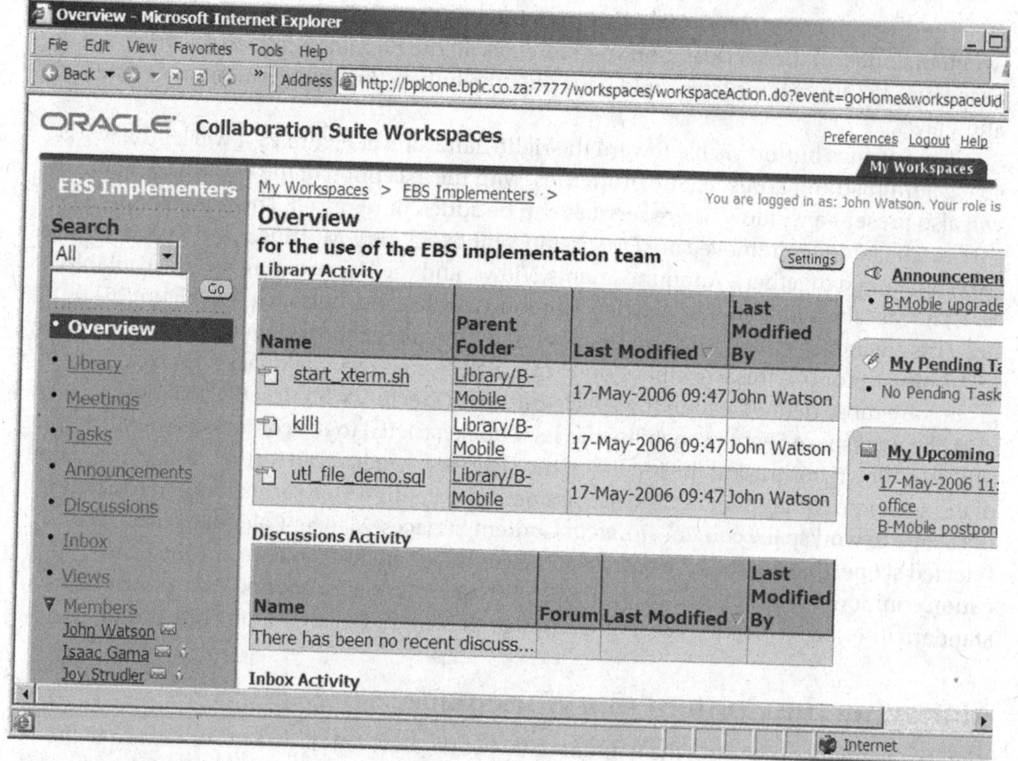

Figure 15-5. *The home page for a workspace with all services configured*

The home page has (in the left-hand menu block) links for the services defined for the workspace. It is through these links that information is added to the workspaces and relationships are defined between items of information. The following is a list of the services and their descriptions:

Library service: Interfaces to data stored within Content Services. A workspace's library contains a set of folders and files created and uploaded by the users. The standard Content Services facilities of document virus checking, versioning, and locking are all available. When connecting to Content Services with the web client, with WebDAV, or with the Oracle Drive Windows client, library folders appear as shared folders in the <domain>/<workspaces>/<workspace_name> folder.

Meetings service: Interfaces to Calendar. When creating a meeting, the user selects whether it is a standard meeting or a web conference and selects a time, a place, resources, and invitees. The resources and invitees need not be restricted to the workspace members (or even to Oracle Collaboration Suite users). Calendar will take care of conflict checking and distributing notifications.

Tasks service: Interfaces to Calendar. Tasks can be created and assigned to one or more workspace members, with start and completion dates and tracking of progress toward completion. Tasks will also be published to users through the Calendar web client, the Calendar Desktop client, and Microsoft Outlook.

Announcements service: Lets users create messages that will be posted on the workspace's home page. They can be configured for automatic expiry after a certain date, defaulting to a lifetime of one month.

Discussions service: Interfaces to Discussions. Forums (but not categories) can be created and used as any other forum.

Inbox service: Provides a Mail account for the workspace. Through this service, any user can send mail to any address, with a copy sent to the workspace Mail account where it will be visible to all workspace members.

Views service: Collates workspace content along dimensions other than the content type. Once a view is created, library files, meetings, tasks, and forums can be selected and grouped within it. Users can thus subdivide a workspace into functional units that contain information drawn from any and all of the other services. One information item can appear in any number of views. The information items do, of course, remain accessible through the Workspaces service to which they belong, as well as through the interfaces native to their application component.

The multidimensional nature of Workspaces is an important feature and occurs at several levels. The creation of a workspace immediately adds a new dimension to Oracle Collaboration Suite's data storage. Information from the various application components can be grouped within a workspace and made easily accessible to the workspace's members. Then within the workspace, views provide another level of subdivision. At any stage there is never any duplication of data. Workspaces is a classification system that creates pointers to information, making it more easily accessible.

The finest level of classification is to create links between workspace items. Any item can be linked to any other items: files, folders, meetings, tasks, and discussions can all be connected in a manner that makes it possible to navigate from one to another. Figure 15-6 shows a meeting that has been linked to a folder, a document, and a task. The links are always point-to-point and bidirectional, making it possible to navigate through the whole of the workspace's content by following whatever links users have set up.

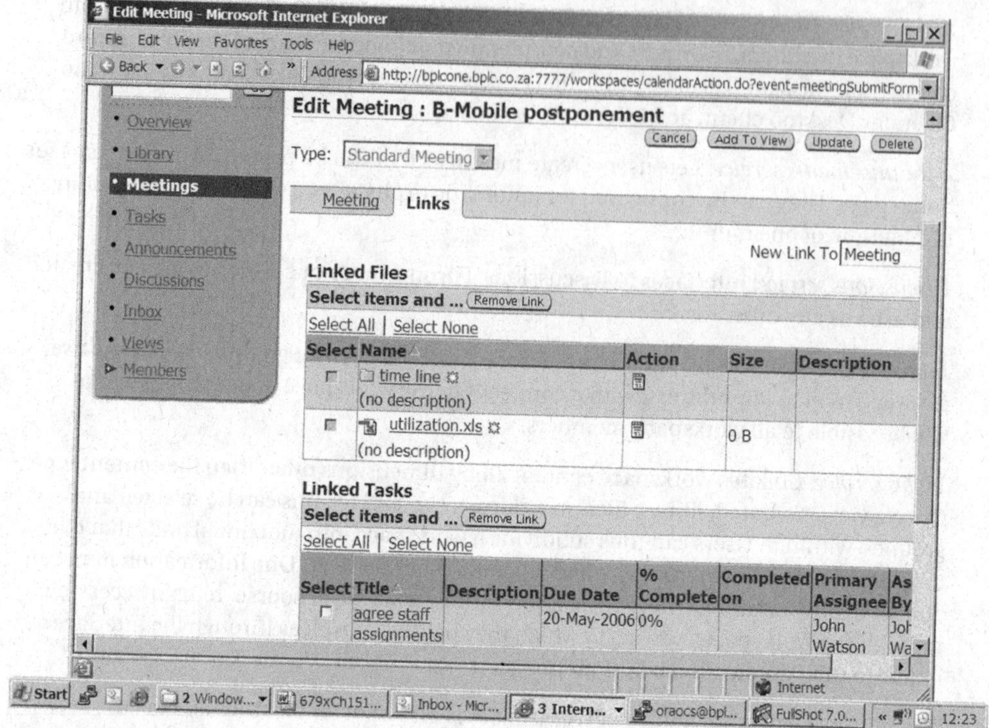

Figure 15-6. *A meeting, with links to other information items in other services*

CHAPTER 16

Logging, Monitoring, Tuning, and Maintenance

Following initial deployment of Oracle Collaboration Suite, the administrator and any component administrators must monitor the use and performance of the installation and make any adjustments necessary. There are many tasks associated with this day-to-day management work, and it may not be possible for one person to manage the entire system; very few people have the breadth of knowledge needed to do this. This chapter is a summary of some of the more important tasks, grouped into broad categories that indicate the areas of concern.

Database Management Tasks

The Oracle Collaboration Suite installation will have at least one Oracle database. While it is possible for one database to provide all the data storage that is necessary, a single database installation will not be suitable for an installation supporting more than a few hundred users. A large-scale installation could have several databases in order to distribute the workload of managing the data maintained by the different components. In some cases it may be necessary to dedicate a database, or possibly several databases, to one component. The components that are candidates for their own databases are the following:

Metadata repository: This stores the configuration data for the Oracle Application Server farm that is hosting the installation. While this is critical to the functioning of the installation, it is comparatively small and static.

Oracle Internet Directory: This stores the tables that make up the directory data. It is theoretically possible to distribute this data across more than one database, and certainly possible to replicate it to another database. The directory may well contain millions of entries and expand to many gigabytes. The data is not very volatile but does tend to have a high query workload.

Content Services: It is not possible for Content Services data to be distributed across multiple databases. The volume of data can expand to terabytes. The I/O operations include large transfers of LOB data as documents are saved and retrieved. The data volumes can be controlled by use of quotas.

Mail: Mail data can be distributed across multiple databases. The volume of data can be terabytes, though this can be controlled by allocating quotas to users. This database also stores the Discussions data and the Voicemail and Fax data.

Real-Time Collaboration: The Real-Time Collaboration data can be stored in its own database, and this may be advisable if there are many web conferences in progress at once.

Portal repository: This data is comparatively static but can have a high query workload.

It is possible to make an initial installation with just one database and subsequently pull component schemas out of this and move them to dedicated databases. However, this may be extremely awkward and will certainly involve downtime. It is therefore advisable to consider use of multiple databases from the beginning.

As can be seen, the pattern of activity on the different component datastores does vary. Apart from data volumes, this is a powerful reason for using separate databases; it may be much easier to tune different databases according to their respective usage than to tune one database for all access patterns.

Oracle databases must be monitored continuously. Performance tuning and space management are to a large extent straightforward tasks, but they must not be ignored. Release 10*g* of the database can simplify and automate a great deal of this work. Use of the alert system, the various tuning wizards, and the tools for running jobs automatically can remove a great deal of the more mundane work from the database administrator.

Alert Log and Trace Files

The most basic monitoring that should be carried out daily is to inspect the alert log and any background trace files. These will be generated in the directory specified by the instance parameter BACKGROUND_DUMP_DEST. The naming convention for these files is

```
alert_<SID>.log
```

for the alert log, where *<SID>* is the instance name, and

```
<SID>_<PROCESS_NAME>_<PID>.trc
```

for background trace files, where *<SID>* is the instance name, *<PROCESS_NAME>* is the name of the process, and *<PID>* is the process number (on UNIX) or thread number (on Windows) of the process that generated the trace file.

The alert log is a continuous sequential log of certain important events. These events include startup and shutdown, log switches and archives, any changes to the physical structure of the database, any changes to instance parameters, and some critical errors. The alert log is a record of major problems and operations and should be kept for audit purposes, but it will become unwieldy as it increases in size. On a regular basis (perhaps weekly) it should be backed up and deleted. The Oracle instance will create a new file as soon as it needs to write out another message.

Trace files are usually generated because a background process detects an error. Depending on the seriousness of the error, the instance may terminate. For example, if any process detects a problem with the controlfile it will write out a trace file describing the problem, and the instance will abort immediately. Conversely, if the log writer detects a problem with one copy of a multiplexed online redo log file it will write a trace file describing the problem, but as this is not considered critical, the instance will continue to run. Trace files should be used to diagnose problems, and the database administrator should take appropriate action.

Space Management

An Oracle database stores data logically in segments, and physically in data files. Segments are visible to users; data files are visible to the system administrators. Only the DBA can see both sides. There are several possible types of segments, such as the *table* segments that hold rows of structured data, and *large object* segments that can hold unstructured data such as word processing documents. The abstraction of the logical structures from the physical structures is accomplished through an entity known as a *tablespace*. One tablespace can contain many segments and be composed of many data files. One segment can be cut across many data files, and one data file can contain parts of many segments. There is no direct relationship between any one segment and any one data file. The other significant storage needs are for the redo data used to guarantee recovery of the database in the event of any failure.

Regular space management tasks include the following:

- Estimating anticipated space needs and sizing segments and data files accordingly.
- Monitoring disk usage and performance and locating data files appropriately.
- Checking segments for wasted space and reorganizing segments when necessary.

The initial installation of Oracle Collaboration Suite includes a database (or more than one, depending on the topology chosen) that is minimally sized. Detail will vary depending on release and platform, but it will have about 70 tablespaces, each consisting of just one file, with 6GB to 7GB of total disk space occupied. Within the tablespaces there will be 2 or 3 gigabytes of space not yet allocated to segments (of which there are more than 12,000).

All the segments will expand as necessary and the data files are defined such that when they fill they will extend automatically. There are no upper limits other than the available disk capacity. However, if it is known that the segments in a tablespace will require a certain amount of space, it is good practice to allocate this space in advance, either by manually increasing the size of a data file or by adding additional data files to the tablespace, rather than relying on automatic extension. The component documentation includes sizing guidelines that will help with estimating how much space may be required in each tablespace depending on anticipated usage.

Space within tablespaces can be preallocated to segments. However, this is generally considered to be very time-consuming work with minimal benefit, and is rarely worth the effort unless certain large-scale operations are planned. It may be worthwhile doing this, for example, before initiating a data load exercise involving uploading many gigabytes of data.

Disk activity needs to be monitored in terms of how full the file systems are, how evenly activity is balanced across the file systems, and how well each file system is performing. Data files should be relocated (a straightforward exercise, though it does require downtime) to optimize the disk usage.

Manipulating data can result in a need to reorganize segments. Typical problems involve waste of space within table segments and a deterioration of the efficiency of index segments. Segments that would benefit from reorganization need to be identified and appropriate action taken.

Space management can be a major part of a database administrator's workload and requires constant attention.

Managing the Redo Log

The redo log is a record of all change vectors applied to the database. A properly configured redo log is a guarantee that no data will ever be lost. Furthermore, the configuration of the redo log is a critical factor for performance and must be monitored closely.

The default installation creates a database with a redo log in need of the following major adjustments:

- The database is, by default, operating in NOARCHIVELOG mode. This means that any damage to data files will result in data loss. The database should be transitioned to ARCHIVELOG mode before the system comes into use.
- The redo log consists of only three log file groups. Most installations will require more groups than this.
- The log file groups are only 10MB each. This is too small (by one or two orders of magnitude) for any production system. The rate of redo generation must be monitored and the groups replaced with groups of appropriate size.
- The log file groups consist of two members but they are on the same file system. Members should be distributed across different file systems to give some fault tolerance.

A related topic is the location of the controlfile. This is multiplexed but (like the log file members) both copies are on the same file system. They should be separated to different file systems for safety.

Use of the Advisors

The 10*g* release of the Oracle database ships with a number of advisors for diagnostic and tuning work. They can be accessed through APIs or through the Enterprise Manager graphical user interface. Use of the advisors does have licensing implications, and all sites must confirm that their licensing is adequate before launching them.

Generally speaking, the advisors do not do anything that a good database administrator cannot do using his own knowledge. They run queries against various historical and current statistics, present the results in an easily comprehensible form, compare the results to expected values, and apply an expert system to attempt a root cause analysis of any deviations. The term *root cause* is important. It is easy to fall into the trap of treating symptoms rather than causes. A basic example of this would be if the analysis shows that disk I/O is a bottleneck in performance. To treat the symptom, one could optimize the disk configuration and perhaps even invest in faster hardware; but this will be merely making an inefficient system run more quickly. An alternative approach would be to ask why there is a need for so much disk I/O. Perhaps adjusting memory settings, so that the data needed is in memory already and therefore doesn't have to be read from disk, would be a better solution. The advisors attempt a root cause analysis for many common problems and can save the database administrator a great deal of work by directing him toward probable solutions, but they do not replace manual instance database tuning. They do make life a great deal easier though, and in many cases they do all that is needed. There are seven advisors:

- Automatic Database Diagnostic Monitor (ADDM)
- SQL Tuning Advisor

- SQL Access Advisor
- Memory Advisor
- Mean Time to Recover (MTTR) Advisor
- Segment Advisor
- Undo Advisor

The ADDM runs automatically by default every hour. It picks up unusual events, makes basic recommendations, and may also suggest running other advisors (which must be invoked manually). The ADDM reports are the first source of information whenever it is believed that there may be any issues with the way the database or the instance are performing, and they should in any case be reviewed regularly.

The SQL Tuning Advisor can investigate high-load SQL statements, the statements that are causing performance issues by, for example, generating excessive disk I/O. Its recommendations can include rewriting the statements or generating additional statistics that will help Oracle develop more efficient execution plans. The SQL Access Advisor can suggest how to improve the running of statements by changing the indexing strategy within the application. These two advisors would not normally be run against an Oracle Collaboration Suite database without discussing the results with Oracle Support Services.

The Memory Advisor should be run against all instances. It will advise on how much memory should be assigned to various memory structures, both the shared memory that makes up the instance, and the memory that is private to each session. An important point is that while memory allocations should (ideally) be at least what the advisor recommends, do not assign more; in some cases, too much memory can be as bad as too little. When allocating memory, the database administrator must work with the system administrator to ensure that the system will not begin to swap; there is little point in giving Oracle more virtual memory than there is physical memory available. This advisor should be run periodically to ensure that changing workloads do not necessitate changes in memory allocations.

The MTTR Advisor will specify certain settings dependent on how much downtime can be tolerated in the event of a failure. This must be monitored in conjunction with relevant service level agreements. The MTTR Advisor will also determine the minimum necessary size for the online redo log file groups; if they are too small for the workload, performance will deteriorate. This advisor should be run periodically to ensure that changing workloads do not necessitate changes in redo configuration.

The Segment Advisor will monitor index and table segments and determine whether they are adequately sized (using historical data to determine growth trends) and whether they would benefit from reorganization. This advisor should be run periodically against all segments; this would be a massive task to initiate manually, but the graphical interface lets the administrator nominate a tablespace, and the report will then cover all objects in that one tablespace highlighting only the ones that need attention.

The Undo Advisor will monitor the rate at which undo data is being generated and compare this with the need for undo data for consistent reads and the available space for storing undo data. This advisor too should be run periodically to ensure that changing workloads do not necessitate changes in undo data configuration.

The Alert System

Release 10*g* of the Oracle database is sometimes described as the *self-monitoring* database. This is because of the Alert system. The Alert system is implemented by a background process that monitors the instance and the database, continually comparing its current state with configured threshold values. Once a threshold is passed, it will report on this. It will also report on certain events. The Alert system can be used through an API or through the Enterprise Manager graphical interface.

The Alert system is preconfigured with thresholds for space usage and for some events. This preconfiguration means that whenever a tablespace becomes 85% full a warning will be issued, and when it reaches 97% full a critical warning will be issued. Events such as transactions failing because of a shortage of undo space will also be reported.

To view the alerts raised, the default configuration requires querying data dictionary views or using Enterprise Manager. However, the Alert system can be configured by the database administrator to generate e-mail or SMS messages when an alert is raised.

As well as the preconfigured alerts, the database administrator can configure thresholds for many other conditions. These include the following:

- CPU usage
- Disk I/O volumes and speed
- Transaction throughput
- Record locking
- Memory access hit rates

By configuring thresholds appropriate to the installation, the database administrator can be made aware of potential problems before they become critical and thus become proactive in his tuning and maintenance work.

The Scheduler

The Oracle database includes two facilities for automating jobs. These are the DBMS_JOB package and the Scheduler. The former has been available for many years; the latter is a new 10*g* feature. DBMS_JOB lets users submit PL/SQL or Java procedure calls to be executed at a certain time, and then repeated at regular intervals subsequently. The Scheduler is much more sophisticated. It can assign priorities to jobs; the jobs can accept runtime parameters; jobs can be configured to retry if they fail, or to abort if they do not complete in a time limit; and perhaps most importantly, the jobs can be operating system commands and shell scripts as well as PL/SQL or Java procedures.

The older DBMS_JOB facility is used extensively by the Oracle Collaboration Suite application components. This is for historical reasons: the components were developed before the Scheduler existed. Examples of this usage are the jobs that update the indexes used by Search. There are only two preconfigured Scheduler jobs: the GATHER_STATS_JOB that will analyze the database in order to give the SQL optimizer the information it needs to run code efficiently, and the PURGE_LOG job that clears out the Scheduler's own logging records.

The database administrator should consider using the Scheduler to automate many day-to-day tasks that would otherwise involve manual intervention or use of complex operating system scheduling and scripting. Suitable work for launching through the Scheduler includes backups, data validation routines, index rebuilding, advisor tasks, and data archiving, and running activity, space usage, and audit reports.

Apache Management Tasks

An Oracle Collaboration Suite instance exists in an Oracle Application Server farm of at least two instances; there will be an infrastructure instance providing support services to applications deployed to one or more middle tier instances. Every Oracle Application Server instance will have an Apache web listener, acting as the HTTP entry point to the application components hosted by the instance. Performance and availability of this web listener is critical to the performance and availability of the whole instance as perceived by end users. There is little point in tuning the application components if the bottleneck in the request flow is the rate at which Apache can receive URLs from end users and transmit responses back to them.

Standard Apache Logging

The default installation of Oracle Collaboration Suite will install Apache configured with standard Apache logging, as opposed to the Oracle Diagnostic Logging. Logging, as with all other aspects of Apache, is controlled with directives in the file

```
$ORACLE_HOME/Apache/Apache/conf/httpd.conf file
```

The directives are `LogLevel` which determines the severity of the condition that must be raised before a log record is written to the error log, and the directives that control the names and locations of the log files. The `LogLevel` options in descending order are the following:

- `emerg`: Conditions that make the listener unusable
- `alert`: Action to be taken immediately
- `crit`: Critical failures
- `error`: Error conditions
- `warn`: Warnings
- `notice`: Normal but significant events
- `info`: Informative messages on activity
- `debug`: Detail of all activity

Setting the directive to a certain level will cause all messages of that level and higher to be reported. The Apache organization recommends `crit` or higher; the default Oracle Collaboration Suite level is `warn`. There are two log files related to user access to the Apache web listener: the transfer log and the error log. The transfer log records every URL received by the listener; the error log records events that do not complete successfully. Always bear in mind that what may appear to an end user as an error may not be an error as far as Apache is concerned. For instance, if a user requests a file that does not exist, Apache will simply return a page to that effect. Apache has no problem with this—it is a successful execution of the request-response cycle—but the user may interpret this as an error. This request-response would appear in the transfer log, not the error log.

The location of the transfer log is determined by the directive `CustomLog`. This can be a hard-coded filename, or it can nominate a program to which to send the logging data. The Oracle default is to send the logging data to the `rotatelogs` program with parameters that will cause it to write records to one file for 12 hours before switching to another file. The files will be named

```
$ORACLE_HOME/Apache/Apache/logs/access_log.<nnnnnnnnnn>
```

where *<nnnnnnnnnn>* is a ten-digit number specifying the number of seconds since the first of January 1970. After 12 hours, the `rotatelogs` program will start writing to a new file with an incremented ten-digit suffix.

A typical transfer log entry is the following:

```
10.10.10.65 - - [27/May/2006:17:44:03 +0200] ➥
"GET /welcome/images/icon16-bullet-right.gif HTTP/1.1" 200 257
```

This shows that a process on a machine with the IP address 10.10.10.65 sent a URL on the 27th of May to the Apache web listener requesting a file called `icon16-bullet-right.gif`. Note that the IP address in the log may not be the address of the actual end user. In this case, it is the IP address of the node where the Web Cache is running, because as far as Apache is concerned that is where the URL came from.

The status code 200 followed by 257 indicates that the file was returned successfully and that it was 257 bytes long. This is in fact one of the GIF files included on the welcome page when users contact Oracle Collaboration Suite. When resolving problems experienced by end users, analyzing the contents of the transfer log to see what URLs they issued and what the status codes were is often a useful starting point. Status codes are three-digit numbers—the codes are grouped into categories determined by the first of the three digits. The groups are shown in Table 16-1.

Table 16-1. *HTTP Status Codes*

Code Range	Category	Example
100–199	Informative messages	101: switching protocol
200–299	Success codes	200: request completed
300–399	Redirection instructions	301: moved permanently
400–499	Client errors	401: authentication required
500–599	Server errors	503: service unavailable

The error log is defined by the directive `ErrorLog`. This is set up in the same manner as the transfer log. The error log files are named `error_log.<nnnnnnnnnn>` with a 12-hour rotation. An example of an error log entry is the following:

```
[Thu May 25 17:21:09 2006] [warn] [client 10.10.10.65] [ecid: 80919500087,1] ➥
MOD_OC4J_0184: Failed to find an oc4j process for destination: OC4J_OCSADMIN
```

This entry indicates that Apache received a URL that it attempted to pass to the OC4J_OCSADMIN component (which is the component that implements the Search application) through the modoc4j module, and that this component was not running. The message is at the "warn" level because, as far as Apache is concerned, nothing is wrong. Of course, the end users will receive errors until the component is started.

Oracle Diagnostic Logging (ODL)

Oracle Application Server provides an alternative to Apache standard logging, which is Oracle Diagnostic Logging (ODL). ODL is not enabled by the Oracle Collaboration Suite installer, but can be enabled subsequently.

ODL creates log records in an XML format that is compatible with the logging format that should be used by all other current Oracle products. To enable ODL, set three directives in the `httpd.conf` file:

- `OraLogMode`: Enables ODL when set to `oracle`
- `OraLogSeverity [module] <msg_type>[:level]`: Determines what to log
- `OraLogDir`: Indicates the directory to which to save the XML files

The directives should be placed in the `httpd.conf` file above the `LoadModule` directives that load the dynamic link libraries that implement Apache modules in order that any module-specific ODL logging will be established before the module is loaded. The syntax of the `OraLogSeverity` directive, which can occur many times in the `httpd.conf` file, lets the administrator specify different settings for different Apache modules. If it is omitted, the setting will apply to all modules that do not have their own settings. The *<msg_type>* argument can be set to one of the following:

- `INTERNAL_ERROR`
- `ERROR`
- `WARNING`
- `NOTIFICATION`
- `TRACE`

which correlate to the Apache standard logging `LogLevel` settings. The optional *<level>* argument can be used as a finer filter if the module assigns error level numbers to its messages.

As an example, these directives

```
OraLogMode oracle
OraLogSeverity WARNING
OraLogSeverity mod_fastcgi.c NOTIFICATION:4
OraLogDir logs/oracle
```

will enable the ODL mechanism with `WARNING` level logging for all modules except the FastCGI module, for which logging will be at the higher level of `NOTIFICATION` level 4. The XML files generated will be written to the nominated directory relative to the Apache root directory.

The XML log files are uploaded to a central repository within Oracle Application Server by the LogLoader process that runs periodically, and can then be viewed through Oracle Application Server Control, along with the log files from all other ODL-enabled products.

Runtime Configuration Issues

End users contact Oracle Collaboration Suite through a Web Cache, which forwards all requests through to the Apache web listener. The Web Cache is a specialized web listener that can handle thousands of concurrent connections; Apache cannot scale to the same level. The number of concurrent requests one Apache listener can manage, and how it manages them, is determined by a set of directives in the `httpd.conf` file. If the demands of end users exceeds Apache's capacity to deliver, performance may degrade and users will receive "500" messages indicating a server error. These will show in the error log with an indication of the problem.

The critical directives, with the default values following an Oracle Collaboration Suite installation on Linux, are the following:

```
KeepAlive on
MaxKeepAliveRequests 100
KeepAliveTimeout 15
MinSpareServers 5
MaxSpareServers 20
StartServers 5
MaxClients 150
```

Apache must spawn a child process (or on Windows launch a child thread) for each concurrent request. It will attempt to keep a number of *spare* processes ready to service new requests. When there are fewer spare processes than `MinSpareServers` it will spawn more; when there are more spares than `MaxSpareServers` some will be killed. The launching and termination of processes can place a strain on the operating system, and ideally the `StartServers` directive will be set to a value that is adequate for the workload. If Apache finds it necessary to spawn more than four child processes a second, a message to this effect will be written to the error log.

The `KeepAlive` directives let Apache take advantage of the HTTP1.1 feature that enables persistent connections between browsers and the listener. If this were set to OFF, each request-response cycle would require instantiating a new level 4 connection between browser and listener. Setting it to ON will certainly improve performance as perceived by end users but means that a child process will be dedicated for a significant period of time (by default at least 15 seconds or 100 requests) to each client. This means that more child processes will be required. Reducing the `KeepAliveTimeout` may let Apache support more users with fewer child processes.

The `MaxClients` directive sets an absolute limit on the number of child processes that will be launched and therefore the number of concurrent requests that can be serviced. It is intended to prevent Apache from crashing the operating system by launching more processes than it can handle effectively. Requests exceeding the setting will be queued until a child process becomes available, up to the value of `ListenBacklog` (which is not set and defaults to 511). Clearly, queuing is not good and implies that there are insufficient child processes or that the `KeepAlive` settings are allowing them to be occupied for too long.

The Server Status Module

A useful tool for monitoring Apache is the module modstatus. This will be accessible through a URL such as the following specifying a virtual path of `server-status`:

```
http://bplcone.bplc.co.za:7777/server-status
```

The output for a healthy web listener is shown in Figure 16-1.

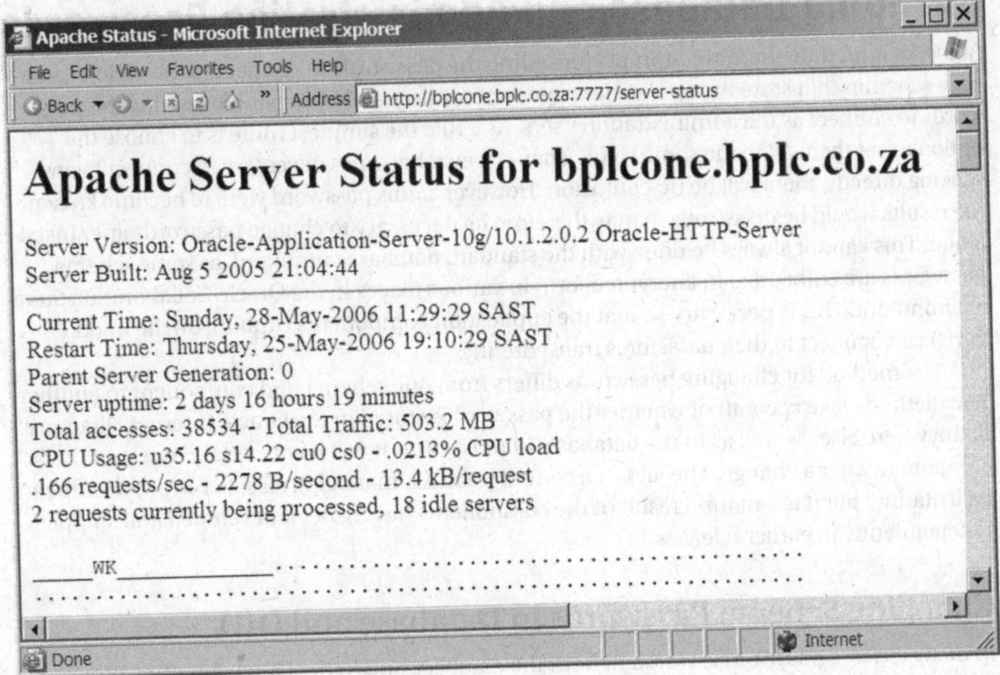

Figure 16-1. *The output of the Server Status module showing a web listener that is feeling no pain*

The Server Status module does give out information that could be of value to malicious users such as those trying to identify security weaknesses or planning denial-of-service attacks and may therefore need some adjustment if it is not to be a security risk. The default configuration is this section in the `httpd.conf` file:

```
<Location /server-status>
    SetHandler server-status
    Order deny,allow
    Deny from all
    Allow from localhost bplcone.bplc.co.za bplcone
</Location>
```

This limits access to URLs originating from the host node (in this case bplcone) which sounds OK but since the Web Cache may well be running on the host node, this does not in fact restrict anyone. This is what has happened in Figure 16-1. The URL has hit the Web Cache on port 7777 and then been routed through to Apache on the same machine, thus bypassing the attempt to restrict access to local users. Adjusting the `Allow` directive to nominate a named list of nodes that does *not* include the local host will prevent this.

Changing Database and Administration Passwords

At installation time there are prompts for setting the passwords to connect to the various database schemas that store the application components data and code, and for setting the passwords to connect as the administration users. As a rule the simplest route is to choose the option to set them all to the same value. Then if it ever becomes necessary to connect to any schema directly, there will be no confusion. However, if this password were to become known, the results would be disastrous. It may therefore be necessary to change passwords after installation. This cannot always be done with the standard database command, as some schema passwords are embedded in encrypted form in various places in the Oracle Collaboration Suite environment. This is necessary so that the application components running on the middle tier(s) can connect to their datastores transparently.

The method for changing passwords differs from one schema and component to another. The methods take account of whether the password is stored in the Oracle Internet Directory or anywhere else, as well as in the database. In most cases it will be necessary to restart the component after a change. The lack of a central point for managing all schema passwords can be irritating, but it is a natural result of the components having been developed and shipped independently in earlier releases.

Changing Schema Passwords in Database and OID

In many cases, a password is stored in both the database and in the Oracle Internet Directory. For some components, Application Server Control provides an interface that will prompt the user for a new password and will then update both locations; but in some cases it will be necessary to set passwords in each environment using the tools SQL*Plus for database passwords, and `oidadmin` for Oracle Internet Directory passwords.

To change a schema password within the database, connect to the instance with SQL*Plus and use the `alter user` command, as in the following example which connects as user SYSTEM and changes the password for the user OWF_MGR to `Oracle`:

```
[oraocs@bplcone oraocs]$ sqlplus system/oracle1@orcl
SQL*Plus: Release 10.1.0.4.2 - Production on Sun May 28 12:54:06 2006
Copyright (c) 1982, 2005, Oracle.  All rights reserved.

Connected to:
Oracle Database 10g Enterprise Edition Release 10.1.0.4.2 - Production
With the Partitioning, OLAP and Data Mining options

SQL> alter user owf_mgr identified by Oracle;
User altered.
SQL>
```

To change the schema password as stored within the Oracle Internet Directory, connect to the directory as the ORACLADMIN user with the `oidadmin` tool (as described in Chapter 6), and in the Entry Management branch navigate to the entry with this distinguished name:

```
orclReferenceName=ocsdb.bplc.co.za,
cn=IAS Infrastructure Databases,
cn=IAS,
cn=Products,
cn=OracleContext
```

Expand the `orclReferenceName` entry and you will find a list of all the Oracle Collaboration Suite database schemas. Select the one to be changed, and adjust the `orclpasswordattribute` attribute. Figure 16-2 shows this being done for the schema OWF_MGR, which is associated with Workflow.

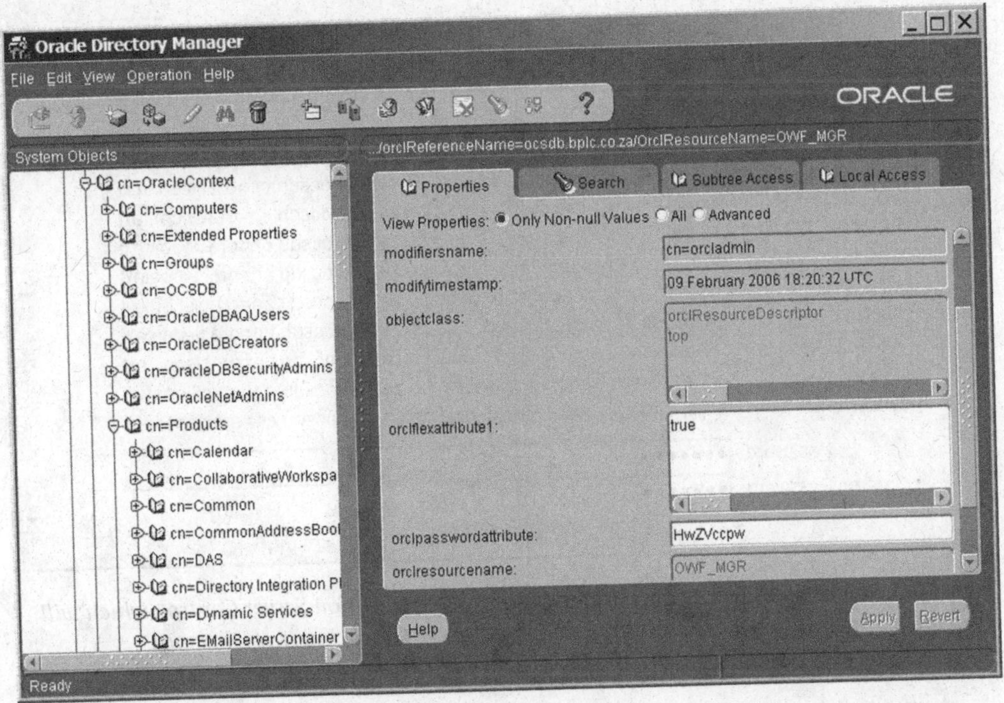

Figure 16-2. *Setting a database schema password in the Oracle Internet Directory with oidadmin*

In Figure 16-2, the schema password being changed is for OWF_MGR, identified by the `orclresourcename` attribute. The current database password is seen to be HwZVccpw. When using SQL*Plus, there is no way to determine the current password.

Passwords within a database are not case sensitive, though within the Oracle Internet Directory they are. Furthermore, there may be some characters that are legal within one environment but not the other. As a general rule, it is sensible to stick to a range of standard characters such as uppercase letters without accents, digits, and the common punctuation marks.

Some application schemas can have their passwords set in both the database and the Oracle Internet Directory through Application Server Control. Connect to the Application Server Control for the middle tier instance, and from the home page click the Infrastructure tab, then the Change Schema Password link. This will bring up the window shown in Figure 16-3, where several schema passwords can be set.

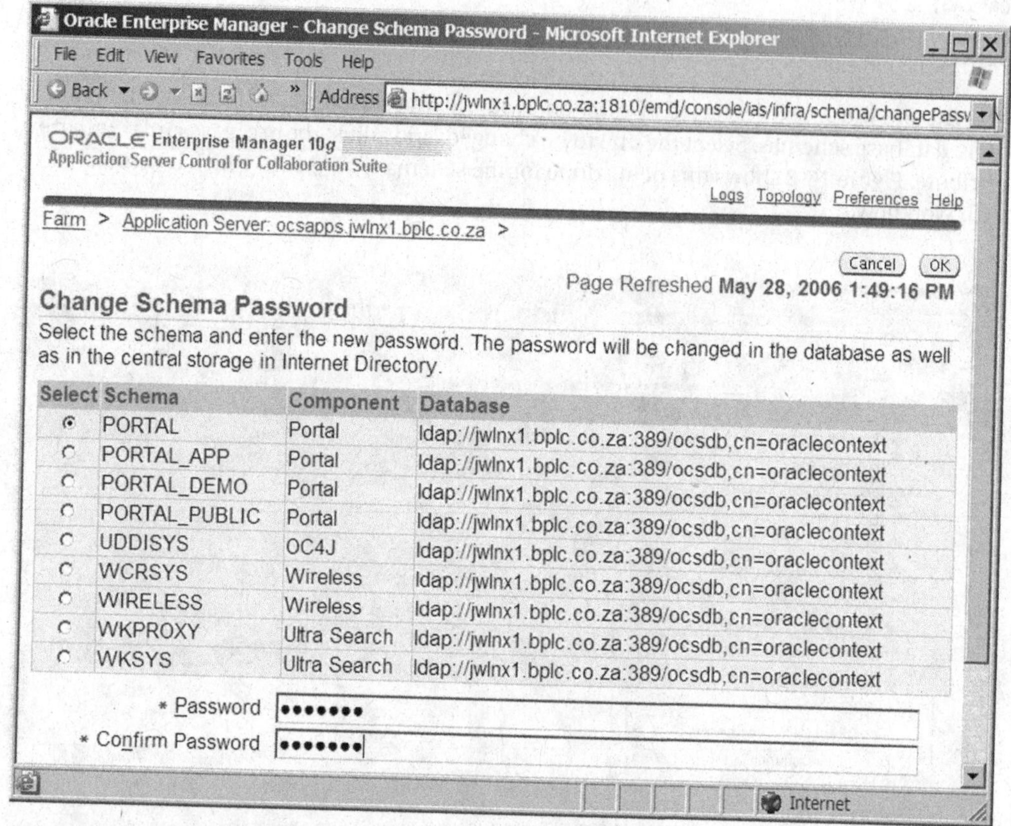

Figure 16-3. *Some schema passwords should be set with Application Server Control, which will keep them synchronized with the passwords stored in the Oracle Internet Directory.*

Taking the same navigation path through Application Server Control for the infrastructure instance will let you change the Single Sign-On schemas' passwords.

The following are the schemas whose passwords can be changed with the techniques described previously:

B2B, DCM, and OWF_MGR schemas: Use SQL*Plus to change the password in the database, and `oidadmin` to change the password stored in the Oracle Internet Directory as shown in Figure 16-2.

The PORTAL_* schemas, UDDISYS, WCRSYS, WIRELESS, WKPROXY, and WKSYS: Use Application Server Control on the middle tier instance.

The ORASSO_* schemas: Use Application Server Control on the infrastructure instance.

SYS, and SYSTEM schemas: Use SQL*Plus only. These passwords are not stored elsewhere.

Other schemas have product-specific techniques.

Changing Application Component Schema Passwords

Some components have component-specific methods for changing database passwords. The following list shows these components and the routines that must be followed or the results will be disastrous:

Oracle Internet Directory: Use the `oidpasswd` command-line utility, specifying the connection identifier for the database. You will then be prompted for the current and the new passwords, as in the following example:

```
oidpasswd connect=ocs_db change_oiddb_pwd=true
```

Note that this is not changing the password for the Oracle Internet Directory `orcladmin` superuser, only the password for the ODM schema.

Calendar: Change the password for the CALENDAR schema within the database with SQL*Plus, then use the `unioidconf` command-line utility specifying the global name of the database as an argument as in the following example:

```
unioidconf -setschemapassword orcl.bplc.co.za -D cn=orcladmin
```

You will be prompted for the `orcladmin` password and then the new password for the CALENDAR schema.

Content Services: In Application Server Control, navigate to the Content Services home page and click the Change Schema Password link in the Administration section. You will have to provide the current SYS password, as well as the new password for the Content Services schemas.

Mail: First, use SQL*Plus to change the password for user ES_MAIL. Second, use `oidadmin` to change the attribute `orclpasswordattribute` for the entry

```
cn=<global_name>,
cn=MailStores,
cn=um_system,
cn=EMailServerContainer,
cn=Products,
cn=OracleContext
```

where *<global_name>* is the global name of the database, such as `orcl.bplc.co.za`. Third, set your CLASSPATH environment variable as follows:

```
CLASSPATH=$ORACLE_HOME/jlib/esinstall.jar:$ORACLE_HOME/jlib/esldap.jar: ➥
$ORACLE_HOME/lib/mail.jar:$ORACLE_HOME/jlib/esadmin.jar: ➥
$ORACLE_HOME/jlib/escommon.jar:$ORACLE_HOME/jlib/repository.jar: ➥
$ORACLE_HOME/jlib/emConfigInstall.jar
```

Last, recompile the relevant Java classes:

```
$ORACLE_HOME/jdk/jre/bin/java oracle.mail.install.EMConfig $ORACLE_HOME
```

Real-Time Collaboration: Use SQL*Plus to change the password for the schema RTC within the database, then use the command-line utility `rtcctl` to change the password stored on the middle tier:

```
rtcctl updatedatabaseinfo -dbpassword=<new_password>
```

The IAS_ADMIN Application Server Control User

All Oracle Application Server instances can be managed with Application Server Control using a preconfigured user called IAS_ADMIN. The password is set at installation. To change this later, use the `emctl` utility:

```
emctl set password <old ias_admin password> <new ias_admin password>
```

The Oracle Internet Directory Superuser

The user ORCLADMIN is preconfigured as the Oracle Internet Directory superuser. The password is set at install time. To change it later, connect to the directory as ORCLADMIN with the `oidadmin` utility and navigate to the System Passwords tab and make the change, as shown in Figure 16-4.

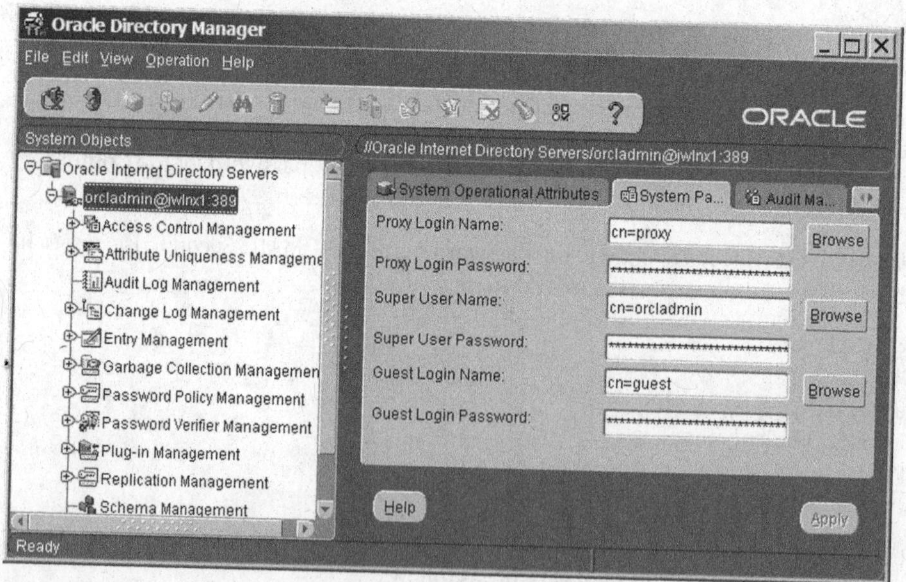

Figure 16-4. *How to change the password for the Oracle Internet Directory superuser with the oidadmin utility*

Changing Ports After Installation

The Oracle Collaboration Suite installation will have assigned a number of ports, selected with defaults based on the content of the `static_ports.ini` file, which can be found on the installation DVD. Following installation, the ports selected are listed in the following file:

```
$ORACLE_HOME/install/portlist.ini
```

One port that cannot be changed at install time is the database listener port. This must be 1521. If any service is already running on that port, it should be stopped while the installation is in progress. All ports, including the database listener port, can be changed later, though there are different techniques depending on the component. In most circumstances, it will be necessary to restart the component after a port change. In some cases (such as changing the database listener port) it will be necessary to restart the whole environment.

In an ideal world it would never be necessary to change ports, but sometimes it is. In some cases communication between OC4J components in different Oracle Application Server instances or between OC4J components and the Apache web listener will have to pass through firewalls that may impose restrictions on which ports are open to various protocols, or there may be other applications running on the machine that have less flexibility in port assignment.

In general, changing ports can be awkward and is best avoided if possible. It is more than likely that no adjustments will ever need to be made. The following sections describe how to change the ports for services that may sometimes need adjustment.

The Application Server Control Port

The default port will be (typically) 1156 or 1810, depending on whether the instance is middle tier or infrastructure. If there are multiple instances on one machine, this default port will be incremented for each instance. To change the port used by any one instance, from an operating system prompt, set the ORACLE_HOME environment variable to point to the instance and use the `emctl` utility:

```
emctl config iasconsole port <new_port_number>
```

OC4J Port Numbers

Every OC4J component (and there will be a number of OC4J components in every Oracle Application Server instance) needs several ports for accepting traffic with the various protocols used to connect to Java applications. These protocols are the following:

- AJP, for communications with modoc4j
- JMS, for messaging between Java applications
- RMI, to invoke methods on JavaBeans
- IIOP, for CORBA messaging

By default there are no fixed values for these ports but rather a range, which will be the same for every OC4J component in the instance. When the component starts, it will pick a free port dynamically from the range. The OPMN process keeps track of which ports have been assigned in its routing table. To adjust the port ranges, use Application Server Control to connect to the instance's home page and click the Ports tab. The display will show the fixed ports for the Calendar Application System, DCM (Distributed Configuration Management), and the Mail listeners (these can be changed by other means) followed by the port ranges for the protocols for each OC4J component in the previous list. If for any reason the ranges are not acceptable, adjustments can be made. When a component is started, this window will show which port from the range has been dynamically assigned for each protocol.

The Apache Listening Port

The Apache web listener will monitor, or listen on, whatever port is nominated by the `Listen` directive in the `httpd.conf` file, or if the directive occurs several times it will listen on all the nominated ports. It is not advisable to change this directive directly, because there are many dependencies between the specification of the port and other components. For instance, the Web Cache configuration must be updated following an Apache listening port change or it will not be able to forward URLs correctly. There will also be issues with redirections for Single Sign-On.

To ease the process of Apache port changes, Oracle has provided a utility that will update all the necessary configuration files in all components: the `portconfig` command. This command does not exist as an executable file but must be created as a macro routine. This is done on UNIX or Linux with the `alias` command, or the `doskey` command on Windows.

To create the `portconfig` macro, on UNIX enter this command from an operating system prompt:

```
alias portconfig '$ORACLE_HOME/jdk/bin/java ➥
-cp $ORACLE_HOME/sysman/webapps/emd/WEB-INF/lib/emd.jar: ➥
$ORACLE_HOME/dcm/lib/dcm.jar: ➥
$ORACLE_HOME/sso/lib/ossoreg.jar ➥
oracle.sysman.ias.sta.tools.PortConfigCmdLine \!*'
```

The equivalent command to create the macro on Windows is the following

```
doskey portconfig=%ORACLE_HOME%\jdk\bin\java
-cp  %ORACLE_HOME%/sysman/webapps/emd/WEB-INF/lib/emd.jar; ➥
%ORACLE_HOME%/dcm/lib/dcm.jar; %ORACLE_HOME%/sso/lib/ossoreg.jar ➥
oracle.sysman.ias.sta.tools.PortConfigCmdLine $*
```

In both cases, the entire string should be entered as one line.

Having created the macro, change listening ports with this syntax:

```
portconfig -oracleHome <oracle_home> -oldPort <old_port> -newPort <new_port> -sso ➥
-url http://<host.domain>:<new_port> -user <apache_user> -webCache
```

The arguments are the following:

- `oracleHome` specifies the instance that is to be adjusted.
- `oldPort` is the existing listening port that is to be changed.

- `newPort` is the new listening port.
- `sso` indicates that the port is protected by Single Sign-On.
- `url` specifies the URL to be used to contact the new port.
- `user` is the operating system account that launches Apache.
- `webCache` indicates that the port can be an origin server for the Web Cache.

Running `portconfig` is not enough; it is also necessary to update entries in the service registry stored in the Oracle Internet Directory with the new port number. The service registry stores all the URLs used internally to connect to the application components, and these will all need to be adjusted. Figure 16-5 shows the navigation path in `oidadmin` to the part of the service registry where the URLs relevant to the Calendar Application System are stored.

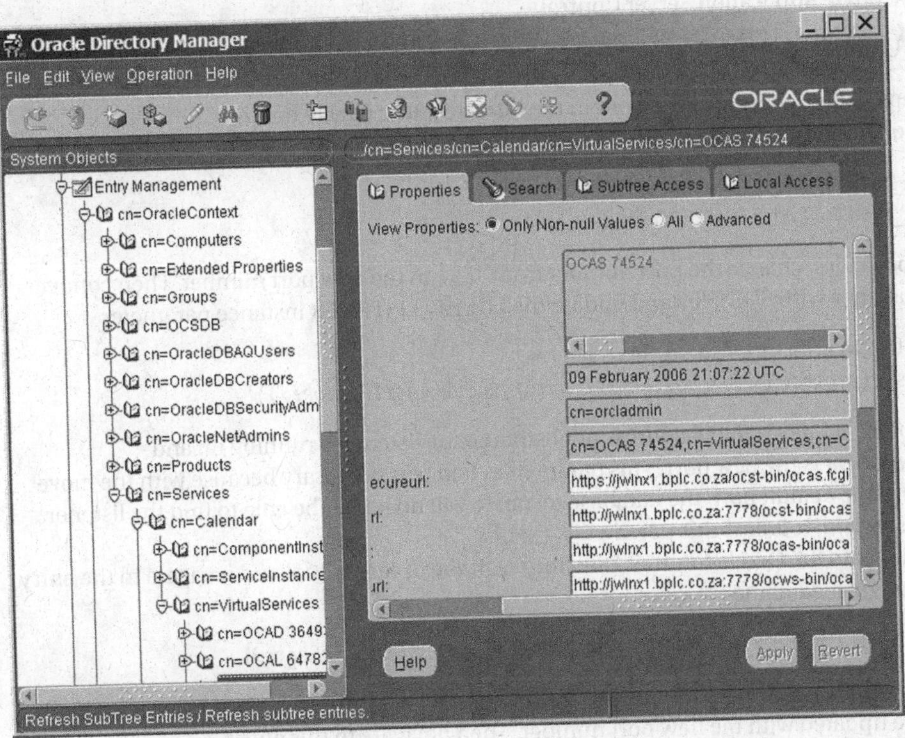

Figure 16-5. *The Calendar application system URLs, as stored in the Oracle Internet Directory*

All applications in `cn=OracleContext,cn=Services` should be inspected and adjustments to the port number made.

The Database Listener Port

The database listener port cannot be specified at installation time, so any process running on the default port of 1521 must be stopped before proceeding with the installation. After installation there may in fact be no need to change the port if the conflicting service is another Oracle database listener. One listener in one Oracle home can connect sessions to any number of database instances in any other Oracle home, provided that certain rules for version compatibility are followed. It may therefore be possible to resolve the conflict by adjusting the listener installed with Oracle Collaboration Suite to handle connections to the other databases as well as connections to the Oracle Collaboration Suite database.

If it really is necessary to change the database listener port, follow these steps:

1. Update the Oracle Net configuration.
2. Update the Oracle Internet Directory.
3. Update Single Sign-On.
4. Update the certificate authority.
5. Update Application Server Control.
6. Update the middle tier instances.

Steps 1 through 5 are carried out in the infrastructure Oracle home.

Two Oracle Net configuration files need to be edited:

```
$ORACLE_HOME/network/admin/listener.ora
$ORACLE_HOME/network/admin/tnsnames.ora
```

In both files, change the port number from 1521 to the new port number. Then connect to the instance with SQL*Plus and update the LOCAL_LISTENER instance parameter

```
SQL> alter system set  local_listener=➥
'(address=(protocol=tcp)(host=<host_name>)(port=<port_number>))'
```

where *<host_name>* is the IP address or hostname the listener is running on and *<port_number>* is the new port. This parameter change is necessary because with the move away from the default port, the database instance will no longer be able to find the listener and register with it unless this parameter is set.

Connect to the Oracle Internet Directory with the `oidadmin` tool and navigate to the entry with distinguished name

```
cn=ADDRESS_0,cn=DESCRIPTION_0,cn=<database_name>,cn=OracleContext
```

where *<database_name>* is the name of the database. The attribute `orclnetaddressstring` should be updated with the new port number. Then navigate to this entry

```
cn=OCSDB,cn=OracleContext
```

and make the same change.

Propagate the change to Single Sign-On by running this command:

```
$ORACLE_HOME/jdk/bin/java -jar $ORACLE_HOME/sso/lib/ossoca.jar ➥
reassoc -repos $ORACLE_HOME
```

Propagate the change to the certificate authority with this command:

```
$ORACLE_HOME/oca/bin/ocactl updateconnection
```

Update Application Server Control by editing this file:

```
$ORACLE_HOME/sysman/emd/targets.xml
```

Search for all occurrences of the old port number in the `ConnectDescriptor` value, and change them.

Switch to the middle tier Oracle home to configure the middle tier instances with the new port. First, edit the `tnsnames.ora` file exactly as in the infrastructure Oracle home. Second, edit the file that defines the database access descriptors used by the Apache PL/SQL gateway, and change any references to the port number. The file is the following:

```
$ORACLE_HOME/Apache/modplsql/conf/dads.conf
```

Third, update Application Server Control by editing the `targets.xml` file in the same way as already described.

Following all these changes, it will be necessary to restart the entire environment.

The Oracle Internet Directory Port

To change the port on which the Oracle Internet Directory listens, follow these steps:

1. Update the directory process to monitor the new port.
2. Update the LDAP configuration.
3. Update the Application Server configuration.
4. Propagate the change to Single Sign-On.
5. Propagate the change to the Certificate Authority.
6. Update the middle tier instance.

Using the `oidadmin` tool, navigate to the branch Server Management➤Directory Server➤Default Configuration Set and adjust the attribute Non SSL Port.

This LDAP configuration file needs to be edited to point to the new port:

```
$ORACLE_HOME/ldap/admin/ldap.ora
```

Edit the `OIDport` property in the Application Server properties in this file:

```
$ORACLE_HOME/config/ias.properties
```

Update Single Sign-On with this command:

```
$ORACLE_HOME/jdk/bin/java -jar $ORACLE_HOME/sso/lib/ossoca.jar ➥
reassoc -repos $ORACLE_HOME
```

Update the certificate authority with this command:

```
ocactl changesecurity -server_auth_port <new_port_number>
```

At this point the Oracle Internet Directory must be restarted. Then, to update the middle tier instance(s), connect to the middle tier's Application Server Control and click the Infrastructure tab. In the Identity Management section click the Change button, and follow the wizard to enter the new port number.

Application Component Log Files

Activity and error logs can be inspected by opening the log files with an editor, or through Application Server Control. The log files are distributed across various directories in the file system. In summary, the log files for each application reside in the directories shown in Table 16-2.

Table 16-2. *Component Log File Locations*

Component	Log File Location
Calendar	`$ORACLE_HOME/ocal/log` `$ORACLE_HOME/ocas/logs`

Content Services	`$ORACLE_HOME/content/log/<content_domain>`
	`$ORACLE_HOME/opmn/logs`
	`$ORACLE_HOME/j2ee/OC4J_Content/application-deployments/Content/OC4J_Content_default_island_1`

Mail	`$ORACLE_HOME//oes/log/um_system` `$ORACLE_HOME/opmn/logs`
Mobile Collaboration	`$ORACLE_HOME//wireless/pimap/logs` `$ORACLE_HOME//wireless/logs`
Real-Time Collaboration	`$ORACLE_HOME//imeeting/logs`
Voicemail and Fax	`%ORACLE_HOME%\um\log`

These log files can be inspected with an editor or through Application Server Control. On each component's home page there is a link, Logs, that will display the log files. There is also a centralized search facility that can search across all the log files. Reach it from the Logs link on the Application Server instance's home page.

Configuring or Removing Components After Installation

At the time of installing an Oracle Collaboration Suite middle tier instance, you will have selected which components to configure. This does not affect which components are installed: every installation will install all the components. If a component is not selected for configuration at install time, it can be configured later.

To reach the component configuration wizard, connect to the middle tier instance with Application Server Control. If any components were not configured at install time, there will be a button Configure Component. Clicking this button will launch the wizard. Figure 16-6 shows the wizard's first window, which prompts for selecting which component to configure.

In Figure 16-6, the component configuration wizard is being run on an instance that was installed specifically for running Voicemail and Fax. For this reason, all the other components are available for selection.

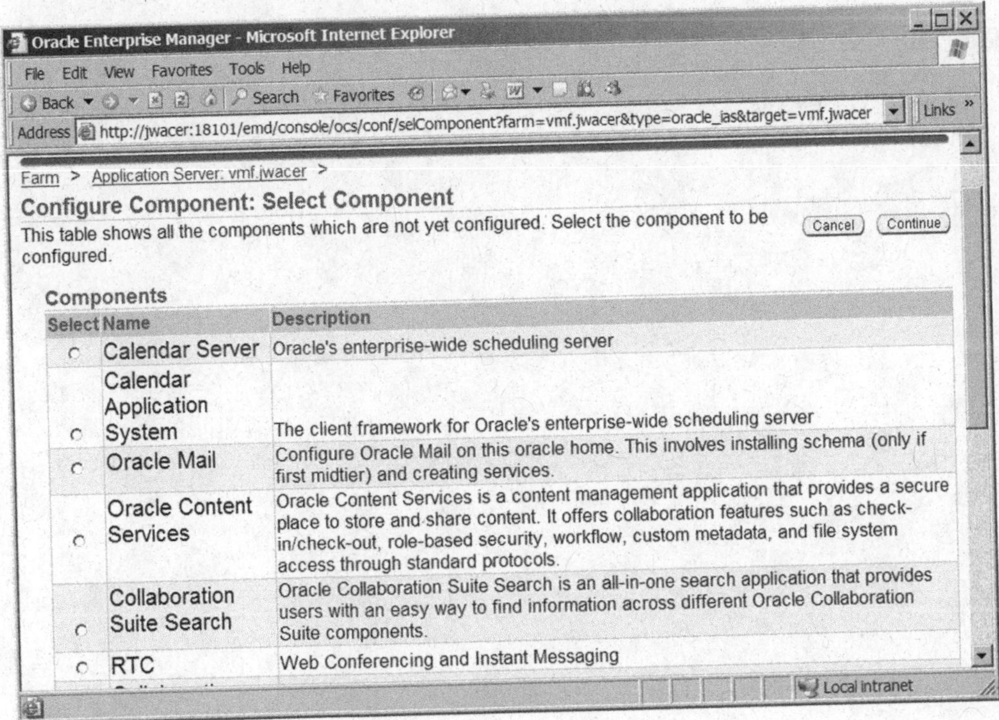

Figure 16-6. *The component configuration wizard*

It is not possible to make a selective installation: all components are installed. Similarly, it is not possible to make a selective deinstallation; the whole Oracle Collaboration Suite middle tier instance must be removed. Use the Oracle Universal Installer to uninstall an instance, but before doing this the instance should be deregistered from the Oracle Internet Directory. If the instance is uninstalled before being deregistered, it can never be deregistered subsequently. Having instances that no longer exist registered in the Oracle Internet Directory is not a technical problem, but it is irritating to see them displayed by Application Server Control, and makes it impossible to install a new instance with the same name. To deregister an instance, run this command:

```
<ORACLE_HOME>/perl/5.6.1/bin/perl <ORACLE_HOME>/bin/deconfig.pl
```

where *<ORACLE_HOME>* is the home directory of the middle tier instance. The script will prompt for the address and port of the Oracle Internet Directory, and the username and password of the directory superuser. Enter the username as cn=orcladmin. The `deconfig.pl` script will remove all references to the instance from the Oracle Internet Directory, the metadata repository, and Application Server Control. Following this, use the Oracle Universal Installer to uninstall the instance.

CHAPTER 17

Backup and Restore, Fault Tolerance, and High Availability

The various datastores and technology stack components that make up an Oracle Collaboration Suite installation must all be backed up on a regular basis. An appropriate regime of backup combined with appropriate configuration options should make it possible to approach the goals of zero data loss and 100% availability. But there is a price to be paid for achieving these goals—often a price that can be quantified financially, and always a price in workload for the administrator.

When designing an operating environment, there is often a play-off between performance on the one hand and data loss and uptime on the other. It is sometimes much easier to tune for maximum performance, if one does not have to worry about the consequences of anything going wrong. The scalability of the environment can also impact on its performance and safety aspects. All these points must be considered when designing the Oracle Collaboration Suite operating environment, preferably when the installation is first planned.

This chapter first investigates the requirement for data security and system availability, and then details the methods whereby they can be provided. Remember that this is not just about data security; for the administrator, this is job security as well. Apart from securing the environment against loss of data, it will also be necessary to protect it against failure. The various components can be protected such that end users should never be aware of any problems. In an ideal world, there would be no single point of failure. All aspects of the Oracle Collaboration Suite must be considered, starting with the database(s), then the infrastructure, the middle tier instance(s), and the Web Cache.

The Service Level Agreement

In the world of IT systems administration, there is no such thing as right or wrong—there is only whether the administration practices conform to what has been agreed upon with the users, and this agreement must be documented.

IT system failures may take several forms: typically, loss of data, breaches of confidentiality, downtime, and poor performance. The users state their tolerance for these and other factors, and the system administrators then plan accordingly. Their plans will come with a price tag, which may result in the users modifying their requirements. Eventually, a process of negotiation will result in an agreement that defines the standards of data security and availability to which the system should conform. It is vital to record these standards in a service level agreement that will define what the system administrators are required to deliver; how the conformance to these standards will be measured; and possibly penalty and reward clauses applicable to levels of conformance. If this is not fully documented and ratified by all concerned, any problems will result in conflict between the parties involved.

Service level agreements for Oracle Collaboration Suite installations are likely to be exceptionally complicated. This is because of the number of components involved in delivering the service to the end user, and it is further complicated because many of these components will be supported by different groups, possibly by different support organizations and by different companies.

To take a simple example, consider the case where an end user cannot access his e-mail account from his browser. In an Oracle Collaboration Suite environment, there could be any number of reasons for this:

- The Mail datastore Oracle instance could fail or reach certain critical limits. This is a problem to be fixed by the database administrator.
- The Mail datastore database could suffer loss of data files due to disk failures. This is a problem to be fixed by the system administrators, or perhaps the hardware support people.
- The network could fail between the browser, the Web Cache, the Apache web listener, the datastore database instance, or the Oracle Application Server infrastructure database instance. This would be a problem for the network support team.
- The Oracle Application Server infrastructure instance's Oracle Internet Directory or Single Sign-On server (which themselves comprise several components) could fail to respond. This could be the responsibility of another support group.

Human nature and financial realities are such that when something goes wrong, the injured party will want to blame a particular service provider, and no one service provider will want to take the responsibility for the problem. An Oracle Collaboration Suite installation needs a service level agreement that consists of a set of interlocking responsibilities with defined interfaces and dependencies between each support group. For example, there is little point in the database administrators guaranteeing 99.9% uptime for the datastore and metadata repository databases if the network administrators only provide support during daytime hours. Or if a database fails because of damage to an online redo log file, is that the fault of the database administrators for not adequately multiplexing the file within the database, or the fault of the system administrators for not protecting the file with a suitable level of RAID mirroring?

Consider a call center using Oracle Collaboration Suite to schedule callouts by engineers and deliver e-mail and SMS notifications. This is done with Mail and Calendar, using Wireless when necessary. A reasonably undemanding service level agreement might be to provide availability for all services between 07:00 and 19:00 Monday through Friday and 07:00 through 13:00 on Saturday, with only 30 minutes unscheduled downtime per month before the first level of penalty charges kicks in. The penalties could escalate after two hours unscheduled downtime. These figures equate to an availability of approximately 99.8% for the first penalty, and 99.25% for the second. Extending the hours to twenty 24 hours a day for each weekday changes the percentages to 99.9% and 99.6% respectively. Many installations will work to at least this standard. An Oracle Collaboration Suite installation will usually be essential to an organization's functioning and it will usually be required at all hours, particularly for organizations that cross time zones.

When you consider that just rebooting a large server and starting the services it runs can take half an hour, it becomes apparent that configuring all components for fault tolerance is essential. All the technology stack components of an Oracle Collaboration Suite installation can be protected with techniques that avoid a single point of failure, but setting up a zero data loss and 100% uptime environment will be far more expensive (in both financial terms and human resources) than setting up an environment where a certain amount of downtime, and even data loss, can be tolerated. There is also a play-off between downtime and data loss; complete data recovery after a failure may mean considerable downtime, whereas accepting a small data loss may sometimes mean that the systems can be made available for use much more quickly.

All these factors and more must be considered when defining the service level agreements between the user community and the various system administration and support groups. In particular, the interdependencies between the various components of an Oracle Collaboration Suite installation and the different groups that support the components must be thoroughly researched and documented.

Database Tier Fault Tolerance

It is absolutely impossible to corrupt an Oracle database. No matter what you do to it, the mechanisms of undo and redo mean that there is no way the database can be corrupted. The definition of *corrupted* in this context is important: a corrupted database is a database that is storing uncommitted changes, or has lost committed changes. This is sometimes referred to as an *inconsistent* database. The undo and redo mechanisms mean that no matter what happens, neither of these situations can occur. As a brutal example, there could be thousands of users logged on and working when the server is rebooted. Oracle won't care. The crash recovery process, which is totally automatic and impossible to avoid, will repair any corruptions when the database is next opened. If anyone has any doubts on this point, he should study the database and instance architecture until he can prove it to his own satisfaction. The crash recovery mechanism assumes no physical damage. Physical damage to files can result in loss of data, but this will never happen if the database administrator takes appropriate precautions. This phenomenal reliability is why people buy Oracle (and why it isn't cheap). It is also why if an Oracle database loses even one row of committed data, the management response will often be to fire the DBA, because everyone knows it is his fault, not Oracle's.

It is possible for a database instance to crash. There are many circumstances that can cause this. After a crash, the database is indeed corrupted, but the instance recovery mechanism, based on redo and undo data, will repair the corruptions and bring the database back to a consistent state before opening. If this instance recovery fails, and it will only fail if the redo or undo data is not available due to physical damage to files, the database cannot be opened until the database administrator has carried out the necessary database restore and recover operations. In the event of physical damage to files caused by disk damage, it will still be impossible to lose data if the database has been protected with an appropriate backup regime. The downtime may, however, be considerable.

Zero data loss and zero downtime are both achievable but require a certain amount of skill and resources to configure. Also, such an environment may perform at a lower level than an environment where the requirements are less demanding.

Configuring a Database for Zero Data Loss

The zero data loss environment is enabled through Data Guard, an Oracle database facility introduced with release 9*i*. There are various possible Data Guard configurations, giving various degrees of performance and fault tolerance, which can be applied to both an infrastructure metadata repository database and to component datastore databases.

To ensure that data cannot be lost, an Oracle database stores rows of data in one set of disk-based data structures, known as *data files*. The change vectors that have been applied to the rows are stored in another set of disk-based data structures: the redo log files. Data files must be backed up periodically, and the online redo log files must be archived. The archive log files thus produced must also be backed up. Both online redo log files and archived redo log files can and should be multiplexed. If this is done, in the event of damage to any data file it will always be possible to restore a backup of the data file and bring it up-to-date by applying changes extracted from the relevant archive and online logs. The only circumstance where this will not be possible is if all backups of the file or all copies of the relevant online and archived redo log files have been lost. The number and locations of the backups and copies, and therefore the degree of fault tolerance, is a matter for negotiation between the system administrators and the users.

The rules to which a relational database (all relational databases, not just an Oracle database) must conform state that once a transaction is committed, it must be absolutely impossible for the database to lose it. Oracle conforms to this rule by writing the change vectors that make up the transaction to the online redo log files in very nearly real time, and when a user issues a `commit` command, the write really is in real time: the session will hang until the database server receives an acknowledgement from the operating system that the write has completed. The only exception to this rule is if a database 10*g* release 2 feature is enabled that allows the write required by a `commit` command to be performed asynchronously. A site would need a very good reason to enable this. Thus, if there are adequate backups of the data files and the online redo logs are available, it will always be possible to repeat the work up to the commit point. But if the online log files are destroyed, this will not be possible. Thus, the one circumstance that a regime of data file and archive log backup and multiplexing of online log file backup cannot protect against is complete loss of the machine. In that case, there will be no problem with the data files and the archived log files because backup copies of these will be available; but all copies of the online redo log files will be gone. It will therefore be possible to restore and recover the database only up to the point at which the last archive log was backed up. All work done subsequently will be lost. It is this circumstance that Data Guard can protect against.

A Data Guard environment consists of two or more databases on two or more machines. One database, known as the *primary*, is open for use; it is this database that users connect to. The other database, known as the *standby*, is based on a copy of the primary. In a zero data loss configuration, the change vectors applied to the primary database by user sessions are also written in real time across the network to the machine hosting the standby database. Once received by the standby database, they can be applied to it, thus keeping the standby database up-to-date with the primary. By this means, even if the primary database is totally destroyed, the standby database will have all the change vectors for every committed transaction and can be opened for use as a replacement for the lost database without any loss of data.

There are many options for a Data Guard environment. The physical standby, described previously, is not available for end user connections under normal circumstances; its function is purely to provide fault tolerance. A physical standby database is byte-for-byte the same as the primary, and it is intended purely for fault tolerance. An alternative type of standby is the *logical* standby database. A logical standby is open for use: users can connect to it and run queries against it. It is called *logical* because while a query run against it will always give the same results as though the query had been run against the primary, the physical structures within a logical standby can be completely different. For example, tables could have different partitioning strategies, additional indexes of different types, or additional materialized views and summary tables. A logical standby is intended for use as a data warehouse; it is based on a copy of the primary, and contains the same data, but is optimized for query processing. This can enhance performance substantially by offloading query work from the primary.

There are also options for how to transmit redo change vectors from the primary to the standby. If it is done in real time, there will be a performance impact. Committing a transaction becomes dependent not only on a write to the local online redo log files, but also on a write across the network to the standby redo log files on the remote machine. So configuring a zero data loss environment will certainly slow down operations, unless the network is set up with this in mind. It is also necessary to consider what the effect will be if the standby database becomes unavailable for any reason. Are you prepared to let it diverge from the primary, or should data inserts, updates, and deletes on the primary cease until the standby becomes accessible again?

An option many sites will settle for is the *maximum performance* configuration. This transmits change vectors to the physical standby asynchronously, not synchronously. When a session commits a transaction on the primary, the change vector is sent to the standby database, but the "commit complete" message is returned to the session as soon as the write to the local online redo logs is complete. It is not delayed until the network write to the remote standby redo logs is complete, so there is no possible impact on performance. Furthermore, if the standby becomes unavailable, the primary will continue to operate and will therefore diverge from the standby. Once the standby becomes available again, all change vectors generated in the interim period get sent to it and it will converge with the primary. This maximum performance configuration means that it is virtually impossible to lose data. If the primary were destroyed, any committed data that was still in transmission to the standby would be lost, but nothing else. And if the standby became unavailable, and subsequently the primary was destroyed, all data from the point at which the standby became unavailable would be lost. This level of fault tolerance is frequently considered adequate, particularly for an Oracle Collaboration Suite site where availability of the components for use is often critical and considered more important than the very faint possibility of losing a very small amount of data.

An important point to remember is that Data Guard cannot provide 100% uptime. In the event of a problem that necessitates switching over from the primary to the standby, there will be several delays. First, the change vectors needed to synchronize the standby with the final state of the primary may not have been applied. Applying the changes may take some time, and until it is done, the standby cannot be opened. It is possible to configure what is known as *real-time apply* to avoid this delay, but there may be performance implications for doing this. A second and unavoidable delay is that the sessions against the primary will have been lost. They must be reinstantiated against the standby. It may be possible to automate this, but it is not possible to do it instantaneously.

Configuring a Database for Zero Downtime

The zero downtime environment is enabled through Real Application Clusters, or RAC. A RAC database is a database that is opened concurrently by two or more instances running on different machines. The database itself, which can be protected by Data Guard (there is no reason not to use RAC and Data Guard together), resides on a shared disk system accessible to all the machines.

RAC is not purely for fault tolerance. Many sites will RAC their databases for reasons of scalability and performance, but it can certainly contribute to the goal of zero downtime by protecting against machine and operating system failure. In the event of one RAC instance failing, the database will remain open and accessible through the surviving instance. Sessions against the failed instance will be reinstantiated against the surviving instance. The effect on the application will depend on how RAC is configured, and how the application will respond to having its database connection broken and then remade.

When a user process requests a connection to a database, the Oracle Net protocol maps this request onto one of the instances that make up the RAC configuration. This is the first layer of fault tolerance; if RAC is appropriately configured, then Oracle Net will ignore any instances that have failed and will not attempt to launch sessions against them. The instance then makes the connection to the database. This *connect time* fault tolerance will be adequate for many sites. A further level of fault tolerance can be enabled to cover the effect of a failure of an instance that has currently connected sessions. This is known as *session failover*. The default configuration is that the sessions will be lost and the process must request a new session, which will be mapped (by the connect time fault tolerance mechanism) to a surviving instance. Configuring session failover will make the reconnection transparently. Theoretically, the process will not be aware that it is now running with a session against a different instance. In practice, there may be problems depending on what the session was actually doing at the time. While it is possible for session failover to allow a SELECT statement to continue to run, if the session were in the middle of a transaction, an error will be returned and the transaction will have to be restarted. Also, configuring session failover may have performance implications.

How components will react to instance failure in a RAC environment is dependent on the session failover configuration and also on the application itself. For example, Oracle Internet Directory server processes, which are spawned on demand, should survive well; processes against the failed instance will detect the problem and terminate, and all new server processes will be launched against a surviving instance. It is only requests that were actually in progress at the time of the failure that may report an error. Other components may not handle the situation so gracefully and users may have to reconnect to the middle tier, or it may even be necessary to restart the middle tier processes.

Apart from allowing the database to remain open following instance failure, RAC can also help with planned maintenance. For example, hardware upgrades can be performed machine by machine, closing down each instance in turn, and always keeping the database open from at least one instance.

Database Backups

Whatever strategy is decided upon for RAC and Data Guard, the database data files, control file, and archive log files must be backed up. The frequency of these backups will have an impact on the downtime in the event of a restore and recover operation being necessary. Note that in Oracle terminology, *restore* means extracting files from a backup, *recover* means applying changes to the restored files to bring them forward in time.

■ **Note** The terms *hot*, *online*, *open*, and *inconsistent* all refer to a backup while the database is in use, without any effect on the users except (possibly) that there may be a performance dip due to the I/O strain on the system. The terms *cold*, *offline*, *closed*, and *consistent* describe a backup while the database is shut down, and imply downtime for the users.

Oracle's approved tool for managing backup-related operations is the Recovery Manager (RMAN), which makes server-managed backups. It is not essential to use it, but most sites will need a very good reason not to. The alternative is to make user-managed backups, which you perform using any operating system utilities you may wish to use. Both techniques can make *hot* backups, meaning that you perform the backup operations while the database is in use without your users being aware of this, but RMAN is a better tool. It provides facilities impossible with user-managed backups, such as the following:

- Incremental backups, which will reduce the time and the size of the output backup files
- Block level restore and recover, which reduces the downtime involved in a recovery operation
- Backups without enabling backup mode on data files, which reduces the redo generation while a backup is in progress
- Backups of data files and archive log files from Automatic Storage Management volumes, if your database administrator has chosen to use them
- Fully automated selection and retrieval of backups to use when performing a recovery operation

To exploit the full power of RMAN, it is necessary to link it to a tape robot, which is an automated tape library. In such an environment, the complete backup-restore-recover cycle can be fully automated.

Database backups are the responsibility of the database administrator rather than the Oracle Collaboration Suite Administrator. But for further pointers or research, the following sections describe some very simple examples of scripts that can be used for hot and cold database backups, using both server-managed backup with RMAN commands and user-managed backup with operating system commands.

RMAN Backup Scripts

The following RMAN script `hotbackup.rmn` will perform a hot backup of the whole database. The line numbers are not part of the script; they have been added for reference purposes. Invoke the script from an operating system prompt with this shell command

```
rman target sys/<sys password>@<database alias> @hotbackup.rmn
```

where *<sys password>* is the password for the SYS database user and *<database alias>* is the connect identifier for the database you wish to back up.

```
1 allocate channel d1 type disk1;
2 backup
3 incremental level 0
4 format '/backup/ocsdb/df_%d_%s_%p'
5 (database include current controlfile);
6 sql 'alter system archive log current';
7 backup
8 format '/backup/ocsdb/ar_%d_%s_%p'
9 (archivelog all delete all input);
10 release channel t1;
```

The lines of this script perform these actions:

1. One channel is launched that is capable of writing files to disk devices. A *channel* is a process that copies files. Depending on the hardware, allocating multiple channels will help performance. Depending on their type, channels can either write to disk or to a tape library.
2. This is the operation to carry out, such as a backup or a restore. This command continues to the end of line 5.
3. A level zero incremental backup will back up everything and can be used as the base for subsequent incremental backups.
4. This is the name of the output file(s) to be written. The % variables will guarantee unique names.
5. This is what to back up: all data files and the controlfile.
6. This forces the database to perform a log switch and an archive. After this, you are no longer dependent on any of the live data structures.
7. This starts another backup operation. The command continues to the end of line 9.
8. This is the name of the output file(s) to be written.
9. This is what to back up: all the archive log files, deleting them from their original locations as they are backed up.
10. Terminate the channel process launched in line 1.

To adjust the script to perform a cold backup, add these lines at the beginning:

```
shutdown immediate
startup mount
```

This will force a clean shutdown (RMAN will not allow you to back up unless the shutdown is clean) and then bring the database back up in mount mode. Then remove line 6, which is not necessary when the database is not open, and add this final line to start the database up once the backup is complete:

```
startup
```

To make subsequent backups (hot or cold) incremental, adjust line 3 to read either

```
incremental level 1
```

or

```
incremental level 1 cumulative
```

depending on whether you wish to back up only those changes since the last incremental level 1 backup or all the changes since the last incremental level 0 backup.

User-Managed Backup Scripts

User-managed backups copy data files with absolutely ordinary operating system commands. If the data files are in use while being copied, the output files will be inconsistent. They will have been copied while being updated, which may result in individual data blocks being damaged in the output file. To get around this problem, tablespaces must be put in *backup mode*. When in backup mode, additional information is written out to the redo log stream that will allow Oracle to repair any blocks that were damaged in this fashion. The need to write out this extra information, which consists of read-consistent copies of updated blocks, puts a great strain on the redo generation system. You may find that your database is log switching every minute instead of every hour when tablespaces are in backup mode. To minimize this strain, only place tablespaces in backup mode for the shortest possible period of time.

If the database is stored on appropriate hardware, it may be possible to back it up by using operating system facilities that can split and reinstantiate mirrors. Before committing to techniques like this, be sure they are supported by Oracle Corporation on that hardware. It may, for example, be necessary to place the whole database in backup mode for the split, or to use the `alter system suspend` command to freeze all disk I/O.

Critical to making reliable user-managed backups is the use of SQL scripts that will interrogate the database's data dictionary to extract details of the files that need to be backed up. The following SQL*Plus script uses PL/SQL to generate a SQL script `hotbackup.sql` that will identify and copy all the data files that make up the database, as well as backing up the controlfile:

```
set serveroutput on
spool hotbackup.sql
declare
   cursor c1 is  select * from dba_tablespaces where contents<>'TEMPORARY';
   cursor c2 (t_name varchar2) is ➥
select * from dba_data_files where tablespace_name = t_name;
begin
 for t in c1 loop
   dbms_output.put_line ➥
('alter tablespace '||t.tablespace_name||' begin backup;');
   for f in c2(t.tablespace_name) loop
      dbms_output.put_line('host cp -p ' || f.file_name  ||' /backup/ocsdb');
   end loop;
   dbms_output.put_line('alter tablespace '||t.tablespace_name||' end backup;');
 end loop;
```

```
14  dbms_output.put_line('alter system archive log current;');
15  dbms_output.put_line('alter database backup controlfile to trace ➥
 as ''/backup/ocsdb/cf.trace '';');
16  dbms_output.put_line('alter database backup controlfile to ➥
''/backup/ocsdb/cf.bak; ''');
17  end;
18  /
19  spool off
```

The lines of the script perform these actions:

1. Enable writing to the terminal device.
2. Create the output file `hotbackup.sql`.
3. Create two variables, which are the cursors that follow.
4. The first cursor will have one row for every tablespace making up the database (excluding temporary tablespaces, which cannot be backed up).
5. The second cursor contains one row for every data file that is part of the tablespace being passed in as a parameter.
6. Begin the executable code.
7. Loop through all the tablespaces listed in the first cursor.
8. Generate the command to place the current tablespace into backup mode.
9. Loop through all the data files that make up the current tablespace.
10. Generate the UNIX command to copy the current data file.
11. Close the loop through the data files.
12. Generate the command to take the current tablespace out of backup mode.
13. Close the loop through the tablespaces.
14. Generate the command to force a log switch and an archive.
15. Generate the command to write out a CREATE CONTROLFILE statement to a trace file.
16. Generate the command to make a binary copy of the controlfile. Note the use of multiple quote characters.
17. Finish the executable code.
18. Run the script.
19. Close the file `hotbackup.sql`.

Having run this script to generate the backup script, run it from an operating system prompt:

```
sqlplus sys/<sys password>@<database alias> @hotbackup.sql
```

This SQL*Plus script, which can be run when the database is either open or mounted, will generate a shell script that will perform a cold backup:

```
spool coldbackup.bat
select 'copy ' || name || ' d:\backup\ocssb' from v$datafile
union all
select 'copy ' || member || ' d:\backup\ocsdb' from v$logfile
union all
select 'copy ' || name || ' d:\backup\ocsdb' from v$controlfile
spool off
```

The lines of the script perform these actions:

1. Create the output file `coldbackup.bat`.
2. Generate the Windows commands to copy all the data files.
3. Generate the Windows commands to copy all the online log files.
4. Generate the Windows commands to copy all the controlfile copies.
5. Close the file `coldbackup.bat`.

Before running the generated shell script, the database should be shut down cleanly.

Calendar Datastore Backup and Restore

Calendar does not use an Oracle database as its datastore; it uses a set of files in each node's directory. The backup and restore facilities are less sophisticated than those for an Oracle database. In particular, there are three limitations that will affect all installations:

- Hot backup of a node is possible, but while in progress the node is locked for updates; data can only be read, not written.
- Node backups must be full: there is no capability for incremental backup.
- There is no transaction logging in a Calendar node database. If a restore is necessary, all work done since the backup will be lost.

Furthermore, unlike an Oracle database, it is not possible to protect a Calendar datastore with techniques such as Data Guard, or to protect the Calendar server with RAC. Such facilities are simply not provided by the technology on which Calendar is based. It is therefore vital to protect the nodes with hardware facilities, such as RAID mirroring. It is not possible to provide perfectly uninterrupted service in the event of a host failure, but if the node databases are on a shared disk device, if one host fails you can start the Calendar server on a surviving host attached to the same disks. This could be a manual procedure, or it can be automated by installing the Calendar server on a cold failover cluster.

The simplest way to back up a node is to shut it down and back up the files with whatever operating system utility you please. The backup should include the node database directory

```
$ORACLE_HOME/ocal/db/nodes/<node_name>
```

and also the configuration files in the directory

```
$ORACLE_HOME/ocal/misc
```

as there will be dependencies between these. However, a cold backup like this will generally not be acceptable to your users. To back up while keeping the Calendar server available for use (at least for read access) use the `unidbbackup` utility:

```
unidbbackup -d <destination> [-n <node_id_list] [-lockall]
```

The *<destination>* is a directory on the local machine to which the backup will be directed. This destination should then be migrated to tertiary storage by whatever operating system utilities you have available.

The *<node_id_list>* is a list of which nodes on the server to back up. By default, all local nodes are backed up in turn, each locked as read-only for the duration of its backup.

The -lockall switch instructs `unidbbackup` to lock as read-only all the nodes being backed up for the duration of the whole operation. This may impact adversely on users but will guarantee consistency between the various node databases. If this is not done, restore of just one node from the set may introduce inconsistencies between the nodes.

This command

```
$ unidbbackup -d /backup/calendar -n 1,2,3
```

will back up the three nodes (identified by number) to the nominated directory. Each node will be made read-only for the duration of its backup.

The complementary utility to `unidbbackup` is the `unidbrestore` utility. Unlike `unidbbackup`, this cannot be run while the Calendar server is running. The syntax is the following:

```
unidbrestore -s <source> [-d <destination>] [-n <node_id_list] -nomisc
```

The *<source>* is the directory from which to read the backup. This must have been created with the `unidbbackup` utility.

The *<destination>* is the target for the restore, which will default to the `$ORACLE_HOME/ocal` directory. By default, any existing files will be overwritten, so you may wish to restore to an alternative location first.

The *<node_id_list>* is a list of nodes to restore. By default, all nodes found in the source directory will be restored.

The -nomisc switch instructs `unidbrestore` not to restore the configuration information in the `$ORACLE_HOME/ocal/misc` directory, only the actual node data.

Oracle Home Backup and Restore

The Oracle home directory is the root of your Oracle software installation. An Oracle Collaboration Suite installation will have at least two Oracle homes: one for the Oracle Application Server infrastructure instance, and one for the Oracle Application Server middle tier instance. The infrastructure instance Oracle home will by default include the Oracle database itself.

As a rule, backup of the Oracle home directories comes within the system administration domain rather than the database administration domain.

The Oracle home is for the most part static files, such as the executable code, but it also contains a number of configuration files. Theoretically, the static files need only be backed up once as they will never change, but the configuration files will be updated as a result of management commands. The default installation also puts the database files in the Oracle home, though your database administrators may well relocate the database files elsewhere after installation for many reasons of performance and security. Generally, you should ensure that the Oracle home directory structure, excluding the database files if they have not been relocated out of the Oracle home, is backed up using operating system utilities following every major configuration change and in any case on a regular schedule (such as weekly). Ideally, this should be a cold backup made when all Oracle Collaboration Suite components are completely shut down. This will ensure that all files backed up are consistent. If it is not possible to perform a cold backup, there are utilities that can back up the configuration files while the system is in use.

Directories that include critical configuration information are the following:

`ORACLE_HOME/network/admin`: Oracle Net configuration files for the database and Mail listeners and for name resolution

`ORACLE_HOME/dbs`: The database instance parameter file

`ORACLE_HOME/j2ee`: The OC4J configuration files and the deployed Java applications

`ORACLE_HOME/dcm`: The Oracle Application Server instance configuration files and the file-based metadata repository

`ORACLE_HOME/opmn/conf`: The `opmn.xml` file and related information

`ORACLE_HOME/Apache`: The configuration files for Apache and all Apache modules, such as modoc4j and modplsql

These can certainly be backed up with operating system utilities while the system is in use, but there is no absolute guarantee that such a backup will be usable, as there is always a possibility that configuration files were being updated while the backup was in progress.

Oracle Application Server Configuration Backup and Restore

The Oracle home directories for Oracle Application Server infrastructure instances contain the configuration files for the various components deployed to the instance. In particular, the Distributed Configuration Management (DCM) repository. This information is also available in the metadata repository of the Oracle Application Server farm and will therefore be backed up when you back up your infrastructure database; but it should always be backed up using the `dcmctl` utility as well, so that it can be restored independently of the database.

A feature of the Oracle database is that it is impossible to restore part of the database in the event of a need to back out some changes. It is all or nothing. Consider the situation where you have done some major reconfiguration work while the system is in use and then wish to revert to the position before you started the work. If you restore the metadata repository database from a backup taken before you commenced work, you will certainly take the configuration back as intended, but you will also take everything else back, such as the Oracle Internet Directory data. This may not be desirable, but there is no way around it. Oracle will not permit the possibility of corruptions that can occur when parts of a database are, in effect, different versions. It is therefore essential to have another means of backing up the metadata repository.

The dcmctl utility is a command-line tool that can be used to configure Oracle Application Server. Its primary purpose is to manage OC4J instances: creating them and deploying Java applications to them. It is unlikely to be used for this purpose in an Oracle Collaboration Suite environment, as the various applications are deployed automatically by the installation procedures, and any subsequent configuration changes will usually be done through the Application Server Control graphical interface. But a secondary function of the utility is to back up the configuration data. This command

```
dcmctl createarchive -arch <archive name> [-i <instance name>]
```

will create an archive of the Oracle Application Server's configuration, naming the archive as *<archive name>*. The optional argument *<instance name>* lets you specify which Oracle Application Server instance you wish to archive; by default, it will be that launched from the Oracle home to which you are currently connected, but it could be any instance in the farm. The default installation will generate archives of all instances automatically whenever any configuration change is made, and the last 15 such archives will be stored and overwritten on a FIFO algorithm. To change the number of archives stored to, for example, 20, use the following command:

```
dcmctl set -arch 20
```

To list the stored archives, run the following:

```
dcmctl listarchives
```

To restore an archive, run the following:

```
dcmctl applyarchiveto -arch <archive name>  [-i <instance name>]
```

This will extract the named archive and overwrite the current instance's configuration (or the named instance, if using the optional *<instance name>* argument).

When an archive is created, it is itself stored within the metadata repository, and in the event of a restore, it is read from the metadata repository. For an external backup, you must first create an archive and then export the archive to an operating system file. This is done with

```
dcmctl exportarchvie -arch <archive name> -f <file name>
```

which will write the archive specified by *<archive name>* to the file specified by *<file name>*. The file will be a .JAR Java archive file. The archive file can be imported into a metadata repository, either the original one from whence it came or the repository of a different farm, with

```
dcmctl importarchive -arch <archive name> -f <file name>
```

and it can then be restored with the applyarchiveto command.

The Oracle Collaboration Suite Recovery Manager

The Oracle Collaboration Suite Recovery Manager is a tool written in Perl that can help automate backup of the Oracle Collaboration Suite database(s), the Calendar node databases, and the Oracle Application Server instances' configurations. It was released with the Oracle Collaboration Suite 10*g* 10.1.2 patch and is based on the `bkp_restore` tool shipped with Oracle Application Server 10*g* release 1.

Before using the tool, it must be configured by running the tool in configuration mode. This should be done in each Oracle Application Server Oracle home. On UNIX, run this command:

```
cd $ORACLE_HOME/backup_restore
./ocs_bkp_restore.sh -m configure
```

or on Windows

```
cd %ORACLE_HOME%\backup_restore
.\ocs_bkp_restore.bat -m configure
```

This will prompt you for the Oracle home you wish to configure for backup, the directories to which to direct the backups of the database and Calendar nodes, the configuration data, the log files generated by the tool, and, if you wish, e-mail notifications, as shown in Figure 17-1. This configuration routine is in fact editing the `config.inp` and `notification.inp` files in the Recovery Manager's `config` directory. The defaults are picked up from the environment variables of the session running the utility.

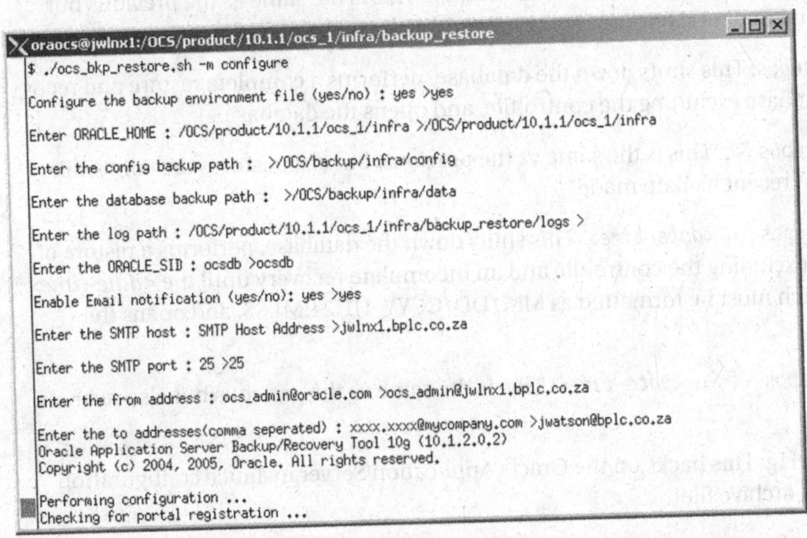

Figure 17-1. *Use of the Recovery Manager configuration tool for an infrastructure instance*

The target directories specified for the backups should exist before using the tool. The database backup directory will require enough space for at least one full backup, plus archive logs. The configuration backups of an infrastructure instance will be dozens of megabytes each; the configuration backups of a middle tier instance will be hundreds of megabytes each. The Calendar node backups also go to the configuration directory, which must be sized accordingly. Clearly, it will be necessary to use operating system utilities to migrate all these backups to tertiary storage.

Then to perform backup and other operations, run the tool with this syntax:

```
ocs_bkp_restore.sh -m <operation> [<arguments>]
```

The *<operation>* can be one of those described in the following list, some of which take an additional *<argument>*. The list is not exhaustive. To list all the possible operations and for some usage notes, run `ocs_bkp_restore.sh` (`ocs_bkp_restore.bat` on Windows) without any arguments. For detail of what the various options do, it is necessary to investigate the Perl scripts and the template files, all located in the `backup_restore` directory. Note that all the database backup and restore operations are carried out with RMAN scripts; all the configuration backup and restore operations are carried out with Distributed Configuration Management archive, export, and import commands; the Calendar node backup and restore operations are carried out with the `unidbbackup` and `unidbrestore` utilities. These are the possible operations:

`-m backup_cold`: This shuts down the database, makes a full backup of the database with any archive logs, and starts the database.

`-m backup_cold_incr -l <incremental level>`: This is the same as the previous but performs an incremental backup. *<incremental level>* can be one of `0`, `1`, or `1 cumulative`.

`-m backup_online`: This makes a full online backup of the database and any archive logs.

`-m backup_online_incr -l <incremental level>`: This is the same as the previous but performs an incremental backup. *<incremental level>* can be one of `0`, `1`, or `1 cumulative`.

`-m restore_repos`: This shuts down the database, performs a complete restore and recovery of the database excluding the controlfile, and opens the database.

`-m restore_repos -c`: This is the same as the previous, but also restores the controlfile from the most recent backup made.

`-m restore_repos -u <date-time>`: This shuts down the database, performs a restore of the database excluding the controlfile and an incomplete recovery until the *<date-time>* specified, which must be formatted as MM/DD/CCYY_HH24:MI:SS, and opens the database.

`-m restore_repos -c -u <date-time>`: This is the same as the previous but also restores the controlfile.

`-m backup_config`: This backs up the Oracle Application Server instance configuration as an exported archive file.

`-m restore_config -t <date-time>`: This restores the Oracle Application Server instance configuration from a backup made at a certain time, specified as CCYY-MM-DD_HH24_MI_SS. The available configuration backups will be in the directory specified during the configuration shown in Figure 17-1, and the filenames include this time stamp.

`-m node_backup -o prepare`: This shuts down the middle tier instance, backs up the configuration, starts the instance, and backs up the Calendar node database files.

`-m node_restore -t <date-time>`: This shuts down the Calendar server and restores the mode databases from the backup taken at the `<date-time>` given.

It will virtually always be necessary to edit the files used by the Recovery Manager tool before use. To do this, identify which files each of the `-m <operation>` options invokes by investigating the `ocs_bkp_restore.pl` Perl script. For example, the `-m restore_repos -c -u` *`<date-time>`* option in fact runs the following RMAN script, `restore_db_pitr_cf.tmpl`, which your database administrators will almost certainly need to adjust:

```
1  set dbid=$dbid;
2  connect target /;
3  shutdown abort;
4  startup nomount;
5  set controlfile autobackup format for device type disk to ➥
   '$database_backup_path/%F';
6  restore controlfile from autobackup until time ➥
   "to_date('$until_time','MM/DD/YYYY_HH24:MI:SS')";
7  startup mount force $pfile;
8  run {
9  set until time "to_date('$until_time','MM/DD/YYYY_HH24:MI:SS')";
10 allocate channel dev1 device type disk format '$database_backup_path/%U';
11 restore database;
12 recover database;
13 release channel dev1;
14 alter database open resetlogs;
15 }
```

The lines of the script perform these actions:

1. Set the database identifier to assist in locating the correct controlfile.
2. Connect to the database with operating system authentication.
3. Shut down the database.
4. Start the instance, but do not read any database files.
5. Set the path for backups to the path configured for the utility.
6. Restore the controlfile from a backup made prior to the time requested.
7. Mount the database with the restored controlfile.
8. Start an RMAN job.
9. Set the time up to which the incomplete recovery will be made.
10. Launch one channel, which will read backups from the configured directory.

11. Restore the database.
12. Recover until the time specified.
13. Terminate the channel process.
14. Open the database with the syntax necessary after an incomplete recovery.
15. Finish the RMAN job.

Remember that the Oracle Collaboration Suite Recovery Manager tool is merely a front end to utilities already available. It is not properly documented and may not always react in the manner that one might expect.

Oracle Application Server and Failover Clusters

An Oracle Collaboration Suite installation can be protected against failure by installing on a failover cluster. This is a capability provided by your hardware and operating system and will be proprietary to your chosen platform vendor. Failover clusters come in two forms: cold failover clusters, and active failover clusters. These can be used to protect both the infrastructure tier of your installation and the middle tier. This section concentrates on protecting the Oracle Application Server infrastructure instance, but is equally applicable to middle tier instances.

A cold failover cluster is two (or more) computers (the *nodes*) connected to a set of shared disks. At any one time, only one node is active; the other is passive. Each node will have a private IP address, but the cluster as a whole is presented to the network by the cluster software through a virtual IP address and a virtual hostname. The `ORACLE_HOME` directory structure is installed on the shared disks. The middle tier instances that make up the rest of the farm do not connect directly to either node; they connect to the virtual address of the entire cluster. If the active node fails, passive node will launch the infrastructure processes and take over the virtual IP address. To the middle tier instances, the now active node appears identical to the previously active node. Thus, failure of the machine running the infrastructure will appear to be nothing more than a brief interruption in availability. The failover will be managed by the vendor's cluster management software, and the exact process followed will be platform-dependent.

At any one moment, the infrastructure is only running on one node of a cold failover cluster. However, that does not necessarily mean that the other node must be idle; it can be running other processes, perhaps even a middle tier instance. You can therefore configure the cluster such that services on each node can fail over to the other node. Clearly, the workload on the surviving node will be high following a failover, but if financial constraints preclude installing redundant hardware, this may be acceptable.

An active failover cluster is more complex in that the infrastructure is running on both nodes concurrently. This provides a much more transparent high-availability service in the event of failure, because there need be no downtime. Both instances are accessible through a network load balancer, and in the event of a failure, the load balance will simply redirect all connections to the surviving instance. This should mean zero downtime, and only requests that were actually in progress at the time of the failure will be affected. Active failover clusters are significantly more complex to set up, and support for their use with Oracle Application

Server is limited. Before committing to using such an environment, it is vital to ensure that Oracle Corporation has certified the configuration for use in this fashion.

Failover clusters provide fault tolerance and high availability through operating system and hardware facilities. If the platform is certified for use with Oracle Application Server, the Oracle environment will survive the failure of a node in the cluster. If you are not running on a certified platform or cannot justify the financial investment required, there are facilities within the Oracle environment that can give similar levels of protection.

Load Balancing Devices

Load balancers are essential to a high-availability environment. Simple in concept, they may be very expensive in practice. A load balancer offers a name and IP address to the public network that will be used by any processes requesting the services for which it is load balancing. The services themselves are provided by two or more servers with different names and IP addresses to which the load balancer will forward the requests it receives. The whole concept relies on deception: users think that they are contacting one machine when in fact they are routed to another. Intelligent use of the worldwide DNS system is vital to this mechanism.

A load balancer will be configured with rules that let it apportion requests across the servers to which it is routing requests. These rules may be very simple, such as random distribution, or they could be based on more complex algorithms related to how busy the servers are and what their relative capacities are. Depending on the nature of the service being requested, there may be more complexities. If the request is stateless, it can be routed to any available server. This would apply to, for example, a simple LDAP request to validate a username and password. The request will hit the load balancer, the load balancer will forward it to any available Oracle Internet Directory selected by whatever algorithm it has been configured to use, the response will be returned to the load balancer, which will return it to the requesting process. The connection will then be dropped. Other requests may be stateful. For example, if the end-user request is for a Java application service that requires a persistent session, only the initial login request can be load balanced. The load balancer can direct the initial request to any server, but all subsequent requests from the same client must go to the same server where the session has been established. This facility is often referred to as *session stickiness.*

The load balancer is vital for two purposes. First, it can scale the environment. Additional server machines can be installed behind the load balancer, and end users will not be aware of this. The entire web site will still be presented to them as one address, and the fact that it is actually being cut over a variable number of servers will be concealed from them. Second, load balancers will have a fault-tolerant capability built into them. As servers join or leave the web site, they will register and deregister with the load balancer. Typically, the load balancer will be configured to ping the servers regularly, and any server that fails to respond will be removed from the load balancer's routing table until it responds again. Thus, end users will not be aware that any one server has ceased to function, though if it was supporting stateful sessions, those sessions may have to be reestablished against a surviving server.

The load balancer itself must be capable of supporting the entire concurrent connection workload of the web site. For this reason, high-performance load balancers are usually implemented with firmware, and they are not cheap. Oracle Application Server (and, with the default installation, Oracle Collaboration Suite) comes with a software load balancer: the Web Cache. This is designed for high-speed routing of HTTP and HTTPS requests across the

Apache web listeners that are the front end of an Oracle Application Server middle tier instance, and it is very effective at this. The Oracle database also comes with a built-in load balancer: Oracle Net. Appropriate configuration of the client and server sides of Oracle Net in a RAC environment will spread connections across all available instances. To load balance other protocols, such as LDAP, you will need third-party devices. A large web site will also require a load balancer as the initial entry point to the web site that will load balance across a number of Web Caches.

High Availability for Identity Management Services

All the Oracle Collaboration Suite application components are critically dependent on the identity management services provided by an Oracle Application Server infrastructure instance. The standard installation will have created an infrastructure instance with the metadata repository database and three identity management components: the Oracle Internet Directory, the Single Sign-On server, and the Certificate Authority. The metadata repository database must be protected with Data Guard and RAC, but the identity management services can be protected by installing multiple instances.

Replicating the Oracle Internet Directory

The Oracle Internet Directory is a source of information on users, privileges, configurations, and much more. Some application components can survive without access to it, but not for very long. At the very least, it must be available for any users to connect. All the Oracle Collaboration Suite components make use of the Single Sign-On capability, and for the user's initial authentication the Single Sign-On server must connect to the Oracle Internet Directory to validate the user's password. It is therefore a single point of failure.

A part of the LDAP standards to which Oracle Internet Directory conforms is *directory replication*. This is a mechanism whereby multiple LDAP directories will contain an identical directory information tree—whichever directory you bind to (*bind* is the LDAP terminology for *connect*) you will see the same data. Note that directory replication is not synonymous with directory synchronization. *Replication* maintains identical content; *synchronization* is a technique for transferring a subset of data between two independent directories. For example, you might have a Microsoft Active Directory that manages users for network access, and an Oracle Internet Directory that manages your Oracle Collaboration Suite. It will be impossible to replicate between them because they use different standards for their object classes. For example, users will be defined with different attributes. But you can synchronize the two, so that creating a user in one directory will cause the user to be created in the other.

To provide fault tolerance and scalability, you can create multiple directories and configure replication between them. Each Oracle Internet Directory will store its data in its own Oracle database. Oracle's implementation of LDAP directory replication is based on database technology: either Advanced Replication or (in later releases) Streams. Both products deliver the same result: any transactions committed against one database will be propagated over an Oracle Net connection to the other database. The propagation is typically asynchronous. You can configure synchronous propagation but this is rarely done, as it tends to impact adversely on performance. The asynchronous schedule can, however, be as frequent as every few seconds. Until transmission, the transactions are stored in a deferred transactions queue. Advanced Replication uses DML triggers to capture the transaction as it occurs, whereas

Streams extracts the transaction from the redo data it generates. Either way, local transactions are stored, then shipped to the remote database(s) and applied. Thus the content of the two databases is kept identical.

It is not necessary to propagate changes to all tables. You can choose just a subset of the database, but any tables that are configured for Advanced Replication or Streams will contain the same rows at both sites, though the data will diverge temporarily, depending on the schedule for transmitting the transactions. This divergence is unlikely to be an issue for an Oracle Internet Directory. The nature of LDAP usage is such that the vast majority of the workload is queries against relatively static data. However, if the two databases lose contact with each other for a prolonged period, perhaps because of a network problem, they will continue to operate independently and the divergence may be significant. Once the communication link is reestablished, the backlog of deferred transactions will be applied and will bring everything back into sync.

A possible problem is that if the same row has been updated independently in both databases, when the deferred transactions are propagated between them there will be a conflict: Which version of the row is the "correct" one? Conflict resolution can be *automatic* or *manual*. Automatic conflict resolution relies on a set of rules that the administrator decides upon. For example, you could instruct the replication system that if two directories have different versions of the same rows, then one directory will always take precedence, and its version will be enforced on the others. Or you could decide to keep the latest version, no matter where it was created. Manual conflict resolution causes the conflicting data to be written to a queue where you can inspect it and choose which version to keep. Conflicts are unlikely to be a problem unless there is a prolonged breakdown in communications; but if they are a concern, it is possible to configure a replication model where updates occur on only one directory, known as the *supplier*, and are propagated to read-only directories, known as *consumers*.

Installing Multiple Identity Management Servers

The default Oracle Collaboration Suite installation will have a single infrastructure instance hosting the metadata repository database, the Oracle Internet Directory, the Single Sign-On server, and the Certificate Authority. The database will contain the Oracle Application Server farm configuration data, and also component repositories such as the Portal repository and the tables that make up the Oracle Internet Directory schema. For a large installation that might support tens of thousands of concurrent users, this is a lot of work for one infrastructure instance. And for any installation, it is a single point of failure.

Undoubtedly the simplest way to add scalability and fault tolerance to the identity management services is to protect the database with Data Guard and RAC, and to launch additional Oracle Internet Directory servers. To launch additional servers, use the `oidctl` utility to instruct the `oidmon` monitor process to start another server, as in the following example:

```
$ oidctl connect=ocsdb server=oidldapd instance=3 configset=3 start
```

The `connect` argument specifies the Oracle Net alias of the database storing the directory data. The `server` argument specifies that the server to be started is the LDAP listener. The instance number must be unique for all servers started, but otherwise has no significance. The `configset` argument instructs the monitor to start the server using a particular set of configuration directives, in this case set number 3. These are the settings stored within the directory that control, among other things, what port the server will listen on, how many child server processes to launch, and how many connections to the database each child process can make. As an alternative to using saved `configset` configurations, you can use the `flags` argument to specify these details dynamically.

This technique will help the scalability of the directory; but if the new server is on the same node and running off the same infrastructure installation as the original server, it does not help with fault tolerance. To launch a server on a different node, you must make an infrastructure installation on the node. To do this, run the installer, click the Advanced option, specify your Oracle home directory, select Infrastructure, and then click the option to install identity management services and an Oracle Collaboration Suite database. The window you will see, shown in Figure 17-2, lets you select services. Select only Internet Directory.

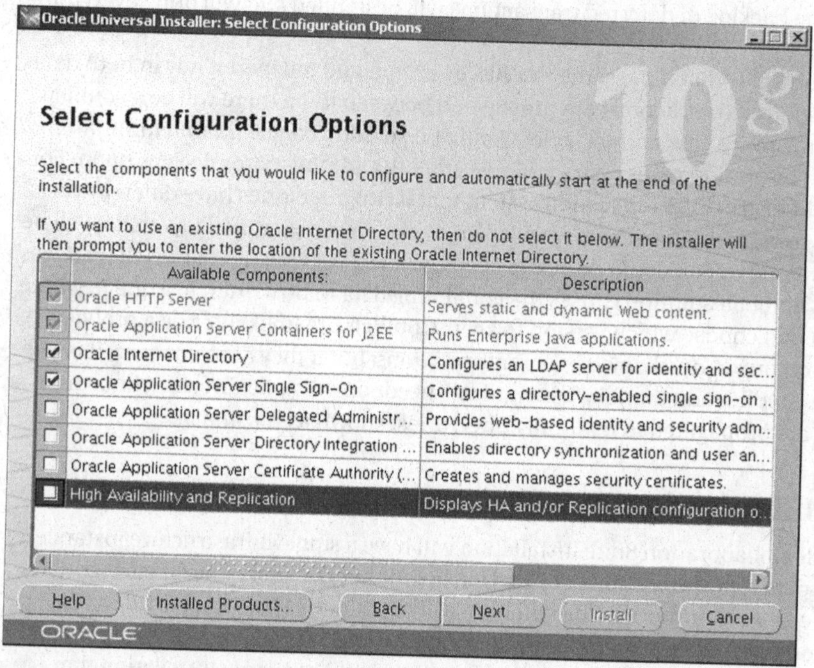

Figure 17-2. *Infrastructure installation options*

After the installation completes, you will have a fully self-contained and independent Oracle Internet Directory running off its own database. This is no use. What you need is to have an additional directory server that reads data from the same source as your original server. To achieve this goal, first shut down all the processes of your new installation. Second, add an entry to the `tnsnames.ora` file that points to the database of your original infrastructure. Then launch the `oidmon` monitor process, specifying the connect string to the original database, and use the `oidctl` utility as before:

```
$ oidmon connect=ocsdb start
$ oidctl connect=ocsdb server=oidldapd instance=3 configset=3 start
```

This will launch a Directory server on the local node, connecting to the database installed with the original infrastructure. A load balancer capable of routing LDAP should be configured with the virtual address for the Oracle Internet Directory that your application processes will use, and it will then apportion the requests across the two directory servers.

To achieve the highest possible level of redundancy, you would leave the new directory server connecting to its own database and configure replication between this new directory and the original one.

Single Sign-On and Certificate Authority Servers

Single Sign-On is a PL/SQL application running in an infrastructure database accessed through an Apache web listener and a DAD. To configure multiple Single Sign-On servers, follow the same technique as that described for installing multiple Oracle Internet Directory servers. Install a new Oracle Application Server infrastructure and stop the database. Then edit the file `dads.conf` to adjust the connect string the DAD uses so that it will find the original infrastructure database. Finally, an HTTP load balancer needs to be configured with a virtual address for Single Sign-On, and it will then balance requests across the two Single Sign-On servers' Apache web listeners.

The Certificate Authority is a far less important component for fault tolerance. If it isn't available, it will not be possible to issue new digital certificates. While this will be irritating, it is not the disaster that failure of the other identity management components would be. However, if necessary, it can be protected by similar techniques.

An Example of a Highly Available Topology

As an example of an environment that should be able to withstand the loss of any one machine, consider a minimal environment, using two load balancers to spread work across a total of four nodes. There are two nodes that each run identity management services and an Oracle database instance opening a RAC database on shared disks. The shared disks must be protected by RAID mirroring. The other two nodes each run a middle tier instance. There must be two load balancers capable of routing the web protocols (HTTP and HTTPS), the mail protocols (SMTP, IMAP, and POP), and LDAP. The DNS system will spread incoming requests across the two load balancers. Should one of them fail, DNS reconfiguration will conceal this failure from the users.

The load balancers are both known to the outside world as the same hostname, `ocs.bplc.com`. The DNS system will distinguish between them. The four server nodes are the following:

- `inf1.bplc.co.za`
- `inf2.bplc.co.za`
- `mid1.bplc.co.za`
- `mid2.bplc.co.za`

The first two nodes run infrastructure identity management services and database instances opening a RAC database on shared disks. The second two nodes run the middle tier applications, including a Web Cache. The virtual server addresses presented to the world by the load balancers might be routed by the load balancers to actual server addresses as in Table 17-1.

Table 17-1. *Virtual Address Routing for a Highly Available Topology*

Virtual Address	Protocol	Requests Forwarded To	Traffic	Traffic Source
ocs.bplc.com:389	LDAP	inf1.bplc.co.za:4389 inf2.bplc.co.za:4389	Directory lookups	Middle tier servers
ocs.bplc.com:636	LDAPS	inf1.bplc.co.za:4636 inf2.bplc.co.za:4636	Directory lookups using SSL	Middle tier servers
ocs.bplc.com:7777	HTTP	inf1.bplc.co.za:7777 inf2.bplc.co.za:7777	Single Sign-On requests	Middle tier servers
ocs.bplc.com:80	HTTP	mid1.bplc.co.za:7777 mid2.bplc.co.za:7777	Web applications	End-user browsers
ocs.bplc.com:443	HTTPS	mid1.bplc.co.za:4443 mid2.bplc.co.za:4443	Web applications using SSL	End-user browsers
ocs.bplc.com:25	SMTP	mid1.bplc.co.za:25 mid2.bplc.co.za:25	Outgoing mail	End-user mail tools
ocs.bplc.com:143	IMAP4	mid1.bplc.co.za:143 mid2.bplc.co.za:143	Mail retrieval	End-user mail tools
ocs.bplc.com:110	POP3	mid1.bplc.co.za:110 mid2.bplc.co.za:110	Mail retrieval	End-user mail tools

The entire web site is presented to the world as one address by the load balancers. The worldwide DNS system will take care of routing incoming connections to the load balancers. The ports the load balancers are listening on are the default ports that users will connect to. As a request flows through the system, whenever a process needs to go to another service, it will go via the load balancers, which will always route it to a functioning server. The ports the servers are listening on are those that will be in use following a default Oracle Collaboration Suite installation.

The following is the traffic flow for a request from a user to access his e-mail through the web client:

1. The end user issues the URL to contact Oracle Collaboration Suite virtual host:

   ```
   http://ocs.bplc.com
   ```

   This will hit one of the load balancers on port 80.

2. The load balancer routes the URL to one of the middle tier nodes, hitting its Web Cache on port 7777.

3. The Web Cache will route the URL to one of the middle tier Apache web listeners on port 7778.

4. The Apache web listener will redirect the user to the Single Sign-On virtual host, hitting one of the load balancers on port 7777.

5. The load balancer will route the SSO request to one of the infrastructure hosts, hitting its Apache web listener on port 7777.

6. The SSO server will generate a login window for the end user and validate the password by issuing an LDAP request to the LDAP virtual host, hitting one of the load balancers on port 389.

7. The load balancer routes the LDAP request to one of the infrastructure hosts, hitting its Oracle Internet Directory listener on port 4389.

8. Following authentication, the SSO cookie is sent back to the browser, and the browser is redirected back to the Oracle Collaboration Suite virtual host, hitting one of the load balancers on port 80.

9. The load balancer, making use of session stickiness, routes the request through to the same middle tier host that was selected in step 2, hitting its Web Cache on port 7777.

10. The Web Cache routes the request to the same middle tier Apache web listener that was selected in step 3, again making use of session identifiers, hitting it on port 7778.

11. The middle tier connects the user to the Webmail client process, which issues a request to the IMAP4 virtual host, hitting one of the load balancers on port 143.

12. The load balancer routes the requests to one of the middle tier hosts, hitting its IMAP listener on port 143.

13. The IMAP listener retrieves the user's mail from the Mail datastore and returns it to the Webmail client.

14. The Webmail client formats the mail for display in a page of HTML and returns the results to the Web Cache from which it received the request.

15. The Web Cache returns the page to the end user's browser.

This mechanism means that no process ever contacts a process on a (possibly) remote node directly; it always goes via an intermediary device, either a load balancer or a Web Cache, that will be aware of the availability status of the various servers. Not included in this example of request flow is the contact with Oracle Databases, which is through an Oracle Net connection to the database instances. This will have occurred three times:

- Step 6, where the Apache web listener makes a call through a DAD to PL/SQL-stored procedures.
- Step 8, where the LDAP server will have connected to a database to read the tables that store the directory information tree.
- Step 13, where the IMAP server retrieves messages from the Mail datastore.

These database connections will be load balanced by Oracle Net across the two database instances running on the two infrastructure nodes. Oracle Net provides load balancing and failure detection mechanisms for RAC database access comparable to those provided by the load balancers and the Web Caches.

Figure 17-3 is a graphical representation of this environment.

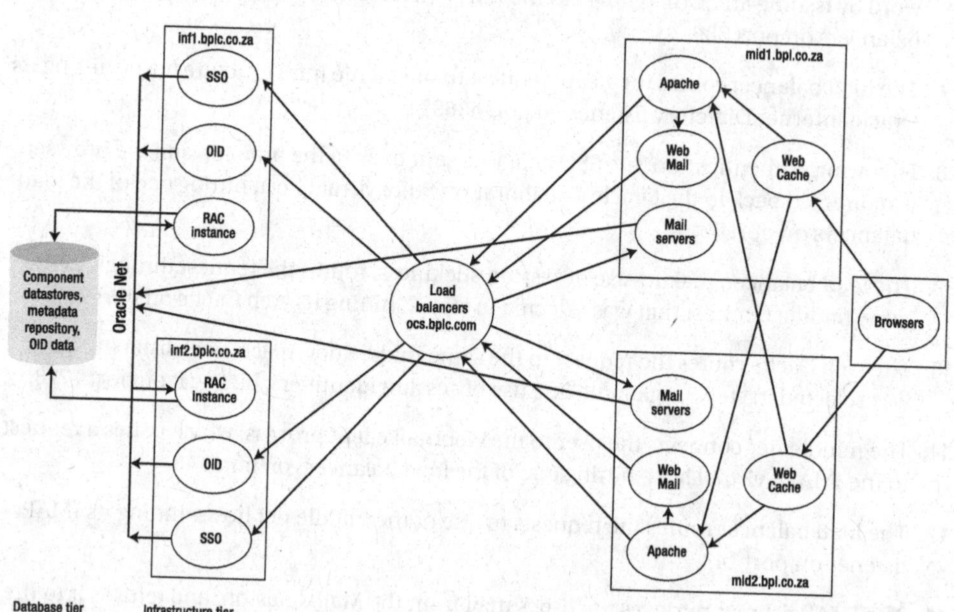

Figure 17-3. *A highly available topology for Mail, based on load balancing*

Points to note are that there are no direct connections between a middle tier process and an infrastructure process; all connections into the Oracle Internet Directory and Single Sign-On processes are through the load balancers, and the connections from the Mail servers to the database instances are load balanced by the Oracle Net layer. The connections to the database instances from the Oracle Internet Directory servers and from the Single Sign-On servers are also balanced by Oracle Net. Within and between the middle tier nodes, the Web Caches balance end-user browser connections across the Apache web listeners; no user connects directly to a web listener. Though not shown in the figure because it would make it look like a pile of spaghetti, the initial connections from browsers to Web Caches go through the load balancers.

The end product of this environment is that any one node can go down and service will continue. It is possible that requests in progress, that are actually being serviced when the node fails, will be lost. Also, any stateful sessions against services on the failed node may also have to be reestablished. But overall, the Oracle Collaboration Suite will remain available at all times, and users should perceive, at worst, a very short break in service and possibly reduced performance subsequently, because the entire workload (which in normal running is spread across both nodes) is supported by only one node until the failed node is brought back into service. This example covers only Mail services, but the principle can be extended to other Oracle Collaboration Suite components.

Index

D

E

I

J

K

L

T

U

V

W